ABOUT THE AUTHOR

James F. Dunnigan, whose books include *From Shield to Storm, Shooting Blanks, A Quick and Dirty Guide to War,* and *The Complete Wargames Handbook,* was codesigner of a war games simulation featured in November 1990 on ABC's *Nightline* that correctly projected every major aspect of the Persian Gulf war. He lives in New York City.

How to Make War

How to
Make War

A COMPREHENSIVE GUIDE
TO MODERN WARFARE IN THE
TWENTY-FIRST CENTURY

Fourth Edition

JAMES F. DUNNIGAN

HARPER

NEW YORK • LONDON • TORONTO • SYDNEY

HARPER

The first edition of this book was published in hardcover in 1982 by William Morrow and Company.

A previous edition of this book was published in 1993.

HOW TO MAKE WAR (Fourth Edition). Copyright © 2003 by James F. Dunnigan. All rights reserved. Printed in the United States of America. No part of this book may be used or reproduced in any manner whatsoever without written permission except in the case of brief quotations embodied in critical articles and reviews. For information, address HarperCollins Publishers, 195 Broadway, New York, NY 10007.

HarperCollins books may be purchased for educational, business, or sales promotional use. For information, please e-mail the Special Markets Department at SPsales@harpercollins.com.

Designed by Nancy B. Field

Library of Congress Cataloging-in-Publication Data
Dunnigan, James F.
    How to make war : a comprehensive guide to modern warfare in the
twenty-first century / by James F. Dunnigan—4th ed.
    p.   cm.
Includes index.
ISBN 0-06-009012-X
    1. Military art and science. 2. Military weapons. 3. War. I. Title.

U102 .D836 2003
355—dc21

2002024547

HB 01.26.2021

Contents

Contents

Foreword to the Fourth Edition

The first edition of *How to Make War* was published 20 years ago, during the last decade of the Cold War. A lot has changed since then. The Cold War ended, lots of little wars sprang up, and the ideas about what war is have changed considerably. A lot of these new ideas have less to do with politics than with technology. The last time this happened was during the two decades between World War I and World War II. Back then everyone was trying to figure out what effect new weapons like tanks and warplanes, and new technology like electronics and operations research, would have on warfare. The changes were enormous, and it was nearly 50 years before another such revolution began to emerge. This is called a "revolution in military affairs," and its extent and impact is not yet known. I'll be providing a lot of information on this revolution, where it came from, what it is at the moment, and where it may be going.

While the revolution in military affairs of the 1920s and 1930s was known for things like mechanized warfare, strategic bombing, electronic warfare, and carrier aviation, the current revolution in military affairs features things like robotic weapons, information systems, and space-based communications and reconnaissance. Welcome to the twenty-first century.

There are lots of changes in this edition, including some new chapters, many rewrites, and new illustrations. As I always enjoy hearing from readers, and carefully consider the comments, you will find several items changed as a result of reader feedback. Modifications are not radical, but incremental. Things change, this book shows it, and it is better for these evolutions. I can be reached via e-mail at jfdunnigan@aol.com, or at jim.dunnigan.com. You can also find updates to *How to Make War* at strategypage.com.

Illustrations are taken from various U.S. Department of Defense and U.S. government sources.

As with previous editions, I am indebted to a number of people for their advice and criticism of the manuscript. Among these are Austin Bay, Albert Nofi, Ray Macedonia, Mike Macedonia, Dan Masterson, Steve Cole, Adam Geibel, Mike Robel, Stephen B. Patrick, Bill Gross, Dave Tschantz, Mark Herman, and many others too numerous to mention (especially the attentive readers on strategypage.com).

How to Make War

1

How to Become
an Effective
Armchair General

With the proliferation of smaller and often more politically complex conflicts, it is becoming more difficult to make sense of wars. The end of the Cold War also has focused more attention on these smaller wars. Yet you can better understand a complex issue like war if you know the details and how they fit together. Warfare is certainly complex. With the spread of nuclear, chemical, and biological weapons, war and terrorism are becoming a more immediate fear in our lives. Still clouded by obscurity and confused by myths, the process of warfare is misunderstood by most of us. The mass media helps create and perpetuate many myths. Often the appointed experts are equally ill-informed.

When a war breaks out, these myths gradually become apparent as distortions. Operating on these misunderstandings, leaders and citizens are much more likely to get involved in wars, or make ones they have forced on them even more expensive. One of the constants of history is that a nation rarely goes to war until it has convinced itself that victory is attainable and worth the cost. In reality, warfare is never worth the cost for those who start them. Instigators of wars invariably come to regret it. Those who resist aggression have a better case. Yet avoiding war typically leaves people feeling they have missed a golden opportunity to right some wrong. Real warfare is ugly, destructive, and remembered fondly only by those who survived it without getting too close. Time dims our memories and conjures up wishful myths. This book removes some of the obscurity and destroys a few of the myths.

The Principles of War

Understanding how the military mind operates requires familiarity with the central "truths" military commanders have learned over the centuries. These principles of war have been distilled from our long history of warfare. They reflect reality. Were they followed to the letter, there would probably be a lot less fighting. The principles of war preach, above all, that you must know what you are doing. Or at least know your business better than your opponent. These principles are codified, and applied, somewhat differently from nation to nation, but the following describes the more common and important ones as I define them.

Mass. This is best summed up by the old American saying "Get there first with the most." While superior troops can enable you to fight outnumbered and win, victory usually goes to the side that masses the most combat power on the battlefield.

Unity of command. Armed forces have always been large organizations and usually larger than one leader can command and control. This principle warns the leader to make arrangements to deal with different parts of the armed forces operating at cross purposes with one another. All the units should know and be ready to execute the same plan, or take previously arranged actions if the plan doesn't work as expected. This principle has always been one of the most difficult to practice.

Maintenance of the objective. This means choosing and sticking with a reason for being on the battlefield. In warfare, the commander regularly operates with very little information about what is going on. As the situation develops, there is a temptation to change objectives. This wastes time and energy. History has shown that the army that consistently pursues its original goal is likely to succeed. An example is found in the Arab-Israeli wars. The Israelis ruthlessly maintained their objectives, ignoring temptations to surround bypassed Arab formations. This straightforward attitude always resulted in the destruction of far larger Arab forces. By contrast, the Egyptians, in 1973, changed their plan after crossing the Suez Canal. Instead of digging in to receive the Israeli counterattack, they launched further attacks of their own. This resulted in heavy Egyptian losses, which set the stage for a successful Israeli crossing of the canal.

Economy of force. Otherwise known as not putting all your eggs in one basket. No one ever has enough resources to accomplish everything. Economy of force dictates carefully parceling out forces for each phase of the operation. This does not mean using nothing but small forces all over the place. For key operations, you will often need massive forces. These are obtained only by using as little as possible everywhere else. Most important is the maintenance of a large reserve, some units that are kept out of the battle to deal with unanticipated emergencies. If nothing else, once all your committed forces get hopelessly tangled up, you will still have control of the reserve. Invariably the reserve snatches survival from the jaws of disaster. During World War II, the German army maintained a reserve no matter how desperate the situation. This habit alone may have prolonged the war by at least a year. Economy of force also allows you to mass sufficient combat power where it will do the most good.

Flexibility. This may seem a contradiction of the maintenance-of-the-objective principle, but it isn't. Flexibility in planning, thought, and action is otherwise known as common sense. Maintenance of the objective does not imply ignoring the obvious. If your orders are to take a town, and you determine that the easiest way to do this would be to surround it and then attack it from all sides instead of charging right in, that's being flexible. If, while moving around the town, you discover that a larger relief force is coming to support the enemy troops in the town, you would go after this new relief force before it could unite with the enemy forces in the town. After the relief force is defeated, you can go back after the town. That's being flexible and maintaining the objective at the same time.

Initiative. Getting there first with the most and taking advantage of the situation is the principal quality of the combat leader, and not all of them have it. Being first off the mark most of the time leaves the other fellow with less opportunity to respond to your moves and plans. Defeat is the likely outcome for a commander who always waits for something to happen. Indeed, surprise is little more than an enormous disparity in initiative between two forces.

Maneuver. If you don't move your troops around, then you can, at best, achieve a stalemate. This may be sufficient, but victory is better, and often necessary. To win, you must outmaneuver your opponent, or cause your opponent to try some fancy maneuver that turns into a disaster. Maneuvering is always dangerous, as the other fellow may turn out to be better at it. For this reason, many otherwise able commanders fail in battle because they do not have the proper mind-set for maneuver warfare. They are not willing to take risks. Successfully moving troops around in battle is the pinnacle of military art and the usual precursor of victory.

Security. It's not sheer bloody-mindedness that causes captured spies to be shot in wartime. Information can usually be calculated in lives saved or lost. If you know what the enemy is up to while concealing your own plans, your chances of success increase immensely. The crucial Battle of Midway in 1942 was won largely because the United States knew of Japanese plans, from having broken their codes, while the Japanese knew little of the U.S. forces' deployment, nor that the Americans were reading their coded messages. Good security capability enables you to achieve the most crucial of combat advantages: surprise.

Surprise. One of the earliest lessons soldiers learn is that it's a lot safer, and potentially more successful, to hit the other guy when he's not expecting it. That's what surprise is, and that's why security is also a principle of war.

Simplicity. Warfare is a chaotic and unpredictable undertaking. Elaborate plans quickly come apart under the stress of combat. Large, elaborate, and complex military organizations do require some planning to keep them going. It's not easy to keep the procedures simple. The key is the quality of your leaders and their ability to do the right thing in unison. Good leaders are another scarce resource. It's no easy thing waging war.

Morale. This is not generally considered one of the principles of war, but morale has always been one of those crucial items that overrule all others. Often taken for granted until it's too late, morale is the attitude of the officers and troops. It is generally much higher at the beginning of a battle than during and after. Once morale declines to a certain point, the troops lose their desire to fight. If this breaking point is reached during a battle, the side suffering from it loses.

Entropy. This is also not generally considered one of the principles of war, but entropy has been a constant throughout military history. In practice, entropy means that after an initial shock, the war or battle will settle down to a steady grind. Once a war gets started, casualty and movement rates become predictable. In combat, personnel losses can average up to a few percent a day per division. Against enemy opposition, even mechanized forces rarely advance farther than some 20 kilometers a day. There are exceptions, and the exceptions may win battles. Over the course of an entire war, however, entropy takes over. A technical way to put it is that "events tend to regress toward the mean." Don't let flashy press reports fool you; exceptions tend to get published far more than day-to-day averages. Commanders who are best able to cope with entropy develop a more realistic, and winning, attitude.

Rules of Thumb

As crass as it might seem, it is possible to boil this book down to a dozen rules of thumb on "how to make war." These are the historical outcomes that consistently repeat themselves.

An armed force's strength is calculated by multiplying numbers of men, weapons, munitions, and equipment by the quality factor. Quality is a seemingly nebulous thing, but it includes the effectiveness of leadership, training, morale, weapons, and equipment. Numbers alone are not the standard by which you can calculate a nation's combat strength. Units with equal numbers of men and equipment can vary substantially in terms of combat effectiveness. In other words, a soldier of one army can be worth several of another. It is also assumed that the armed forces in question have the proper ratios of infantry, tanks, aircraft, artillery, ships, trucks, etc. This is often a rash assumption, because the force with a higher quality rating possesses proportionately more weapons and equipment.

Attack strength ratios. An attacker needs three or more times as much combat strength (not just troops and weapons) in order to overcome a defender at the point of attack. This varies with the size of the forces. At the platoon level, the required ratio can go as high as 10:1. At the theater level, where up to a million or more troops are involved, anything between 1:1 and 2:1 will often suffice because only a small part of the terrain in the theater will be fought over at any one time. You also have to take time into account. The larger the advantage, the less time it will take to win. Keep in mind that the historical record from the last century has shown some armies with troops six or more times effective than their opponents. There have been smaller wars where the ratio is even larger. Remember, it's not the number of troops that count, but combat power (number of troops times the quality factor).

Climate and terrain have a severe effect on the tempo and effects of combat. Rough terrain, darkness, and winter all slow down operations and reduce the casualty rate from combat, while increasing the losses from disease and sickness. The cumulative effects can slow down operations by over 50 percent and reduce casualties even more. Chemical weapons have the same general effect as bad weather, although with a slightly higher casualty rate. Flat, open terrain speeds up operations, particularly if the defender cannot put up substantial opposition. Such conditions can also reduce attackers' losses while enormously increasing those of the hapless defender.

Modern ground combat causes average losses of 1–5 percent casualties per day of sustained combat per division (of 10,000–20,000 troops). Losses vary enormously depending on the soldiers' jobs. The infantry units' casualty rate is two to three times the overall rate. Tank-unit losses are about the same as the overall rate. Artillery units suffer half the overall rate, and all other troops are lost at about one-sixth the rate of the division as a whole. Keep in mind that smaller combat units like battalions will have over 50 percent of their strength exposed to enemy fire, while a larger unit like a division will expose only

10–15 percent. You don't have to be a mathematician to figure out that a battalion will have a much higher rate of loss than a division. If you have enough of a numeric and quality edge over your opponent, as did the United States over Iraq in 1991, your losses will be even lower.

Combat vehicles (tanks and personnel carriers) are lost in combat at a rate of 5–10 times the personnel loss rate. If a division loses 2 percent of its troops a day in battle, it will lose over 10 percent of its armored vehicles. Highly mechanized forces tend to grind to a halt over time as their equipment breaks down. Low-tech forces can continue killing each other longer without being stopped by equipment failure. When low-tech troops (such as the Afghan resistance in the 1980s) engage high-tech troops (such as the Soviets), the low-tech force can keep going a lot longer on fewer resources. This is why guerrilla warfare is so difficult for a high-tech force, and why most of the wars in the twenty-first century will be resistant to high-tech solutions.

The ratio of dead to wounded is about 1:4 in most armies. This varies according to how much medical resources you have. Armies with substantial medical resources get the ratio up to 1 dead for 5–10 wounded. Most of the wounded can be returned to service in less than a month. Noncombat losses per month vary from 1–40 percent depending on living conditions, climate, and medical facilities available. Wars in the twenty-first century will generally be in unhealthful places. Noncombat losses are liable to be higher than combat losses.

All things being equal, defending is easier than attacking. This is especially true if the defender is within fortifications that the attacker cannot bypass. By defending, a force doubles or triples its combat power. A stalemate can be achieved if both sides are too strong for the other to attack. World War I was a classic example, and many other campaigns in the past century suffered from this problem. Guerrilla wars often end up as stalemates. This favors the guerrillas, as the other side is usually spending a lot more money and will go broke first.

Modern air combat causes losses averaging 1–5 aircraft lost per 1,000 sorties. The American experience in Vietnam and the Soviet record in Afghanistan demonstrated that noncombat losses amount to between 1–5 percent of all aircraft per month. If you manage to shut down the enemy air defenses right away, as happened in the 1991 Gulf War, you can get the losses down to less than one per 1,000 sorties (it was about .4 per 1,000 sorties in the 1991 Gulf War and none in the 1999 Kosovo campaign).

Naval warfare consists mostly of nations dependent on maritime trade protecting their merchant shipping, or preventing the enemy from using theirs. Naval warfare is largely a defensive exercise, more so than air or ground combat. The

Gulf War was yet another example of this, with allied naval forces shutting down Iraqi ports. The allied naval forces then had to devote considerable resources to protecting themselves from possible Iraqi air or missile attack.

Surprise in battle can increase one side's combat power by a factor of three or more. The effect wears off after one to three days. This is one of the key factors in battlefield success and is regularly underestimated or ignored.

Troops that have not been in combat, or have not undergone intensive and realistic training, underestimate how much time, effort, and casualties it will take to accomplish anything in battle. It is very difficult to break out of this habit. For most armies, only combat experience will provide a realistic attitude toward warfare. A welcome exception was the experience of U.S. forces in the Gulf War. America had spent millions of hours and billions of dollars on realistic training exercises. This preparation was close enough to real warfare to make the operations against Iraq highly successful. One aspect of this that went unnoticed by the American public was that U.S. ground troops, because of their intense and realistic training over the years, knew how to make use of the months of time spent in the Saudi Arabian desert. Here they perfected their techniques with more training on the local terrain and detailed rehearsals for the advance north. As the U.S. experience in World War II demonstrated, spending a lot of time on inappropriate training is counterproductive when the shooting starts.

Warfare is expensive. Depending on how wealthy a nation is, and how many weapons and munitions it can buy, each enemy soldier killed can cost from several thousand to several million dollars. Just moving a lot of troops to an area where there might be a war, but none occurs, can cost billions of dollars. There's no such thing as a cheap war.

How to Find the Right Questions

Warfare, to put it bluntly, is just a job. There are techniques the successful practitioners must learn and tools they must master. As in any other profession, conditions change constantly. Practitioners must adapt to these changes by answering correctly the questions raised by changed conditions. But warfare cannot easily be practiced. This makes it difficult to determine the important questions, much less the answers. Here are some of the ones that are raised in this book.

How many armed forces do we need as we enter the twenty-first century? Not a whole lot. After finishing the analysis of the world's armed forces (at the end of the book), it becomes clear that there are no other nations powerful enough or angry enough to drag the United States into a major war. The world is a more peaceful place (in relative terms) than it has been in over a century. One of the benefits of the Cold War was the unity created among the industrialized nations (the "West," which includes several Asian states). In previous centuries, the major powers were always at odds with one another, and often at war as well. The Cold War and its nuclear stalemate changed all that. Thus, it is not up to the United States alone to take care of military emergencies threatening many other nations as well as the United States. If America had not promptly responded to the Iraqi invasion of Kuwait in 1990, the other industrialized nations had more than sufficient military means to go there and sort things out. They would not have been able to do it as expeditiously as the United States, but the matter would have been cleared up. Before World War II, the United States spent about 2 percent of gross national product on defense. That is a two-thirds of what is being spent now. Could we go back to that level? Voters must study the matter and decide.

What were the lessons of the Gulf War? The principal lesson was that training pays large dividends. U.S. troops underwent unprecedented (for peacetime American forces) training during the 1980s. Moreover, the troops were now all volunteers and carefully selected. This has been the traditional method of creating a highly effective armed force. The Iraqis were largely an army of ill-trained, -led, and -motivated conscripts. These training and troop quality factors, not superior equipment, were what made the victory so lopsided. The lesson yet to be learned is if the U.S. armed forces will choose to maintain their training levels or, as has happened during the 1990s, cut back training in favor of developing and producing new equipment. The choice is hard, as U.S. defense budgets always suffer considerable shrinkage when a war ends. There were several other lessons from the Gulf War. Some of the more prominent ones were:

Spare parts and munitions were not at "big war" levels. The Gulf War was a medium-size short war, and if it had gone on much longer, there would have been embarrassing shortages of spare parts and munitions. This situation got worse during the 1990s and only started to get fixed after the 2001 war on terrorism got started.

Combat service support was not up to wartime standards. Although U.S. Army doctrine had preached maneuverability for over a decade, there were not enough trucks available to support it. Last-minute scrounging to improvise sufficient transportation was still not able to prevent supply shortages once the three-day ground offensive got under way. This problem was never fixed.

The Navy floats better than it fights. The U.S. Navy was revealed to have overlooked some key technologies during its 1980s expansion. The U.S. Air Force had a superior bombing technology that the Navy knew about but had declined to get involved with because of the expense, and the feeling that the Navy way was the right way. This can be seen as either good news or bad news for inter-service rivalry. The good news is that while one service took the wrong path, the Air Force went another way that proved more efficient. The bad news is that the United States had two quite independent air forces, one operating from land and another from carriers. In any event, one of them got it right. The Navy has since adopted a lot of the Air Force technology.

Massive amounts of money spent in peacetime can save lives. The low U.S. casualty rate in the Gulf War was a direct result of the money spent on training and equipment during the 1980s. This spending was cut back in the 1990s, but no major war came along to show how this increases casualties. This pattern of post-victory cutbacks is ancient. There's a pragmatic reason for this: defense spending, no matter how essential, hurts the economy. Non-defense spending builds the economy and provides more jobs. A run-down economy and unemployment cause lower living standards, increased disease, and shorter life spans. It's always been tough getting money for the troops in peacetime, and always will be.

You can't see everything from the air in the desert. As spectacular as the Air Force performance was in the Gulf War, it was a typical experience for an air force in a desert. Yet the Air Force was stymied in finding and stopping the Scud missile attacks, or even hitting a lot of targets it thought it had hit. This has dire consequences for future war as missile technology continues to spread. More potential enemies will have missiles and exotic warheads (chemical or nuclear), which means that not finding a few missiles can lead to large losses. The large gap between what the warplanes thought they hit, and what they actually hit, was seen again in the 1999 Kosovo campaign.

Gee, that was easy. No, it wasn't. The chapters on combat and logistics show that the conditions under which the Gulf War was fought were unique. Change those conditions a little and you can change the results a lot.

What does war cost? Are you appalled by the size of this year's defense budget? With annual worldwide arms spending still in the neighborhood of $800 billion, you have plenty of company. The end of the Cold War did not bring about as much of a cut in defense spending as many people thought. Worldwide, spending only went down about a third by 1998. After that, spending began to rise again. But there are still wars, and wars are not getting any cheaper. The chapters on combat operations rate the relative worth of the various weapons bought. Chapter 23, on logistics, gives more details on the material needed to carry on a war. Using the chapters on the cost of war, logistics, and attrition (Chapter 24), you can do your own calculations on the cost of a current or a future war (Chapter 25). Although the cost of war is not frequently mentioned in the press, governments are well aware of it. This cost is a major element in the decision to wage war or to seek a less expensive means of achieving national goals. These chapters explain why modern wars are either short or eventually bankrupt the participants. The Iran-Iraq war is a good example of a "war of bankruptcy." And even the 1991 Gulf War cost the winners $60 billion, and the losers much more.

What entity controls two-thirds of the planet? The U.S. Navy does, as 75 percent of the world's surface area is water and most of that is international waters, where the strongest naval power holds sway. The U.S. Navy is now more powerful than all the other navies of the world combined. No likely combination of foreign navies can challenge the U.S. Navy. Not now, not for the rest of the century. Chapters 9, 10, 11, and 26, on naval power, explain why and demonstrate how the growth of the U.S. Navy since before World War II has resulted in the ultimate victory at sea.

Is the threat of nuclear war increasing? Chapter 20, on strategic nuclear weapons, reveals a few surprises about what might happen: for example, use of ICBMs (Intercontinental Ballistic Missiles) with nerve-gas warheads. What probably won't happen is the end of the world. The reasons? Primarily fear of massive use of the weapons and the unlikelihood that the weapons will actually work. Yet anything is possible. Read and study the details and decide for yourself. The chapters on nuclear weapons point out a number of factors influencing weapons reliability and effects that are not normally published in the open press. Nuclear weapons may well be used in the future, but not in ways we currently anticipate. Read Chapters 19, 20, and 21, and draw your own conclusions.

Who's on first in Europe, the Middle East, Africa, and Asia? Chapter 29, on the armed forces of the world, puts this topic into perspective. The information on each nation's armed forces indicates the potential resolution of such conflicts. Other chapters can be consulted to gain a more complete understanding of the possible outcomes. All countries have armed forces, but not all have an effective military organization. Except for the top ten military nations in the world, effective offensive warfare is not a realistic possibility. Iraq thought otherwise, and look what happened to it. The most pressing danger is that more militarily competent countries will be drawn into a local squabble. With the information contained in this chapter you can quickly assess who might do what to whom.

Who gets hurt? In modern warfare, few people in the combat zone are exposed to enemy fire, and fewer still actually fight. They rarely even see an enemy soldier, except as a corpse or a prisoner. The sections on ground, naval, and air combat demonstrate this in detail. These sections also add accurate detail to frequently misleading news accounts of combat. How are current wars being fought? The chapters on various aspects of military operations give details not ordinarily found in other sources. The chapters on the human factors are also crucial, as these items are repeatedly ignored or misinterpreted.

What is all this talk about electronic warfare? Chapter 18 lays it all out, step by step. The widespread introduction of electronics has profoundly changed the ways in which wars are fought. This electronic equipment has led to overconfidence and overspending, and sometimes increased military effectiveness. More than anything else, electronics have led to uncertainty, as there is no practical experience with these devices in a major war. It is important to understand their potential, limitations, and current status.

Information warfare? This is a modern variation on deception, and now has a chapter of its own.

International terrorism? This was a twentieth-century invention that has become more deadly in the twenty-first century. Again, another new item that now has its own chapter (Chapter 21).

A Few Notes on Approach

A half-serious maxim among military historians contends that you can determine which army is more effective by looking at their uniforms. The best-dressed army is generally the least effective. A fresh coat of paint makes any weapon appear awesome. How, then, do we determine which weapon is better than the other?

My solution is to combine historical trends and aggregation of these trends to produce a numerical evaluation of weapons and the units that use them. What this means is that there are identifiable trends in military affairs, and that if you collect enough data on enough nations over enough years, you get a very accurate picture of current and future military capabilities. This approach works well if combined with a study of the trends in leadership and manpower quality. You may not agree with some of my evaluations, but at least you'll have a point from which to start your argument. This book is for people who ask questions rather than simply accept the obvious answer. Because much of this book's subject matter is normally classified secret, or worse, information had to be obtained from whatever sources were open. Because of my long experience with this type of information gathering, I am confident that this is as accurate a picture of modern warfare as you are going to get. Even access to classified information is shaded by doubts about its trustworthiness. But that's another story (see Chapter 14 on intelligence). Any errors in fact or interpretation are my own.

The metric system of measurements has been used in most instances. Units of distance are measured in kilometers. To convert to statute (British/American) miles, divide kilometers (or km) by 1.6. To convert to nautical miles (or knots), divide by 1.8. Weights are in metric tons (2,240 pounds). Nonmetric measures are sometimes used to enable British or American readers to grasp scale better.

PART ONE

GROUND COMBAT

Wars are decided on the ground. A war isn't over until your infantry, the ultimate arbiter of victory, walks into the other fellow's cities and takes up residence. You can win a war with bombers or blockading and bombarding ships. But that doesn't end the war. Only infantry can do that. Ground combat uses the majority of troops and accounts for most of the casualties.

2
The Poor Bloody Infantry

Want to imagine what it's like to be in the infantry? Try this. You are in the outskirts of a largely abandoned town. The few remaining inhabitants take an occasional shot at you. A little more excitement comes from the seemingly random explosions caused by shells falling from the sky, or from earlier falling objects equipped with time-delay fuses. Your only protection is to seek shelter in half-wrecked buildings or dig a hole in the rain-sodden ground. You have not had a hot meal or bath for five weeks and are living on cold food out of a can or pouch. Your small group of ragged companions waits for instructions to come over a radio. You will be told either to move toward an area experiencing more explosions, or in the other direction, where the mayhem level is a bit less. Your only escape from this nightmare is to be injured or killed.

The above is not science fiction, just the life of the average infantryman. Those who have not been through it find the appalling stories of what infantrymen must endure hard to believe. It's tough on the people involved, as well. Studies during World War II indicated that after as few as 100–200 days of combat, and the stress that goes with it, the average infantryman was a mental and physical wreck, incapable of further performance. Most infantrymen didn't survive that long. With an average daily casualty rate of 2 percent, the chances of keeping body and soul together for 100–200 days were slim. The infantry, by definition, takes the brunt of the fighting. It's always been that way, and, despite giving the grunts armored vehicles to ride around in and body armor, this won't change.

Candidates for the Infantry

For several generations, it's been known that the more effective infantryman was a fellow of average or better intelligence, with good mechanical skills and in good physical shape. These were the same skills needed in the artillery, or to operate armored vehicles. Because armies have become more technical, there is less capable manpower available for the infantry. As complex infantry weapons have become more common, the demand for high-quality troops in the infantry has increased. It is impossible to get good infantry if you get only the stupid or inept recruits. The leaders of infantry units must also be of good quality; otherwise, the infantry is completely lost. These leaders, particularly the NCOs (sergeants), come from the ranks. The net result is that the infantry takes the recruits it can get and makes the best of it. Effective training of NCOs and officers will compensate for inept troops. The ancient truism, "There are no bad troops, only bad officers," applies especially to the infantry.

· Although the industrialized countries have greater demands for the best and the brightest recruits, they also tend to have a higher level of education in their population. These nations also use relatively more firepower and less infantry. The solution of many industrialized nations is to have smaller, professional armies that can obtain carefully screened volunteers. This solution has worked but cannot provide sufficient high-quality infantry for mass armies. But then perhaps we don't need mass armies anymore.

The Infantry Unit

Every infantryman depends on his unit for physical, moral, mental, and medical support. During World War I, it was noticed that most of the firepower of an infantry unit is in its crew-served heavy weapons, not the individual soldiers' rifles. A weapon requiring operation by more than one person, such as a machine gun that needs another man to feed the ammunition and look out for targets, is more likely to be fired while an isolated solider will tend to not fire. The close proximity of another soldier, and the greater firepower of their weapon, reassures the troops and helps suppress anxiety. Loneliness and the presence of death are a devastating combination that plunges many isolated soldiers into a frozen panic. Under the stress and uncertainty of combat, individual infantrymen will tend to seek cover and not use their weapons, or at best fire blindly. It is not unusual for units new to combat to hit the ground en masse at the sound of a few rifle shots. Once on the ground, out of sight of its leaders, an entire battalion could take hours to get up and start moving again. Technology is addressing this problem, as individual radios for each infantryman become more common. But knowledgeable leadership, a spirit of cooperation, and mutual support have long proved capable of turning an infantry unit from a panic-stricken mob into a cohesive, effective combat unit. Wartime surveys have consistently shown that the infantry fight not for mom and the flag, but for the guys they are with every day in combat: the "band of brothers," so to speak.

Infantry Organization

One of the few things that have become standardized throughout the world is the organization of infantry units. What follows is a list of infantry units, from the smallest to the largest.

Fire teams have two to six men and are sometimes called a section. They are based on the operation of a crew-served weapon such as a machine gun, mortar, or antiaircraft or antitank missile. This recognizes that men in combat perform better when working closely together. While only one man may be needed to operate the weapon, and another to assist with ammunition, the other members of the team provide security and replacements if the machine-gunner is wounded. Heavy losses in combat will often shrink fire teams down to a minimal size of two men. Fire teams are commanded by the lowest grade of noncommissioned officer (NCO). When attacking, a fire team spreads out on a frontage under 50 meters. In defense, a fire team is responsible for an area that can be covered effectively by their primary weapon: if a machine gun or automatic rifle, this means a range of over 500 meters on an open plain to a few meters in jungles. More important is the range at which the troops can detect, by eye or ear, the presence of enemy troops. Detection capability gets worse after a few hundred meters and is also reduced by rain, fog, night, and heavy winds. Fire teams use positions containing at least two men, and sometimes the entire team. These units are the foundation of any infantry force, whether or not they operate from armored personnel carriers (IFVs). If the fire teams are not efficient, the larger units will never be.

Squads have two or three fire teams (8–15 men) and are commanded by an NCO. In the attack, they advance on a front of 50–100 meters. In defense, they are responsible for an area generally 200 meters wide and deep. The squad is the largest unit consisting of nothing but infantrymen. That is, all the troops in a squad have a job classification as infantry (in the U.S. Army, the classification code is 11B, or "eleven bush").

Platoons have three or four squads (30–50 men) and are commanded by an NCO or the lowest grade of commissioned officer. Typically, if there is a fourth squad, it contains special weapons, normally machine guns or mortars.

Platoons attack on a front of 100–150 meters, normally with two platoons side by side and a third behind in reserve. A platoon defends two or three times that area (up to 500 meters' frontage) generally by concentrating several squads for all-round defense. The platoon is the smallest unit with non-infantry specialists such as radio operators or medics. It still consists of 80–95 percent infantry.

Companies have three or four platoons (100–250 men) and are always commanded by an officer, assisted by a senior NCO. The fourth platoon typically contains mortars, heavy machine guns, and sometimes antitank and/or antiaircraft missiles. Wealthier armies have electronic sensors and other special equipment. A company attacks on a front of 500–1,000 meters. In defense, it holds twice that frontage. A company is 60–90 percent infantry.

Battalions have three to five companies (400–1,500 men), are commanded by a major or lieutenant colonel, and have small staffs. Battalions sometimes have tanks and artillery and are the smallest combined arms unit capable of independent operations. In effect, a battalion is outfitted as a miniature army. In the attack, a battalion advances on a frontage of 1–3 kilometers and defends twice that. A battalion is 40–80 percent infantry.

Regiments (often called brigades) have three or four battalions (1,500–2,500 men) and are commanded by a lieutenant colonel or colonel. They usually have small contingents of artillery, tanks, engineers, and other support units. Most Western nations no longer have infantry regiments, but instead form brigades with smaller proportions of infantry in them. These brigades have their own support units, which turn them into miniature divisions. A regiment is 25–60 percent infantry.

Larger units. Brigades, divisions, and armies contain smaller proportions of infantry and are frequently not referred to as infantry units. The proportion of infantry declines rapidly as unit size increases. Most infantry divisions are less than 10 percent infantry, the remainder being combat and noncombat support troops.

Combat engineers. Called "pioneers" or "sappers" by most armies, combat engineers are specialists in exotic weapons and engineering equipment. They are also expected to be infantry-trained and in emergencies are used just like infantry. Their weapons include mines, special explosives, flamethrowers, and any new device that seems to fall within their area of expertise. Their specialty is setting up an elaborate defense quickly. Engineers are also expert at demolishing enemy defenses quickly, which qualifies them as combat troops. They are highly respected by the infantry. This is primarily because of their activities in front of the infantry when assisting in an assault on dense enemy defenses, specifically concrete-reinforced "fixed" defenses. Because of their specialists' training, combat engineers are used as regular infantry only in emergencies. They are highly trained and not as easily replaced as regular infantry.

Special Operations Forces (SOF). Otherwise known as commandos, raiders, Rangers, Spetsnaz, or Special Forces. SOF are highly trained infantry who operate quietly in small groups. In theory, small groups of well-prepared infantry should be much more efficient. In practice, many nations try to have it both ways and use these troops in large groups. Under these conditions they usually attract too much attention, and enemy firepower. These guys are good, but not bulletproof. SOF earn their keep when doing what they do best—raids, reconnaissance, and other special operations. These actions are expensive to support with the required aircraft, ships, and staging areas. Moreover, there are few of these tasks to be done compared to the more massive operations of a major war.

The Infantryman's Job

Once a soldier is inducted, given some training, and sent to the combat zone, he can expect to encounter the following activities:

Reserve. Not in contact with the enemy, but still available for combat. New units arriving at the front are put in reserve until things quiet down. Then they can be given a "quiet" sector of the front to ease them into the horrors of combat. Reserve status is also an opportunity to rest units that have been in heavy fighting. The troops catch up on sleep, clean themselves up, send and receive mail, get hot food, receive replacements for lost men and equipment, and train. Normally, but not always, all this occurs in an area that is not under enemy fire. Often the accommodations aren't much better than those at the front. Most of the units sent to Saudi Arabia in 1990 were, in effect, in reserve status until the fighting began.

Movement. Until the 1950s, the majority of the infantrymen walked. Some still do. Today, infantry ride in armored personnel carriers (infantry fighting vehicles, or IFVs), trucks, or helicopters. Movement affords a good opportunity to sleep, so veterans learn this quickly and practice it diligently. It is not easy to sleep in an IFV, especially cramped Russian ones, but it can be done. This is one reason why troops spend over 90 percent of their time outside their vehicles. But when the units are on the move, the troops practically live in their vehicles. The vehicle drivers are only human, and if great care is not taken, they also will doze off during long drives at night. A characteristic of mechanized units moving around a lot is frequent accidents as driver fatigue increases. The risk of ambush from the air or ground has also increased considerably, partially as a result of the greater fluidity of the battlefield and partially because air and ground sensors are more capable. Aircraft were always a problem, but now we have "smart" artillery munitions that can quickly pounce on the unsuspecting convoy and, at the very least, wake everyone up. These nasties operate at all times, even during weather conditions that ground aircraft. Some smart munitions even land and wait for a vehicle to pass by before detonating. Troop movements will never be as restful as they once were.

Meeting engagement. In the early stages of a war, a lot of "meeting engagements" are anticipated between advancing units. They are expected to be spirited and hectic. Since the 1970s, many armies have come to believe that this will be the common form of combat in future wars. In any case, the infantryman will find himself either ambushed or, after a warning, sent off in some direction as if on patrol to ambush someone else. Only the most confident and experienced troops look forward to this form of combat. Too many things can go wrong in such chaotic engagements.

Construction. A soldier's best friend is not his weapon, but his shovel. Once a soldier gets a taste of infantry combat, he quickly develops protective attitudes. Even in an inactive situation, the infantry still has daily casualties from stray enemy and friendly fire. When this fire increases, so does the risk to life and limb. This provides a constant incentive to obtain better protection. This is where the shovel comes in. Even with the widespread use of armored personnel carriers and infantry fighting vehicles, troops still dig. The armored carriers are not immune to all shells and bullets, and a disabled IFV means the crew has to do without the amenities it provides. The IFV's are dug in if time and resources, such as a bulldozer blade on some armored vehicles, permit. When a combat unit halts for more than a few hours, it works diligently to get "wired in" and "dug in." Preparing trenches and other protective positions comes first. The wiring consists of putting out sensors (trip flares, sound and motion detectors, ground radars, etc.) and laying, and sometimes burying, telephone wires. If resources are available, mines are emplaced, barbed wire is laid down, and barricades are erected on vehicle routes. Weapons are positioned so that they can be fired quickly—and "blind" at night or in bad weather—and can cover all likely avenues of enemy movement. Supporting artillery, tactics, air force, and ground operations units are contacted and arrangements made for their firepower to be delivered to key locations if needed. More important, these distant units are alerted where not to fire, so as to avoid hitting friendly units.

All of this is not enough. Enemy fire can cut the telephone wires, and jammers render the radios useless. Preparations must be made to use alternate forms of communication, such as colored flares or messengers. The emphasis is on making the defenders capable of executing defensive operations as quickly and tersely as possible. This is accomplished through considerable efforts by the troops. All troops in a position must be drilled on where everything is, including supplies. Routes protected from enemy fire are marked so that people can move safely, especially if a retreat is called for. Provision must be made for things going from bad to worse. The routes for withdrawal to another defensive position, and the new position itself, must be identified. The troops must be drilled on the sequence of a withdrawal; otherwise, it can easily turn into a rout and a great slaughter. These arrangements increase survivability during the chaos of an enemy attack. During the heat of battle it is difficult to perform the simplest actions, such as moving 10 meters, pulling a trigger, or getting a fire request back to an artillery unit. All this preparation takes some skill, considerable diligence, and not that much time. Twenty-four hours of effort will do wonders to prepare these safety measures. An ancient saying has it that "the more you sweat before the battle, the less you will bleed during it."

Patrol. Superior information gives you a lifesaving edge in combat. Patrolling is how you obtain it. Patrolling is also a tense and dangerous activity. Troops go into enemy territory to look around and often try to capture one or more of the enemy troops for interrogation. Friendly and enemy forces are typically separated by a few hundred meters or up to a few kilometers of no-man's-land. This is the site of most patrol actions. Each side struggles to hide details of its own situation while discovering what its opponent is up to. Patrols attempt to prevent the enemy from gaining surprise. The patrol's biggest danger is an enemy ambush. Modern electronic sensors have helped somewhat—microphones or, more recently, devices that recognize the sound or heat signature of men and equipment. Battlefield radars also are used if the area is open enough. Troops on foot, however, remain difficult-to-detect targets. Also, it's dangerous to patrol wooded or built-up areas, where detection ranges are lowest.

Night is the preferred time for patrols. In the dark it is possible to remain undetected longer, or more easily escape from an encounter. Ambushes are typically set up at night, as are booby traps and mines. At night, attempts are also made to remove the enemy traps and mines. Patrols generally do not go looking for a fight; they just want information. But each side will fight to preserve their own secrets. Patrolling comprises most of a soldier's time in combat. It is a terror-filled time of deadly hide-and-seek. Just sitting in your hole can be dangerous enough; getting out and patrolling is very unhealthy.

The tactics of patrolling are simple enough. The size of a patrol averages from fire team to platoon strength. At the head of the patrol are one or two men who constitute the "point." Their job is to spot the enemy before the enemy spots them. Even if the point man is hit, the rest of the patrol, 30–100 meters behind, will have time, and space, to deploy to face the enemy on more even terms. Depending on the size of the patrol, the nature of the terrain, and the expected enemy opposition, additional points may be sent to the flanks and even to the rear. Ideally, the rest of the troops try to maintain a distance of five meters from each other to minimize casualties should they be shelled, run across booby traps, or suffer automatic weapons fire. Patrols are conducted very systematically, or should be. The primary purpose of patrolling is finding the enemy and determining what he is up to. You also seek any other useful information about the local geography and population. Patrols often have a secondary mission to seek out and destroy enemy patrols and outposts. Before the patrol goes out, available information is reviewed, and a route is plotted on the map.

Sometimes the patrol is assigned an ambush position, or just a location from which to observe. Some patrols go out to set up booby traps, listening devices, or mines. Patrols last from a few hours to a few days. Sometimes the patrol goes out by helicopter and walks back, or is picked up and brought back by air. Artillery and air-power support are sometimes arranged, although this requires that the patrol continually know where it is and stick closely to the assigned route. Otherwise, the supporting fire will hit nothing, or perhaps even the patrol itself. Technology, in the form of GPS (Global Positioning System) handheld locating devices (showing where you are via satellite signals, to within 50 meters or less), makes patrolling a lot safer for those who have them. The GPS devices were very welcome among the combat troops during their first battlefield use in the Gulf War.

Multiple patrols will support each other, or additional forces will be held ready to go after an endangered patrol. Patrolling is done day and night. Round-the-clock patrolling is an indicator that a force has good control over an area. Troops that know how to patrol effectively have mastered the most difficult aspect of soldiering and are usually superior in other ways to their opponents.

Defense. Soldiers sometimes attack, frequently patrol, but always defend. When the other fellow attacks, you might have received some warning from your patrols. Typically the attack is announced by incoming artillery fire, which might include poison gas or nuclear weapons (gas shells have been used, but not nukes, though the capability is still there). Survivors of this must quickly get out of the bottom of their holes or dugouts and set up antitank and other heavy weapons. These weapons are normally concealed to prevent damage during the initial enemy fire. The defenders must also emerge to observe the advancing enemy and direct the fire of their own artillery. Although now exposed to some enemy fire, the defenders are still in their positions and have a chance of surviving. Their prospects are further improved by the spread-out nature of modern warfare.

As part of a platoon strong point, you would occupy one of ten or so holes in the ground in a circular area 100–200 meters in diameter. The enemy might not even be coming your way. Instead, enemy artillery would be fired to prevent you from going to the aid of your comrades who are being overrun in the distance. If you have the misfortune of being in the way, you can only hope that your firepower, and that of your artillery, will stop them. You may survive being overrun, because the attack's initial goal is getting through your front-line positions and into the rear area to shoot up supply and artillery units. In the chaos of battle, it is easy enough to crawl off somewhere and hide, or just keep your head down as the enemy's armored vehicles rumble past. Fighting to the death exists more as a fiction than as an infantryman's goal in battle.

Surrender is always a possibility, assuming the battered attacker is in a compassionate mood. However, given the fact that 70 percent of attacking troops in destroyed IFVs are killed or injured, the enemy might be bloody-minded. Although it is not often written about, prisoners are usually not taken during opposed attacks, especially if individuals or small groups are trying to give up. The attacker doesn't want to spare any troops to guard prisoners, par-ticularly since he needs all the help he can get to complete the attack success-fully. And then there are all those troops who are wounded and are in need of more attention than enemy prisoners. This is why defeated defenders attempt to hide or sneak away rather than test the questionable mercies of surrender. Veteran troops know this; otherwise, they wouldn't be veterans. The 1991 Gulf War was not exceptional in this respect. The Iraqis, for the most part, did not resist. The attacking coalition troops soon realized that they had achieved the soldier's rarely realized dream: a dug-in defender who didn't want to fight. The coalition troops celebrated by taking prisoner just about any Iraqi who wanted to surrender.

On the other hand, the defender has a number of advantages. First, he is under cover, customarily dug in. He is difficult to see. The attacker is nerv-ously aware of this invisibility, and this frequently leads to an attack disinte-grating due to panic. The attackers see their companions being hit by unseen defenders. The defender also sees this and is encouraged. Moreover, defender casualties are generally not seen by the attackers or defenders, further widen-ing the gap in morale. The defender knows that safety is as close as the bottom of his hole.

When attackers go for cover, the attack breaks down. You can't attack when you are flat on your face. Therefore, attacks succeed only if the troops are well trained and well led (a rare combination), and/or the defender has been all but obliterated by artillery, infantry attack support, and other firepower (also rare). If the defender cannot maintain a continuous front of firepower, the attacker will be stopped only in front of the surviving positions. These posi-tions can then be hit from all sides and eliminated more easily. However, a con-tinuous front does not require a large number of troops: in open terrain, one functioning machine gun can hold up infantry on a front of 200 meters or more. Defense rarely produces victory, only various degrees of defeat. If you stop the enemy attack once, there will likely be another one. If you do manage to really clobber the attacker, you are often rewarded with an order to counterattack. An astute commander attempts to have defending troops fall back before the next attack hits, especially if he calculates that this next attack will overwhelm his defenses. Even if he feels he can hold, a successful and well-timed fallback will force the enemy to waste a lot of firepower, fuel, and energy attacking an empty position, thus weakening the enemy for the next attack.

Attacking. Think of this as a large-scale patrol where you are almost certain to be ambushed. This is the most dreaded of infantry operations. No matter how well planned, an attack means that you must get up and expose yourself to enemy fire. Ideally, the artillery smashes the defender to the point where the infantry simply walks in, takes a few prisoners, and keeps on going. It rarely works out that way.

If patrolling and information gathering are first rate, you will know the position of most, but never all, of the enemy positions. If the artillery fire is plentiful and accurate (it rarely is), you can destroy many of these positions. If the leaders planning and leading the attack are skillful enough, they can destroy the key positions, allowing troops to bypass many of the remaining ones. This way, the assault can be carried out with minimal losses to the attacker. If the attacking troops are adept enough, they work as a deadly team, avoiding enemy fire and eliminating defending positions systematically. If, if, if . . .

The key ingredients are skill, preparation, and, above all, information. History demonstrates that a successful attack is won before it begins. The norm is not enough time, not enough resources, not enough skill, and not enough information. Even against an unskilled defender, everything must go right to achieve minimal losses. Keep in mind that the defender can fire off a shot in relative safety and not even be detected. The attackers may get him, but not before they've had a few more casualties. Historically, the only way truly to "soften up" a defender is to destroy his morale. This is generally achieved more through psychological means than with firepower. It can be done, it is often done, but depends a great deal on who the defender is. Defenders fighting for something they believe in are very difficult to demoralize.

In the attack, the quality of the troops is the critical factor. Poorly trained, poorly led troops do not press home an attack against even inept opposition, and when they do, they take heavy casualties. Some things never change, and this is one of them. Reckless bravery does not help, as it just gets more attackers killed. The security of infantry fighting vehicles has also proven to be false; most armies have reverted to infantry attacking on foot, with their tanks and IFVs behind them providing fire support. The Arab-Israeli wars showed this, just as the Japanese banzai attacks in World War II showed the futility of blind courage. But attacks can be enormously successful. The most recent example was the allied ground offensive in the Gulf War. The attacking troops, largely

Americans, made all the right moves described above. They did it professionally, thoroughly, and relentlessly. Their reward was the quick defeat of the Iraqis, and an unprecedented low casualty rate among the attacking troops.

Pursuit. Once the enemy is on the run, you must chase down the defeated remnants before they can reform and defend again. Pursuit is deceptively dangerous. You never know when the enemy will stop and ambush you, or with what. The resistance might be just a few die-hards unable, or unwilling, to retreat any farther. It might also be fresh enemy units, strong enough to stop the pursuer cold. The watchword of pursuit is speed. Go so fast that you overtake the fleeing defender, along a parallel route if possible. The ideal situation is to set up your own ambush, then collect more prisoners or kill off the enemy in comparative safety. Again, the deciding factors are skill in patrolling and intelligence gathering, as well as the ability to deploy rapidly against any resistance despite fatigue.

Urban warfare. In 1998, the Pentagon conducted a war game concerning a possible Iranian invasion of Saudi Arabia. This has been done before; such war games are played out regularly. But this one had a very disturbing outcome. The Iranians managed to capture the Saudi capital, Riyadh. Because of decades of oil revenue, Riyadh has grown from a dusty desert town to an urban megalopolis similar to Los Angeles. NATO troops suffered 40,000 casualties (dead, wounded, and missing) taking the place. The city was destroyed in the process, but everyone realized that there would be a major political stink because of those 40,000 casualties. There was nothing wrong with the war game, either. For decades, U.S. war-game designers have been incorporating data from half a century of urban warfare.

Soldiers don't like to attack cities. The defenders have enormous advantages, even if they are surrounded. Defenders have more places to hide in a city, and the fact that they are resisting indicates that they will fight hard. The first thing you do when approaching a defended city is attempt to get it to surrender. When you are told to take a hike, you do what the Russians recently did in Grozny. Note how much bad press the Russians got for their heavy use of artillery and bombs in their battle for that city. The Russians suffered only about 4,000 casualties, but then the city really was a large town and apparently was held by only a few thousand lightly armed Chechens. Put 10 times as many defenders in a city 10 times larger, like Riyadh, and you can easily get 40,000 casualties.

So what do you do? In America, the emphasis is on trying to develop technology that will make it easier for the attackers. There is actually some potential in this approach. Heat, seismic, and acoustic sensors have become much more effective and cheaper. The military is already using a lot of these sensors for early warning on the front lines. In fact, acoustic (glorified microphones) and heat sensors have been used since Vietnam, and acoustic sensors were used during World War I. Current heat sensors can let you look inside a building for the presence of people. Seismic (microphones that listen through the ground) and acoustic sensors can be fired like tear-gas grenades into buildings to detect the presence of defenders and monitor the enemy troops until the enemy, or the sensors, are discovered and destroyed. Even computers come into play, interpreting the sometimes far-off (at the other end of a building) sounds to let the troops know if they are up against troops, civilians, or stray dogs.

Another innovation taken from the civilian sector is the remote-control robot that can be sent into a building to check it out and dispense tear gas or grenades to deal with unfriendlies. Actually, the U.S. military has been working on such combat robots since the early 1980s, but mainly with an eye toward developing antitank weapons that crawl around the battlefield. The same technology could be used to turn loose killer "droids" inside a building. Stick a wireless "battlecam" on it and let the robot show you what's around the corner or in the basement. These little droids can be made bulletproof (or -resistant). An infantry officer will quickly remind you that he won't have to write letters home to the parents of dead droids.

Most of the likely future battlefields for Americans are built-up areas, either cities or just urban sprawl. This has been known for some time. But since the Gulf War, American losses have become a no-no. Not that we have been indifferent to American combat losses in the past, it's just that such casualties are more painful with live TV coverage of wars, and a feeling among politicians that any military victory will be tainted (along with their political reputation) if there are a lot of U.S. dead and wounded. So now word is out: take those cities without generating a lot of American body bags.

Everybody, especially the troops, goes for this. The only problem is making it work. Not all nations train their troops with equal intensity for all the above activities. Some emphasize the offense at the expense of the others. Many less powerful nations emphasize the defense. Some nations simply have strange priorities for any number of reasons. The U.S. Army, for example, does not train for "pursuit" operations. Why they don't is a long story, but the point is that "well-trained troops" can have quite different capabilities from one nation to the next.

The Standard of Living at the Front

It is very low, and the overriding goal is to not get hit by flying objects. This requires being inconspicuous, as what the enemy can't see he is less likely to shoot at. Shellfire is less deliberate and more difficult to hide from. For this reason infantry become like hobbits, living underground. Even so, it's an uneasy life. There's much work to be done. Defensive positions must be prepared and maintained. Equipment must be looked after, which is now a major chore since the infantry has been given armored vehicles. Enemy fire and Mother Nature conspire to keep everyone dirty, damaged, and generally on the verge of a breakdown.

Security is the major consideration. From 20 to 50 percent of the troops are on guard at all times, doing little more than manning their weapons and watching for the enemy to do something. Some of this guard time is spent in working on fortifications, an endless task. Depending on how aggressive and capable a unit is, 10 percent of the guard duty time will be spent outside the unit positions setting up ambushes and listening posts. This is a form of patrol work, in addition to the normal patrols that regularly go out and move around a lot. These activities are immediate, essential, and a matter of life and death. Competent armies have set routines for troops in the field, with the work divided up so that the troops have some time to eat and sleep, and little else. There are always emergencies and distractions to disrupt those not "at work"—from an enemy attack to random shellfire.

The uneasy nature of life under enemy fire is not conducive to rest and relaxation. About 10 percent of all casualties are attributed to combat fatigue, the cumulative effect of little sleep, poor food (typically cold and consumed in an unappetizing atmosphere), dreary living conditions, and the constant threat of random death or mutilation. If it rains, you normally get wet. If it's cold, you bundle up as best you can. If it stays damp, you are in constant danger of maladies like trench foot (your toes literally rot). If it's a tropical climate, you can rot all over, plus contract numerous tropical diseases. These afflictions can be avoided only by energetic measures to keep dry and medicated, which requires discipline and the availability of medicines and dry clothing. Staying clean is nearly impossible, as you are living in the dirt. But a certain level of cleanliness (or "field sanitation") is critical; otherwise, the troops get sick. Eventually most of the troops get sick and some begin to die. Normally the only solution to the constant threat of wastage from these living conditions is rotating troops out of the front line periodically. Two weeks in, one week out is ideal. Rarely are there enough troops to go around; the ratio is often lower, and sometimes there is no relief for the infantry. Such a situation means that hardly any troops will survive prolonged combat alive or uninjured.

Even without the immediate presence of the enemy, life in the field in wartime is an ultimately degenerating experience. Modern infantry units have to maintain enormous quantities of equipment. A 700-man U.S. mechanized infantry battalion has over 100 vehicles, mostly armored personnel carriers. These heavy, tracklaying (bulldozer-like) vehicles require at least four manhours of maintenance a day to keep them going. Add over 100 machine guns, 50 antitank guided missiles, over 100 major electronic items (radios and sensors), plus generators, stoves, maintenance supplies, personal weapons, and other gear. When living in barracks, the troops can spend over 20 hours a week per man just keeping their equipment in shape. The troops are capable of only so much. Eventually they and their equipment begin to waste away. It's an eternal truth of warfare that when campaigning, even without deadly contact with the enemy, an army will eventually wear itself out.

Infantry and Nonlethal Warfare

One new kind of warfare the troops aren't crazy about is fought with nonlethal weapons, but they have been urged to come up with a lot of them because dead civilians make politicians unhappy. The involvement of U.S. troops in peace-keeping has been the major force creating the demand for nonlethal weapons. Work in this area increased in the 1990s even while other areas of military research were being cut back. The military points out that the term "nonlethal" is misleading, and that the devices should be called "less lethal," as they can kill, just not as often. The generals are concerned that calling this stuff "non-lethal" will cause more problems when people get killed by these devices anyway. Lots of work produced some 57 "nonlethal" devices (many of which have been around for quite a while). These include: riot batons, shields, various types of nonlethal ammunition, and pepper spray. Troops are now expected to be able to switch quickly between lethal and nonlethal fighting. However, nonlethal weapons are difficult to use. It's impractical for a soldier to carry both nonlethal and lethal weapons. This means having some troops armed with lethal weapons, and others carrying nonlethals. Commanders have to keep a close eye on the situation and know when to order the use of which type of weapon. The theory is that nonlethal weapons are for use in low-intensity situations where killing a civilian could trigger a mass violent reaction from a mob. But large-scale use of nonlethal weapons against a violent crowd could kill and send the situation out of control, anyway. Nevertheless, more new nonlethal weapons are in development and scheduled for release:

Bullet mine. A claymore mine that fires a barrage of rubber projectiles (instead of metal balls) to an effective distance of a hundred feet.

40mm crowd dispersal round. Operates like a shotgun shell, spewing a wide pattern of rubber projectiles.

Portable Vehicle Arresting Barrier. Looks like a speed bump but ejects a net strong enough to stop a 3.5-ton vehicle going at 40 miles an hour. The net traps the occupants inside.

Ridged foam. A rapid aerosol foam that hardens when exposed to air and used to block doorways, stop vehicles, or otherwise create barriers.

Nonlethal 81mm mortar round. This would provide long-range indirect fire support. The shell detonates over a crowd, showering the people with fast-moving rubber pellets or beanbags.

66mm grenade launcher. Mounted on a vehicle, this is a long-range weapon that fires a flash-bang grenade or a shell that showers the crowd with rubber pellets.

Vehicle-Mounted Active Denial System. Looks like a searchlight, but what is broadcast are radio waves that make people in the way feel an intense burning sensation in their skin.

Many other nonlethal weapons have been around for years, used with varying degress of success. Slippery surface coatings are designed to block crowds by getting everyone off their feet. Flash-bang grenades scare people, not to mention temporarily blinding them and making them deaf. Related to these are concussion grenades, which cause shock and temporary deafness. The acoustic Dazzler creates a 150-decibel sound for 45 seconds and is more disorienting than the concussion grenade. There are also various types of tear gas, water cannon, and sticky substances.

Combat Robots

Finally, robots have joined the infantry. Robots have been serving in the armed forces for over a century. In the nineteenth century there was the torpedo, which moved at high speed just below the surface, making it harder for ships to spot and avoid. Modern torpedoes are "fire and forget," able to look for targets on their own. Then came naval and land mines, some now equipped with computers, sensors, and some mobility. The Air Force has had cruise missiles for several decades, and the Navy has missiles that seek out enemy ships on their own. The Air Force has used robot reconnaissance aircraft since the 1970s and now has models that can cross oceans and stay aloft longer than any manned aircraft. Robot bombers and fighters are being designed. Everyone has gotten into the robotic warrior business, including finally the Army.

Armies have always taken more casualties than air forces or navies. So why hasn't the ground-combat crowd acquired robots for their more dangerous work? Because land warfare is a lot more complicated and messy than in the air or at sea. The most dangerous infantry work is sneaking around forests or buildings, never knowing exactly where the enemy is or when a firefight will break out. By far the most dangerous job is "point," the guy who goes ahead to prevent ambushes. Often he just gets shot. Even when defending, there has to be some troops out front to provide some warning of an attack. Dangerous business. Perfect for robots.

The U.S. Marines are buying two models of robots for fighting in urban areas, a type of combat more dangerous than out in the countryside. The K-8 weighs 30 pounds (so it can be carried to buildings where it is needed) and is small (24×20×7 inches). It carries video, infrared (for seeing in the dark), and still cameras, as well as microphones. It broadcasts what it sees and hears to nearby troops. Using tracked paddles to get around, the K-8 can climb stairs and rubble. If it gets knocked over, its paddles can right it. It's also built to survive a six-foot drop, for often the troops will have to throw the K-8 through a window or a door to check out a potentially dangerous situation. The other marine robot is the Lemming. Roughly the same size as the K-8, it has an arm that can carry a camera so a picture can be obtained without exposing the entire robot to possible enemy fire. The Lemming can also operate underwater, making it perfect for checking out sewers.

The Army looked into mobile (like the K-8) antitank robots in the 1980s but never went past the discussion stage. Relatively cheap civilian technology was increasingly suitable for things like combat robots. And the technology was getting better every year. The Israelis had long been taking advantage of cheap civilian technology to develop successful robotic recon aircraft. But the United States stumbled along doing it the old-fashioned way (sort of reinventing the wheel, rather than buying a better and cheaper one at Wal-Mart). Yet the 1970s U.S. cruise missile had boasted extensive use of off-the-shelf technology. There was a trend of using newer and cheaper material instead of milspec (military specification, meaning too expensive, obsolete, or both).

Gradually, there developed the idea of making combat droids that were "fast, cheap, and out of control." Not fast in terms of speed, but more in terms of thought, artificial thought. They were cheap in terms of making many thousands of the robots. They were out of control in that you just turned them loose and overwhelmed the enemy's ability to cope. ("Out of control" is more commonly known as "fire and forget.") Faster microcomputer technology had made missiles, radars, and navigation equipment smarter and faster. Electronics became so cheap that tanks now have dozens of microprocessors, and individual soldiers carry a few around in GPS or radio sets. All this is coming together in the design of infantry robots. The battle droids have to think fast to find their way around the battlefield. During the first attempts at driving a truck (or tank) using a computer, it was obvious you needed a very powerful microprocessor to deal with all the decisions we take for granted when roaring down the highway or cross-country. But there is sufficient cheap computing power for a slow-moving robot, under some degree of human control, to be made cheaply and lightly. Inexpensive digital video, batteries, and miniature electric motors, as well as the wireless technology that provides cheap cameras, toys, and cell phones, also combine to make possible combat robots. Police have long used large, tracked robots for going into buildings containing bombs or armed criminals. The Navy is now building underwater droids to find and disarm naval mines.

There is one complication, however. There is a widespread and growing fear of arming robotic soldiers. When the army tried to build mobile antitank robots in the 1980s, the project was canceled because of a feared public backlash against armed robots. The treaty to eliminate land mines, no matter how misguided and futile, showed how popular the robot disarmament movement is. But there is still plenty of dangerous work for unarmed robots. Information is a powerful weapon on the battlefield, and robots can snoop around without getting your troops killed. Small droids can be dropped from the air deep into enemy territory. You program these droids to use their radio only when they have something important to report, then send them quickly and move away before enemy troops use the transmission to find them. The side with scout droids has a big edge in combat. Knowing where the other guy is first lets you get in the first shot. And any infantryman will tell you that's often the difference between surviving and dying.

Theory and Practice

Being in the infantry means you are most likely to get hurt, will have the worst living conditions, and, to make a bad situation even worse, will get the least attention when it comes to new equipment. It's not that armies don't try to equip their infantry well, it's just that these efforts so often fail. And such failure is often fatal for the ground pounders.

Idiotic equipment is less likely to be developed during wartime, but even then you get some real beauties. Consider, for example, where the steel helmet came from. Shortly after World War I began, everyone began to notice a very high proportion of head wounds. World War I was the first war that used a lot of artillery, which put a lot of metal fragments in the air and into any soldiers in the vicinity. Up until then, soldiers didn't wear metal helmets, because bullets or large, nonexplosive shells were the most common objects running into the infantry. A helmet was not practical. But with all the new shells and their smaller, more numerous fragments, a steel helmet loomed as a cheap way to prevent a lot of injuries. So Britain, France, and Germany proceeded, each in its own way, to develop some protection for their infantry. The French, being fashion minded, consulted experts in medieval armor and came up with a tasteful, elegant helmet that would not have been out of place in the fifteenth century. Unfortunately, it was now the twentieth century, and many needless French casualties resulted. The British formed a committee. They came up with a flat (literally) helmet that was vastly inferior to the German helmet, which looked a coal bucket but provided the best protection. The Germans had looked at what parts of the head needed the most protection and created a design that was eventually adopted by most of the world's nations—including the United States, whose version is called "the Fritz."

While the Germans do manage to lose wars, they also have a knack for taking better care of their infantry. Consider the idea of giving the infantry automatic weapons (what we now call "assault rifles"). The Germans were the first to do this, noting that machine guns were the most lethal weapon the grunts had. So before World War I ended, some 18,000 MP-18 "submachine guns" (assault rifles firing 9mm pistol ammunition) were issued. By the time World War II rolled around, the Germans had a lot more submachine guns, but most of the infantry were still equipped with bolt-action rifles. The Russians, however, gave their troops a lot more submachine guns, and the Germans noticed the impact of entire units of attacking or defending submachine gun–armed Russians. By 1943, the Germans were producing the StG (SturmGewehr, or assault rifle) 44 and tested it on the Russian front that year. The extensive reports of these tests, captured by U.S. troops at the end of the war, made dramatic reading. The StG 44 was basically the same design as the later Russian AK-47. The StG 44 used a "short" rifle cartridge instead of the pistol round used by submachine guns. This gave the StG 44 more range, hitting power, and accuracy. The troops loved it. The Germans made as many as they could through the rest of the war. But only the Russians developed their own assault rifle, the AK-47, right after the war. Everyone else felt the infantry did just fine with a semiautomatic (one shot at a time) rifle.

Eventually, in the 1960s and later, the United States, and most other nations, developed their own assault rifles (the M-16 and clones). Why the delay? Simple: the generals didn't trust the troops to watch their ammunition supply and were obsessed with long-range rifle fire (which required the larger cartridge). It was an old problem. The same thing happened during the American Civil War, when the brass resisted adopting repeating rifles.

And just in case you think the brass has finally gotten the message, keep in mind that the U.S. M-16 was modified after the Vietnam War to fire three-round bursts instead of full automatic. The troops would really, really like to get full automatic again. But, hey, that might waste ammunition.

The list of lost opportunities goes on and on. Take something as simple as the backpacks ("web gear" in milspeak) the grunts use to haul around all their gear. Since World War II, the Army has made several attempts to catch up with the outfits that make gear for civilians who like to hike and camp out. Again, the troops would often buy the better civilian gear with their own money. This became common during Vietnam, when there was a big civilian market for hiking, and, since there was a war going on, officers were less likely to stop the troops from equipping themselves with better web gear and boots. The U.S. Army is still trying to get decent web gear to the troops.

In peacetime, anyone can be an expert on what the infantry needs, especially if you are a general. So the troops get high-tech portable antiaircraft missiles (the Stinger), despite the fact that the U.S. Air Force has kept enemy warplanes away from our infantry for over half a century. What they really want is a decent portable rocket that will blast a bunker or enemy troops barricaded inside a building. In practice, the troops often use antitank missiles for that, but it would be real nice if something cheaper (so you could have more of them) and more effective were available. And let us not forget some of the pathetic missiles the troops have been stuck with. The Dragon antitank missile, in service for some twenty years, was widely considered the first item to be "lost" when a shooting war came.

Being a grunt has never been easy.

Another problem with infantry is that there is a lot less of it. A Western mechanized infantry division of 16,000 men has less than 1,000 infantrymen. Even many Third World infantry divisions have the same number of infantry. The chief cause of this is the introduction of the infantry fighting vehicle (IFV), and a lot of other equipment that must be taken care of. The IFVs are actually light tanks equipped with small cannon and ATGMs (Anti-Tank Guided Missiles). A crew is required to operate all this equipment, and the operators come from the infantry squad.

Numerous other problems intrude. The vehicle and its additional equipment require a lot of attention, leaving less time for infantry training. The armored IFV also prompts troops to stay near their vehicle, making them more vulnerable to enemy fire. IFVs are very vulnerable to a large number of modern weapons. Each IFV carries a cannon that is effective against other IFVs. All antitank weapons can destroy IFVs. Worst of all, IFVs have not seen a lot of action. It is not yet known, from actual experience, which tactics are most efficient for IFVs. The experience with Russian IFVs (BMPs) in Middle Eastern wars has not been encouraging. The experience of U.S. IFVs in the Gulf War was not conclusive because the IFVs did not get a sustained workout. Finding out what IFVs are best at is likely to be a painful and expensive process. The experience to date is not encouraging. After all, Israel went out of its way to produce a new tank but saw no compelling reason to develop an IFV. Armies are not unmindful of the many problems created by the numerous armored vehicles their infantry now has.

The Future

While the Third World nations attempt to catch up with Western levels of infantry equipment, Western nations keep moving forward. The United States, in particular, is still keen on giving its infantry every possible edge. This involves moving U.S. infantry into the realm of what is currently considered science fiction. The overall "infantryman of the future" project is called Land

Warrior. In addition to more effective protective clothing, the most significant new equipment will be electronic. In particular, miniaturized electronics and high-capacity batteries make it possible to put a short-range communications and navigation system in a soldier's helmet without unduly increasing weight. This would enable troops to keep in touch with each other, and know where everyone else is, when visual contact is not possible. As battlefields and troops become more spread out, this form of contact becomes more critical. Navigation aids, based on GPS technology, will be carried by platoon or even squad leaders.

Some weapons already have special electronic sighting equipment for improved accuracy. These are either mounted on the weapons (infrared or laser) or in the helmet (image enhancement for seeing through dark and smoke). A laser-spotting device can indicate where the weapon will hit out to 800 meters, which saves a lot of ammunition when you are trying to hit something. Also available for deployment is a thermal sight for rifles and machine guns. These sights have a range of 400–1,000 meters (depending on weather conditions) and would make high-tech infantry a devastating force at night. The U.S. Army plans to equip each soldier, sometime in the next decade or so, with a lightweight microcomputer that would work with a helmet display to show position, navigation, and other information and link to a battlefield intranet. We saw a preview of these technical advantages in the 1991 Gulf War, when only the armored vehicles had GPS navigation systems. It is now possible to equip individual infantrymen in the same way. While the cost of the U.S. infantryman's equipment is currently about $1,400, the high-tech grunt's gear is expected to cost 10 times that amount. However, the new equipment would provide an edge in battlefield situations.

Naturally, all this electronic gear can be a liability if the opposition also has access to sophisticated electronics. For example, because of the signals broadcast by the U.S. infantry gear, off-the-shelf electronics could easily be fashioned to provide low-tech infantry with a warning that the high-tech troops are in the vicinity. This is not a guaranteed countermeasure, but a potential and possible one. With the end of the Cold War, the Western nations have something of a monopoly on this stuff and are likely to arrive at a future battlefield with their technical advantages intact.

Work continues on the U.S. Army's replacement for the 40-year-old M-16 rifle: the OICW (they've got a catchier name for this thing: SABR). The much-criticized weapon is not due for service until the end of the decade. This will give the M-16 the longest career of any U.S. infantry rifle. Before the OICW reaches the troops, the Army says it will get the weight down from 18 pounds to 14. This is still much heavier than the current eight-pound M-16. The troops will not be happy unless the OICW does what its developers promise. What the OICW has set out to do is enable our troops to get at enemy infantry who are hiding behind cover (walls, trenches, trees, etc.). This is done using a 20mm shell that will explode over, or next to, the enemy troops. It does this using a laser range finder and microelectronics in the shell. The system works, at least in tests. No one will know until it's tried in combat how effective it will actually be. The M-16 has long used an add-on 40mm grenade launcher that was able to get at hidden enemy troops about 10 percent of the time. The Army feels the OICW will improve this to 50 percent. But, as always with weapons like this, the only real test is on the battlefield. The Army has also pointed out that the $24,000 cost of the OICW is not that outrageous. U.S. infantry can currently use an M-16 with 40mm grenade launcher and night-sight add-ons. This costs over about $3,000 a system and weighs as much as the 14-pound OICW. Moreover, the army plans to buy only 22,000 OICWs, equipping a third to half of each infantry squad with the weapon. In the past, only about 20 percent of infantry were equipped with the M-16s/ 40mm grenade launcher attachment combination. Expect to see the Army get some OICW prototypes to the troops as soon as possible, so that when there is an opportunity, the weapon can get some combat experience to settle the current uncertainty about its effectiveness.

By 2001, the Army was testing prototypes of Land Warrior body armor with a computer inside. The armor component, with its ceramic plates, is lighter than the current "Ranger" armor and can handle several 7.62mm hits. The computer, however, is still primitive. This early version used a 133 MHz Pentium processor, which required as long as six minutes to boot up. The computer worked with much-improved sensors. There is a TV camera in the rifle that displays a picture in the soldier's eyepiece. This allows shooting around corners or looking for the enemy without getting shot at. A major known problem is batteries. The current system includes two 12-hour batteries. Now running out of ammunition will take on a whole new meaning.

After years of design, field testing, adjustments, and redesign, the U.S. Army finally issued new MOLLE rucksacks in 2001. The Modular Lightweight Load-carrying Equipment (MOLLE) system consists of several components (which don't have to be worn all at once):

- A load-bearing vest with room for six rifle magazines, two grenades, and two canteens. This is what the soldier would wear in combat.
- A rucksack that carries most of the soldier's stuff. But troops still complain that MOLLE won't stand upright like the earlier ALICE pack and is actually a little smaller.
- A smaller patrol pack that can carry three days of food (or other stuff). When the soldier is carrying the MOLLE rucksack as well, these two items are actually carrying more than the older ALICE system. As its name implies, the patrol pack can be carried alone, or along with the vest for actual combat operations.
- A small waist pack that can be used on its own or snapped to the rucksack.
- A bedroll bag that snaps to the frame of the MOLLE rucksack.

- A camelback water system similar to commercial designs, with a drinking tube. This arrangement is more popular than canteens with the troops.
- A specially designed bandolier that carries another six magazines of rifle ammunition. The bandolier can be snapped inside the patrol pack or rucksack or carried on its own strap.

The troops also like the fact that MOLLE can be adjusted to fit each soldier. The straps can be adjusted to fit the smaller (and differently shaped) shoulders of women. The only problem with the adjustability is that if two soldiers end up swapping packs in mid-battle, they may be uncomfortable until they make adjustments. The old ALICE system allowed for few adjustments.

While the new MOLLE carries stuff more efficiently, it still carries more than the troops would like to lug around. The army is trying to reduce the load from the current 88 pounds to a more manageable 55 pounds.

Even snipers are getting dramatically new equipment. The Barrett firm has, since the 1980s, been producing a line of .50 (12.7mm) caliber rifles. These weapons range from 25 to 40 pounds in weight. The lightest (at 25 pounds) and cheapest (at $3,000, plus another thousand for a scope) is a single-shot model. It's 50.4 inches long with a 33-inch barrel. The heavier, and more expensive, models have a 10-round magazine. What makes a beast like this work is a patented device that reduces the recoil by 69 percent. Marines used Barretts to shoot up Iraqi artillery pieces in the 1991 Gulf War. The Barrett is not for killing people, but taking out trucks, artillery, radars, and the like that are up to a mile (1,600 meters) away.

Giving each grunt a short-range radio has been increasingly popular with the troops. Commandos have used these devices successfully for years. During training exercises, troops have been caught using their cell phones (set on vibrate, not ring) to communicate with each other. Observing how popular and successful these are, many armies are working on battlefield intranet technologies that will allow for a "soldier's cell phone." In the meantime, short-range radio setups are being tested for infantry use.

The troops also appreciate the U.S. Army's new camouflage face paint. In addition to some extra colors, the new stuff has insect repellent mixed in.

Another area that has gotten a lot of attention is urban fighting. World War II showed that this was the most dangerous form of infantry combat. Going into the twenty-first century, the U.S. Army and Marines have developed a number of new tools to make city fighting more survivable.

The most useful developments are for getting through walls (doors and windows are often covered by enemy troops). Explosive Cutting Tape is a relatively small device that blows a man-size hole through a brick wall. Another version of this is BEAST (Breachers Explosive Access Selectable Tool), a 2×5-foot item that is attached to a brick or masonry wall, also to blow a man-size hole in it. Just the thing needed to surprise the bad guys on the other side.

For long-distance work there is RLEM (Rifle-Launched Entry Munition). The long metal tail of this device slips into the barrel of an M-16 and is propelled by a grenade-launching blank round. The metal tail behind the warhead provides for very accurate shots at up to about 100 feet. The explosive will blow down a door.

Other new tools include new portable ladders, more effective hand tools for breaking down doors, flash-bang grenades (to stun people in a room, in case they are just civilians, or if you want to take prisoners), elbow and knee pads, and disposable handcuffs.

The Marines have also developed mobile robots with built-in cameras and microphones that can climb stairs and rubble to check out buildings. Also developed in the 1990s, and since improved, are lightweight (10 pounds or so) recon aircraft. The built-in camera broadcasts images to a laptop and gives the troops instant information.

The twenty-first century infantryman, if he comes from a wealthy country, has a lot more tools. But this requires that more time be spent training on how to use all the new stuff. It also puts a premium on getting bright, quick learners into the infantry. This has not been a problem in the United States, as many of the volunteers for the infantry are college-bound kids looking for a little excitement before they hit the books.

Tools of the Trade

Light infantry weapons. These are the infantryman's personal weapons. They are called light because the weapons and their ammunition are carried by the individual soldier and used without any assistance. These weapons include pistols (generally useless), bayonets (useful for domestic chores), grenades, and rifles. The most effective weapon is the rifle, now called an assault rifle. These are generally of small caliber (5.56mm), the same as the American .22, but with a high-powered propellant charge. Although capable of fully automatic fire, these weapons carry only 20–40 bullets in a box magazine rather than the over-100-bullet belts used by the heavier machine guns. On full automatic they fire off 30 rounds in less than three seconds. Also unlike heavier machine guns, the rifles have lighter barrels that will overheat after 100 rounds are fired in less than a few minutes. This will cause jams, premature firing, or worse. Infantrymen customarily carry no more than a dozen 20-round magazines, each weighing about a pound. The real killing is done with heavier weapons, and firefights rarely last long enough for the infantry to exhaust its ammunition.

The characteristics of grenades, the infantryman's "personal artillery," have been vastly distorted by the media. Fragmentation grenades weigh about a pound, can be thrown a maximum of 40 meters (10–20 meters is more common), and injure about 50 percent of those within six meters of the explosion. Less than 10 percent of the wounded will die, thus making grenades one of the least lethal weapons in the infantryman's arsenal. In theory, grenades have a 3–5-second fuze. Quality control being what it is, these fuzes are sometimes a little longer or shorter, usually longer for safety reasons. Some grenades use a contact fuze, exploding when they strike something hard. These can be used only if your target is not soft, which will cause the grenade to bounce harmlessly. Grenades are favored when fighting at night or in cluttered areas like forests and buildings. Grenades are rarely thrown large distances, as the thrower is generally prone or otherwise not in a position to do a proper windup. Tossing them around corners or over an obstacle is more common. American troops have been using grenade launchers for over twenty years. Originally it looked like a large-barrel shotgun, but it has gradually evolved into an extra barrel that can be attached to assault rifles. This 40mm grenade can be propelled over 300 meters, although accurate use is rarely beyond 100 meters. A full range of grenades is available. More details are found in the section at the end of this chapter describing infantry weapons.

Heavy infantry weapons. These are infantry weapons requiring more than one man to operate, although most can be used without assistance in a pinch. Principal weapons of this type are:

- Machine guns, which need an extra man to carry the ammunition.
- Antitank and antiaircraft missiles, which require two or more men to carry the system.
- Mortars, whose weapon and ammunition weight requires several men.

Ideally, all infantrymen should be adept with these weapons. In practice, everyone specializes. In particular, the mortars and missiles tend to be used only by specialists. All infantrymen are given some training in the use of machine guns, grenade launchers, and antitank rockets. This is called "familiarization training" and is just that. Any real proficiency with these weapons has to be gained in combat.

Special equipment. Some types of equipment are handled by most infantrymen, even if supervision by experts is required. Minefields and booby traps can be installed by experienced infantrymen. These explosive devices can be dangerous to handle, and it is more effective to have a few practiced individuals do the work. If no experienced people are available and the job must be done, you tend to have some accidents.

Other specialist devices are dangerous only if they don't work, such as sensors and communications equipment (radios, telephones, and flares). These gadgets are particularly essential for successful defense, along with mines and booby traps. Sensors warn you of the enemy's approach. Communications equipment coordinates your actions and is the vital link with supporting artillery and aircraft.

Personal equipment. More mundane but essential tools are the vital entrenching tool (folding shovel), a bayonet (used for everything but stabbing someone), a gas mask, and other chemical protectors like ointments, antidotes, and special clothing. The most respected articles of protective clothing are the flak vest and helmet.

The United States has finally produced a lightweight bulletproof vest. For the first time since the introduction of firearms five centuries ago, the infantry has some real protection from bullets. Between 1999 and 2003, the U.S. Army will distribute 54,000 of the $1,700 Interceptor vests to infantry units. Another 22,500 CBA (Concealable Body Armor) vests (that can be worn under civilian or military clothing) are also being distributed to Special Forces, MPs, and security personnel. The CBA is basically a lighter version of the Interceptor, without the ceramic plates to stop high-power rifle bullets. The CBA will stop most pistol bullets.

The Germans developed the first modern protective vests during World War I. These weighed about 20 pounds, restricted movement, and were mainly used by troops who stayed put a lot (like machine-gunners.) During World War II, the United States developed a similar "flak jacket" for bomber crews. While not bulletproof, they did offer protection from exploding German antiaircraft shells ("flak"), which caused most of the wounds for bomber crews. These jackets, which were too heavy and bulky for the infantry, used layers of the new "synthetic silk," nylon, for added protection. By the end of World War II, the army had developed a 12-pound vest, using aluminum plates and nylon fabric. It was still bulky, and restricted movement, but it was a lot lighter. During the Korean War, an eight-pound protective vest, using layers of nylon and a nylon-type material called Doron, was provided starting in 1952. While it was still not bulletproof, it was able to stop two-thirds of fragments (which caused 75 percent of wounds) and some 20 percent of bullets (which caused 25 percent of wounds). Wound injuries to the torso were also reduced by two-thirds. And those fragments and bullets that did penetrate did a third less damage. These T-52 vests cost about $280 (in current dollars). Improved versions of the T-52 were later used with success in Vietnam, although these things were very hot in tropical climates. Often, troops did not wear them if they knew they would be moving around a lot.

In the early 1970s, Kevlar vests were produced. Kevlar was a much stronger material than Doron and provided more protection. Although the Doron and Kevlar vests were not called "bulletproof," they could stop many pistol rounds, and even rifle rounds that were ricochets or had been fired a long distance. The tougher Kevlar fiber and better layout of the vest reduced casualties of wounds to the torso by over 70 percent (as compared to troops without vests). But the troops wearing a vest were still vulnerable to high-velocity bullets (from AK-47s, M-16s, and 7.62mm machine guns). Being "bulletproof" was important in a different way than having all that protection from fragments. The biggest danger from bullets was when you were attacking, when the enemy could actually see you and shoot at you. This is the scariest part of being an infantryman. It's bad enough when you're in a foxhole or behind a wall getting shelled. At least you have some protection, and the older, fragment-proof protective vests were much appreciated in these situations. But when you were out in the open, being even a little bit bulletproof makes a big difference to morale and motivation.

By the late 1980s, it was possible to make truly bulletproof vests using metallic inserts. But the inserts were heavy and so were the vests (about 25 pounds). Great for SWAT teams, but not of much use to the infantry. In the 1990s, additional research produced lighter, bulletproof ceramic materials, and by 1999, the U.S. Army began distributing a 16-pound "Interceptor" vest that provided both fragment and bullet protection. This, plus the 3.3 pound Kevlar helmet (available since the 1980s), gave the infantry the best combination of protection and mobility. And just in time: since the end of the Cold War, more of the situations U.S. infantry find themselves in involve lightly-armed irregulars who rely more on bullets than bombs. The bulletproof vest eliminates most of the damage done by the 30 percent of wounds inflicted to the trunk (of which about 40 percent tend to be fatal without a vest). The Kevlar helmet is also virtually bulletproof, but it doesn't cover all of the head (the face and part of the neck are still exposed). Even so, the reduction in deaths is significant. Some 15–20 percent of all wounds are head wounds, and about 45 percent of these are fatal without a helmet. The Kevlar helmet reduces these deaths by at least half, reducing many wounds to the status of bumps, sprains, and headaches. Half the wounds occur in the arms and legs, but only 5–10 percent of these are fatal. That won't change anytime soon. Thus, since Vietnam, improved body armor has reduced casualties by about a third. The protective vests used in Vietnam and late in the Korean War reduced casualties by about 25 percent compared with World War II figures, so the risk of being killed or wounded has been cut in half since World War II because of improved body armor. Much better medical care (especially rapid evacuation of casualties by helicopter) has also helped reduce the ratio of wounded to dead from 3:1 during World War II to 5:1 today.

The Interceptor vest was an improvement in other ways. It was easier to wear and was cooler in hot climates because you could more easily adjust it to let some air circulate. You could also hang gear from the vest, making it a more functional piece of clothing. It's still uncomfortable wearing the vest in hot weather. But if you're expecting a firefight, the decision to wear the vest is easy: you know it will stop bullets. U.S. troops who have fought in Afghanistan and who have been hit with rifle bullets that would have penetrated earlier vests are already spreading the word throughout the ground-combat community.

Because of their expense, only a few armies use any kind of protective vests. These include the United States and most of the industrialized nations. Russia began issuing them in the 1980s, first to commando units. In most armies the helmets are made of steel. The newer ones are of plastic and offer better protection and more comfort.

And then there is the first-aid kit, a mini-drugstore with pep pills, aspirin, antibiotics, bandages, painkillers, and other controlled substances. Not everything that goes into the first-aid pouch is official issue, or even legal. Experienced infantrymen learn to equip themselves as best they can.

Speaking of unofficial equipment, veteran infantrymen often obtain a pistol or even a shotgun. The pistol makes the soldier feel a little more secure, and the shotgun is very useful in close-range combat. Transistor radios continue to be present, along with cell phones, providing another way to find out what really's happening, assuming that you are in range of a signal. For personal comfort we find sleeping bags (or just blankets in the low-tech armies), spare clothing (notably socks), sunglasses (good for safely viewing distant nuclear explosions), canteens (more than one in hot climates), mess kits, and food (junk food is favored over the official rations). As troops now move around in IFVs, the amount of equipment has increased. Losing the IFV, therefore, has a greater adverse effect on morale.

Combat Values and Unit Organization

For much of the last century, military analysts have tried to come up with ways to place values on weapons. There is only so much money for the army, and you want, so to speak, to get the most bang for the buck. Without going into the math (which can get pretty complex), you can take two different approaches. One is to calculate how much firepower a weapon has. This isn't as simple as it sounds, because it's not just how many shells or bullets you can fire a minute, or how much the shells weigh, or what special effect the shells have (explosive, armor piercing, electronic fuse, etc.). What counts is the weapon's effect in specific kinds of combat situations. A tank is great for killing other armored vehicles, but much less useful fighting infantry in a city. Artillery is good for blowing apart buildings and killing infantry out in the open, but much less useful against infantry that have had hours or days to dig themselves in. Artillery is also much less effective against tanks and other armored vehicles. Actual combat power must also take into account the quality of training and leadership, as well as a host of other situational factors. This is generally referred to as the "quality factor." Historically, these training and leadership factors can increase unit effectiveness by several hundred percent. A 20–30 percent advantage is normal for most wars, and in some cases the advantage is 200–300 percent. Such was the case in the 1991 Gulf War, where U.S. units had a nearly 200 percent quality advantage. Once all the equipment and quality factors have been accounted for, the attacker needs a 3:1 advantage in combat power to have a reasonable chance of success. Six to one or better is preferred. See Chapter 24 on attrition for more details.

The other approach is used by war-game designers. Using battles already fought, you can calculate what overall combat values different types of units have had. This approach has been much more effective. When you go look at the historical factors, you find that the weapons are not as important as how well-trained and -led the troops are, and what the situation is. For example, while mortars can fire explosive shells many kilometers, they are really useful only if the enemy is not well dug in. But if you do catch the enemy out in the open, as when they are attacking you, a lot of damage is done. This makes mortars a better defensive weapon. Tanks, however, are armored and mobile. They are a better offensive weapon. This is what tanks were first designed for back in 1915, to advance into rifle and machine-gun fire and destroy enemy machine guns. Except for the addition of missiles, infantry unit organization has not changed much in the past century. Below is a description of the quantity and type of weapons you will find in infantry units throughout the world.

Infantry Battalions

These units come in two main types, mechanized and non-mechanized. The former have armored vehicles (IFVs, or infantry fighting vehicles), and the latter do not (the troops either walk or ride about in trucks). Guerrilla units are the lightest of all, usually having no trucks and not a lot of heavier weapons. But most armies are mechanized, and each battalion will have 400–1,500 troops and one IFV for every 8–10 men. Each man has an assault rifle, and there is one machine gun for every 6–8 men. Mech infantry usually has a large supply of ATGM (Anti-Tank Guided Missile) launchers, one for every 6–8 men. Most of the ATGM launchers are carried on the IFVs. In addition to the ATGMs, there are usually one-shot, shoulder-fired antitank rocket launchers, one for every 5–10 troops. Most mech battalions have some mortars, 6–12 of them and either 81mm or 120mm caliber. Shoulder-fired antiaircraft missiles are also increasingly popular, but each battalion rarely has more than a dozen of these. There are several dozen trucks to carry ammunition, tents, and other equipment.

Infantry battalions usually have three infantry companies (100–200 men each), a headquarters company (100–200 men, often larger by incorporating stuff like mortars or other heavy weapons), and perhaps another company for some heavy weapon (like antitank, which would mean 60–70 troops and 6–12 ATGM launchers). Each mechanized infantry platoon contains a platoon headquarters (sometimes just the platoon commander, but often up to six men in their own IFV) and three infantry squads (each with 8–10 men, 1 IFV, 1–3 machine guns). This organization is subject to change every few years, principally because reorganizing infantry platoons is a favorite peacetime activity in many armies. Many armies issue single-shot antitank rocket launchers as rounds of ammunition. Machine guns are distributed, for all practical purposes, on the basis of one for every 12 men in a division, with higher concentrations in combat battalions. Each IFV has a machine gun mounted on it. Experienced troops tend to "acquire" many more machine guns. Practically all armored vehicles, and several non-armored ones, have radios. The mechanized infantry battalion has approximately 20–60 trucks of various sizes, with wealthier armies providing a few armored support vehicles. All these trucks and armored combat vehicles carry combat and non-combat troops, maintenance tools, special equipment, supplies, and special weapons (SAMs, flamethrowers, etc.). Supplies include up to three days or more of food, fuel, and ammunition, as well as spare parts. Your average infantry battalion has over a hundred vehicles. Poor nations can "motorize" their smaller (400 men) infantry battalions with 20–25 trucks.

Infantry Regiments and Brigades

Infantry battalions are usually grouped together into regiments or brigades. Regiments tend to be fixed organizations with the same number of infantry battalions, usually three. Brigades have usually been more flexible, having more than three infantry battalions, plus more additional units than regiments. In addition to its infantry battalion, a regiment or brigade will often have a tank and artillery battalion, plus smaller (usually company-level) engineer, antiaircraft, and supply units. The manpower in a regiment or brigade is usually 150–200 percent the infantry strength. Thus, an infantry regiment with three 500-man infantry battalions will have (with the extra units) a total strength of some 2,200 men. A brigade with three 700-man infantry battalions will often have a total manpower of 4,200 troops.

In Russian-style armies (still popular with less wealthy nations), the regiment serves the same function as the battalion in Western armies. Non-Russian armies that use Russian equipment and doctrine often call these regiments "brigades." Whatever the name, these units are capable of supporting themselves in the field. To do this they must have various support capabilities, such as signal, maintenance, supply, and specialist combat units. Because support from other specialized units is an all-or-nothing situation in the Russian army, the regiment contains a little of everything in the way of support. Generally, the only support the regiment will get is what it has with it. The Russian mechanized rifle regiment (at the end of the Cold War) contained three mechanized rifle battalions, a regimental headquarters (65 men, three APCs), a tank battalion (165 men, 40 tanks, two APCs), an artillery battalion (220 men, 18 122mm self-propelled howitzers), an air-defense battery (60 men, 4 23mm automatic cannon systems, and 4 SA-13 missile systems), a reconnaissance company (57 men, 12 IFVs), an antitank battery (55 men, eight APCs mounting a total of 45 AT-5 ATGMs), an engineer company (70 men with two self-propelled bridges), a maintenance company (65 men), a medical company (25 men), a transportation company (70 men with 40 4.5-ton trucks, each with a 10-ton trailer), a chemical-defense company (35 men with three decontamination rigs on trucks), a traffic control platoon (20 men), and a supply and service platoon (20 men). The other regimental equipment is similar to that carried by the U.S. battalion. The regiment has 149 trucks and a total of over 500 vehicles of all types. Poor nations generally have fewer vehicles and special weapons (ATGMs, antiaircraft guns, and missiles).

Note that most Western armies have field kitchens at the company or battalion level. The Russian-style army has them only at the regimental level. In general, the quality of life for these soldiers is lower. This puts these soldiers closer to the edge of survival on the battlefield. They have less food and less medical, shelter, and equipment maintenance support. Compared with their counterparts in Western armies, these soldiers are less experienced and less capable, at least in the peacetime conscript army. In wartime these soldiers become as proficient as their Western counterparts. But this method is wasteful of human life and equipment. Many Third World nations have adopted this organization, mainly because it is cheaper and more suitable to their needs.

Centralization Versus Decentralization

There is another major difference in how infantry battalions are organized, and that is centralization of heavy weapons. For example, the 12 infantry platoons of the U.S. infantry battalion possess over half of the battalion's combat power (guys with weapons). The remaining combat power is in the battalion and company support units. One immediately obvious fact is that while Russians and Americans put about the same percentage of their manpower in the infantry platoons, Americans place more of their combat power directly in these platoons. The 12 infantry platoons of a U.S. infantry battalion contain about 40 percent of the battalion's manpower but some 60 percent of its combat power.

At the other extreme we have the system pioneered by the Russians nearly a century ago. Russia put about a third of its manpower in the 27 infantry platoons of its infantry regiment, but only about 30 percent of the combat power. The Russian system keeps a larger portion of the superior unit's combat under central control. This combat power is applied, typically in large doses, by attaching numerous specialist units to a few of the regiment's nine infantry companies. The advantage of this central control is primarily just that: control. The Russian system does not rely on sophisticated communications as much as Western armies. If the Russian regimental commander wants to get his reserve—over half the regiment's combat power—into action, he sends a messenger down the road to deliver the message, or leads it himself. This central control is also practical. It eases supply and maintenance problems, with all of the complex gear concentrated in one place instead of dispersed among the numerous infantry units. On the minus side, combat units get fewer opportunities to train with the specialist units. A lot of last minute "mix and match" places the specialist troops next to infantrymen they know little about. The infantrymen tend to be uncomfortable about trusting their lives to these strangers from the headquarters reserve.

Western units also indulge in this practice in a different form. This is called "cross attachment," where a tank battalion will send one company of its tanks to a neighboring infantry battalion and receive an infantry company in return. The Russians also do this by breaking up their tank units and sending a tank platoon to each infantry company while attaching an infantry platoon or squad to a tank company. However, the Russians prefer to use their specialists as a large mass. This Russian approach has great appeal for Third World armies because they, even more than the Russians, lack the technically competent personnel to provide skilled troops for all combat units. These differences in organization are typical depending on how much money a nation has and how well-educated and -trained its people are.

The U.S. system, a variation of Western European systems, uses larger, more heavily armed units. Most nations, including the United States, Germany (in 1945 and the 1970s), Israel, and other major Western military powers have recognized that the leaner organization of the Russians is superior in combat. The Russian type of organization dates from the late 1940s, when they adopted many organizational ideas the Germans had used at the end of World War II. Many Western armies have used the leaner combat unit organization in conjunction with the more abundant combat support units typically found in the armies of industrialized nations.

Infantry Divisions

Infantry divisions follow the same pattern, each having three regiments or brigades plus a lot of additional units (usually battalions of reconnaissance, intelligence, transportation, maintenance, antiaircraft, intelligence, and so on).

The basic unit of ground forces is the division, a force of 8,000–18,000 men. The Russian-style organization still represents over half of these divisions. Chinese-style infantry divisions, very similar to the Russian type, represent most of the remainder. There are over 500 combat divisions in service worldwide. Most are infantry divisions, although many of the mechanized infantry divisions have over 100 tanks each. There are also numerous specialized infantry units. The United States also has light infantry, infantry, air mobile, and airborne divisions in active service as similar units for its reserve and National Guard forces. Adding Marine divisions, we have a very diverse force.

The "combat power" of these divisions varies considerably, even before you get into aspects that define quality. These numeric values are derived from work done on combat simulations. There are actually different numbers depending on what the division is doing (attacking, defending), where it is (armored units do better on plains, infantry divisions do better in cities and forested mountains), and how much air power is involved (infantry units are harder to hammer from the air). Lower-quality Russian-style divisions have a combat power of about 4. Give these units better equipment and you can bump combat power up to about 7. Equipment and weapons quality does make a difference, as the Iraqis discovered in 1991 when they found U.S. M-1 tanks invulnerable to fire from their older T-72 tanks. Western-style division combat power ranges from about 7 for light infantry divisions, to 11 for mechanized divisions, 12 for armored divisions, and 14 for U.S. Marine divisions (which have a lot of extra stuff). American reserve and National Guard divisions, with older equipment, come in 10–20 percent lower. These numbers do not take into account the sometimes considerable qualitative differences resulting from:

Quality and quantity of support equipment. Obvious items enhance combat ability, like engineer, signal, and transportation support, plus more exotic things such as devices for electronic warfare, data processing, and fire control. Also important are procedures for the effective movement of supply and maintenance and repair of equipment before, during, and after combat.

Training and doctrinal differences. Different nations can use identical organization and equipment, but because of different approaches to the selection and training of troops, or the application of the doctrine, there will be substantial qualitative differences. Take, for example, the Argentine and British ground forces in the 1982 Falklands war, where both sides used similar and sometimes identical equipment, organization, and doctrine. Another example is the Libyan and Egyptian armies. In 1973 Egypt finally did what no other Arab army was capable of and stood up to the Israeli army for a while. The Libyan army, also equipped with Russian equipment and doctrine, fell to less heavily armed and less numerous Chadian tribesmen in 1987.

Differences within a national army. Iraq, like many nations, has a smaller number of elite (and politically reliable) units, such as the Republican Guard. Many nations also have reserve divisions that are manned by a small number of full-time troops (5–30 percent of full strength) and use older, less well maintained equipment. The Soviet Union maintained a force of some 200 divisions for nearly 40 years. But only about 60 of these divisions were ready to go at any time. The rest were maintained as reserve divisions. After the Cold War ended, it was revealed that most of these reserve divisions were in very bad shape. Their equipment was poorly maintained, and the reservists who were to join them in wartime were not really ready for combat.

Russia After the Fall of the Soviet Union

One symptom of the USSR's collapse was the spreading refusal of young men to do their compulsory military service. Reservists also were reluctant to cooperate in maintaining the readiness of reserve divisions. Actually, this last phenomenon was seen as early as 1979, when divisions mobilized in Soviet Asia for service in Afghanistan performed with a notable lack of enthusiasm and effectiveness. More problems appeared in 1980, when Russia attempted to mobilize reserve divisions on Poland's border in response to the quickening collapse of Communism in Poland. That mobilization had to be called off. Without willing or at least docile conscripts and reservists, the 200-division force of the former USSR crumbled down to a fraction of its former size. While Russia and Ukraine have grabbed the majority of the USSR's armed forces, only Russia came away with a significant armed force. The Russian army now has 30 divisions (plus 17 reserve divisions), and only about 20 of them are near the level of the former Soviet Union's first-line divisions.

Russia did maintain a force of 50,000 airborne, air mobile, commando, and marine troops of the former USSR. The Spetsnaz (commandos) are particularly good. These troops are a rough bunch, even though largely conscripts. They are selected carefully from volunteers, rigorously trained, and well rewarded with higher pay and many privileges.

Russia plans eventually to have a professional force, relying much less on conscription. The sheer mass of equipment that characterized the Soviet army has been sharply reduced by a shortage of money and conscripts, and by the various treaties negotiated as the Soviet empire was crumbling in the late 1980s and early 1990s. Tens of thousands of tanks and other armored vehicles were destroyed or moved into the Ural Mountains east of Moscow. The treaties allowed them to move the equipment away from Europe and still use it to defend the Asian portion of their territory. However, as the USSR collapsed, these vehicles were orphaned. Most of them lie unattended, out in the open. A few Siberian winters and a lack of maintenance reduced these vehicles to scrap. Aware of this, local governments, as well as the central government, have been selling the newer weapons to other nations and using the older ones for spare parts or scrap metal.

The Soviet-era Russian Motor Rifle Division (often called a Mechanized Infantry Division, which is a more accurate term, anyway) was organized in a fashion still common with many less wealthy nations. The division consisted of a division headquarters (320 men), three motor rifle regiments (2,700 men each), one tank regiment (1,101 men, no motor rifle battalion), an artillery group (1,800 men, 12 100mm guns, 24 122mm rocket launchers, 12 AT-5 ATGM IFVs, 4 SS-21 missile launchers, 72 152mm self-propelled howitzers), an air defense, a ground regiment (302 men, 20 SA-8B or 6 SA-6 SAM launchers), an independent tank battalion (241 men, 51 tanks), a reconnaissance battalion (300 men, 28 IFVs, six tanks, motorcycles), an engineer battalion (380 men), a signal battalion (294 men), a chemical-defense battalion (150 men), and support troops consisting of a maintenance battalion (294 men), a medical battalion (158 men), a transportation battalion (217 men), an aviation company (220 men; 6 Mi-2, 8 Mi-8, and 8 Mi-24 helicopters), and a traffic control company (60 men).

The Soviet-era Russian Tank Division was organized in a fashion still common with many less wealthy nations. It was organized identically to the Motor Rifle Division except for the following changes: three tank regiments (1,580 men, 94 tanks, 51 IFVs, 4 ZSU-23s, 4 SA-13s, 24 122mm self-propelled howitzers, six self-propelled bridges, one motor rifle battalion), one motor rifle regiment, no antitank battalion, and no independent tank battalion.

U.S. and Western Divisions

American and other Western nations have similar divisions in totals of men and equipment. There is one major difference in how they use their divisions. Many nations are using their brigades more as independent units. In effect, the brigades become little divisions, much like the Russian regiments. This has a major advantage in that the battalions in the brigade are a permanent part of the brigade and therefore train regularly. In peacetime the U.S. brigades do keep their battalions together, although combat doctrine stipulates that battalions be shifted freely to other brigades. Another significant difference is the less lavish use of IFVs and ATGMs. The rationale is that, with limited funds, it is better to put the money into fewer and better weapons. Some nations are more lavish with artillery and ammunition.

Overall, the similarities are more prominent than the differences. Western divisions use variations on the U.S. "base" system for their divisions, where support units are common for all divisions. Only the mix of combat battalions differentiates the types of divisions, and the light and airborne divisions use lighter artillery and fewer support battalions. Each divisions has a division headquarters (100–200 troops), three brigade headquarters (100–150 troops each), a variable number of tank and mechanized infantry battalions (six tank and five infantry for an armored division, four tank and six infantry for a mechanized infantry division, all infantry for the light and airborne infantry divisions), a divisional artillery brigade (about 100 guns and rocket launchers, counter-battery radars, and 2,000–3,000 troops), an air-defense battalion (about 600 troops), an engineer battalion (800–900 troops), a Combat Aviation Brigade (1,000–1,500 troops, 150–200 helicopters), a signal battalion (500–600 troops), a military police company (200 troops), a chemical-defense company (150–200 troops), a combat electronic warfare intelligence battalion (about 500 troops), and support troops (2,000–2,500). The support troops total varies a bit as unit organizations are modified, but are the same for infantry and armored divisions. The number of men in the combat battalions is about the same (some 7,000 troops) in the armored and mechanized infantry divisions. The tank division only has about 30 more tanks than the mechanized division.

The U.S. combat division organization underwent many changes in the 1990s as a result of 1980s experiments, the 1991 Gulf War, and the end of the Cold War. For example, in the Gulf War, the engineers were organized into a brigade of three 400-man battalions. This allowed one or two engineer battalions to be assigned to the division's combat brigades. The Combat Aviation Brigade structure is constantly tinkered with, and more heavy truck units are being added to the division.

Germany has tank and infantry battalions similar in size to Russian battalions. Instead of three of these battalions per brigade, there are five (two tank battalions in the infantry brigade, three in the tank brigade). The British and French have a "brigade-oriented" organization. They have, in effect, 4,000–8,000-man divisions that are simply slightly larger versions of the German brigades.

Americans and Germans have relatively few reserve and mobilization divisions. The U.S. reserves are identical to the active units. The German reserves are similar but not identical. Any mobilization of reserves depends on trained manpower and usable equipment.

During World War II, Germany raised the equivalent of 50 mechanized and armored divisions, plus more than 200 Chinese-style infantry divisions (see below). This was done with a similar population and a smaller industrial capacity than Germany possesses today. Most Western nations, particularly the United States, France, and Britain, maintain lighter, non-mechanized units suitable for rapid-air movement units. These are suitable for intervention in faraway places and rugged terrain.

China

The Chinese divisions are actually closely related to the pre-1950 Russian infantry divisions, before Russia mechanized all of these units. The Chinese system does have several advantages. The majority of the troops are long-term volunteers. Promotion is still possible from within the ranks. Troops tend to remain in one regiment for their entire career. Marriage is allowed only for officers and senior noncommissioned officers. There are now 30 pay grades from the lowest recruit to the highest officer, along with more spiffy uniforms. Until the late 1980s, there were no formal ranks, only jobs based on position held (platoon leader, division commander, etc.). Since the early 1980s, China has reduced its troop strength by over a million men, and these reductions continue.

Many of the less efficient infantry divisions were disbanded. More money has been put into buying modern equipment overseas and building more of it in China. After the political crackdowns in 1989, the military received even less money, but then the military budget increased and continues to increase. Better opportunities in the liberalized civilian economy have made it more difficult to obtain high-quality volunteers. This has led to poor morale, lower living conditions, and reduced combat effectiveness. Because the Chinese government looks to the army to protect it from an increasingly restive population, the military budgets were increased in the early 1990s. Much of this increased funding went to higher pay and benefits, but a lot also went to more modern equipment. The Chinese have taken advantage of the collapse of the Soviet Union to purchase Soviet military equipment at fire-sale prices. This has enabled the Chinese to get the most modern Soviet aircraft and technology for

Shoulder-Launched Multipurpose Assault Weapon (SMAW)

the first time. More infantry divisions are being motorized and mechanized using Chinese-built trucks and armored vehicles.

Moreover, there are more obvious disadvantages. In most Chinese divisions, only heavy equipment moves by truck; the infantry walks. There is also a pervasive lack of equipment. Most of what they do have is still outdated by Western and Russian standards. They are further hampered by a lack of recent combat experience. Senior officers are somewhat debased by the use of political reliability as a promotion criterion. This has produced mediocre performance in border battles with combat-experienced Vietnamese troops. Chinese combat power was enhanced by the training, quality, and superior morale of the troops, perhaps an increase of 10–30 percent, depending on the unit. But much of this advantage has been dissipated in recent years. Because of its lack of strategic mobility, the Chinese army is primarily a defensive force. China is trying to change this during the twenty-first century, and this is making its neighbors justifiably nervous.

Infantry Weapons

The chart shows the most common small arms used worldwide. The various other weapons utilized by the infantry will also be described in this section.

Weapon is the weapon's official designation.

Primary user is the nation that is the principal user of the weapon as well as its designer and major manufacturer.

Weapon	Primary user	Caliber	Weapon weight (lbs)	Ammo weight (lbs/100)	Ammo in weapon	Pract. rate of fire/RPM	Eff. range (m)	Used for
M-4	U.S.	7.62	7.5	5.5	25	75	800	Standard infantry rifle
AK-47/M	Russia	7.62	8.8	6.2	30	90	400	Standard infantry rifle
M-16A2	U.S.	5.56	8.8	3.5	30	45	600	Standard infantry rifle
AK-74	Russia	5.45	8.8	4.7	30	100	500	Standard infantry rifle
MG3	Germany	7.62	39.6	6.1	200	200	1,200	Standard LMG
M-240B LMG	U.S.	7.62	27.6	6.1	100	200	1,200	Standard LMG
PKM	Russia	7.62	18.4	6.1	250	200	1,200	Standard LMG
RPK	Russia	7.62	13.5	6.1	40	120	800	Standard Squad LMG
RPK-74	Russia	5.45	13.2	6.1	40	120	600	Standard Squad LMG
M-249 SAW	U.S.	5.56	19.4	5.6	200	200	800	Standard Squad LMG
Barrett 82	U.S.	12.7	33	24	10	15	1,500	Anti-Vehicle Sniper Rifle
SVD	Russia	7.62	10.1	7.3	10	20	800	Standard sniper rifle

Caliber is the diameter of the weapon's projectile, in millimeters (1 inch = 25.4mm).

Weapon weight (lbs) is the weapon's loaded weight in pounds. This is more meaningful than the empty weight, as the weapon can be used only when loaded with ammunition.

Ammo weight (lbs/100) is the weight of 100 rounds of ammunition. This includes the magazine, or metal link weight. Rifles typically have ammunition in magazines; machine-gun rounds are linked together with metal fasteners. Without magazines or links, ammunition has the following weights (rounds per pound): Russian 5.45mm, 43; U.S. 5.56mm, 40; Western 7.62mm, 19; Russian, 7.62mm (short, AK-47), 42; 7.62mm (long, used in PKM and SVD), 32. The .50 caliber stuff is heavy enough (about four ounces per round) that you could do some damage just throwing it at someone.

Ammo in weapon is the number of rounds normally loaded in the weapon. Machine guns fire ammo in theoretically endless belts of linked rounds. As a practical matter, the belt is long enough to carry in a box hanging from the weapon (up to 100 rounds). This allows the machine gun to be portable and handled by one man.

Pract. rate of fire/RPM is the practical rate of fire per minute. These weapons have theoretical rates of fire between 600–1,300 rounds per minute. Several factors make the practical rate lower:

- *Impaired accuracy at high rates of fire is the major limitation.* As an automatic weapon fires, it recoils. Although modern weapons have reduced this recoil considerably, it still exists and throws off the aim. Bursts of 5–10 rounds are generally more effective than a steady stream of bullets. Don't believe what you see in the movies when the actor fires a weapon at full automatic and constantly hits something. In practice, a machine gun with a high rate of fire, used with small bursts, is used as a long-range shotgun. This has proved to be the most effective way of killing people with machine guns.
- *Barrel overheating is a more common, and serious, problem.* Depending on the weather, especially tropical temperatures and exposure to the sun, a machine-gun barrel quickly overheats if the practical rate of fire is exceeded for a few minutes. The result is that rounds fire without the trigger being pulled ("cooking off") because the excessive heat ignites the propellant without the firing pin hitting the tiny explosive "igniter" at the base of the cartridge. Rounds also become jammed due to heat expansion, and the weapon becomes useless. For this reason, water-

cooled machine guns were used up through the Korean War, and some nations still use them. The water jacket around the barrel was heavy and prone to failure, but the constant stream of steam escaping from the jacket assured the gunner that he could keep firing. The water cooling also reduced barrel wear and maintained the accuracy of the machine gun. A better solution for the heat problem was removable barrels, a technique the Germans pioneered during World War II and others adopted. However, the overheating problem was most frequently solved by the gunners exercising discipline when using their weapons. Those who did not were frequently found dead next to a jammed machine gun.

- *Ammunition supply.* Under the best of conditions, it takes a least a few seconds to change magazines. More time is required to load a new belt. Care must be taken during these operations to prevent jams. You can also run out of ammo.
- *Dirt and fouling.* A machine gun is a precision piece of machinery designed to work under severe stress (a rapid succession of bullets exploding their propellant and forcing a bullet through the barrel at high speed). Dirt can get in any of the moving parts and jam the mechanical parts. Each bullet fired leaves some of its propellant in the barrel, "fouling" it and reducing accuracy. Dust and dirt can also enter the barrel, or other portions of the weapon, also fouling the barrel. You can often tell if troops are well trained by how well they take care of their weapons when not using them. If you see troops marching along with their weapons wrapped in cloth or plastic, and sometimes with a condom fitted over the barrel, you are looking at pros. These guys will have cleaner and more effective weapons when they actually have to use them. These troops will also take their weapons apart and clean them at every opportunity. Professional troops know that clean weapons can be a matter of life and death.

Eff. range (meters) is the average effective range of the weapon in meters. With any weapon, a superb marksman can obtain hits at twice the average ranges. As a practical matter, there aren't many marksmen in the ranks. Even if there were, the opportunities for accurate shooting are rare in combat. Most firing is done in bursts at fleeting targets. On the battlefield, you keep your head down and move quickly. If you don't, you get killed. Other major factors in the effective range are the design of the weapons and their ammunition, as well as troop training. A weapon that is designed to remain steady when fired will produce greater accuracy. This was one of the major reasons for the move to the smaller but faster 5.56mm round. Ammunition design can also produce greater accuracy and more lethal results. The latest types of 5.56mm rounds can pierce 15mm (.6 inch) IFV armor at 100 meters. Although a larger 7.62mm round can do this at 400 meters, most shooting opportunities are at the shorter range. Aimed fire is possible out to 800 meters (half a mile), and both 5.56mm and

7.62mm rounds are capable of this range. The probability of deliberately hitting anything at the range is quite low. This is where machine guns come in, as they can put dozens of bullets near the target at ranges of 1,000 meters for 5.56mm rounds and 2,000 meters for 7.62mm. Battlefield experience in the last century has shown that 1,000 meters is sufficient range for infantry weapons. Most bullets' strikes cannot be spotted beyond the range of the tracer burnout, which is about 900 meters with most 7.62mm bullets. Beyond that, you need another fellow with powerful binoculars to spot the landmarks for the gunners to aim for. Note that all the above ranges are for bullets hitting an unprotected man. Flak jackets and some of the newer helmets will make nonfatal, if not harmless, hits. One still finds all those unprotected arms, legs, and faces to be injured. Accuracy is about the same for both calibers. Firing two- or three-round bursts at a six-foot-diameter target and using a bipod, the following percentage of hits were obtained with 30 rounds (5.56mm/7.62mm): 300 meters, 81 percent /81 percent; 400 meters, 73 percent /77 percent; 600 meters, 55 percent /41 percent. Contrary to popular myth, the lighter 5.56mm rounds are no more likely to be deflected by underbrush than the heavier and slower 7.62mm bullets.

The weapons shown in the chart are representative of hundreds of similar models in use throughout the world. The infantry rifle or "assault rifle" is the weapon most commonly used in any army. The AK-47 is a copy of the German SG-44 assault rifle. The SG-44 saw extensive use during the last year of World War II, and the Soviets wisely adopted it. It uses a shorter 7.62mm round. Over 50 million have been produced, and most are still in working order somewhere. The M-16 is a high-velocity .22 caliber (5.56mm) weapon that was first proposed in the late 1930s. World War II intervened, and it took thirty years for the idea finally to be accepted. Gradually, nations are converting to this new caliber. The AK-74 is a Soviet version of the M-16, developed about 10 years after the M-16 was first introduced during the Vietnam war. The two AKs are good examples of how the Russians observe the success of military technology and then adopt it themselves. China is still a major manufacturer of AK-47s (and M-16s, also). The Chinese can manufacture an AK-47 for under $20 and are still exporting hundreds of thousands a year in order to obtain hard currency. There are dozens of M-16-type weapons produced around the world. One recent innovation is the M-4, which is basically a lightweight version of the M-16 for commandos.

The next most common weapon is the LMG (light machine gun). These weapons are widely used by the infantry and are often mounted on vehicles. Although the 5.56mm round was quickly adopted as the infantryman's personal weapon, it took a few years for most armies to accept the fact that this round was adequate for machine gun use, also. Another factor influencing the decision to adopt the smaller-caliber LMG was the problem of supplying two types of ammunition. However, the changeover is not complete in any army. Partially, this is because armies have a large investment in 7.62mm machine guns, which are expensive (over $1,000) and last a long time (easily over 20 years). Another reason for holding on to the 7.62mm LMG is that it is easier to design an effective armor-piercing round for this weapon. Only the light armor of IFVs can be defeated, but that can be a significant capability. Most of the current 7.62 LMGs (MG-3, M-60, and PKM) are derived from the German World War II MG-42, the first widely used machine gun with an easily replaceable barrel.

The lighter squad LMG is a Russian innovation. The Russians solved the problem of having two sizes of ammunition by issuing the infantry squads LMGs that use the same lighter round that the AKs use. These LMGs are heavy-duty versions of the assault rifle with a heavier barrel and capable of using magazine or belted ammunition. The United States eventually adopted this practice, while the Russians came out with a new squad LMG to complement their 5.45mm assault rifle. The United States soon followed with a similar weapon, as have many other nations.

Sniper rifles are commonly used in a specialized form of combat. In many armies, 2 or 3 percent of the infantry are trained and equipped as snipers. Their weapon is generally a nonautomatic rifle using a full-size (7.62mm) round. In most cases, these weapons are standard rifles that are rebuilt to higher standards of reliability and accuracy and equipped with special sights and other features. A good marksman can also be quite deadly with the standard assault rifle and its

M-82A1A .50 caliber sniper rifle

lighter round. A new development has been the .50 caliber (12.7mm) sniper rifle, based on the old reliable M-2 .50 caliber machine gun. The "lightweight" sniper version of the .50 caliber is not for killing people at 2,500 meters on human targets. It takes special ammo, a finely tuned weapon, and a scope to hit a man-size target at 2,500 meters. The main reason for the .50 caliber sniper rifles is to hit hard targets (Scud launchers, light armored vehicles, trucks, radar gear, etc.) at long range. This was done by the British Special Air Service (SAS) during the 1991 Gulf War. Moreover, a sniper armed with a .50 caliber rifle is at a disadvantage at closer ranges, for normally a sniper is only a hundred meters or so away from his targets and must be able to move around a bit. This is not easy with a 30-pound rifle. But at 500 meters or more behind the front line, a .50 caliber rifle using armor-piercing or incendiary rounds can do a lot of damage to trucks and light armored vehicles. You can also get match (highly accurate at long range) rounds, but these are more expensive. As it is, a normal round costs a couple of bucks, and an armor-piercing round (the discarding sabot kind the Marine Corps uses) costs $7.50 each.

Other Infantry Weapons

Heavy machine guns. These are not exactly infantry weapons, as they are not portable and are usually mounted on vehicles. Because most infantry now operates with its own IFVs, these weapons do qualify as infantry weapons. Except for their larger caliber (12.7mm–30mm), they operate much like infantry machine guns. These weapons have a longer range and more hitting power and tend to concentrate their fire on vehicles or aircraft. These heavy machine guns are also capable of using more effective armor-piercing projectiles. In a pinch, the infantry does not hesitate to turn such awesome firepower against two-legged targets. In some cases, the heavy machine guns are taken from the vehicles and installed within fortifications.

Automatic grenade launchers. To provide heavier firepower for the infantry, the automatic grenade launcher was developed in the 1960s. This was a slower-firing machine gun whose slower-moving, high-explosive shells had the effect of covering an area with exploding "grenades" (the shells). This weapon fires a 30mm–40mm shell similar to the one used in the shotgun-like attachment for U.S. and Russian assault rifles. The United States first deployed an automatic version on helicopters during the Vietnam War. In the late 1960s, a ground-based version, the M-19 machine gun, was deployed. Russia came out with a 30mm copy in the early 1970s. The U.S. ground version weighs 140 pounds and fires a 9-ounce shell as far as 2,000 meters. It takes 17 seconds for shells to travel this distance. An armor-piercing shell can penetrate over 60mm of armor. In other words, IFVs can be knocked out with the M-19's 40mm shell.

During the 1980s, various night sights were added, making the M-19 a powerful weapon for attacking or defending at night. The Russian version, the 30mm AGS-17, weighs only 90 pounds and has a maximum range of 1,700 meters. Each 30mm round weighs about 6 ounces and is not guaranteed to penetrate IFV armor. Both U.S. and Russian weapons have an effective rate of fire of 100 rounds a minute. The U.S. M-19 jams once every 5,000 rounds or so. The cruder Russian model jams once every 1,000 rounds, and the shell often explodes in the process. These accidents are not always fatal but must have an adverse effect on users' attitudes toward the weapon. The first major user of the U.S. weapon was the Marines, which equips each battalion with 10 weapons. The U.S. Army now uses them nearly as much as the Marines, and Army troops and commanders were impressed with the weapon's performance in combat during the 1991 Gulf War. Russia deploys eight AGS-17s to each infantry battalion. The grenade launchers have proved more effective than the older, and still widely used, 12mm–15mm heavy machine guns.

Pistols. These are rather useless on the battlefield, although handy in tunnels and buildings. They are generally carried by officers and operators of heavy weapons and equipment. Combat officers prefer an assault rifle. The primary problem with pistols is poor accuracy, it being difficult to hit a man-size target beyond 25 meters. Even if you hit someone, pistols don't have the same stopping power as rifles. Moreover, pistols carry less than half as many rounds as assault rifles. One solution to the shortcomings of pistols was the machine pistol (also known as a "submachine gun"). This is a magazine-fed pistol with a longer barrel. Still not much stopping power, but you can fire more rounds with more accuracy. Out to 100 meters, these weapons are pretty effective. The success of these weapons in World War II (the Sten gun and the MP-40) led to the development of the SG-44, AK-47, and M-16 assault rifles. At present, machine pistols are used primarily by police.

Grenades. Grenades are small bombs weighing about a pound. Upon detonation, the common fragmentation grenade releases projectiles that can wound exposed personnel out to a radius of up to 15 meters. Most modern fragmentation grenades release hundreds of light, high-speed fragments that are readily stopped by obstacles a bullet would easily pass through. Although movies show a large explosion and bodies flying through the air, real grenades carry a small explosive charge that will throw up dust and knock a man down if he is very close. Noise is the prominent characteristic, plus a drizzle of tiny spent fragments. And don't try to pull the arming pin with your teeth, unless a dentist is handy to repair the damage. The most common grenade is the fragmentation type, good only against people. Other important types are smoke (for some concealment, depending on the wind), high explosive (for blast effect, to stun someone close by without worrying about fragments), thermite (for burning things up, including metal), illumination (turns night into day), riot control (tear gas, good for clearing out bunkers or otherwise discomforting the opposition), and marker (colored smoke, to show aircraft where to land or drop, or not drop, something).

The most commonly used grenade is the "defensive grenade," so called because it throws fragments as far as possible and is thus best employed when the user is hiding behind some cover. "Offensive grenades" are largely explosive with few fragments. This is so the user can throw them short distances while they are in the open and not have to worry about getting hit by fragments. The average fragmentation grenade injures nearly everyone within 2 meters of the explosion, 75 percent of those within 4 meters, 50 percent of those within 6 meters, 25 percent of those within 10 meters, 5–10 percent of those 15 meters away, and less than 1 percent of those 20 meters away. Older grenades, of World War II vintage, were less effective because their fragments were larger, fewer, and slower, and much of their destructive effect tended to hit the ground harmlessly. Grenades were first developed several hundred years ago to solve the problem of delivering firepower around or over an obstacle without exposing the user. Fighting in built-up areas would be more costly for the attacker were it not for grenades. The easiest way to clear out a cave, bunker, trench, or roomful of enemy troops is to heave in a grenade. Grenades can be thrown no more than 40 meters, with 20–30 meters being a more common extreme range. Most grenades are of the fragmentation type, with four or five ounces of explosive and a 3–5-second fuse.

Variations on the grenade include rifle-launched grenades. These are not widely used by American or Russian forces, but are popular with many other armies. The bullet is used to propel various types of grenades from the barrel. Their range is over 100 meters, although accuracy is acquired only after practice. Grenade launchers, which are quite different from rifle-launched grenades, are popular with U.S. forces, sending 40mm projectiles ("grenades") out over 300 meters from a shotgun-like weapon, or about 100 meters from a tube-like device fitted under the barrel of an M-16. Rifle-launched grenades are about as effective as thrown grenades, while the 40mm version is about half as powerful.

Mortars. Mortars are the artillery infantry carry with them, so mortars must be kept light. Although capable of high rates of fire (up to 30 rounds a minute), little ammunition can be hauled. The infantry has to maintain its mobility and cannot afford to go into battle weighed down with a lot of extra equipment. With all these restrictions, the chief virtue of mortars is their ability to respond rapidly and accurately to the infantry's need for additional firepower. An additional advantage is the mortar's ability to hit targets behind obstacles. Mortars' shells are fired at a sharp angle (sometimes almost straight up). The most common infantry mortars are 81mm. They weigh about 100 pounds and fire shells

M-19 40mm automatic grenade launcher

weighing 12–15 pounds at maximum ranges of 3,000–4,000 meters. The heavier 120mm mortar weighs 700 pounds and fires a 33-pound shell out to 6,000 meters. These are almost always mounted inside APCs, as are many of the 81mm types. This allows these mortars to carry more ammo with them, but not as much as the regular artillery units farther back. To alleviate this problem, some armies are using mortar rounds with sensor and maneuver control mechanisms in them. This allows the mortar round to find armored vehicles and guide themselves to the target. A lot more expensive than the usual high-explosive or ICM mortar round, the guided round vastly improves the anti-armor capability of mortars. The 60mm mortar continues to be used by non-mechanized infantry. It weighs 50 pounds and, like the 81mm version, can be broken down into two or three components for carrying. Shells weigh less than 10 pounds and can be fired out to 3,500 meters.

Mines and other surprises. Land mines and their cousins, booby traps, are classic infantry weapons. These are defensive weapons and enable the infantry to resist more effectively larger forces and armored vehicles. In more mobile situations, mines are used to encourage the enemy to move in another direction (where you have set up an ambush). Mines are also used to guard an area when you don't have troops available for the job. The chief limitations of mines are their weight and the time required to emplace them. As a rule of thumb, it takes 1 ton of mines to cover every 100 meters of front, and 10 man-hours per ton to emplace them. You can use special machines to plant them, but such equipment is not always available. Mines should be emplaced while the enemy isn't looking, in order to maintain the element of surprise. To overcome these limitations, lightweight "scatterable" mines are becoming more common. Mines are surprise weapons; they are customarily laid in areas covered by the fire of other infantry weapons to prevent the enemy from discovering their presence until it is too late, and then the covering fire makes it more difficult for the attacker to clear the mines. Mines are also laid (dropped on the ground) quickly by artillery shell or aircraft. There is currently an international treaty prohibiting the manufacture or use of antipersonnel land mines. But the largest manufacturers and users of these mines (the United States, Russia, and China) have not signed on. The treaty is largely a protest and public relations exercise against the use of mines by rebel and terrorist organizations. These folks are not going to stop using them.

Similar to mines are booby traps, which are grenades, mines, or other explosives rigged with trip wires or other devices to make them detonate when the victim stumbles over them. The casualties are bad enough; the effects on troop morale are worse. A land mine planted under an inch or so of dirt is just another form of booby trap. Some mines are meant to be dug up and reused if the enemy never encounters them. This takes three or four times as long as it took to lay them. Many mines are now made of plastic, which makes them much more difficult to clear, as you have to use a portable radar to search

M-18 (claymore) mine

under the dirt. Such was the case in the Falklands and, to a lesser extent, Kuwait, where uncleared plastic mines will continue to kill wayward people and animals for many years to come. Considering the dozens of people killed each year in Europe because of uncleared World War I and II mines and shells, we have to assume that any major modern war will keep on killing for a century after the fighting officially stopped.

Mine technology has taken tremendous strides since the 1960s. Microelectronics and other technical advances have spawned new generations of smaller, lighter, and more lethal mines. The first of these were the track-buster mines. Weighing 2–5 pounds each, they are not buried but are dropped in the path of advancing armored vehicles. The mines can only blow the track off an armored vehicle, but this is enough to immobilize it temporarily. Should this happen in combat, the crippled vehicle is in great peril and usually abandoned by its crew. Another version of the scatterable mine has a magnetic sensor that causes a shaped charge to explode upward when a large metal object passes overhead. This does not blow the track but penetrates the thin bottom armor of tanks and IFVs. This will do some damage and may ignite ammo or fuel and destroy the vehicle. Along with the antitank mines come antipersonnel devices, making a quick exit from crippled tanks on the battlefield, or searching for antitank mines, a risky endeavor. Many Western mines have a self-destruct feature, which takes effect from several hours to several days after they are deployed. This makes them less of a menace to your own troops, who later must travel the same ground. As expected (by the troops, not the manufacturers), a large number of the self-destruct devices did not work when first used on a wide scale in Kuwait. About 10 percent of the mines stayed active beyond their self-destruct deadline, causing casualties long after the fighting had been successfully concluded. Worse yet, many of these smaller mines are not laid carefully in the ground but are scattered from bombs, artillery shells, and dispensers on aircraft and helicopter. This gives the combat troops yet another cause of random mayhem to worry about.

We now have robotic mines (an American innovation), with their own sensors and computer and the ability to sense, track, and fire on armored vehicles. These smaller mines also can be delivered quickly by artillery or aircraft. This makes artillery and air support against an armored attack more efficient than before, when high-explosive shells were the most common weapon available. Other developments in mine warfare have been more efficient remote-control mines, which can be detonated by the defending infantry on command. Some of these smart mines are specifically designed to attack helicopters flying nearby. All of this activity in mine development springs from the historical record. In past wars, mines accounted for up to 50 percent of armored vehicle losses in some battles. The percentage appears to be headed upward, much to the infantryman's relief.

Electronic aids and other gadgets. The revolution in electronics has assisted the infantry in many ways. The most useful tools are observation devices. The infantry now has its own radar and, even more useful, passive night-vision equipment. The latter are called "starlight scopes"—vision devices that electronically magnify available light so that night no longer covers enemy movement. These are attached to weapons and vehicles or are simply used to detect troops that can be attacked with mortars or artillery. These devices proved enormously useful in Vietnam and particularly in their first mobile use during the 1991 Gulf War. Other sensors are covered in more detail in Chapter 19 (electronic warfare).

3

Tanks: The Arm of Decision

Tanks possess a lot of firepower (about a third of a mechanized division's firepower), are hard to kill, and cost a lot ($2–5 million each). Yet their crews represent less than 8 percent of an armored division's manpower. Tanks usually spend most of their time hiding or looking for a place to hide. They must do this because their considerable firepower makes them a prime target. However, the concentrated combat power of tanks makes them, alone of all the combat arms, capable of forcing a decision quickly and decisively.

The "arm of decision" hasn't always operated this way. Traditionally there have been three distinct combat forces in land warfare. First there was the infantry, which took a lot of abuse and was absolutely necessary. Then came the missile troops—spear throwers, slingers, archers, and artillery—who were protected by the infantry because the missile troops were better at killing the enemy at a distance than they were at defending themselves. Finally, there was the cavalry: infantry or missile troops on horses. Better armed, trained, and motivated than their unmounted associates, the cavalry were the shock troops. Normally the cavalry was held back either to turn a stalemate into a victory or to mitigate a defeat.

When horse cavalry became obsolete in the early part of the twentieth century, its functions and traditions were transferred to the tank troops, sometimes with strange results. Initially, particularly during the early stages of World War II, many armor units attempted to storm their way through the opposition. They soon learned that the opposition could shoot back with deadly effect. Sitting behind all that armor, many tank crews feel invulnerable. Experienced tankers know better. They also know that if they are careful, they can avoid getting hurt.

    The importance of being careful is a lesson the mounted troops have had
to relearn many times over the centuries. The 1991 Gulf War risks giving U.S.
tank crews a false sense of invulnerability. In that war, most U.S. tanks were of
the latest design and fought against a previous generation of Russian tanks
equipped with ineffective Iraqi-made tank shells. Fortunately, today's U.S.
Army tank crews are the most professional America has ever had in peacetime.
The officers and NCOs are already spending a lot of time disabusing the troops
of any illusions of invulnerability. The next opponent is likely to be better prepared and equipped.

What Tanks Cannot Do

World War II destroyed, at great cost, the various myths about what tanks could
do. Each one of the tank no-nos in turn define what a tanker's life is all about.
Tanks cannot advance on the enemy without thorough and continuous ground
reconnaissance. Tanks are delicate beasts and cannot go just anywhere. Their
movements should be planned to take advantage of cover from enemy observation. Tanks are large (25 feet long, 12 feet wide, and 8–10 feet high). Tanks can
often be heard a long way off, as they sound like a bulldozer, except louder.
The tracklaying mechanism is there to move the 40–60-ton vehicle over rough
terrain without getting stuck. But armored vehicles can have problems, anyway, when they encounter excessively steep slopes and overly soft ground.
Terrain that is very broken up with rocks and tree stumps will cause the tank's
track to pop off. It usually takes several hours to replace the track.

Tanks cannot operate by themselves. When the tank is "buttoned up" with all
hatches closed, the crew can see only through slits, gun sights, and periscopes.
They cannot see very much, and the crew spends most of its time running the
tank, not looking for some foot soldier sneaking up on it. This makes tanks
very vulnerable to infantry, especially in close terrain or built-up areas. Tanks
may look dangerous, but since they can only shoot at what they can see, a nimble infantryman can usually stay out of harm's way. The infantry knows this
and strives to defend in broken terrain when facing tanks. One survival technique for tanks facing infantry is the U.S. Army's "overwatch." Half a tank unit
gets into a position from which it can observe the advance of the other half.
The moving group then advances into positions to observe the movement of
the other group. This is actually the ancient "you advance and I'll cover you"
technique. This "moving by bounds" is safer, but slower. In combat, time is a
luxury. If tanks cannot be accompanied by infantry, which usually slows them
down, its only other recourse is for the commander of every tank to keep his
head out of the hatch. The Israelis use this technique. You win a lot of battles,
but you lose a lot of tank commanders.

Ideally, tanks support infantry. The exception is when the combat is on flat, featureless terrain, where the tank commanders can see any enemy infantry a long way off. In terrain with cover (forests, hills, buildings, etc.), the infantry advances on foot just ahead of the tanks. When your infantry encounters opposition, it keeps the enemy infantry from getting at your tanks. The tanks then use their firepower to assist their infantry in clearing out the opposing foot soldiers. The infantry's eyes and ears are thus complemented by the tanks' massive firepower. Against good infantry in "busy" (forested or urban) terrain, tanks cannot operate efficiently by themselves. As the U.S. Marines put it, "Hunting tanks is fun and easy," ever more so when the tanks charge ahead of their own infantry. Well-trained tank units do not do this. The tanks would prefer to take a shot at the enemy but can do this only in a fluid battlefield where their speed and long-range weapons can operate to best effect. Most of the time, the tanks creep forward under the infantry's protection. In any case, the infantry will be killed off more easily than the tanks. Even with its own armored personnel carriers, the infantry is more vulnerable. But to be effective, the infantry must dismount and expose itself to enemy fire. Even if infantry and tanks operate together efficiently, tanks will still be around after most of the infantry has been lost. At that point the tanks advance only at greater risk.

It's gotten worse of late as infantry has gotten in the habit of staying in its IFVs rather than getting out and walking along with the tanks. This situation developed when tanks became more mobile over rough ground in the 1980s and 1990s. Tanks got in the habit of moving out faster than foot troops could keep up. So the infantry rode along in its IFVs. All this was possible because American troops have not had to take tanks into cities since Vietnam. The Russians know better because of their recent experience, and American tank officers have been studying this. But there has been no change in the way American, or most non-Russian, tank units operate.

Tanks cannot operate in massed formations. A massed formation is tanks operating closer than 100 meters from one another. Bunched-up tanks only attract fire from artillery and antitank weapons. Typically, artillery will not destroy a tank, but it can put it out of action by damaging the engine or tracks, not to mention the external components of the tank's sensors. The tank's fire-control equipment is particularly vulnerable, as are defensive items like smoke dispensers and the antiaircraft machine gun atop the turret.

No one has perfected a really cost-effective artillery shell that can home in on individual tanks. But even old-fashioned high-explosive shells can wreck a tank unit if enough shells are fired. The shells can't destroy the tanks, but they can damage enough tank equipment to make the tanks ineffective until repaired. The repairs can take days or weeks. Artillery and air strikes attack small areas and will harm only tanks that are in that area. The more the tanks spread out, the less likely they are to get hit. ATGMs also do better if they find a lot of targets close to one another. If one ATGM target momentarily ducks behind some smoke or other cover, the missile operator can quickly shift to another target. Tanks that keep their distance on the battlefield last longer.

Tanks cannot survive with untrained crews. An effective tank crew operates as a team. A team is created by allowing a crew to operate with its tank for about six months together. This is not always accomplished, even in peacetime. During a war, the attrition among less capable crews is very high. It's not uncommon for over 50 percent of inadequately trained crews to be lost in their first battle. The slaughter is especially intense if ill-trained crews are attacking. A grim example occurred in the Golan Heights during the 1973 war. Hundreds of poorly trained Syrian armored vehicles advanced against far fewer Israeli tanks. The Israelis were better trained and made few mistakes. The Syrians were advancing in formation and were paying little attention to advantageous terrain or Israeli maneuvers. The Israelis noted this and methodically fell back from one piece of defensive terrain to the next, picking off a few Syrian vehicles between each move. The Syrians lost 10 vehicles for each Israeli one lost. The Israelis knew their terrain, and their crews knew how to move and shoot effectively. The Syrians were deficient in both respects and blindly followed the Soviet doctrine they had been taught. Better-trained Syrian crews would have been more effective at avoiding Israeli fire and more accurate in their own shooting. The Syrians demonstrated the effects of better training in the 1982 Lebanon war, where the ratio of destroyed Israeli and Syrian tanks was not nearly as lopsided as in 1973. History is full of similar examples.

Unfortunately, training is expensive. Tank crews using Russian training methods are at a considerable disadvantage because they typically use their vehicles very little in training. Russian vehicles are built inexpensively and wear out quickly. The Russians have observed that combat vehicles don't survive long in battle, so why build them to last? In peacetime, the crews train with crude simulators and spend less time in their vehicles than do Western crews. In addition, Western armies have more effective crew simulators and training equipment. As the performance of U.S. tank crews in the Gulf War demonstrated, these differences in training levels were very evident on the battlefield.

Tanks cannot move long distances without running into serious maintenance problems. Long movements require careful planning. If you run tanks too hard, most of them will break down. There have been many tank campaigns since 1939 where most of the losses have come from mechanical failure, not enemy action. Such losses can be reduced considerably by checking the route you plan to send tanks over and making provisions for regular maintenance. Tanks are simply not built to move more than a few hundred kilometers without stopping for maintenance. Weighing 40–70 tons and moving on tracks, they are designed for speeds of up to 60 kilometers per hour but not for long periods. Russian tanks break down, on average, every 250 kilometers. Western vehicles last about 300 kilometers. With adequate maintenance support, most of these breakdowns can be repaired in less than an hour, or a few hours at most. Even so, a division of 300 tanks moving 100 kilometers (three hours' marching) will average 100 or more breakdowns. At the very beginning of a campaign, when all the vehicles are fresh, the rate will be much less but will increase later to compensate for the initial free ride. In other words, the breakdowns will increase about the same time you make contact with the enemy. Breakdowns will also increase as you stress the vehicles, as you would while maneuvering against the opposition. Depending on the tanks' condition, the crews' maintenance training, and the efficiency of the tank-maintenance units, a division will lose 2 to over 20 percent of its vehicles per hour of movement. Most of these crippled vehicles will get going again and catch up, but the effect will be disorganized units, run-down vehicles and crews, and generally less effective combat divisions. Normally, tanks are moved long distances overland by train or truck. If tanks have to march long distances, there will be a price paid in spare parts and man-hours. Both may not be available, resulting in a lot of broken-down vehicles along the march route. Losses can easily exceed 50 percent. As far as the enemy is concerned, a tank lost to a worn-out transmission is just as advantageous as one hit by an antitank missile. Tanks cannot neglect routine maintenance.

Maintenance is one of the less glamorous aspects of working with tanks. Tanks require a lot of it to keep them in top shape. Eight man-hours a day is not unusual if you use the vehicle a lot and want to maintain it in excellent condition. Keeping tanks in such good shape is becoming more difficult. The amount of equipment being added to tanks is increasing, especially electronics. At the same time, there is a trend toward smaller crews (three instead of four). The smaller crew is achieved by installing an automatic gun-loading mechanism. One possible solution is that "ground crews" be made available to tanks, to service them the way aircraft are after each flight. Unfortunately, tanks don't fly back to a relatively secure airbase after each combat mission. They are always at risk when in a combat zone. The maintenance problem is worse for Russian-type tank units, as they have more three-man tanks and crews that are less capable and diligent about maintenance in the first place. This was a key factor in the low readiness level of Iraqi tanks in the Gulf War. Tanks cannot operate successfully without adequate recovery and repair units. As pointed out above, armored vehicles are prone to breakdown. During and after battles, tank repair crews go out to get damaged vehicles running again. Tanks are basically robust but have many things that can fail and immobilize them. After a battle it is possible to repair over 50 percent of the vehicles knocked out by enemy action. For noncombat losses, recovery approaches 100 percent.

Frequently, damaged vehicles must be hauled back to a repair facility. This is done by recovery vehicles that are turretless, unarmed tanks. The proportion of vehicles returned to service depends on the number and skill of your repair and recovery units.

To appreciate the scope of the repair and recovery problem, consider the number of things that can go wrong in a tank. These vehicles have numerous major failure-prone systems:

- First there is the tracklaying mechanism upon which the tank travels. Hit an obstacle at the wrong angle and the track falls off. This is a common problem with inexperienced, or fatigued, drivers. It can take a few hours to get the track back on. Tracks also wear out. After anywhere from 1,000–3,000 kilometers, it's replacement time. All those wheels and rollers associated with the tracks require lubrication and inspection for wear and tear. More so than with an automobile, the driving controls, transmission, brakes, and so on must be inspected frequently and maintained to avoid complete failure. Otherwise, failure tends to come when you can least afford it.
- The tank engine is also in a class by itself. Typically a diesel, although the U.S. M-1 uses a gas turbine (the heart of a jet engine), these mechanisms generate 500–1,500 horsepower and are under considerable stress.
- Although there's plenty of work required just to keep the tank moving, it's all for nothing if the vehicle's weapons are not maintained. A tank's weapons are mounted in a 10-ton turret, which is moved about by another complex mechanism of electric motors and bearings. The main gun and machine guns must be cleaned and resighted periodically, usually after much firing or hard movement. Ignore weapons maintenance and you steadily lose accuracy.
- Finally, we must deal with the electronics. A fire-control system contains precision optics and frequently one or more computers. Most modern tanks use a laser range finder that is very accurate, but very complex. To assist the main gun there is an infrared searchlight and/or a light amplification system. Most tanks also have smoke-grenade dischargers (small mortars), radios, an intercom system, and sometimes air conditioning and an automatic fire-extinguishing system. Many Russian tanks are now supplied with shells that are actually guided missiles, which require a separate fire-control system. Supporting all this is an extensive electrical system.

To assist maintenance, crews use checklists, tool kits, manuals, and some test equipment. The complexity of some tanks exceeds that of many aircraft. But it all comes down to the people. If the crew is attentive to maintenance, and is backed up by adequate repair and recovery units, you will have more tanks on the battlefield and recover more once the combat is over. No tank unit is perfect, and some of the above rules will always be broken under the best of conditions. On average, the situation is quite bad.

The urgency of wartime conditions regularly forces commanders and troops to forego observation of the above maintenance rules. Combat and non-combat losses can be very heavy. World War II and recent experience indicate that tank losses will be five to six times personnel losses during heavy combat. That is, if a unit losses 10 percent of its personnel, it will lose 50–60 percent of its tanks and other armored fighting vehicles. However, past experience shows that up to 60 percent of combat tank losses and nearly all noncombat losses can be repaired. Depending on the repair facilities available, a division could return half its disabled vehicles back to service in less than a week. A lot depends on availability of spare parts, which are scarce, even though destroyed or damaged vehicles are stripped of useable components. Another critical factor is the mechanical capabilities of the tank crewmen. All this assumes that the wrecked vehicles could be recovered. The side that is driven from the battlefield loses more than the battle.

Tank Units

Tanks almost always operate with infantry but actually belong to purely tank units. These tank battalions are largely administrative organizations, to make the enormous maintenance load easier to handle. Tanks are organized into platoons of three to five vehicles. A company is three or four platoons plus one or two headquarters tanks. A battalion has three companies, plus a few tanks in a headquarters, for a total of 33–60 tanks. Tactical experience has shown that the three-tank platoon is most efficient. In this respect, tanks are used like fighter aircraft, using a "loose deuce" formation where one tank is the lead element supported by one or more "wingmen" behind and off to the side. Tank units rarely remain at full strength long in combat, so two-tank platoons are common. Tank battalions usually have small ATGM, reconnaissance, mortar, headquarters, ammunition, fuel, and maintenance units added, placing the battalion strength 50–300 men above the tank crews alone. Russian-type armies add most of these specialist units to the tank regiment.

Tank Tactics

Unlike the infantry, a tank cannot easily sneak up on anyone, although in some cases it can get within a few hundred meters of enemy infantry undetected. Even during an artillery barrage, a tank tends to announce its imminent arrival with a cacophony of distinctive noises. Tanks produce two noises, the engine roar and the track squeak. The squeak and squeal of the tracks is louder and easier to pinpoint. The gas turbines on the U.S. M-1 make remarkably little noise.

What a tank can do is survive a lot of punishment and still deliver substantial firepower. And through all this, tanks are able to flit about the battlefield at better than 500 meters a minute. Tanks are not invulnerable, just tough to kill. With all the firepower they attract, the crew tends to hunker down inside, making their view of the outside world somewhat limited. As described elsewhere, the foot soldiers and tanks work with each other. This ordinarily means the tanks spend most of their time moving at speeds closer to 20–30 meters a minute. Tanks do not have their own tactics, only procedures for tanks working with infantry. The best way to integrate tanks with infantry has not yet been agreed upon. For over 50 years a debate has raged over whether it is better for the tanks or infantry to lead the attack. At the moment, a majority of opinion opts for infantry first, but a lot depends on the situation. There are situations where a company or even a battalion of tanks can successfully operate independently. Some armies use both methods, depending on the situation, with tanks in front, infantry right behind or beside them, and light armored vehicles (IFVs) a hundred meters or so to the rear. Because the infantry has their own IFVs to ride in, it is possible for both tanks and infantry to move quickly when the enemy is not in the immediate vicinity. Under such conditions, the long columns of tanks and IFVs (and self-propelled artillery plus antiaircraft and other support vehicles) stand ready to go through a multiphase deployment maneuver if the enemy is detected nearby. Assuming the reconnaissance units are able to find the enemy before your columns get ambushed, the armored columns will first deploy into several smaller columns, moving cross-country.

Just before the enemy comes into sight, these smaller columns will form lines, with tanks in front and IFVs directly behind. Artillery will be farther back, and antiaircraft vehicles will be with the IFVs. If there are woods or built-up areas involved, at 500–1,000 meters from the suspected enemy positions, the infantry will dismount and move forward. Otherwise, the infantry will stay in their vehicles until needed to dig the enemy infantry out of any concealed location. At the same time, the tank guns and artillery may be pounding suspected or confirmed enemy positions. At this point, the attacking units will begin to take fire. Ideally, you are not attacking the front of an enemy position, but the side or rear. The mobility of armored vehicles is supposed to make this possible. But everything depends on accurate information. If you lack precise information of where the enemy is, attacks are always fraught with surprises. If the attack goes right up against the front of a strong enemy position, the attackers may be shot up and forced to withdraw. Because the enemy is also mobile, and capable of reinforcing the position you are attacking, speed is critical. If you wait too long to find out exactly what's in front of you, there is liable to be a lot more opposition once you get the assault going.

Information is the key ingredient in tank tactics. The whole point of putting vulnerable infantry in front of the tanks during the final assault is so the infantry can provide the tanks with better information and keep the equally nimble enemy infantry at bay. Once tanks are committed to an attack, they are exposed to enemy observation and not easily withdrawn from view. Specifically during the final assault, when the infantry is dismounted, the tanks cannot use their superior mobility to withdraw without risking loss of their infantry. Tanks without infantry are less capable in combat. Tanks can obtain a higher degree of information if the tank commander stands up in the turret, with his head and half his chest exposed. From that vantage point, 8–10 feet above the ground, much can be seen. Unfortunately, the visibility works both ways, and tank commanders who habitually stand up to see can also be seen, and shot at. The only solution to this problem is to get the battle over with as quickly as possible.

While tanks have problems attacking, they are superb in defense, especially against other armored vehicles. Tanks have firepower, mobility, and protection. The key to defense is surprise. Surprise consists of hitting the enemy when they don't expect it, hitting them hard, and then getting out of the way before you get hit. Defense is most efficient when it is successful against a larger force. In this respect, tanks excel. The classic "mobile defense" relies on good planning and reconnaissance. The planning involves picking out several positions for each tank unit to fall back to as they shoot up the advancing enemy. The reconnaissance ensures that you don't lose track of the larger enemy force. If that happens, your tanks are liable to being ambushed themselves.

Although tanks are large and noisy, they regularly find places to hide. The favored position is on the reverse slope of a hill. This is called "defilade." The tank depresses its gun and, while facing the direction of enemy advance, backs down that slope until all the enemy can see is the gun and top of the turret. Even this much need not be shown until the enemy is in range, as it only takes a few seconds for the tank to move up the slope and into firing position. It is equally easy to back down and move off to the next firing position when the enemy gets too close. Note that Western tanks can depress their main guns farther than Russian tanks, which means Russian tanks must expose more turret when in defilade. If a defilade position is not available, any other concealment will do. The important thing is to get off the first shot, if not the first few shots. The defender will have to try to spot you while sitting among burning vehicles and growing panic. Some units may set off their smoke grenades immediately and pull back. This can be done from inside the tank by simply pushing a button. Such protection from observation allows the defender to stay in position, and perhaps call in some artillery fire. Historically, such engagements have resulted in disproportionate losses, with the defender often getting away unharmed. This tactic is ironic, in that it cancels the tanks' mobility advantage in the attack. As long as the defender does not completely collapse, a handful of tanks, with some infantry and artillery, can delay a larger force by forcing them to deploy from their road-bound columns to overwhelm the defender. An attacker would have to be some 10 times more numerous and able to maneuver in order to brush aside a tank-based defense.

Tanks are not as efficient in defending against infantry. The 40–60 shells carried for the tank's cannon are primarily (and often exclusively) armor-piercing, with only a dozen or so antipersonnel shells at most. U.S. tanks carry nothing but antitank shells. One or more machine guns, one in the turret alongside the main gun and/or another atop the turret, comprise most of the tank's anti-infantry armament. In the defense, the tanks are always placed behind the infantry. It is frequently tank commanders who are given the task of calling for artillery fire or maintaining communication with support units. There is typically a lot of artillery fire on defending units, and tanks are largely immune to it. The presence of friendly tanks typically provides more confidence than firepower for the infantry, but the positive effects of this morale boost should not be underestimated. The grunts like the additional firepower potential, not to mention the implied protection from enemy tanks.

Some tanks are equipped with special weapons. A common one is ATGMs fired through the main gun barrel. Russia has long used this weapon. As noted above, tanks are equipped to generate smoke for concealment. In addition to smoke-grenade dischargers, some tanks have a mechanism that sprays diesel oil over a hot engine part and produces a lot of smoke quickly. What they enemy can't see, they have a hard time hitting. This gets us into some of the more interesting aspects of antitank warfare.

Antitank Tactics

Tanks were originally developed to assist the infantry. This they still do, but primarily as a defense against enemy armored vehicles. Their maneuverability and firepower make then the most effective antitank weapon, but not the most efficient. Tanks are expensive and difficult to maintain. Other antitank weapons are cheaper and nearly as effective. Until the 1960s, the most cost-effective weapon was a tank gun without the tank. These were either towed, at one-tenth the cost of a tank, or in a lightly armored vehicle, at one-third the cost. Then along came the ATGM (Anti-Tank Guided Missile), which changed the rules for antitank warfare. Cheaper, fairly accurate, potent, long-ranged and lightweight, they did have some shortcomings. They had a slower rate of fire, two or three rounds a minute versus up to a dozen for a gun. A prominent back blast was more likely to give away the crew's position. The missiles are slow, taking up to 30 seconds to reach their target, which could take evasive action or fire on the missile operator and spoil his aim. Many ATGMs, particularly the early Russian ones, were inaccurate under 500 meters. As this is the average engagement range with tanks, this was a serious deficiency. World War II experience and German army tests found that, in nondesert areas, you will spot a tank at 500 meters 40 percent of the time, 500–1,000 meters 25 percent of the time, 1,000–2,000 meters 20 percent, and over 2,000 meters 15 percent. Even in open areas, the longer-range possibilities are compromised by tanks taking advantage of undulations in the ground or cover created by huge dust clouds generated in dry weather.

To better appreciate the problems of using ATGMs, consider the following situation. Armored vehicles are first seen approaching 800 meters away. They are moving at 30 kilometers an hour (eight meters a second). Your ATGM crews can get off a maximum of three or four missiles before surviving vehicles are on top of them. The missile crews may not survive that long, as their first shot can easily reveal their position. The tanks' machine gun fire will not make the missile operators any more efficient, as it will often spoil the missile operators' aim. The tanks also can throw a smoke screen in front of themselves, or call artillery or mortar fire on the exposed missile operators. Even APCs are vulnerable, as their sighting and tracking equipment is exposed, as are their missiles before they are fired.

With these deficiencies, why have ATGMs proliferated? Simple: The missiles are light enough for the infantry to carry and operate. Moreover, 20 years of use and development have made them more effective. Most ATGMs can now hit a tank at short range (under 100 meters.) Back blast has been reduced somewhat. Speed is still a problem, however, as it is controlled by the ability of wire to be unspooled and time required for the operator to get the missile squarely on the target. Unlike tanks, missile crews are not always as mobile or as well protected. Tanks can pull out under an artillery barrage. Missile crews, in trucks or IFVs, are at greater risk. Pulling back under enemy pressure is always a tricky maneuver and is made more difficult when you are taking a lot of casualties. The least effective antitank weapon is the light rocket launcher. Carried by the infantry and most other ground troops, these weapons are useful attacking bunkers and IFVs. Against tanks, a lucky hit on the tracks is about the best you can hope for.

The Threat from Below

The most feared antitank weapon is not guns or missiles, but mines. These are the ultimate antitank weapons. Mines exist for no other purpose than to destroy any vehicle that rolls over them. Mines are cheap and require no crew to make them work. Just place them in or on the ground and they are ready. Being machines, mines are fearless and unflinching in the performance of their mission. In World War II over 20 percent of tank losses were due to mines. Since then, mines have become more effective, and the percentage shows signs of increasing with the introduction of robotic mines.

The Threat from Above

Aircraft are generally overrated and overpriced as antitank weapons. But they do play an important role in warfare. The Persian Gulf war was an exception because the enemy was in the desert and not enthusiastic about fighting back. Helicopters and certain fixed-wing aircraft are more lethal than your average fighter-bomber. Helicopters use the same ATGMs the infantry use. Specialized fixed-wing aircraft (the U.S. A-10) use automatic cannon. All aircraft can be exceptionally effective in the antitank role simply by delivering mines. Unless, of course, the enemy tanks are dug in and not moving. But most aircraft do not have the weapons or fire-control systems that are effective enough to hit armored vehicles on the ground. In the Persian Gulf, the Iraqis cooperated by putting thousands of armored vehicles out in the desert and staying there for months so they could be pinpointed and bombed efficiently by aircraft that normally would not be so effective going after armored vehicles.

While combat aircraft are expensive to operate, so are effective counter-measures against them. Armies spend considerable sums to field effective anti-aircraft weapons for their combat units. Even so, aircraft are difficult to hit, and helicopters are perhaps the most difficult of all. Helicopters lurk, dropping down behind trees and hills or flitting around close to the ground at over a hundred miles an hour. Attack helicopters use friendly ground units and scout helicopters to locate the enemy. The attack helicopters then move to an ambush position and try to hit their targets at maximum range (over 3,000 meters) with ATGMs. The helicopters are at greatest risk when they accidentally overfly enemy forces. A modern tank with a laser range finder can do a quick number on a slow-moving helicopter. Battlefields are not neat places, and accidental ambushes happen frequently.

Helicopters' relatively slow speed exposes them to the risk of ambush, while the faster fixed-wing craft use speed as a form of protection. Planes come in low and fast and can speed away at over 400 miles an hour. They make their attack runs at about 100 meters a second, using 20mm–30mm cannon against the thinner top armor of tanks. If the battlefield is quiet, which it rarely is, you can hear them 20–30 seconds away. Unfortunately, you can't always tell what direction the attack is coming from. Ground-attack aircraft are also armored and built to take a lot of abuse, except from enemy interceptors. Tank crews are instructed to stand and slug it out with aircraft. Sometimes this works, but frequently the primordial urge to run the tanks into the woods takes over. The aircraft have an interest in self preservation and typically make only one or two passes and then depart before their victims can get organized.

Advances in cluster-bomb technology have made aircraft more lethal, but not as much as the Air Force people expected. The most devastating antitank cluster bomb is the one that carries trackbuster mines. A 500-pound cluster bomb carries over a hundred of these mines. A fighter-bomber can carry over a dozen cluster bombs, enabling it to spread trackbusters to cover an area over 100 meters long with each bomb. A ton of trackbusters (1,200 mines) can cover an area 1,000 by 100 meters. Each tank entering such a minefield would have a 70 percent chance of losing a track. The mines are small, flat, and painted camouflage colors. A tank that loses a track while under fire is likely to be finished off by some other antitank weapon. At night or during combat, armored vehicles don't have an opportunity to check the ground for these small mines. Losses can quickly mount, particularly when antipersonnel mines are mixed in with the trackbusters. A blown track under more peaceful circumstances will halt the vehicle for several hours and fatigue the crew. Antipersonnel mines mixed with the trackbusters will make the crew reluctant to move around to repair the tank and will also eliminate the accompanying infantry. The only reliable countermeasure to trackbusters is to equip the lead tanks with plows, which will literally plow any trackbusters out of the way. This slows the advance considerably and makes the advancing tank unit more vulnerable to other antitank weapons.

Another form of cluster bomb deploys bomblets that descend and pierce the thinner top armor of tanks. Such weapons are easier for aircraft to use as they do not require aiming at a single armored vehicle. Unlike the trackbusters, which can be dropped before the enemy arrives, the antitank bomblets have to be dropped on the enemy tank formation.

Individual troops, or even a member of the tank crew, can also eyeball the trackbusters and other cluster bomblets and either avoid them or shoot them up with an assault rifle. The 1991 Gulf War demonstrated that the Iraqi troops, like troops everywhere, used their sense of self-preservation and resourcefulness to overcome much of the anticipated effect of cluster bombs.

Despite their expense, and the battlefield shortcomings of new aircraft weapons, aircraft still have the considerable advantage of being able to concentrate a lot of firepower on a distant battlefield on short notice. They are the antitank weapon of last resort, and this justifies their expense.

Changes in Tank Design

Advances in antitank weapons do not take place without improvements in tank design. Until recently, more powerful antitank weapons resulted in thicker tank armor. You can only go so far making heavier tanks. Once you get over 60 tons, the weight of the vehicle becomes a handicap. Many bridges cannot be used, and the wheels and tracks wear out much more quickly. Armor had to be made better instead of thicker. Composite armor was developed, consisting of layers of metal and other materials. This made solid projectiles break up. Spaced armor can be added, an extra thin layer of armor mounted a few inches from the hull. This weakened the effect of shaped charges. Spaced armor, and an additional layer bolted on to key parts of the tank, have been in use since World War II.

As projectiles were improved, reactive armor was developed in response. Reactive armor is not really armor but a layer of explosive panels mounted on the tank's armor. When hit by a HEAT (shaped charge) shell, the reactive armor explodes, weakening the HEAT shell's effects. All of these new developments have several major problems. No one knows just how well they will work with the various different HEAT warheads. The new armor is more expensive. The reactive armor, because it is an explosive, cannot be mounted at all times and is installed only prior to combat or special training sessions. This stuff is dangerous, as when it explodes it is dangerous to any friendly troops near the tank.

Many other measures have been taken to increase the survivability of tanks, such as automatic fire extinguishers, smoke generators, and the like. The net result has been to make the tanks more expensive and difficult to maintain.

Perfect antitank weapons do not exist, only more or less destructive ones. One trend is certain in antitank warfare: It is becoming increasingly difficult for armored vehicles to survive on the battlefield. But then, it is becoming more difficult for anything to survive on the battlefield.

The Life of a Tanker

Crews do not live in their tanks; they spend less than 10 percent of their time inside their tanks or APCs. Moreover, 25 percent of their casualties occur while outside the vehicle. Armored vehicle crewmen are servants to their machines, providing at least eight hours a day of maintenance to keep things running. If the climate or geography is bad, it's worse for the vehicles. You either provide more maintenance or lose more vehicles to breakdowns. In combat, systems are stressed to the maximum. If the vehicles are not in peak condition when they enter combat, they are more likely to break down when they can least afford it. Inside the tank, there is very little space. A smaller tank means a lighter and cheaper tank. France and Russia require their tank crewmen to be less than five feet six inches tall, allowing them to build smaller vehicles with the same capabilities of tanks a larger crewman will fit into. This means that the crews can be selected from only 5 percent of the population. Even larger tanks are cramped.

The inside of a tank is not safe. The turret slews around, the main gun recoils, and fifty-plus-pound shells are tossed about. Fractures, lacerations, and amputations regularly occur among careless, fatigued, or untrained crewmen. The turret generally has two or three men in it. The gunner sits in a small seat next to the main gun with his face pressed against a range finder that displays data on the gun's bearing and the range of the viewed objects. Connected to the tank's range finder is a computer that adjusts the aim of the gun and tells the gunner when he can fire. The quality of these systems varies, as does the skill of the operators. Skillful gunners operating high-quality equipment can obtain first-round hits over 90 percent of the time. Poorly trained and motivated gunners can get only 10 percent (or less) first-round hits. Assisting the gunner is a human or mechanical loader. The human loader is most liable to injury, the mechanical loader likely to fail under stress. Most Russian tanks use a mechanical loader and three-man crews. With only three men to maintain even more machinery, you can imagine the readiness problems. Western armies aren't the only ones in love with new gadgets.

The third man in the turret is the vehicle commander. His seat is just below the turret hatch. Usually the commander stands up with his head and chest out the hatch. This provides better visibility. When all the hatches are closed, visibility is limited to a few small slits and a periscope. If the commander is wounded, which frequently happens, everyone gets upset until the wounded man quiets down or the corpse is allowed to fall to the floor of the tank or is thrown overboard. At that point the gunner takes over command of the tank from the gunner's seat. The result is a tank that can see much less because the gunner cannot work the cannon with his head outside the turret. Ideally, the tank commander should be able to replace any other crew member, especially the gunner. The current U.S. tank, the M-1, gives the tank commander equal access to the fire control system, and a better view of the outside when the tank is zipped up. But cross training to allow crew members to replace each other is an ideal that is rarely achieved. The tank commander is usually a former gunner, theoretically the most highly skilled member of the crew. Despite the obvious benefits, there is rarely sufficient time to cross train. Without cross training, the loss of one or two crewmen will reduce the tank's capabilities considerably. The only crew member not in the turret is the driver. Squeezed into the front part of the tank, the driver sees through a few slits. At best, he can open a small hatch and stick his head out. He takes direction from the commander, who typically has a better view of where they are going. It's no wonder that tanks in combat appear to move blindly. Most of the time, they are doing just that.

Another critical crew skill is speedy restocking of ammunition and fuel. With some tanks, this can take over an hour. Tanks carry up to a ton of munitions, and nearly as much fuel. If you run low on these items during combat, the speed at which you replenish can be critical. Israeli experience during their wars led them to design the Merkava tank. This vehicle has large doors in the rear for rapid loading of larger quantities of ammunition. In defense, the tank can stay buttoned up with less loss of control. A good crew will have surveyed the surrounding terrain carefully and will be able to manage without the commander exposing himself to enemy artillery and small-arms fire. At this point, the biggest danger often comes from fatigue and nausea caused by engine gases that leak into the crew compartment, as well as gases from the fired shells. This is most often the case with older Western and Russian tanks that are not well ventilated: the crews suffer accordingly. In hot climates Russian crews become, for all practical purposes, nonfunctional after an hour of combat because of the lack of ventilation. Western vehicles will last longer because many have some form of air conditioning. Fortunately, combat normally doesn't last that long. When tanks get into a firefight, they are either quickly hit, or withdraw to a safer position. Tanks spend a long time waiting for the other fellow to make a false move. The brutal business of fighting is usually over quickly. Night fighting has become more common with the widespread introduction of thermal sights and sighting devices that amplify available light. With these, tanks can see nearly as well as in daylight. These devices favor the defender more than the attacker. The defender can sight his night-viewing devices at the likely avenues of approach.

Infantrymen with IFVs live with their armored vehicles much the same way tank crews do with their tanks. The maintenance load for IFVs is lighter because 9–12 men are assigned to a mechanically simpler vehicle. Another major difference is that in combat the infantrymen spend most of their time outside their vehicle. It wasn't meant to be that way, as the second generation of IFVs (from the 1960s on) were designed so that the infantry could use their weapons from inside. Subsequent combat experience showed this to be ineffective. This is another example of why you must be wary of new doctrine developed in peacetime.

One final note on IFVs: Because they are lighter and less stable than tanks, they cannot move as quickly cross-country as tanks without injuring the passengers. Tank crews are more securely seated in their heavier and more stable vehicles. Depending on the quality of the suspension system, a modern tank can move 30–40 kilometers an hour cross-country, while IFVs can move about half that speed safely. The heavier IFVs, such as the German Marder and the American M-2, are better able to keep up. As you can see, there's one problem after another.

Theory and Practice

Throughout their short history, tanks have struggled to survive in combat. Although the most heavily protected vehicles on the battlefield, tanks are also the most likely to be shot at. Each tank confronts three or four antitank weapons, including every other tank. But the situation gets more complex in peacetime. Tanks and antitank weapons are very high tech. As more gadgets are added, the situation is guaranteed to become more unpredictable when all this new stuff meets in combat. Experience in the last 60 years has shown that such systems rarely work as anticipated in war. On the bright side, everyone's systems will perform in unexpected ways. The only problem with this is that peacetime planners have a difficult time calculating what their position is versus their opponent. Consider the situation in the 1980s, as tanks were equipped with composite and reactive armor. Even though ATGM warheads and tank shells have become more effective, the tank partisans now sense a chance to recapture the lead on the battlefield. This has been the case with the U.S. M-1 (and the better armored German and British tanks). To get around this, more nations are using top-attack HEAT warheads. These detonate shaped charges that go through the thinner top armor. Western tanks have not had to face this sort of thing yet, but it will happen eventually and remind U.S. tankers that they are not invulnerable.

Tanks cannot win battles by themselves and are not as invulnerable as some would think based on the record of U.S. tanks in the 1991 Gulf War. Tanks are still vulnerable to attack from the rear, from above, and from below. Trackbuster mines may prove to be the most robust tanks' undoing. Meanwhile, the maelstrom of other weapons rips away the accompanying infantry and light armored vehicles. Tanks may be the most powerful system on the battlefield, yet they may not be powerful enough.

The experience of U.S. M-1 tanks rolling, virtually unscathed, right through Iraqi tank units in the 1991 Gulf War was a result of several unique conditions. The M-1 version used was the most modern tank in the world and incorporated a more advanced type of composite armor. The Iraqis were using armor-piercing shells of their own manufacture. These Iraqi shells were inferior to the ones Russia made for the Russian-built tanks the Iraqis were using. As a result, the U.S. tanks were virtually invulnerable to Iraqi tank fire. As most U.S. tanks were maneuvering around the open flank of the Iraqi positions, they encountered few mines. Because the battles were in a desert, the long-range guns of the U.S. tanks were able to operate at peak efficiency, and it was rarely necessary to send infantry ahead to clear out enemy infantry and antitank weapons. For the allied troops, it was an ideal tank battle, fought under ideal conditions and with ideal results. These situations have occurred in previous desert tank battles, but they are the exception, not the rule.

The Future

Battlefield survival for tanks against an equal opponent becomes increasingly difficult. Armored fighting vehicles have long been caught up in competition between tank protection and tank destruction. At one point in the late 1980s, there was a proposal for a new reactive armor that explodes before being hit, thanks to sensors that detect the approaching projectile. The Soviets took this idea one better by developing and deploying a turret-mounted system that used a millimeter-wave radar to detect incoming missiles, and then fire one of eight shotgun-type weapons that would use a pattern of steel pellets to damage the missile sufficiently to render the shaped-charge warhead useless. Systems like this have been under development in the West, and it appears that the Russian one is fairly effective.

Armor itself is no longer slabs of high-grade steel, but many layers of different materials, designed to defeat better an increasing variety of antitank weapons. No one is really sure what will kill a tank anymore and probably won't find out for certain until there is another major tank battle.

Meanwhile, Western nations have developed missile warheads that can penetrate the new "composite plus reactive armor" on many Russian tanks. Russia has equipped thousands of its older T-62s and T-55s to wear reactive armor, and this technology is being sold to any nation that has the hard currency to pay for it. Many of these older tanks have also been equipped with laser range finders and modern fire-control equipment. The Russians really believe in tanks and will equip any other nation that thinks likewise.

Russia and the United States are planning several variants of a new "future technology" tank, one with a very small turret containing the main gun and fire-control sensors. There is no "top" armor in the usual sense: the frontal armor slopes up and toward the back of the tank, with engine heat vented out the back instead of the top rear. This design adds some protection against conventional weapons that attack the top armor and/or home in on heat. The tank also puts most of the protection to the front. Tank battles in the past 30 years have shown that two-thirds of hits are in the front, less than 10 percent in the rear, and the rest on the sides. The future-technology tank is supposed to have a 140mm gun better able to penetrate improved armor designs (more complex, and expensive, composite armor). However, the larger round will reduce the tank's ammunition load and rate of fire. Since the 1980s, work has been underway to develop higher-velocity liquid propellant (which is lighter and safer) and electrically propelled guns for tanks. These are at least 10 years away. In fact, these technologies are probably more than 10 years away because of the end of the Cold War. Liquid propellant is likely to appear in lower-velocity artillery before a high-velocity, liquid-propellant tank gun is introduced. These new technologies are being worked on to ultimately create higher-velocity shells. The higher velocity not only penetrates exotic armor more efficiently, but makes countermeasures more difficult. Current high-speed shells move at about 1,500 meters a second. The future-technology shells are expected to achieve 3,000–5,000-meter-a-second speeds. At over 3,500 meters a second, the shells will leave a glowing trail behind them and show where they came from.

Another problem is how the two-man crew will efficiently keep in touch with the outside world. Throughout the tank's history, the commander standing with his head and chest outside the turret has been the most effective means of control. The future-technology solution appears to be equipping these new tanks with sensors similar to those now found in attack helicopters. This increases the cost enormously and doesn't help much, as most of the time attack helicopters are still notoriously blind to what's happening on the ground. Other features proposed include an armored capsule for the two-man crew for additional protection, and blowout panels for ammunition and fuel storage areas so that the crew doesn't get cooked when these vital areas are hit. Another innovation, previously tried and discarded by Western armies in the early 1970s, is an ATGM fired from the tank gun tube. An even more immediate problem presents itself: maintenance. A more complex tank with an even smaller crew brings to a head tank commanders' growing demand for more maintenance personnel. When you have a tank as complex as an aircraft, you need a "ground crew" to keep it going, and more highly skilled "pilots" to operate it. Current Western tank battalions contain about one technician for every tank crewman, and that ratio will eventually be greater than 1:1. With all the gadgets proposed for the future-technology tanks, these vehicles are still vulnerable to mines, the eternal bane of armored vehicles and something aircraft don't have to worry about. These future-technology tanks have been in development for some time, a common situation as they move toward increasingly complex and expensive technology for their basic weapons. The end of the Cold War has eliminated most enthusiasm for building any of these future-technology tanks anytime soon. Sharp budget cuts on both sides of the former Iron Curtain have made it impossible even to maintain current stocks of tanks. Future-technology tanks will have to wait for the next arms race.

Most worrisome to all the tank-owning nations, and to tank crews in general, are the forthcoming "smart" robotic weapons, which use sensors and warheads that can automatically be lobbed 100 yards in any direction to penetrate the thinner top armor of tanks. These weapons have already entered production in Western armies. Several nations are introducing new features for their ATGMs, in addition to modified warheads, to penetrate reactive armor. The most popular innovations are top-attack and wireless guidance. These "fire and forget" ATGMs use multiple sensors to home in on armored vehicles. The missile's onboard computer sorts out the battlefield clutter and goes for still-functional tanks, despite countermeasures. The top-attack warhead, first introduced in the Swedish BILL system, passes over the armored vehicle and fires its shaped charge down at the thinner top armor. Reactive armor on the top of the tank can defeat these unless the ATGM warheads are designed to take on reactive armor, which the new ones are. A more brute-force approach is embodied in hyper-velocity rockets fired from aircraft or ground vehicles. Also ready for production are electronic weapons that attack the more numerous sensors and electronics of current armored vehicles. If you can't kill them, then blind them or inflict electronic amnesia.

Adjusting for inflation, your average tank today costs more than three times what you paid during World War II. Yet it is still a very inefficient system. Only recently have tank tracks been made sturdy enough to last more than a thousand kilometers. Most Russian-made tanks are still equipped with tracks that wear out after less than a thousand kilometers of use.

Russia, and many of the customers for its tanks, have made a large wager on the success of the tank. Western nations have shown greater preference for cheaper countermeasures. It was Western nations that developed and perfected the ATGM, ATRL (bazooka), and trackbuster mine. Ironically, better armor, main guns, and other tank components were also developed in the West, but introduced on a larger scale by the Russians. As history has shown, the defense (antitank weapons) tends to stay in the lead against offensive weapons (tanks). Despite the success of the U.S. M-1 tank in Kuwait, the future holds a horde of cheap, electronics-based, "smart" antitank weapons. While it's easy for the U.S. to control export of its 60-ton M-1 tank, many nations have the electronics technology needed for the new generations of antitank weapons.

Principal Main Battle Tanks

Vehicle. The official designation of the vehicle. Vehicles are grouped by their nation of origin manufacture. In some cases, the vehicle is also manufactured in other nations. Russia used to account for the majority of armored vehicles built annually, but no more. Russia still makes some replacement parts and upgrade kits. Other major manufacturers are the United States, Britain, France, China, and Israel. Several other nations with steel industries and other technological resources also build their own tanks. Original designs are often used. These smaller-scale manufacturers include Japan, South Korea, and Brazil.

Firepower. This is the numerical evaluation of the vehicle's firepower. It is calculated by taking into account the following factors:

- *The "proving ground" performance of the vehicle's main gun and the various types of ammunition.* The type of shell used can have a vastly different effect on the target. Tanks carry various types of shells among the 40–50 rounds typically carried. The types carried depend on what opposition they expect to encounter and how large their ammunition budget is. Some shells are more expensive than others. The cheapest shell is HE (High Explosive), useful only against soft targets. Next comes your economy-model, armor-piercing APS (Armor Piercing Shot) shell, which is little more than a pointed hunk of high-grade steel. The

Vehicle	Fire-power	Pro-tect	Range (km)	HP:WT	Wght (tons)	Max spd (km)	Hght (m)	Main gun	Max range	In use	Intro-duced
Russia											
T-90	12	10	650	21	47	65	2.3	125	3,000	500	1993
T-80	11	9	400	24	42	60	2.3	125	3,000	5,000	1981
T-64	10	8	400	24	42	60	2.3	125	3,000	4,000	1971
T-72	9	7	500	25	40	60	2.5	125	2,000	14,000	1972
T-62	8	6	480	19	37	59	2.4	115	1,500	4,000	1962
T-55	6	4	300	16	36	50	2.4	100	1,000	5,000	1957
U.S.											
M-1	12	10	560	26	60	72	2.4	105	4,000	1,000	1984
M-1A1	14	12	560	22	67	67	2.4	120	4,000	3,800	1986
M-1A2	16	12	560	22	70	67	2.4	120	4,000	1,000	1999
M-60A3	10	7	300	19	48	48	3.2	105	3,000	8,000	1977
Germany											
Leopard II	13	10	350	30	50	68	2.5	120	3,500	2,100	1978
Leopard I	9	7	375	23	40	65	2.6	105	2,500	2,500	1965
France											
Leclerc	11	9	550	27	55	70	2.5	120	4,000	400	1991
Israel											
Merkava 3	12	10	500	18	55	58	2.8	105	3,000	1,200	1990
China											
Type 59	6	4	300	16	36	58	2.4	100	1,000	6,000	1957
Type 69	8	6	430	19	38	58	2.8	105	3,000	1,200	1962
Type 80	8	6	430	14	38	60	2.2	105	3,000	500	1988
Type 85	9	7	700	17	42	57	2.3	125	3,000	300	1991
Type 90	10	8	600	25	48	60	2.2	125	3,000	100	1999

most expensive "shot" shells are APDS (Armor Piercing Discarding Sabot) and APFSDS (Armor Piercing Fin Stabilized Discarding Sabot, for smooth-bore guns). The armor-piercing element of discarding sabot rounds is less than half the diameter of the shell and made of very expensive, high-density metal. Its smaller size enables it to hit the target at very high speed, up to 1,600 meters a second. This is the most common shell and is constantly being improved. The United States purchased a recent version that uses a penetrator of depleted (nonradioactive) uranium. Most armies are installing 120mm smooth-bore tank guns that have the same penetrating power as the depleted-uranium APDS, plus the ability to use future shell designs that require a larger projectile. These would be the "smart" shells with their own sensors and guidance systems. Composite armor was developed to defeat APDS, but it is not always successful. HEAT (High Explosive Anti-Tank) rounds have fallen from favor because their success depends on hitting a flat surface on the tank. Modern tanks have few flat surfaces. On the plus side, HEAT shells must be fired at lower speeds, are good at any range, and many are now built with a fragmentation capability to make them useful for antipersonnel work. The AP-type shells are less effective at longer ranges. Similar to HEAT, more expensive and still in use, is the HESH (High Explosive Squash Head) shell. After this item hits the tank, the explosive warhead squashes, and then it explodes. The force of the explosion goes through the armor and causes things to come lose and fly about the inside of the tank (the "spall" effect). The vehicle may appear unharmed, but the crew and much of its equipment are not. It works at any range but is somewhat defeated by spaced and composite armor. The most expensive tank shell currently is used by the Russians in their tanks equipped with 125mm tank guns—an ATGM. The United States tried this in the 1960s and 1970s but dropped it. It's unclear yet if the Russians will be any more successful. The price range on the above shells goes from several hundred (HE) to several thousand dollars (ATGM) per round.

- *The fire-control system.* This includes the type of range finder (see below) as well as the computing system. The more recent electronic fire-control computers on tanks have proved to be more effective than the older mechanical types. Unfortunately, the fancy gadgets are usually less reliable, although they are improving.
- *The internal layout and organization of the tank.* This includes how the ammunition is stored and how easily the various crew members can reach and operate their equipment. The cramped Russian tanks suffer in this respect. Tanks lacking air conditioning are also a problem. Tanks that have been upgraded to the point that their interior is crowded also have problems.
- *Gun stabilization and platform stability.* The tank must be sufficiently

stable so that the main gun can be fired accurately while the vehicle is moving, or immediately after a halt. This has been something of a Holy Grail for tank builders since World War II. Some of the current systems actually do the deed some of the time.

- *Ammunition carried.* The more you have, the more you can use to hit the other fellow.
- *Rate of fire.* The ability to get off the first shot accurately and—in these days of voodoo (reactive and composite) armor—the second shot. Experienced crews can fire faster than the number indicated. The chart merely indicates the tank's normal rate of fire they can maintain without overheating the barrel or wearing the crew out.

Protect is the numerical evaluation of the vehicle's ability to defend itself. This is a combination of the following factors:

- *Quantity and quality of armor.* How thick is the armor, and how well it is laid out? Armor that has no sharp edges and offers only a "slope" for enemy shells to hit is more effective. Antitank shells are just very large bullets. If they hit sloping armor, they have a tendency to ricochet off. When hitting four inches of armor at an angle rather than head on, they will have to go through more metal. This is why modern tanks have such a smooth appearance. Armor thickness counts for less today than what it is made of. The best armor since the 1980s is composite (or "Chobham," after the British organization that developed it). This material is an expensive combination of layers of armor, plastics, and ceramics. It absorbs and breaks up shot-type shells before they can penetrate. It is also effective against HEAT and HESH high-explosive shells. Spaced armor has come back into vogue to defeat ATGM HEAT warheads. This is nothing more than thin armor sheets mounted a few inches from the main armor. Basically, it causes the HEAT shell to detonate prematurely and form its penetrating plasma jet inefficiently. Spaced armor, in turn, can be defeated with a special fuze. And so it goes. The latest wrinkle is reactive armor, which is composed of explosive material. When struck, it explodes and makes HEAT shells' penetration much less efficient. This stuff is only mounted in wartime, for obvious reasons. Most nations can, or do, use spaced armor. The M-1, Leopard II, T-80, and British tanks use composite armor. The Russians and Israelis have installed reactive armor. Composite armor can also be installed as add-on protection, although this increases the weight of the vehicle somewhat.
- *Speed of the vehicle.* This is a combination of actual top speed, vehicle power (see HP:WT below), ground pressure, and quality of the suspension system and other machinery required to drive the vehicle. Power and speed enable the vehicle to get out of the way quickly. Higher ground

pressure makes it more likely that the vehicle will get stuck in soft ground. A better suspension system prevents the crew from being knocked about during high-speed, cross-country movement.

- *Ability to lay smoke.* Some vehicles have smoke-grenade dischargers. Others form smoke by spraying diesel fuel on hot engine parts. Some vehicles cannot produce any smoke, leaving them unable to produce a place to hide when they most need it.
- *Size.* All armored vehicles are large. Height is the best indicator of a vehicle's ability to remain unseen.
- *Main gun depression.* The greater this is, the less the tank is exposed when it goes into defilade behind a slope, with only its gun and turret visible to the enemy.
- *Viewing devices from inside the tank.* Ideally the tank commander should have his head outside the tank. But this is not always possible. Various arrangements are made in tanks to provide viewing slits protected by bulletproof glass. The quality of the gunner's sight is also considered.
- *Damage control.* This includes fire-extinguishing system, location of explosive items, and layout of crew compartment to protect the crew in case these items are hit. Chemical warfare protection system and escape capability are also considered.
- *Communications.* Russian-type tanks typically have many vehicle radios capable only of receiving. It's cheaper and avoids the problem of useless chatter. It does make information gathering more difficult. Quality of internal communication also varies. Timely information can save your life in a tank battle.

Range is the unrefueled range of the vehicle in kilometers. Generally, in combat, 100 kilometers of range equals 3–5 hours of running time (assuming 40 percent off the road, 20 percent on the road, and 40 percent stationary with the engine running). This will vary with the season: more time in the summer when the ground is dry and firm, less when it is very hot (air conditioning), cold (snow), or muddy. Cruising speed is generally 30–40 kilometers per hour.

HP:WT is the horsepower-to-weight ratio (the horsepower of the engine divided by the vehicle weight). The higher this is, the more "lively" the vehicle will move. This is more important for acceleration and moving up slopes than for pure speed.

Wght is the full-load weight of the tank in metric tons. Ground pressure (in pounds per square inch) varies from 11 (for most Russian tanks) to 15 (for the Merkava). The lower this is, the more easily the vehicle can cross soft ground like mud, ice, snow, or sand. An infantryman's weight produces 2–10 pounds per square inch.

Max spd (in kilometers per hour) is the maximum speed of the vehicle on a road. Cross-country speed is limited by vehicle weight and the effectiveness of the suspension system. Heavier vehicles actually have an easier time of it. It's the same difference in rider comfort experienced between a Cadillac and a compact.

Hght is the height of the vehicle in meters (one meter equals 3.3 feet). It is measured to the top of the turret. The taller a tank, the easier it is for the enemy to spot it.

Main gun is the caliber of the main gun in millimeters. One little-recognized aspect of gun design is the gun depression in degrees. The greater the depression, the better. A tank defends most effectively from defilade. That is, it backs up behind a hill as far as it can go and sights its gun over the top of the hill. Depending on how steep the slope is, very little of the vehicle is visible to the enemy. At best, all the enemy sees are the gun and the top of the turret. On gentle slopes, a small depression is adequate. Steeper slopes require more depression, unless you want to expose more of the tank. American tanks have 10-degree depression; most other tanks have about half that. Most tanks have about 50 main gun rounds on board, normally a mix of armor-piercing (over 75 percent) and antipersonnel rounds (the rest). The rate of fire is also important. Highly skilled crews can get off as many as 50 percent more rounds per minute. They cannot do this for long, as the barrel will overheat. Less adept crews can manage a high rate of fire, but the aim is often way off. Most tanks also carry one or two machine guns in addition to the main gun. One is usually 7.62mm, the other 12.7mm or 14.5mm. One machine gun is customarily mounted next to the main gun and can be fired in its place (using the same viewing system the main gun uses). The second (larger caliber) machine gun is mounted on the top of the turret for use against aircraft or ground targets.

Max range is the maximum effective range of the main gun in meters. The farther the better. As was mentioned elsewhere in this chapter, the average shot is between 500 and 1,000 meters.

In use is the number of this type in use as of 2002. Few tanks are still in production, although many are getting upgrades in their electronic equipment. In the late 1980s, the annual production for each was approximately: BMP, 2,500; BMD, 200; M-2/M-3, 1,400; T-80, 400; T-72, 1,800; T-64, 1,000; M-1, 800; Leopard II, 400. By the early 1990s, this production had fallen by more than half. By 2000, this decline had reached the point where about the only armored vehicles being made were wheeled ones intended for peacekeeping missions. China is still producing clones of Russian tanks. There will always be some production of armored vehicles. But the end of the Cold War eliminated the

M-2 Bradley Fighting Vehicle

major source of demand for them. Right about now, armor vehicle production will be at their lowest level since the end of World War II.

China has been building its own tanks for many years—fortunately, not very good ones. After receiving some Russian T-55s in the 1950s, China began turning out copies, and later variants, of that Soviet-era design. The first copy of the T-55 was the T-59, and this was built into the 1990s. China still has over 5,000 of them, and thousands more are in use in nations that can't afford anything better. In the early 1980s, China introduced an improved (in many small details) T-59. The T-69 is still in production, but mostly for export. China has only about 500 of them. Later in the 1980s, China introduced the T-80. This was a new design that used a NATO standard 105mm gun and better fire control. Few were built, and China has only 400. A further development of this tank, the T-85, had a Russian-type 125mm gun and an auto-loader. This tank was developed in cooperation with Pakistan. Roughly comparable to the 1960s U.S. M-60 and Russian T-72, the T-85 is still in low-level production. China has a few hundred of them.

Armored Personnel Carriers and Infantry Fighting Vehicles

APCs (armored personnel carriers) are also referred to as IFVs (infantry fighting vehicles). An IFV is basically an APC with a turret and a higher price tag. IFVs are also used widely as reconnaissance vehicles. In this case, they carry

368 High Mobility Multi-Purpose Wheeled Vehicle (HMMWV) with TOW missile

more weapons and fuel, and fewer men. Many of the terms used in this chart are the same as those previously used in the tank chart. These lighter vehicles have a ground pressure of 7–9 pounds per square inch, except for the heavy German Marder, which is 12.

Passengers is the number of passengers the vehicle was designed to carry. You can crowd a third or more people in, but at substantial loss in livability.

Crew size for tanks is four, except for the T-72/64/80 series, which is three. These vehicles have an automatic loader that replaces one man, leaving a vehicle commander, gunner, and driver. IFVs have a minimal crew of two (commander/gunner and driver). Some have a third man assigned as a gunner if there are more on-board weapons.

There are certain characteristics all IFVs share. They all can float (with the exception of the German Marder). Speed through the water is 6–10 kilometers per hour (with the exception of the USMC LVTP, which can do 13). But these vehicles just barely float and cannot manage rough water. Many of these vehicles originally had gun ports, which allowed the passengers to engage targets with their rifles. This sort of thing never really worked too well in practice. Most new vehicles do not have the ports, and older ones had the ports closed up. All APCs/IFVs/LAVs have machine guns. Most have at least two, and the more current ones also mount an ATGM launcher.

Vehicle	Fire-power	Pro-tect	HP: WT	Passen-gers	Wght (tons)	Max spd (km)	Hght (m)	Max range (km)	In use	First used
Russia										
BMD	6	3	42	9	6.7	55	1.9	300	900	1969
BRDM*	2	2	20	3	7	100	2.3	750	2,500	1966
BTR-60*	2	2	18	16	10	80	2.3	500	3,000	1961
BMP-1	7	3	22	11	13.5	65	2.1	600	5,000	1967
BMP-2	7	3	20	10	14.5	65	2.5	600	4,000	1982
BMP-3	7	3	26	10	18.7	70	2.3	600	1,000	1990
U.S.										
M-2	8	5	22	9	22.5	68	2.6	480	3,200	1981
M-3	8	5	22	5	22.5	68	2.6	480	1,400	1981
LVTP-7	3	3	17	28	24	60	3.3	480	940	1972
M-113	2	2	20	13	11	65	2.5	480	25,000	1960
LAV-25*†	4	2		8	12.8	99	2.7	660	2,000	1982
France										
AMX-10P	6	4	20	11	14	65	2.5	600	1,500	1973
Germany										
Marder	7	5	21	9	29	75	2.9	520	1,200	1971

*Vehicle uses wheels instead of tracks.
†LAV is Light Armored Vehicle.

VEHICLE NOTES

Each nation tends to have its own philosophy on armored warfare, which carries over to its vehicle designs. Russia has gone for massive numbers of effective yet expendable tanks. Their tanks have had large guns, but incomplete fire-control systems and shoddy ammunition. Armor has been thick, but crude. Externally, the armor is well sloped to deflect hits. Their tanks are low and wide to present less of a target. They go for a high horsepower-to-weight ratio. Their tanks are cramped, uncomfortable, difficult to maintain, and numerous. Since the 1970s, their tanks have gradually approached Western designs in number and complexity of gadgets. Most of these new items have been copies of similar Western devices. Russia has built over 60,000 tanks since the mid-1960s. Until 1991, most of them were still in use, as they are operated infrequently so as to make the maximum number available for combat. The oldest model is the T-55, a direct descendant of their famous T-34 of World War II fame. Most of these had been scrapped by 2000. China still makes a T-55 variant, the T-59. The T-55 had a lot of flaws, however. It caught fire too easily, particularly with fuel tanks in the front of the vehicle. It had a larger, for the time, 100mm gun and crude fire control. It was fast and simple. Those used in the Middle East and other areas were not popular with their crews. In the early

1960s the T-62 came along. This model had a larger gun (115mm), and better armor and fire control. It also had numerous mechanical problems and was replaced earlier than expected in the late 1960s by the T-64/72. The "64" was a more advanced model used only by the Russian army, the "72" a cheaper version of the "64," also used for export. Both models had a larger gun (125mm), thicker armor, better fire control, and an automatic loader. This resulted in a three-man crew. Further development led to the current T-80 and T-90, both of which feature laser range finders and ATGMs fired from the 125mm smoothbore gun. Both also have composite armor. Reactive armor can be added to all tanks, the primary limitation being expense.

In the late 1940s, the Soviets introduced wheeled APCs for their infantry. In the 1950s they began making tracked APCs that could keep up with their tanks. In the late 1960s came the BMP-1 and phasing out of many of the wheeled APCs for the infantry. The older wheeled models were passed on to combat support units. The BMP was a mixed success. It was cramped and gave a rough ride. The passengers were in poor shape to do any fighting after a high-speed romp with the tanks. The 73mm gun of the BMP-1 had a weak shell and low rate of fire. The ATGM carried was one of the less effective models. The BMP caught fire easily and was difficult to maintain. The vehicle looked impressive as hell, though. During the 1980s, the BMP-2 appeared, with an automatic 30mm cannon replacing the 73mm gun.

The huge inventory of Russian armored vehicles shrank in the late 1980s when the Soviet Union, facing economic ruin from the arms race and internal mismanagement, signed a series of arms-control treaties. The collapse of the Soviet Union in 1991 rendered still more of their armored vehicles unusable as the units they belonged to shrank or fell apart.

The United States never had a reputation for outstanding armored-vehicle designs. After World War II, the United States built tanks that tried to have the best of everything: thick armor, heavy firepower, crew comfort, advanced fire control. In most particulars, these objectives were achieved. Although much is made about the larger size of U.S. tanks, this does not appear to have seriously compromised their combat performance. The biggest problem was maintenance. American troops are accustomed to using their vehicles a lot in peacetime, resulting in a heavy maintenance workload. United States tanks were built to last, largely because of extensive peacetime use. Running a tank is also expensive, making money a limiting factor. Out of this has come electronic devices to enable more realistic training in the field and back at the barracks. In the field, weapons are equipped with lasers and vehicles with sensors so that you can hit targets without hurting anyone. Back in the barracks, one finds elaborate simulators that often approach aircraft simulators in their realism and complexity.

The M-48 was developed in the late 1940s from World War II experience, both U.S. and German. The M-60 was basically an upgrade of the M-48. Many

M-48s were subsequently upgraded to M-60 standards in terms of gun size, fire control, and engine power. The M-1 is a more radical development in tank design than the M-60, notably because of its composite armor, propulsion system, and lavish use of electronics.

U.S. APCs were originally built just for transport. The primary stimulus of building the U.S. IFV (M-2/M-3) was the Soviet BMP. The IFV concept, especially fighting from the vehicle, has not been particularly successful in practice. The M-2 is basically an APC with a turret and 25mm cannon. The latest version of the BMP now has a 30mm cannon in its turret. The M-3 is a reconnaissance version of the M-2. The M-113 continues to be widely used in support roles. Several hundred World War II half-track vehicles are still in use. The LVTP-7 is the U.S. Marine Corps amphibious IVF. Other nations adhered to a slightly different tank-design formula. Germany, with loads of World War II experience, came out with a series of tanks somewhat between those of the United States and Russia in philosophy. The Germans stressed quality, high firepower, and speed. They accepted lower weight and less protection. The French went for an even lighter tank, while the British opted for less speed and more protection. The British designs have been less successful, and for a while they were shopping around in Germany and the United States for their next generation of tanks. Israel, after years of using other people's tanks, designed their own, the Merkava, for defensive warfare. It is heavily protected, and its larger-than-usual storage compartment is easy to resupply through large doors.

Non U.S./Russian IFVs normally follow the Russian model. The French AMX-10P and the German Marder both resemble the BMP. With few exceptions, nations that manufacture tanks do not use those of another nation. Most less wealthy nations have Russian tanks. These vehicles are the easiest to maintain and use. Russian tanks have always been the most inexpensive, and since the end of the Cold War, the prices have sunk even further. Still, purchasing armored vehicles appears to have more to do with political arrangements than with technical merit.

Portable Antitank Weapons: Missiles and Rockets

Currently, three broad classes of antitank weapons exist: guns, mines, and the others. These "others" are the more exotic missiles, rockets, and submunitions. Most antitank guns are found on tanks, although some armies, including Russia's, still use towed antitank guns (although these may finally disappear in the twenty-first century). Most guns rely primarily on kinetic (high-velocity) shells, which allow for rapid firing. These shells travel at over 1,000 meters a second. Contrast this with ATGMs' slower 200 meters a second. Mines are one of the more effective antivehicle weapons and are discussed in greater detail on page 59–61. Mines are passive weapons; they must be placed in the path of enemy vehicles. Mines are also heavy, particularly in useful quantities. The other antitank weapons are of more recent vintage and were developed to give troops without tanks and minefields some protection against armored forces. The ATRL (Anti-Tank Rocket Launcher) was an American development during World War II. These weapons were to give the infantry some defense against tanks. Their effectiveness has been overrated, perhaps because unsuccessful users rarely survived to report their failure. An example of this occurred in the early 1970s, when an American adviser to South Vietnamese troops survived an encounter with North Vietnamese T-55 tanks. Over a dozen of the latest American ATRLs (the LAW) were fired at these older Russian-made tanks to no effect, and a few of the LAW users escaped to report their experience. The LAW had been around for nearly 10 years at that point, and it was only after this incident that attention was paid to the actual (as opposed to announced) effectiveness of these weapons. This was not the first time this happened to the Americans. In 1950, U.S. troops faced Russian-made T-34 tanks with their 60mm bazooka ATRL (of World War II fame). The T-34s were immune. It had been discovered in 1943 that some German tanks were also immune, so the American army began developing an 88mm (3.5 inch) ATRL and was finally able to send some of these more effective weapons to the front in 1950. The problem was that that 60mm version was thought to be sufficient. The problem with ATRLs is not just their dubious penetrating power, but also their accuracy and ease of use. Their accuracy is dependent on steady nerves and some experience. The rocket-propelled warhead is actually lobbed at the target at low speed. A pretty good marksman is required to hit a moving vehicle at one hundred meters. It ain't like the movies at all. Despite these shortcomings, ATRLs are issued in the millions. They do give the infantry a chance, at least against lighter armored vehicles like IFVs. The rockets are also quite useful against enemy fortifications, whether in buildings or the field.

The ATRL's deficiencies brought about the development of the Anti-Tank Guided Missile (ATGM). Actually, the Germans invented the ATGM toward the end of World War II but never got many of them into action. Currently, over 50,000 ATGM launchers are in use, each launcher having up to ten missiles. These launchers and several million ATRLs are defensive weapons arrayed against nearly 100,000 tanks and several hundred thousand IFVs. Naturally, friendly tanks will also be used as antitank weapons. The odds might appear to be against armored vehicles. ATGMs have had mixed success on the battlefield. Over 30 years of use have brought numerous improvements to ATGM design and use. Yet, for all that, on the battlefield the tank still looms larger than life to the infantryman. ATGMs are no guarantee of survival, just another chance.

Antitank Weapons

Name is the official designation of the weapon. The chart contains the vast majority of weapon types currently in use. For example, over 500,000 TOW missiles have been produced since 1970. The improved TOW-2 entered production in 1981, with a TOW-3 (or TOW-2A) coming on line in 1987. Each new model was more lethal and reliable than its predecessor. The Dragon is a smaller and less effective ATGM. About 100,000 of these have been produced, and a replacement is being developed. The Milan, HOT, and Swingfire are all European missiles similar to the U.S. TOW (HOT, Swingfire) and Javelin (Milan). Only the Milan has been produced in large quantities (over 200,000), mainly because of its superiority to the Dragon. The TOW is slowly taking over the market in the West for heavy ATGMs. For over 10 years, work has proceeded on a "fire and forget" ATGM that would not require operator guidance to hit its target. The technical problems have proved daunting, and the only system deployed so far is the U.S. Hellfire. This is not a pure fire-and-forget system, as most of the 50,000 missiles deployed use a laser guidance system that requires that the target be illuminated by a laser device on the helicopter or ground. The system can, however, be fitted with a self-contained target seeker once one is perfected. The Sagger was Russia's first widely used ATGM; more than a quarter million were probably produced. It is no longer made but apparently is still in use. It has been replaced by the Spigot and other models. This points out a peculiar problem with missile weapons: they are expensive, costing $5,000 and up. The Russians paid a high price for missiles, as these high-tech systems took a lot out of their technology-starved economy. These weapons degrade with time, especially the solid-fuel rocket motor, batteries, and the warhead explosives. These components must be replaced periodically; otherwise, a growing percentage of your missiles become duds. You won't know which ones will fail until you try to use them. The Russians had a difficult time maintaining inventories of high-tech items. They are also reluctant to fire many for training. They rely on simulators, which are not as effective as those used in the West. In the West, far more missiles are fired in training. Most of the over 25,000 TOW missiles fired have been for training. Missiles are updated and refurbished regularly to improve their effectiveness. In combat, reliability will be higher, making for significantly more effective weapons.

The AT-4 is a one-shot rocket launcher that replaced the less successful LAW. The RPG-18/22 is a similar Russian weapon. All the other RPGs are highly successful copies of a World War II German antitank rocket launcher (the Panzerfaust). This weapon was a small-diameter tube (about two inches) with a 3.5 inch (88mm) HEAT warhead sticking out one end. Behind the warhead was the propelling charge and a longer, narrower extension of the warhead that stabilized the rocket in flight. The German weapon was a one-shot

Name	Accuracy: % probability of hit					Armor pen. (mm)	Effective range (meters)		Speed (mps)	Back blast	Missile weight (lbs)	Launch system weight (lbs)
	>100m	>500m	>1,000m	>1,500m	>max		Min	Max				
U.S.												
TOW	20	90	90	90	90	750	65	3,000	360	Yes	40	184
TOW-2	80	90	90	90	90	1,200	65	3,750	360	Yes	47	191
TOW-3	80	90	90	90	90	1,500	65	3,750	360	Yes	50	194
Dragon	0	50	80	80	0	500	300	1,000	100	No	30	32
Javelin	20	60	90	90	90	700	75	2,000	100	No	61	50
Hellfire	0	20	70	80	80	900	500	6,000	300	No	95	
Copperhead	0	0	0	0	70	Top	3,000	17,000	800	No	140	
AT-4	30	0	0	0	90	400	10	300	100	Yes	4	11
Russia												
AT-3 Sagger	0	0	50	60	70	400	500	3,000	120	No	25	40
AT-4 Spigot	0	60	70	80	80	500	150	2,000	200	Yes	26	40
AT-5 Spandrel	0	70	80	90	90	500	150	4,000	200	No	37	50
AT-9 Spiral*	0	0	80	80	80	750	500	4,000	300	No	66	
AT-13 Saxhorn	0	50	80	80	0	400	300	2,000	100	Yes	40	40
AT-8 Songster†	0	0	80	80	80	750	500	5,000	400	No	80	
AT-10 Stabber†	0	0	80	80	80	800	500	4,000	400	No	54	
AT-11 Sniper†	0	0	80	80	80	800	500	5,000	400	No	61	
RPG-7V	30	30	0	0	0	320	5	300	200	Yes	5	15.4
RPG-18	30	0	0	0	0	375	5	200	110	Yes	4.4	
RPG-22	40	0	0	0	0	390	5	250	100	Yes	6	12
RPG-16	30	40	0	0	0	375	5	800	200	Yes	6	
France												
Milan 2	70	90	90	90	90	800	25	2,000	180	Yes	32	105
HOT 2	80	90	90	90	90	1,100	75	4,000	200	Yes	46	
Sweden												
BILL	0	70	90	90	90	Top	150	2,000	200	Yes	24	23

* For use on aircraft
† For use from tank gun barrels

affair. The Russian innovation was to give it a better sight, more powerful rocket, and make it reloadable. The RPG is still manufactured in large numbers and is very popular among poor and untrained troops in Third World civil wars, rebellions, and disorders. The RPG has become the "poor man's artillery" and is used mostly against everything but tanks. RPGs have even brought down helicopters. Recognizing the popularity, Russian manufacturers have come out with several more effective antipersonnel warheads. Perhaps the most interesting one uses Fuel Air Explosive. This provides a very large bang for a small warhead and is very effective against troops in houses, bunkers, or caves. Several other weapons are not shown on the chart but seem destined to become decisive antitank weapons. Currently available in increasing quantities are the trackbuster mines. These are small, weigh 2–5 pounds, and can be scattered about where enemy vehicles will pass. Trackbusters can be delivered by hand, artillery shell, aircraft, or helicopter. These small mines lie on the ground and can be spotted. However, for vehicles moving at night or under enemy fire, these small, camouflaged mines are easily missed. They blow the tracks off armored vehicles and immobilize them for at least several hours. Two other weapons are to be deployed by the United States and other Western forces in the next few years. HEAT SM are submunitions used in bombs and artillery, and now also in mines. These fall to the ground and, if there is an armored vehicle beneath them, will strike the thinner top armor and penetrate.

The HEAT (High Explosive Anti-Tank) SFW (Self-Forging Warhead) is a more deadly variant now entering use. It uses a high-explosive warhead that forms a thin stream of fast-moving molten metal (the "self-forging warhead"). The advantage of this is that it is effective for several hundred feet from where the warhead detonates. This enables the submunition to descend more slowly by parachute (or other similar device), scan the ground for targets, and then detonate only when it detects something to hit. This weapon is worrisome to the Russians (and to Third World nations in general) because it uses existing technology and industrial capabilities the West has and Russia lacks (microcomputers, sensors, precision machining, etc.). Moreover, these weapons are dangerous to the side with the larger number of armored vehicles to hit. There is no easy way to counter the molten-metal HEAT.

Accuracy is the percentage probability of hitting a target at various ranges. Destroying the target depends on armor penetration. The hit probability is given for each distance under ideal conditions. Many older systems require a few seconds after launch for coordinating the guidance system and the rapidly moving missile. This accounts for the sometimes lengthy minimum range. The maximum range is often a function of the reach of the guidance system. Many systems are wire-guided, with a thin wire fed out from a spool in the launcher to the missile. When you're out of wire, you're out of control. Missiles also run out of momentum. The missile propellant is burned up a few seconds after launch. This, plus visual limitations, limits range and accuracy. Poor visibility and enemy fire will reduce this probability by more than half. To obtain the listed hit probabilities, you need a stationary or slowly moving target in plain sight, in clear weather, and not shooting back. A rapidly maneuvering target (30–40 kilometers an hour; that is, 8–11 meters a second) heading for cover will be more difficult to hit. At longer ranges, where the missile can spend up to 20 seconds in flight, the tiny speck in the gunner's sight can easily disappear. Fog, smoke, or dust make seeing and hitting the target more difficult. If aware of the situation, the target often objects to being fired on and shoots back before the gunner can complete guiding the missile to the target. This actually happens, largely because in dry weather the missile launch will throw up a lot of dust. A well-trained tank crew will be on the lookout for such launches, and a lot can be done in 10 seconds when your life depends on it. The missiles can be seen in flight, and firing at the point of launch can easily spoil the gunner's aim.

There are four methods for guiding a missile to its target. The most primitive is used by the rocket launchers (RPG, AT-4). Since the projectiles have no guidance system, you simply aim the weapon, pull the trigger, and hope for the best. The earliest ATGMs allowed the operator to maneuver the missile to the target with a joystick. Speed could not be controlled, only altitude and direction. If the operator got nervous, or lacked skill, accuracy suffered. Only the Sagger and Swingfire still use this system. The next generation (TOW, Dragon, Milan, HOT, etc.) required only that the operator keep the target in his sights for the missile to home in on it. Enemy fire can still make the operator wince and, as the sight shifts, so does the flight of the missile.

The newer, not yet perfected, fire-and-forget missiles use a terminal homing system. The missiles are launched in the general direction of the target. The missile has a seeker in it that homes in on the target once the missile is 1,000–2,000 meters away. Aside from the expense of these seekers, there is the problem of getting the missiles to hit undamaged targets and not go for burning (or non-burning) wrecks. Potential targets have several characteristics that a seeker can home in on. Heat sources can be picked up by infrared seekers, and images of targets can be picked out of the clutter with the aid of an onboard computer. Large masses of metal can be detected, as can the movement of large objects. For best results, the warhead should have two or more different types of sensor. But this gets very expensive. An example of this is the U.S. Copperhead artillery shell, which only has one sensor. Using a HEAT warhead, it is guided to the target by a seeker that looks for reflected laser light. The laser light is bounced off enemy armored vehicles by front-line troops equipped with laser devices. Unfortunately, the laser is degraded by bad weather. The laser operator is often degraded by enemy fire, as the laser light can be seen by anyone using a special viewing device. Worst of all, the cost of the Copperhead round escalated, preventing more than a few thousand of the shells to be manufactured and distributed.

For aircraft, the high cost is less of a factor. From the air, a larger variety of targets are available, many of them far more valuable than individual armored vehicles. Aircraft are more exposed anyway, so the added visibility of their laser equipment is not as dangerous as it is for the man on the ground. The aircraft are also capable of using the laser farther away and can get out of harm's way more quickly. But for destroying individual armored vehicles, laser guided missiles from the air are also too expensive.

The West does have a considerable advantage in microcomputers, miniature sensors, and the ability to produce these things on a large scale and relatively inexpensively. Fire-and-forget missiles that work at an affordable price will eventually arrive, perhaps in the next five or ten years, depending on how much money the military has in the post–Cold War world. When they do arrive in quantity, a major watershed will have been reached. Man will be fighting effective robots. A desperate sense of self-preservation has nullified new weapons in the past. Against thinking robotic missiles whose only function is to seek out and kill, man will encounter a unique adversary.

Armor pen is the number of millimeters of armor the warhead will penetrate if the armor is hit directly at a right angle. The angle of hit is an important consideration. High-velocity, solid-shot rounds tend to ricochet off armor if they hit at too radical an angle. HEAT rounds have even more problems dealing with angles. These shaped-charge rounds operate by "focused explosion." The front part of the round is hollow, and the rear half is an explosive with a cone-shaped depression, open on the side facing the front of the shell. When the warhead hits, a detonator is set off at the rear of the explosive. This creates a metal-penetrating stream of superhot gas. This plasma jet burns a small hole in the armor and, once inside the tank, will ignite something else like ammunition, fuel, and/or crew. It is not always fatal, as the plasma jet is only 10–20 percent the width of the warhead and dissipates quickly. The rule of thumb is that a shaped charge can penetrate armor equal to five times the warhead diameter (a 100mm-wide warhead goes through 500mm of armor). Shaped charges can be defeated in several ways:

- *Spaced armor.* The plasma jet exists for only a fraction of a second, burning through whatever is in front of it. If thin armor (or even cyclone fencing as in Vietnam) is placed 300mm from the tank's main armor, the warhead explodes and burns through 300mm of air before it reaches the armor. Shaped-charge warheads also need a fraction of a second for the explosion to form the plasma jet.
- *Sloped armor.* This also is used to make high-speed, solid-shot rounds skip off the armor without penetrating. Shaped-charge rounds may do the same, or they may explode and the plasma jet will hit the armor at an angle and end facing a greater thickness of armor. Modern tanks have few flat surfaces, so the average slope encountered will degrade shaped

charges from 25–50 percent. Thus, a normal penetration of 500mm becomes 375mm or 250mm, which is often not sufficient to penetrate the hull or do any serious damage.

- *Composite armor.* Instead of just 50mm to 200mm of armor, an equal or greater thickness of lighter, layered materials is used. This combination of metal, plastic, and ceramic layers absorbs the plasma jet's energy without allowing complete penetration. Good composite (or Chobham) armor can degrade a shaped charge's penetration by a factor of two or more. It is very expensive, though.
- *Reactive armor.* Blocks of high-speed explosive are mounted on the tank's armor. When a high-energy object strikes one of these blocks, it explodes. This diminishes the effectiveness of HESH and HEAT. Drawbacks are that it's expensive and only works once as it self-destructs. This is dangerous to any infantry close by. But then a stricken tank, with its ammunition blowing up and fuel catching fire, isn't very safe to be around, either. It cannot be used safely on lighter armored vehicles. It is only mounted in wartime, thus giving your opponent another warning that war is on the way.
- *Soft layer.* A thin layer of a soft metal, like lead, on the top of the tank is used by some Russian vehicles to defeat the fusing mechanism of HEAT submunitions from cluster bombs. Their calculation is that this will cause these munitions to not detonate because the detonator will not make hard enough contact. Soft layer protection is known to have been tested by the Soviets, but not deployed on a large scale.

The above defenses combine to make HEAT shells very ineffective. Tanks like the M-1, with some 600mm of sloped, composite armor and some thin metal skirts, can withstand most hits by warheads capable of penetrating over 1,000mm of normal armor. This does not make a tank invulnerable. Even non-penetrating hits can damage other components, like the running gear, engine, weapons, and sensors. One or more damaging hits can make a tank ineffective without destroying it. For comparison purposes, the maximum armor thickness of other modern tanks is: T-55/62, 200mm; M-48/60, 250mm; Leopard I, 170mm; AMX-30, 150mm; Chieftain, 400mm. Western tanks have thicker armor on the sides and rear. Russian tanks are thinly armored in these areas and depend on not letting the enemy fire at anything but their front. The above thicknesses should be multiplied by 1.3–1.5 to reflect the effect of sloping. Using composite armor adds 40–70 percent to their effective armor protection (or "armor basis") against AP, and 200–250 percent against HEAT. The variation depends on whose composite armor is being used. The Western stuff is much better. There is no additional weight for composite armor, but the stuff takes up more space.

Meanwhile, the technology of shaped-charge warheads goes forward. The latest wrinkle is combining two shaped charges in the same warhead plus a long metal "penetrator" in the front of the projectile. These two charges go off one behind the other, thus increasing the penetration to 10 times the warhead diameter. Still another approach is used by the Swedish BILL system: the warhead flies over the target and detonates downward into the thin top armor of the tank. Other existing ATGMs have been fitted with downward-firing warheads, also. The Copperhead shell has a similar effect as it plunges earthward.

Effective range is expressed in minimum and maximum. The minimum is necessary to arm the warhead and get the missile under operator control after launch. The control time varies with the sophistication of the missile system. Maximum range is also a matter of control. A HEAT round is effective at any range, as long as it hits a target. Although most ATGMs depend on wire for operator control, newer types do not use wire but rather laser or infrared signals to sensors in the rear of the missile. This type of control is less reliable because of atmospheric conditions but does allow for much faster missiles.

Speed (meters per second). This is limited primarily by the speed with which wire can be unspooled. That limitation is about 200 meters a second. Another limitation is the reaction time of the operator and the guidance system. HEAT rounds also perform better if they strike their targets at a low speed, although higher-speed rounds can be made. These fast HEAT rounds are more expensive. The long flight time of ATGMs (15–20 seconds) has proved sufficient to allow an alert target to react.

Back blast. All missiles have a back blast. In some cases it is very prominent. These are indicated with a Yes. The back blast warns an alert opponent that ATGMs are on the way. Even the Sagger, with its relatively small back blast, was spotted by Israeli tankers in the 1973 war. They were able to take evasive action and avoid many missiles.

Missile weight (pounds). This is the missile, rocket, or projectile weight and shows the relative portability of the system.

Launch system weight (pounds). Many systems have a reusable launcher containing a launch tube and guidance system. This often includes a power supply, also. The AT-4-type weapons are self-contained. The launcher is thrown away once the rocket is launched.

4

Artillery: The Killer

When asked which weapons they fear most, soldiers always put artillery at the top of the list. Artillery causes the most casualties and is the most unpredictable danger on the battlefield. Worst of all, you can't fight back. Even tanks can be shot at, but artillery is out of sight and always ready to deliver death and mutilation.

Artillery is large-caliber guns firing projectiles or rockets containing explosive and, increasingly, more diverse implements of destruction. From the user's point of view, artillery is an ideal weapon. It does enormous destruction without exposing the user to much risk. Better still, the users rarely suffer the dismay of seeing their mangled victims. However, artillery is a rich man's weapon. A less wealthy army can be just as destructive, but at greater human cost to itself. Throwing shells instead of infantry at the enemy is preferable, if you can afford it.

During World War II, artillery caused nearly 60 percent of all casualties. World War II still holds the record for the most artillery fire thrown at the most troops. During World War II, it was found that artillery's effects varied by terrain type. In open plains and deserts, about 75 percent of the casualties were from artillery. In mixed terrain, about 60 percent of casualties were from artillery, and in forests and built-up areas it was 50 percent or less. The trend was clear: troops will take full advantage of any place to hide. Today's combat troops have armored transport, providing them with more abundant protection from anything but a direct hit. However, artillery has also improved its efficiency. The munitions, in particular, have gotten more deadly. Another crucial change is greater reliance on large supplies of fuel, ammunition, and other items. All of these are carried by unarmored vehicles that are more vulnerable than in the past. Even modern tank divisions consist of over two-thirds unarmored vehicles. The longer range and improved fire control of modern artillery put combat support at risk almost as much as the infantry.

Artillery Fire and Missions

Modern artillery came of age in the first 20 years of this century. The guns have gotten bigger and acquired more gadgets. Yet the same basic techniques are still used over 70 years later—artillerymen from 1918 would feel right at home. The big change nearly a century ago was the development of accurate indirect fire: that is, artillery fire that could hit targets they could not see. For 600 years previously, the vast majority of fire was at targets the gunners were looking at. Modern indirect fire is delivered in two forms: barrage and concentration. Beyond this are many variations, but they are of interest only to artillerymen. A barrage is literally a wall of fire—shells exploding in a line—that is employed to screen troops from enemy observation or to prevent enemy movement. A rolling barrage moves forward at a preplanned speed in front of an advance. If this is done properly, the advancing troops will reach the defending positions right behind the exploding shells, leaving the enemy little opportunity to fire back. A concentration is high-density fire for the purpose of destroying a specific target. Barrages and concentrations are fired at three levels of intensity:

- *Harassment.* Up to 10 percent destruction, enough to keep the troops' heads down.
- *Neutralization.* About 30 percent destruction, causing a temporary inability of the unit to perform.
- *Destruction.* Fifty to 60 percent destruction, resulting in disintegration of the unit or long-term ineffectiveness.

"Temporary" means from a few hours to a day. Destruction fire depends on a higher level of casualties breaking the morale of the survivors and completely disrupting the organization of the bombarded unit. More resolute and well-led units will not always break under destruction fire. Indeed, the effects of all three intensities of fire can be compromised by the quality of the defender's fortification, as well as the quality of the units. Artillery effects are never a sure thing.

Musical metaphors are often used in describing the use of artillery. One "conducts" or "orchestrates" artillery fire in the hope that the composition will have the desired effect on its victims. The above types of fires are organized into a pattern of missions. Artillery fire requires a lot of expensive equipment plus large supplies of munitions. It is not done in a haphazard manner unless you want to waste it.

Each time a group of guns fires a particular type of fire they are performing a mission. There are several basic types of missions:

- *Preplanned.* Guns are assigned to fire a specific number of shells at a specific target according to a schedule.
- *On call.* A preplanned mission that is fired as often as called for.
- *Target of opportunity.* An observer works out the details on the spot, talking directly to the gunners.

Offensive and defensive barrages are preplanned fires to assist attacking or defending troops by providing a wall of fire. Usually of neutralization or destruction intensity, they may be either stationary or rolling (moving every few minutes). These barrages often use smoke and high-explosive shells together to keep the other side in the dark as much as possible.

Standing barrages are screens to prevent enemy movement or observation. Conducted at harassment intensity, it often includes smoke and poison-gas shells. It guards the flank of an advance or cuts the enemy's retreat or route for reinforcements. It is almost always preplanned or on call.

Fire assaults concentrate against specific targets in the hope that the defender will be destroyed. It is customarily preplanned, but defenders often use it as on-call fire once the position of the attacker is known. This is the heaviest intensity of fire.

Harassment is usually random fire on enemy positions to keep the enemy from functioning at full efficiency. This type of fire will force the enemy to be careful moving around and prevent them from getting sleep, regular resupply, and so on. It is normally very light fire, a few shells at a time in a small area. Depending on how sloppy, or unlucky, the defender is, there will be little or no damage. When the fire is placed on roads behind the enemy lines, it is more likely to catch some hapless vehicle loaded with fuel or ammunition, with spectacular results.

Interdiction is similar to, but a heavier form of, harassment fire. It is frequently employed on roads or routes behind enemy lines for the purpose of stopping or slowing down movement. Varying degrees of intensity are used, depending on your ammunition supply and how badly you want to interdict.

Counterbattery is fire at enemy artillery to suppress or destroy the enemy guns. This has become more effective of late, as sensors to spot artillery positions quickly become more common and efficient.

Techniques of Artillery Use

Artillery is warfare by the numbers. Even aircraft, for all their technical sophistication, are successful in combat largely because of the skill and talent of a human pilot. Artillery is more a matter of mathematics and formulas. Artillerymen cannot see their targets; all they have are references on a map and perhaps the voice of an observer over the phone. To make this work, surveyors first plot the precise location of the guns. Detailed weather reports, as well as how worn out the gun barrel is, are also taken into account. A computer calculates the precise direction and elevation of the guns, as well as how much propellant to use and what adjustments to make to the fuze. Humans do the less cerebral tasks, like carrying the ammunition and firing the gun. All of this is becoming increasingly automated, including the loading of ammunition and the reports from the front. An observer at the front can now point a laser at a target and have the information automatically radioed back to the guns, which then fire. All of this automation is for a purpose. Gunfire must be accurate; otherwise, your own troops will be hit, not to mention the even greater chance of missing the enemy. Losses from friendly fire are all too frequent because of observer error rather than faulty calculations. Automation also solves an increasingly difficult problem with round the clock combat. Artillery is often on call 24 hours a day. Gun crews easily make fatal mistakes when suddenly called to provide unplanned fire support at 3:00 A.M. Automatic loaders and firing computers can eliminate many of these predawn errors. Development continues on guns that would aim, load, and fire automatically.

It was during World War I (1914–18) that artillery fire became largely indirect. The gunners could no longer see the effects of their fire. They had to rely on trigonometry, ballistics, maps, electronic communications, observers, and registration by fire to direct the shells to their target. Despite these difficulties, the gunners didn't mind. If they couldn't see the enemy, the enemy couldn't see and shoot back at them. Unlike previous wars, where the artillery was a primary target, the guns now survived longer while their targets perished with greater frequency. When I was in the army, I was in the artillery, and I greatly appreciated the development of indirect fire.

The scientific techniques behind modern artillery are quite simple. First, the flight of shells is fairly predictable if you take into account all of the elements that can alter their path: the minute differences in the composition of different batches of propellant, wear and tear on the gun barrel, humidity, wind direction, speed, and so on. The precise location of guns and targets is taken care of by using accurate maps and surveying equipment. Triangulation is used to determine the direction and elevation the guns will fire. Often a few rounds are fired and adjustments made before unleashing the entire barrage or concentration. During World War II, the United States perfected techniques that allowed one observer to control hundreds of guns: "every gun within range," as the saying went. Before this, each observer talked to, and controlled, one unit of guns. More complex and efficient communications and plotting systems were required to tie in a large number of artillery units and observers. The U.S. Army first developed this system in the 1930s and continues to lead in this development.

Because artillery units themselves are spread over a wide area, determining the bearing (direction) and elevation of the guns is not only a very complex problem but one that must be solved quickly before the target moves or some of the guns are fired upon. Western armies can have shells on the way in less than a minute, often as little as 15 seconds. The major flaw in all this is the increasing use of electronic jamming. Without reliable communications, the guns might as well go back to direct fire. Good training and imagination can overcome the damage caused by electronic warfare. The common workaround is to do what they did in World War I under similar conditions. You use flares, messengers, and rigidly preplanned fires.

The Russian-trained (and less well-trained troops in general) armies still employ nearly half their artillery for direct fire. This solves the communications problems. It also allows the enemy to shoot back more easily at the artillery. Although direct fire is two to three times as effective as indirect fire, your gun losses go up by a factor of 10. This is not surprising when you consider that direct-fire guns must be used within 1,500 meters of their targets. Although an increasing portion of Russian (and non-Western) artillery is mounted on armored vehicles, the majority is still towed. Non-Western artillery is becoming more sophisticated, But it still does not operate as spontaneously as Western guns. Non-Western artillery also suffers from more problems with defective ammunition. Many Third World nations take pride in producing their own artillery ammunition, but they often do it badly and don't discover their mistakes until they use a lot of their defective shells during a war. The Russians, and their artillery equipment customers, place greater faith in mass than in gadgets and fancy footwork.

Counterbattery fire, shooting at the other fellow's artillery, has always been a tricky business. In the last 20 years, advances in computer and radar technology have given the Western nations very effective counterbattery capability. Previously, one had to estimate the guns' positions by observing the sound and flash fire and then doing some crude calculations. At best, this technique was not very accurate. Vast quantities of shells were then expended in the hope that some of the enemy guns were where your calculations predicted. Western counterbattery radars, and the use of MLRS (Multiple Launch Rocket Systems) with ICM (Improved Conventional Munitions) rounds, can quickly eliminate enemy radar. But just as Western technology has come up with an effective counterbattery weapon, they have also developed a solution to it. The U.S. Army has developed a ceramic artillery shell that is invisible to radar. The ceramic shell is more expensive than metal shells and, because of the post–Cold War budget cuts, was not produced in significant quantity. Third World and Russian counterbattery technology is not up to the Western standard, but it is effective enough to encourage frequent changes in firing positions. The age of "shoot and scoot" has arrived, but only if the troops can use and maintain the gadgets effectively.

Electronic warfare has complicated the picture. If the guns are running around shooting and scooting, they are very dependent on radio contact with their front-line observers. If the enemy is blasting away with his jammers, communications are unreliable. At best, this slows down the process of requesting fire and getting it. At worst, there is no communication between the users and providers of artillery fire. These problems can be circumvented in a number of ways. Arrangements can be made for the infantry to use certain combinations of colored flares to call for prearranged fire. This eliminates targets of opportunity and slows things down in general. But it is preferable to no artillery support at all. If distances are not too great, and time and resources permit, you can lay telephone wire. The wires may get cut, but then you still have your flares. You can also use jamming against the counterbattery radars, or antiradiation rockets to knock them out. Things never become impossible, just more difficult. And accidents happen. The infantry takes a dim view of getting hit by friendly fire. This is accepted more philosophically in the Russian army, whose artillery fire tends to be rigid, preplanned, and massive, and very closely coordinated with the advancing infantry and tanks. Losses from friendly fire are considered preferable to leaving the infantry unprotected as they approach the enemy positions. Most Third World nations have adopted the Russian approach, largely because the Russian approach allows you to get the most out of poorly trained and inexperienced gun crews.

LIFE ON THE GUN CREW

Like tank crews, gunners have a lot of equipment to maintain. If the guns are self-propelled, as most are, the maintenance load is about the same as a tank. Self-propelled artillery are about the same size as tanks but have light armor like IFVs. They normally mount a larger gun (152mm and up) than tanks and have more room inside to accommodate a larger crew and more activity. Self-propelled artillery fire a lot more shells, in less time, than tanks. The other difference from tank guns is that artillery guns fire their shells at a lower velocity. This is done for several good reasons. Low-velocity shells allow the barrel to last longer and fire more shells before overheating. Lower-velocity shells put less stress on the other gun components, allowing them to last longer while making maintenance easier and cheaper. Indeed, the only reason tanks need high-velocity shells is to achieve maximum armor penetration and accuracy.

M-198 Towed 155mm artillery

Gunners have a lot more precombat work than tankers. To avoid counter-battery fire, or simply to support a complex fire plan for a major offensive or defensive operation, they have to prepare a number of alternate firing sites. Teams of gunners and surveyors are sent to positions chosen from a map to mark firing positions for the guns and determine their precise location. Access routes must be checked and storage sites for ammunition laid out. Sometimes ammunition is moved to the firing positions ahead of time. When the firing position is used, the guns drive in and move into their previously marked locations. Each gun's sights are lined up on the surveyors' marker poles, and the guns are rotated and elevated to align them with their distant targets. Then the signal is given to load, fire, load, fire, etc., until the required number of shells have been sent on their way. Most guns can fire six or more shells a minute for a few minutes. After that they have to slow down to two or three a minute to avoid overheating the barrel.

Firing the gun is a well-trained drill. The gunner keeps the gun lined up properly, shifting the alignment according to the fire plan so that the proper number of shells falls on the right targets in the right sequence. The loader gets the shells into the gun. The ammo crew, the "gun bunnies," keep the supply of shells moving. These shells weigh 90 pounds for 155mm guns, plus the lighter propellant charge that is loaded separately. The gun chief keeps checking that the right type of shell is being loaded, that the right fuze and fuze settings are being used, and that things are going well in general. A lot can go wrong. He also keeps the gun log, which is important for maintenance and adjusting gun aim to take account of barrel wear. During a major operation, as many as 500 shells per gun per day may be fired. That could be over four hours of steady firing, but it's rarely all at once. Usually bursts of a few shells, or a few dozen, are fired interrupted by displacement to new positions, maintenance, and, if the front is close by or the enemy has broken through, defense against ground attack. The crews must always be alert to the danger of air attack, and the dreaded counterbattery fire. In a defensive situation, the guns may be on call at all hours. You just wait, day and night, for the "fire mission" call. Then you scramble through the drill as quickly as possible. An infantryman's life depends on the gunner's prompt and accurate delivery of the requested fire.

ORGANIZATION OF ARTILLERY

Almost all artillery units are organized into battalions—typically of 12–24 guns, containing guns of the same type and caliber. The typical battalion has three firing batteries, each with a third of the battalion's guns. A headquarters battery contains the communications and fire-control specialists and their equipment. Some Western armies have a fifth ("detail") battery that takes care of ammunition supply, maintenance, and other details. The actual gun crews of an 18-gun battalion number under 200 men. Ammunition supply troops add another 100, while the fire-control and support troops can be 100–200 men. Western armies average some 500 men per battalion, and Russian-style battalions about 300, although they place the equivalent of another 100 men per battalion under the control of the next-higher headquarters (divisional artillery, artillery regiment, etc.). These troops perform the same jobs as specialists belonging to Western battalions. Artillery battalions are assigned to combat divisions as "divisional" artillery, or to corps and armies as "non-divisional" artillery. Divisional artillery uses lighter guns and usually consists of three to five battalions. Three of these battalions would be some standard caliber (105mm, 122mm, or larger), while the other units would have heavier guns or rockets. Your typical U.S. divisional artillery has 155mm guns and rocket launchers. Russian divisions typically contain 122mm or 152mm guns plus rockets (unlike Western divisions, usually two or more different calibers of launchers). All other armies have variations on the above, and it generally comes down to 80–100 large-caliber artillery pieces and rocket launchers per division. These weapons expend some 80 percent of the ammunition used by the division. There are a lot of additional artillery weapons in the division. Everything from a 81mm mortar to a 125mm tank gun is technically artillery. If you count all this other "artillery," you find 400–500 pieces for each Western or Russian division. Third World divisions average less than half to three-quarters this amount of artillery weapons. Only a 100 years ago, few armies had as many as six guns per 1,000 men, while today the average is about 30 per 1,000. The standard of dying has gone up along with the standard of living.

The non-divisional artillery is assigned to divisions as needed and contains the heavier-caliber weapons. Few guns are larger than 203mm (eight inches). Non-divisional artillery units include the long-range (up to 800 kilometers) missiles. These are frequently armed with nuclear or chemical warheads. However, the trend is toward conventional warheads for these missiles, using warheads carrying submunitions. The United States and Russia eventually realized that nuclear and chemical weapons would be more costly for both sides than they are worth.

The rule of thumb is to have one non-divisional gun or rocket launcher for each one in the divisions. This is a wartime standard, using many guns normally manned by reservists during peacetime. For example, in wartime, a corps with three divisions and 12 battalions of divisional artillery would have an additional 12 battalions of non-divisional artillery.

Artillery assigned to smaller units in a division has less available ammunition. It is not practical to deliver vast quantities of ammunition to front-line units. Divisional artillery normally operates at least a few kilometers from the fighting. This is to prevent ammunition resupply from being interrupted. Without a substantial and steady supply of ammunition, artillery is much less useful. With adequate supply, a battalion of 155mm guns can fire over 500 tons of munitions a day at the enemy. That tonnage has to reach the guns before it can be sent off to the enemy. Indirect (mortars) and direct (tank guns) fire weapons are used near the front because of the need for quick response to enemy activity. If used properly, the front-line artillery fires only when necessary. Limited ammunition supplies are not an insurmountable problem if the divisional and non-divisional artillery, and their better access to munitions, is available.

SHELLS SMART AND DUMB

Guns use many kinds of artillery shells:

High Explosive (HE). Still the standard artillery shell; basically a shell container with an explosive charge of five to over 20 pounds, depending on the shell's caliber. Despite the introduction of ICM (Improved Conventional Munitions), HE still comprises the vast majority of the world's artillery stocks.

Smoke. Creates a smoke cloud lasting from 10 to over 20 minutes. The most common non-HE type shell, it represents less than 5 percent of all shells.

Star shell. An illuminating flare, with a parachute to delay its fall so that the light will last 5–10 minutes or more. It creates daylight in an area several hundred meters in diameter, depending on climatic conditions (fog, cloud height, humidity).

Chemical. Loaded with one of several poison gases (see Chapter 20 on chemical weapons). This is often a variation on the HE shell, with half or more of the explosive replaced with poison.

Nuclear. In guns 152mm and larger. It has an explosive power up to five kilotons. About 8,000 of these existed at the end of the Cold War. Over half were destroyed during the 1990s. More recent models cost over $2 million each.

HEAT. High Explosive Anti-Tank shell. It generally can penetrate armor equal to five times the shell's diameter (caliber).

Beehive. A large shotgun shell filled with thousands of metal darts. Used to defend against infantry that gets too close, it is fired directly at its target, just like a shotgun.

Each shell can use a variety of fuzes, whose function is to make the shell explode. The fuze is a separate component in guns larger than 105mm; it is screwed into the tip of the shell. Fuzes come in the following varieties:

Contact. The simplest kind, it ignites the shell when the fuze strikes anything.

Delayed action. Delays ignition for up to a few seconds after contact so the shell may penetrate first; it is used for destroying fortifications, creating deep craters, etc.

Proximity. Has a radar range finder that ignites the shell when it is at a preset distance from a solid object. It is good for getting an airburst. This is necessary for Improved Conventional Munitions (ICM) that use submunitions. It also increases the effectiveness of HE, smoke, chemical, and nuclear shells. Most of these shells explode on contact and will promptly bury much of their effectiveness into the ground. The ICMs often use smaller submunitions that must be dispersed before they explode. These fuzes have been in use for over 40 years and are quite reliable, although still expensive. They were originally designed for use against aircraft, for which they are still employed.

VT (Variable Time). The poor man's proximity fuze. Gunners can preset fuze to ignite a certain number of seconds after being fired. If the calculations are correct, this has the same effect as a proximity fuze. Obviously, it is not as useful against moving targets.

ICMs (Improved Conventional Munitions)

During the 1970s, there was a significant revolution in ammunition design. So dramatic were the performance increases that this new generation was called Improved Conventional Munitions. On the downside, the ICMs were also more expensive (over $5,000 for an ICM round, versus a few hundred dollars for a conventional HE shell). This was a minor drawback, as the ability to deliver more destructive power with the same weight of munitions proved an enormous battlefield advantage. Despite the advantages of ICMs, most munitions are of the older type in nearly all armies. ICMs are simply too expensive to become the standard. In the U.S. artillery, however, over half the shells are of the ICM type, with traditional HE comprising less than a quarter of munitions available, and various other specialized types comprising an even smaller fraction. All classes of shells were improved, but only those that showed a dramatic improvement are properly called ICM. The current ICM features include:

Cargo shell. Hollow shells designed to carry a variety of submunitions (loaded at the factory). The submunitions are either antipersonnel, anti-armor, or DPICM (Dual Purpose ICM for use against troops and vehicles). These smaller warheads (about the size of a flashlight battery) are ejected before the shell hits the ground and are spread over a wide area before they detonate. Sometimes they don't go off right away, but detonate later or act as mines. Antipersonnel and trackbuster mines are often used and simply lie on the ground until stepped on or passed over by a soldier or vehicle. Other antipersonnel submunitions function like hand grenades, while antitank munitions also come in the form of small HEAT warheads that hit and penetrate the thin top armor of tanks. There is continuous development of deadlier submunitions. The principal current types (and the number of bomblets carried) are 155mm shells (88), 203mm shells (180), MLRS rockets (688), and ATACMS (Army Tactical Missile Systems) (950).

Rocket boosters. An add-on for shells that, as the name implies, boosts the range of shells up to 50 percent. There is some loss of accuracy and payload.

Guidance systems. These have not worked out too well. The only shell in use that has a guidance system is the U.S. Copperhead. It's too expensive, requires someone at the front to bounce a laser off the target, and fog and smoke can interfere with this process. Something like this will work effectively eventually.

General improvements. Most other types of shells are also being dramatically improved with regard to effectiveness. You can see from this that the number of guns is less important than shell quality and quantity.

Artillery is basically a delivery service. It delivers ammunition in large quantities to targets designated by the combat units.

SELF-PROPELLED VERSUS TOWED

Throughout artillery's history, there has been "foot artillery" and "horse artillery." The more numerous "foot" had the gunners walking and the guns dragged along by horses. In the "horse artillery" everyone rode on a horse or a high-speed wagon. This unit was organized and equipped for speed of movement and action. Modern self-propelled artillery follows that tradition, with a few twists. The first tanks were intended to be self-propelled artillery. The armor was added to give protection against enemy fire. The tracklaying mechanism (like a bulldozer) was used to get this heavy contraption over the torn-up battlefield. The primary purpose of all this was clearing out enemy machine guns so that the friendly foot soldiers could make some headway. Soon both sides had tanks, and the tanks were soon pounding away at each other. This left the infantry in the lurch once more. Some 25 years after the tank was first used, artillery was mounted on a tank chassis and used as mobile artillery. The purpose was to avoid direct fire and enemy tanks. The new "horse artillery" proved highly successful. Today, the self-propelled (SP) artillery is mounted on a lightly armored chassis of similar size to tanks. Although three or more times as expensive as towed artillery, it has several important advantages:

- SP artillery can keep up with mechanized units and go places towed artillery cannot.
- Its armor makes it more resistant to enemy artillery, and more capable of delivering direct fire and surviving.
- Each SP gun is a self-contained unit, so emplacing the gun is faster. Towed artillery takes about 30 minutes to prepare for firing; SP guns need about half that time. Most time-consuming is calculating the precise position of the gun relative to its target. Recent developments in electronic navigation systems allow some SP guns to halt and fire within minutes of the order. The satellite-based GPS navigation system now allows this to be done even more quickly.
- SP guns are also faster moving out of a firing position, taking a minute or two. Towed guns have to load gear back onto trucks, hook the guns on to their tractors, and generally stay in one place long enough to get hit by counterbattery fire.

SP guns have their drawbacks:

- Being tracked vehicles, they are more prone to breakdowns.
- Traveling along with fast-moving mechanized units exposes them to more enemy fire. Their armor notwithstanding, they take heavier losses.
- Supply is more difficult for the SP guns. Most of the ammo is carried on trucks, although some armored vehicles are used.
- These weapons are expensive. While Western armies have had them since World War II, Russia and many Third World nations are still in the process of equipping their divisions with SP guns.

Overall, SP guns are still superior to the towed variety, despite their shortcomings. But SP guns are a wealthy nation's advantage, another example of how you can buy a battlefield advantage.

ROCKETS AND MISSILES

Modern field-artillery rockets were a Soviet innovation during World War II. Western armies have recently begun using these again. The rockets were initially developed to provide a large amount of firepower quickly. Accuracy and range were not critical, just the ability to saturate an area with explosions. These weapons were also relatively cheap. Because the Soviets lost so much conventional artillery in 1941, these rocket launchers were the right weapon at the right time. Rockets had other advantages. Against an opponent with good counterbattery capability, rockets can get into position, fire all their rockets, and get out before enemy counterbattery can hit them. Rockets are inaccurate but get around this by being launched in large numbers, simultaneously, at the same area. As a result, they are called "area fire weapons." You fire a lot of them in the general direction of the target and hit whatever is in the area before the enemy troops have a chance to seek cover.

In the last 60 years, rockets have gained accuracy and range. They are still crude compared to conventional artillery. For example, 50 percent of rockets fired can be expected to land in a 100–200 meter circle. Ranges now go up to 40 kilometers. Rockets are still useful in modern warfare and have numerous advantages:

- They are a surprise weapon. You inflict more casualties when you catch troops outside their tanks, IFVs, and fortifications. The first shell to land sends everyone diving for cover. When several dozen rockets arrive all at once, there is little opportunity to duck.
- When using chemical weapons, rockets are the ideal delivery system. Gas is an area weapon, and surprise is important to prevent troops from putting on their masks.

- For the Russians and many Third World nations, rockets still compensate for several of their shortcomings. A lack of high-quality fire-control equipment is overcome with barrages of rockets. This makes rockets an ideal counterbattery weapon for these lower-tech armies.
- Fear. The sudden and massive firepower delivered by rockets often demoralizes troops on the receiving end. This was the case when rockets were first used against the Germans in 1941, and half a century later Iraqi troops were equally terrified by the U.S.-made MLRS rockets.

As an example of what rockets can do, consider a Russian battalion of 18 BM-21 rocket launchers, with 40 tubes per launcher. The unit can fire 720 rockets in a few seconds to a range of 20 kilometers. The launchers are mounted on trucks and can be on their way in under 10 minutes. It takes 15–30 minutes to occupy a new position, depending on time of day. A launcher can be reloaded in 10 minutes with three tons of rockets. An automatic loader is being used in some units, which cuts the reload time to two minutes. This makes it possible for a unit to fire two salvos before moving on. Units usually carry only two loads of rockets with them. A 720-round volley of 122mm BM-21 rockets will devastate an area as large as 2,000 by 500 meters. It would take a battalion of guns six minutes of rapid fire to do the same damage. The rocket warheads are no more lethal than equivalent-caliber artillery shells. However, the effect on troop morale is more pronounced. For this reason, rockets are preferred when you want to achieve surprise and overcome the enemy quickly. Western rockets are more accurate, have longer range, and carry more exotic warheads (submunitions) than Russian models. The Russians have copied some of these developments, although their less capable manufacturing prevents them from achieving parity. The U.S.-made MLRS rocket system proved the value of the high-tech Western rocket launchers in the Gulf War. The improved accuracy, cluster-bomb warhead, and longer range of the MLRS had a devastating effect on Iraqi units, particularly artillery units.

The only disadvantages of rockets is their minimum range of a few kilometers and the rather prominent cloud of dust and smoke that pinpoints the launchers' position when the rockets are fired.

Field-artillery missiles are a post–World War II development. These were originally intended for one purpose: delivering nuclear weapons. These weapons have longer ranges and greater accuracy than rockets. Most now have inertial guidance systems, and some have ranges of over 1,000 kilometers. The shorter-range weapons (under 200 kilometers) are more often being equipped to deliver chemical or ICM loads. The Western MLRS can fire either 16 conventional artillery rockets or two longer-range missiles (ATACMS).

Long seen as a supplement to regular artillery, the introduction of the high-tech U.S. MLRS rocket system in the 1980s began to make a lot of conventional artillery obsolete. Of course, artillery has always been ripe for innovation. The U.S. 175mm gun, introduced in the 1960s, was rendered obsolete in the 1980s with the introduction of special long-range ammo for the 203mm (8-inch) howitzer. When the MLRS entered service, one of the three batteries in each division's 203mm howitzer battalion was equipped with MLRS units instead. But MLRS proved so effective that the 203mm howitzer battalion became an MLRS battalion. There were always non-divisional MLRS battalions, as the MLRS was seen, from the beginning, as an ideal weapon for massed artillery fire. The Gulf War allowed the MLRS to show off what a potent weapon it could be. The larger rockets also provided room for more complex payloads (cluster and "smart" munitions) and guidance systems. This was another example of how technology can transform an old weapon. While the Russians have been using rocket launchers for over 60 years, they never got around to enhancing their effectiveness.

HELICOPTERS

What has really replaced the fast-moving horse artillery of old is the helicopter. Fixed-wing bombers deliver their bombs while moving along at 200–400 miles an hour. Helicopters can hover and deliver their weapons with artillery-like accuracy. All helicopters can be equipped with weapons. Most nations build special gunships that can carry rockets, automatic cannon, machine guns, or ATGM. Some now carry air-to-air missiles. Unarmed helicopters often drop mines. Although helicopters are aircraft, armies use them as very mobile artillery, sending them wherever the danger is greatest.

Theory and Practice

Most Western divisions have one or more artillery-spotting radars. Even Russia, and some Third World nations, have begun to deploy them. These devices track mortar and artillery shells in flight and determine where they were fired from. This information is passed back to friendly artillery, which then does a little counterbattery number on the opposition. Soviet doctrine long assumed that any of their guns would be targeted and shot at within minutes of firing at a Western unit. These developments have changed the way artillery operates. There is more decentralization: regiments and brigades have their own artillery. These may be a few batteries or a few battalions. Divisions and armies have their own artillery groups, which are used to reinforce the brigades and regiments. Forward observers from the artillery units still travel with the infantry and tanks. These observers do not expect to have the kind of good radio communications that they have had in the past. Electronic warfare has forced this move away from massed fires.

Many armies still use massed artillery attacks, but only as carefully pre-planned operations. These set-piece operations will not require radio, they will go according to the plan. Any armies that are in the wrong place at the wrong time yet use these set-piece tactics will get smashed by their own guns. Many new developments work against future use of mass fire: more effective counterbattery fire, electronic warfare, a more fluid battlefield, and more effective munitions. The Iraqis received a demonstration of this in 1991.

Artillery was originally developed to tear up unprotected troops. Most front-line soldiers are now in or near an armored vehicle. Artillery is not all that cost-effective against armored vehicles. Electronic warfare makes quick communication between infantry and artillery unreliable. Counterbattery has become so effective that massing guns together is risky. With all combat units on wheels, troops will be spread all over the place. As a result, artillery has been greatly decentralized. A regiment or brigade has its own artillery battalion, while the division retains a few battalions, which often get attached to a brigade, anyway. Cargo shells carrying antitank or antipersonnel submunitions are a more effective use of limited transportation resources. The emphasis is on responsiveness and speed.

All industrialized nations now use computers for field-artillery-driven fire-control systems. Widely available are lightweight laser range finders that also compute the location of the target. Working with this gadget are the GPS receivers that receive signals from navigation satellites so that the user always knows their position to within 20 meters or so. These two items got their first major workout in the Gulf War and performed very effectively. They were not seriously degraded by Iraqi ECM (electronic countermeasures), although the Iraqis tried.

When ICM got their first widespread workout in the 1991 Gulf War, one ugly side effect was discovered. As reports from Russian use of ICM in Afghanistan confirmed, not all the bomblets in cluster bombs would detonate when desired. This left the battlefield covered with "dud" bomblets that would still go off if a vehicle, or even a person, came upon them—a nasty surprise for which a solution will have to be found.

While nearly all artillery fired in the vicinity of friendly troops is spotted by artillery observers at the front, some 90 percent of the spotting of targets in the enemy rear is by aircraft. This has been the case since 1917. But now RPVs (Remotely Powered Vehicles) and satellites are becoming more common.

The Future

After several decades of stagnation, the last 20 years of developments in guns and ammunition have increased artillery's effectiveness considerably. These improvements are only now maturing and spreading to many nations. The most important new developments will be sensors, guidance, and the increased effectiveness of submunitions. For example, your average 155mm HE shell creates fires 1–2 meters from the point of detonation. Some 2,000–4,000 fragments spray out, traveling 500–1,700 meters a second. The average fragment weight is two-thirds of an ounce, and most fly harmlessly into the air or ground. ICMs can, for the same weight of shell, deliver several times the number of effective fragments and fire-producing capability by using sensors and computers in the shell to determine the optimal position and altitude for detonation. Also, GPS receivers are getting cheaper and smaller. Experiments have been conducted with GPS-guided shells, although we'll see GPS-guided rockets first.

Principal Artillery in Use

The artillery, systems-in-use weapons shown in the chart represent over 90 percent of what is currently in use worldwide. The United States and Russia provide much of what is used by other nations, either in the form of exports or designs. Some other Western nations manufacture their own, but these holdings are minor. China manufactures copies of Russian equipment and exports some of it. Weapons are sorted by nation and caliber.

Caliber (mm)	Name	Range (km)	ROF per min	Radius (m)	Shell (kg)	Protection	AT cap. mm pen.	Mobility	Weight (tons)
U.S.									
105	M102	11.5	3	175	15	0	102	Towed	1.15
105	M101A1	11	3	175	15	0	102	Towed	2.26
155	M198	30	2	360	44	0	800	Towed	7.20
155	M109A6	30	2	360	44	7	800	SP	32.00
155	M114A1	14.6	2	360	44	0	800	Towed	5.80
175	M107	32.7	0.5	520	67	0	0	SP	28.20
203	M110A2	29	0.5	470	91	0	0	SP	28.20
227	MLRS A1	41	4	750	400	6	0	SP	25.00
Russia									
122	M55/D74	24	6	210	22	0	460	Towed	5.50
122	BM-21	20.5	4	2,000	46	0	0	SP	11.50
122	2S1	15.3	8	240	26	5	460	SP	16.00
122	M63/D30	15.3	8	240	26	0	230	Towed	3.20
130	M46	33	6	280	33	0	230	Towed	7.70
140	RPU-14	9.8	4	750	40	0	0	Towed	1.20
152	2S5	28	1	350	44	3	800	SP	21.40
152	2S3	24	2	350	44	3	800	SP	28.00
152	M55/D20	24	1	350	44	0	800	Towed	5.70
203	2S7	30	1	470	91	3	0	SP	30.00
220	BM-27	40	1	750	360	0	0	SP	22.70
240	2S4	9.7	1	350	100	3	800	SP	32.00
300	9A52-2	70	0.3	800	235	0	0	SP	44.00

Caliber is the diameter of the projectile in millimeters.

Name is the designation of the weapon. The 105mm (4.1-inch) guns were standard during World War II but now are used only by Western airborne units. All 122mm weapons are of Russian design. The D74 is a long-range gun, while the D30 is the Russians' standard towed howitzer. The SP guns are generally SP versions of towed weapons like the D30. The BM-21 is the standard, but not the only, rocket launcher. The 130mm M46 is the most widely used Russian long-range gun. The RPU-14 is the standard rocket launcher in airborne units. The D20 and the SP version are the standard 152mm artillery and are identical except that one is self-propelled. The M-114A1 is out of production but still widely used. It is being replaced by the 155mm M198. The M110A2 (203mm) is found in many Western armies. The 2S series is the new generation of Russian self-propelled artillery. The Russians use missiles and larger rockets like the BM-24, 9A52-2, and BM-27.

Range is the extreme range of the gun in kilometers. In practice, the best accuracy is achieved at two-thirds this range. Although the chart does not state it, you can see which artillery is the short-barreled howitzers and which are guns. Howitzers are designed to fire at high angles and hit targets behind obstacles like hills. Guns have longer barrels, a higher shell velocity, and a flatter trajec-

M-109A3 self-propelled 155mm artillery

tory. Although unable to hit targets behind hills, guns have longer ranges. This wears out the barrel more quickly, often after fewer than 500 rounds are fired. Howitzer barrels will last for thousands of rounds. Near the end of a barrel's useful life, wear and tear have an increasingly detrimental effect on accuracy. Range can be increased with RAP (Rocket Assisted Propellant) shells. Although RAP increases range 40–50 percent, there is a considerable loss in accuracy. At these extreme ranges, half the shells will fall outside a 150-meter circle. You then have to either fire more shells at the target, or use a nuclear warhead. The use of submunitions also makes RAP shells more effective, although there is less space in the shell because of the need to make room for the RAP rocket motor itself.

ROF per min is the sustained rate of fire per minute. Guns can fire double to triple that rate for a minute or so. Maintaining a higher rate of fire for any longer will overheat the barrel. For rockets, the number of rockets per reload cycle is given. The rocket launchers fire their projectiles in seconds and take about 10 minutes to reload unless special fast-reload equipment is available. The BM-21 launcher has 40 tubes, the RPU-14 has sixteen, the BM-27 has 16, the 9A52-2 has twelve.

Radius (in meters) is the area covered by the battery volley (one shell each from a battery of six guns) of HE (High Explosive). In this area there is a 50 percent chance of an exposed individual being hit. ICM (Improved Conventional Munitions) used by Western, and increasingly by Russian, armies increase this area by two or three times and the probability of getting hit by up to 90 percent. The ICM customarily use hundreds of smaller bomblets that scatter over a large area before exploding.

Shell is the weight of the standard HE shell in kilograms (2.2 pounds). A complete round also includes propellant and packing material. This increases total weight 30–50 percent. An increasing number of shell types are becoming available. Their weight varies from that of the standard shell for that caliber by no more than 20 percent either way.

Protection is the degree of armored protection. A zero indicates no protection at all.

AT cap. mm pen. is the armor-piercing capability of the weapon using available armor-piercing shells, in millimeters.

Mobility indicates if the gun is towed by a truck or tractor or self-propelled on a tank or IFV chassis.

Weight is the weight of the system in tons (without tractor if towed).

Artillery Destruction Table

This chart shows how much artillery ammunition must be used to inflict various levels of damage on armored and unarmored units. The casualty figures are averages. Actual losses can be more than doubled or halved depending on the luck and skill of the attackers and defenders. Using conventional HE (High Explosive) shells against armored targets is an expensive and questionable process. Each ton of HE costs about $12,000. Modern armored vehicles (tanks, IFVs, and specialized types) cost an average of over $1 million each. The units in the chart have some $60 million worth of vehicles. To destroy a unit, you must destroy or disable 50 or 60 percent of its vehicles. That comes to about $35 million worth of damage. On the average, you can do this using less than $35 million worth of artillery shells. However, accountants do not determine who wins on the battlefield. The biggest problem with calculations of this sort is how thousands of tons of munitions are to reach their targets. A division in a major attack might have 200 or 300 guns available, with access to large ammunition supplies. Three hundred guns could fire, on a sustained basis, 600 shells a minute. That's about 35 tons a minute. If the division is attacking three battalions, a destruction bombardment will take from one to five hours. Because of the faster reaction times and more accurate counterbattery fire, a gun that fires more than five minutes from the same position is inviting destruction. The other problem is logistical. Providing large quantities of ammunition on the modern battlefield is an uncertain business. All this has not gone unnoticed. Several solutions can be applied. Fewer shells can be fired, using ICMs (Improved Conventional Munitions). These were calculated to be 3–10 times as effective as HE shells. ICMs proved to be slightly less effective after receiving some extensive combat use. But ICM is the future, especially for MLRS rockets (which can carry large quantities of submunitions). ICM in artillery shells is too expensive because of the restricted space in shells and the difficultly in making electronics work in fast moving shells. Destruction fires will

| Activity of defending unit | Area covered (sq km) | % casualties per 100 tons of ammo | | Tons of ammunition expended to: | | | |
| | | | | Neutralize | | Destroy | |
		Armor unit	Soft unit	Armor unit	Soft unit	Armor unit	Soft unit
Hasty attack	1	31	109	96	28	160	46
Prepared attack	1	21	75	143	40	239	67
Assembly	1.7	30	49	99	61	165	101
Hasty defense	3.6	9	18	345	169	576	282
Prepared defense	3.6	3	6	1,043	517	1,739	862
Dispersed defense	7	1	3	2,029	1,005	3,381	1,676

be used only if enemy counterbattery is not a threat. Neutralization fires will be the norm.

Activity of defending unit indicates how men and equipment are deployed. The unit represented is a reinforced battalion with 500–1,000 men and 50 or 60 combat vehicles if an armored unit.

Hasty attack is a quick movement from column on a road to lines of vehicles moving cross-country to the attack.

Prepared attack is more deliberate, with troops and vehicles taking advantage of terrain to minimize artillery damage.

Assembly is troops gathered together before engaging in some other activity, or simply resting.

Hasty defense is similar to hasty attack, except that the troops seek cover and prepare to defend.

Prepared defense is when troops have time to dig in and prepare to defend.

Dispersed defense is similar to prepared defense, except that the troops are spread over a wider area.

Area covered is the area occupied by the unit. It is the area into which the artillery falls. It is roughly square-shaped and measured in square kilometers.

% casualties per 100 tons of ammo is the percentage of the units' troops and/or vehicles that will be killed, destroyed, or disabled. The two classes of targets are:

Armor, a unit consisting primarily of tanks, IFVs, and other armored vehicles.

Soft, a unit consisting only of troops and/or unarmored vehicles.

The traditional rule of thumb for neutralization fire with HE shells is 1 round per 100 square meters for armored units and 1 per 1,000 square meters for soft targets. A Western-type division carries over 3,000–5,000 tons of artillery munitions, a Russian or Third World division about half that. These numbers can be increased when transportation and munitions are available. The other problem is time. If you spend too much time blasting away at a unit to soften it up, you give the defender an opportunity to bring up reinforcements. Artillery fires on the modern battlefield will be of short duration, probably no more than 15 minutes.

Tons of ammunition expended to neutralize or destroy indicates how much ammunition will be needed to neutralize (destroy one-quarter to one-third) or destroy (about 50 percent) of the unit. The tonnages shown are for HE shells. About one-fifth that amount will be needed if ICMs (Improved Conventional Munitions) are used.

5

Combat Support

Combat troops need all the support they can get. The battlefield is not occupied solely by infantry, tank crews, and artillerymen. There are a large number of specialist troops there, also. These combat-support troops are not there to fight, but to support those who do.

The Multiplier Effect of Combat Support

By themselves, combat troops can be quite effective. But in many special situations, their effectiveness can be increased considerably with the addition of specialist troops. Engineer support makes it easier to take enemy fortifications or cross natural and man-made obstacles. Some natural barriers, like rivers, are impassable to tanks without the engineers and their portable bridges. These same bridges will get you across antitank ditches dug by the opposition. Enemy minefields and fortifications can be made less lethal by combat engineers. Signal troops ensure that there is communication between combat troops and their supply sources, headquarters, and support units to the rear. Transportation troops keep the fuel, ammunition, and other supplies coming. Without this, combat troops will be out of supply within days. Military police control traffic, guard prisoners, and maintain security just behind the combat zone. Many more combat troops would be required to do what the military police are trained to do. Chemical troops provide assistance in decontaminating vehicles and troops exposed to chemical weapons. Otherwise, chemical-warfare losses would be several times higher. Electronic-warfare troops reduce the effect of enemy jamming and in turn debilitate enemy communications.

Headquarters troops coordinate everything. Without them there would be more chaos than already exists on the battlefield.

Centralized Versus Decentralized

There are two ways to use combat support. Because support units are expensive and difficult to create and maintain, nations with fewer resources keep most of the combat support troops out of the combat divisions in order to preserve them as much as possible. This makes the combat divisions less efficient but enables the entire armed forces to stay in combat longer. Nations with larger degrees of industrialization and technology development have an easier time creating support units. Less developed nations must depend more on pure combat units to fight a short war. An army with slender support resources will not be able to replace combat and noncombat losses as quickly as more technologically advanced states. Without combat support, battlefield losses increase. Western armies are trained and equipped to keep men and machines operational longer. Russia, for example, has long created equipment and units designed and deployed to fight a short, intense war. For a long war, their equipment would break down rapidly, and they would have difficulty rebuilding their shattered arms.

All armies have specialist support units. Each division has them, with others available at the army level, much like divisional and non-divisional artillery. Keep in mind that Western armies have about twice as much combat support as Third World forces. Below is a description of each combat support unit's function. The size of the unit shows the differences between Western and Third World armies. The larger units are typically Western. Also given is the average percentage each specialist group takes up in a division. Typically, a division is one-third combat troops, the rest combat support. Depending on the type of division and nationality, infantry comprises 8–30 percent of division strength, tank crews 1–10 percent, and artillery (including antiaircraft and antitank weapons) 6–12 percent. Combat troops comprise an even smaller portion of non-divisional forces, something like 5–10 percent. Since combat divisions account for 20–50 percent of army manpower, combat troops comprise only 10–25 percent of all personnel. In all armies, combat support troops are very much the majority.

Engineers

Engineers comprise 2–10 percent of a division's manpower. Each division has at least a battalion (400–1,100 men) of engineers. Often regiments and brigades have their own engineer company (100–300 men). The United States has experimented with giving each combat division an engineer brigade. Non-divisional engineer battalions are supplied to armies in a ratio of one or more battalions for each division in the army. Whenever something has to be built or torn down, the engineers are called in. Many of the troops in divisional engineers' battalions are actually combat troops doing demolition or construction work while under enemy fire. The U.S. army engineers see their job as twofold: mobility enhancement (keeping things moving) of their own forces and counter-mobility work to slow down the opposition. The engineers are a hard-working crew, as the following list of their major responsibilities indicates:

Bridges. Most engineers are builders, in this case bridge builders. About one-third of a divisional engineer battalion consists of bridge-building troops. They use various self-propelled and truck-carried bridging equipment. The former are 15–20-meter bridges mounted on an unarmored tank chassis or a truck. These can support up to 50 tons or more (one tank). Longer bridge sections, which can also double as ferries, are carried on trucks.

Digging and minelaying. Engineers also supervise or control all construction equipment. The Russians went even further, providing each division with sufficient excavation equipment to entrench one of the division's four regiments in a day. Each Russian combat regiment has enough engineer equipment to entrench one battalion a day. Minelaying machines (Russian) can lay at least 800 mines (eight tons) per hour. Depending on how many mines are carried, ten kilometers of minefields are laid down for each regiment. Such a lavish use of mines is generally unlikely in the opening stages of a war because when on the offensive, a division carries less than 100 tons of mines. Western armies depend more upon trackbuster mines delivered by aircraft and artillery. Stored at the air bases, these weigh less than five pounds each, one-tenth as much as conventional mines.

Defensive positions. Engineers have found the "speed bump" approach to be effective on the battlefield. Anything that slows down the enemy is an advantage. This entails more than mines and trenches. Other engineer chores are constructing road barricades and laying out markers to show where defending units will deploy and where roads will be built and camouflage constructed. This planning and supervisory function is one of the more important ones engineers provide. Many of the earliest military academies, including the United States' West Point, were founded to train engineer officers for this kind of work.

Mine clearing. Infantrymen can clear mines, but engineers can do it more quickly and safely. Their training and specialized equipment make engineers critical if you must get through a minefield quickly. Many new plastic mines are very difficult to detect and clear. In this case, the engineers are responsible for finding and marking these areas. The first large-scale clearing of plastic mines took place after the 1991 Gulf War. There are several such fields remaining in the Falklands, Cambodia, and Afghanistan. Those are gradually being cleared by wayward animals and pedestrians.

Demolition. What goes up, demolition brings down. Handling tons of explosives to demolish large structures requires expert knowledge and proficiency. Bridges are particularly difficult to bring down. Airfields, roads, rail lines, and structures of all kinds may have to be destroyed by engineer troops. Such jobs take longer if the proper equipment and specialists are not at hand. For example, clearing a 75-meter abatis (large earthen obstacle laden with barbed wire, logs, and booby traps) can take 16 hours with just chain saws and hand tools. The same squad of engineers with a combat engineer vehicle (CEV) can do it in less than four hours.

Construction and repair. Aside from field fortifications dug out of the ground, engineers can also quickly put up one-story prefabricated buildings, large tents, and inflatable structures, and build roads, runways, and railroads. Special engineer construction battalions do most of the construction, and most other engineer units can do the maintenance. For example, repairing a large road crater (30 by 20 by 10 feet deep) takes an hour with a CEV. Air forces maintain special engineer units to repair airfield damage quickly. Navies have their own engineers who specialize in building, maintaining, operating, and repairing port facilities.

Maps. You can't fight a proper war without a timely supply of accurate maps. Normally, the engineers are responsible for creating, reproducing, and distributing maps. Increasingly, the maps are digital and are delivered electronically via CD-ROM to units, and less frequently printed on paper.

Utilities. Engineers are responsible for generating power in the field. Any large plant, such as a field bakery, decontamination equipment, or field baths is often maintained and operated by engineers. It simplifies the question of whom to call when something breaks down.

Engineers in combat units handle largely combat-related tasks. The noncombat engineer tasks are taken up by non-divisional engineer units.

Signal

Between 3–12 percent of a division's personnel are assigned to signal troops. Divisional signal battalions (400–1,000 men) are not the only signal units in a division. Every unit down to a company or platoon has some signal troops.

Nondivisional signal units exist in a ratio of one per division. Modern armies are held together with electronic signal equipment. Armored vehicles have an internal intercom system and one or more radios for outside communications. Defensive and noncombat positions make extensive use of telephones. All this equipment is maintained, and often installed and manned, by signal troops. Non-divisional signal battalions take on many aspects and responsibilities of civilian telephone companies. These units set up and maintain long-distance communications, especially satellite links. They set up hundreds of radio and telephone "nets" (party lines) and look after the security and efficiency of these nets. Western armies are making increasing use of satellite and cellular-phone technology, also. Signal troops also assist the intelligence and elec-tronic-warfare troops. The dozens of radio nets in a division can easily lapse into chaos without the efficient efforts of the signal troops. Many units have multiple nets. Typical communication-net types are for combat units (com-pany's battalions, brigades) as well as different types of units (an artillery net, a supply net, an aircraft net, etc.). At headquarters, the nets are connected to one another with multiple radio sets or special equipment. Signal troops assist in maintaining radio and net discipline. That is, no useless chatter, unauthorized breaking in on another net, or transmitting in other than the rigid, authorized format. All of this is being revolutionized by the introduction of intranet tech-nology to the battlefield—not just "battlefield intranet," but the same kind of networking for voice communications.

Chemical

Chemical troops comprise 1–4 percent of a division's strength. Most divisions now have a chemical company or battalion. Smaller units often have their own chemical unit, such as a chemical platoon for a regiment or brigade. The pri-mary responsibility of the chemical troops' portion in a division is detection of chemical, nuclear, or biological weapons. They often have decontamination equipment. More information on this is given in Chapter 21.

Transport

Between 8–16 percent of a division's troops are involved in transportation, including the drivers of combat unit supply vehicles. Most divisions have a transport battalion. Otherwise, transport vehicles are scattered through the division and/or the transport units belong to a higher headquarters. Battalions and regiments follow the same pattern. Non-divisional transport units are usu-ally available in a ratio of two or three transport battalions for each division in an army. No matter how they are organized, there are a lot of trucks running around the battle area with supplies. Transport units move supplies. They are typically equipped with trucks, but some have railroad equipment or even coastal and river boats. A typical medium truck battalion has about 200 five-ton trucks, each capable of pulling a 10-ton trailer. Allowing for out-of-service vehicles and variable load size, this gives the unit a maximum practical carrying capacity of 2,000 tons. A transport company has a 500-ton capacity, a platoon 150 tons. Western armies have introduced a new generation of heavier 10-ton (and up) trucks that are designed to handle pallets and containers while also being able to move more easily off roads. These vehicles got their first wartime workout in the 1991 Gulf War and performed well. This was essential, it turned out, because the older-type trucks were not able to deliver fuel and supplies fast enough and in adequate quantity cross-country. The latest generation of tanks uses much more fuel. The Gulf War operations were in the desert, requiring nearly as much water as fuel to be moved. Because of the flat desert terrain, the combat units were able to move more rapidly, putting even more stress on the supply transport units. Without the new generation of trucks, the battle would have proceeded more slowly, and with more coalition losses.

While transport units will carry anything, some specialize. For example, tank transporter units consist of 30–60 heavy tractor-trailers, each with a 50–70-ton capacity. Other heavy units have tanker trucks for carrying fuel. Most divisions and all armies have air-transportation units. These are helicopters and light fixed-wing aircraft. The trend is toward one aviation battalion per division, although this unit is used more as a taxi/delivery/ambulance/scouting service than as a transportation unit. Army-level aviation units are more likely to be used for transport. For more details, see the chapters on logistics (Chapter 23), air transport (Chapter 27), and naval transport (Chapter 26).

Military Police

Between 1–2 percent of a division's strength are military police (MPs)—traffic-control and security troops. Most divisions have at least a company (100–200 men). At army level, there is often a battalion or more, usually including criminal investigators (detectives) and lawyers. The main function of MPs in wartime is traffic control. In rear areas, especially just behind the fighting troops, they are also used to maintain order, guard against saboteurs, and handle prisoners.

Medical

Some 2–5 percent of a division's strength are medical personnel. In addition to a medical unit (300–900 men), all combat units have medical personnel attached. Non-divisional units typically number one battalion per division in an army. At and below division level, the medical troops give first aid and evacuate wounded troops as quickly as possible. Because two-thirds of combat casualties can be returned to duty eventually, it is essential to prevent wounds from worsening and evacuate the wounded to rear areas for recuperation as quickly as possible. An equally important task of medical units is the supervision of preventive medicine. In cold climates, this means treating and monitoring exposure casualties. The chief medical officer alerts the unit commanders when these losses get out of hand. In disease-prone locales, like the tropics, the medical troops distribute medicines and eradicate pests. In any area with a lot of civilians, venereal disease will be a major problem, often the number-one cause of days lost to noncombat casualties. At all times, medical troops monitor the purity of food and water and keep an eye on living conditions in general. Because noncombat losses have historically been higher than combat casualties, the medical troops are a critical force in maintaining unit strength.

Maintenance

From 3–10 percent of a division's troops are mechanics and technicians who perform equipment repair and maintenance. Most divisions have a maintenance unit (400–1,000 men). Depending on the number of vehicles and equipment, smaller units will have up to 20 percent of their personnel specializing in maintenance tasks. Non-divisional units also have 10 percent of their troops engaged in maintenance tasks. Although military equipment is built to take a lot of punishment, the breakdown rate in the field is high. The maintenance units wage, at best, a holding action. See Chapter 24 (on attrition) for more details. Western armies have historically been more proficient at keeping things operational. Russian and Third World armies take a more brute-force approach and abandon broken equipment so that follow-up maintenance units can recover and repair what they find. Like medical units, maintenance troops devote a lot of their efforts toward performing and supervising regular and preventive maintenance. This function, in the long run, has more impact than the ability to perform many repairs quickly during combat.

Headquarters

Between 5–15 percent of a division's manpower is assigned to headquarters tasks. Every unit has a headquarters, even if it consists of one man (a squad or platoon leader). Larger units have larger headquarters; at the division level, the headquarters comprises several hundred men. Non-divisional forces have the same proportion of their manpower devoted to headquarters tasks. Headquarters administers, leads, plans, coordinates, and supports. It includes intelligence units that often send detachments to combat units to screen prisoners, examine captured equipment, and generally gather information firsthand. Headquarters collects information from subordinate units, analyzes it, and issues appropriate orders. Headquarters controls the flow of supplies; it also contains the cooks and other personal-service troops like chaplains or political officers. Without a functioning headquarters, units lose the ability to function effectively and work with other units. Many armies have headquarters that are too large. A dose of combat often indicates how small the headquarters can be to be effective.

Electronics

Between 1–3 percent of a unit's troops are operators of electronic warfare, support, and intelligence-gathering tasks. Although these troops could be considered signal troops, their work and equipment is so different as to make them a different category. The trend is toward having one electronic-warfare battalion (400–700 men) per division. Each army may have an additional battalion or two. These battalions monitor enemy signal traffic and, where appropriate, jam enemy communications. See Chapter 18, "The Electronic Battlefield," for more details.

Theory and Practice

Anyone entering the armed forces is more likely to become a clerk or technician than a combatant. However, many support personnel, particularly in the Navy, are as much at risk in combat as those manning the weapons. During peacetime, the ratio of clerks to fighters tends to grow in favor of the clerks. When the fighting starts, the trend rapidly reverses. Western armies, especially the United States, are criticized for having too many support personnel. Part of the criticism is warranted. America has developed a style of warfare that uses complex and often capable weapons. When working properly, this high-tech war machine is an awesome combat force. To keep it functioning requires prodigious personnel and material support. All nations accept that aircraft require large ground crews and masses of support equipment and supplies. Some ground weapons, like tanks and artillery, are approaching aircraft in complexity and capability. This trend comes from the realization that few troops are injured by hand-to-hand fighting, but rather through massive application of firepower. Although mountains of munitions and spare parts are built up in peacetime, these are rarely sufficient to match the capacity of weapons to consume munitions and spare parts during the initial phases of combat. Running out of ammo and spares adds to the uncertainty of battles. The complexity of current weapons will compound these concerns more so than in the past. Many high-performance weapons require enormous amounts of spare parts when they are used intensively. This has long been accepted for aircraft and ships but is now common with land weapons like tanks and missile systems. Moreover, the higher mobility of current armored vehicles has not been matched by the vehicles that must carry supplies to them. There have not yet been any wars between forces equipped with high-tech weapons. Nor have a sufficient number of technicians been trained to maintain all these new systems. It's quite common in Western armed forces to have civilian technicians from the manufacturer assigned to combat units in order to keep the equipment functioning.

In those wars where a high-tech power went after a lesser power, the initial technical confusion was compensated by the major power's numerical superiority. The Gulf War of 1990–91 demonstrated how this works. Iraq quickly exhausted its meager supply of spare parts before the fighting even began. The United States itself only had sufficient spare parts for a few weeks' combat. Many combat units had to resort to cannibalization (taking parts from one vehicle or weapon to repair several others) before the fighting began. The United States had to borrow, buy, or lease hundreds of heavy trucks to keep the troops supplied, and even that was not adequate to support an advance of more than a few hundred miles. What goes around, comes around.

The Future

Maintenance will become more automated; it has to. A shortage of experienced repair people and larger numbers of more complex equipment force greater use of computer-controlled diagnostic equipment. Since the last major war 60 years ago, the quantity of tonnage and different items needed to wage a "modern" war has increased severalfold. The means to physically move the needed supplies to the troops is easily recognized, although the problem itself never seems to be completely solved. A more subtle problem is the mix of items that will be available, or actually needed, when the shooting starts. There are vital expendable items such as hundreds of different batteries, filters, and exotic munitions. Both the combat-support and the fighting troops will have to make a lot of adjustments when a war starts. Things will not be as the planners thought they would be.

Engineer troops are already highly automated in major nations. More countries are adding items like automatic mine layers and combat-engineering equipment. Because there is less infantry, automated entrenching equipment is becoming a necessity. What infantry remains is kept busy maintaining its own growing inventory of complex gear. Mapmaking is becoming more automated, with major nations maintaining master maps on computers for quick updating and reproduction. Signal equipment will become more capable and more automated. People will be needed primarily to install the automated signal stations and antijamming equipment.

One largely unnoticed but vital function, weather forecasting, will become more accurate as more accurate radars and powerful computers are installed. More accurate and timely weather prediction can have decisive military results. Chemical equipment will see more effective detection and decontamination gear. The most startling new developments will be in the availability and use of computers and similar electronic gear. A lot of this additional computer power is taking over clerical tasks. An unfortunate side effect of this is a growing inability to perform essential clerical tasks without the computer. More prosaic tasks may become difficult without upcoming technology.

6

Paramilitary Forces and Reserves

Paramilitary troops do more fighting than regular armed forces, typically against their own people. In a major war, these paramilitary types often get involved in a major way, although the reserves (partially trained civilians) usually do most of the fighting.

Police Armies

Police forces for keeping the peace and pursuing criminals are a recent development, being practically unknown two centuries ago. Before that, police functions were performed by a combination of semiofficial vigilantes and the armed forces. When a nation is undergoing internal disorder, or the government rules with a heavy hand, special infantry forces are maintained to supplement the police. As the disorder increases, or a major war starts, these police armies grow larger and more active. Many countries organize their national police forces along military lines, making it easier to expand them and go over to more purely military operations. With the glaring exception of the United States, Canada, and several other European nations, most countries maintain substantial forces of light infantry whose primary purpose is to protect the government from its own citizens. The Soviet Union was a classic example of the paramilitary police state, as are most dictatorships. Until its collapse, the Soviet Union maintained 200,000 KGB border troops. This "army" had armored units, naval ships, and combat aircraft. These forces served the same functions as the United States Coast Guard and Border Patrol. But in America these forces amount to fewer than 50,000 men and women. In addition, the

133

Soviet Union had 260,000 MVD (Ministry of Internal Affairs) internal security troops organized into combat units. There was nothing comparable to this in Western nations, where at most you have a few thousand riot-control troops. The successor states of the Soviet Union did not disband all of these paramilitary troops, and nearly half were retained in some police or military function. The uncertain political situation in these nations may cause the number of paramilitary troops to increase to their previous Soviet levels. As the twenty-first century dawned, the Russians had more infantry in their paramilitary forces than in their army.

Some Western nations do, in fact, use the regular military to wage war against their own citizens, making these troops less capable of performing their traditional role. An example of the effects of this was seen in the Falklands in 1982. The Argentine army had spent many years making war against the Argentine people. It was in no shape to face the more professional British troops. Paramilitary forces often have little to do but stand around watching people. Such a large group of armed, bored soldiers generally leads to abuse of their police powers and declining military capabilities. The paramilitary police then become part of the problem and use their police and military power to become a self-perpetuating institution. To the government, these troops are basically an expensive insurance policy against the chance of civil disorder. We saw another example of this in Iraq in the wake of the Gulf War, as Iraqi troops spent more time fighting their own people than they did the Kuwaitis or coalition troops. This use of paramilitary and regular troops is one of the heavy costs borne by undemocratic governments.

Military Reserves

Some 200 years ago, several major European nations began conscripting civilians for the military on a regular basis. These soldiers served for only two or three years before being released. Shortly thereafter, clever staff officers in several nations came up with the notion of bringing some of these former soldiers back to the army in times of national danger. Thus began the infamous "reserve system," which enabled enormous armies to be created quickly and relatively inexpensively. World Wars I and II would not have been possible without the reserve system. These former soldiers are used in a variety of ways:

To bring skeleton peacetime units up to strength during mobilization. This is an essential element of the Russian reserve system. The former Soviet Union's army was an extreme application of the reserve system, where only a third of the divisions were at full strength in peacetime. Even the United States maintains only 55 percent of its divisions at full strength in peacetime.

The Soviets were prepared to mobilize over 2 million men to fill out their divisions in wartime. America requires a million reservists to bring all units up to strength. About half of all reserves are required for non-divisional (largely support) units. The new Russian army will probably have a system closer to that of the United States. In any event, the U.S. system worked quite well in the Gulf War, particularly with regard to the noncombat support units. The United States is also reducing its reserve forces with the end of the Cold War. But reserves will remain, as they are too effective a concept to discard entirely.

For maintenance of active units. The former Soviet Union maintained many of its reserve divisions with but a skeleton crew of active-duty soldiers. The United States maintains its reserve divisions primarily with reserve soldiers who serve full time several days a month and two weeks during the summer. In 1914, the Germans demonstrated to their disbelieving opponents that reserves could be as effective in wartime as regulars. The Germans did this by requiring their reserves to train regularly, much like the current American system. The Soviet Union could not afford this, although attempts were made to do some training. Most Soviet reservists were assigned to a unit they had never seen, and never would see unless called up. The Soviet Union did activate its reservists in this manner when it invaded Afghanistan in 1979, but quickly removed these reserve troops and replaced them with regulars. The successor states to the Soviet Union are abandoning the traditional Soviet reserve system and are trying to emulate the U.S. system. One reason to emulate the U.S. system is that the U.S. system obviously works. The other reason is to eliminate the Soviet Union's reserve obligations, which were very unpopular with the millions of reservists.

As replacements for combat losses. During heavy combat, tank and infantry battalions can lose 10–20 percent of their men a day. Half these losses will be permanent or long term. Other units in the divisions will lose smaller amounts. Three weeks of heavy combat with 20 divisions means over 200 battalions losing 40 or 50 men a day. That adds up—in this case, it amounts to over 150,000 troops who have to be replaced quickly. The reserve troops are the most readily available source.

For the formation of new units. Forming a new division requires non-divisional troops as well, for a total of at least 20,000 men per new division. You need troops possessing a variety of technical skills. Some of these specialists have a civilian counterpart and can often be taken directly from the civilian population. Specialists for whom there is no civilian equivalent, primarily combat ones, must come from the reserves. Starting new divisions from scratch, without a pool of trained manpower, can take a year. With sufficient former soldiers, you can do it in a few months. The former Soviet Union maintained an additional 50 divisions on paper, to be raised in wartime from reserves and obsolete equipment held in storage. These units, with troops in their 30s and 40s using equipment as old as they were, would have been no match for an equal number of active divisions. But such "mobilization" divisions did make a difference during World War II. The successor states to the Soviet Union will probably maintain some paper divisions, if only on paper. There isn't much useable equipment left for these units.

Israel provides an example of very extensive use of a reserve system. Mobilization calls up over 15 percent of the Jewish and Druze population and severely disrupts the economy. Other nations, Sweden and Switzerland, also have reserve armies whose mobilization would shut down their economies. However, these two nations are neutral and depend more on the threat of mobilization. Israel has had to mobilize many times in the past and will probably have to do it again. Economic disruption is not the only problem mobilization armies face. Many of these armies tend to rely heavily on conscripts, to the extent that 75 percent of their manpower are two- or three-year draftees. This is typical in nations that rely on conscription. In Russian-style armies, most of the noncommissioned officers are senior conscripts of dubious quality. The officers in these armies are generally all volunteers and graduates of military academies. These officers perform the tasks normally assigned to NCOs in Western armed forces.

The U.S. System

The U.S. reserve system grew out of the pre-Revolution militia, now represented by the National Guard system. These units provide 40 percent of the infantry and armor battalions. Although the Guard has a longstanding reputation as a social club and fiefdom of local politicians, its performance in this century has demonstrated that it can fight, too. Active army units that have "fought" Guard units in maneuvers have learned not to underestimate their skill and effectiveness.

The official reserve units are under the direct control of their respective services. Like the Guard, the reserves use both former active-duty troops and personnel recruited directly into reserve units. Together, the Guard and reserves accounted for over 50 percent of ground combat and 60 percent of combat-support units just before the Cold War ended. This militia system is used by several other nations. Britain, for example, has its territorial troops who operate much like the U.S. National Guard. Germany has a territorial army whose wartime task is maintaining order and guarding against saboteurs and raids. Most nations have small navy and air force reserve units. The United States maintains major portions of its naval and air force strength in the reserves. Hundreds of aircraft, including the most modern combat planes, are manned by reservists. Again, the reserve pilots often show up the regulars. This should not be surprising, as the reserve pilots are former regulars who continue to pile up flying hours as a hobby. The

U.S. naval reserve maintains scores of support and escort ships, participating in maneuvers on an equal basis with regular navy units.

The U.S. reserve system is a recent development. Only a wealthy economy can provide enough skilled people with enough leisure time to become effective part-time soldiers. The average reservist spends five weeks a year training. In addition, he can be called up for longer periods in the event of civil or military emergencies. A few nations have gone the United States one better. Sweden, Switzerland, and Israel maintain similar but proportionately larger reserve systems. Indeed, Sweden and Switzerland have practically no regular forces to speak of and depend on their huge reserve armies to deter potential aggressors. So far, this appears to have worked.

The U.S. system is not without its disadvantages. Although over half of U.S. Army combat strength is from the reserve and National Guard forces, these received only 10 percent of the Army's budget at the end of the Cold War. While this might be enough if there were reasonable spending goals, the U.S. Army goes for building combat units that, in wartime, would have to be supported by reserve units that lack much essential equipment. On paper, National Guard brigades are part of regular Army divisions that would fight together in the event of a war. However, the National Guard units do not have complete sets of equipment like the regular units. It would take over 30 days longer to ship the National Guard units to a war because of the time required to obtain the missing equipment. These discrepancies are regularly glossed over. Indeed, the National Guard officers are told not to report equipment shortages if the discrepancy is major. This approach only shows minor shortages and simply ignores the major ones. Moreover, during the Gulf War, the regulars simply didn't want the three National Guard brigades that were technically part of divisions sent to the Gulf. There was a considerable scandal over how this was handled, and we haven't heard the last of it.

The only bright spot in this situation is that every other nation probably has a similar situation with understrength reserve units. The chief advantage of the U.S.-style reserve system is the existence of fully formed and trained units. The quality of these units is what makes the system work. Training together over many years, these reserve units achieve a degree of cohesion and professionalism that often surpass regular units. It's a rich man's system that less affluent nations like Russia cannot afford to match.

The Uncounted Reserves

When war breaks out, a lot of civilians find themselves in uniform doing pretty much the same work they performed in peacetime. As warfare becomes more technological, the skills of the support soldier become more important. Complex skills are retained only through practice. A soldier who learned a technical skill in the service and went on to another career as a civilian rapidly loses those military skills. The regularly practiced skill of a civilian electronics technician becomes immediately useful in the military. The ability of a nation to make civilian expertise a military asset depends on the quantity and quality of these skills available. The Western nations have a distinct advantage in this respect. These nations have a surplus of these skills because of their higher standard of living. Poor nations live closer to the threshold of survival. Current examples are the many poor colonies that lost their thin reserve of technicians in the postcolonial period. Starvation, economic collapse, and a general inability to make any massive efforts, like industrialization or a major war, resulted. Russia suffered in this fashion during World War II. Much of Russia's industrial base was overrun by the Germans in 1941–42. Most of the aid given to Russia during the war was not war material, but industrial goods, raw materials, and other supplies. These were lacking because too many Russian technicians were at the front getting killed. Soviet industrial and technical resources were not sufficient to keep their armed forces going without external assistance. Russians remember this trauma better than most Westerners realize. Despite the demise of the Soviet Union, Russians will continue to implement their traditional solutions. Their equipment will be kept quite simple by Western standards. Russian designers will readily sacrifice performance in order to field a weapon that can be used effectively with minimal training. This is not always possible, but it is pursued diligently enough to make Russian weapons attractive to Third World nations lacking a large pool of technically skilled people.

Theory and Practice

Paramilitary and reserve forces are a case of theory and practice often falling far apart when reality hits. Most of the paramilitary forces in the world, whether they be formally organized as such or merely the regular armed forces performing the function, generally perform poorly. There is always the temptation to substitute quantity for quality in paramilitary forces. These are troops who are usually lightly armed and poorly trained, leading the government to seek safety in quantity. But by using a lot of ill-trained and poorly paid troops to buck up an unpopular government, it's only a matter of time before the paramilitary troops become a fertile recruiting ground for rebellious elements. This has become a pattern in Third World nations. Even tightly disciplined and well-trained paramilitary forces, such as those the Communist nations developed, proved more loyal to the population than to the bureaucrats.

Reserves are another case of "if I don't see anything, it's not happening." Reserves are very difficult to maintain at any level of wartime usefulness. This the United States learned during the Gulf War. Many deficiencies in reserve manning and training became starkly evident under the pressures of wartime demands. While the performance of U.S. reserves in that war was among the highest of any reserve force in history, it was not always up to what Congress had been promised. But the quantity of the resources available to the United States allowed many of these shortcomings to be shunted into the shadows. Until the next time.

The Future

More nations are training and equipping their reserve troops to handle civil disorder better. Technology is changing the nature and effectiveness of reserve troops. As more complex weapons become the norm, the degree to which reserve troops retain their technical skills after release from active duty becomes more critical. This has been less a problem in the West, where reserves undergo regular training in complex skills. What is becoming more of a problem is creating effective reserves for the increasing number of combat jobs that require technical skills. Less than a century ago, most combat jobs could be quickly taught to physically fit young men. This is no longer the case. Even the infantry must master dozens of unique technical skills to become highly effective fighters. Increasingly, the solution is to use more civilians or uniformed women in combat-support jobs for the active forces and to maximize the number of well-trained men in combat units. The reserve system that developed in the nineteenth century to provide masses of infantry is now seen as counterproductive. Mass is no longer as effective as it once was in the face of high-tech weapons.

Increasing automation may eventually make it possible to field large armies from reserves, but this development will have to wait for the next century.

Only the United States and Israel have quickly fielded large, modern reserve forces to good effect. But each of these nations exists in special circumstances. While this is seen as a pattern that works, it is one that few nations can afford to emulate.

PART TWO

AIR OPERATIONS

Air warfare is a creature of the twentieth century. This is high-tech warfare, very expensive and arguably the most destructive.

7

The Air Force: Fighters, Bombers, and Snoopers

Air forces get very touchy when anyone suggests that their primary purpose is to obtain information. In the beginning, warplanes were used exclusively to gather information for land and naval forces. Despite constant attempts to diversify into other areas, air forces still pay their keep by getting information, or preventing the enemy from doing so. Yes, there is a problem with air forces in that they would rather be fighting the war on their own, without getting mixed up with the grubby work of the infantry. This is something of a dirty little secret in the armed forces. Yet you don't have to observe the infighting between the air forces and other services for long to figure out what the flyers would rather be doing. They would rather be fighting other air forces. Air-force people know aircraft; they know less about what goes on in the trenches. It's dirty and dangerous work flying down into the flak zone to support ground troops. Although many pilots prefer this kind of work, the majority don't.

There is also the sense of self-preservation. An air force's most likely enemy is another air force. The air bases are usually far away from the ground fighting, reachable only by enemy aircraft. If the air force can't stop those enemy planes, their bases will be hit, leaving friendly aircraft cut off from their vital lifeline.

There is a lot not to like when supporting ground forces. In the air, it's either missiles from the ground or aircraft from all over. The missiles are easier to get away from. Attacking ground targets in the combat zone, the hostile fire comes from every direction, in three dimensions.

This ground-support situation varies from air force to air force. In many armed forces, the ground-support aircraft are under army control. In the United States, control of ground-support aircraft was taken away from the Army when the independent Air Force was created after World War II. The U.S. Air Force has had mixed feelings about this move, and the current growth of U.S. Army helicopter forces makes the Air Force's shrinking number of ground-support aircraft look embarrassing at times. The message from the ground forces seems to be, "If the air force won't give us support, we'll get it any way we can." The U.S. Marine Corps has its own air force and receives superb ground support from it, and this experience is not lost on the Army.

Air forces still spend a lot of time snooping around, but satellites have taken some of that work away. Given a free hand, an air force would consist largely of fighters, with some recon and bomber aircraft to cover those specialties. Air forces prefer to pick their own targets, specifically ones deep in the enemy rear. An air force survives by controlling the air and keeping its bases free of enemy attacks. An air force's first priority is to destroy the other fellow's air force. There is never enough air force to go around. This is because aircraft are, pound for pound, the most expensive weapon available. The air force is also much in demand. Aircraft can be where they are needed quickly, and with a lot of firepower. Although aircraft cannot occupy ground or replace ground forces, they can give one side a decisive edge by wresting control of the air from their opponents early in the war.

What air forces do has not changed in 90 years. Aircraft take pictures, fight other aircraft, or carry things (bombs or cargo). Their missions are simple; their means are not.

Ground Control and Support

Aircraft give the illusion of freedom to their crews, but they are always very much attached to the ground. Aircraft ultimately answer to someone on the ground, and to the ground all planes must return every few hours to refuel and rearm. Commanders on the ground use radar and radio to maintain control over their airborne subordinates. Ground-based command and control radars are increasingly replaced by airborne systems, but these are vulnerable and backed up by ground installations. Russian-style air forces attempt to overcome lower pilot skill and aircraft quality by enforcing more strict ground control on their planes. Western air forces equip their aircraft with more capable radar and electronics, train their pilots more intensively, and expect more initiative in the air.

Increasingly, since the 1930s, radar has dominated air warfare. Radars look not only for enemy aircraft, but keep an eye on where friendly ones are. Today you can have hundreds of radars sending information to a small number of headquarters, which then issue orders to their far-flung aircraft. The high speeds and vast range of aircraft mean that the air battlefield covers a far larger area than the ground fighting. Aircraft are told when to take off; what direction, speed, and altitude to fly; and when to engage the enemy. They are then guided back to their base. Pilots are also expected to adapt to unexpected conditions. There is always something unexpected in warfare. Pilot skill is still a crucial edge, even with all the directions warplanes now get from ground-based or airborne command centers.

Reconnaissance Missions

Reconnaissance has always been the primary mission of air power. The use of satellites has not changed this. Looking at reconnaissance from the viewpoint of the consumer, the ground-forces commander, it appears as follows:

Tactical reconnaissance. This is for the troops in a combat division, or the area immediately around a naval task force. Much of this is done by low-performance aircraft, prop-driven planes, and helicopters, and increasingly UAVs (Unmanned Aerial Vehicles). This task involves constant monitoring of the enemy when the bad guys are in contact with friendly forces. Most of the observation is done through various forms of photography. Observers in the aircraft are used less often, largely because of more intense ground fire and the superiority of electromechanical observation devices. UAVs are also gradually replacing manned aircraft. Film is also being replaced by TV cameras and sensors that detect heat, electronic signals, movement, and large metal objects. Infrared cameras, for example, can detect camouflaged positions through the unnatural pattern of heat from inorganic or dead vegetation used as camouflage material, and warm yet hidden vehicles. Especially in Western air forces, these cameras can obtain accurate pictures even though the aircraft is fifty or more miles away from the target. This is done using a lot of computer power to reconstruct the off-angle image obtained. This technique makes it possible to observe heavily defended targets safely. Most non-Western recon aircraft must still fly over the target. This greatly diminishes recon ability because of the generally more capable Western antiaircraft weapons. Sometimes smaller sensors are dropped in enemy territory. In special situations, recon patrols are dropped, either to make their way back on foot or be picked up later. In all cases, information is often broadcast back to friendly forces from patrols, aircraft, and sensors. Tactical reconnaissance loses its value in a short time, often in hours. Tactical reconnaissance missions are usually flown close to the ground to increase the quality of information and, sometimes, to draw enemy fire so as to reveal his positions.

The major shortcoming of aircraft reconnaissance in the Gulf War was that there was not enough of it. There was more than enough aircraft to fight enemy aircraft, but not enough to keep track of what was on the ground before and after the bombers did their work.

The latest generation of satellites (improved KH-11) that allow for real-time TV pictures of the battlefield have become an important aspect of tactical reconnaissance. The only drawback is that these birds are enormously expensive, and in peacetime no more than two or three will be up at one time. In wartime, these satellites are prime targets, which may mean that none of them will be available. Moreover, these are not stationary satellites, but orbit around the planet. Although the orbits can be changed, the satellites will make only a few passes over the ground below each day.

The information sought by tactical reconnaissance includes location, strength, identification, and activities of enemy units. It is important to evaluate the results of an air strike, ground attack, or artillery barrage. All of the information is passed back to a headquarters where intelligence people sort it out, give the divisional commander something to chew on, and pass useful material onto the combat units. This frequently prompts requests for more information, which starts the cycle anew. Often, the demands for operational and strategic recon, used by higher-ranking commanders, push aside the requests for tactical recon.

Operational reconnaissance. This is longer range and less urgent; it's for army and theater commanders. Tactical reconnaissance extends from right in front of your combat troops to about 20 kilometers behind the enemy lines. Operational reconnaissance may extend hundreds of kilometers into the enemy's rear area, as well as your own if the situation is fluid. The information required is the same as is needed for tactical recon. Because most of the enemy forces you are scouting are not in contact with your troops, there is less immediacy, at least for friendly ground forces. Such is not the case for your air forces and senior ground commanders. Enemy forces not yet in contact can be attacked from the air, and senior commanders must plan how they will deal with these uncommitted enemy forces. Enemy air forces also fall into this area of reconnaissance. Enemy surface-to-surface missile forces must be watched constantly for signs of imminent use. Operational recon uses specially equipped fighter and strike aircraft to perform these missions deep into enemy territory. Special recon aircraft, like the TR-1, are also sometimes used, as well as satellites and longer range UAVs. Operational recon flights are considered dangerous combat missions because of the large number of enemy defenses that must be penetrated. These recon aircraft typically carry no weapons but instead load up on fuel (for range, and quick acceleration out of a tight spot), ECM (electronic countermeasures), as well as cameras and sensors. Recon aircraft depend primarily on good planning, speed, ECM, and pilot skill to get in and out in one piece. Sometimes there is a fighter escort, but usually it is solo. Flying is customarily at high speed and low altitude, with radio and radar turned off. Using onboard sensors and computers to monitor enemy radars and radio, the recon pilot roars low and fast over enemy terrain. More advanced recon aircraft use a terrain-following system that automatically guides them quickly at altitudes of a few hundred feet. A computer chooses the safest path through the thicket of enemy defenses. Recon pilots are often combat veterans with superb flying skills and steel nerves to get them through these missions. The only thing a recon pilot fights against is detection. The aircraft must often pop up to a higher altitude to get a better look at its objective, or make an extended high-altitude run over an area to get good photographs. Every enemy fighter pilot in the area would love to bag a recon plane. Pilots know that it requires no little courage to go in alone just to take pictures. These pilots are often the best. They have to be, for without their information, the armed forces are blind.

Strategic reconnaissance. This covers global information. This includes everything that a nation uses to wage war: armed forces, economic strength and resources, etc. In addition, strategic reconnaissance gathers the same types of information gathered by tactical and operational recon. This is long-term and long-range information. This is the type of reconnaissance that takes place most frequently during peacetime. Major nations use satellites for most of this work (see Chapter 19). More traditional means are still heavily used. These include long-range aircraft and electronic eavesdropping. In wartime, many of the aircraft will be vulnerable and therefore useless unless they have sufficient electronic countermeasures to render them invisible to enemy radars. Peacetime use of these aircraft is intensive, with Russian planes operating throughout the world. Only the United States has high-altitude aircraft (TR-1) that can hope to survive over enemy territory in wartime conditions. The United States retired its high-speed, high-altitude SR-71s in 1990, but there is a secret program to develop a replacement for the SR-71 (which was expensive to operate).

JSTARS. The E-8 JSTARS (Joint Surveillance and Target Attack Radar System), first used during the 1991 Gulf War, ushered in a new era of air reconnaissance. The "joint" stems from the fact that it is both a U.S. Air Force and U.S. Army system. This is an airborne command and control aircraft. It was not scheduled for regular troop use until 1993–94. But the two prototype models were undergoing testing at the time of the Iraqi invasion. These two developmental aircraft were quickly brought up to active service status and sent from Europe (where they were being tested) to the Gulf. Unlike the AWACS (Airborne Warning and Control System), which handles only air operations, the JSTARS' primary job is tracking ground activity and was designed to better integrate air and ground operations by quickly locating targets for our aircraft and coordinating those attacks with friendly ground operations. The radar is built into the underbelly of a B-707 aircraft. The radar has two modes:

wide area (showing a 25 by 20 kilometer area) and detailed (4,000 by 5,000 meters). Each E-8 had 10 radar displays on board plus 15 more on the ground with Army headquarters units. All the radar displays could communicate with each other. The radar simultaneously supported both modes and several different chunks of terrain being watched. While an operator might have to wait a minute or two for an update on his screen, this was not a problem because of the relatively slow pace of ground operations. The radar could see out to several hundred kilometers, and each screen full of information could be saved and brought back later to compare to another view. In this manner, operators could track movement of ground units. Operators could also use the detail mode to pick out specific details of ground units (fortifications, buildings, vehicle deployments, etc.). For the first time in history, commanders were able to see and control mechanized forces over a wide area in real time. JSTARS could also pass data directly to radar screens in specially equipped strike aircraft (in this case, F-15Es). This allowed quicker and more accurate air strikes.

During the Persian Gulf war, JSTARS performed its designed mission well and speeded up the development process (and guaranteed the spending of billions of dollars on additional JSTARS aircraft). The two E-8s flew 49 missions during Desert Shield and (mostly) Desert Storm, each lasting about 11 hours.

JSTARS (or J-STARS) is now established as the favored means of controlling large ground operations. Combined with ground-based navigation and communications systems like GPS and PLRS (Position Location Reporting System), and linked with friendly strike aircraft, JSTARS allows air and ground forces to work together, everyone sharing the same information. Naturally, the JSTARS picture of the ground situation won't be as clear in forested or mountainous terrain, but the data will still be abundant enough to show commanders where major units are.

After the Gulf War, work continued, with eight aircraft available at the end of the century and another 10 or so planned.

Interception Missions

Soon after reconnaissance was discovered, air-to-air combat followed. Rifle and pistol fire between passing recon planes soon escalated to fighter aircraft battling each other to gain control of the air. Control meant access for your own recon forces and exclusion of the enemy's. In other words, the successful air warrior gained an all-seeing eye while rendering his opponents blind. This work was called interception: meeting and defeating enemy aircraft before they could return the favor. The basic rules for this air-to-air combat were established over 80 years ago and have not changed since. In World War I, pilots soon discovered that the key to success and survival was to gain surprise and get the first shot. Dogfighting—high maneuverability, tighter turning, and greater speed—was a poor second choice and typically ended up in a stalemate or random losses. Today the same basic tactics apply, with a number of important additions and modifications. While individual pilot skill is important, modern air combat is more a matter of teamwork and technology. Longer-range weapons and better communications enable pilots to detect and attack enemy aircraft at longer distances. Today's 30mm automatic cannon allows 800-meter shots compared to 100 meters with 7.62mm machine guns 80 years ago. Missiles allow kills at ranges of up to 200 kilometers, with highly reliable missile kills at ranges of 10–40 kilometers.

From the beginning of air combat, spotting the other fellow first has remained the key to success. Some 80 percent of air kills are the result of the attacker surprising the defender. The victim usually never even sees his attacker. The cardinal rule of air-to-air combat is: hit the other fellow while he isn't looking. Obtain the favorable position (usually high and behind the enemy) and get in the first shot. The average plane-to-plane combat is over in less than 90 seconds. It's not enough to be good; you must be good in a short space of time. When fighter goes up against fighter, the orderly, planned routine of other air operations goes out the window. Successful interception requires aircraft that are technically capable of staying up with the opposition. Pilot skill often becomes the critical factor. Superior aircraft and inferior pilots generally equal defeat. You don't need a lot of good pilots to prevail. Historical experience has shown that 5 percent of combat pilots account for the majority of the enemy aircraft destroyed. This is a common pattern in all combat situations. Competence is not enough; you need as many of these exceptional pilots as you can muster in order to win control of the air.

All pilots require a wide range of flying skills. Some are obvious, like knowing how to efficiently take an aircraft through a wide range of maneuvers, from tricky landings and takeoffs under bad weather conditions to reacting to unexpected changes in flying conditions and equipment failures. Other skills are seemingly mundane, such as how to do a thorough preflight check on your aircraft. A loose component or an erratic instrument can lead to flying problems. Such problems during combat can be fatal. A very common combat-flying problem is fuel management. As a rule of thumb, a fighter can take its total flying range and divide it into thirds: one third for going out ("operating radius"), one third for coming back, and one third for combat. A typical modern fighter can cruise at 900 kilometers per hour. It might have an extreme range of 2,700 kilometers. That gives it a theoretical flying time of three hours. However, high-performance fighters obtain their speed by having an engine that can increase its fuel consumption enormously for short periods. For example, at cruise speed, this fighter burns about .56 percent of its fuel per minute. By kicking in the afterburner, cruise speed can be more than tripled, and fuel consumption increased more than 20 times. At full "war power," an F-15 can burn up a third of its fuel in less than three minutes. It can also escape from unfavorable situations because of this sudden increase in speed. A less-experienced pilot will abuse the high performance of his aircraft to get him out of one tight situation after another. Once a fighter reaches BINGO fuel (just enough to get home), combat must cease. Otherwise the aircraft will likely run out of fuel before reaching its base and be just as useless as if shot down by the enemy. It's a common tactic to try to force the other guy into more high-fuel-consumption maneuvers. Eventually he will run low on fuel and try to break away. At this point he becomes desperate and vulnerable.

Several decisive factors must be considered when on an interception mission. Each of these elements multiplies the effectiveness of your aircraft, enabling you to achieve a multiplier effect that makes one of your aircraft equal to two or more of the enemy's:

- The side with superior detection devices and ECM often gets superior position. This is often in the form of airborne warning radar and control systems (AWACS) and superior electronics in the combat aircraft. This can double or triple aircraft effectiveness.
- Everything being equal, the side with superior tactics gains an advantage or mitigates the other side's electronic advantages. The opening stages of any war provide numerous examples of tactics surprise. The Gulf War was a good example. Some air forces are better able to figure out how to best use their aircraft in combat before the fighting starts. The ability to adapt quickly to new conditions can be an advantage throughout a war, but especially at the beginning. At the beginning of a war, this can double or triple aircraft effectiveness, although it is less of an advantage later in a war.
- The side with more skilled and resourceful pilots gains a substantial advantage. This can multiply aircraft effectiveness by a factor of four or more.
- The defender has an advantage in requiring less fuel. The defending interceptor can hang around longer and have more fuel to burn in combat. The defender is closer to his bases and can thus land, refuel, and rearm, and get back into the battle more quickly.
- And then there is the quantity of aircraft multiplied by aircraft quality. Sheer numbers can prevail if the disparity is too great.
- Excellence in combat aircraft design is more than higher speed. Maneuverability is the key.

If one side has a combination of these factor in its favor giving it a 5–10 multiplier effect, it can win a virtually bloodless victory. This has happened quite often in the last 60 years. Examples are the Gulf War and the Arab-Israeli wars. Customarily, the results of one side's superiority are manifested by an exchange ratio: how many aircraft are shot down for each one lost. Western aircraft have nearly always achieved a ratio of 5:1 or better against Russian equipment. This is not a guarantee of future success, but an indicator of past performance.

Electronic warfare is becoming an increasingly critical element. In the past, one could get past radar and missiles by coming in "low and fast." During the 1980s, the Soviets and the United States deployed airborne "look down" radars for waiting interceptors and AWACS aircraft circling hundreds of kilometers inside friendly territory. Western air forces have the edge in this area because of their general technical lead and the need for substantial computing power to pick aircraft out from everything else seen up by the radar. The Soviet Union countered a technical disadvantage with numbers; they maintained more interceptors than the West and could saturate an area with aircraft if need be. Interceptors that can wait on the ground until they are needed have a substantial advantage. This was first shown when the German air force attacked Britain in late 1940. The British had the first large-scale radar warning system in place and were able to conserve their outnumbered interceptors. The British took off only when they knew where the Germans were and thus could mass and outnumber separate groups of German aircraft. The Germans were beaten piecemeal, without being able to use their numerical and qualitative superiority effectively. Western air forces have long planned to do the same thing to Russia, or any other opponent, in any future war. Thus far, it appears the West was able to do what it planned to do—at least as far as the Gulf War was concerned.

Strike Missions

Pilots call these "air to mud" missions, and for good reason. Going after ground targets is dangerous and unpredictable. There is danger from enemy interceptors, plus all manner of firepower hidden in the landscape below. Finally, there is the ground itself. Fly too low and you can make an involuntary fatal contact with the ground. At 400 miles an hour, this is not a pretty sight. Aircraft can't hang around long waiting for someone to request their firepower. Air forces prefer to leave fighting ground units to their own devices. Helicopters have increasingly become the favored ground-attack system for front-line combat support. Therefore, most strike missions by fixed-wing aircraft are arranged in advance by intelligence and planning staffs against objectives behind enemy lines. Targets, in approximate order of priority, are aircraft on the ground (where they can't shoot back), air bases, nuclear-weapons systems, radars, antiaircraft systems, fuel and ammo supplies, transportation systems, combat units, and support units.

Flying into enemy airspace is a risky business. High- and low-altitude antiaircraft defenses are numerous. Radars are all over the place. One approach is to sneak in with small (one to four) groups of planes. Coming in low, a few hundred meters high or low enough to singe the treetops, the enemy has little time to react before you are past him. Zipping along at 200 meters a second, there is not much for the enemy to see or shoot at. Using electronic mapping and navigation devices, the target is found (most of the time), the munitions released, and an equally rapid exit made. Few aircraft are capable of this approach. The electronics are expensive. However, by designing an aircraft for maximum resistance to detection, you end up with a stealth aircraft. Such an airplane has a reasonable chance of penetrating enemy defenses to hit targets with a high degree of surprise. This is important, as the damage done goes down with the amount of warning the target has. Five minutes of warning can reduce air-base damage 40 to 80 percent, depending on how many concrete aircraft shelters the base has.

Without stealth aircraft, you must send in larger groups of aircraft led by lavishly equipped electronics warfare planes. This approach will usually succeed in destroying a lot of enemy ground defenses along the way, which makes it easier for subsequent raids. Such a large operation also attracts enemy attention and sometimes is expected to develop into a major air battle. Surprise is lost, and you end up using up to 10 support aircraft for every one going after the primary target. The aircraft that lead such raids are called "Wild Weasels." They have radar detection and jamming equipment that can either hide the group from enemy radar or prevent the enemy from making accurate use of their ground-to-air missiles. You will need fighters to deal with enemy interceptors. Thus, the battle can range from 10,000 meters up down to ground level. The Wild Weasels carry missiles that home in on enemy ground radars. The most dangerous opposition comes from enemy guns, which often can fire without radar in clear weather. For this reason, raids at night and in bad weather are often preferred. If all goes according to plan, the Weasels will protect the electronically less sophisticated strike aircraft to the targets, where they release their loads. Everyone then fights their way home past a thoroughly alerted enemy.

The stealth aircraft are well suited to perform the Wild Weasel role. This would be a common mission, as there will be a lot of non-stealth strike aircraft and a need to suppress antiaircraft defenses. For targets where surprise is not critical, stealth-led raids are the norm. This was the case in the Gulf War. Russia was striving, with some success until the collapse of the Soviet Union in 1991, to catch up with Western strike aircraft in overall sophistication and effectiveness. None of their new generation of strike planes has been used under combat conditions, so there is no way of knowing how effective they are. They are already into their generation of AWACS, and their Wild Weasel aircraft are somewhat tame compared to Western models. Russian pilots, by and large, are not as expert, experienced, or audacious as their Western counterparts. Israel, however, is producing a quite capable AWACS, mainly for export.

Fire Control

The major innovation of the 1980s, validated in the 1991 Gulf War, was the precision fire-control systems on strike aircraft. These systems were pioneered in the U.S. F-111 aircraft, where they were built in. The systems consist of FLIR (Forward Looking Infrared Radar) sensors, laser designators, and guided bombs. The system works like this:

- The FLIR detects differences in the temperature of objects on the ground and presents a picture of this on a TV screen in the cockpit. These were the black-and-white images you saw from precision bombing runs during the Gulf War. These images are remarkably sharp. Current FLIRs have a range of 10–15 km; by the end of the decade some of these may have twice that range. The pilot uses a joystick to select the target on the TV screen and releases the bomb.
- When the pilot releases the bomb, a laser light is directed at the spot that the pilot's crosshairs cover. The pilot either manually keeps the cross hairs on the target, or more complex systems memorize the target shape and "lock" on to the target.
- The bomb has a sensor in its nose that can detect laser light reflected from the target. The bomb has a set of controllable fins that keep the bomb heading for the reflected laser light until the bomb hits the target.

The first of these precision bombing systems cost millions of dollars each. But by the end of the 1980s, the FLIR and laser were packaged into pods the size of small bombs and weighing 100–500 pounds. These pods cost $500,000–$1,000,000. The price comes down with experience and the general reduction of electronic component costs. Cheaper pods can be made by using a TV set instead of a FLIR, but these are only good for daylight bombing. The U.S. LANTIRN (Low Altitude Navigation and Targeting Infrared for Night) system is the most famous of these pods, but several European nations have built their own. Future developments will put the targeting information on the pilots' HUD (Head Up Display) or displays mounted in the pilots' helmets. These developments are needed to allow single-seat aircraft to use precision bombing more easily. This is because of the short amount of time available to spot the target, put the cross hairs on it, and release the bomb. Coming in at 200–300 meters a second, and having to release the bomb at least a few kilometers from the target, the 10–15 kilometer range of the FLIR gives the pilot only 20–50 seconds to do the job. One pilot can do it, as the US F-117A demonstrated. But a very easy-to-use system is required.

A further step in error-proof fire control is the use of GPS-guided bombs. GPS has gotten a lot cheaper since its introduction in the early 1990s. It's gotten to the point where commercial receivers can be had for $100 or less. GPS is now in smart bombs. Aside from the danger of jamming (which can be blocked to a certain extent), you can equip any aircraft with GPS-guided smart bombs. All the pilot has to do is drop them close enough to the target so the bombs can glide to the preprogrammed target. There are somewhat more expensive (and a bit less accurate) guidance systems that can be (and are) used in some GPS smart bombs as a backup in case the GPS fails or is jammed. The downside of this is that these cheaper smart bombs make it possible for less affluent nations to build smart bombs. Before GPS, smart bombs were a tool largely restricted to wealthy nations.

The Revolution in Close Air Support

The war in Afghanistan revealed a new and very useful way to supply close air support (CAS) for ground troops. CAS had something of a golden age during World War II, when there were plenty of fighter-bombers overhead and they all belonged to the Army (the separate air force did not arrive until after World War II). The single-engine fighter-bombers were often in radio contact with the ground troops, having been assigned to support a specific unit. The aircraft would provide information about what was up ahead, and the ground troops could call for specific ground targets to be strafed (attacked with the aircraft's machine guns) or bombed (most fighter-bombers of that era could carry two or four 500-pound bombs). After World War II, the air force became a separate organization and replaced its slower prop-driven fighters with faster jets. While the jets could carry more bombs, their higher speed made it more difficult to drop the bombs precisely. This was especially true when enemy ground troops were around, often firing at you as your jet fighter-bomber came in at nearly 200 meters a second as you tried to fly the plane, find the target, and avoid ground fire all at once. The Air Force began to move away from providing this kind of support. The Army was buying more helicopters, and jet fighter-bombers became more expensive and fewer. By the end of the twentieth century, the U.S. Air Force rarely delivered World War II–style CAS, and usually only with their shrinking number of A-10 aircraft.

All this changed during the 2001 Afghanistan war. U.S. Special Forces troops with the anti-Taliban forces were in constant communication with aircraft overhead, ready to bring down bombs when encountering Taliban resistance. The 2,000-pound bombs were favored, as past experience going back to World War II showed that only very thick cement fortifications could withstand such a weapon. The Taliban had neither the resources nor the time to build such fortifications, so they were systematically blown out of their earthen bunkers and trenches. Unlike World War II, where 2,000-pound bombs dropped by heavy bombers landed hundreds of meters from their intended target, smart bombs hit within 30 meters of their targets over 95 percent of the time—and not much farther than 30 meters when they "miss." Thus, during World War II, it took several dozen 2,000-pound bombs to do what one can do now. Moreover, back then, you had to keep friendly troops farther away to avoid getting hit by the wayward bombs. During World War II, low-flying fighter-bombers like the P-47 could drop 500-pound and 1,000-pound bombs with more accuracy, but those smaller bombs were less likely to take out enemy fortifications, and the aircraft were more likely to be damaged or shot down by ground fire. Smart bombs using GPS, or guided by laser designators on the ground, are a lot more accurate than even the low-flying P-47s (which were, in turn, more accurate than the low-flying jet fighter-bombers that had to move at a higher speed during their bomb runs).

This new technique was enormously effective. Because the friendly troops could be as close as half a kilometer from the enemy target, they could quickly move in and take the enemy position before the foe could rush in reinforcements. But it got better. The bombs could be dropped by heavy bombers far overhead, out of range of enemy guns or portable missiles. A B-52 or B-1 can carry two dozen 2,000-pound GPS-guided bombs. The guys on the ground can move up to an enemy position, call in a few bombs to blow away the entrenched enemy, and then go in and finish off the dazed survivors. No more problems with overworked pilots coming in fast, trying to figure out who is where, and getting shot at in the process. Moreover, a 2,000-pound bomb will also disable (if not outright destroy) tanks and other armored vehicles.

All this makes life a lot more difficult for enemy ground forces who don't have any air force or long-range surface-to-air missiles in working condition. The U.S. Air Force still has to begin any war by going after these targets. Once they are gone, the guys on the ground can pound the enemy with the one-ton bombs. This approach cracked ground defenses time after time in Afghanistan, and there's no countermeasure for the technique on the horizon.

RPVs, UAVs, and Drones

RPVs (Remotely Piloted Vehicles, now officially known in the United States as UAVs, or Unmanned Aerial Vehicles) and drones (robot pilots) are increasingly popular for their low cost and inability to get human pilots killed. The lack of a pilot saves a lot of weight, making drones and UAVs cheaper than normal aircraft. Moreover, a lot of the UAVs now work as advertised. This was not always the case in the past. For extremely dangerous missions, they are ideal. UAVs are cheaper, but they must be guided by a ground-based pilot and can be jammed. Drones don't need external guidance but still have a way to go before they can completely take care of themselves in the air. Right now, drones are slowly overtaking UAVs and may soon replace them. During the Vietnam War, some 2,000 drones were used. Overall, each drone survived five missions, although by the end of the war this rose to 30 flights. Flak accounted for 12 percent of losses. This is high but reflects the policy of sending drones into risky areas. Another 10 percent were lost during recovery, which reflects the difficulty of landing any aircraft, especially one without a pilot on board. System failure was 5 percent. Again this was high; a human pilot could have taken care of some of these problems. Israel has improved on this experience throughout the last twenty years.

The Gulf War was the most recent, and most revealing, opportunity for UAVs to strut their stuff. The results were impressive. Here are the experiences of each major UAV deployed in the Gulf:

Pioneer UAV. This is a small, propeller-driven aircraft carrying either a TV or infrared (for night work) cameras and flown by a pilot on the ground by remote control (up to 150–200 kilometers away). Israel has used this UAV for over a decade, and the Pioneer is an adaptation of the Israeli UAV first used by the U.S. Navy on its battleships to spot targets for the big 16-inch guns. As a result of the Pioneer's success with the Israelis and the U.S. Navy, it was adopted by the Marines and the U.S. Army. Pioneer weighs only 420 pounds, has a top speed of 180 kilometers an hour, and a usual operating range of 160 kilometers. It can stay in the air about four hours and flies as high as 15,000 feet, which takes it out of range of small antiaircraft weapons. It's very difficult to spot on a radar and usually cannot be heard on the ground. During the Gulf War, only about 40 Pioneer UAVs were available for use. Two-thirds were used by the ground force, mostly the Marines. The Pioneers were used as much as their limited supply of spare parts would allow, flying 533 sorties. Each sortie lasted about three hours. Twenty-six Pioneers were damaged and 12 were destroyed. Two were lost to enemy fire; the rest were lost to accidents. One ran out of fuel and crashed while shadowing a Scud launcher. Several Pioneers were sent over 100 kilometers into Iraq to search for aircraft on the ground and Scud launchers. The Pioneers were principally used to look for enemy artillery positions and troop bunkers. The Iraqis soon got wise to this, and, although the Pioneer's engine sounded like a chain saw, it couldn't be heard very well when the UAV was flying at altitudes of 2,000 feet or higher. When the Pioneer did come lower for a better look, the Iraqis got their licks in as best they could. The Pioneer's advantage was that it was under the control of the ground troops and could thus be sent up quickly when the local ground commander felt he needed to get a look at what was going on over enemy territory. In areas where there are a lot of enemy ground troops who could shoot at helicopters, the UAV can go in, look around, and survive. This proved a significant advantage against Iraqi ground units on the Saudi border. The loss rate of UAVs is high compared to manned aircraft, plus an even higher noncombat loss rate. But then, no pilots were lost, and each Pioneer cost less than 10 percent as much as the cheapest manned reconnaissance aircraft.

Pointer UAV. This is a shorter-range UAV tested by U.S. Army troops during the summer of 1990. Although the tests were successful, in the Gulf it was not as effective as expected. This was due to a short operating time of one hour and a maximum range of five kilometers from the operator. Altitude was limited to 500–1,000 feet. The light weight of the Pointer (50 pounds) caused it to be blown around by any but the lightest breeze. In the desert, the troops could often see up to five kilometers, obviating the need for the Pointer. However, had the fighting continued into built-up areas, the Pointer would have been very useful. The light weight had some advantages; it can be taken anywhere by the troops. The control unit for the Pointer weighs only 50 pounds, making a complete unit only 100 pounds. The troops called it "a 200-foot-tall observer with binoculars." With only black-and-white TV cameras available in the Gulf, it was difficult to pick out distant items in the monochrome desert. In the future, a color TV model is expected to solve that problem.

Several other UAVs were used in the Gulf, including British and French systems used for artillery fire control. One of the more interesting UAVs deployed was the little-known ExDrone. The Marines used about 55 of these "expendable drones," and they performed somewhat like the Pointer. The system worked well, as another 110 were purchased after the war. The TV-equipped ExDrone was used extensively in scouting the way for the Marine advance into Kuwait. The Marines attributed their fast advance and low casualty rate to timely information from ExDrones.

Originally, drones and UAVs were used largely as targets to give aircraft and antiaircraft weapons realistic practice. More and more, the primary mission of drones and UAVs is reconnaissance, including electronic warfare. Sensors are lighter than bomb loads, and are reusable. Small, flying low and slow, these aircraft are difficult to detect. Target acquisition is a form of reconnaissance and has become a distinct mission. Advances in electronics have made it possible for the artillery to see what the UAV sees. High flight endurance enables the UAVs to stay over the battle area and give the artillery continuous information on new targets and the effectiveness of fire. Drones and UAVs also have an important role in air combat, even without being armed. Electronic gear can be carried that will detect enemy radars. Piloted aircraft can then fire antiradiation missiles, or other munitions, to destroy the enemy radars and missiles. New drones are being developed that will perform the antiradiation mission itself.

While the original research work was done by the United States, Israel has taken the lead in use and development of UAVs. Other nations are now developing their own. This is happening because rapid advances in technology make it possible to build very capable UAVs at relatively low cost. The West appears to have maintained an increasing advantage in this area. There has not been a lot of drone and UAV activity in the former Soviet Union until the 1980s. During the late 1980s, Russian drones are being used by Syria, but not with a lot of success.

There is still a major problem with drones, and to a lesser extent UAVs: these machines have the potential for taking away pilots' jobs. One man's technological breakthrough is another man's career threat. Few people in the Air Force will come right out and admit this. Yet halfhearted enthusiasm for drones in many air forces can be traced back to pilots' unease over their becoming too effective. This is ironic, as the air forces themselves had to fight similar prejudice from the cavalry, artillery, and navy in the early years of combat aviation.

Theory and Practice

There have been two kinds of air war with modern equipment. The most common is a situation where not a lot of aircraft are available. Operations are sporadic, and often one side does not even have an air force. The Falklands, Lebanon, the 1980–88 Persian Gulf war, Kosovo in 1999, and the Afghanistan wars are examples of sporadic air war. Afghanistan and other counterinsurgency conflicts are typical situations in which only one side has an air force. The other kind of air war is the one most air force money and energy are spent on. The premier example of this was the effort the allies put forth in the 1991 Gulf War. That war saw over 2,000 allied combat aircraft flying over 100,000 sorties in six weeks in the most intense air campaign since World War II. These air forces had been preparing since the late 1940s to fight an even larger air battle in Central Europe, where on either side of a 500-kilometer border were 2,600 NATO and 3,000 Warsaw Pact combat aircraft. In addition, the former Soviet Union had nearly 4,000 additional combat aircraft between Moscow and Russia's western borders. NATO had a smaller number available as reinforcement. This battle was never fought, but the 1991 Gulf War demonstrated how well prepared Western air forces were to fight it.

Another rather emerging situation exists with long-range air-to-air missiles. This weapon has existed for over 40 years and has finally overcome the problem of obtaining positive identification of targets the pilot cannot see with his own eyes. For over half a century, each aircraft carried an IFF (Identification, Friend or Foe) device that made it easier to sort out the good guys and bad guys. Until the Gulf War, and the first use of AWACS control aircraft, pilots preferred to trust their eyeballs and get in close with cannon or short-range missiles. In the Gulf War, pilots felt confident enough to use long-range missiles and did so with good effect. BVR (Beyond Visual Range) missiles are now considered a common and reliable weapon.

The Future

The combat power of bombing is becoming more decisive. In World War II, the British bomber force, attacking mainly at night (without escorts) over a six-year period (1939–45), dropped 955,000 tons of bombs in 199,000 sorties, losing 6,400 aircraft in the process. During Vietnam, a much smaller number of aircraft flew 100,000 sorties and dropped 226,000 tons of bombs with much smaller losses in 1966. In 1991, 2,000 aircraft flew 108,000 sorties to drop 88,000 tons of bombs in six weeks with minuscule losses. Moreover, the accuracy of the bombing has increased dramatically since 1966, after making little progress since World War II. The accuracy of bombing continued to make greater strides during the 1990s as the computerized bombing systems got cheaper, more capable, and equipped more aircraft.

Until 1991, the primary focus of future developments was the new generation of U.S. fighters and the "stealth" aircraft. Principal among these is the F-22, which will replace the F-14 and F-15 in the next decade. Before 1991, the F-22 was scheduled for introduction during the mid-1990s, but now it's looking more like another 10 years. Among the new features of the F-22 are more "stealth," easier maintainance, improved electronics, and "supercruise" (allows high-speed cruising at relatively low fuel consumption).

The Navy had to cancel its new attack aircraft, largely because of budget problems. But along came the JSF (Joint Strike Fighter, now the F-35), which is right behind the F-22 in the development pipeline. The Europeans also managed to get their own advanced fighter, the Eurofighter, into production.

The other big initiative is stealth aircraft. The United States has already deployed the F-117A attack aircraft, while the more ambitious B-2 stealth bomber is unlikely to get beyond the 20 already built. There are said to be some highly secret stealth aircraft still in development, but decades of sleuthing by the aviation trade press has not brought forth any detail. The F-22 and F-35 are very stealthy.

More uses were found for the venerable B-52. In Afghanistan, B-52s developed some new tactics. Instead of just the carpet bombing that was so successful during Vietnam, the heavy bombers were carrying fewer, heavier (1,000- and 2,000-pound) smart bombs. They now often circled above the target area (like Kunduz) and waited for Special Forces troops on the ground to spot targets and identify them with their lasers. Then the B-52 dropped one large bomb that tore up a specific trench or bunker. This is similar to what was done during World War II, when spotters on shore would spot targets for the large (and quite accurate) big guns of offshore battleships. Many of the battleship shells weighed over 2,000 pounds. Smaller fighter-bombers have always been able to deliver this kind of support, but they have to come in low and risk getting hit by ground fire. In Afghanistan, smaller aircraft could carry only one

B-52 Heavy bomber

or two large bombs. The B-52s could carry two dozen or more and have
enough fuel to circle the battlefield for an hour or more. The success of this
technique is going to generate a lot of study and rethinking of how bombers
and ground troops can operate together.

The Afghanistan war gave a graphic view of future warfare. One compelling aspect of that conflict was that fact that 72 percent of the bomb tonnage
was dropped by just 18 aircraft (10 B-52s and 8 B-1s). On most days, four B-1s
and five B-52s took off from Diego Garcia for Afghanistan. Because of their
long range (and in-flight refueling), these aircraft were able to circle the combat areas for several hours. On most days, the flights of these bombers were
staggered so that one was over Afghanistan 24 hours a day. Some 90 percent of
the missions were against targets to be designated by U.S. Special Forces
troops on the ground, or recon aircraft and UAVs. The bombers carried combinations of 2,000- and 500-pound JDAMs (Joint Direct Attack Munitions),
cluster bombs, and unguided 500-pound bombs. Most cluster bombs also use
guidance kits. When unguided bombs were used, it was usually by the B-52,
which uses its ground radar to drop a tight pattern of these bombs with devastating effect. Each B-1 has three bomb bays. Each bay can carry either ten
cluster bombs, 28 unguided 500-pound bombs, or eight 2,000-pound JDAM.
The B-52s can carry a dozen 2,000-pound JDAMs, or 51 unguided 500-pound
bombs. Some B-52s carry guided cluster bombs (Wind Corrected Munitions
Dispenser). Communicating directly with troops on the ground (using GPS

units to locate the targets and enable the aircraft to program the bombs with a precise location), the bombers were usually able to get a bomb on target within 10 minutes of a request. The Air Force wants to improve that time but needs newer communications equipment and satellite links. This stuff exists; it's just a matter of getting the money to buy and install it. The money will probably be forthcoming because of the performance of the bombers. B-2 bombers were also used, but they were a lot more expensive to operate. The B-2s carry the 5,000-pound bunker buster as well as all the bombs the B-52 and B-1 carry.

In terms of individual bombs, the heavy bombers dropped 72 percent of them, with smaller Air Force aircraft (F-15Es and F-16s flying in from the Persian Gulf) dropping 8 percent. Carrier aircraft dropped the other 20 percent.

The U.S. Army continues to upgrade its attack helicopter (the AH-64) and has rebuilt several hundred of its current models to include the "Longbow" millimeter-wave radar system and a more powerful fire-control system and "fire and forget" Hellfire missiles to go along with it. This will make the AH-64 an all-weather attack aircraft on a par with anything any air force has. While budget cuts may slow this project down, the R&D has been completed, and all that is required to produce the new AH-64 is the money to rebuild old ones.

Russia began introducing its latest generation of combat aircraft in the late 1980s, about 10–15 years behind the West. As is their custom, the Russian aircraft are larger, heavier, and less efficient. For example, the Su-27, introduced

B-1B Heavy bomber

in 1987 after nine years of flight testing, is roughly equivalent to the F-15 and F-14. However, the Su-27 is 20-percent heavier than the F-15, much less reliable, and carries missiles heavier than their more effective Western equivalents. The next Russian generation of aircraft, the SU-37, was originally planned for introduction a few years after the F-22 (ATF). But new aircraft research has atrophied in the economic upheaval that followed the collapse of the Soviet Union. Russian air force officers speak gamely of their next generation of aircraft appearing "sometime in the near future." Russia continues to develop versions of the Su-27, but shortage of money and customers is hindering progress.

While improvements in combat performance are being stressed in the new generation of aircraft, greater emphasis is being placed on the more mundane areas of maintainability, reliability, and ease of use. There is good reason for emphasis on getting more out of these new planes, as their cost will be almost double that of the current models, so there will be fewer of them. For example, F-15/16-class aircraft must spend 30 minutes on the ground between combat sorties; the F-22 is looking to cut that in half. The same applies for the number of aircraft unavailable because of repairs. The current rate is about 15 percent; the F-22 is aiming for 2 percent. The speed with which malfunctioning aircraft can be repaired is also critical. Currently only about 45 percent of malfunctions can be fixed in under four hours. The F-22 hopes to increase this to 75

F-16 Fighting Falcon

F-14 Tomcat

percent. Compared to aircraft 20 years ago, or current Russian aircraft, improvements like these are not unreasonable. For example, current U.S. carrier aircraft have accidents at a rate giving pilots a 5–10 percent chance of being killed or disabled in a major accident during their flying careers. Twenty years ago, pilots had a better than 50 percent chance of coming to grief. These experiences carry over into combat, where minor accidents often become major during the heat of battle. These improvements also make more aircraft available for combat, and an often decisive edge in battle.

Ease of use has become a key factor in combat performance. For years, aircraft cockpits have increasingly come to look like video arcades. But as useful as all these displays have become, the pilot still had to be facing forward to use them. The latest wrinkle is to build a display inside the helmet's visor. Testing has shown this technique more than doubles the number of air-to-air kills. Israel and Russia are using this system. New sensors that can be built into the skin of aircraft will further multiply the effectiveness of better displays. These trends also show that pilots are gradually being replaced by automation. Aircraft crews have been reduced over 50 percent in the last 40 years. World War II heavy bombers had a crew of 12. The 1950s B-52 needs six crewmen, the 1970s B-1 needs four, and the B-2 needs only a pilot and weapons operator. Advances in computer technology, sensors, robotics, and artificial intelligence have made a pilotless drone interceptor possible and likely in the next decade. Meanwhile, Western air forces are beginning to equip aircraft with "pilot associates," computer-based systems that take over the more routine and technical aspects of flying and communicate with the pilot in a spoken language. Many tasks that previously required a button push can now be executed with a spoken command. Tests in actual cockpits have demonstrated accuracy of 98 percent, which is higher than many human crews are capable of. Typical tasks for spoken commands and electronic ears are requests for information on aircraft condition, or changing the status of a sensor or weapon system. A typical speech system can recognize three dozen commands, including seven in slurred speech common during high-stress maneuvers. Silicon copilots also constantly collect and examine information from the dozens of sensors on board. These sensors range from the familiar fuel gage to radar and radar-warning devices. Often overlooked are the numerous calculations and decisions pilots must make in flight. For example, on an interception mission, the pilot must decide how best to approach distant enemy aircraft. Radar will usually spot other aircraft long before weapons can be used or the target can be seen visually. There may also be ground-based missile systems aiming radars at you. These conditions present several options: should you go after the enemy aircraft with long-range missiles? Or speed up and engage with more accurate cannon and short-range missiles? You also have to worry about your own fuel situation, and which of your systems might be malfunctioning. The AI (artificial intelligence) computer's memory contains the experiences of many more experienced pilots as well as instant information on the rapidly changing situation. You can ask your electronic assistant what the options are and which one has the best chance of success. The pilot can then make decisions more quickly and accurately. When enemy aircraft are sighted, the electronic assistant can suggest which of the many maneuvers available are likely to work. If the aircraft is damaged, the electronic copilot can rapidly report what the new options are. One becomes quite fond of computers once they have saved your bacon a few times. Once the robotic copilot is in use, someone will calculate the expense of training human pilots ($5–$10 million) and making space (another $1–$5 million) for them in costly aircraft and decide to go with all-silicon air crew. More pressing reasons exist for getting rid of human pilots: they restrict the capabilities of the aircraft. When high-performance aircraft twist and turn violently, there is always the possibility that the pilot will black out and lose consciousness from the stress. This "black out" factor is currently a major limitation in aircraft design. Before robotic combat aircraft come into use, there will be more capable reconnaissance and attack drones. There are now long-range recon drones using navigation satellites, which enable them to fly in complete electronic silence. Western cruise missiles are the prototypical robotic strike aircraft, while air-to-air homing missiles increasingly contain the technology needed for robotic interceptors. Upcoming antiradar missiles will loiter in the area for up to an hour, waiting for enemy radar to come on. The U.S. Navy is particularly keen on robotic aircraft to take the recon load off increasingly expensive manned aircraft. Current trends indicate that robotic pilots will drift casually into use. All of a sudden, they will be all over the place. The first nation to get effective robotic pilots into the air will have a considerable advantage. Such advantages win battles and wars. The U.S. Air Force and Navy have begun developing robotic strike aircraft.

Robots on the ground are also playing a greater role in air warfare. Mission planning has long been the bane of combat operations. This planning consists of working out all the mundane navigation and fuel/weapons load questions before the aircraft take off. This mission planning was, in turn, driven by which overall strategy the air commander was pursuing, and this, in turn, was modified by what was known about the enemy capabilities and intentions. During the 1980s, the U.S. Air Force (USAF) took the lead in this area and developed two techniques that have changed the way air campaigns are conducted:

Air Tasking Order (ATO). This is a computer-supported system that enables the commander to sort out quickly the targets to be hit and the aircraft available. The completed ATO efficiently combines the high command's decisions on what they want air power to do on a particular day, and the air commander's appraisal of what would be available and how these resources could best be used. Creating the entire ATO by computer and issuing it to the units a day before it is to be used is a recent innovation. An interconnected system of computers figures out all the tedious (and complex) details such as:

- Where and when each aircraft would fly.
- How much fuel it would take off with (and where and when it would refuel in the air with a tanker).
- What weapons would be carried.
- What targets would be attacked.
- Which aircraft would fly together in a mission package.

Details of which pilots would be in the aircraft are left to the air units. Units report the percentage of their aircraft that are available to fly (usually between 80 and 95 percent), and the ATO computer program would take care of this.

Currently, an ATO is transmitted to the air units in electronic form at least 24 hours before the day the ATO is to be used. Most people using the ATO will see it only on a computer screen. The AWACS aircraft will often be the heaviest users of the ATO, as they must make sure aircraft in the air are where they are supposed to be, when they are supposed to be there.

The ATO controls nearly all U.S. Air Force, Navy, Marines, and, if available, allied fixed-wing aircraft. Helicopters, with a few exceptions, are not included in the ATO. Some marine aircraft and all attack helicopters are controlled by the ground combat units they belong to. The U.S. Air Force would like to get the attack helicopters and Marines fighter-bombers under ATO control, but the Army and Marines insist that the current ATO requires too much time (48 hours) to prepare. This question of ATO control is a quasipolitical one, and when the ATO gets its preparation time down to hours, more attack helicopters and marine aircraft will probably make use of it.

Mission Planning System (MPS). This provides pilots with essential mission information before they climb into their aircraft. Current MPS developed, during the 1980s, from a basically manual system to a largely automated one. The basics of mission planning consist of information the pilot needs to find the target, how to attack it, and how to avoid the enemy. Eighty-five years ago, pilots were told roughly what the situation was, then aircraft would go out individually or in small groups to engage enemy air and ground forces. This impromptu approach rapidly escalated over the next 25 years into "mission planning." From the 1950s, the U.S. Air Force used a complex and largely manual planning procedure for preparing pilots and aircraft for their increasingly complex missions. This planning includes items like:

- How much fuel can be carried (less fuel means more munitions).
- Where air refueling will take place (if needed).
- The best approach to the target.
- The best weapons to carry.
- Which aircraft will be in what position to the others during the flight.
- Who will do what under different circumstances.
- Potential enemy opposition is taken into account.

In the 1980s, the microcomputer revolution entered the process, and in 1986 the Air Force began installing computer-based MSS ("Mission Support Systems"). Aside from taking a large workload off the pilots, MSS allows for more effective mission planning and execution. For most aircraft, pilots can work out their flight plan on a computer, take a tape of the computer-generated plan, insert the tape into the aircraft computer, and eliminate a lot of the guesswork and rough calculation. Going into the 1990s, the USAF introduced more powerful microcomputers and workstations, as well as new software, that allowed the pilot to simulate flying the combat mission. This looks much like the air-combat simulators you can buy for personal computers. Thus, pilots combined training, practice, and planning on the same machine. The new MSS allowed pilots to:

- See graphically what the target will look like on radar, as well as a computer-generated color "movie" of what the mission will look like from the cockpit. Pilots prefer the movie.
- Make the hundreds of instrument settings (required before takeoff) on the

MSS and then insert the MSS tape into the aircraft computer and have all the settings made automatically. This allows for faster takeoff.

- Practice the bomb runs, taking into account the nature of the target and weapons used. For example, the MSS will calculate the safe altitude and speed to avoid damaging the bomber when the target is hit.
- Transfer the data electronically to the aircraft's computer (as with the older systems).

JTIDS (Joint Tactical Integrated Data System). This is the glue that will tie together U.S. Air Force, Navy, and Army aircraft control systems. JTIDS is basically a computer workstation and data network that takes data from AWACS, ship radars, ground radars, and combat aircraft systems and passes it to everyone in the network (which can cover over a million square miles). This will enable everyone to have all information available, including the status of friendly aircraft in the air (fuel and weapons available, etc.). JTIDS became operational by the late 1990s. Over a thousand JTIDS systems are being purchased, at a cost of over half a million dollars each.

A big breakthrough this decade will be in passive radar. This type of system is based on infrared (IR) or passive millimeter-wave technology and fast signal processing. The ability to sense other characteristics besides heat (IR), such as magnetism and sound, is also being developed. For the moment, however, IR "passive radars" are already performing quite well in the laboratory, and the Russians have equipped their MiG-29 fighter with one that apparently works. The current generation of Western IR air-to-air missiles uses a reliable IR radar that can track the heat from an aircraft at any angle and over several kilometers, although problems persist with clouds degrading the heat signal. For this reason, the first passive IR radars will be used in conjunction with conventional radars. There is a great urgency in this area, because missiles that home in on active radars are becoming more common and effective. Passive radars are also an important component of the new generation of air-to-air missiles. A short-range passive sensor, the IR homing device in short-range missiles, has been used for over 40 years. Longer-range missiles have always required guidance from the aircraft or extremely expensive and space-consuming active radars. Neither of these solutions has been very effective. Progress marches on, however, and smaller components and more powerful microcomputers have made possible missiles like the AMRAAM (Advanced Medium-Range Air-to-Air Missile). Aside from being much lighter than the AIM-7 Sparrow missile it replaces, AMRAAM can find the target on its own without constant guidance from the launching aircraft. AMRAAM has several ways to find its target. In addition to its own search radar, its onboard computer can be told the predicted position of its target. Once launched, the AMRAAM speeds off to this position and, if the target is not immediately found, searches for it. This is what torpedoes have been doing for over 60 years. But then torpedoes weigh several tons and move a lot more slowly.

Without exception, most air forces see "BVR (Beyond Visual Range) engagements" as the primary means of future victories. Both air-to-air and air-to-ground weapons stress BVR capability. In the air, this requires pilots to trust their sensors to sort out friend from foe. Historically, they have been reluctant to do this. As a fallback, more effective short-range missiles are being developed. The latest version of the U.S. Sidewinder can be fired at a target from any angle and has proven very effective in combat. The longer-range BVR missiles will probably end up being used sporadically for well-planned aerial ambushes. On the ground, the situation is even more dependent on sensors. Hitting ground targets from the air has always been more art than science, and there were never enough artists to go around. In the last 30 years, the technology has come of age, as the 1986 U.S. raid on Tripoli and the 1991 Gulf War demonstrated. These operations also confirmed that accuracy is relative no matter how mature these weapons are. The navigation systems on attack aircraft are becoming quite accurate and reliable. But moving along near the ground at 100–200 meters a second leaves little room for timely pilot action. If the target's position is stationary and known, you can literally program it into the automatic pilot and go along for the ride. This is becoming more common. The "standoff," or BVR, weapons also have their own guidance systems, or use other sensors, to actually hit the target. Acknowledging still more inaccuracy, cluster weapons are more common, thus ensuring that the target will be hit with something. Easy-to-locate targets like bridges, airfields, and other installations are still the favorite prey of fixed-wing aircraft. On the battlefield itself, helicopters are becoming the air-to-ground weapon of choice. Another innovation is the "look and shoot" helmet, which has a display built into the visor and linked to cannon and rocket pods. When the pilot sees something worth hitting, he just looks and pushes a button, and that's it.

Another continuing problem with long-range engagements is making sure you are not firing at your own people. IFF (Identify, Friend or Foe) devices have never really worked as intended, and pilots don't trust them. These gadgets will, on pilot command, send a signal to a suspected target. If the target is a friendly aircraft, its IFF device will respond with the correct code. This system has several serious flaws. If the IFF device fails or malfunctions, you get shot at. The aircraft using IFF is sending out signals that enable the enemy to find you. ECM can be used to deceive IFF devices. All these problems are being addressed in the laboratory. It may be a while before an IFF device that pilots will use appears. While long-range engagements are preferred, all previous predictions of long-range ambush taking over the air have proven premature until the first combat use of the AWACS aircraft. These radar-equipped control aircraft can more effectively direct friendly aircraft over enemy territory and give the pilots confidence that their far distant aerial targets are not friendlies. The Gulf War was the first opportunity to test this system. The system worked, and air combat will never be the same.

Close-range combat continues to be a possibility, however, and success depends on agility. Opposing the streamlined stealth shapes are designs that feature a lot of extra little wings, fins, and other devices that allow unheard-of maneuvers. To give aircraft more agility, microcomputing power is again called upon to control the aircraft flaps and control surfaces more rapidly than any human pilot possibly could. This maneuverability also allows more efficiency in landing, taking off, and flying at high speed with high fuel efficiency. A fighter that can turn on a dime and tilt up 45 degrees without falling like a rock equals a formidable dogfighter. The key to these designs is enough computing power to prevent the aircraft from spinning out of control. A major loss of F-4 aircraft in Vietnam was from early model F-4s trying to keep up with more nimble MiGs. Various Western high-maneuverability aircraft designs are in development, and many forms of computer-driven "stability control" are already deployed. The B-2 takes full advantage of this approach, as its flying-wing shape is inherently unstable. Other aircraft that make partial use of this technology are the F-16 (in pitch, anyway), EFA, Rafale, ATF, and the Swedish Grippen. An additional advantage of this technology is the ability to operate from shorter, or damaged, airfields. A new generation of engines will allow combat aircraft to fly very high and fast, like the SR-71, without requiring enormous quantities of fuel. Combining this with stealth technology makes these high and fast aircraft more difficult to spot with radar, or hit with radar guided missiles. The replacement for the SR-71 will basically be a high-altitude and high-speed stealth aircraft. Without an announced replacement, the SR-71 was retired in 1990. It is too expensive to operate, over five times the cost of a fighter, and most of its missions can be undertaken by satellites.

Helicopters have finally arrived, as they are now being used for nearly every task that fixed-wing aircraft perform. Helicopter gunships are being equipped with air-to-air missiles for use against other helicopters as well as fixed-wing fighters. Helicopters loaded with electronics wage electronic warfare. This last task is being complemented in the United States by a new version of Vietnam-era gunship based on the C-130 transport. This version carries 20mm and 40mm automatic cannon as well as a 105mm howitzer and, as needed, Hellfire missiles. Multiplying the effect of this firepower is a full load of sensors and electronic warfare equipment. The crew sits in air-conditioned, armored comfort while unleashing all that firepower. There are only about a dozen aircraft available, and they will be risky to use in areas where the targets have much antiaircraft capability. Against poorly armed insurgents, however, they can be devastating. The U.S. Army is also modifying several dozen of its helicopters by adding more sensors and weapons so that they can more effectively support commando operations.

C-130 tanker refuels a helicopter

Developing new aircraft is becoming more difficult. An obvious problem is the greater expense needed for increasingly complex technology. The other problem is managing the complex technology and equally intricate development projects. Western nations are finding that increasingly they can't afford the neat new goodies they are developing.

The number of combat aircraft available has been steadily declining since 1945. The next generation of combat jets will cost over a $100 million each, with the number built up to half as much as the current generation. Attack helicopters are also escalating in price, with a subsequent plunge in numbers. All of this shrinkage is a result of more expensive models. The overall capabilities of aircraft fleets have increased, along with a decline in operational accidents. Indications are that the robotic aircraft will be a natural end product of these trends.

An effective, although not entirely popular, method of increasing aircraft performance is the installation of new components. Because engines wear out relatively quickly, upgrading these is a favorite exercise. Electronics tend to get smaller and lighter, so new items are not difficult to fit in. Helicopters, in particular, have always been upgraded over time to the point where they were practically rebuilt. Western firms are having a good time upgrading Third World nations' Russian aircraft, which have sturdy structures but unreliable engines and substandard electronics. Another option increasingly favored by rich and poor nations alike is to use more low-performance aircraft for specific missions. This has been done for several decades, with jet trainers being con-

EA-6B Prowler electronic warfare aircraft

verted to ground-attack or interception aircraft. Another future trend is for
many Third World nations to design and build their own low-performance aircraft, thereby depriving the major arms producers of export markets and driving up the cost of the already expensive high-performance aircraft because of
smaller production runs.

One thing that will not change is the enormous lead Western aircraft possess over those built in Russia or Third World nations. There is another new
development that may realistically enable us to fight the next war without actually doing so. Dissimilar training and simulation have become an ever more
crucial advantage in Western air forces. Flight simulators have been used for
over 60 years, but in the last decade increases in computer power have made
possible highly realistic combat aircraft simulators. Although these machines
cost nearly as much as the aircraft they simulate, they are much cheaper to
operate. Upcoming are much cheaper simulators, for the same reason that
microcomputer prices are declining. Already, over a dozen simulators can be
electronically linked so that groups of aircraft can fight each other. Of more
import is the new ability to operate against accurate aircraft and tactics used by
other nations. This works well with a 20-year-old U.S. program to train pilots
in the air against "aggressor" aircraft and pilots, using the different equipment
and tactics pilots can expect in wartime. These training advantages, added to
the greater flying time Western pilots get, have proven a critical advantage for
Western pilots in recent wars.

Fighters, Bombers, and Recon Aircraft

This chart shows the capabilities of some 25,000 combat aircraft. These comprise over 90 percent of those available worldwide. Included are helicopters possessing some combat capability. Increasingly, helicopters are taking over ground-support duties. Moreover, helicopters are being armed with air-to-air missiles so they may attack other helicopters and fixed-wing aircraft. Long regarded as little more than flying trucks, helicopters are making the lower altitudes their own exclusive territory. The only helicopter types shown are U.S. and Russian, as these represent over 75 percent of those in use. The

Designation	By	Capability ratings		Max wght	Normal combat radius (km)	Year introduced	No. in use 2002
		Air	Ground				
Air Superiority							
Ching Kuo	TW	20	15	12.2	1,200	1975	130
EF-2000 (Typhoon)	NT	46	53	21.0	400	2002	40
F-1	JP	11	14	13.7	400	1976	40
F-4 (Phantom)	U.S.	19	21	28.0	1,100	1963	768
F-5E (Tiger)	U.S.	7	9	11.1	1,000	1972	1,177
F-14A (Tomcat)	U.S.	29	10	33.7	1,000	1970	140
F-14b/D (Bombcat)	U.S.	19	42	33.7	1,100	1990	110
F-15 (Eagle)	U.S.	54	24	25.0	990	1977	870
F-16 (Falcon)	U.S.	32	40	16.0	900	1980	2,565
F-18A (Hornet)	U.S.	29	44	28.8	600	1982	850
F-18D (Super Hornet)	U.S.	45	69	22.0	800	1999	120
F-22 (Lightning)	U.S.	100	11	32.0	990	2004	12
F-104 (Starfighter)	U.S.	6	2	14.0	1,200	1958	102
J-6 (MiG-19)	CH	5	1	8.7	680	1970	2,083
J-7 (MiG-21)	CH	6	2	9.4	1,100	1965	1,116
J-8	CH	7	2	18.0	800	1969	260
J-10 (Lavi)	CH	16	13	19.0	1,100	2005	0
Kfir C2	IS	14	13	14.7	780	1974	147
MiG-21J (Fishbed)	RU	8	1	9.4	700	1956	1,769
MiG-23 (Flogger-B)	RU	14	4	18.0	960	1971	747
MiG-25 (Foxbat)	RU	4	0	37.5	900	1970	81
MiG-29 (Fulcrum)	RU	24	16	17.0	1,300	1984	808
MiG-31 (Foxhound)	RU	6	0	41.0	1,100	1982	200
MiG-33 (Fulcrum+)	RU	35	14	17.0	1,100	1992	0
Mirage III	FR	9	6	13.7	1,300	1963	152
Mirage F1	FR	13	13	15.2	1,000	1973	340
Mirage 2000	FR	24	24	16.5	1,600	1983	408
Mirage V	FR	23	26	17.0	1,600	1992	169
Rafale	FR	32	18	14.5	700	1998	10
Su-27 (Flanker)	RU	26	9	27.0	900	1983	594
Su-37 (Terminator)	RU	32	14	34.0	1,500	1999	10
Tornado	NT	25	54	24.0	1,300	1980	800

remaining machines are manufactured by other Western nations (Britain, France, Italy, etc.) and tend to follow American design practice. The helicopters of these nations have been added to similar types shown in the chart. Not included are training, supply, and reconnaissance aircraft. This gets a bit tricky, as these other aircraft can, and sometimes do, serve as combat vehicles. Indeed, many of the helicopters shown on the chart are primarily transports. However, because they operate so close to the combat zone, transport helicopters are usually armed and frequently have ample opportunities to use their weapons.

Designation	By	Capability ratings		Max wght	Normal combat radius (km)	Year introduced	No. in use 2002
		Air	Ground				
Bombers							
A-4 (Skyhawk)	U.S.	4	12	20.0	1,500	1960	184
A-10 (Warthog)	U.S.	6	59	23.0	500	1977	210
AC-130U (Spooky)	U.S.	1	23	70.0	1400	1966	21
Alpha	NT	4	11	7.5	520	1979	267
AMX	IT	3	19	14.0	700	1986	80
AV-8 (Harrier)	UK	9	15	11.0	400	1969	394
B-1	U.S.	1	96	217.0	5,800	1984	90
B-2	U.S.	3	100	181.0	7,200	1992	21
B-52 (BUFF)	U.S.	1	54	225.0	1,600	1955	90
EA-6E (Intruder)	U.S.	6	36	27.0	750	1963	110
F-15E (Strike Eagle)	U.S.	24	70	32.0	990	1988	190
F-35 (JSF)	U.S.	22	88	25.0	1,200	2008	0
F-35N (Navy JSF)	U.S.	18	94	29.0	1,200	2008	0
F-111F (Aardvark)	U.S.	5	56	45.0	2,000	1967	32
F-117A	U.S.	7	38	16.0	700	1981	44
H-5 (IL-28)	CH	1	3	21.0	800	1950	260
H-6 (Tu-16)	CH	1	10	79.0	1,800	1955	100
Jaguar	NT	6	36	18.0	1,300	1972	166
MiG-27 (Flogger-C-D)	RU	9	13	20.0	400	1973	140
Q-5	CH	2	3	17.7	600	1972	430
Su-17 (Fitter-C)	RU	1	4	17.7	600	1972	566
Su-24 (Fencer)	RU	7	33	41.0	1,200	1974	639
Su-25 (Frogfoot)	RU	2	18	19.0	500	1983	357
Su-30 (Flanker)	RU	25	40	33.0	1,200	1983	16
Tu-22 (Blinder)	RU	1	16	83.4	1,500	1962	5
Tu-22M (Backfire)	RU	1	40	130.0	2,500	1974	220
Tu-95 (Bear)	RU	0	10	188.0	5,000	1955	90
Tu-160 (Blackjack)	RU	2	26	250.0	5,200	1985	16
Helicopters							
AH-1S (Cobra)	U.S.	3	9	5.0	180	1984	650
AH-1W (SeaCobra)	U.S.	3	6	6.6	400	1987	247
AH-64 (Apache)	U.S.	19	35	9.5	300	1985	806
Ka-50 (Havoc)	RU	4	29	10.8	400	1992	10
Mi-24 (Hind)	RU	2	8	11.0	160	1972	1,048
OH-58 (Kiowa)	U.S.	0	7	1.5	200	1969	360

Designation. The official designation of the aircraft, followed (in parentheses) by the more common name. Some aircraft have no common name. The ones for most Russian aircraft are the old names NATO used to assign to Soviet Union warplanes.

By. The nation that designed, and generally manufactures, the aircraft. It is common for widely produced aircraft (F-16, MiG-21) to be built in several nations. Nation abbreviations used are: U.S.=United States, NT=NATO (consortium of NATO countries), FR=France, TW=Taiwan, IT=Italy, JP=Japan, IS=Israel, RU=Russia, CH=China, UK=United Kingdom.

Capability ratings, Air. All aircraft are given a numerical rating to show their ability to fight other aircraft. This is commonly called "air superiority" and includes evaluating a number of other aircraft characteristics and equipment, as well as the sortie rate and readiness rate (how many, on average, are ready for action). A more detailed discussion of what creates air-to-air combat capability follows:

- *Pilot skill.* Perhaps the most decisive factor, once an aircraft is armed and in the air, is pilot skill. And these skills are obtained mainly by allowing pilots to fly their warplanes a lot. This lesson was driven home decisively in World War II, when performance records of over 100,000 combat pilots could be examined. There was a direct relationship between a pilot's success in combat and the number of hours he had spent flying before joining a combat unit. At the beginning of World War II, Japanese pilots got 700 hours of flying time before going off to war. U.S. pilots got only 305 hours. By 1943, the growing demands on Japan's meager resources forced them to cut training hours back to 500. At the same time, America was able to increase its training time to 500 hours. Japanese pilots were not nearly as successful in 1943 as they were in late 1941. In 1944, U.S. hours went up to 525 and Japanese fell to 275. At that point, the superiority of U.S. warplanes was obvious. By 1945, Japanese pilots got only 90 hours, and the air battles had become decidedly one-sided. Most new Japanese pilots were used to fly kamikaze suicide missions. Today, complex modern warplanes require pilots to spend at least 100 hours a year to maintain minimal skills. Better yet, 200–300 hours, but the new jet aircraft are expensive to run, and for the last half-century it's been a struggle to get the money for pilots to fly a lot of training hours. Simulators, even computer-based ones, help. But you've got to spend time in the air. A lot also depends on how the pilots spend their time in the air. During World War II and Korea, U.S. pilots trained to deal with the different tactics and techniques of their opponents. But in the late 1950s, American pilots fell into the bad habit of training against one another. The Vietnam War showed that to be false economy, and out of that experience came the Top Gun training program, where realism in air combat training was stressed. Not every nation gives their pilots a hundred hours a year in the air, and fewer still have programs like Top Gun. So even if a nation gets modern fighters, such as MiG-29s in North Korea or Su-27s in China, if they don't spend the money to keep their pilots in the air a lot, and build a realistic training program, these high-performance jets will just be expensive targets for more experienced pilots in less capable aircraft. Over the last 60 years, better-trained pilots (even when flying inferior aircraft) have regularly shot down 10 or more enemy aircraft for each one their own side has lost. For the purpose of this chart, pilot skill has been assumed to be the same for all aircraft. But in the real world, the wealthier nations have better pilots even if all they do is let them fly more. In many cases, like Israel and the U.S., pilots also have the advantage of well-thought-out training programs. So if there's ever a war in the Taiwan Straits or Korea, don't be surprised if you see a disproportionate number of Chinese or North Korean aircraft going down in flames.

• *Electronic equipment.* This includes radar (for finding distant targets and using long-range missiles), fire-control equipment (enables pilot to control guns and missiles), and countermeasures (detects enemy radar use and approaching missiles as well as, in some cases, deceiving enemy radar and missiles). Different models of the same aircraft can have very different quality electronics. When aircraft are sold to a foreign air force, they often don't have the most powerful electronics available. Another aspect of electronics capability is not entirely electronic, and that is stealth, the ability to hide from enemy radar. While some stealth can be achieved with electronic gadgets, the most successful stealth effects come from clever design of the aircraft's shape and the use of materials that will absorb radar signals. Other design tricks can reduce the amount of heat the aircraft's engines will make available to infrared detectors. If the enemy can't find you, he can't hurt you.

• *Weapons.* In the last half-century, missiles have replaced guns as the principal air-to-air combat weapon. The capabilities of air-to-air missiles vary enormously. They all depend on some of the aircraft's electronic equipment, especially the long-range missiles. These require the aircraft radar to find distant targets for the missile before launch, and some of the older missiles use the aircraft radar to stay in contact with the target. To put it more bluntly, two identical aircraft with pilots of identical skill can have very different air-to-air combat capabilities depending on the quality of missiles carried. The warplane with the better missiles and onboard electronics will be at least twice as effective as the aircraft with the lesser weapons.

GBU-15 smart bomb (guided via TV camera in nose of bomb)

- *Maneuverability.* This is not as important as it once was, given the growing importance of radars and missiles. With long-range missiles, very little maneuverability is required. But when it comes to avoiding enemy missiles, and getting into position to return fire, maneuverability becomes an issue. Speed is not as important as it once was. With missiles, you rarely have enough of a speed advantage to escape a superior enemy, and enemy missiles. The most recent Russian aircraft (MiG-29, Su-27, and Su-37) have put a lot more emphasis on mobility. But many pilots, particularly those who have flown the MiG-29 and Western aircraft, feel the increased mobility will mean little in combat. On the other hand, the new U.S. fighter, the F-22, has a "super cruise" feature that enables it to cruise at supersonic speed without quickly using up all its fuel. Super cruise enables a few F-22s, guided by long-range radar on the ground or in airborne AWACS, to cover a much larger chunk of air space.
- *Durability and maintainability.* Car owners have noted that some models can take more punishment and require less maintenance and repairs than others. It's the same with combat aircraft. You can build a warplane with lots of range, maneuverability, and other qualities, yet it may be a bitch to keep flying. Put another way, a warplane that is able to fly only once every three days will be less useful than one that can fly several times a day. Each time an aircraft takes off and performs a mission, it has performed what is called a "sortie." The overall measure of an aircraft's

durability and maintainability is its sortie rate. This is the number of sorties that can be flown over a certain period of time. Between sorties, an aircraft must be checked out visually and electronically to see if all key components are operational or approaching failure. Fuel and munitions are loaded. The pilot must be briefed on the mission, which can take from a few minutes to over an hour. After a sortie, the same cycle must be repeated before another takeoff. You can cut corners in maintenance, which increases the risk of losing the aircraft and/or sending it up with some capabilities crippled. All aircraft have, in theory, the ability to fly several times a day. How many times a day they can actually fly depends on how the aircraft was designed, maintained, and what kind of ground crew is currently tending to it. And then there is the sortie rate. There are basically two types of sortie rates: surge and sustained. Surge rate is flying as many times a day as you can and is typically used early in an air campaign to capitalize on the element of surprise. The sustained rate is what you can fly day after day for weeks or months. In a typical campaign, you would have two days of surge and many more days of sustained sorties. You might slow down to catch up on bypassed maintenance so you can surge again for a few days. Aircraft units often practice surging. A typical example is one American F-16 squadron, which used its 20 aircraft, 40 pilots, and very energetic and well-trained ground crews to fly 160 sorties in 12 hours. This was an exceptional performance and not representative of combat conditions, where many aircraft would come back with combat damage. This also points out the need to have more pilots than aircraft, as the pilots are more fragile than the aircraft they fly. Most Western aircraft can fly three or more sorties per day for two or three days, and one or two per day indefinitely as long as the spare parts and ground crews hold out. Western air forces practice high sortie surge tactics far more than less-affluent nations. Israel has demonstrated the effectiveness of this practice in all its wars, as did the U.S. Air Force during the 1991 Gulf War. For this reason, the number of aircraft and the quality of pilots are not the only factors that determine which aircraft are superior. Western air forces have long used high sortie rates as a key component of their air power. This is one reason why Western warplanes are so expensive. They are built to fly a lot, especially in combat. This means they are easier to maintain, despite their heavy use of electronics. It's a style of aircraft design that works. During World War II, the most glaring example of how well it worked was in the Pacific. Japanese aircraft were built for maneuverability and long range. But American warplanes were a lot more rugged, and more dependable. Early in the war, American pilots had to adjust their tactics to compensate for the better maneuverability of the Japanese aircraft. Russia also developed a unique style of aircraft design during World War II. Not having as many people familiar with mechanics as Germany and America, they built aircraft that were simpler to maintain (and thus requiring fewer technicians). While simpler aircraft were somewhat less capable, this worked for the Russians. They believed quantity could make up for quality and managed to make that work. But many poorer nations bought Russian aircraft over the last half century because of the easier maintenance. These nations were willing to sacrifice quality in order to keep costs down. This is one reason why Western warplanes tend to make short work of these air forces (Israel versus Arabs, United States versus Iraq, and so on).

Capability ratings, Ground. All the items that make for air superiority in aircraft apply to ground attack. But there are a few differences. Bombing depends a lot more on electronics and carrying capacity. How many bombs an aircraft could carry used to be the main factor, but no more. Beginning in World War II, more emphasis was placed on fire control: instruments that help you put the bombs exactly where you want them. The two major innovations that came out of World War II were precision bomb sights and electronic aids. The bomb sights were precision instruments that controlled for factors like the speed of the aircraft, wind, and the types of bombs carried. Some calculation was done, but this was limited by the technology available. Electronic devices were most useful for bombing at unseen (because of clouds, darkness, or smoke) targets. Radar that was pointed at the ground and showed the shape of things down there was a big breakthrough. For the last sixty years, these primitive (by today's standards) tools have been steadily improved. In World War II, half the bombs would, on average, land within 3,000 feet of the target. By the 1950s, you could get half your bombs within 400 feet. By the 1980s, this was down to 40 feet. Another factor is the electronics on the bomb itself. Again, beginning in World War II, guided bombs were developed and used. These were controlled by radio, with a controller in the aircraft manipulating the fins on the bomb. By the 1970s, lasers were used to bounce laser light off the target. Such specially equipped bombs had a sensor that could see the reflected laser light and automatically manipulate the small wings on the bomb to crash into the target. With these guided bombs, you could hit ten feet or less from the target. The downside of this is that the more precise fire-control systems, as well as the guided bombs, cost a lot more (about 20 times more). The fire-control equipment for laser-guided bombs is also very expensive, $1 million or more per aircraft. As a result, many air forces have resisted buying the more expensive, and more accurate, bombing gear. Eventually, most aviators realized that this was false economy. Better bombing accuracy saves you a lot of money in lost aircraft, and the expense of flying more missions to take out a target.

Max wght. This is the maximum takeoff weight for the aircraft, in tons. This is a good indicator of the size of the aircraft. The maximum takeoff weight is, on average, about twice the empty weight for Western aircraft and only about 1.5 times the empty weight for Russian-designed aircraft. The difference is because of better Western engines and greater use of lighter composite materials in Western aircraft. One result of this is that Western warplanes tend to have a longer range and larger bomb load than Russian aircraft (which are also used by China and many less affluent nations).

Normal combat radius. This represents how far, in kilometers, the aircraft can normally travel from its base and perform its mission (air superiority or ground attack). The rule of thumb is that the combat radius is one-third the distance an aircraft can fly in a straight line on a full load of fuel. This assumes a trip out and back, plus one-third of fuel for combat operations. But for that handful of nations with a lot of aerial tanker aircraft, the situation is quite different, and rather more complicated. With tankers you can have combat aircraft top off their fuel tanks just before they enter hostile airspace, and do the same when they return. This can more than double the normal range of warplanes. But it gets more complicated than that. Aircraft have a maximum takeoff weight, but bombers can take off with more bombs and less fuel. After flying a long distance to just outside enemy territory, they can take on more fuel, deliver their bombs, and tank up again on the way home. Aircraft can also carry more weight in flight than they do when taking off. So refueling in the air can as much as double the normal bomb load. This technique is particularly useful with heavy bombers like the B-52, B-1, and B-2. But even smaller bombers make use of the technique, especially the F-117. America has the largest aerial tanker fleet and is the most frequent user of tankers to extend range and increase bomb load. Another factor affecting range is the use of speed to avoid enemy warplanes or ground fire. Normally, aircraft burn about .5 percent of fuel per minute when cruising at the economical speed (600–800 kilometers an hour). When enemy warplanes or ground fire are encountered, maximum speed is used. These high-speed maneuvers will often get you away from danger or are sometimes used to catch up with enemy fighters. But maximum speed burns up a lot more fuel. Fighters can consume 10–15 percent of fuel per minute at maximum speed. Even strike aircraft will frequently crank it up to 2–3 percent of fuel per minute while maneuvering toward or away from their targets. The average aircraft has sufficient fuel for 2–3 hours of cruising and up to 15 minutes of high-speed maneuvering during combat. Strike aircraft prefer to conserve their fuel so they can circle the battlefield waiting for the opportune moment to go down and hit a target. Fuel is a weapon. If one aircraft has more fuel, it can force another into a situation where the disadvantaged plane will crash with empty gas tanks. When the low-fuel aircraft realizes that it only has enough to get back to base, it can be more easily outmaneuvered by its opponent, who can be more generous with fuel and speed. Fuel is also a handy defense. Recon aircraft, in particular, use bursts of speed to avoid danger from aircraft above or missiles below. Combat aircraft often fly off to their objectives with one or more large fuel tanks hanging from them. These tanks slow down the aircraft and decrease maneuverability. Before entering combat, these tanks are normally dropped. A common tactic is to force the other fellow to jettison his drop tanks before the fuel they carry has been used. This is done by attacking the enemy formation with missiles or interceptors before it has reached its objective. The attack does not have to be serious, just enough to force those partially full tanks to the ground. Once more, aerial tankers are a crucial advantage. Aircraft coming out of hostile airspace with nearly empty tanks are often rescued by waiting tankers. Other nations often lose aircraft when pilots have to choose between getting shot down and using so much fuel that they could not make it to a landing strip in friendly territory. Russian aircraft were built with this in mind and are rugged enough to land on any long, flat surface that's reasonably firm.

Year introduced. This is the year the aircraft type was first delivered to a combat unit. Aircraft that have been in service for a long time (10 years or more) will have a lot of variation. The longer a type is in service, the more it will be improved and modified. Later versions have substantially improved, or at least different, performance. This is not difficult to do, as aircraft must be overhauled frequently. Depending on the type, and country of origin, every 500–3,000 flight hours the aircraft must be practically taken apart. During this process, improved components can be installed. The combat values given for each aircraft are thus averages for that type. If an aircraft changes enough, it is listed separately as another aircraft.

No. in use 2002. This is the number of the type of aircraft estimated to be in use during 2002. There may be some small errors due to increased accident/war losses or production changes. Earlier retirement of older planes, as well as the secret nature of some of this information, also makes these values approximations. Most air forces are still shedding older aircraft, and order fewer new planes, in light of the Cold War's end. Each year, hundreds of military aircraft are lost to accidents and other noncombat causes.

Aircraft Types Found in Chart

A-10. U.S. ground support aircraft. The Air Force loves to bomb, but not in a combat zone. Enemy troops shoot back, and an aircraft has to be armored to survive. The A-10 was the U.S. Air Force solution to this problem. It carries 7.2 tons of bombs and missiles. Although the Air Force would prefer to sidestep direct support of combat troops, they are reluctant to let the Army have fixed-wing combat aircraft. Although the A-10 did exceptionally well in its combat debut during the Gulf War, its slow speed and ground-attack weapons make it different from other Air Force combat aircraft. The Air Force is reluctant to build a replacement and has even expressed a willingness to transfer its A-10s to the Army. All this may be moot, as the helicopter is increasingly the primary source of air support for ground troops.

A-4. Predecessor of the A-6, this is a lightweight carrier bomber. It carries 3.5 tons of bombs. It saw extensive combat in Vietnam and in the Israeli air force. It is still used by many nations as an inexpensive but effective (if elderly) ground-attack aircraft.

AC-130U. First developed for the Vietnam War, this is a unique combat aircraft. This gunship can slowly circle a combat area at low altitude. Communicating by radio with troops on the ground, the gunship can deliver pinpoint fire as needed. The infantry love "Spooky" (the original nickname for Vietnam-era gunships). The current aircraft is a four-engine C-130. It is equipped with 25mm and 40mm automatic cannon and a 105mm howitzer. It also can carry four Hellfire missiles. It has an extensive array of electronics, allowing it to operate in any kind of weather. Aerial refueling allows the AC-130 to go just about anywhere and hang around until its ammunition is used up.

AH-1S. This is a substantially improved version of the AH-1G (the first helicopter gunship, which was, in fact, a heavily modified UH-1). It carries 1.6 tons of rockets and missiles. There are still quite a few of these in service. It is particularly useful when armed with TOW antitank missiles.

AH-1W. This is the USMC version of the AH-1. It is a much-enhanced AH-1S, particularly in the use of two engines instead of one. It carries 2.3 tons of rockets and missiles.

AH-64. This is the second-generation U.S. helicopter gunship. It carries two tons of rockets and missiles. It has much more powerful fire-control systems than earlier gunships.

Alpha. An inexpensive light bomber. It carries 2.5 tons of bombs.

AMX. This is a ground-attack aircraft built by Brazil and Italy with the hope of selling this low-cost warplane to the Cold War market. But the Cold War ended, and export sales are hard to come by. It can carry 3.8 tons of bombs and missiles.

AV-8B. The original STOL (Short Takeoff and Landing) fighter-bomber, it can also take off like a helicopter. It saw its first action in the 1982 Falklands war, where it proved even more capable than originally predicted. It carries 4.8 tons of bombs.

B-1. A U.S. long-range bomber designed to use low flying and ECM to penetrate heavy defenses. It is a very complex system that has had a lot of growing pains. It carries up to 60 tons of bombs, which makes it a replacement for the B-52. But the B-1 is a more complex aircraft and is likely to be retired before the B-52.

B-2. The "stealth bomber." The first aircraft to cost more than most warships. It carries up to 22 tons of bombs and is equipped with excellent fire-control capabilities. But the B-2 is very expensive to maintain. The special antiradar coating has to be touched up after each flight. As a result, the B-2 is likely to be retired before the B-52.

B-52. The basic U.S. long-range bomber since the 1950s. Its electronics have been vastly upgraded, and many now carry cruise missiles. Its maximum bomb load is 24 tons. A late 1940s design that proved remarkably sturdy and easy to maintain, it is expected to serve into the 2030s.

Ching Kuo. When Taiwan was faced with the prospect of no source for modern jet fighters in the 1980s, they decided to build their own. This was the result, an aircraft somewhere between the F-5 and F-16 in capability (carrying 3.8 tons of bombs). When foreign sources of modern jets reappeared in the early 1990s, production of the Ching Kuo was cut back to 130. The project is a good example of what an industrialized nation, lacking much of an aviation industry, can do to produce its own high-performance warplanes.

EA-6E. Until the 1990s, the main U.S. Navy bomber. It is now used as the principal electronic-warfare aircraft for the Navy and Air Force. Long range and large carrying capacity (4.5 tons) make it an excellent performer in this role. But the remaining aircraft are old, and the heavy workload demanded contributes to the rapid wearing-out of the remaining aircraft.

EF-2000 Typhoon. Also known as the Eurofighter. Britain, Germany, Italy, and Spain joined forces to design and build this multipurpose warplane. It is roughly equivalent to the F-18E. It can carry 6.5 tons of bombs and missiles.

F-1. Produced more out of national pride than for any practical reason, it's actually an upgraded version of the Japanese-built T-1 jet trainer (similar to the U.S. T-33 jet trainer). It is intended as a ground-support aircraft but carries only 2.7 tons of bombs. Only 77 were ever built.

F-104. A 1950s design, it was a contemporary of the MiG-21, but not as successful. It is still used by some U.S. allies who have not been able to afford a replacement yet. It can carry about three tons of bombs but is not very stable at low altitudes. All F-104s will probably be out of service by 2010.

F-111. This was the principal U.S. medium-range bomber and electronic-warfare aircraft (the "Spark Vark," after its unofficial nickname, the "Aardvark"). It can carry up to 13 tons of bombs, is still used by Australia, and was the model for the larger B-1.

F-117A. Otherwise known as the stealth fighter. This is a rarity in the West, a secret aircraft development project. The Russians probably knew more about it than the American public, assuming they were able to get a photo satellite into position when these things were flying. This is not really a fighter in the same sense as the F-16, F-18, and F-15. Its function is more akin to the A-6. In addition to a heavy load of electronic devices, largely passive, the F-117A is designed to present a very small target to radar. Like the human eye, radar can see larger targets farther away. A B-52 is the aerial equivalent of an aircraft carrier to a radar; the F-117A appears as a small speedboat. Typical missions for the F-117A are destroying SAM sites or heavily defended targets. Reconnaissance is also an ideal mission. As a fighter, the F-117A would, and probably could, have to get the first shot in if equipped with the right sensors and missiles. This is not a very fast or particularly maneuverable aircraft, so it would have to hit first and then slink away. Veteran fighter pilots prefer this approach anyway, which is why they are veterans. The very accurate fire-control system is necessary because the F-117 only carries two tons of bombs (usually just two bombs).

F-14A. Until the arrival of the F-18D, this was the principal U.S. Navy interceptor. It was actually designed around its expensive long-range Phoenix missiles. Until recently, its primary job was defending the fleet, especially the carriers. The A model was hampered by an underpowered engine (the result of budget problems). Because it carried the Phoenix missile, this was not much of a problem.

F-14B/D. The B model arrived in the late 1980s, with the more powerful engine the A version never got. This allowed a number of upgrades not possible before. But one of the more important features of the new engines was the ability of the F-14 to take off without using its afterburner. During night launches, the afterburner could been seen 80 kilometers away at sea. The B model was followed a few years later by the D model, with many improvements in the aircraft's electronics. This made it possible for the F-14 to drop smart bombs, resulting in many B and D models shifting to ground-attack missions as the "Bombcat." It can carry 6.5 tons of bombs.

F-15. The most effective Western interceptor. It can also be used as a fighter-bomber (carrying ten tons of bombs).

F-15E. This two-seat version of the F-15 was developed primarily for ground attack. It carries eleven tons of bombs. The F-15E did very well in the Gulf War.

F-16. The most numerous Western interceptor, with over 4,000 built, and still in production. It can also function as a bomber and ground-attack aircraft, although it's not as effective as the air force folks would have you believe. It can carry four tons of bombs. In air-to-air combat, it has shot down 69 aircraft so far, without losing anything to enemy warplanes. It was originally designed as a cheaper alternative to the heavier F-15 but has since been provided with numerous upgrades and additional equipment. It was originally designed to be a 8.5–13-ton aircraft (depending on the various proposals). The first production version was 8.1 tons empty, the latest is 10 tons. Not a great increase in weight, but improvements in technology make the current version a much more capable aircraft.

F-18A. Replaces the A-7 aboard U.S. carriers (as the "F/A-18," with the "A" indicating ground attack capability). It functions as both an interceptor and bomber, carrying seven tons of bombs. It is basically a two-engine version of the F-16, which is why the Navy took the F-18 and the Air Force the cheaper F-16. The Navy prefers two-engine aircraft for carrier operations; they're safer when operating over water. The one major shortcoming of the F-18 is relatively short range. The Navy has few aerial tankers, forcing the F-18 to use drop tanks (replacing bombs) when more range is needed.

F-18D. A considerable redesign of the original F-18. The D model is larger than the A model, allowing it to carry 40 percent more internal fuel, as well as providing sufficient space for additional electronics. Most nations would give the F-18E a separate designation (like F-23 or something), but the Navy ran a bit of a scam to get the F-18D built, steadfastly maintaining that the D model was simply an upgrade of the A model. It worked, even though the "upgrade" cost billions more than similar programs for other aircraft. By the time Congress caught on, it was too late. Its bomb load is only four tons, but its range is longer. For all practical purposes, the F-18E can carry the same tonnage of bombs as far as the F-18A. The F-18D also has some stealth characteristics, and better maneuverability and electronics than the earlier version.

F-22. The U.S. ATF (Advanced Tactical Fighter) is to be the premier fighter for the early twenty-first century. Because of its stealth features, weapons have to be carried internally. This limits its bomb load to two half-ton bombs. But the

F-22 is equipped to deliver precision munitions, so the two (or more smaller) bombs are likely to hit what they are aimed at. One reason for the development of smaller (250- and 500-pound) guided bombs is to give stealthy aircraft like the F-22 better bombing capability. At over $60 million each, the United States probably won't be able to afford more than a few hundred (less than half what the Air Force is asking for). Russia and a consortium of Western European nations are each working on their own version, but because of the cost, neither project is likely to threaten the technical superiority of the F-22. While not invincible, the F-22 is capable enough to dominate any air battle it enters.

F-35 (the JSF, or Joint Strike Fighter). An attack aircraft (light bomber) still in development. This is the Air Force version, which can carry six tons of bombs. It has some stealth ability, and a variant (for the U.S. Marines and the British navy) of this version will be able to take off vertically (like the Harrier). The F-35 will have the most modern fire control and all-weather electronics. The F-35 will also be a very expensive light bomber, costing some $50 million each.

F-35N (Navy JSF). Heavier and sturdier (to withstand carrier landings) than the U.S. Air Force version, it still shares some 80 percent of the components of the Air Force JSF and has much the same characteristics. It carries eight tons of bombs.

F-4. The predecessor of the F-15. The F-4 is an early 1960s design that has been upgraded considerably. It is one of the most widely used warplanes of the late twentieth century (over 5,000 built). It is still a capable aircraft, with many in use. Some will probably be in use at the end of the decade. A classic design that proved very capable in combat, the F-4 was very capable as a ground-attack aircraft, carrying seven tons of bombs.

F-5. Designed and built by the United States as an inexpensive interceptor for nations with tight budgets and insufficient technical manpower to support more complex aircraft. It is roughly equal to the MiG-21. For this reason, many less affluent nations facing neighbors equipped with MiG-21s feel much better when they have a few dozen F-5s in their air force. It is also useful for ground attack, carrying three tons of bombs. It is being phased out, and many that are still in use are poorly maintained or otherwise not really ready for combat.

H-5. A Chinese-built Russian Il-28. Although the Il-28 design is 50 years old, China has continued to rely on their H-5s as one of their principal bombers.

H-6. A Chinese-built Russian Tu-16. After nearly 40 years, this bomber still serves, mainly as China's heavy bomber. Many are gradually being converted to electronic-warfare duties. It can carry nine tons of bombs.

J-6. A Chinese-built copy of the MiG-19. This is an inexpensive alternative for less wealthy nations, including China. It carries only a half ton of bombs.

J-7. A Chinese-built copy of the MiG-21. Many are being equipped with Western electronics and engines. This makes it a considerably improved MiG-21. It can carry 1.5 tons of bombs.

J-8. A Chinese two-engine variant of the MiG-21. This was China's first attempt at building its own aircraft. But it was not a very original or successful effort. It can carry about three tons of bombs.

J-9. A development project based on MiG-29 technology. The Chinese aircraft industry is pushing this one, but the air force is resisting. Officially, the project is still underway, but nothing has flown yet. The tentative plan is to have it enter service by 2005.

J-10. Basically the Israeli Lavi (a F-16 clone Israel was forced to abandon in the 1980s because of money problems). China appears to have obtained the technology from Israel, and from an F-16 obtained from Pakistan. China is obtaining the high-performance jet engine from Russia. The electronics may be obtained from Israel (secretly, as the U.S. will raise a stink if the Israelis try to do it openly), or from Russia. America has the best stuff, but this technology will have to be stolen.

J-11. The Chinese designation for the Russian Su-27. China is also assembling Su-27s from Russian parts. Some modifications already apparent are a greater emphasis on the Su-27's bombing capability.

J-12. A new Chinese design, not expected to enter service until 2015. The J-12 is an attempt to design and build an F-22 class fighter. The Chinese will have to acquire a lot of new technology (legally from Russia, illegally from the U.S., and semi-legally from Israel) to pull this off. If they do it, this will be the first home-grown Chinese warplane.

Jaguar. A British-French joint effort. This is basically a ground-attack bomber. It carries 4.7 tons of bombs. It was originally designed as a trainer but kind of just grew.

Ka-50. The latest Russian attack helicopter. It is unique in that it has a crew of one. Western helicopter designers are dubious that the Russians can achieve enough onboard automation to allow one pilot to do it all. Apparently they were right, as there is now a two-seat version. It is not likely to be produced in large numbers unless foreign customers can be found. Russian armed forces have bought only about a dozen. It can carry three tons of rockets and missiles.

Kfir. An upgraded version of the original Mirage V. It carries six tons of bombs and was designed and manufactured by Israel.

Mi-24. A Russian helicopter gunship. Originally designed primarily as an armed transport, it was soon modified to emphasize the gunship role. It can carry 2.4 tons, which can include up to eight troops.

MiG-21. A 1950s design, the most widely produced post–World War II fighter. Many nations keep it in service because it is cheap and easy to maintain, and because a wide range of avionics and weapons upgrades are available. It is not really designed for ground attack but can carry 1.5 tons of bombs.

MiG-23. The Russian equivalent of the F-4, equipped for air-to-air combat. It can carry three tons of bombs.

MiG-25. Originally designed as a high-altitude interceptor, this ended up as a reconnaissance aircraft with secondary air-defense duties. Built around two huge engines so that it could fly very fast, it's very expensive to operate, and few are in service anymore. It has no ground-attack capability; it only carries air-to-air missiles.

MiG-27. The Russian equivalent of the F-4, equipped for ground attack. It can carry four tons of bombs.

MiG-29. The Russian equivalent of the F-16. Many variants have been produced to satisfy export customer needs. It can carry three tons of bombs. When the Cold War ended, the Russian air force realized it could not afford to buy many new aircraft. It had to choose between supporting the MiG-29 or the Su-27. The MiG lost and must depend on export orders to stay alive.

MiG-31. An upgraded version of MiG-25, with much better radar, other electronics, and engines. It is primarily for air defense and is still very expensive to operate. It has no ground attack capability; it only carries air-to-air missiles.

MiG-33. It looks like the MiG-29 but is built of different materials, uses a different engine, and has a much improved set of avionics. It can carry 4.5 tons of bombs. It is much more effective in ground attack than MiG-29. This project was an attempt to get something into the air to counter the U.S. F-22. Unfortunately, no customers can be found yet. Much of the MiG-33 technology was sold to China, which is developing the J-9 (or FC-1) for itself and Pakistan.

Mirage 2000. Roughly equivalent to the F-16. It carries 6.3 tons of bombs. A few two-seat versions were built to carry a nuclear stand-off missile. In the

1990s, both the single- and two-seat versions received better electronics. Like most French aircraft, few were built; in this case, not quite 600 of all Mirage 2000 types.

Mirage F1. This replaced the Mirage III interceptor. It is basically a fighter-bomber in the F-4 class. It did not use the delta wings of most French aircraft, giving it better control close to the ground (and making it a better ground-attack aircraft). It can carry four tons of bombs.

Mirage III. The original French lightweight interceptor. Basically a superior Western version of the MiG-21 type, it was a very capable aircraft in its time. Mirage V and Mirage 50 are ground-attack versions. It can carry four tons of bombs.

Mirage V. A ground-attack version of the Mirage III. It carries four tons of bombs.

OH-58. The current U.S. scout helicopter. It can carry about a ton of rockets and missiles but is mainly used to find targets for gunships and to illuminate targets with a laser so the larger gunships don't have to get so close to launch antitank missiles.

Q-5. A clever Chinese modification of the Russian MiG-19. The front of the aircraft was redesigned to allow for a radar dome. It can only carry two tons of bombs.

Rafale. The latest French lightweight interceptor. It can carry six tons of bombs.

Su-17. Basically a swing-wing version of the older Su-7 ground-attack aircraft. It is exported in less capable versions designated Su-20 and Su-22. It can carry 3.1 tons of bombs. It is being phased out.

Su-24. The Russian version of F-111 and Tornado. It carries 8 tons of bombs and has a good fire control and electronics.

Su-25. The Russian version of the A-10. It carries 4.4 tons of bombs. Kinks were worked out during the 1980s Afghan war.

Su-27. The Russian version of the F-15. It is used primarily for air defense. It is also a navalized version of Russia's only heavy aircraft carrier. It has ground attack capability and can carry four tons of bombs.

Su-30. The Russian version of the F-15E bomber. It can carry eight tons of bombs and has two crew (one a weapons officer). All will be upgraded with the vector-thrust engine, making the aircraft much more maneuverable.

Su-37. Basically a single-seat version of the Su-30, optimized for air-to-air combat. No customers in sight, but the "Terminator" is available. It can carry eight tons of bombs.

Tornado. A multipurpose aircraft, most versions are optimized for medium-range bombing, although the British developed an interceptor variant. It is a British-German-Italian joint effort. It can carry 8.5 tons of bombs.

Tu-160 (Blackjack). The Russian version of the U.S. B-1. This aircraft has been under development for over 10 years, indicating that the Russians are having a difficult time getting it to perform as they would like. Considering the problems with the B-1, this is understandable. It went into service in 1990, but only 36 were built. It can carry 16 tons of bombs.

Tu-22. An older Russian medium bomber, a category that no longer exists in the West. Designed to carry cruise missiles, it can carry 12 tons of bombs and missiles.

Tu-22M. The replacement for the Tu-22 (although the Tu-22M is a completely new design). It is the backbone of Russia's long-range bomber force and can carry 24 tons of bombs.

Tu-95. A Russian heavy bomber that entered service about the same time as the U.S. B-52. It serves as a recon aircraft as well as a cruise-missile carrier. It can carry 11 tons of bombs and other weapons (like depth charges in the Tu-142 anti-submarine version).

Aircraft Weapons

Air-to-air missiles are of two basic types: infrared homing (IR) and radar homing (RH). The most widely used are the U.S.-made Sidewinder (IR) and AMRAAM (RH). Other Western and Russian missiles are derived from these two designs. The Phoenix is ahead of its time in that it has its own radar which, when the missile is 16 kilometers from the target, seeks it out on its own. The new generation of RH missiles, like the AMRAAM, use the same technique. The new missiles, however, are more expensive. Each Phoenix costs $3 million, and the Sparrow replacement had to be a lot cheaper than that. The Sparrow costs less than $250,000, and the Sidewinder is less than $100,000. The AMRAAM ended up costing about $500,000 each, which was in the ball-

Weapon	Made by	Target detection	Aspect	Range (km)	Weight (lbs)	Speed (mps)	Guid-ance	Rank
Air-to-Air Missiles								
Phoenix AIM-54	U.S.	Active	All	200	1,024	1,600	9	9
AMRAAM AIM-120	U.S.	Active	All	100	335	1,200	8	9
Sky Flash	UK	Active	All	45	425	1,000	7	8
R-77 (AA-12)	RU	Active	All	100	386	1,400	7	7
Sparrow AIM-7P	U.S.	Active	All	40	514	1,200	6	6
Python 4	IS	Passive	All	15	265	1,100	7	8
Sidewinder AIM-9X	U.S.	Passive	All	18	188	820	8	7
Sidewinder AIM-9M	U.S.	Passive	All	14	190	820	7	8
Magic R550	FR	Passive	All	13	196	1,000	7	7
Sidewinder AIM-9J	U.S.	Passive	Rear	10	185	820	4	6
ASRAAM	UK	Passive	All	15	221	1,000	8	7
R-33 (AA-9)	RU	Active	All	100	800	1,100	5	5
R-72 (AA-11)	RU	Passive	All	20	232	1,000	7	6
R-27TE (AA-10)	RU	Active	All	120	755	1,000	6	6
R-13M (AA-2)	RU	Passive	Rear	7	155	700	1	2
Air-to-Surface Missiles								
AGM-84H SLAM	U.S.	Active	All	270	1,488	280	9	9
Kormoran 2	GE	Both	All	37	1,320	300	7	9
HARM AGM-88C	U.S.	Passive	All	50	807	1,200	8	9
Harpoon AGM-84D	U.S.	Active	All	130	1,498	280	7	9
Exocet	FR	Active	All	60	1,442	300	7	9
Kh-59 (AS-13)	RU	Passive	All	40	1,672	285	6	6
ALCM AGM-86	U.S.	Active	All	2,500	3,150	240	7	8
Kh-41	RU	Active	All	250	9,900	750	6	6
Kh-31P (AS-12)	RU	Passive	All	100	1,600	330	5	7
Kh-59m (AS-18)	RU	Passive	All	115	2,046	285	7	6
Kh-58 HARM	RU	Active	All	120	1,408	1,100	7	7
Kh-25MP (AS-9)	RU	Passive	All	40	704	260	6	5
Kh-55 (AS-15)	RU	Active	All	3000	3,500	240	6	6
Maverick AGM-65G	U.S.	Passive	All	27	630	670	7	7
Kh-15 (AS-16)	RU	Active	All	150	2,640	1,500	6	6
Paveway	U.S.	Passive	All	15	2,100	200	7	8
JDAM	U.S.	Passive	All	30	2,100	200	9	9
SRAM AGM-69A	U.S.	Active	All	100	2,240	1,000	8	8
9M127 Vikhr	RU	Passive	All	10	132	600	7	6
Walleye AGM-62A	U.S.	Passive	All	4	2,400	200	9	8
Kh-29TE (AS-14)	RU	Passive	All	30	1,514	200	5	5
Kh-35 (AS-17)	RU	Active	All	130	1,056	300	5	4
Cannon								
GAU-8 30mm	U.S.	Both	Chase	1	57	1,020	3	9
M-61A1 20mm	U.S.	Both	Chase	1	28	1,036	3	8
ADEN 30mm	UK	Both	Chase	1	10	790	2	7
Gsh-23 23mm	RU	Both	Chase	1	27	950	1	6
NR-30 30mm	RU	Both	Chase	1	14	780	1	6

park. Meanwhile, the cheapest missile has proven to be the most lethal. The Sidewinder has been in service for over 40 years. It has knocked down more warplanes (at least 270) than any other air-to-air missile. Its first kills were by

Taiwanese pilots fighting Chinese MiGs in 1958 (four confirmed kills). Next came the Vietnam War (1965–73) with 82 kills. Then there was the Six Day War in 1967, with at least 20 kills. The Indo-Pakistan war of 1971 resulted in three kills. The October War (Middle East) of 1973 resulted in at least 75 Sidewinder kills. In 1981, the U.S. Navy took down two Libyan jets with Sidewinders. In 1982, Britain downed 18 Argentine warplanes with Sidewinders. Later in that year, there was a short war between Syria and Israel that saw 51 Syrian warplanes downed by Sidewinders. In 1991, Iraq lost 12 warplanes to Sidewinders, and over Bosnia in 1994, Yugoslavia lost three aircraft. The Sidewinder has constantly been upgraded over the years. The current model (AIM-9X) can turn and chase a passing aircraft. During recent tests, a pilot fired an AIM-9X against a passing drone. The pilot was surprised to see the missile pass less than 100 feet in front of him as it chased down the drone. It's this kind of capability that is causing the U.S. Air Force to get away from short-range missiles like Sidewinder. Longer-range missiles are now preferred, and they have had a good record in the last few years. But it will be a long time, if ever, that one missile matches the record of the Sidewinder.

Air-to-surface missiles come in four types:

- *Homing missiles* are launched in the general direction of the target. Thereafter the missiles' own sensors take over, enabling the launching aircraft to get to safety. These missiles are expensive, most costing around $1 million each. Most air-to-surface missiles are of this type.
- *Antiradar missiles (ARM)* are specialized to home in on and hit radars. This is an electronic-warfare weapon with an onboard computer and considerable agility. As the radars and their operators become more clever at avoiding these weapons, the ARMs themselves gain more features and capabilities. It's just like everything else in the ECM area. HARM, Shrike (now obsolete), and AS-9 are ARMs.
- *Guided missiles* are controlled by an operator in the aircraft via a TV camera in the missile, or simply by eyeballing missile and target. More recent versions require only that you get the target on the TV screen; the missile then remembers that image and homes in on it. As microcomputers become cheaper and more popular, this approach becomes more cost-effective and popular. This type of missile normally hits within three meters of the target. This system can also be used on guided bombs.
- *Guided bombs* are like the guided missiles, except they have no power. A bomb is fitted with wings and fins and a power supply to control these. This was the original air-to-ground guided-weapon concept first used in 1943. It was used extensively during the Gulf War because there were more aircraft equipped to handle them. The U.S. GBU series and the Walleye are examples of these systems. In the 1990s, GPS guidance was

added, as well as cheaper and more effective inertial guidance systems. This has revolutionized the use of bombs. GPS allows you to enter the coordinates of the target electronically. All the bomber has to do is get within range of the target and release the bomb. The latest kit for bombs, JDAM, enables a bomb to glide up to 30 kilometers to a target. This puts the aircraft out of range of many antiaircraft weapons and is almost as accurate as the earlier laser-guided Paveway series. The laser-guided bombs could hit within eight meters of the target (which had to be continuously illuminated by a laser). GPS gets to within 13 meters. If the GPS fails or is jammed, an inertial guidance system puts the bomb within 30 meters of the target.

Cannon shown are representative of the more common types. The GAU-8 is the only aircraft cannon designed solely for destroying armored vehicles. It could be devastating against aircraft except for the fact that it weighs nearly two tons, 10 times as heavy as any other aircraft cannon. Next to the name of each cannon is its caliber in millimeters.

Made by is the nation that designed the weapon, and often the sole source of that weapon. GE-Germany, RU-Russia, IS-Isreal, and FR-France.

Target detection indicates whether the using aircraft must emit an electronic signal in order to guide the weapon. *Active* means that a radar signal is sent and can be detected and possibly defeated by countermeasures. *Passive* means that no signals are transmitted; the missile sensors just listen or look and are more difficult to defeat with countermeasures. *Both* means that active and passive means are used.

Aspect shows the direction from which the aircraft may make an attack with that weapon. *All* means that an enemy aircraft, or ground target, may be attacked from any direction. *Rear* means that the enemy aircraft may be attacked only from the rear. *Chase* indicates that although the weapon can be used to attack from all directions, it is far more effective when used from the rear during a chase of the target aircraft. This is the case with cannon.

Range (in kilometers) is the maximum effective range. This will be more or less—for exceptionally large or small targets. Longer range is largely a function of the size and efficiency of the propulsion system and the range of the radar. Cannon range is longer when these same cannon are used in ground-based vehicles because of the great loss of accuracy from a rapidly moving platform.

Weight (in pounds) of the missile. Missiles possess four components:

- Airframe (shell).
- Propulsion system.
- Guidance system.
- Warhead.

The warhead generally comprises 15 percent of missile weight. Propulsion system weight is a function of range, while airframe weight is a function of missile size. The largest variable is the guidance system, including fins and other control surfaces as well as the flight computer, radio gear, and sensors. Western missiles' more efficient technology allows for lighter and more capable guidance systems. The weight given for cannon is the weight of shell the cannon fires per second.

Speed (in meters per second). Higher speed is always desirable. It can be obtained only when the guidance system can handle it. Air-to-air missiles have solid-fuel motors that burn out quickly (in 2 to over 10 seconds), leaving only momentum to carry them to the end of their mission. The high initial speed thus accounts for the minimum range of missiles, as the higher speeds are more difficult to control. It also limits the range of highly maneuverable missiles intended for use at close range. Too high a speed and the minimum range will be too long. Ideally, minimum range should be no more than a few hundred meters. Using cannon, aircraft have been brought down at under 100 meters. This is dangerous with missiles, as the destruction is generally more catastrophic and the debris has been known to take the attacker down with it. The speed given is the highest attained at motor burnout.

Guidance is an evaluation—from 1 (poor) to 9 (excellent)—of the missile's guidance-system quality. The evaluation includes the accuracy and dependability of the system as well as its resistance to countermeasures. Even passive systems, specifically infrared ones, have a number of weaknesses. Because infrared missiles home in on heat, they can be confused by such natural phenomena as the sun or the hot surface of the desert. Also, clouds can mask the heat source, not to mention flares. Radar-guided systems are very sensitive to jamming, especially with chaff. This is often circumvented by having the missiles hone in on the jamming source.

Rank indicates comparative effectiveness within the classes, taking all factors discussed into account.

Notes on Iron Bombs and Unguided Missiles

Air-to-ground operations have traditionally used a wide range of gravity bombs and unguided missiles. These have not been eclipsed by guided air-to-ground munitions. During the 1991 Gulf War, only 7 percent of the bomb tonnage consisted of "smart" bombs and missiles. As the list below demonstrates, iron bombs have become a lot smarter and deadlier. Iron bombs are the traditional high-explosive filled containers dropped by aircraft for the last 85 years. Largely unchanged in the last 60 years, they come in numerous sizes, weighing from a few pounds to over a ton.

CBU (Cluster Bomb Units) saw widespread and effective use during the Vietnam War. First deployed in the 1960s, they are containers of smaller bombs. When the container is dropped, it breaks open and distributes the smaller bombs over a wider area. A typical 600-pound CBU contains 150 smaller (three-pound) bombs that would fall over an area 50 meters wide and 200 meters long. Often the pilot can select a smaller or larger pattern. Any unprotected people with this 50-by-200-meter area have a better than 50 percent chance of being injured. The CBUs can carry a variety of loads: antitank, incendiary, and chemical. The bomblet weight varies from a few ounces to over 20 pounds. In addition, the bomblets can be equipped with timers or sensors that turn them into mines and booby traps. Moreover, as many as 10 percent of the bomblets would not go off and would remain to explode later when disturbed by civilians. That was about 10 years ago. Today's CBU uses the same smart-bomb technology to hit targets more accurately. The dud rate was reduced to less than 1 percent.

When these high dud-rate problems were first discovered in the early 1980s, several solutions were at hand. More complex, expensive, and reliable fuzes were a possibility. But research showed that to halve the dud rate would double the cost of a submunition. To bring the dud rate down to 1 percent would quadruple the cost. At the time, submunitions cost about $6 (in current dollars). In the United States, the largest manufacturer of submunitions, no change was made through the 1980s. To use the more expensive fuzes would mean buying fewer munitions. But the Gulf War of 1991 showed that all those dud submunitions tended to cause a lot of casualties among your own troops. The reason was simple: as you fired a lot of submunitions at the enemy, and then overran the enemy positions, your troops would suddenly find themselves amid all those duds, and friendly casualties were the result.

Israel and Germany, which both manufactured their own submunitions, went for the safer fuze. Better designs brought the cost down, and they ended up paying $10–$15 for each submunition. But they achieved dud rates of less than 1 percent. The safer fuze was basically a self-destruct device. If the submunition did not explode as it was supposed to, another fuze detonated it within 14–18 seconds.

Even with the better fuzes, submunitions are still more dangerous after the battle than older shells. Fire 10,000 artillery shells (a typical quantity for a battle in an area covering a square mile or so), and you end up with a minimum of 200 dud shells, or as many as 3,000 if you are using old, poorly made stuff. But if you use the most modern submunition-equipped shells, you are putting 200,000 or more submunitions into the area, and a minimum of 2,000 duds. Fight this battle in the winter, with the older fuzes, and you end up with over 50,000 duds. And the bomblets are on the surface, not buried like most artillery shell duds. It's no wonder that most submunition fuzes are now of the more expensive, and more reliable, variety.

FAE (fuel air explosive) is a variation on the napalm bomb (thickened gasoline). An FAE hits the ground, breaks open, and creates a mist of flammable liquid. A small delayed-action explosive then goes off, causing the cloud to ignite. The pressure of the blast is sufficient to wreck vehicles, ships, and equipment, as well as being fatal to personnel. The only other device to produce similar results are nuclear weapons. Pound for pound, FAE weapons are three to five times as destructive as high explosive. For example, an 1,100-pound FAE would destroy most equipment and injure all personnel within 250 meters of the impact point. These devices are also used in CBUs. Because of their area effect, FAE bombs have been successful in clearing mines. In Vietnam, large FAEs were used to clear helicopter landing sites in the jungle. FAEs are effective against entrenched troops, as the blast is severe and will enter any position that is not airtight. Unfortunately, FAEs are not as reliable as other types of bombs. The "explosive mist" must form just so to be effective. Weather conditions can seriously degrade the effect of FAE. Russia has developed a new formula for FAE weapons that the United States may end up licensing for a new generation of FAE bombs.

The U.S. Air Force also has a rather unique weapon: the 15,000-pound "daisy cutter" bomb. This weapon, developed during the Vietnam War to clear jungle areas for helicopter landing areas, uses a unique method to create a huge explosion. The bomb contains ammonium nitrate and aluminum, which form a mist that is detonated. It creates an effect similar to a nuclear explosion. A powerful shock wave, and removal of most oxygen from the area, kill nearly everyone within about 500 meters. There is often a mushroom-shaped cloud rising from the detonation, which makes people nearby think that nuclear weapons are being used. Another unique aspect of the daisy cutter is that it is shoved out the back of a C-130 transport. Unfortunately, the C-130 must come in at 6,000 feet to get the bomb on target, and this makes it vulnerable to ground fire.

Incendiaries are the familiar napalm bombs (no longer used) plus an assortment of other flammable items. These are being supplanted by more effective and reliable FAEs.

Special-purpose bombs fulfill a variety of specialized needs. Concrete-piercing bombs are used to crater airfields and destroy heavy structures. Also in this category are chemical and nuclear weapons.

Unguided missiles, or free-flight rockets (FFRs), are still used. They have a variety of loads: fragmentation, illumination, smoke, armor piercing. Their range is several kilometers. They are usually carried in pods containing 7–32 rockets each.

UAVs (Drones and RPVs)

The former are self-guided aircraft; the latter are controlled by human pilots in the air or on the ground. *Duration* is in hours; *Load* is in pounds.

The Israelis were the first nation to do a lot of work on UAVs and produce systems that were militarily effective. Finally, after much agitation by Congress and people in the U.S. military, Israeli technology and experience were applied to American UAV development, and the United States ended up with some decent UAVs. But American manufacturers continue to have problems, with projects spending a lot of time in development and having a lot of teething woes.

Going into the twenty-first century, the American UAV inventory looked like this:

GNAT-750 Lofty View. It has been in use since 1989, but is being phased out. The GNAT can stay in the air for up to 48 hours and has a range of 800 kilometers. This aircraft is 16.4 feet long with a 35.3-foot wingspan.

Prowler II is a scaled-down version of the GNAT that is still in development and has had some problems.

System	Made by	Duration	Load	Range (km)	Weight (lbs)	Speed (mps)	Guidance	Rank
Pioneer	Israel	9	100	185	430	51	4	4
Searcher II	Israel	16	150	144	950	55	6	6
Scout	Israel	7	84	100	350	50	3	3
Hunter	Israel	11	150	260	1,600	60	5	5
Prowler II	U.S.	24	50	249	250	50	6	5
Predator	U.S.	24	450	720	2,250	60	6	5
Shadow 600	U.S.	14	100	200	600	60	6	4
Global Hawk	U.S.	36	1,950	3,000	25,600	200	7	7
GNAT	U.S.	40	140	450	1,125	60	5	5

Hunter UAV was an unsuccessful predecessor of the Predator. The Hunter system had a lot of operational and software problems. The military stopped buying them in 1996, although a few are still in inventory. It is 23 feet long with a 29-foot wingspan.

RQ-1 Predator. Built to replace the GNAT, it can operate in any weather and stay up for 40 hours. It can bounce its data off satellites and provide near-real-time video. The RW-1 carries two color video cameras and is 26.7 feet long with a wingspan of 48.2 feet.

RQ-2 Pioneer. It was built for use off warships and was first used in 1986. It saw service in the Persian Gulf war, where it flew over 300 missions. It is used for spotting targets, and reconnaissance for ground troops. Eventually, it will be replaced by the Navy's Tactical UAV system. RQ-2 is 9.6 feet long with a wingspan of 17.1 feet.

Shadow 600. This is an upgraded RQ-2 that can fly longer (up to 14 hours) and can carry 17 different sensors. It was widely used during the Gulf War, flying over 700 hours. It is 15.4 feet long with a 22.4-foot wingspan.

RQ-4A Global Hawk. It is still in development, but several are available for service. RQ-4A is a jet-powered, high-altitude, very-long-range aircraft. Global Hawk carries a variety of different recon equipment, including cameras, infrared sensors, and radar. It can stay in the air for as long as four days at an altitude of 66,000 feet. It also can carry jamming equipment and electronic countermeasures to defeat SAM attacks. Global Hawk can be programmed to fly an entire mission, from takeoff to landing, without any human assistance. It has crossed the Pacific to Australia, performed a recon mission, and landed all by itself. It is a large aircraft, 44.4 feet long with a wingspan of 116.2 feet.

There were several other shorter-range UAVs in development, as well.

8

Air Defense

During the last 20 years, not a lot of aircraft have been shot down by antiaircraft weapons. This is because most of the battles involve American-made warplanes equipped with weapons and tactics that have proven very good at defeating, and destroying, antiaircraft systems (usually made by Russia).

It's been 50 years since U.S. troops were attacked from the air (a few times early in the Korean war), so the U.S. Army is now convinced it doesn't really need short-range air defense. Shoulder-fired Stinger antiaircraft missiles and Patriot antiaircraft missiles remain in use. But the idea of having air-defense weapons with capabilities between Stinger and Patriot is gone. The Patriot, in use for over a decade, has never had an opportunity to shoot down an aircraft. The U.S. Air Force has been quick to grab, and keep, air superiority over the last 60 years, and the Army now believes this will not change for the foreseeable future.

That's quite a change from what was predicted early on. When it was first suggested that aircraft be used for military purposes, a common reaction was that these fragile machines would soon be blown out of the sky. They could easily be seen, and shot at, by troops on the ground. The first 25 years of air combat demonstrated that they were not that easy to bring down. Even so, in 1939, the Germans thought that only 50 of their 88mm antiaircraft gun shells would be needed to shoot down one enemy aircraft. Allied aircraft turned out to be both elusive and resistant to the vaunted "88." Over 12,000 shells were needed for each aircraft destroyed.

When antiaircraft missiles appeared in the 1950s, it was thought that aircraft were again doomed. No such luck: experience over Vietnam and the Middle East in the 1960s and 1970s saw an average of 50 missiles required to kill one airplane. This was not as large an improvement as it might appear to be, as the 50 missiles cost more than the 12,000 cannon shells needed during

World War II. Moreover, the aircraft developed an unpleasant habit of attacking the air-defense units. This only made the task of antiaircraft units more difficult. Air defense has always proved an impediment, at times even a deterrent, to air attacks. But air defense has not been able to stop aerial assaults in the long run. Although aircraft have been touted as the ultimate weapon by many, they too have failed to be overpowering, not because of air defense, but because of limitations in aircraft weapons and the performance limitations of the aircraft themselves. Aircraft are not superweapons, and neither are the antiaircraft systems that attack them.

In the light of these limitations, air-defense units learned to strive for attrition and deterrence. Air-defense attempts to force aircraft either to abort their missions or take heavy losses. Surface-to-air missiles often force aircraft to fly low enough so they can be shot at by the smaller caliber, but much more numerous, machine guns and automatic cannons. At least then the gunners can see what they are shooting at. Indeed, it is at these lower altitudes where most aircraft losses to air-defense forces take place. Over North Vietnam, some 80 percent of aircraft losses were due to low-altitude machine guns, while in the 1973 Arab-Israeli war, between 30–50 percent of aircraft losses were due to machine guns (Israelis claimed the higher number). On the other hand, over 10,000 small-caliber cannon shells were required for each plane downed. Finally, as in other forms of warfare, the results depended on the quantity and quality of the air defenses and the aircraft they fought.

The most dangerous antiaircraft weapon against helicopters is not shoulder-fired SAMs, but RPG rockets and machine-gun fire. Portable antiaircraft missiles are often not effective against low-flying aircraft and helicopters because these aircraft have defensive systems that easily defeat missiles by using flares and missile detectors. There is no defense against the RPG rockets. Of course, the RPGs only work if many (over a dozen, if possible) are fired at a chopper from close range (a hundred or so meters away). These conditions are rare, but they do occur, and helicopters have been brought down by RPGs. Rifle fire, particularly from larger-caliber machine guns (14.5mm and larger), have also brought down choppers, although more commonly the result is just a lot of damage. But all that damage often leads to a helicopter being forced down in enemy territory. Not a pleasant prospect.

Naturally, pilots have developed ways to avoid getting nailed by a barrage of RPG rockets:

- Do not fly low along streets, roads, canyons, or river lines for a long time.
- Don't always take off and land from the same direction. This is often done because of weather conditions or the lay of the land (fewer obstacles on one direction). Don't do it, for the bad guys can mass their RPGs along your usual flight path.

- If possible, drop a fuel-air bomb on a new LZ (landing zone) before landing the first time.
- Never fly the same pattern or formation while on patrol. Again, this makes it easier for an ambush to be set up.
- Never use predictable patterns of operations (by time, formation, or sequence of events).
- Send in pathfinders (ground scouts) on any LZ before sending in the full landing force.
- When two or more helicopters are flying together, always keep 500 meters between helicopters. This allows each chopper enough room to use its weapons against RPG gunners.

For fast-moving jet bombers, there is no easy cure for the gunfire encountered at low altitudes. So the practice thus far has been to destroy the enemy radars and high-altitude missiles, and then keep the bombers high (15,000 feet or higher). This has become practical if you use mostly smart bombs. This was demonstrated in the 1991 Gulf War and the 2001 war in Afghanistan.

Detect, Acquire, Track, Destroy

Whatever the antiaircraft weapon being used, be it powerful long-range missile or a machine gun, the same procedures are employed. Air defense has learned to go through a four-step drill in its attempts to bring down aircraft. First, an aircraft must be detected; then, you must acquire a precise idea of where it is. You track the target long enough for your weapons to find it and, hopefully, destroy it. Each of these steps provides ample opportunity for failure. Pilots also have a keen sense of self-preservation and diligently respond to whatever temporary advantage the air-defense crowd might acquire. The four steps are:

Detection. Aircraft, no matter how large, are small objects in the vastness of the sky. Early air-defense forces learned that the best method for detection was to examine carefully the situation from the enemy pilot's point of view. The always-scarce detection resources were then placed where the enemy planes were likely to come from. There are never enough radars or human observers to cover every possible direction. Pilots are aware of this problem—or opportunity, from their point of view. Electronic warfare and low flying are the favorite ploys for avoiding detection. Attacking aircraft have sensors that tell them when they are being "painted" by enemy radars. If their ECM (Electronic Countermeasures) is good enough, they may be able to "play Space Invaders on the enemy radar screen," as one U.S. pilot put it. ECM can make detection either impossible or dubious. If ECM does not do the trick, the old "on the deck" solution usually works. Flying a hundred meters or less from the ground evades most radars, but at the price of considerable pilot fatigue. A third solution to avoiding detection is the "stealth" aircraft, which is designed and equipped to defeat radar as much as possible. The solution to low fly-ers, and to a lesser extent stealth, has been airborne radars. During the 1960s, the United States developed the AWACS (Airborne Warning and Control System), a large radar-and-command center in a four-engine commercial jet. The Russians followed with their own version a decade later. AWACS aircraft are only as good as their computers. Everyone has problems getting enough AWACS to cover every-thing. The U.S. AWACS can only stay on station for six hours, unless it gets an inflight refueling. Twelve hours in the air is the usual maximum because of the need for ground maintenance on the aircraft and the complex radars and computers.

Acquire. Once an aircraft has been detected, it must be "acquired." That is, you must confirm that it is an enemy aircraft and determine exactly where it is and where it is going. You want to know when the aircraft will be within range of your weapons. The detection and acquisition radar always have a longer range than your weapons so that you can hit the target as far away as possible. This is important for two reasons. First, the air-defense system deploys behind the fighting front. The target aircraft are often attacking targets on the front line or are using long-range missiles. If the aircraft gets too close before being shot at, it may launch its weapons before it can be hit. Second, the aircraft will likely be traveling at high speed, between 200–700 meters a second. For a tactical air-defense system with a maximum weapon range of 20,000 meters, every second counts. All of this occurs in an atmosphere of uncertainty. A typical ground radar can spot aircraft up to 550-kilometers out and 30 kilometers high. However, at the 550-kilometer range, the probability of making a positive detection is only 50 percent. At 370 kilometers the probability is still only 90 percent. A daring pilot can take advantage of this uncertainty to fly most of his mission at high altitude before descending to the more dangerous and nerve-wracking flying at treetop level for the final approach to target.

Tracking. Successful target detection and acquisition can take less than a minute. Often only seconds are needed. If those two steps are successful, you now go through the white-knuckle phase of the operation. You have to maintain your "track" of the enemy aircraft long enough for your guns or missiles to do their job. Tracking generally commences outside the range of the weapons it serves. Missiles, with their longer range, are fired soon after tracking begins. Missiles without independent guidance systems (that is, most of them) depend on continually successful tracking. Guns, because of their short range, must track the longest before they get a shot off. While all this tracking and shooting is going on, the target is trying desperately, and often successfully, to "break the track." Violent maneuvers and/or ECM will often succeed. Other counter-measures include diving down to treetop level and dropping flares to draw off heat-seeking missiles and chaff (strips of foil) to befog the radar.

Destroy. Even if an air-defense weapon manages to succeed in detecting, acquiring, and tracking a target, a hit does not always result in destruction, or even significant damage. Modern aircraft are overbuilt and made to last. They have many duplicate and triplicate systems. The warheads of many missiles are under 12 pounds. Even a direct hit has to hit a vital component to do the job. Larger warheads explode when they get close, but even here the damage is often not any greater than a direct hit by a smaller warhead.

Air-Defense Weapons

Air-defense weapons range from small-caliber projectiles to nuclear explosives. The size and design of these various warheads combine in different ways to attack their targets.

Small warheads. It is possible to destroy an aircraft with a small warhead. An aircraft moving along some 100 meters from the ground at 200 meters a second is very susceptible to the slightest damage. When more massive missile damage occurs at the higher altitudes, the aircraft has more distance, and time, to sort things out. Smaller missiles, primarily the low-altitude portable ones, have only five-pound warheads. Half the Israeli A-4 aircraft hit by these warheads in 1973 returned and landed. These missiles are limited by their small size and lack of a proximity fuze, a radar device that allows the warhead to explode in a near-miss situation. The small missiles are heat seekers that, in most cases, can be fired only when behind the target. Their targets tend to fly in low, fast, and unexpectedly. This gives the missile operator about 10 seconds to get off a shot. Many aircraft have sensors that warn of approaching missiles. A sharp pilot will eject flares or zip behind a hill in frequently successful maneuvers to avoid the missile. Often, however, the low-flying pilot never sees the missile.

At these low altitudes, under 1,000 meters, guns are still the most effective antiaircraft weapon. Many missiles exist because they are portable, and weapons designers and manufacturers think they are neat. Guns have shells ranging from 20mm to 57mm in size. These shells require a direct hit to do any damage, and one hit is rarely fatal. But these shells are used in large quantities. The damage adds up, if not to a downed aircraft, then to an increased workload on the already overburdened aircraft maintenance crews. Shell weight varies considerably. A 20mm shell weighs only 3.5 ounces. The 57mm weighs in at 100 ounces, over 6 pounds. Commonly used are 20mm, 23mm (7 ounces), 35mm (20 ounces), 40mm (30 ounces), and 57mm. These weapons are often used in multiple-barrel turrets. The Swiss-developed Gepard (two 35mm guns) can deliver 18 35mm shells a second for its German users. The Russian ZSU-23 mounts four 23mm guns and can deliver 60 shells a second. These light antiaircraft guns are increasingly deployed primarily against helicopters. And helicopters are being armored and protected so that they can withstand 20mm and 23mm shells. Although calibers are being upgraded, the real damage is being done by larger weapons. The lighter guns can damage, but increasingly they cannot kill.

While portable SAMs like the Stinger can be defeated by flares, they can still be dangerous when they show up unexpectedly. During the Afghan war with the Russians in the 1980s, Afghans fired 340 U.S.-supplied Stinger missiles at Russian aircraft and helicopters, bringing 269 of the Russian aircraft down. The CIA also supplied the Afghans with a lot of less-portable 20mm antiaircraft guns. These did less damage, but between the guns and Stingers, the Russians began to avoid bringing their aircraft and choppers in low. While the CIA bought back most of these missiles in the 1990s, some are still in Afghanistan. Their special batteries are dead, and the missiles are useless. But it was found that when the batteries were replaced in the repurchased missiles, most of the Stingers still worked. During the 1991 Gulf War, Iraqis fired 2–3 portable SAMs a day once the ground war began and U.S. aircraft flew lower. A-10s were hit several times, but these aircraft were designed to take such hits and keep going. One A-10 was thought to be brought down by portable SAMs. Four Navy F-18s were also hit but managed to return to their carriers. In the last 30 years, some three dozen civilian transports were hit with Russian-made portable SAMs, bringing down 29 of these aircraft. Most of these incidents took place in war-torn areas, particularly Africa. All air forces, particularly the U.S. Air Force, have developed new methods of protecting their aircraft from portable SAMs. Usually this involves more and better flares to distract the missiles. Some aircraft have had their engines modified to better survive getting hit by these missiles.

Larger warheads. Larger missiles have warheads that are often quite elaborate and weigh hundreds of pounds. The design of these warheads strives for flexibility and the ability to destroy or inflict damage even for misses. Direct hits are difficult to obtain and quite rare. A near miss with the right kind of warhead can cripple or kill. Using shaped charges to direct a flight of high-velocity fragments, these warheads can be fatal to many aircraft 100 or more meters away from the explosion. Proximity fuzes calculate the most effective detonation point. Western warheads are the most elaborate and lethal. An unexpected form of antiaircraft missile has been found in antitank missiles. Because helicopters fly slowly and close to the ground, it has been found theoretically possible to down them with antitank missiles. There has been no use of this technique yet, but several armies have investigated the possibility. In combat, troops will take advantage of whatever edge is available to them. And in this case it comes full circle, as during World War II the Germans turned their principal antiaircraft weapon, the 88mm gun, into the most deadly antitank weapon of that war.

Larger caliber (75mm and up) antiaircraft guns. These also use proximity fuzes and specially designed fragmentation warheads. These shells are expensive and are used less often than simpler ones. The reason is that a large number of the elaborate shells are still needed to obtain a hit. A new generation of even "smarter" shells is proposed, to give large-caliber antiaircraft guns many of the same capabilities of surface-to-air missiles. However, missiles are more expensive still but are more flexible and easier to upgrade. Large-caliber guns are still used by Russia and its client states. The guns are used as they were during World War II (1939–45) and in Vietnam (1966–75). A barrage of shells is thrown up where the radar predicts the approaching aircraft will be. In clear weather, when the radars are blinded by ECM, they can still perform well. Navies still make extensive use of large (and small) antiaircraft guns. Part of this is due to the lack of obstacles at sea.

Guns can shoot at what they can see, and on the ocean you can see more. Special small-caliber guns have been developed against high-speed cruise missiles. Once turned on, these radar-guided weapons will automatically attack any object in the vicinity that resembles a cruise missile. As these missiles come in at up to 1,000 meters a second, there is no time for human intervention.

Very-small-caliber antiaircraft guns. Although not decisive weapons, machine guns and rifles can have an effect. During World War II, the Soviets developed the tactic of having ground troops firing into the air when under attack by aircraft. This not only damaged some aircraft, but also maintained the morale of the troops. Doing something, anything, to fight back is better than simply diving for cover. Most tanks, and many other vehicles, have a heavy-caliber machine gun (12.7mm–14.5mm) that is effective to an altitude of 1,000 meters. Enough of this small-caliber fire in the air will not discourage aircraft—they usually won't even see it—but damage will be done. In rare instances, aircraft have even been brought down. Normally, however, just more damage is created, and the damage adds up.

Tactical Deployment

Air-defense weapons are deployed according to their range and mobility. The short-range and mobile systems travel with the combat units. The longer-range and less-mobile equipment is set up as far back as 100 kilometers behind the fighting front to protect rear-area installations and give additional high-altitude protection to front-line units. Ideally, air-defense units should be stationed on high ground to allow the greatest coverage by radar or visually controlled missiles. This is often not practical, especially in a mobile battle, where everyone will be on the road when the aircraft attack. In a defensive situation, or when attacking a rear area, the aircraft are more cautious and come in with the primary intention of first destroying air-defense units. As the latter are usually unarmored and full of explosive and flammable materials, they are very vulnerable targets. ICMs (Improved Conventional Munitions) include cluster bombs that spread dozens (or hundreds) of smaller bombs (up to 200 incendiaries from one bomb) over a few hundred thousand square meters. Air-defense systems are fragile things and usually don't survive a cluster bomb.

The key to successful air defense is layers of defense at multiple depths and altitudes. The extreme example of this was the Russian technique employed at the end of the Cold War. The Russians expected to lose the war for control of the air, so they developed a multilayered air-defense system. This started with the ZSU-23 (2-kilometer range) cannon, portable missiles, and SA-9 (8-kilometer range) missiles right up with the combat troops. In addition, the troops have shoulder-fired surface-to-air missiles (SA-7/14, 4-kilometer range). A few kilometers behind the front are SA-8 (12 kilometers), SA-11 (25 kilometers), and SA-6 (30 kilometers) missiles. The SA-4 (75 kilometers) and SA-10 (50 kilometers) systems provide defense farther back, with only some of them extending their coverage beyond the leading units. Today, most nations have only three or four air-defense systems (portable SAMs, medium-range SAMs, long-range SAMs, and maybe some cannon). For Western nations, air superiority is seen as the primary air-defense technique. Less-wealthy nations put more of their air-defense strength on the ground.

The Ultimate Air Defense: Air Superiority

The only sure protection from enemy air attack is to destroy or suppress the enemy air force. In other words, the best air defense is air superiority. While this sounds nice in theory, several potential problems exist in practice. The successful destruction of enemy air forces in World War II has made Western armies slow to realize that they may not always have air superiority. During the last 50 years, America has made belated and desultory attempts to develop air defenses to deal with a possible loss of air superiority. These efforts were dealt a double blow when the Soviet Union (with the largest air force in the world) collapsed, followed shortly by the triumph of U.S. air power in the Gulf War. It is now, and for the foreseeable future, assumed that U.S. ground forces won't have to worry too much about defending themselves from enemy air attack. There is no air power on the planet to contest Western air forces attaining general air superiority in a future war. But if this air superiority is not obtained, or until it is, the burden of defense will be on the guns and missiles of the antiaircraft units. Even when air superiority is achieved, the enemy may be able to muster sufficient aircraft to obtain temporary air superiority in one area or another.

Air defenses have never been as omnipresent as they are today. In the past, air defenses had shorter ranges and lower altitudes. Today, SAM systems can cover areas over a hundred kilometers from the missiles, and over 10,000 meters high. Sufficient systems are available to cover an entire theater of operations containing up to a million square miles of real estate.

One of the more difficult aspects of air defense is keeping your missiles from shooting down your own aircraft. The key here is careful planning, and trying to maintain control of all the air-defense units. Unfortunately, warfare is a messy process, and confusion is the rule. Whichever side has the initiative will be able to maintain a semblance of order in their SAM and aircraft coordination. However, once things start to get busy, not everyone is going to get their orders in time. Friendly aircraft have been, and will continue to be, shot down by their own air-defense weapons. Unfortunately, the situation will no doubt be worse in the future because of the larger number of air-defense systems on the battlefield. In effect, two quite separate air-defense systems exist. One is based on aircraft and has its own radars and control systems. The other is based on missiles and guns and also has its own radars and overall command. No one has put two of these interrelated systems against each other on a large scale. The side most at risk is the one that has air superiority only some of the time. The many ground troops with machine guns and their own portable missiles are difficult to control. It's going to be an interesting mess.

Theory and Practice

One of the curious aspects of air defense is that in the past 55 years, most of the action has been between Western aircraft and Soviet-made air-defense systems. This has given the impression that air defense is not very efficient. During this period, at least 50 Soviet SAMs were fired for each aircraft hit. The lackadaisical performance of Russian air-defense systems was typical of the low effectiveness of Russian high-tech weapons. Western systems are customarily more effective. In the few instances when Western air-defense systems have been used against Russian aircraft, the SAMs performed better. Israel has used their U.S.-built Hawk antiaircraft missiles against Soviet-built Arab jets and required fewer than five missiles for each aircraft hit. Western portable antiaircraft missiles (Stingers) proved far more effective in Afghanistan than similar Soviet-built systems. The U.S. Stinger missile has a 90 percent hit rate during testing and over 50 percent on the battlefield. This is a typical pattern between test and combat conditions. The Russian SA-7/14 results have been less impressive. Historically, air-defense weapons have had to fire enormous quantities of munitions to hit an aircraft. During World War II, between 5,000 and 12,000 88mm or 105mm shells were fired to hit one aircraft. In theory, far fewer shells should be needed. In practice, the aircraft are never that easy to find, and the aircraft are eager to avoid destruction. Even the seeming success of the portable Stinger SAMs in Afghanistan was possible because the Russians have not had time to develop effective defensive measures. During the first year of heavy air combat in World War II, fewer than 2,000 artillery antiaircraft shells were needed to hit an aircraft. After a year of this, the U.S. and British bombers changed their tactics and raised the shell count three to six times. Effective air defenses often perform like mines, attacking friendly and enemy aircraft alike. Incorrect identification causes serious problems. During the 1973 Arab-Israeli war, the Arabs fired 2,100 missiles and destroyed 85 aircraft, 45 of which were Arab. This is not supposed to happen. All aircraft carry an electronic gizmo called IFF (Identification, Friend or Foe) that gives a coded electronic response when interrogated by radar. But codes can be broken, and responses can be ignored or misinterpreted. The Arab air-defense people and at least 45 Arab pilots know all about this problem. It plagues all air forces in all wars. Target acquisition is no trivial task.

Another important aspect of air defense is the tendency of aircraft to avoid heavily defended areas. Going after air-defense systems, otherwise known as SEAD (suppression of enemy air defenses) or "flak suppression," is an expensive task. Shutting down air defenses is only undertaken if the target being defended is important enough to warrant such an expensive application of air power. Increasingly, missiles shape up as a more efficient way to go after heavily defended targets. This has spurred development of air-defense systems that can hit missiles. The U.S. Patriot SAMs' ability to intercept Scud missiles was the first combat example of this technique. While crude, the Patriot showed that it could be done. That said, all the allied aircraft losses in combat during the Gulf War were from low-tech weapons like machine guns and small SAMs. As in the past, air defenses will spend most of their time waiting for targets that never appear.

The Future

Smaller and more powerful electronics make it possible to put powerful radars in missiles and even artillery shells, providing aircraft with more things to worry about. It is increasingly common for missiles and radars to have guidance computers that can be reprogrammed, allowing pilots to develop new defensive techniques. It is also possible for missile computers to learn on the spot and outthink their prey. High-tech antiaircraft weapons are even coming to the aid of ground troops, as the new generations of shoulder-fired missiles pack a lot more electronic intelligence. Pilots will have to choose increasingly between avoiding heavily defended areas, using massive resources to destroy anti-air systems, or accepting high losses to complete their missions. Naval air defense has additional problems. Over a dozen ships in a task force are spread over several hundred square miles. Each is capable of air defense. But if they coordinate their activities, their defense will be even stronger. The traditional solution has been passive coordination, assigning each ship a sector to defend. Currently being introduced is active coordination, where computers on each ship talk to other ships and instantly decide who will shoot at what. This rapid coordination is becoming mandatory in the face of possible massive cruise-missile attacks. The key is not so much the computers but the communications. If the right types of satellites are available, this coordination becomes even more effective. Electronic warfare prowess then becomes critical, no matter which side of this battle you are on. In one case—the use of lasers to intercept artillery shells and rockets—air defenses have become completely electronic. The laser system, developed by the United States and Israel, has a short range, but it's worked during all its tests through 2001. Once reliability problems are fixed, it will be deployed in Israel, where rocket and missile attacks against civilians are common. As laser technology improves, so will range and hitting power. Eventually, this weapon will be used against aircraft.

It is still questionable just how effective antiaircraft defenses are, at least those built using Russian equipment. The United States shut down the Iraqi air-defense system in 1991, and the Afghan one in 2001. Israel has regularly suppressed Russian-supplied air-defense systems used by its Arab neighbors. Even when the Russians themselves build an air-defense system, they get clobbered. An example of this occurred in Angola, during the late 1980s, when the Soviets constructed the most elaborate air-defense system found outside Europe. Over 70 radars and two dozen missile bases were supported by nearly 100 interceptors. Most of this was maintained by East German mercenaries. Yet South African aircraft regularly penetrated this system. Some things never change, and many potential buyers of Russian weapons took notice. The embarrassments that Russian-made air-defense forces have suffered over the years are having their effect. The collapse of Soviet military power, the 1991 Gulf War, and the air campaign over Kosovo in 1999 all had enormous impact on the future of the air-defense weapons. With the enormous Soviet military establishment now a fraction of its former size, there is no longer an easy justification for additional research on more capable air-defense weapons. Yet the Gulf War demonstrated what the low-tech (Iraqi) and high-tech (U.S.) air-defense weapons were capable of. The technological lead the West has in air defense will remain for some time, even without a lot of additional R&D. While military research may not get a lot more money, civilian research on computers and other electronic components will keep the military supplied with affordable upgrades to existing weapons. The only dark spot in all this is that, as high-tech air-defense weapons become cheaper and more dependent on purely civilian technology, these weapons will more easily spread to many different nations. Thus the next war involving Western air forces may find these aircraft facing more capable weapons that are, in many respects, first cousins to the electronic consumer goods that have always been so abundant.

Air-Defense Weapons

The following chart shows the characteristics of the world's air-defense weapons. Shown are the most widely used weapons, which are representative of the ones not included. As it is a relatively easy matter for an industrial nation to manufacture most air-defense weapons, a few nations do not have a monopoly on their manufacture, as is the case with aircraft, tanks, and similar weapons.

Type gives the designation of the weapon. For Russian weapons, the Russian and NATO designations are given. See below for notes on the systems. Weapons are organized by nation, in alphabetical order.

Effectiveness is a general evaluation of the relative capabilities of the weapon on a 1–100 scale. These are estimates, as many of these weapons have not been used in combat. Those that have been used against real targets have since undergone modification. All air-defense weapons constantly undergo upgrading. In addition, the primarily electronic countermeasures of potential targets have a considerable influence on their effectiveness and have been taken into account. The ratings also take into account systems reliability, quality of target acquisition system, and lethality of warhead.

Effective altitude, Maximum is the maximum altitude (in meters) at which the weapon can reasonably be expected to hit a target. This limit is imposed primarily by the weapon's ability to reach that height. Missiles operate best at high altitudes. Guns tend to do better closer to the ground.

Type	Effectiveness	Effective altitude (meters)		Range (km)	AWC	Caliber	Mobility
		Min	Max				
Britain							
Rapier	28	10	3,000	7	4	133	SP
France							
AMX-30SA	27	0	2,000	4	4	30	SP
Crotale	29	50	3,600	9	5	156	SP
Germany							
Roland	39	10	3,000	6	6	163	SP
Many .50 caliber	5	0	1,000	1	0	12.7	SP

Type	Effectiveness	Effective altitude (meters)		Range (km)	AWC	Caliber	Mobility
		Min	Max				
Russia							
3M9M4 (SA-6)	36	25	24,000	28	6	335	SP
9K31M (SA-9)	12	30	6,100	8	0	110	SP
9K32M (SA-7)	11	18	4,500	6	0	70	Port
9K331 (SA-15)	21	100	6,000	12	0	235	SP
9K33M3 (SA-8)	26	10	12,000	15	4	210	SP
9K34 (SA-14)	16	50	6,000	6	0	75	Port
9K37M1 (SA-11)	48	30	14,000	30	6	400	SP
9K38 (SA-18)	25	10	3,500	5	0	120	Port
9K40BUK (SA-17)	31	10	3,500	32	0	420	SP
9K310 (SA-16)	20	10	3,500	5	0	120	Port
9M8M2 (SA-4)	32	300	20,000	50	5	860	Mob
9M37 (SA-13)	20	10	3,500	5	0	120	SP
9M111 (SA-19)	24	5	8,000	12	0	170	SP
ADMG-630	28	0	2,000	2	5	30	Ship
S-125 (SA-3)	32	100	25,000	25	4	600	SP
S-200 (SA-5)	65	100	30,500	250	4	860	SP
S-300P (SA-10)	45	25	30,000	45	6	450	Mob
S-300PMU1 (SA-10)	60	30	30,000	90	7	500	SP
S-300PMU2 (SA-10)	94	25	24,000	200	7	500	SP
S-300V (SA-12)	36	1,000	25,000	100	6	450	Mob
SA-N-3	35	150	25,000	30	6	305	Ship
SA-N-3 Improved	38	150	25,000	55	6	600	Ship
V-75 (SA-2)	23	1,000	24,000	50	4	750	Mob
ZPU-4	10	0	1,400	1	0	14.5	SP
ZSU-23	19	0	2,000	3	3	23	SP
ZSU-30	21	0	2,500	4	4	30	SP
ZSU-57	14	0	4,000	6	3	57	SP
Switzerland							
Gepard	23	0	2,000	4	6	35	SP
U.S.							
Avenger	36	0	4,800	5	2	70/12.7	SP
Chaparral	18	100	1,000	5	0	127	SP
Hawk	45	100	11,000	30	6	350	Mob
Improved Hawk	70	30	18,000	40	6	370	Mob
M-42	10	0	1,500	3	0	40	SP
Nike-Hercules	51	1,000	50,000	150	6	800	Mob
Patriot	100	100	24,000	60	7	410	SP
Phalanx	47	0	2,000	2	7	20	Ship
Sea Sparrow RIM7H	32	15	5,000	5	6	200	Ship
SM-2 ER Aegis	104	25	28,000	180	6	343	Ship
SM-2 MR	94	50	25,000	150	6	305	Ship
Stinger	31	0	4,800	5	0	70	Mob
Tartar RIM24B	33	50	20,000	20	6	300	Ship
Vulcan	10	0	2,000	2	0	20	SP

Stinger shoulder-fired surface-to-air guided missile

Effective altitude, Minimum indicates the minimum altitude (in meters) at which the weapon can reasonably be expected to hit a target. For missiles, this represents the distance traveled after launch before the warhead is armed and the guidance system can figure out where it is and where the target is. Most missile systems cannot hit targets very near ground level because radar has difficulty spotting a target among the clutter of objects on the ground. The degree to which targets are moving about near the ground also degrades missile system performance. Because of these problems, the minimum is optimistic and depends on how ideal the situation is for the missile system.

Range is the maximum horizontal range of the weapon in kilometers. This limit is dictated largely by the system's target-acquisition ability.

All-Weather Capability (AWC) is a numerical rating of the system's ability to operate at night and in bad weather. However, even the most sophisticated systems often have manual backups. This is because missile- and radar-guided gun systems are quite complex and subject to failure. The manual backup capability allows the system to be used in clear weather if the all-weather system fails. The higher rating indicates better all-weather capability and higher system reliability.

Caliber is the diameter of the shell or missile in millimeters (25.4mm = 1 inch).

Mobility. SP means self-propelled; the entire system moves on one or more vehicles and can be used while equipment is still on the vehicles. *Mobile* means the entire system can be moved on vehicles and put into action after a minimum of unloading and preparation. *Portable* means that the system can be moved but requires extensive setup. *Fixed* means the system operates from permanent sites. *Ship* is a system that is normally mounted on a ship. All naval versions operate from a ship.

THE MISSILE SYSTEMS

ADMG-630 is the Russian equivalent of Phalanx. Its capability is somewhat less, which is not very encouraging considering the problems Phalanx has had. There is an earlier version of this weapon that is nothing more than twin 30mm guns. This is basically the small-caliber air-defense cannon developed about 60 years ago. Many navies still use such weapons, although it is unlikely that major-nation aircraft would approach close enough for these to be used. The more advanced air forces use standoff missiles to keep the aircraft away from ship defenses. Unless automated, like Phalanx, it is difficult for such weapons to successfully engage missiles coming in at over 500 meters a second.

Hawk is the original U.S. missile system for defense against low-flying aircraft. It is still used by many nations that cannot afford the upgraded version (see below).

Nike-Hercules is the standard long-range air-defense missile system used by nations that cannot afford Patriot and similar systems. Obsolete.

.50 caliber (12.7mm) is a machine gun commonly found mounted on armored vehicles and trucks for air defense. Often multi-gun arrangements are used—dual or quad are most common. Each barrel can put out about 10 rounds per second.

3M9M4 was once the principal Russian battlefield air-defense missile system for which there is no Western equivalent. It is still used by a lot of Third World nations.

9K31M is similar in concept to Chaparral, although it uses a missile more similar to the portable 9K34 than to an air-to-air type.

9K32M is the Russian version of the U.S. Redeye.

9K331 is a more modern self-propelled system with a missile more agile and resistant to countermeasures.

9K33M3 is the Russian equivalent of Roland.

9K34 is an improved replacement for the 9K32M. This is a clear-weather system with good capability against low-flying aircraft. It is considered to be essentially an attempt to clone the U.S. Stinger.

9K37M1 is a battlefield missile system intended to complement and eventually replace the 3M9M4. It has increased reliability and accuracy against low-flying aircraft.

9K38 is the latest portable missile, with improvements that keep it competitive with the latest version of the Stinger.

9M111 is a system that incorporates 30mm guns and SA-19 surface-to-air missiles. Radar and fire-control equipment are available for both weapons.

9M37 replaced the 9K31M and serves the same purpose.

9M8M2 is the Russian heavy battlefield missile. It is primarily used for long-range, high-flying aircraft. Although it is the Russian equivalent of the now-defunct U.S. Nike-Hercules, it is not as capable.

AMX-30SA is a battlefield air-defense cannon. Each of its twin barrels can put out about 10 rounds per second.

Avenger is a U.S. system first deployed in the late 1980s. It consists of a powered turret on a Hummer vehicle. The turret has eight Stinger SAMs and a 12.7mm multi-barrel machine gun. There is a FLIR system for spotting targets at night and bad weather. But target acquisition normally is visual. Each barrel can put out about 10 rounds per second.

Chaparral is an air-to-air missile (the Sidewinder) used as a battlefield air-defense system.

Crotale is similar to the Rapier and Roland systems.

Gepard is a battlefield air-defense cannon. Developed in Switzerland, it is used primarily by Germany. Each barrel can put out about 10 rounds per second.

Improved Hawk is an extensively upgraded version of the original Hawk. This is the primary air-defense missile system for the United States and many Western ground forces.

M-42 is a World War II–era battlefield air-defense cannon that is still found in many armies. Each barrel can put out about 10 rounds per second.

Patriot was introduced in the early 1980s after over 20 years of development. It replaced Nike-Hercules and Hawk. Current versions of the missile can intercept ballistic missiles. This capability was just being introduced when the Patriot was used during the 1991 Gulf War, and the missile is much better at it these days.

Phalanx is a "last chance" automatic defense system against surface-to-surface missiles and low-flying aircraft. It is used on ships only. Each barrel can put out about 10 rounds per second.

Rapier is a battlefield missile system. It is used extensively for airfield defense against low-flying aircraft.

Roland is a battlefield missile system used by many Western nations.

S-125 is an older system still used by nations that cannot afford anything better.

S-300 is the standard system for the defense of Russia's borders. Its principal features are quick reaction time of the detection and acquisition systems, and high speed of the missiles (2,000 meters a second). It is effective against low-flying aircraft and missiles. It has been steadily improved and now exists in four different versions (S-300P, S-300PMU1, S-300PMU2, and S-300V). The S-300V is designed to have some antimissile capability, making it similar to the current version of the Patriot. Yet another antimissile system, the S-400, has been in development for some time.

SA-N-3 Improved is the latest version of the Standard heavy naval air-defense missile system and the Russian equivalent of the U.S. Standard.

SA-N-3 is an older version of the improved model.

Sea Sparrow is an air-to-air missile used in an air-defense system adapted for shipboard use.

Standard SM-2 ER (extended range) is the standard shipboard missile system for the U.S. Navy.

Standard SM-2 MR (medium range) is a shorter-range version of the Standard ER (see above).

Stinger is an air-defense missile system carried and fired by one man. It replaces the similar Redeye. Stinger is also used as an air-to-air weapon on helicopters (AH-64).

Tartar is an older U.S. Navy missile system that was replaced in the U.S. fleet during the 1980s by the Standard system.

V-75 is an obsolete missile system still used in places like China and nations that cannot afford more modern systems. Numerous upgrades have made it a still-lethal system against aircraft that do not have countermeasures.

Vulcan is a battlefield air-defense cannon. Each barrel can put out about 10 rounds per second.

ZPU-4 is typical of the multiple machine guns used for air defense. It is generally only used by less-well-equipped armies or reserve formations. It puts out about 40 rounds a second.

ZSU-23 is a battlefield air-defense cannon. It is still widely used by Third World armies. It puts out about 65 rounds a second.

ZSU-30 replaced the ZSU-23, with 30mm guns and better electronics. It puts out about 40 rounds a second.

ZSU-57 is an older battlefield air-defense cannon that has been replaced by missiles and the ZSU-23. It puts out about four rounds a second.

PART THREE

NAVAL OPERATIONS

Naval warfare has always been the least seen, and least understood, form of combat. It is slow, tedious, and expensive warfare. For nations dependent on maritime commerce, naval warfare is almost as important as ground combat.

9

The Navy:
On the Surface

America rules the waves. The only credible opponent the U.S. Navy has had since the 1950s is now no more. The Soviet navy has, since the late 1980s, been wasting away at anchor, starved of the resources that keep a navy viable. One could say that not only is the Soviet navy history, but it always was more history than substance. However, a lot of the Russian Navy remains and will continue to exist for some years to come.

If there is a major naval war in the future, two conspicuously different styles of maritime warfare will collide. The two major naval powers are still Russia and the United States. Each has markedly different attitudes toward the use of naval forces. The U.S. Navy is unquestionably the largest and most powerful navy in the world and has adopted a style of naval warfare that is unique, yet befitting the Navy's singular structure and composition. Moreover, the Russian naval doctrine is widely used by many Third World navies. To understand what the Russians and like-minded navies might do, you must understand what the Russians have done.

Lessons from the Past

There is nothing more instructive than defeat. The Russian navy has taken lessons not only from its own defeats, but from those of its enemies. Adopting the submarine doctrine of Germany, which failed in World Wars I and II, and the kamikaze doctrine of the Japanese, which failed in 1945, the Russians developed a style of warfare widely regarded as potentially successful. The Russian style has been adopted by most of the smaller navies of the world, including many Western ones, as well as China. This style depends on the stealth of submarines, sheer numbers of cruise missiles, and vast minefields. This last element, mines, victimized the Russian navy three times in this century. First there was the Russo-Japanese War (1904–5), then the two World Wars (1914–17 and 1941–45). The Russians have a lot of experience in how not to do it. Out of this experience they have developed a set of guidelines they trust will change their naval fortunes.

Surprise is essential. Get in the first shot and make it count. Hit the other fellow before he knows there's a war on. The bulk of the Russian navy was built and trained for this type of operation and was not organized for a long war. Anything beyond a few months was beyond its planned capabilities.

Construct ships for maximum "one-shot" capability. The Russian navy's targets were, in order of importance, ballistic missile submarines, aircraft carriers, nuclear attack submarines, and enemy shipping. The Russian navy had a lot of small, heavily armed ships so that it can hit as many of these targets as possible in the shortest time.

Learn from the Japanese kamikaze experience. A multitude of aircraft that crash themselves into ships can overcome massive defense systems. This was reflected in the large number of naval cruise missiles in the Russian navy.

Arleigh Burke (DDG 51) class destroyer

Learn from the German experience with submarines. Send enough submarines against the West before it can mobilize its forces, and you can deny it use of the oceans. The Germans almost succeeded in 1914–17 and 1939–45. Germany began World War II with only 57 submarines to counter some 16,000 Allied merchant ships. If the third of those ships controlled by Great Britain could have been quickly decimated, victory would have been within sight. At the end of the Cold War, Russia was prepared to unleash some 200 submarines against 20,000 merchant ships.

The victor in World War II, the United States, also used its experience to develop basic attitudes toward naval war. These can be summarized as follows:

No matter what you thought before the war, new weapons systems will soon assert themselves with superior or unexpected performance. Before World War II, it was still assumed that the battleship was the decisive naval weapon. The aircraft carrier was seen as just another support system for the big-gun battlewagons, and an untried one at that. Today the carriers are seen as the decisive naval weapon, and nuclear submarines are the untried system supporting the carriers. The situation is similar to the pre–World War II one in that the older system (battleships) did prove useful in supporting amphibious landings and protecting task forces from enemy aircraft. The primary function of a capital ship is to go after the other guy's capital ships. So today we have nuclear subs going after one another to decide who rules the seas, while carriers support amphibious operations and help protect the fleet from enemy subs. The United States covers its bets by attempting to maintain strength in both areas. Unlike the 1930s, when the carriers had to scramble for every dollar, nuclear submarines still receive more resources than any other ship type.

Nations that depend on merchant shipping can win a war only if they maintain control of the oceans. The Western allies did this during World Wars I and II and were victorious. The Japanese were not able to withstand the onslaught of American submarines in World War II and collapsed when their economy was strangled by this blockade. Merchant shipping powers like Japan, the United States, and Britain have spent a lot of money on antisubmarine warfare since then. Surprise will not guarantee any future submarine user a victory if its intended victims remain alert and wary. Japan launched a number of surprise attacks in 1941, including Pearl Harbor. Numerous ships and aircraft were destroyed. Yet America recovered. Rather than depending on eventual recovery, the United States and her allies maintain a high degree of vigilance against future surprise attacks. Any future naval aggressor's prime chance for success in a future war depends on surprise.

Superior information-gathering ability is not the same as knowing what the other fellow will do. Cracking the enemy's codes and keeping him under observation at all times will not allow you to get inside his head. Too much information, incorrectly interpreted, can lead to fatally wrong conclusions. This is one of the most ignored lessons of World War II, Korea, and Vietnam.

Techniques of Modern Surface Warfare

Although fleets continue adding more submarines to their rosters, it is still surface forces that call the shots. There are few independent operations that submarines can undertake. In most cases, subs are a supporting force, albeit a crucial one. The following description of techniques assumes the participation of submarine and antisubmarine forces:

Deployment. During peacetime, about 80–90 percent of most Third World navies and 65 percent of Western navies are in port. Ships go to sea to practice, and to keep an eye on potential opponents. Nearly every navy organizes its fleet into task forces of up to a dozen or so ships. The core of these task forces are aircraft carriers or large ships carrying cruise missiles. Normally, there is one major ship (a carrier or large cruiser/battleship) plus 6–10 cruisers, destroyers, and frigates, plus one or more subs. These ships move in a pattern that gets the best effect from their differing capabilities in antiair, anti-surface, and antisubmarine warfare. The task forces are based together at naval installations, which contain supply and repair facilities as well as housing for families. When ships go to sea, they are sustained by a network of supply ships. Some travel with the task force, while others shuttle back and forth to restore their supplies. These supply ships are always a weak point in naval deployments. Not only are these ships liable to destruction, but their detection often gives an indication of where the warships they support are located.

Detection. If you want to destroy the other fleet, find it first. The United States uses satellite reconnaissance and a worldwide network of intelligence-collection ships, aircraft, and shore-based observers. In peacetime, some smaller navies shadow major Western task forces with combat and/or surveillance ships. If war comes suddenly, these shadows may be quickly blown away before they can make a suicide attack. A gradual escalation to war would involve attempts to reinforce these shadows, while the Western ships would attempt to elude them. Both these techniques are practiced in peacetime. Generally, Western fleets have the edge in detection with their larger land- and carrier-based air reconnaissance forces. In addition, the United States maintains a worldwide network of underwater sensors.

Attack. The most noticeable change since World War II is the standoff weapons, guided missiles launched from ships and aircraft at distances of nearly 1,000 kilometers. Submarines also carry some versions of these missiles, as well as long-range guided torpedoes (over 40 kilometers). Another result of this shift to missiles is a reduction in the striking power of each hit because of the smaller warheads, compared to large-caliber guns and torpedoes.

Defense. Basic techniques vary, depending on the resources of the task force. An aircraft carrier uses a more elaborate defense than a noncarrier force. This defense system is described in Chapter 11, on naval air operations. Noncarrier task forces use ship-based helicopters to give additional detection capability, as well as whatever land-based and satellite reconnaissance resources are available to all naval vessels. Electronic warfare plays a large role in defense, as it is possible to hide yourself by deceiving the enemy's sensors.

Damage control. Battle damage is inevitable. How quickly ships are able to recover from this becomes a decisive factor, particularly when one side is more capable in this area. Western navies have an edge in damage control. This edge is not absolute, as all navies that have not been in combat for a decade or so lose their edge in this area. The reasons are the usual ones: situations that do not occur regularly tend to get less attention than those that do. Although accidents occur during peacetime, few are as catastrophic as combat damage. As new equipment and ship designs are introduced during peacetime, there is little opportunity to determine how damage-control equipment and procedures should be changed. Peacetime practice rarely catches up with wartime reality until after there have been several disasters. See also the section below on ship design.

The Strategy and Tactics of the Weak

Most Western navies have long and successful naval traditions. Russia, and most smaller navies, have had a shorter and less distinguished experience at sea. Neither World War I nor World War II was a glorious chapter in Russia's naval history. While Soviet ground forces have regularly come back from initial defeat to gain ultimate victory, the Soviet navy has begun and ended its wars on equally sour notes. In light of this experience, Russia attempted to rewrite the book on naval practice. Russia began its "new navy" in the 1950s. The Russians have been perceptive, imaginative, resourceful, and desperate. Although the United States had taken the lead in nuclear-attack submarine development, Russia was the first to push ahead in the development of surface-to-surface missiles and electronic warfare. Withal, Russia has clung to its traditional concept of putting all their power up front. Another tradition retained was the building of large numbers of smaller but heavily armed ships. The theory was that this provided more targets and made it more difficult and expensive for their opponents to hunt them all down. All of this was to increase the ability of Russia to defend its maritime borders more efficiently.

Belatedly, the West caught on to the potential of the Soviet innovations. Russia was then faced with two problems. As its fleet grew larger, Russia saw the potential for projecting its naval power beyond its own coastal waters. The second problem was the West's increasing ability to go after the numerous small targets the Soviet fleet provided. This brought about a second shift of Soviet naval planning in the 1960s. They began building larger ships, better able to take punishment and effectively move thousands of miles from their own waters. By the 1980s, they had carriers and battle cruisers, as well as the world's largest cruise-missile submarines. Both sides were becoming more like each other, but fundamental differences remained. These dissimilarities are most prominent in the following areas:

Ship design. Russia (and now China) favored a larger number of smaller, somewhat cheaper, and, ton for ton, less-effective ships. These vessels appear to bristle with weapons, especially when compared with Western ships. Indeed, Russian ships do carry more weapons. But they also carry some serious liabilities as well. There is less work space and equipment access than in Western ships. This makes it very difficult to get at anything that breaks down. Russian crews were primarily three-year conscripts, so they were short on skilled technicians. Inaccessibility and unskilled crews mean most repairs must await a return to port. In the meantime, the ship must depend on duplicate systems, if they are available. The multiplicity of weapons and other equipment also served to ensure that something would be working when the battle begins. Even then, an additional problem exists, as most missile systems have no reloads. One salvo, and that's it. More serious problems are a lack of vibration damping and onboard repair facilities. Electronic systems are very prone to vibration damage. Equipment that would be fixed quickly in Western ships would remain broken on Russian vessels. No tools, spares, technicians, or easy access makes command of a Russian warship a struggle against progressive decay. Moreover, combat would reveal that a relative lack of compartmentalization makes damaging hits catastrophic ones. On the plus side, Russian ships tend to have more modern propulsion systems and better sea-keeping capabilities. This is just as well, as the crew quarters are cramped and uncomfortable. Keep in mind that the above is suitable for a coastal navy, where ships rarely spend more than a week or so away from port. When the Russian fleet headed for the high seas, the problems multiplied.

Command and control. Western ships developed the combat information center (CIC) concept. The CIC is a room, often in the bowels of the ship, where all sensor and fire-control information is centralized. During combat, the captain or watch officer commands from the CIC while the executive officer, the second in command, mans the bridge topside. CICs and radar displays allow the commander to grasp the entire battle from the CIC. Radars and other ship sensors cover an area beyond what any human being can grasp without electronic assistance. The CIC recognizes this fact and brings the over 100 kilometer range of air and surface radars, as well as underwater sensor data, together where one officer can make sense out of it. The CIC became essential once ships became dependent on sensors that saw beyond visual range. Commanders could no longer command from the bridge, relying only on their eyes for battle information. Each ship sends data to the task force flagship where it is coordinated, and analysis is sent back to each ship. All of this takes place at a close to real-time pace, thanks to the development of a "battlefield intranet" approach to communications. Everyone is plugged into everyone else's information. The task-force commander can make more effective decisions for the entire task force. At the same time, the individual ship commanders can still operate independently as needed. In a fast-moving naval situation, the side that is best able to cope with new situations will prevail. Following longstanding practice, Russian operations were carefully planned and executed under centralized control. Little room is left for individual initiative or deviations from the plan. The command layout of Russian ships reflects this. The Russian captain normally commands from the bridge. The navigation, early-warning and fire-control radar sections, sonar antisubmarine warfare, and other sections report to him from a room full of consoles deep within the ship. Unlike CIC systems, all this information is combined only in the captain's head. The Russian task-force commander issues more detailed orders before an operation, leaving less latitude for individual initiative. This works fine if the previously prepared plan is carried out. Things begin to fall apart when unexpected events occur. Only among some of their submarine captains do the Russians give the individual commanders free rein.

Concept of mission. Not all navies have the same purpose and mission. Russia, as a continental nation fighting oceanic powers, has the obvious mission of denying sea access to the oceanic powers. The U.S. mission is to maintain sea access. Merely presenting a potential danger to oceanic powers lessens the use of the oceans for moving goods. If, in addition, sufficient quantities of merchant shipping can be destroyed, then the economic and military power of the oceanic nations is diminished. This makes Russia, and any other continental power like China, relatively stronger. The attacker in this case is similar to a guerrilla fighter. He doesn't have to be everywhere at once; he can pick and choose his strikes. As Russia's fleet grew more numerous, and its ships larger, it began to look like the navy of an oceanic power. A large fleet must be protected. Trying to be two kinds of fleet does little to concentrate your attention.

Deployment. Only 15 percent of Soviet ships (and most Third World navies) were at sea at any time, versus 35 percent for Western navies. This reflected a longstanding tradition in the Russian armed forces to not use equipment until war breaks out. This guarantees that there will be somewhat more equipment available, and that no one will know how to use it very well. Practical reasons exist for this. With 75 percent of the Russian sailors being draftees, there were not enough technicians to maintain heavily used equipment. The ships are cramped and uncomfortable during long cruises. The nuclear-powered ships produce many cases of radiation poisoning. There were several mutinies on Soviet ships, and they didn't want to encourage more. The money saved by not operating ships enabled them to build more ships. These Soviet practices allowed them to put more ships to sea when war came. Quantity is preferred to quality because, historically, Russia has been more successful with quantity. There is always the danger that the fleet won't make it very far or won't be able to do much when they get to where they are going. This is another reason why Russia's move toward a high-seas fleet was such a risky undertaking. The Western practice, also based on long experience, is to keep the crews at sea as long as possible. Practice, it has been found, makes for more effective crews. As the majority of sailors are technicians, their skills can be maintained only through constant use. The majority of Western sailors are long-term veterans. There is no substitute for high-seas experience.

Attack techniques. Ambush is the preferred technique in all navies. This has become easier to pull off with the growth of electronic warfare and long-range missiles. Beyond this, the major difference is that the smaller navies must stay out of the way of the more powerful Western task forces while preparing their attacks. Western ships are better equipped to come looking for the smaller opponents. In peacetime, ship locations of potential enemies are monitored more accurately by Western forces than the other way around. This is particularly true with submarines.

U.S. submariners openly proclaim their ability to detect foreign (particularly Russian) subs at 10 times the range of foreign sensors. This is less true as more recent foreign subs have obtained more effective silencing. Many navies attempt to overcome their deficiencies by maintaining small surface combat ships or submarines as "escorts" for all major Western task forces. These ships not only maintain location information for other friendly ships, but are expected to get in the first shot themselves. However, these escort ships will likely be destroyed whether they get off any missiles or not. Western task forces are often able to evade these escorts. Once these escorts and their up-to-date information are gone, the location of the enemy task force becomes a mystery very rapidly. For example, in six hours of 30-knot steaming, a task force can travel 320 kilometers in any direction. This search circle includes 320,000 square kilometers. Lacking air-search capability, a noncarrier task force can search only 2,000 square kilometers per hour. A U.S. carrier task force can search over 100,000 square kilometers per hour. Both sides can use helicopters to increase search area when they lack carrier-based fixed-wing aircraft. Under the best conditions, this won't increase the hourly search area beyond 30,000 square kilometers. Satellite and electronic surveillance can work if the satellites remain and/or the enemy task force has sloppy signal discipline. These means are available to both sides, although not continuously.

The search capability that really counts is that of the combat ships. Finding the enemy is of little use if you can't attack him. When the non-Western navy has located a U.S. task force, it attempts to launch a saturation attack of cruise missiles launched from land-based aircraft, surface ships, and submarines. First it attempts to hit the carriers with its longest-range cruise missiles. These are launched from whatever platforms can get close enough. But first the targets must be located. This is often left to slow-moving naval aircraft. These aircraft make attractive targets to the enemy and may have a difficult time surviving long enough to do their job. Once the carriers are crippled, the enemy waits a few hours until all U.S. aircraft aloft are out of fuel. Then it goes in against the remaining ships with all the surface-ship- and submarine-launched missiles it can muster. Enemy aircraft armed with cruise missiles would not have an easy time of it. The longest range non-U.S. antiship missiles travel only 550 kilometers. A carrier has early-warning aircraft that can spot air and surface targets 700 kilometers away. Carriers can launch air attacks at targets over 1,000 kilometers distant. Land-based aircraft can attempt to fight their way through if they have friendly interceptors with them. On the high seas, the Russian solution was (and still is) enormous cruise-missile submarines. The subs still have a problem in finding out where the carrier is. Submarines must depend on aircraft and surface ships for most of their reconnaissance information. They rely on stealth to sneak in close enough (500 or so kilometers) to launch their missiles. Other submarines have shorter-range cruise missiles. Cruise missiles from any platform must get to within 30 or 40 kilometers of their targets before they can use their search-radar, heat-seeking, or radar-homing systems. The homing radar ideally is turned on as close to the target as possible, a few kilometers at most, to avoid jamming. These missiles can be defeated by electronic countermeasures, gunfire, or missiles. Against a task force, there will be dozens of these defensive systems to get by. Against a noncarrier task force, the attacker will have an easier time of it. The basic attack strategy is the same except for more aggressive air observation. The recon aircraft only have to track the task forces' radar emissions. Even helicopters can be used for this, as long as they stay out of surface-to-air missile range.

Many navies still use a number of older, shorter-range missiles with more primitive guidance systems. These missiles need all the targeting information they can get. From the attacker's point of view, the more missiles you can send in the direction of the enemy, the more their opponents have to contend with.

Western navies have antiship cruise missiles, including the longer-range Tomahawk (450 kilometers). They face the same problems of finding out approximately where the target ships are. Their carrier-based strike aircraft carry cruise missiles so they can avoid going in close enough to face the surface-to-air missiles. Another key weapon in defense and attack are the Western nuclear-attack submarines. These are quieter and have better sensors than those of any other nations. Non-Western antisubmarine capabilities in general are below those of Western navies. Non-Western ships and subs must be wary at all times of Western subs. Most Western shipping routes are close to their potentially hostile naval bases. But several key areas are not. It is for this reason that the West is so dependent on carrier air power to defend these distant links in their economic chain. The carriers are also vital if the hostile naval forces are to be defeated in their sometimes remote bases. As long as a significant number of hostile ships survive in a future war, they pose a threat to Western commerce and economic survival. The "fleet in being" has long been a viable tactic for a weaker naval power. To guard against the depredations of a less numerous fleet requires substantial effort. The only way to eliminate this burden is to go after the weaker opponent where he will be strongest: his naval bases. This is a risky undertaking but always offers a chance of success for a capable carrier fleet.

The United States maintains a dozen attack carriers, of which as many as 10 can be put to sea at any one time. The other Western allies can contribute as many as six smaller carriers. An American aircraft carrier, with its 60 combat and 20 or so support aircraft, is capable of detecting enemy surface ships, submarines, and aircraft over 700 kilometers away. Attack and support aircraft can launch cruise-missile attacks without much risk. A typical attack would include three electronic-warfare aircraft and 12 strike aircraft carrying 24 cruise missiles plus other weapons like guided bombs and radar-homing missiles. They could, at worst, encounter half a dozen hostile ships mounting about 30 surface-to-air launchers with 500 to 600 functioning missiles. The attacking aircraft don't even have to get within range of the these hostile SAMs in order to launch their cruise missiles. The odds are against the defending ships.

The Sailor's Life

Most sailors are technicians. There is little work on a modern warship for the unskilled. Although housekeeping chores still exist, seamen spend most of their time maintaining, repairing, and operating complex equipment. Considerable effort is spent in perfecting combat skills. These consist of practice on weapons and damage-control drills. It is difficult to practice wartime activities in peacetime. The sailors who can become proficient at this "making believe" will likely survive during the real thing. A sailor's career alternates between sea duty and going ashore for additional schooling. While at sea, a third of the crew is on duty at all times. When combat is possible, half the crew is at work, with the critical combat systems manned. A general quarters (combat) alert puts everyone at battle stations. This can only be maintained for so long before fatigue takes over. Although sea duty means being assigned to a ship, it doesn't mean you're going to spend most of your time steaming around some ocean. U.S. ships outside the United States spend about 70 percent of their time at anchor, although not always in a port. Ships in the United States spend over 80 percent of their time stationary. Russian ships spend even less time at sea.

Combat also comes in several flavors. There is active and passive combat. Passive combat is more common and occurs even in peacetime. This consists of looking for the enemy and/or waiting to be found. Active combat is actually exchanging fire. In peacetime, ships often go looking for those of potential opponents under conditions closely approximating wartime. This is primarily true with submarines, which spend a lot of time stalking surface ships and submarines of potential opponents. In wartime, sailors would spend from two-thirds to three-quarters of their time in passive combat. Active combat would occupy less time, perhaps a few hours a week at most, on the average. When it comes, you wish it hadn't.

Mine Warfare

Mines are the weapon nobody wants, but no one can avoid. Mines are a deadly nuisance. They are considered vaguely unseemly in a violent undertaking that otherwise knows few limits. Perhaps naval officers are uncomfortable commanding warriors that don't salute. Mines are also cheap. They can be employed with relatively little risk to the user. Their effect on their victims is paralyzing. This last item may explain why many navies shun mines. It reduces warfare to the plodding drudgery of a siege. If you are a fast-moving, dynamic navy, the last thing you want to think about is mines. But they won't go away. Mines are the weapon of choice for the little guy. If you are about to get clobbered by a larger navy, you build and use a lot of mines. You don't have much choice. Russia, no matter how large its fleet got, always maintained the world's largest stock of naval mines.

THE HISTORICAL EXPERIENCE

Modern naval mines were widely used for the first time during the Russo-Japanese war (1904–5). These were contact mines, floating in shallow water and kept in place with an anchor and chain. When the tide was right, they would be just below the surface, ready to explode whenever struck by a ship. Some 2,000 of these mines were used to destroy 16 ships. This experience pointed out how important it was to keep track of your own mines. A number of ships were sunk by their own mines, often while moving through a supposedly clear lane in a friendly minefield. During and after the war, several ships were sunk by free-floating mines as well as anchored (moored) ones that had broken free. Thereafter, more care was taken to reduce the number of loose mines floating about. This illustrates another unsavory aspect of mine warfare: mines are indiscriminate, blowing up friend and foe alike.

During World War I, modern mine tactics were further developed. Thousands of mines were laid to provide defensive barriers against enemy movement. Mines were used offensively by secretly placing them across known enemy sea routes. More than 1,000 merchant ships and warships were lost because of the 230,000 mines used.

During World War II, mine warfare came of age. A total of 2,665 ships were lost or damaged to 100,000 offensive mines. That's one ship for every 37 mines. Some 208,000 mines were used defensively to inhibit enemy movement and tie up his resources. Most of this went on in the North Sea between German and British anti-mine forces, which totaled 2,400 ships and aircraft operated by 99,000 men. Using mines achieved several striking successes. In the Pacific, naval mines proved more destructive to the Japanese war effort than the atom bombs. During a 10-week period between April and August 1945, 12,000 mines were delivered by American bombers. These accounted for 1,250,000 tons of Japanese shipping (670 hit, 431 destroyed). That's 18 mines for each ship hit. The Americans had air superiority, so losses during these 1,500 missions amounted to only 15 planes, most of them to accidents. Had these missions been flown against opposition, losses would have been between 30 and 60 aircraft, plus similar losses to their fighter escorts. This was siege warfare, and the Japanese people were starving along with their war industries. Unfortunately, without the shock of the atomic bomb attacks, the Japanese government might have continued resistance throughout the winter of 1945–46. This would have caused over a million civilian deaths to starvation, disease, and exposure. Mine warfare can win in the long run, but the long run is not pretty when starving civilians are involved. A conventional submarine campaign was also waged against Japanese shipping. Comparisons to the mine campaign are interesting. A hundred submarines were involved in a campaign that ran for 45 months from December 1941 to August 1945. Some 4.8 million tons of enemy shipping were sunk. For every U.S. submarine sailor lost using submarine-launched torpedoes, 560 tons were sunk. During the mine campaign, 3,500 tons were sunk for each U.S. fatality. On a cost basis, the difference was equally stark. Counting the cost of lost mine-laying aircraft (B-29s at $500,000 each) or torpedo-armed submarines ($5 million each), we find that each ton of sunk shipping cost $6 when using mines and $55 when using submarines. These data were classified as secret until the 1970s. It indicates that mines might have been more effective than torpedoes even if the mines were delivered by submarine.

The Germans waged a mine-laying campaign off the east coast of the United States between 1942 and 1944. Only 317 mines were used, which sank or damaged 11 ships. This was a ratio of 29 mines used for each ship hit. In addition, eight ports were closed for a total of 40 days. One port, Charleston, South Carolina, was closed for 16 days, tying up not only merchant shipping but the thousands of men, warships, and aircraft dealing with the situation. American submarines also waged a limited mine campaign in the Pacific. For 658 mines used, 54 ships were sunk or damaged (12 mines per ship). No subs were lost. Considerable Japanese resources were tied up dealing with the mines. On the Palau atoll, the port was closed by the mines and not reopened until the war ended. Even surface ships were used to lay mines. Three thousand mines were laid by destroyer. Only 12 ships were hit, but these were barrier fields, not the ambush-type minefields that a submarine can create by sneaking into an enemy-held area.

In Korea during the early 1950s, the Soviets provided North Korea with 3,000 mines, many of 1904 vintage. These were used to defend Wonson Harbor. It took several weeks for UN forces to clear these, at a loss of a dozen ships hit. Half of these ships were destroyed. During the Vietnam War, over 300,000 naval mines were used, primarily in rivers. The vast majority were not built as mines but were aerial bombs equipped with magnetic sensors instead of fuzes. These bombs/mines used a small parachute to ensure that no damage occurred on landing. In shallow water, these makeshift weapons sat on the bottom and performed as well as mines. Haiphong Harbor was actually mined with 11,000 of these "destructors," as the U.S. Air Force called them, and less than a hundred conventional mines. A complete tally of the ships destroyed by these mines could not be obtained because neither side was able to keep track of losses. Based on fragmentary reports, the mines performed quite well.

During the 1991 Gulf War, the Iraqis laid over 1,000 mines off the Iraqi and Kuwaiti coast. The predominantly U.S. naval forces did not have sufficient mine-sweeping resources to deal with this situation and had a helicopter carrier and cruiser hit and damaged while trying to clear the area. This effectively prevented any U.S. amphibious operations, although the Marines were not going to be used for a landing, anyway. It took over a month of mine-clearing after the fighting ceased to eliminate all the mines.

NAVAL MINE DESIGN

Currently, naval mines weigh between 1,000–2,000 pounds. Normally, a submarine can carry two mines in place of one torpedo. Naval mines have several characteristics that make for different types:

Free-floating mines are just that, mines that are floating freely. This type was abandoned early on when it was discovered that they would eventually be a danger to friend and foe. The winds and tides are not predictable, leaving these mines to go where you don't want them to. This type is still encountered when moored mines break loose, as they sometimes do. Terrorists also find this approach to their liking. Only Russia is known to have developed and stockpiled free-floating mines. They have a mechanism that keeps them at a set depth. Once their batteries give out, they deactivate.

Moored mines drop anchor and float either near the surface or up to several hundred feet down (to hit subs). The original moored mines were detonated by contact. Current models are more sensitive and merely require that a ship pass close by. These can be deployed in water up to 6,000 feet deep and are called "rising mines" because the mine, or torpedo, that contains the explosive must rise toward the surface to hit its target.

Mobile mines can move under their own power. They can be either moored or bottom mines. Some simply move a set distance and then settle on the bottom. This makes it safer to lay mines in heavily guarded waterways. The means of delivery is often a modified torpedo. Another type is the U.S. CAPTOR mine. This is a moored mine equipped with a Mk 46 lightweight torpedo. It was developed to provide a quickly deployed (by air) minefield that could cover a very large area. The mine is equipped with a powerful acoustic sensor and is supposed to be able to detect subs at a range of several kilometers. Once detection is confirmed and the course of the target plotted, the torpedo is released to home in on and destroy the sub.

Contact mines. Another distinguishing characteristic of mines is their target-detection system. This area has produced the largest number of new developments in the last few decades. The earliest system was remote-control, where a human observer would detonate the mine when a target came close enough. This is still used, although often just to turn on other sensors in mines or to deactivate mines so your ships can pass. Several nations have remote-control mines in key waterways, ready to be switched on when needed. The most widely used sensor in the early part of this century was the contact fuze. This is the familiar form of mine to most people, a spherical object with long rods protruding from it. These rods are the contact fuzes. If a ship hit and breaks one of these rods, the mine detonates. Contact mines are not often used anymore because it is so easy to clear them. They are moored and near the surface. Once spotted, you can shoot them up with rifle or machine gun fire. However, these mines are easy to manufacture and are readily available on the world arms market with no questions asked. These cheap mines can be, and sometimes still are, rigged as command mines.

Influence. These mines detect ships over a distance. First came the magnetic influence mine. A ship is a large hunk of metal that will "influence" a mechanism within the mine that contains small magnets. This was first used as a bottom mine that must lie no more than 100 feet below the surface. Then came the acoustic mine. Ships make noise. A sound detector in the mine will sense this and explode when a ship passes overhead. Acoustic and magnetic mines can also be floating mines held at a certain depth by a cable and anchor. Then came the pressure mine, which senses the change in water pressure when a ship passes overhead. These must lie on the bottom and must also have a sensitive mechanism to account for the pressure generated by the local tides. Some modern mines use two or three of these influences. This makes these mines very difficult to disable. You can't easily fool them into exploding because the mine is programmed to get positive responses from all of its sensors before exploding. Microcomputers can now be put into mines to detect ships by weight and even type (warship or merchantman). If you want to destroy only submarines, the mine will be programmed accordingly. The mine can be programmed to let one or more ships pass by before detonating. Or the mine can activate for a while, then deactivate for a different period of time. This makes clearing mines even more nerve-wracking than it has been in the past. When you think you've cleared a channel, you haven't. All you did was get the mines that were active. This deactivation technique also allows for the use of dummy mines—light, empty shells that just lie there. An additional feature of the programmable mine is its ability to self-destruct, either according to a timer or upon command. This saves the hassle of clearing your own mines, particularly if they are a very difficult type.

MINE CLEARING

Mines are at best a deadly nuisance, and at worst an impenetrable barrier to ships. Western navies have a greater technical capability to clear them, while other navies simply have more mine-clearing boats. No nation has the resources to clear the number of mines available. Pressure mines, the most difficult to clear, are detected by a mine-sweeping boat (called, naturally, a "minesweeper") equipped with a special sonar. Then a remote-control miniature submarine goes down to confirm the mine's presence and to plant an explosive to destroy the mine. It's a slow and tedious process, but at least it's a solution. Work goes on to develop quicker methods, but so far mine clearing has resisted assembly-line procedures. Moreover, sweeping techniques are not 100-percent effective. Worse yet, a new minefield typically announces itself by sinking a few ships. The ideal situation for clearing pressure and other bottom mines is to use the sonar to identify all objects underneath a shipping channel. This can be done in peacetime, although it has to be updated periodically depending on how much turnover there is on the bottom. When war, and the possibility of bottom mines, arrives, the sweepers can quickly go over the cleared shipping channel. They only have to stop and send down the mini-sub if they spot something not seen last time around. Not all minesweepers have bottom-scanning sonar. Most still use the technique that gave them their name, a cable between two boats that "sweeps" forward looking for the cables of moored mines. The minesweeping boats are light and built of nonmetallic material (wood or fiberglass) so as not to detonate magnetic mines. Traveling slowly and posting lookouts to spot contact mines, their light weight and non-metallic construction protected them from most pressure and magnetic mines. Against magnetic mines, they would sweep with a magnetized cable, or some similar device. To set off acoustic mines, a noisemaker would be towed over the suspect area. The United States pioneered the use of helicopter-towed "sleds" that could search for magnetic, contact, and acoustic mines at high speed. These sleds had the advantage of being easily sent anywhere in the world by aircraft. They are a lot safer for their crews and cover a larger area more quickly. Despite constant improvements, they are still incapable of clearing out pressure mines. Another disadvantage is that the helicopters can stay in the air only four hours at a time. The only known way to sweep all known mines is a technique developed by the U.S. Navy in the 1960s. An old merchant ship is stripped of all equipment and filled with styrofoam. The ship moves slowly, using what are essentially large outboard engines. A minimal crew runs the ship from a shock-mounted pilot house. Such a rig can take quite a few hits before coming apart. The United States eventually adopted the more practical, second-best approach to clearing all known mines. In the late 1980s, the United States began building specialized minesweeping boats, as their European allies had been doing for several decades. Going one step further, the United States developed an airborne mine-detector pod ("Magic Lantern") that can be carried on helicopters or jets. This allows a quick sweep of sea areas to detect if mines are present. Then, at least, you know where to send your minesweepers.

As always, the best way to deal with mines is to prevent the enemy from using them. When they do get used, mines announce their general location dramatically. Most will be in shallow water near heavily used naval routes. Bottom mines, the weapon of choice these days, are dropped no deeper than 30 or 40 meters (against surface ships) or 200 meters (against subs) because of sensor limitations. Even then, they will have to rise to the surface before exploding. Otherwise, their explosive force will be smothered by the intervening water. Barriers of moored antisubmarine mines can be placed in waters up to 6,000 feet deep. These barriers are expensive where there is a wide area for subs to maneuver in. Moreover, such a minefield must be three-dimensional. Although you can equip mines with their own passive sensors and nuclear explosives, this is extremely expensive (over $1 million per mine), and you still need two of them for every kilometer of sea you want to guard. This assumes a 20-kiloton nuclear charge with a kill range of 700 meters. It can cause varying degrees of damage for about twice that range. Again, when the batteries wear out, the mine becomes useless. The life of such a field would not likely be more than a year at most, and typically only a few months.

Mines are becoming more flexible and reliable as technology, most notably electronics, improves. Western nations have an edge, although it is largely confined to the laboratory. The Russians build more mines; their peak inventory (at the end of the Cold War) was estimated at 50,000. Western navies had about a third that number. These inventories have shrunk by more than half since the Cold War ended. Surprises can be expected when mines are again used in earnest.

WHY AREN'T MINES USED MORE?

Mines are not good examples of military discipline and decorum. There's nothing sexy and exciting about them. Mines loiter in dark corners waiting for the unwary victim to wander by. Their fighting habits are more similar to muggers than trained sailors. They are insubordinate, attacking friend and foe alike. Thus none of the traditional naval services, surface, submarine, or air, will lay claim to them. Mines are tolerated because they work. Even this is not given full recognition till a war breaks out and the superiority of mine weapons becomes difficult, and dangerous, to ignore. The U.S. Navy is one of the more extreme examples of military loathing of mines. Remember that the reports of mine efficiency against Japan were kept classified until the 1970s. Only recently has the U.S. Navy taken any measures to deal with pressure mines, a type that has been around since the 1940s. Now that many Third World nations see naval mines as a useful way to attack other nations, the United States has finally begun to take mine warfare, and mine clearing, more seriously.

MINES IN THE NEXT WAR

World War II, Korea, Vietnam, and the 1991 Gulf War suggested how effective mines can be. These wars also demonstrated that the side with control of the air and sea was less exposed to mine damage, while their opponents would be devastated. Until one side gains the upper hand, mines could be used heavily in a number of critical areas. Indeed, it is quite possible the mines will be put to work even before a future war starts. While mines are heavy (1,000 to 2,000 pounds) and bulky (over 10 cubic feet each), numerous techniques are available for getting them were you want them. In wartime, mines are delivered by a variety of means: ships, submarines, mines, aircraft, missiles. More worrisome is the laying of mines in peacetime or just before the start of hostilities. Peacetime minefields are quite common. Key harbors or sea passages are routinely mined with devices that can be quickly activated when hostilities are imminent. These are generally bottom mines with a cable connection to a control center. The cable is used for monitoring the mines' readiness as well as for activation. These mines must periodically be retrieved for repair or maintenance. Another form of prepositioned mines is not talked about. These are the ones placed secretly in a potential opponent's harbors or seaways. The Soviets were long suspected of doing this, although it is unlikely that they are guilty of anything more than practicing surreptitious mine laying. Leaving mines in foreign waters is a risky business. The mines must be activated remotely, which is not an easy task for underwater objects. Prolonged submersion may lead to malfunctions, and batteries may last for years but not forever. Finally, these mines may be discovered, causing potentially disastrous diplomatic repercussions. You do not have to place mines in too many places to have a dramatic effect. The Western powers have a short list of key locations that opponents might mine. These include the Persian Gulf, the Djakarta and Singapore straits, the east coast Japanese ports, the English Channel ports, and the three largest ports on the east and west costs of North America. Mine the majority of these areas and keep them mined, and you paralyze the Western war and industrial effort.

The most potent mine-laying vehicles in the early stages of a war may be merchant vessels. Fitting these ships with mines is not difficult. A coded radio message in a time of imminent conflict could lead to minefields springing up quickly in the wake of such ships. The world had a taste of this in the summer of 1986 when a Libyan merchant ship secretly dropped a number of Soviet mines in the Red Sea. This was done as an act of terrorism. Multiply this even a few dozen times and you have a decisive act of war. Missiles, both cruise and ballistic, are another means of placing naval mines in far distant waters. As the major powers continue to back off from the use of nuclear weapons, their missiles become available for other tasks. Already, many battlefield missiles are having many of their nuclear warheads replaced with ones containing land mines or chemical weapons. Missiles are an expensive way to deliver naval mines, but when one considers the impact these mines can have in the early stages of a war, it is not such a bad bargain.

Theory and Practice

Theory is closer to practice in naval operations than in any other area of warfare. Ships at sea get ample experience just coping with the elements and the complexity of their temperamental equipment. But there have been no major actions between naval forces since 1945. Large American task forces have seen extensive action, but always against land forces, and never against significant air forces. Smaller actions have been instructive, particularly the Falklands battles of 1982. The big lesson has been that antiship missiles have to be respected and that air attacks are still a substantial threat. Unlike fleets of the 1940s, fewer of today's ships are armored. The norm is ill-protected ships crammed with explosive munitions and flammable materials. The "burning aluminum" delusion that came out of the Falklands had some basis in fact. The aluminum did not burn; it did collapse from heat stress more quickly than steel. This also exposed serious deficiencies in damage-control procedures. No one had really given these issues adequate attention until it was too late. Similar surprises are waiting to be found the old-fashioned way: by accident. Among the questions to be resolved only through large-scale combat are: nuclear submarines used on a large scale and in cooperation with other ships, mass use of cruise missiles, viability of attack carriers, impact of electronic warfare, and the effectiveness of ASW against modern submarines. All of these surprises are typical of what happens to navies that go to war with significantly new weapons after decades of peace. The next major battle between naval forces will be noted for its surprises.

The Future

There will be fewer ships, fewer sailors, and slower development of new technologies. All this is a result of the collapse of the Soviet navy. Since the 1950s, the primary reason for building warships frequently and abundantly has been the threat of Soviet naval operations in wartime. As the Soviet navy continued to grow during the 1960s, 1970s, and 1980s, Western navies kept pace. This resulted in the largest peacetime warship building in history. With no more hostile Soviet fleet to contend with, naval budgets, ship-building programs, and R&D are falling and will continue to decline for the foreseeable future. Attention now concentrates on the naval threats posed by smaller navies. Most of these will be quite local. This makes the U.S. Navy's job more complex, if smaller in scale. Meanwhile, some technical trends will continue to move forward, if at a slower pace.

Continuing a trend that has been ongoing for centuries, ships are becoming more automated. During World War II, each thousand tons of warship required over 80 crewmen. Current ships require a third less. On the drawing boards are designs that will again dramatically reduce crew size, taking the men per thousand tons down to under 20. This is the result of a number of different technological trends. Sensors are becoming more automated. Missiles are more common and are often delivered in storage containers from which they are fired, thus requiring little maintenance. Engines are increasingly automated, just like the industrial machinery from which they are derived. The ships are more frequently built of low-maintenance materials that do not require constant scraping and painting. In addition, more naval designers are taking into account the advantages of stealth ship-design technology. Submarines have long recognized the need for silence and general unobtrusiveness as a means of avoiding attack. For the past decade, new surface ships have attempted to suppress onboard noise to assist ASW operations. The success of stealth aircraft designs in reducing radar observation has been carried over to warships. The U.S. Navy spent several billion dollars over the last two decades working on stealthy ship design. This is resulting in ships with lots of smooth corners topside and a lot less clutter. A potentially troublesome side effect of smaller crews will be fewer men available for damage control duty and greater potential for reduced capability when key personnel are injured.

An understandably unheralded future development is the perfection of many recently installed weapons and systems. Combat technology that has not seen combat has an alarming tendency to not work very well when it is first made operational. It's more than the unexpected cracks appearing in new aircraft. Systems where performance is more difficult to determine, like missile-guidance systems and ASW equipment, are prime offenders. There are always several examples of these systems being unable to function as designed and the users being unaware of it. Eventually, these items get fixed, but only at great expense if the flaws are exposed during combat. The expense of these new systems and the shrinking budgets of the post-Soviet era, are forcing another practice on navies: upgrading older ships instead of building new ones. The design of warship structures has stabilized in the last 60 years. Meanwhile, weapons and sensors have become smaller as they have also gotten more powerful. If a ship is not heavily stressed, its hull and superstructure are good for 40 or more years of use. New weapons, sensors, and even engines can be added at half the cost of building new ships of equal capability. Even navies that use their ships heavily, like the United States', still get 30 years of use out of their hulls. Extensive upgrades are becoming an accepted practice and can be expected to grow in the future.

The 1991 Gulf War did not give navies as much of a workout as it did the air and ground forces. U.S. carrier aviation was shown to be capable, but behind the regular air forces in using the latest technology. That experience jarred the U.S. Navy into cooperating more energetically with the Air Force.

Most of the larger navies are looking more to their own territorial waters, something the U.S. Navy calls "littoral warfare." Since no one can challenge the American fleet on the high seas, any fighting is likely to take place close to shore. This means even the U.S. Navy is considering building new, smaller ships better able to deal with fighting in the shallow and crowded inshore waters.

Radical innovations in naval technology will be slow in coming. Meanwhile, the surface navy has yet to come to grips with nuclear submarines. It will take a major naval war to resolve the many unsettling questions raised by these new weapons. Until then, it will be more of the same, along with gradual innovations.

Naval Forces

SHIPS

Shown are the classes of combat ships in the U.S. and Russian navies, as well as selected ship classes from other navies for comparative purposes. The list is organized by class type and then each class alphabetically within the class.

Class type is a code indicating the size and function of the ship. Each nation tends to have a slightly different interpretation of what the commonly used (as least in the West) codes stand for. In order to bring a little order to this chaos, a single classification criterion has been applied the same way to ships of all nations. The more conventional letter designations are given in parentheses.

- *A* indicates aircraft carriers (CV, CVL, CVN, CVA, CVH), which vary in size from 12,000 displacement tons up to over 90,000 tons. These are the largest surface warships and are usually the centerpiece of a task force. Included are the helicopter carriers assigned to amphibious and antisubmarine operations. Normally, these ships carry helicopters for transporting Marines and their equipment ashore. But most of the helicopters have some weapons, and a few are heavily armed. It is also common to base some vertical takeoff fighters (Harriers) on these carriers.
- *B* is battleship (BB), displacing over 20,000 tons of water and capable of independent operation, although these are often the primary ship of a task force. This class of ships is likely finally to disappear in the next decade or so, about a century after they were first conceived and built.
- *C* is a cruiser-class ship (CA, CG, CL) of 5,000–20,000 tons displacement. Most are between 6,000–12,000 tons. Basically, these are smaller battleships with less of everything except speed. Cruisers also tend to specialize in something like antisubmarine, antiair, or surface combat. Cruisers sometimes operate with one or more other cruisers or destroyers in a small task force.
- *D* are destroyers (DD, DDG, FF, FFG), or 2,000–5,000 tons. These are escort ships for task forces and merchant ship convoys, ordinarily having an orientation toward anti-air or antisubmarine work. As antiship missiles have gotten smaller, the more recent destroyers usually have them.
- *E* are escort and patrol ships (DE, PH, PT, etc.), under 2,000 tons and typically found in coastal waters.
- *M* are ballistic missile boats (SSB, SSBN). These are almost all nuclear, as are an increasing percentage of the attack subs. Indeed, you can always tell if a ship is nuclear-powered by looking at its range. Those with the larger ranges are nuclear. Ms have torpedoes and sensors and can fight other ships but are not intended to do so except in emergencies.

Class type		Class name	# in class	Combat values Surf	Sub	Air	Prot.	Long	Wght
A	TH	Chakri Naruebet	1	11	10	10	6	182	11.5
A	FR	Clemenceau	1	30	0	12	6	265	33
A	FR	De Gaulle	1	35	0	25	7	262	41
A	U.S.	Enterprise	1	85	24	90	10	332	92
A	IT	Garibaldi	1	14	12	10	6	180	13.8
A	UK	Invincible	3	12	15	12	6	209	20.6
A	U.S.	Iwo Jima	0	2	0	6	3	183	18
A	U.S.	JFK	1	85	24	85	10	327	81
A	U.S.	Kitty Hawk	2	85	24	85	10	326	82
A	RU	Kuznetsov	1	54	22	8	8	306	59
A	BZ	Minas Gerais	1	8	8	10	5	212	19.9
A	U.S.	Nimitz	3	100	24	100	10	335	95
A	SP	Principe de Asturias	1	12	14	12	8	196	17.2
A	U.S.	Tarawa	5	4	0	8	4	254	40
A	U.S.	Theodore Roosevelt	5	100	24	100	10	333	98
A	IN	Viraat	1	10	12	8	5	209	28.7
A	U.S.	Wasp	6	4	0	8	4	257	40
B	RU	Kirov	1	30	10	10	5	251	26
C	PE	Almirante Grau	1	3	6	6	3	190	12.2
C	U.S.	Arleigh Burke	28	6	16	12	4	154	8.8
C	U.S.	Arleigh Burke II	2	6	16	12	4	155	9.2
C	U.S.	Belknap	0	4	10	5	2	167	7.9
C	U.S.	California	0	14	9	8	2	182	11.1
C	IT	De La Penne	2	6	4	3	3	148	5.4
C	IN	Delhi	3	5	4	2	2	163	6.7
C	JP	Haruna	2	4	3	3	2	153	5
C	JP	Hatakaze	2	6	3	3	2	150	5.5
C	CA	Iroquois	4	1	4	3	2	130	5.1
C	RU	Kara	1	3	6	4	2	174	8.5
C	U.S.	Kidd	0	4	14	4	2	161	8.4
C	JP	Kongo	4	24	12	18	3	161	9.4
C	RU	Krivak II	0	40	22	6	6	273	3.6
C	RU	Kynda	1	5	2	1	1	143	5.3
C	U.S.	Leahy	0	3	6	5	2	162	7.8
C	U.S.	Long Beach	0	3	8	4	4	220	17.1
C	CH	Luhai	2	5	3	1	3	143	6.6
C	JP	Murasame	3	4	3	3	2	151	5.1
C	JP	Shirane	2	1	3	3	2	159	5.2
C	RU	Slava	3	3	10	6	2	186	11.2
C	RU	Sovremenny	7	6	7	3	2	156	8.5
C	U.S.	Spruance	24	6	16	2	2	172	9.2
C	FR	Suffern	2	2	5	4	2	158	6.9
C	U.S.	Ticonderoga	27	30	14	20	3	172	9.5
C	FR	Tourville	3	6	3	3	3	153	5.9
C	RU	Udaloy	7	3	12	6	2	163	8.4
C	RU	Udaloy II	1	3	12	6	2	150	8.9
C	U.S.	Virginia	0	12	12	8	2	178	10

Speed	Range	EW	Guns	Air-craft	SAM	SSM	TT	Class end build	Crew
52	20	4	4	12	4	0	0	1997	1,375
64	12	5	0	36	4	0	0	1963	1,338
54	200	7	8	40	6	0	0	2000	1,950
61	200	8	3	70	3	0	0	1961	5,800
60	11	5	6	11	2	8	6	1985	825
56	14	6	8	27	0	0	0	1985	1,050
41	18	2	6	25	2	0	0	1970	685
54	8	8	3	70	3	0	0	1968	5,000
54	16	8	3	71	3	0	0	1961	5,100
58	24	7	8	45	32	12	0	1991	2,626
48	24	5	0	16	2	0	0	1945	1,300
56	200	9	3	70	3	0	0	1982	5,900
50	13	6	4	18	0	0	0	1988	760
43	20	4	2	26	2	0	0	1980	940
56	200	9	4	71	3	0	0	1998	5,900
56	20	4	4	20	0	0	0	1959	1,350
43	19	4	5	38	2	0	0	1994	1,080
64	28	8	10	3	14	20	10	1998	655
64	14	3	16	0	8	0	0	1953	953
60	8.8	9	3	0	61	37	6	1999	337
60	8.8	9	3	2	48	48	6	2000	380
57	14	5	5	1	2	8	8	1967	477
54	200	6	4	0	2	8	12	1975	600
62	14	6	4	2	1	8	6	1993	377
56	13	6	5	2	2	16	5	2001	360
62	NA	5	4	3	1	0	14	1973	340
60	NA	5	4	1	1	8	14	1987	260
54	9	4	2	2	1	0	6	1973	322
65	14	4	8	1	4	8	10	1974	380.
59	12	6	4	0	4	8	10	1982	360
60	9	7	3	1	1	8	7	1998	340
60	23	7	12	35	4	8	36	1988	840
68	12	2	4	0	1	2	6	1964	304
57	14	4	6	0	4	8	14	1964	423
54	200	4	4	1	4	8	14	1961	958
58	28	5	6	2	1	16	6	2001	250
60	9	6	3	1	1	8	7	2002	170
62	NA	4	4	3	1	0	14	1981	360
65	12	6	8	1	12	16	8	1989	481
66	12	5	8	1	2	8	4	1994	296
64	16	7	4	1	1	61	6	1983	334
68	6.9	4	6	0	2	4	4	1970	355
58	12	8	4	2	2	8	6	1994	364
64	10	5	4	2	1	6	2	1977	300
59.4	12	6	6	2	8	8	8	1991	220
59.4	12	6	4	2	8	8	8	1999	296
58	200	7	2	2	4	8	4	1980	570

Class type		Class name	# in class	Combat values		Air	Prot.	Long	Wght
				Surf	Sub				
D	AR	Almirante Brown	4	3	3	3	1	126	3.4
D	JP	Asagiri	8	3	3	3	2	137	4.2
D	IT	Audace	2	3	3	3	1	137	4.4
D	FR	Cassard	2	3	3	3	2	139	4.7
D	JP	Hatsuyuki	12	3	4	3	1	130	3.8
D	RU	Kashin	1	3	3	2	1	132	4.5
D	RU	Kashin II	1	3	3	2	1	146	4.9
D	U.S.	Knox	0	2	20	3	1	134	3.9
D	RU	Krivak	7	0	1	3	1	123	3.4
D	RU	Krivak II	7	0	1	3	1	125	3.3
D	FR	Leygues	7	2	3	2	2	139	4.6
D	CH	Luda I	13	3	1	1	1	132	3.5
D	CH	Luda II	2	3	2	2	1	132	3.5
D	CH	Luda III	1	3	1	1	1	132	3.5
D	CH	Luhu	2	3	3	2	1	143	4.2
D	RU	Neustrashimyy	1	3	5	3	2	130	4.2
D	U.S.	Perry	25	2	12	3	1	139	3.6
D	JP	Tachikaze	3	3	2	2	2	143	3.9
D	JP	Takasuki	2	3	3	3	1	136	3.5
D	JP	Yamagumo	3	1	2	1	1	115	2.3
E	RU	Dergach	2	3	2	1	1	65	0.9
E	RU	Grisha II	27	0	1	1	1	71	1.1
E	RU	Matka	0	0	1	0	1	82	1.2
E	RU	Mirka II	0	0	2	0	1	82	1.1
E	RU	Nanuchka	20	3	0	1	1	59	0.7
E	RU	Parchim II	12	2	0	1	1	75	0.9
E	RU	Tarantul	29	2	0	1	1	56	0.5
M	RU	Delta I	2	2	8	0	6	155	10.5
M	RU	Delta III	8	2	8	0	6	155	10.6
M	RU	Delta IV	7	2	8	0	6	167	11.7
M	U.S.	Franklin	1	8	16	0	9	130	7.3
M	U.S.	Lafayette	0	8	16	0	9	130	7.2
M	U.S.	Ohio	18	8	14	0	9	171	16.7
M	RU	Typhoon	2	0	8	0	6	173	23.2
N	RU	Akula	8	20	24	0	8	110	8
N	RU	Foxtrot	0	2	10	0	2	92	2
N	RU	Kilo	12	2	9	1	2	74	2.4
N	U.S.	Los Angeles 688	20	10	20	0	8	110	6.1
N	U.S.	Los Angeles 719	8	20	40	0	10	110	6.2
N	U.S.	Los Angeles 751	23	24	48	0	10	110	6.3
N	RU	Oscar II	8	20	8	0	6	154	14.7
N	U.S.	Seawolf	2	30	60	0	12	108	7.5
N	RU	Sierra	3	20	8	0	6	107	6.3
N	U.S.	Sturgeon	0	16	25	0	9	89	4.3
N	RU	Tango	0	2	9	1	2	73	2.4
N	RU	Victor III	7	10	16	0	8	106	7
N	RU	Yankee	1	12	7	0	4	103	4.3

Speed	Range	EW	Guns	Air-craft	SAM	SSM	TT	Class end build	Crew
61	9	3	5	2	1	8	6	1984	200
60	NA	5	3	1	1	8	10	1991	220
68	6	4	4	2	1	8	6	1972	380
59	16	5	3	1	3	8	2	1991	244
60	NA	5	3	1	1	8	14	1987	170
68	7	1	2	0	2	0	5	1969	288
64	10	1	8	0	2	4	5	1974	330
48	8	5	1	1	1	1	12	1974	280
61	10	1	4	0	2	4	8	1980	190
61	8	1	2	0	2	4	8	1981	181
60	17	5	5	2	1	4	2	1990	244
72	6	3	12	0	0	6	8	1991	280
72	6	3	8	2	1	6	8	1991	280
72	6	3	12	0	2	6	8	1991	280
62	10	6	6	2	1	8	8	1995	230
64	12	3	3	1	4	0	6	1993	210
58	10	6	4	1	1	1	6	1989	214
64	NA	5	4	0	1	8	14	1983	250
62	14	3	2	0	1	8	14	1968	260
54	14	3	4	0	0	0	14	1978	220
106	5	1	3	0	1	8	0	1986	65
64	8	1	2	0	1	0	4	1994	86
54	9	1	4	0	0	0	14	1972	100
61.2	9	1	4	0	0	0	12	1967	100
68	8	1	2	0	1	6	0	1991	51
49	4	1	2	0	2	0	4	1995	80
63	5	1	3	0	1	4	0	1995	41
43.2	200	6	0	0	0	16	6	1982	120
48	200	6	0	0	0	16	6	1979	130
48	200	6	0	0	0	16	4	1992	135
45	200	6	0	0	0	0	4	1974	211
45	200	6	0	0	0	16	4	1974	143
45	200	6	0	0	0	24	4	1996	163
50	200	6	0	0	0	20	6	1989	179
66	200	6	0	0	1	0	8	2000	73
32.4	36	1	0	0	0	0	10	1973	75
40	15	2	0	0	1	0	6	1993	52
54	200	6	0	0	0	0	4	1985	141
72	200	9	0	0	0	12	4	1989	164
72	200	9	0	0	0	16	4	1996	164
62	200	6	0	0	0	24	6	1997	107
80	200	12	0	0	0	0	8	1998	133
66	200	6	0	0	1	0	8	1993	60
63	200	7	0	0	0	4	4	1975	129
36	24	2	0	0	2	0	6	1995	53
62	200	2	0	0	0	0	6	1992	96
54	200	5	0	0	0	8	6	1985	90

- *N* are nuclear and nonnuclear attack submarines, types SS, SSG, SSN, and SSGN.

Not included are ships under 100 tons (including minesweepers and minelayers, which are sometimes larger). These are little more than seagoing police cars. What antisubmarine gear some of them have is largely ineffective against modern subs. Some also have lightweight surface-to-air missiles. Russia and China have the largest number of these small boats, several hundred, in fact. Some boats in this class have antiship missiles. These are included in the E class above.

Class name is the name of the lead ship of a group of generally identical ships. The ships of that class are normally referred to by the name of the first ship built. For example, a "*Spruance*-class ship" is a reference to a class of U.S. destroyers in which the first one built was called the *Spruance*. Although ships in a class are built according to the same set of plans, modifications occur to individual ships as the class gets larger and/or older. When the differences become too large, a new class is created. This is shown on the chart.

 # in class is the number in that class as of 2001. In some cases, a number of the ships in a class are in reserve—no crew, just a minimal number of technicians to do essential maintenance, like ensuring that key components remain in working order and any weather damage is quickly repaired.

Combat values are numerical evaluations of the ship's combat capabilities against surface ships (SURF), submarines (SUB), and air (AIR) targets. These values take into account the quality and quantity of onboard weapons, equipment, and crew, as well as past performance. The most critical factor is the quality of crew training and leadership.

Prot. is the protection value of that ship against attacks from enemy weapons. For submarines, this includes the difficulty other ships and subs have in detecting it. This is a function of sub quietness, diving depth, displacement, hull arrangement, and countermeasures. For surface ships, these values suggest the number of major weapon hits the ship would have to receive before it was no longer capable of combat.

Long is the ship's length in meters. This and weight (below) pretty much define how large the ship is.

Wght (weight) is the ship's full-load displacement in thousands of tons. For submarines, it is surface displacement. The term displacement refers to the weight of water the ship displaces when it is floating on the surface. I know it sounds complicated, but it is the common term used. If you want to deal with the Navy, learn to speak its language.

Speed is top speed in kilometers per hour. Rarely used except in emergencies it is also rarely achieved except when the engines and hull are in top shape. These conditions decline the longer a ship is at sea and/or in action. At that point, top speed declines 10–20 percent. Efficient cruising speed tends to be one-half to two-thirds of top speed.

Range is the unrefueled range in thousands of kilometers, at a cruise speed of between 20–30 kilometers an hour. This is quite slow for wartime activities, and task forces normally cruise at 50 kilometers an hour or even faster. This can reduce range by up to 50 percent. Nuclear ships' range is shown as 200,000 kilometers. In many cases it can be up to five times this before the nuclear reactor's fuel must be replaced. The range given is what most nuclear boats would have at the beginning of a war. Note that the Navy has their own units of distance (nautical mile, which equals 1.8 kilometers) and speed (knot, equal to one nautical mile per hour). Most landlubbers (and some sailors) use kilometers. So will we.

EW is the effectiveness of the ship's electronics in general and its electronic-warfare capabilities in particular. The higher the number, the better.

Guns is the number of gun systems the ship mounts. Multibarrel Gatling types (used against cruise missiles) count as one gun. Almost all guns are under 128mm and are used primarily for air defense.

Aircraft is the number of helicopters and fixed-wing aircraft on board. Smaller ships only carry helicopters.

SAM is surface-to-air missile launchers carried. This is sometimes misleading, as most launchers have magazines, and the launcher is capable of firing a dozen or more missiles in one engagement.

SSM is surface-to-surface missile launchers. These are usually one-shot affairs.

TT is the number of tubes for launching torpedoes (TT). Modern submarines have 4–10 torpedo tubes on board, with twice as many on surface ships armed with torpedoes. Many Russian ships still use depth charge throwers (DCT), a remarkably ineffective weapon against nuclear subs, although still of some use against Russia's own large fleet of nonnuclear subs. Figure that one out.

Class end build is the year in which the last ship of that class was built. This indicates how up-to-date that class is. This is very true with Russian and non-Western ships, as Western navies tend to upgrade their ships every 10 years or so. The Russians simply build a new class in most cases. Dates later than 2001 usually indicate that the class is still being built.

Crew is the number of sailors in the crew.

WARSHIP DESIGN

Warship design is a game of compromises. You never have enough money to get everything you want out of a new ship design. From a designer's point of view, three classes of ship exist; submarines, aircraft carriers, and surface combat ships. This last class also includes lightly armed supply and amphibious ships. All warships are basically cargo vessels in which weapons replace wheat and iron ore. Aircraft carriers carry tremendous quantities of fuel and munitions (over 10,000 tons), plus up to a hundred aircraft. Submarines require a large number of mechanical and hydraulic systems to allow them to operate under water.

As an example of the compromises you must make when designing a warship, let us consider the tradeoffs that go into designing your typical surface combat vessel. You must consider:

Weight. Metal costs money, as does the labor to assemble it. Normally, 40–45 percent of the ship's weight goes to the structure: the hull and superstructure. This is up to 40 percent more than merchant ships, largely because of greater compartmentalization and, sometimes, armor.

Power plant. Another 20–25 percent goes to the main power plant. This is more than twice what a merchant ship requires, as a combat ship requires more speed. Some 15–30 percent goes to auxiliary machinery and equipment. Merchant ships have very little of this because combat ships have a lot of additional equipment to support.

Weapons. From 6–14 percent goes to an item merchantmen completely dispense with: weapons. For a warship, this last item is the cargo. For a merchant ship, over 50 percent of the ship weight will be cargo.

The distribution of cost is quite different from weight, primarily because silicon for electronics is more expensive than metal. The structure normally accounts for 15–20 percent of the total ship cost. The main power plant takes up 10–15 percent. Weapons and sensors amount to between 50–65 percent of cost. And that is why a warship will cost three or more times a ton as much as a merchant ship. Ways can be found to save money, if you are willing to sacrifice certain features. The most obvious area is space: make the ship smaller without reducing the equipment and weapons you want to put in it. The catch is that what is in the ship must be squeezed more closely together. A typical Western ship has 20 percent more internal volume than a comparable Russian-designed vessel. The Russians coped by putting more weapons topside, on the deck. They allot less space for equipment access, passageways, internal bulkheads, and work areas. This has serious repercussions in combat as well as during peacetime operations. A U.S. vessel allocates 12 percent of its space to access versus 8 percent for a Russian ship. Stores occupy 12 percent versus between 2–4 percent in Russian ships. Fifty percent (3 versus 2 percent) more space is allocated to ship control. Ironically, Western ships devote somewhat less space to personnel. Western ships tend to have smaller crews because of greater automation. The Western crew quarters are more comfortable, with amenities like air conditioning. Even though the Russians devote a bit more space to crew quarters, it is less efficiently laid out and less comfortable.

The Western warship design tradition is based on extensive World War II experience, particularly that of the U.S. and British navies. This experience showed what would work and what wouldn't. However, experience is perishable. New technology and conditions intrude. To not change is to court disaster. Yet every change made without combat experience is a risk, a risk that must be taken. Many things have not changed since World War II. Ships still require a lot of space to store spares, test equipment, and tools. While at sea, even the availability of helicopters to rush in critical parts and supplies is not always adequate. For most of this century, sailors have had to be very resourceful just to keep the increasing amount of equipment functioning.

The Russians have tried to rewrite the book in this area by cutting out a lot of the space used for workshops and parts storage. Part of the reason for this move is the lack of skilled sailors to allow them to operate at the same level as Western navies. Most Russian sailors are short-term draftees; most Western sailors are careerists. As a result, it's long been a common sight to see a Russian ship riding at anchor in the middle of nowhere because critical systems are broken and incapable of repair with the resources at hand. When it's a submarine, we sometimes hear about it. But it happens just as frequently with their surface ships and aircraft. But this problem is worse than it appears. This additional space in Western ships is also used in combat to give access to damaged areas. This makes damage control easier and can spell the difference between saving or losing the ship. Some of this "extra" space is also devoted to more watertight compartments, additional pumps, and redundant plumbing and power-control systems. At the end of the Cold War, some of the new Russian ship designs showed acceptance of Western ideas. Ships were more spacious and built for more sea time and reliability. But the demise of the Soviet Union meant that far fewer Russian ships could afford to go anywhere anymore. By 2001, Russian warships were again making long voyages. The only area of warship building that remains active in Russia is for submarines, and here the Russians are producing stuff that is similar to, and often competitive with, Western boats.

A major departure from World War II ship design is the near disappearance of armor. This freed up a substantial amount of space on the larger (than destroyer) ships. Western ships took up this space for additional damage control and maintenance facilities. The Russians added a few more weapons. All of this gives them what appear to be smaller and more heavily armed ships. On the minus side, these ships are less capable of keeping all their equipment functional in peacetime or recovering from battle damage. All this is in line with the doctrine developed by Russia over the centuries. It is their land forces' doctrine transferred to the sea. It maintains that initial all-out attacks are more important than the ability to carry on a protracted conflict. It is a risky gamble. But then, defeat at sea is less calamitous for a land-based power like Russia. This "risky gamble" approach, however, does appeal to many smaller nations that simply cannot afford a protracted war. These countries buy Russian ships because they are cheaper, are built to be run by less skillful sailors, and give the biggest bang for the buck in a short war.

The latest trend in ship design is the automated ship. This approach uses the automation techniques developed for commercial ships over the last few decades. This allows the crews to be quite minimal, as in a few dozen for the largest container ships or tankers (over 250,000 tons). Russia and several European navies have been applying these automation technologies to warships, a few at a time. One problem is that you need more skilled sailors to run an automated ship. Since the Russians still use conscripts, they have had to man their most automated ships (like their newer subs) primarily with officers (including warrant officers, technical guys with no command responsibilities). The Akula-class nuclear subs have a crew of about 80 that is 40 percent officers, 40 percent warrant officers, and 20 percent enlisted men (to do the cooking and cleaning). The one problem with smaller crews on more automated warships is damage control. When a ship is damaged in combat, by definition, a lot of the equipment is destroyed or damaged. You need a lot of manpower to save the ship (putting out fires, patching holes in the hull, and repairing essential systems like engines and electricity). In theory, you can automate a lot of the damage control. This is what is done on commercial ships. But those vessels do not receive the same kind of abuse that warships get. What bothers naval officers is that automated damage control is new and not battle-tested. It's very expensive (too expensive for any navy to afford) to test thoroughly such a radical change in warship design. But a growing shortage of sailors is forcing the issue. Even merchant ships are having a hard time finding enough sailors. So more automation is coming, like it or not.

Naval Weapons

This chart shows the principal weapons used by naval vessels. Except for missiles, no attempt is made to show every example of each weapon type. This list is adequate because most other naval weapons have very similar characteristics and effects.

Weapon is the designation of the weapon. Most of the weapons are missiles, but some torpedoes, depth charge launchers, and guns are also shown. Each category is discussed in greater detail below. Weapons are grouped according to their country of origin. Most of these weapons are used by allies of the manufacturing country.

Range is the effective range of the weapon in kilometers. Anything over 40–50 kilometers is "over the (radar) horizon" and needs to have its target located accurately (by someone closer to the target than the missile launcher) before launching the missile. The "line of sight" from the uppermost part of a ship to the horizon varies with the size of the ship. For smaller ships, it's 10–12 kilometers. For the largest ships, it's 24–30 kilometers. Aircraft and the tops of large ships can be seen farther away because they "pop up" from "below the horizon."

Weight is the launch weight of the weapon in pounds. The lighter it is, more a ship or aircraft can carry, or the smaller a vehicle can carry it. With the exception of guns, these weapons are launched from a rather light apparatus, either a container or a rail.

Speed is the average speed of the projectile in meters per second. The faster a weapon, the more difficult it is to evade or destroy. One hundred meters per second equals 360 kilometers an hour, or 225 miles per hour, or 330 feet per second. A rifle bullet travels at about 1,000 meters per second.

Guidance is an evaluation of the weapon's guidance system on a 1-to-9 scale. The higher the better. These evaluations also take into account the sensors of the launch vehicle, as well as those in the missile itself, if any.

Impact power is the destructive power of the weapon, taking into account the accuracy of the guidance system and the destructive power of a nonnuclear, nonchemical warhead. Nuclear warheads will almost always destroy their target, even in a near miss. Missiles that always carry a nuclear warhead are indicated with an N. Chemical weapons will not destroy a ship, but will make the crew uncomfortable or dead if the poison chemicals are not promptly dealt with. Most missile weapons have a warhead containing 100–500 pounds of

Weapon	Range (km)	Weight (lbs)	Speed (mps)	Guid- ance	Impact power	Launched from	Torpedo tube	IOC
Russia								
P-15 SSN-2B	40	5,500	250	2	12	S	No	1958
P-21 SSN-2C	80	6,000	250	3	14	S	No	1967
P-35 SSN-3B	190	12,000	450	3	45	S,U	No	1962
P-70 SSN-7	65	7,700	250	4	38	U	No	1968
P-120 SSN-9	80	6,600	250	5	16	S	No	1969
P-500 SSN-12	500	11,000	800	4	36	U	No	1973
RPK-3 SSN-14	50	3,500	300	3	10	S	No	1969
RPK-4 SSN-15	45	4,000	400	3	23	U	Yes	1972
RPK-6 SSN-16	100	4,000	400	4	23	U	Yes	1972
P-700 SSN-19	500	10,000	800	6	23	S,U	No	1981
3K10 SSN-21	1600	3,800	210	5	15	U	Yes	1990
P-270 SSN-22	110	6,000	800	6	21	S	No	1981
Kh-35 SSN-25	120	1,600	300	6	16	S	No	1988
P-800 SSN-27	300	5,900	210	6	22	S	Yes	1997
MBU 1200	1.2	400	200	2	4	S	No	1964
MBU 6000	6	500	200	2	5	S	No	1970
China								
HY-1 CSSC-2	40	5,000	250	2	15	S	No	1974
HY-2 CSSC-3	95	6,500	250	3	16	S	No	1975
YJ-16 CSSC-5	100	4,000	570	4	16	A,S	No	1996
HY-3 CSSC-6	150	7,500	560	4	22	S	No	2003
HY-4 CSSC-7	120	3,800	500	4	16	A,S	No	1982
YJ-2 CSSC-8	120	1,500	250	5	16	A,S,U	Yes	1990
France								
Exocet	40	1,620	300	7	15	A,S	No	1981
U.S.								
Tomahawk	450	2,700	240	8	30	S,U	Yes	1984
Harpoon	110	3,200	280	8	21	A,S,U	Yes	1977
ASROC	10	959	400	4	15	S	No	1961
Torpedo Mk 48	46	3,500	25	8	20	U	Yes	1972
Torpedo Mk 46	8	565	25	6	8	S,A	Yes	1965
Torpedo Mk 50	12	750	22	8	15	S,A	Yes	2000
Various								
Gun, 76mm	15	14	900	2	1	S	No	NA
Gun, 127mm	23	70	800	2	5	S	No	NA

explosives. A 4,000-pound missile causes considerable damage even if its warhead does not explode. Cruise missiles have an additional advantage in that some of them have rocket motors that keep burning over most of the missile's flight. If the missile is fired at a shorter range, and the missile hits a ship while the motor is still burning, the motor acts like a blowtorch inside the target ship and adds an incendiary effect to the damage done by the exploding warhead. In some cases, where the cruise missile's warhead failed to explode, the missile's still-burning rocket motor caused considerable damage. Even in U.S. cruise missiles, which use small jet engines, there is often unburned fuel remaining when they hit.

Launched from indicates the type of platforms the weapon can be launched from. S = surface ship; U = submarine; A = aircraft. The same weapon launched from an aircraft will have a slightly longer range than a surface launch because it starts at a higher altitude. The air-launched versions are covered in the aircraft-weapons chart. Many of these weapons also have coastal defense versions, which are essentially the naval launcher mounted on land.

Torpedo tube indicates whether a weapon can be launched from a submarine torpedo tube. This is largely a Western concept, which allows a greater variety of weapons to be used in a submarine without additional modification. Most Soviet submarine missiles have special launch facilities in their subs. Often the boat is specially built for a particular missile. Note that American subs can launch torpedoes, mines, tactical and strategic cruise missiles, and antisubmarine rockets from their torpedo tubes.

IOC (Initial Operational Capability) indicates the year the weapon was first in service.

Weapon Types

Missiles. The Soviet Union pioneered the use of antiship missiles. Once the Western nations awoke to the potential of these new weapons, they soon overwhelmed the Soviet models with superior technology. Despite this, the Soviets persisted and left the successor states of the Soviet Union with a wide variety of systems. For example, the P-15 first went to sea in 1958, and the improved P-21 is still in use in some less affluent nations. The follow-up on the P-21 was the P-70 and P-120. These were initially developed for specially designed submarines, although the P-120 replaced the P-21 in new classes of small missile boats since 1969. In 1981, another short-range antiship missile, the P-270, entered service. In 1988, an Exocet clone, the Kh-35, appeared. As the Soviets realized the tactical problems of short-range missiles, they devoted most of their efforts to longer-range models. The first long-range missile, the P-35, was first deployed in 1962 as a strategic weapon. It was replaced in this role by ballistic missiles in the 1960s and 1970s. The P-35 continues in use to this day as an antiship missile. In 1973, the P-70 was deployed on Echo-class submarines, and later on Kiev- and Slava-class surface ships. In 1981, the P-700 was deployed on the large Oscar-class submarines and Kirov-class battleships. In 1987, the Soviets began deploying land-attack cruise missiles (3K10) that could be launched from torpedo tubes (26-inch, rather the U.S. standard 21-inch tubes). A longer-range cruise missile (Kh-35) appeared in 1990 but was too large for torpedo tubes. The United States deployed its first antiship missile (Harpoon) in 1977, although it had a superior version of the P-35 in service before the P-35 appeared. America refrained for doctrinal reasons from producing these missiles. They didn't think they needed antiship missiles. They did produce missiles for going after submarines (ASROC and SUBROC), which the Soviets were not able to duplicate for over 10 years.

Other Western nations produced antiship missiles before the United States. Western antiship missiles quickly surpassed their Soviet counterparts. Aside from being smaller, lighter, and more reliable, Western missiles could be launched from a wider variety of platforms. The Harpoon and Tomahawk can be launched from aircraft, surface ships, and submarines. This keeps the cost of production down and makes training and maintenance easier. By the late 1980s, the U.S. Navy had over 1,500 antiship missile launchers. Despite post–Cold War cutbacks, the number of antiship missiles in use has stayed about the same. Allied U.S. navies have nearly as many. Western missiles, in general, are more reliable and have longer range and greater accuracy than Russian designs.

While most Russian missiles are inferior to Western models, they are still lethal against a ship that is not well defended. Most exported Russian missiles equip small coastal patrol boats in Third World navies. This can be a lethal combination against unprepared Western warships. The most modern Russian missiles have long enough range and high enough speed to make an attack on enemy ships a real threat. In the face of such an attack, the best defense is countermeasures. This is accomplished by jamming the three forms of terminal homing that missiles use to hit their target. For example, an active radar spots the shape of a ship and homes in on it. Radar can be jammed by sending signals to it making the target appear somewhere else. A more crude form of jamming simply electronically fuzzes up the signal, or throws up a cloud of metal foil strips (chaff) for the same effect. The missile may detect this form of jamming and switch to a radar homing system. This, in turn, can also be confused by turning the ship's radars off, or having a helicopter hover near the ship with an electronic "noisemaker" hanging below it. If the missile detects these deceptions, it can use infrared homing to home in on the heat thrown off by a ship. The ship can fox the infrared by firing off flares. Last, the target ship can use high-speed cannon to shoot the missile down during its last few seconds of flight. All of this seeking and jamming goes on during the last five or ten seconds of a missile's flight. With so much to be done in so little time, speed, accuracy, miniaturization, and reliability become the arbiters of success. The one item most used on both sides of this contest is a computer. In this area the West holds a commanding and increasing lead. Evidence of this can be seen in smaller Western nations developing credible antiship missiles. Both Norway and Israel have done this. Larger nations like France have created Exocet.

Russia is energetically selling its antiship missiles to anyone who will pay cash. The market isn't that large, as most nations prefer Western missiles, which have better reputations. Moreover, it's no secret that Russian missile manufacturers are in dire financial shape. Countries like Iran and China take advantage of this by buying lots of Russian missiles at very attractive prices. The Chinese also bought manufacturing rights and build their own. All of the Chinese missiles make heavy use of Russian technology. The HY series is often referred to in the press as "Silkworm" missiles.

Subroc (for use by submarines, withdrawn from service in 1990) and ASROC (for surface ships) are really nothing but rockets carrying torpedoes or depth charges. Sensors give an approximate location of the submarine, hopefully out of torpedo range. The missile is programmed to fly to the location and then, depending on the type of missile, release a nuclear depth charge or a homing torpedo. The depth charge has to be nuclear because a conventional depth charge can damage a sub only within 30 meters of its detonation. A nuclear depth charge is good for 300 meters. Homing torpedoes are even better, as these can run search patterns in a circle several kilometers in diameter. Russia introduced its own versions of ASROC and SUBROC in the 1970s and 1980s. Only the ASROC remains in service, but only with non-U.S. navies.

Torpedoes. These were the first ship-to-ship missiles. They first sliced through the water over a century ago, maintaining a steady course toward their typically unaware targets. Eight years later, in 1877, they were first used in combat. Another 16 years were to pass before they actually hit anything in combat. Considering this record, we may consider torpedoes the first high-tech weapon. Nearly 60 years ago, torpedoes acquired the ability to home in on the propeller noise of their targets. Torpedoes have steadily become more capable ever since. The three models shown are all of U.S. manufacture and are representative of most torpedoes in use today. The top of the line is the Mk 48. This is an exceptionally capable weapon, and no other navy is likely to have anything like it. The Mk 48 is the current outer limit of torpedo technology. The range can be increased, but this is only useful if the torpedo's sensors can detect the target at that range. This problem is currently solved by a wire extending from the torpedo to the launching ship. The ship guides the torpedo until it is close enough for the torpedo's own sensors to finish the job. This is a common mode of operation for the long-range Mk 48. Against submarines that can travel as fast as a regular torpedo, you need a weapon that is extremely fast, accurate, and quiet. Although torpedoes are still nominally useful against surface ships, in most cases warships will not allow a submarine close enough to launch. More and more, torpedoes are seen as a weapon against submarines or merchant shipping. Through the 1980s, a troublesome problem with using torpedoes against submarines was the increasing bulk and multiple hulls of recent subs. The Russians experimented with titanium hulls, strong enough to withstand enormous depths. This strength may also allow a sub to take one or more torpedo hits and keep going. All of this is theoretical and/or speculative. Only actual combat circumstances will reveal what the true situation is, and that is now unlikely for some time to come. The Mk 46 and Mk 50 are light-weight torpedoes used by helicopters and surface ships. These are generally used against submarines.

Depth-charge launchers (MBU 1200, MBU 6000). These are an elderly but still effective means of destroying submarines, especially diesel-electric boats. They are less effective against nuclear subs. The operation of depth charges is quite simple. A barrel of explosive, set to explode at a certain depth, is dropped from the rear of a ship or fired outward by rocket. The charges are used in quantity, according to a pattern thought likely to hit the sub. These weapons are highly dependent on the ship's sensors locating where the sub is and, more important, where it will be once the charges are launched. Nuclear subs are rather sturdy creatures and would require a lot more hits by depth charges before they succumbed. They are still used by less well-equipped navies.

Guns. With the proliferation of rather bulky missiles, not much space has been left on ships for the more traditional guns. Those that remain are generally 20mm–40mm, 3-inch (76mm) or 5-inch (127mm) weapons. The smaller ones are often made completely automatic and are actually machine cannon. These weapons are turned on when there is danger of enemy cruise missiles. The automatic cannon will seek out and shoot at any object that moves, like a cruise missile. See the chart on air-defense weapons for more details. Otherwise, guns can still be effective if you can get close enough to use them.

10

The Navy:
Run Silent, Run Deep

If you have the faith of a true believer and the passion of a zealot, you have the makings of a submariner. Consider the working conditions. You never see, hear, or smell the enemy. Everything is done through instruments. If you make a mistake and the enemy gains an advantage, there's no place to run. Your battlefield is a metal cylinder tapered at both ends. It is 200–600 feet long and 20–40 feet in diameter. You can move in only one-third of this volume; the rest is crammed with equipment, weapons, supplies, and the rest of the crew. In spite of the above, submarines have become the premier naval weapon in the last 50 years. Why? There are a number of key reasons:

Ability to hide. Once submerged, a submarine cannot be easily detected. Even other submarines have a hard time of it. The sea is an excellent place to get lost, and stay lost.

Nuclear power. Until nuclear power came along, only a small-capacity power plant could be crammed into a submarine's limited space. Nuclear power plants were compact and generated enormous power. Nuclear subs could stay submerged as long as they wanted. Power was available to extract air and drinkable water from the sea. Indeed, one of the few drawbacks of nuclear engines was that there was too much power. The noise of the pumps needed to keep the power plant cool made nuclear subs nosier, and easier to detect, than the older diesel-electric boats. This has changed with some of the more recent nuclear boats, especially British ones.

Improved sensors. About the same time combat nuclear-power plants were developed, technology made similar breakthroughs in electronics, computers, and sensors. Submarines were no longer half-blind. Surface ships could now be detected farther away than radar could spot them.

Improved weapons. More accurate and longer-range torpedoes, as well as missiles, have extended the submarines' reach. No longer is it necessary to look through a periscope before firing.

Modern Submarine Design

Submarines are seagoing ships capable of moving and fighting underwater. They are designed around a pressure hull, a steel tube strong enough to withstand water pressure at depths from 200–1,000 meters or more. Outside the pressure hull are water tanks that are filled and emptied to lower and raise the sub in the water. A metal shell, which is what we usually see when we look at a sub, covers the pressure hull and water tanks. Submarines differ in the following characteristics:

Size. Size is a disadvantage. Bigger boats are easier to find. When the mission of the sub and the size of the required equipment are large, you end up with a large boat. Larger boats are also harder to kill. The largest Soviet boats have double hulls and wide distance between the hulls. It's not known how effective Western torpedoes will be in getting one-shot kills. Other Soviet subs have been built with titanium hulls to obtain deeper diving performance. These hulls may also provide some invulnerability to lightweight torpedoes. Weights of modern subs range from under 1,000 tons to over 16,000 tons of surface displacement. The heaviest subs are nearly 600 feet long and 40 feet in diameter. The smallest are 180 feet long and 20 feet in diameter. Crew sizes range from 30–140 men.

Propulsion. Although nuclear power revolutionized submarine design, it did not completely displace the older diesel-electric-powered subs. These boats, first introduced at the turn of the century, used a diesel engine for surface cruising and batteries for underwater work. The diesels require a lot of fuel, and the batteries are heavy, dangerous, and require recharging on or near the surface at least six or eight hours a day. Recent models do have the capacity to run silently underwater for up to 72 hours. Up through World War II, submarines spent nearly all their time on the surface and could not travel underwater for more than a few hours. Diesel-electric boats are not very fast. Nuclear boats can stay at sea longer than diesel-electric subs, which are cramped and uncomfortable. A nuclear boat can steam over 200,000 kilometers before needing to replenish its nuclear fuel. The chief advantage of diesel-electric boats is that they are cheaper, smaller, and generally superior for coastal defense. They carry the same torpedoes and, if they get off the first shot, can defeat a nuclear boat.

Weapons and sensors. Western submarines have the usual technical advantages over Soviet boats. Beyond that, not everyone can afford the best that money can buy. The most modern sensor system on U.S. subs weighs over 40 tons and costs over $200 million. Substantial differences exist between the nuclear boats of a nation. New classes often implement vastly improved systems that are too expensive to refit older boats with. A big problem with diesel-electric boats is that they cannot use all their sensors as often as the nuclear subs. Nonnuclear boats can cruise underwater for a short time, and that's the only time they can use their more effective underwater sensors. In 1943 the snort (snorkel) was introduced. This allowed subs to cruise at periscope depth. This made the subs harder to spot, but running on the noisy diesels made sensors ineffective and the crew uncomfortable.

A Submarine's Weapons

The earliest subs used torpedoes, mines, and a deck gun as their main weapons. The gun was a practical recognition of the diesel-electric boat's status as a small surface ship that could submerge briefly to sneak up on its victims or evade a more powerful adversary. The introduction of better sensors and torpedoes has eliminated the need for a deck gun. Mines are still carried whenever the situation calls for them. Currently, "torpedoes with brains" and missiles are the principal submarine weapons. Improved technology allows underwater sensors to detect targets over 100 kilometers away. At ranges of up to 50 kilometers, accuracy is sufficient for wire-guided torpedoes to be driven into a moving target. One reason for the U.S. Mk 48 wire-guided torpedo was the longer range of American submarine sensors. Torpedoes that depend on their own sensors, generally acoustic, might find their target gone once they reached the position it had been in when the torpedo was launched. This can be 30 or 40 kilometers from the launching sub.

Torpedo sensors cannot be as powerful as those on a submarine. A partial solution to this problem is to have the torpedo run a search pattern when it arrives where it was supposed to find a target and detects nothing. Russia favors this type of torpedo, mainly because it is cheaper, and its long-range sensors are not as accurate. The Western subs are quieter and harder to detect, anyway. Submarines always had a problem with the range of their weapons. Until 40 years ago, that range was under 10 kilometers, the extreme range of a torpedo or deck gun. Modern torpedoes can't go more than 50 kilometers. This was not too shabby, as this was the extreme range of battleship guns.

This was all made moot with the widespread introduction of the aircraft carrier 70 years ago. Aircraft could project their firepower for hundreds of kilometers. All of this meant little until subs acquired the capability to detect targets at distances in excess of a few kilometers. Thirty-five years ago the American Navy deployed a large number of subs with long-range sensors. About the same time, they deployed a rocket-propelled nuclear depth charge (SUBROC) for use by submarines. These SUBROCs were launched from a torpedo tube, surfaced, and took off and flew for 50 kilometers and then released a warhead that sinks to a predetermined depth and detonates. Depending on the size of the charge, any sub within a 300–900-meter radius will be destroyed. The total range was only 55 kilometers, about the same as the Mk 48. SUBROC was cheaper, and the Mk 48 hadn't come along yet. With the introduction of the Mk 48 in the 1970s and the increasing reluctance to be dependent on nuclear weapons, SUBROC was withdrawn in 1990.

The Mk 48 torpedo has a rough equivalent in Russian service, although this system is apparently not yet perfected. Besides, the Russians do not see their subs as primarily antisubmarine weapons. Most Russian submarines are designed for using missiles to attack land or naval targets. This has caused first Russia and then the United States to introduce a number of long-range, submarine-launched missiles. There is a significant difference in the way each side uses these missiles. The United States has longer-range underwater sensors and can use its Harpoon missiles to engage surface targets over a hundred kilometers away. Tomahawk cruise missiles can be sent over 2,000 kilometers at land targets or several hundred kilometers at surface ships. Sending submarine missiles at moving targets beyond the range of your sensors is a problem with the Tomahawk, and with all Russian missiles. ·

For launching missiles beyond the range of the sub's own sensors, the submarine must approach the surface, extend a radio antenna, and receive targeting information from friendly air or surface units. Normally, a nuclear submarine stays away from the surface. The closer it gets to the surface, the easier it is to detect from the air. The U.S. subs have less of a problem because the Russian antisubmarine forces are less of a threat. Russia must use nonsubmarine sensors to give its subs adequate targeting data. This makes Russian missile-firing subs more vulnerable to an already very capable Western submarine detection system. Under the circumstances, the Russians don't have a lot of choice.

Sensors

The key to combat success or survival in underwater warfare is the ability to detect other ships before they detect you. This is done with sensors. Submarines of different classes vary enormously in their sensor capability.

American submariners openly proclaim their ability to detect most Russian submarines at 10 times the range that U.S. subs can be detected. There is ample opportunity in peacetime to test this claim. Although the Soviets made vigorous efforts to close the gap, they never quite made it and remain at a grave disadvantage to this day. Technical inferiority in electronics and computers is the primary reason for the Soviet shortfall. But no one yet has equipment that can make the sea transparent. Although sonar (underwater sound-detection equipment) has made great strides in the last eighty years, it still has a lot of problems sorting out the multitude of underwater sounds.

Sonar interference. Sonar equipment is similar to radar in that it broadcasts a signal, in this case sound, and listens for that signal as it bounces off distant objects. Because water is thicker and "busier" than air, long-range sonar requires a computer to sort out the returning signals. Depending on the quality and power of the sonar equipment, accurate detection can take place at ranges from 1 to over 50 kilometers. The biggest problem is that there are so many other factors that can affect range. In deep water, varying temperatures and salinity in different layers of water distort and misdirect signals. Water tends to form layers of different temperatures, and these layers fluctuate. The deeper the water, the greater the number of layers encountered. Each layer is a potential hiding place. Submarines detect the different layers by dropping a long cable with water analysis sensors attached to it. This gives the sonar some idea of the temperature "geography" in the area and allows adjustments to be made to returning signals.

Another method of dealing with layers is to lower a sonar transmitter and receiver so that the conditions of different layers can be measured and a more accurate picture of the area formed. Sound tends to travel through a layer, even if the layer has a lot of ups and downs. Very few layers are straight. Moreover, several layers normally exist between you and your target. The signals will bend and slow down as each layer is encountered. Unless you know the nature of the layers, your sonar information will be inaccurate at best and misleading at worst. Noise caused by your own vessel also causes problems. This is also taken care of by surface ships and submarines towing a sonar array behind you on a cable. The local sea noises of fish and whales are taken care of with signal processing. The level of noise given off by the target must also be considered. If the target is making enough noise, he will have a harder time hiding in thermal layers. All of this noise and interference makes accurate information a sometime and uncertain thing.

Signal processing. Sorting out all the noise your sonar hears is a data-processing job best handled by a computer. Many nations cannot afford this approach and still rely on human operators. But trained and effective operators are difficult to come by. Some people have the ears and mind for it; most don't. It's a bit of an art, because the sounds are often so subtle. Even with computers, the operator still has decisions to make. But a powerful computer and a library of sounds enables you to classify sounds quickly and accurately most of the time. The simplest sonar puts a blip on a TV screen to show the contact. The more powerful your sonar transmitter is, the farther away you will detect targets. Because of all the interference, the farther away the target, the less accurate its indicated location.

Without signal processing, your best approach to solving the problem is to use more than one sonar set in ships a few kilometers from each other. Triangulation will then provide a more accurate fix. This method is widely used by Russian surface ships. They attempt to use as many sonar-equipped ships as possible when hunting enemy subs. However, this method is not possible for submarines. The sonar ships and aircraft must constantly communicate, and subs cannot do this. A more accurate approach, and one useable by submarines, is to collect as much data as possible on temperature layers, salinity, and other aspects of the underwater geography, as well as recordings of sea noises and other ships. Identify and classify as many of these as possible. Take into account whatever noise your own ship makes. Put all of this on a tape that can be loaded into the sonar-sets computer. When you use the sonar, it compares the signals it received with its signal library and makes a more accurate estimate of what is out there and where it is. This will only work instantaneously with very powerful computers. Western nations have them, the Russians and non-Western nations do not. The Soviets tried to catch up but never quite made it. Last, these data libraries are updated periodically and new tapes distributed to the submarines and surface ships. Apparently, individual ships and submarines can be identified by their noise "signature," at least until they undergo some modification which changes their sound. This brings us to the most effective use of sonar: passive mode.

Active versus passive sonar. If your opponent is noisy enough, you can use your sonar in the passive mode and gain an enormous advantage. Passive means not broadcasting any signals (as in active mode), just listening. One major disadvantage of sonar is that you can hear someone else using it, even without a receiver. With your reception equipment you can locate the other fellow quite accurately. A powerful passive sonar can detect a noisy ship or submarine three to five times farther away than with active sonar. Passive sonar works best with a fast computer, signal processing, and a large library of ocean sounds. This is called a signal processor. The least capable passive sonar can pick up loud targets, like fast-moving ships, at ranges of over 300 kilometers, or quiet submarines at up to 5 or 10 kilometers. More capable equipment can triple these ranges. Some targets are almost impossible to detect. A motionless diesel-electric submarine is almost soundless. Such a target can be picked up only with active sonar. Unfortunately, a motionless diesel-electric boat is sitting there with its passive sonar on waiting for just such an opportunity. Sensor superiority is the key to survival. Active sonars vary enormously according to type. Some can be very effective under the right conditions.

Sonars come in a number of different forms: ·

- *Towed arrays*. Ships and subs tow a sonar set behind them. This gets it away from ship noise. These can also be sent down to a different thermal layer for better results (variable depth sonar). Again, the world's most capable sonar boat, the U.S. *Los Angeles*-class, has a towed array that can detect targets over 100 kilometers away.
- *Sonobuoys*. These are small, portable sonars that are dropped from aircraft. In active mode, they have a range of up to two kilometers. In passive mode they have a range of 10–20 kilometers.
- *Dunking sonar*. Helicopters can hover and "dunk" a sonar into the water. In passive mode, it is good out to 8 kilometers. It also has an active mode, but this lets the sub know it is being tracked.
- *Hull-mounted sonar*. This is the most common form. Ships and submarines use it. The best of these, in modern U.S. subs, are good out to 50 kilometers. Less effective rigs, poorly maintained and used by inexperienced operators, are effective only out to 5–10 kilometers at best.

Run Silent, Run Deep

Active sonar range can vary from 1–100 kilometers. In passive mode, the spread is from 5 to over 1,000 kilometers. Differences are attributable to equipment and operator quality. But the nature of the target plays a large role, particularly the amount of noise your prey throws off. To take advantage of the noise factor, submarines and ships engage in as much silencing as they can. Silencing is the art of making your boat as quiet as possible. The old submariner's expression, "Run silent, run deep," pays homage to this life-saving practice. The deeper you are, the less sound gets to searching surface ships. Many things can create noise in a sub, such as the water rushing past the hull, either from movement or currents. The less streamlined hull of a diesel-electric boat creates more potential for this kind of noise. Inside and outside the boat, soundproofing materials are used extensively. Vibration-damping mounts for propellers and other machinery eliminate telltale sounds. Nuclear subs require constantly operating pumps to cool their nuclear power plants (except at low power levels, when some subs can use convection cooling). For this reason, diesel-electric boats, when operating on batteries and stationary, are inherently quieter. Even the crew moving around can make noise. Everyone wears rubber-soled shoes and practices "noise discipline" at all times, just so they don't develop bad habits. Active sonar isn't the only thing

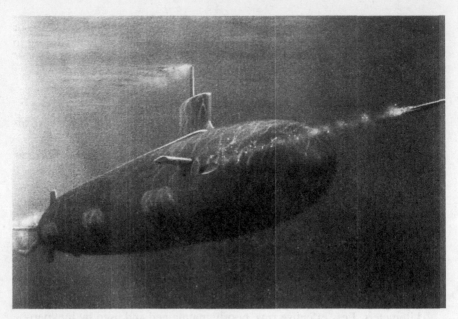

Seawolf (SSN 21) class attack submarine

that produces dangerous sound. A coughing crewman can give you away to a sensitive passive sonar.

Antisubmarine warfare (ASW). Although friendly submarines are the best defense against hostile subs, surface ships cannot always depend on having one handy. This problem is solved with a mixture of surface ships and aircraft equipped with sensors and antisubmarine weapons. Surface ships and aircraft wage antisubmarine warfare using a large number of tools. Already mentioned are the tactical sensors, which are similar to those used by submarines. Added to these are strategic sensors.

Strategic sensors. The United States has a system of passive sonars in key ocean areas: SOSUS (Sound Surveillance System) is on the continental shelf areas bordering the North Atlantic (the Caesar network) and the North Pacific (Colossus), plus a few in the Indian Ocean. They listen to everything and send their data via cable to land stations. There it is sent back to a central processing facility, often via satellite link. Currently this system is accurate enough to locate a submarine within a circle no wider than 100 kilometers. That's a large area, but depending on the quality of the contact, the circle may be reduced down to a tenth of that size. The major drawback of the system is that it does not cover deep-water areas more than 500 kilometers from the edge of the continental shelf. The Soviets knew this and tried to stay in the deep water as much as possible.

The deep water zones are covered intermittently with SURTASS (Surveillance Towed Array System). This system is a large "sled" containing passive sonar and towed by tugs in areas needing coverage. Data is sent via satellite to the signal-processing centers. The only other potential worldwide sensor system would use low-flying satellites with special sensors linked to powerful signal processors on the ground. These would cover all ocean regions, including deep water areas.

Both the United States and Russia have been working on these systems for nearly 30 years, although Russia's work has slowed appreciably in the 1990s. The sensors look for large metal objects and heat and water disturbances caused by ships passing through the water, or under it. These systems have had some success finding surface ships and may eventually be able to track submarines. However, to a greater degree than SOSUS, these systems are subject to prompt destruction during the opening stages of a major war. A further complication is that these satellites orbit the earth, preventing them from maintaining the steady surveillance provided by SOSUS. Both the satellite and SOSUS systems are very expensive to maintain. SOSUS has managed to survive the end of the Cold War by making its sensors available for civilian research and by using cheaper and more powerful electronic technology. While many parts of SOSUS have been shut down, additional portable SOSUS gear has been put in service. Thus, if there were another war involving subs, there would still be a SOSUS capability.

Once the strategic sensors detect a likely target, surface ships, subs, and aircraft can be sent within hours. These use a variety of tactical sensors. Sonar is the principal sensor for surface ships and aircraft. In addition, radar is used against surfaced submarines, and fixed-wing aircraft (and some helicopters) can use Magnetic Anomaly Detectors (MAD). These devices sense disturbances in the magnetic field caused by the sub's large metal hull passing through the water. Helicopters use a dunking sonar that is lowered into the sea on a cable. All aircraft use sonobuoys, miniature sonar sets that are dropped into the water and float around transmitting whatever they have detected. Ships and aircraft have their own signal-processing equipment; helicopters pass data to a ship for complex signal processing. Russian sensors lack the degree of computer and signal-processing support of Western equipment.

The Crew

More so than with any other type of ship, the quality and attitudes of the crew are essential to making a modern submarine an effective weapon. In most navies, submariners (or "squids") are volunteers. They are highly trained, especially on nuclear boats. The crews are small, usually 100–150 men on nuclear boats and half that on diesel-electric boats. The majority of the crew have a college education, or the equivalent in years of technical training. Over half the sub crews are career sailors; the remainder are usually in on long (six-year) enlistments. The long enlistments are necessary to provide sufficient time to train the sailors before they join their boat.

The duty is the hardest part of the job. When nuclear subs go on patrol, they are out for from one to three months. Normally, they are underwater the entire time. The crew members work 12-hour shifts much of the time. They work and live in a crowded environment, affording little privacy. There is constant low-level noise from machinery, plumbing, and fans. The odors of a hundred men and tons of operating machinery confined to a small area soon dull the taste buds. Many squids note a sensory shock when they first encounter the surface world after 30–90 days underwater.

These long absences from family and friends on shore put additional strains on the squids. This problem has been eased with the introduction of e-mail service for submariners. But navies with nuclear boats have a difficult time retaining crews for this silent and arduous service.

Tactics

Destroying a submarine is not impossible, just difficult. First you've got to find it. This is usually accomplished in two ways, either through strategic sensors or because the sub attacked you. Either way, you rarely get a precise fix on the sub's location. Antisubmarine tactics consist largely of converting a general location into a precise one and then attacking.

A general location for a sub may be a circular area over 100 kilometers in diameter, or as small as a few kilometers. The first task is to prevent the sub from escaping, by setting up lines of sonar detectors. Naturally, you will never have enough ships or aircraft to cover the entire area quickly. In this case you use probability theory to lay out a search pattern that will give you the highest potential for pinpointing the sub's location. Western nations have an enormous advantage with their hundreds of long-range ASW aircraft. The aircraft can be concentrated quickly before a sub escapes. Of course, escape is a relative matter. If the sub speeds up it will generate more noise, thus making it easier to track. If it slows down or stops, the searching ASW units will get a crack at finding it. In many cases, the class the sub belongs to determines what it will do. Older nuclear boats are noisy even when stationary. However, they are still fast. So running for it makes sense. The newer Russian boats are quieter, dive deeper, and are just as fast. They come close to Western boats in overall capability, and many are now for sale to whoever has hard currency.

Sometimes strategic sensors or intelligence can identify the type of sub being pursued. This will cause more resources to be directed against the more capable boats. The first units on the scene are frequently aircraft. They drop lines of sonobuoys and listen for a contact. The sonobuoys use their sonar in passive mode, initially. They will only go to active mode when a sub has been located and a more precise fix is needed for torpedo launch. Surface ASW units will proceed to an assigned area where they will stop or slow down to use their passive sonar. ASW ships also have helicopters with dunking sonar, radar, sonobuoys, and MAD. These will take off and move off up to 50 or more kilometers from their ship and lay down sonobuoys. The helicopters enable the ship to spread its sonar net around without moving the ship. A moving surface ship makes a lot of noise to a sub. A missile or long-range torpedo from the sub can quickly turn the tables. Once the sub passes close enough to a sonobuoy, the aircraft rush to that spot. A helicopter deploys a dunking sonar to confirm the sub's location. MAD gear is also used to pinpoint the sub's location. At this point, one or more homing torpedoes are dropped, and the sub is in big trouble. If the sonobuoys do not detect an explosion but still indicate a sub, more torpedoes are used and reinforcements called for. Improvements in electronic and battery technology have resulted in more sensitive and longer-lasting sonobuoys, making these little cylindrical items (36 by 5 inches, weighing under 40 pounds) an increasingly popular antisubmarine weapon.

Subs are not defenseless. Against sonar and MAD, they can go deep and take advantage of the underwater terrain to evade their hunters. The MAD is only effective for about a kilometer, and an aircraft must be lower than 200 meters to use it. While using dunking sonar, the noise of a helicopter's rotors can be heard by a sub. During the 1980s, navies were moving toward equipping their subs with antiaircraft missiles. These could be encapsulated in a torpedo, launched from the torpedo tubes, and take off and run a search pattern for nearby helicopters or fixed-wing aircraft. Other devices were more similar to Stinger or Redeye missiles.

Some subs, largely Russian and British ones, have insulating tiles on their hulls to make the limited passive sonar of homing torpedoes less effective. These tiles reduce the accuracy of other sonars somewhat less. Subs also can deceive homing torpedoes by ejecting noisemakers when they hear a torpedo approach. Surface ships use the same type of decoy. Recent Russian subs can, under some circumstances, outdive and outrun many types of torpedoes. Moreover, some of the larger Russian subs may be of sufficiently massive construction to survive one or more torpedo hits. All the hunter can do is try to keep the torpedoes up to the task through constant upgrades. This cat-and-mouse game may go into several rounds. The aircraft do not have inexhaustible resources. They can stay on station for several hours, depending on how far they had to travel to the search area.

Aircraft carry over a hundred sonobuoys and four or more torpedoes. The sonobuoys themselves last at least eight hours. But you can run out of sonobuoys. The larger P-3 aircraft must return to a land base. Longer-term weapons can be left behind to harry the subs. Antisubmarine mines can be dropped. These are too far down to detect or harm surface ships. They can be set to deactivate after a certain time so that friendly subs can also use the area. If the search is abandoned, it can be turned over to friendly subs. This, however, raises a number of additional problems. It is difficult to tell friendly from enemy subs when they are underwater. It is not unlikely that there will be cases where friendly subs will be hit.

The above description of hypothetical antisubmarine combat is a unique situation because there has not yet been a major naval war involving nuclear subs. In the past, subs spent most of their time on the surface, where positive identification was easier. This is just another complication in what is shaping up to be a unique and nerve-wracking new form of naval warfare.

There have been some antisubmarine operations in the past 40 years. U.S. and Russian nuclear subs have been stalking each other, for practice and bragging rights, since the 1960s. Sweden and Norway have found Soviet nuclear and diesel subs lurking in their coastal waters and have had a hard time nailing these interlopers. This highlights the most likely antisubmarine warfare of the future. Many nations have diesel subs and will most likely use them close to shore. This is the worst possible situation for antisubmarine warfare. Diesel boats are quieter underwater, and the closer to land you get, the more chaotic the underwater landscape is for sonar and other ASW sensors.

Who Is Hunting Whom?

Before nuclear submarines came along, it was rare for submarines to turn on pursuing ASW forces successfully. Nuclear submarines are different. They never have to surface. They are as fast as, and often faster than, ASW ships. Equipped with missiles and long-range torpedoes, they can attack as decisively as surface ships. Submarines have superior sensors. Surface ships cannot hide as easily as subs, nor can they find their underwater opponents as easily. Nuclear subs are seen as solitary predators. They must operate independently because of the lack of communications underwater, not to mention the need for silence to maintain their cover. Submarines have inertial guidance systems that enable them to keep precise track of their position. To avoid fatal contact with friendly ASW forces, the subs will follow a precise route and schedule to their area of operations. Then, like a lion stalking a herd of antelope, the submarine slowly patrols its sector until it detects enemy ships or submarines. The sub then moves close enough to use one of its weapons, fires, and then dives quietly to avoid retribution. Run silent, run deep.

No one knows just how easy it will be to detect submarine weapons being fired under combat conditions. Peacetime exercises in the West assume the worst, that detection of submarine weapons being launched will be difficult. Under these conditions, the nuclear subs have done great damage, even to the point of putting carriers out of action during war-game exercises. This is one reason why every major fleet has some nuclear-attack submarines. A late-model Russian cruise-missile sub has yet to go up against a U.S. carrier group and probably never will in our time, so no one knows for sure what will happen. Meanwhile, each U.S. carrier group has a dozen fixed-wing and helicopter ASW aircraft. Every escort ship has its own ASW gear. Everyone has a strong urge to not get hit by a Russian, or any other, sub. Nonnuclear subs could, and probably would, operate in groups because they must be on or near the surface most of the time. At the very least they could have their periscope, breathing apparatus, and radio antennae on the surface. These boats are easier to find and sink and would be used effectively close to shore in largely defensive operations. Until better sensors come along, the tables appear to have been turned. It is now the surface warships that must always steam in fear of the superior threat beneath the waves.

Theory and Practice

The underwater world is dark, murky, and full of distracting sounds. U.S. submarine war games have shown that up to 40 percent of potential targets were not even detected, and 20 percent of those that were could not be successfully tracked and attacked. Experience with Russian-made subs indicates that their record was (and still is) even worse. The much-feared Russian cruise-missile submarines would have been highly dependent on this blind-man's-bluff atmosphere in order to have had a chance to get close enough to U.S. ships to fire missiles. But then, Russian subs may have had a hard time even finding surface ships. The weapons always have problems. Wire-guided torpedoes can be very effective because they have at their disposal all the sub's sensors as they are steered toward their target. However, the wire must remain intact, and the tube cannot be reloaded until the torpedo has hit something or run out of fuel. This means that the firing sub cannot move around violently lest the wire be broken. Depending on how far the torpedo has to go, it will spend 10–20 minutes running. Meanwhile, the target may detect the torpedo launch and fire off one of its own. Or the target may dive fast and deep and escape. This is definitely a nail-biting exercise. The current submarine scare is from nations like Iran, North Korea, and China, with Russian-made diesel boats. The reality here is that while these subs may be the latest models, the crews are usually poorly trained and spend little time at sea. While diesel boats can often be tough to find in coastal waters, inept crews can make stupid mistakes that get their boat detected and destroyed.

The Future

The future is moving somewhat backward. With the former Soviet sub fleet in disarray and disintegration, the focus of undersea warfare shifts back to the nearly 200 diesel-electric submarines held by unstable Third World nations. While this is a formidable technical challenge, the extent of the threat is small, with fewer than a dozen nations possessing these subs. This has not prevented a lot of anxious talk about the new submarine "threat."

Whatever excitement the Third World submarine threat generates will not balance the rapid decline of the former Soviet submarine fleet. Even before the collapse of the Soviet Union in 1991, the Soviet submarine fleet was suffering from a shrinking pool of resources. Less money was allocated for maintaining and operating its existing subs. This led to an accelerated retirement of the older boats, both diesel and nuclear. But this wasn't enough. Qualified sailors for sub crews became more difficult to obtain. Budgets shrank, and, after the Soviet Union collapsed in 1991, the navy's budget shrank even further. Moreover, the introduction of market pricing in Russia took away the ability of the military to grab resources at bargain prices. Since the mid-1980s, the combat value of the former Soviet submarine fleet has dropped about 80 percent. There is no relief in sight for the Russian sub fleet. The Russians have taken over most of the Soviet submarines but simply can't support them. This has turned out to be a debilitating prospect for Western, and particularly U.S., submariners. The U.S. sub fleet was created in response to the perceived Soviet sub threat. With that threat now rapidly wasting away, it is difficult to justify the tens of billions of dollars spent each year on U.S. subs. However, even after drastic cuts in the U.S. submarine and ASW forces, it will be a while before any other nation comes up with a credible submarine threat to the U.S. Navy.

Underwater "threats" are still with us. China is the current one. The Chinese sub fleet is large (about 65 boats), but only half a dozen are nuclear boats. And China has been having problems getting its nuclear subs to operate effectively. China will keep trying, and Russia will probably eventually sell a lot of its extensive nuclear submarine technology to China. Eventually, China will be a major submarine threat to seagoing nations.

The weapons of submarine warfare are changing. Sensor technology also seems ready for a major leap forward. Part of this may be propelled by the recent breakthroughs in superconductivity. Meanwhile, large increases in computing power make for more efficient analysis of data already being collected. More computing power also makes some types of sensors more practical. Sensors that detect neutrinos, heat, color, and other subtle submarine characteristics may indeed make the oceans transparent. Just installing state-of-the-art computers can increase detection probability by several times. More prosaic changes include putting active sonars into towed arrays. This eliminates one problem with active sonar, that it gives the user's position away. Many Western nuclear subs have towed passive arrays, wormlike devices linked to the sub with a cable. Western technology has made it possible to get the more complex electronics needed by active sonar into the "worm." Better communications also allows for greater use of multistatic sensors. This system depends on one or more active sensors working in coordination with many more passive sensors. Communications coordinates all the information, sorts it out, and more rapidly pinpoints the location of enemy subs. Once more, computer signal-processing power is the key to making this work. This research will lose a lot of steam as the major rationale for it—finding the numerous subs of the former Soviet Union—has disappeared.

11

The Navy: In the Air

Aircraft have revolutionized naval operations and become the key system in all major fleets. The Navy first used aircraft for reconnaissance. It still does. This started before World War I (1914–18). During that war and the 1920s, it was realized that aircraft could be used for naval combat. Once planes became powerful enough to lift a torpedo or large bomb, they could sink the largest warship. Shortly after that revelation, aircraft carriers started appearing in significant numbers. Combat experience in World War II (1939–45) confirmed the predictions, as carriers replaced the large-gun battleship as the "capital ship." The nuclear submarine is touted by some as the replacement for the aircraft carrier. That may be so, but it will not replace aircraft. Indeed, the most potent new weapon on submarines is the cruise missile, which is little more than an aircraft flown by a robot. Most subs can't carry more than a few dozen cruise missiles, and, unlike carriers, they cannot reuse them or obtain reconnaissance from them. Moreover, a submarine's persistent enemies are the various types of ASW aircraft that hound them constantly. Submarines may supplant or replace various types of surface ships. Nothing on the horizon will replace aircraft in their various forms.

Carrier-Task-Force Defense System

The modern (U.S.) aircraft carrier may yet prove to be a dinosaur overstaying its welcome. But for the moment it is one of the more lethal and flexible weapons systems available. The key to carrier operations is the ability of the carrier to defend itself. It does this by putting up a multizone defense extending out for over 700 kilometers from the carrier and its escorts.

The inner zone. The primary or vital zone extends 10–20 kilometers from the carrier and is monitored by shipboard sensors. This zone is defended primarily by electronic weapons, naval missiles, and guns. Electronic jammers blind cruise missile homing systems. "Blip" enhancers make low-flying helicopters appear like carriers to the missiles and decoy the missiles from their intended targets. Electronic pulses can even detonate the missile warhead prematurely. Nonelectronic defenses include chaff—a cloud of metal foil blinds a radar. Last-ditch defenses are fully automatic machine cannon that shoot automatically at anything that looks like an approaching missile.

The middle zone. Covering the area 10–160 kilometers from the carrier, this zone is monitored by the carrier task force's AEGIS cruiser and antisubmarine ships. The AEGIS ships are built around a powerful radar system and hundreds of surface-to-air missiles (SAMs) carried by the AEGIS cruiser and the other escort ships. The AEGIS radars and fire-control systems can coordinate the use of hundreds of SAMs fired at incoming aircraft and cruise missiles. Other escorts will monitor the ocean for the telltale sounds of approaching enemy subs.

The outer zone. This zone is for threats over 160 kilometers away and is monitored by patrol aircraft from the carrier. They can spot surface ships nearly 400 kilometers away and aircraft over 700 kilometers distant. This zone is defended by aircraft and detachments of surface ships and submarines. These detachments of one to four ships use the same techniques as the ships in the primary and middle zones. In addition, these ships may get an opportunity to use their antiship missiles against enemy vessels that come into range. The major drawback is that these ships cannot always take up their positions fast enough. The carrier's F-14 aircraft also have missiles with a range of 200 kilometers that are effective against cruise missiles and aircraft. Their primary targets are enemy aircraft carrying cruise missiles. Other aircraft have air-to-surface antiship missiles with a range of nearly 200 kilometers. Six to twelve F-14s with six Phoenix missiles each should be able to stop most cruise-missile attacks, or at least chop them up so that the primary and middle zone defenses are not overwhelmed. Timing is a critical consideration. U.S. carrier aircraft normally spend about 100 minutes in the air. Few aerial tankers are available for refueling, and you still have to land to rearm. The only alternative is to put up the aircraft in shifts, leaving yourself with a less than maximum defense. The F-14 is being retired, and in ten years it will no longer be around; nor will its Phoenix missiles. F-18s armed with AMRAAM missiles will fill in. Neither the F-18 nor the AMRAAM is as capable as the F-14/Phoenix combination, but they are close enough to deal with post–Cold War threats in the foreseeable future.

The strategic zone. Beyond 700 kilometers from the carrier is the strategic zone. This zone is monitored by satellites, land-based aircraft, and SOSUS.

This demonstrates how vulnerable fleets are to having their satellites destroyed. Not only do the satellites provide some of the reconnaissance, they are vital for passing all information between the fleet and far-distant land and naval units. Once something is spotted, strike aircraft are sent after targets in this zone. The maximum range of aircraft strikes is about 2,000 kilometers. This is the zone in which enemy recon aircraft are hit.

Many navies model their long-range naval aviation doctrine after the one developed by the former Soviet navy. The Soviet navy had over 100 long-range bombers used as naval recon aircraft. In addition to a heavy load of EW and ECM equipment, they could also carry one or more long-range cruise missiles. These aircraft were also responsible for providing targeting information for less well-equipped aircraft. This is critical, as cruise missiles need accurate target location updates if they are fired over the horizon, as most are. Without the assistance of the recon planes, many cruise missiles will miss their targets. Indeed, without a current and precise location of the enemy ships, other aircraft and ships will often not even fire at targets they cannot see. Because of all the electronic warfare used, it is critical that the autopilots on the cruise missiles get their missiles as close to the targets as possible before turning on their terminal homing radar or sensors. This requirement will not soon be eliminated. The sensors needed to enable a missile to find an over-the-horizon target by itself are extremely complex.

This strategic zone is quite possibly the most important. It presents the best opportunities for destroying cruise-missile carriers before they can launch. Enemy aircraft can carry one or two missiles each. Each surface warship or submarine carries up to 10 or more cruise missiles. Once these missiles are launched, they provide a greater number of targets to shoot down. A cruise missile is more difficult to detect and hit than an aircraft or ship. This was one reason the Soviets built over 50 cruise missile submarines (most of which are no longer in service).

The carrier defense system has two modes, passive and active. The passive mode is used in peacetime and in wartime when an attack is not imminent. In this mode, most of the escort ships are within a few kilometers of each other and the task-force carrier. The one or two nuclear-attack subs attached to the task force generally travel out in front of the task force, using their sensors to detect other submarines the task force may encounter.

Active mode is used when an attack is expected. The escort ships spread out, with several taking up position in the middle zone. The carrier's aircraft fly more frequently and are kept ready to concentrate in the direction an attack comes from. The task force's nuclear subs take up position in the rear of the task force to watch for enemy subs coming from that direction. You don't want your own subs maneuvering in the direction of an enemy attack, as that is also the direction enemy subs may come from and there is no way to sort out the enemy and friendly subs when your antisubmarine forces go into action.

Antisubmarine Warfare

Helicopters are the most common ASW aircraft. Ships of over 3,000 tons can usually carry at least one, and often two. Helicopters can extend a ship's ASW capabilities over 100 kilometers. Helicopters can pursue a submarine contact diligently and enable surface ships to keep up with swifter nuclear submarines. Many navies have small aircraft carriers that use nothing but helicopters. The U.S. Navy also maintains a large fleet of P-3 four-engine maritime-patrol/ASW aircraft. Other nations have similar aircraft. These planes enable large ocean areas to be patrolled and subs to be attacked wherever they are found.

Organization of Carrier Aircraft

Large U.S. carriers had, until the end of the Cold War, between 85–90 aircraft. These consisted of 24 fighters (F-14s), 34 strike planes (F-18s, for the most part, 6 plus some A-6s), 10 ASW aircraft (S-3s), 6 ASW helicopters, 4 ECM (EA-6Bs), 4 radar (E-2Cs), and 4 tankers (Ka-6Ds). A few of the F-14s were equipped as recon aircraft. Since the late 1990s, the carriers carry 10 F-14s, 36 F-18s, 4 EA-6Bs, 4 E-2Cs, 6 S-3Bs, and 2 ES-3As. Plus 6 ASW helicopters and 2 HH-60s for odd jobs. The S-3s can stay aloft for 6 hours and carry sonobuoys, torpedoes, and air-to-surface missiles. The E-2C radar aircraft can search out to 700 kilometers. No other nation has anything quite like these carriers. The Soviets built one and scrapped two others before they could be finished. The Soviet carrier was not as capable as the U.S. ones, and, because of economic problems, eventually the Soviets fell out of the carrier business (selling some of them to China and India). The U.S. Navy also has smaller helicopter carriers. These carry a combination of vertical takeoff jets and helicopters. These are used by the Marines for amphibious operations. Other nations, like Britain, France, Italy, and several others, use these vessels for antisubmarine and surface-combat operations.

Land-Based Naval Aircraft Operations

Few navies have aircraft carriers, but nearly all have land-based aircraft. These planes are used for patrolling their coastlines and, in most cases, to attack hostile ships. Western nations have over 500 multiengine, long-range patrol aircraft. These are primarily U.S. P-3 Orion aircraft, which can also carry cruise missiles. In addition, the U.S. Air Force has trained some of its B-52 bomber crews to drop naval mines (CAPTORs) and use Harpoon antiship missiles. A substantial number of naval aircraft are interceptors. As was learned in World War II, naval patrol aircraft are vulnerable to interceptors. China is a strong proponent of defending its coastline and naval bases with interceptors. Against a defended shore, patrol aircraft are increasingly at risk if they approach closer than 500 kilometers to the enemy coast.

Worldwide, navies have over 3,000 fixed-wing aircraft and helicopters operating from land bases. The majority are equipped to hunt submarines. Many of the antisubmarine weapons on these aircraft can also be used against surface ships. It's becoming more common to see ASW aircraft with long-range cruise missiles. This allows the slow patrol planes to get out of harm's way after launching an attack. If a nation has access to enough land bases, these long-range aircraft can be nearly as flexible as carrier-based patrol planes. Carrying an impressive array of sensors and weapons and moving at over 400 kilometers an hour, these aircraft form a fast-moving reserve of naval power. They are able to detect and attack ships far more rapidly than any other vessel. So why have ships at all? Patrol aircraft eventually have to land; ships can sit where they wish for as long as they want. Although some aircraft can stay aloft for over 12 hours, they must eventually land to rearm, refuel, and perform maintenance. Depending on the skill and efficiency of the ground crews, a patrol aircraft can fly one sortie a day for several weeks. After that, things will start to fall apart. Aircraft would replace ships if only they were as durable.

Patrol-Aircraft Missions

Surface ship search. This is the simplest form of patrol and is normally performed with radar-equipped aircraft. The most capable of these aircraft, the P-3, can spot large aircraft carriers or tankers 350 kilometers away. Smaller ships must be closer to be spotted; 200 kilometers for cruisers, 100 kilometers for destroyers, and 50 kilometers for trawlers and surfaced submarines. The cheaper E-2s can spot large ships 180 kilometers away while the aircraft moves along at a speed of 400 kilometers an hour. Other aircraft surface-search radars have shorter ranges, up to 200 kilometers for fixed-wing aircraft and up to 100 kilometers for helicopters. By comparison, human observers can see 20–30 kilometers during clear weather. Searches are performed offensively or defensively. That is, the aircraft can either establish a barrier of observation to prevent the undetected intrusion of enemy ships, or scour an area looking for the something to shoot at. Whenever enemy ships are found, strike aircraft or warships are directed toward the target.

Antisubmarine search. This is not as efficient as searching for surface ships. Aircraft are used to pinpoint a sub that has been reported in an area. These reports come either from an attack by the sub or a SOSUS detection. See previous chapter for details.

Strike. Most aircraft can carry at least one air-to-surface missile. Only the long-range cruise missiles on U.S. (and some Western) aircraft are likely to be used against enemy task forces lacking air cover. Many Russian-made antiship missiles are sold to just about anyone who can pay. These are now made available so that they can operate from just about any type of aircraft. While the Cold War is over, Russian weapons are still the most likely threat to American warships.

Theory and Practice

Cruise missiles, because they are the cheapest and most widely available antiship weapon, are likely to be the biggest threat to ships for some time to come. Although cruise missiles have not been used on a mass scale yet, there was a parallel experience during World War II. American task forces encountered massive kamikaze attacks by Japanese aircraft crewed by hastily trained suicide pilots. The Okinawa campaign saw 1,900 aircraft attacking over a period of 100 days (March–June 1945). Under attack were 587 ships, of which 320 were warships. Each attack averaged 150 aircraft. One had as many as 350 planes. Defending were carrier-based interceptors and antiaircraft guns. Only 7 percent of the suicide aircraft scored hits. Eighteen percent of the ships hit were sunk or put out of action. Although the kamikaze tactic was unexpected, the defending fleet had the usual strong sense of self-preservation. The Americans were also heavily armed. The kamikazes were, in effect, cruise missiles. Because they initially had the element of surprise, they were more successful during this first use. Twenty-two years later, electronic pilots were developed to replace human ones, and Israel lost a destroyer to Egyptian cruise missiles. Over the next five years the cruise missile was used a number of times, severely damaging over a dozen ships. During the 1973 Arab-Israeli war, Israel demonstrated that the cruise missile could be stopped cold with a combination of electronic warfare, gunfire, and evasive maneuvers. Over 50 Arab cruise missiles were fired without scoring a hit. Fifty percent of the Israeli cruise missiles scored hits. It would appear than an unsuspecting target has a 90 percent chance of being hit by a modern cruise missile. Various defensive measures—guns, missiles, electronics, maneuvers—can bring this hit probability down close to zero percent.

The crucial question is, what would be the percentage of hits by future attackers on defending ships? Based on historical experience, between 0–10 percent. This assumes an alert defender. Considering the previously demonstrated ineffectiveness of non-Western nations' antiaircraft and cruise missiles, 1–3 percent is more likely. If the attackers achieve surprise, the probability can easily increase by a factor of three or more. Western cruise missiles will probably hit 3–10 times as often (3–30 percent) if they are the attacker against a non-Western defender.

What, then, would be the outcome of a large-scale use of cruise missiles? It depends on what type of missile is used and against what kind of target. Russia has several kinds of cruise missiles that have ended up on the international arms market. Their most formidable missile is P-700 ("Shipwreck"). These missiles have a range of 500 kilometers and home in on the target's radars. The missiles travel close to the water at over 800 meters a second. The tricky part is discovering the precise position of the defending task force and then getting close enough to launch. Let us assume that ships carrying P-700s get within 100 kilometers of a task force without being discovered, perhaps by sitting in the right place until the task force steamed into range. Suppose the attacker got off 20 missiles. In two minutes they will hit the task force. An American task force has at least six ships, most with their sensors turned on. There might be time to activate all the Phalanx gun systems, chaff, and flares. The task force might even be practiced in turning off all radars quickly. There might still be one or more radar aircraft in the air that could keep their radars on. This would deny the missiles any surface targets to hone in on. If these P-700s also have heat-seeking or active radar guidance, they could be deceived by the chaff and flares. There would be 10 operational Phalanx units. Some of the missiles would malfunction before they reached their targets. Between all of these defensive measures, and making allowances for human error, perhaps one or two missiles would hit a ship. This might not include the carrier. This is in line with the World War II kamikaze experience and might be too high, considering that such are not a surprise this time around. Meanwhile, the attacking ships could be in big trouble if it were attacking a U.S. carrier task force. Spotted when its missiles were launched, it now has a nuclear-attack sub stalking it.

A more likely scenario is some Third World nation (like Iran or Iraq) using a combination of air- and land-based cruise missiles, plus some launched from small ships, delivering something resembling a coordinated attack. If the naval task force were caught napping, this kind of attack could cause serious damage. If the task force were alert, a few of the missiles would still get through. Argentina demonstrated this in 1982, as did Iraq in 1986. We won't know who will try it in the twenty-first century, but someone probably will.

The last major naval war saw aircraft carriers dominate the action, with a strong assist from shore-based aircraft, submarines, and mines. It's uncertain which mix of weapons will be decisive in a future major naval war. It would appear that aircraft will continue to dominate, mines will be as effective as in the past, and that submarines will be more effective. Where does that leave aircraft carriers? The United States, with over 20 large and smaller carriers, has the largest investment in this ship type. American carriers outnumber those of all other fleets combined, even with all the budget cuts in the 1990s. This points out that U.S. carriers will not be needed primarily for anticarrier operations, as in World War II. With their large complement of long-range aircraft, U.S. carriers would be lethal against enemy surface ships and, to a lesser extent, against land-based aircraft. Any ship equipped with cruise missiles is also something of an aircraft carrier, but the shorter range and/or need for targeting data make cruise missiles decidedly second-rate. Submarines and mines are the biggest question mark.

No navy has ever had to deploy over 50 nuclear subs, or defend against such a force. Although nuclear subs are larger and more robust because of it, they are not very well protected. Although much is made about their sturdy waterproof hulls, the least amount of damage can ruin this underwater capability. On the surface, nuclear subs are extremely vulnerable, especially against aircraft. Moreover, when underwater, subs have a very difficult time communicating. When they do, they come near the surface. Again, this makes subs vulnerable to aircraft detection. Communications problems make coordinated operations difficult to the point of impossibility. While the Germans used large "wolf packs" of subs during World War II, these boats were operating on the surface most of the time. Modern aircraft and electronic monitoring devices make it risky for current subs to spend too much time on the surface or communicating openly. Operating individually, nuclear subs will close off their operating areas to friendly forces. This will create a killing zone where any ships are considered hostile.

Mines are another increasing danger. The current models are very difficult to find. They often remain on the ocean floor and require diligent and time-consuming searches. Moreover, mines laying on the bottom cannot be cleared easily using helicopters. The problem with mines is getting them to where they can threaten enemy shipping. Aircraft can be effective if they have sufficient range and air superiority. More likely is the use of submarines to deliver mines, if the subs can survive the gauntlet of antisubmarine aircraft.

The question of whether aircraft carriers are worthwhile rests on their ability to stay afloat. Submarines may or may not be able to get after them. Whatever the case, air-delivered weapons will continue to dominate naval warfare. Even submarines depend on cruise missiles for most of their firepower against surface ships.

The Future

The war in Afghanistan demonstrated once more the usefulness of carrier aviation. Although naval aircraft dropped only about 20 percent of the bombs (Air Force heavy bombers accounted for most of the rest), the carrier aircraft were the first ones on the scene and did most of the work early in the campaign. One carrier was also turned over to the Army for use by helicopters used to support commando operations.

But naval aviation is still threatened by longer-range Air Force planes. The B-2 bomber, also fighting for its fiscal life, is touted as a cheaper way to put bombs on distant targets without the expense of a carrier group. Much to the Air Force's embarrassment, the 50-year-old B-52 proved to be the cheapest and most reliable way to get bombs on Afghan targets. Naval aircraft have already felt the heat. Budget problems have destroyed the U.S. Navy's plans for building a new attack aircraft (to replace the A-6 and F/A-18); they had to use a Navy version of the Air Force's F-35 instead. There will be no immediate replacement for the 1950s-era P-3 recon aircraft, either. More such damage will be felt through the early twenty-first century.

While carriers can still get to the scene of a hot spot first, they are increasingly being pushed out of the way by long-range aircraft. While this won't eliminate the carrier in the short term, the long-term situation does not look good.

Patrol Aircraft Characteristics

This chart shows the patrol aircraft and helicopters among the major maritime powers in the world. This includes AWACS-type planes, as their function is basically one of surveillance. Most of the word's surface is water, and these areas are largely unobserved most of the time. Understandably, navies have taken the lead in developing reconnaissance and patrol aircraft. The United States represents over half the patrol capability, mainly due to its fleet of 260 P-3 aircraft (including some modified for electronic surveillance) and hundreds of helicopters and aircraft operating off ships and carriers. In the 1990s, these aircraft became a lot more capable because of lighter and more powerful radars and heat sensors. This made it possible for less affluent nations to obtain powerful naval-search capability using inexpensive smaller aircraft carrying the new sensors. But for constant surveillance over a wide area, you still can't beat the P-3.

This chart shows the characteristics and capabilities of most of the principal patrol aircraft in service today. Reconnaissance, especially for fleets, is a critical capability. The navy that has the edge in this area is considered to possess a force multiplier, or the equivalent of additional combat ships. In practical terms, the multiplier can often come to a 50 or 100 percent increase in combat capability. Patrol aircraft in navies became even more efficient when they received radar in the early 1940s. This made these aircraft effective when the weather was bad and fog or mist covered the water's surface. Equipped with bombs, depth charges, and rockets, these aircraft could not only find but also attack submarines and light surface ships. You no longer required ships to con-

Aircraft	Index	Search			Attack			From	Cruise	Rng	Time	IFR	Wght	Crew
		Surf	Sub	Air	Surf	Sub	Air							
P-3 Orion	100	6	10	2	6	10	0	U.S.	600	7,600	13	N	64	12
P-2H Neptune	61	4	6	1	4	8	0	U.S.	400	4,500	11	N	34	7
E-3A AWACS	62	8	2	10	0	0	10	U.S.	800	8,000	10	Y	147	17
1150 Atlantic	55	5	6	1	3	6	0	FR	550	6,400	12	N	43	14
S-3A Viking	54	4	7	2	6	8	0	U.S.	680	5,500	8	Y	25	4
Tu-142	54	4	6	1	7	0	2	RU	800	12,500	16	Y	188	10
Il-38 May	39	3	2	1	4	6	0	RU	645	7,200	11	Y	61	12
Tu-22M Backfire	37	3	0	3	3	0	2	RU	900	8,000	9	Y	130	7
Il-76 Mainstay	32	5	0	8	0	0	5	RU	750	4,000	8	N	190	12
S-2E	31	4	4	2	4	6	0	U.S.	440	2,100	5	N	13	4
SH-60B LAMPS 3	28	6	4	0	6	9	0	U.S.	240	250	2.5	N	9	3
Ka-27 Helix	28	5	3	0	5	6	0	RU	230	250	4.5	N	11	3
SH-3 Sea King	27	4	5	0	4	8	0	U.S.	220	350	4	N	8	4
Tu-16 Badger	24	3	0	2	3	0	2	RU	900	5,700	6	N	72	6
M-12 Mail	22	1	4	1	2	4	0	RU	550	4,000	7	N	29	5
NIMROD	94	6	10	2	8	10	0	UK	800	8,000	12	N	87	12
SH-2F LAMPS 2	21	4	5	0	3	6	0	U.S.	210	300	3	N	5.8	3
Mi-14 Haze	21	4	5	0	3	5	0	RU	180	300	4	N	14	3
E-9 JSTARS	18	12	2	0	0	0	0	U.S.	800	8,000	12	Y	145	18
Ka-26 Hormone	15	3	4	0	2	5	0	RU	120	250	2	N	8	4
E-2	12	8	0	0	0	0	0	U.S.	500	4,000	8	N	23	5
TR-1 (U-2)	12	8	0	0	0	0	0	U.S.	650	4,800	8	N	13	1

trol large portions of the ocean. Except where the larger warships or interceptors held sway, the armed patrol aircraft ruled the waves. This search capability
was eventually extended to land operations, where the complex jumble of
objects on the ground required a more intelligent radar. Being able to pick out
aircraft flying close to the ground beneath you was an important breakthrough
for Western armed forces in the 1970s. Few other countries (mostly American
allies) have been able to keep up with this development. The U.S. E-2 and E-3
are the principal aircraft with this feature. The Russians have developed several
aircraft along these lines, although in a less reliable form. The development of
exotic metals and engine technologies led to the development of the TR-1
(U-2) in the 1950s, the SR-71 in the 1960s, and a new aircraft in the 1980s.
These aircraft fly so high (30,000 meters) and fast that most antiaircraft
weapons cannot reach them. Constantly improved and upgraded, no one has
been able to match these strategic patrol aircraft. Naval helicopters are used for
search missions and for transport from sea to land. Except for transport helicopters of the U.S. Marine Corps, most of the world's naval helicopters are
used primarily for search. Often flying from ships at sea, these helicopters look
for surface ships or submarines.

In peacetime, many search helicopters do a lot of patrol and rescue work.
When going after surface ships, the purpose is not just to find the enemy ship,
but often to keep it in sight to help guide missiles from the launching ship. This
type of mission allows ships to fire missiles over the horizon. The helicopter
remains out of antiaircraft range of the target ships, if possible. Against a navy
with carriers, the "spotter" helicopter has a more difficult time avoiding
destruction. The most common combat use of naval helicopters is antisubmarine work. In this role, helicopters are quite effective. The sensors and weapons
required cost more than the helicopter but provide the ability to convert easily
just about any cargo-carrying helicopter to an effective antisubmarine system.
The equipment needed includes sonobuoys, dunking sonar, MAD (Magnetic
Anomaly Detectors), computers, radios, and lightweight torpedoes. Search
radar can also be added to track surfaced subs or other warships. Most of these
weapons and sensors weigh less than 600 pounds each. This is important, as
helicopters do not possess great lifting power. The adaptability of helicopters
through the installation of specialized equipment provides a wide variety of
capabilities for the same model. This is very true of the UH-60 and Sea King
types.

A coming innovation is the increased use of UAVs, including some flown
off carriers and ships.

How to Read the Chart of Patrol Aircraft Characteristics

Index is an evaluation of each aircraft. The chart shows to what extent each aircraft varies in capability. Most of these aircraft specialize in antisubmarine operations. The remainder either have, or can be equipped to have, attack capability against surface shipping. All these aircraft have search capability. In an attempt to show the general qualitative differences between all these types, a value has been assigned to each. The highest value ("100") has been given to the P-3. This aircraft is generally considered the most capable all-round patrol aircraft, despite the fact that it was designed primarily as an antisubmarine aircraft. Note that several different versions of the P-3 exist, largely newer models or rebuilds of older aircraft. The P-3 value given is an average.

Capability ratings are the various capabilities of the aircraft expressed on a scale of 0 (nonexistent) to 10 (best available). Where a certain capability on this chart does not have a 10 rating, it means that some other type of aircraft is the best available. Improvements in aircraft weapons and equipment can increase an aircraft's rating by a point or two. Sometimes improvements have a negative effect because they are markedly less reliable that whatever they replaced. The skill and training of the aircraft and ground crews can modify these ratings by more than half.

Surface search is the ability to detect objects on the land or water. Generally, this means radar search. Other sensors can detect heat, engine exhaust (from diesel-electric subs), electronic transmissions, etc. Visual search is also used but is limited by the need for clear weather. Special viewing devices that can see at night are available.

Submarine search is the ability to detect submerged subs through MAD (Magnetic Anomaly Detectors) and sonobuoys.

Air search is the ability to detect aircraft, especially those flying close to the ground. This is done primarily with radar.

Surface attack is the ability to attack surface targets. The most effective weapon is the air-to-surface missile. Other weapons include torpedoes, rockets, bombs, and cannon. Also taken into account in this evaluation is the quality of the aircraft's fire-control system.

Submarine attack is the ability to attack submerged subs with homing torpedoes or depth charges. Therefore, submarine attack ability is highly dependent on submarine search ability.

Air attack is the ability to attack, not just defend against, other aircraft. This is a rare quality in patrol aircraft. These planes are designed for long periods of relatively slow cruising. The fast, violent maneuvers of air-to-air combat are not possible with most of these aircraft. However, aircraft equipped to control other aircraft (AWACS) do obtain high ratings in this category because of their ability to spot potential attackers and direct defending fighters to these attackers as a means of protection.

From. This is the primary nation of manufacture.

Cruise (in kilometers per hour) is the most fuel-efficient flying speed (for maximum time in the air). Often the aircraft must move slower to use certain equipment, like MAD. The TR-1 is essentially a powered glider that can shut off its jet engine and glide if the situation permits.

Rng (range in kilometers) is the maximum distance the aircraft can fly in one trip without refueling.

Time (in hours) is the maximum flying time at cruising speed. For antisubmarine work, this will be 10–20 percent less to account for time spent on maneuvering during attacks on subs.

IFR (In Flight Refueling). If the aircraft can be refueled in flight, it can greatly increase its range. At this point, the limiting factor becomes crew endurance. If two crews are carried, as is the case with some large aircraft, endurance can be extended to 24 hours.

Wght (tons) is the aircraft's maximum takeoff weight. This is an indicator of size.

Crew is the number of crew carried. This number will sometimes vary with the mission. Generally, the crew is divided into two sections: *flight* (to operate the aircraft) and *operations* (to take care of the sensors and weapons).

One final note: Thousands of other aircraft are used for reconnaissance, largely over land. These are usually fighters without weapons, often equipped with a large array of sensors and electronic countermeasures. Indeed, this special equipment typically comes in the form of pods. These pods are in the shape of bombs and hang from the aircraft just as a bomb would. Western air forces are quite advanced in this area.

The Aircraft

The aircraft are arranged in order of ability. At the top of each column is the nation owning the aircraft (see notes on patrol aircraft for nation abbreviations). The first column shows the aircraft designation. The second column is the total of each type. The second row gives the total aircraft for each nation. Unless otherwise noted, all are primarily antisubmarine aircraft. The listing below is in alphabetical order.

1150 Atlantic (France) is similar to, but smaller than, the P-2.

E-2 (U.S.) is a patrol version of the S-2.

E-3A AWACS (U.S.) is a more powerful version of the E-2. The E-3 is a Boeing 707 crammed with electronics. It can track over 1,000 enemy aircraft at once while controlling over 100 friendly aircraft. It is capable of tracking land traffic and ships.

Il-38 (Russia) is similar to the P-2.

Il-76 Mainstay (Russia) is the second Russian version of AWACS. It is much better than the Il-38, but not up to the standard of U.S. AWACS.

Ka-26 Hormone is the standard Russian shipboard antisubmarine helicopter.

Ka-27 Helix is the "heavy" Russian shipboard antisubmarine helicopter.

M-12 (Russia) is an amphibious patrol aircraft.

Mi-14 Haze is a naval version of the Russian Mi-8 Hip helicopter.

Nimrod (UK) is a British version of the U.S. P-3.

P-2H (U.S.) was the predecessor of the P-3 and is still in use.

P-3 Orion (U.S.) is the most powerful patrol aircraft currently in service. It is excellent as a surface search patrol aircraft as well as for antisubmarine work. EP-3 is an electronic reconnaissance version of the P-3.

S-2E (U.S.) was the predecessor of the S-3 and is still used by many nations as a land-based aircraft.

S-3A (US) is a carrier-based antisubmarine aircraft.

SH-2F LAMPS 2 is an antisubmarine helicopter operating from ships.

SH-3 Sea King is a U.S. helicopter design manufactured by many other Western nations (Italy, Britain, Japan, etc.). It is primarily used for search and patrol, as well as ASW.

SH-60 LAMPS 3 is a naval version of the U.S. Army UH-60 helicopter. The 3 model is replacing the earlier 2 model.

SR-71 (U.S.) is the premier patrol and recon aircraft. It covers land areas from an altitude of 30,000 meters and speeds of up to 900 meters a second. Protected by speed, altitude, and electronic devices, the SR-71 collects information with a wide range of sensors and delivers the data to users in less than two hours. It was withdrawn from service in 1990 and has not yet been replaced by an aircraft of the same type.

TR-1 (U.S.) is an updated version of the 1950s U-2. It is capable of staying aloft for 12 hours. Max altitude is 27,000 meters. It flies along the edge of a battle area looking for enemy electronic installations and other data.

Tu-126 MOSS (Russia) is first Russian version of AWACS. Not very successful, it is rapidly being replaced by MOSS 76.

Tu-142 (Russia) is a long-range bomber used as a naval patrol aircraft. The bomber version is called the Tu-95.

Tu-16 (Russia). Originally designed as a bomber, many are now used for naval patrol and attack work. Some also serve as aerial tankers.

Tu-22M (Russia) is a long-range bomber that does double duty as a naval patrol aircraft.

PART FOUR

HUMAN FACTORS

Often overlooked, frequently underestimated, but never ignored for long.
When it comes to the fighting, warfare is not waged by the numbers, but
through the courage, determination, skill, and leadership of individuals.

12

Getting Psyched: Why Soldiers Fight

Convincing people to fight, and getting them to do it well, is one of the more essential and less noticed aspects of maintaining an armed force. Illusions must be created, and maintained, often unto death. Few individuals, once aware what combat is all about, want to spend any time at it.

It Won't Happen to Me

Anyone induced or forced into combat service is not told how dangerous it is. If potential recruits knew their chances, it would be more difficult to get anyone into the infantry. During this century, the odds of serving in the infantry during combat and escaping injury have been less than one in three. Given a choice, most new soldiers will avoid the infantry by volunteering for any other branch of the armed forces. Most other military jobs are no more dangerous than civilian occupations. Even troops in combat-support units like armor and artillery offer better than even chances of seeing the war's end uninjured. To get people into the infantry, first convince them that they have a good chance of surviving in one piece. Better yet, ignore the concept of surviving or not surviving. Modern combat doesn't work that way. It's always a deadly business for at least one side.

Indoctrination

Those selected for the infantry are customarily subjected to an ancient indoctrination routine that stresses the following points:

Pride. The recruit is told that the infantry is the premier branch of the armed forces, the most noble calling, and the most respected and patriotic service one can render one's country. This is all true, particularly if getting killed or injured for one's fellow citizens is recognized as the highest form of patriotism. The pride taken in the dangerous business of infantry fighting is reinforced by the respect given to combat veterans. Like many other bad experiences, the memories lose their hard edges over time. Hearing the veterans' stories, the potential recruits tend to fixate on the glory instead of the death and terror. This is human nature, and it is drawn on generously to get troops into the fighting without losing them to panic. During times of international tension, when journalists interview combat troops about their eagerness to get to it, the young troops are eager, while the older veterans long for a more diplomatic solution. No one who's been shot at retains the enthusiasm of the uninitiated.

Effective preparation. The combat soldiers are constantly told that they have the best equipment, training, and leadership available. The message is that these advantages will allow the troops to carry out their admittedly dangerous tasks as effectively and safely as possible. This is only rarely true. These tales are often believed by many infantry recruits, who tend to have less education and a more accepting attitude than your average college graduate. Moreover, if a nation has a winning tradition, one has reason to believe that it will turn out all right. In peacetime, when there is no contradictory evidence like body bags and maimed veterans, the official line gets accepted. It is far more comfortable to believe that you will survive. A nation without a military tradition, or one noted for defeat, will have problems from the start. There will be a feeling of inferiority among the troops. The 1982 Argentine infantry collapsing in the face of the highly regarded British troops was a typical example. Another is the attitudes of the various combat forces during the 1979–89 Afghanistan war. The rebels had their track record of no defeats and a zealous religious belief. The Russian troops' attitudes ranged from a well-founded fear among the regular troops to a sense of cocky superiority within the small contingents of Spetsnaz commandos. On the positive side, a reluctant attitude is more realistic than blind optimism. Such unfounded optimism can lead to rashly aggressive action in combat. The opening stages of World War I were infamous for this. Hundreds of thousands of troops were needlessly killed charging into machine-gun and artillery fire. A latter-day example is the reckless courage of the Iranian Revolutionary Guards. Raw, unthinking courage is no match for firepower. But such attitudes are common on the battlefield. This has a lot to do with the generally reckless spirits of young males. These lads seem to think that nothing can hurt them. Well, at least this helps in recruiting them for combat units.

Friends. A vastly underestimated influence in combat performance is the "primary group." This is nothing more than the smallest unit of soldiers, 5–40 men, organized for mutual support. Not all armies see to it that effective primary groups are formed. The primary group must be well trained and well led and, most important, must know and trust one another personally and professionally. The troops must believe in their own skills and the abilities of their leaders. The members of the group must serve together for at least a few months before entering combat. New members should not be brought in until the unit is taken out of combat. Experienced troops do not want to be introduced to replacements while being shot at. In life-and-death situations, you want to know people you work with pretty well. The transformation from green troops to battle-hardened ones is nothing more than the creation of these primary groups among trained soldiers. Just getting men in and out of combat does not form primary groups; leaders make it happen. Some armies are more effective at producing combat leaders. The Germans may have lost World War II, but they were more successful at the troop level. They consistently inflicted more casualties per man than their opponents. This occurred because they took good care of their combat soldiers and paid attention to preparing troop leaders. During World War II, the Germans gave their NCOs more training (six months) than the U.S. Army gave junior officers (the "90-day wonders"). Right up until the end of the war, German officers received a one-year training course before being let loose with troops. The Germans found it was preferable to have a shortage of leaders than to have any that were not well prepared. The logic of this was that troops knew that any officer or NCO was the real thing, not someone who was hastily appointed to a position they could not handle. Studies after the war demonstrated the universal validity of this system. This is not to say that the United States did not have any well-prepared combat units. However, this occurred only because exceptional senior leaders made it happen. One U.S. infantry division had a commander who set up training schools for officers and NCOs and basically duplicated the German system. The results were noticeable, especially to the Germans. It wasn't until the 1980s that the high command of the U.S. Army picked up on this wisdom.

Fight or else. A very ancient and still effective motivating tool is fear. As one general put it, "My soldiers will fight well because they are more afraid of their officers than they are of the enemy." This fear takes many forms. Most cultures apply great social pressure to get out there and fight. Tribal armies, like those in Somalia and Afghanistan, have a warrior tradition in which the greatest humiliation is to fail in combat. Many armies use more severe disciplinary measures. Russian officers have long had the authority to shoot their men on the spot for slack discipline in a combat zone. Other measures include posting a line of military police behind advancing units to discourage any reluctant troops from moving in the wrong direction. This approach was used by the U.S. Army in Korea and was a standard practice for the Soviets during many World War II battles. A U.S. innovation in Vietnam was landing troops by helicopter in hostile territory. They had a choice of fighting their way out or getting killed by the enemy. This unofficial policy was very effective as a motivator. The troops, however, were not fooled; some would refuse to board the helicopters.

What Works

Superior motivation, leadership, and training have consistently proved the formula that produces victorious armies. Leaders who are willing to get out front and get shot at, and often killed, are respected and followed. Officers who stay to the rear find their troops following them in that direction, also. Training that draws from experience, not untried theories, produces the most competent troops. Equipment that works most of the time, and does what needs to be done, is the most effective. Men will start fighting for any number of reasons but will continue fighting, and do so successfully, only if they have confidence in their leaders, equipment, training, and themselves.

Conviction. When a soldier believes he should be fighting, he has conviction. Such an attitude is not easily acquired. Too often, men are simply put in uniform, armed, and called a military force. As Napoleon put it, "The moral is to the physical as two is to one." Moral force, morale, conviction: they are all interrelated and serve as the most powerful motivator a soldier can possess. There are three sources for this motivation: loyalty, personal gain, and desire for adventure. This last one is a chronic defect among the young. Loyalty is more commonly a form of patriotism. Patriotism can come in many forms. The loyalty can be to nation, region, ethnic group, family, organization, or group of friends. Often, loyalty is owed to several of these groups. Patriotism tends to be a group endeavor. If enough individuals are so motivated, they will inspire one another as well as the less motivated members of the group. History has shown that patriotism propels people into situations of almost certain death or injury. The opening stages of wars between patriotic groups are always bloodier than the later stages. As the fighting grinds on, convictions begin to waver. Taken away from the good things one is fighting for, soldiers justify the fight by the prospect of victory and the end of combat. Eventually one side senses its own weakness and looming defeat. The less determined individuals begin to shrink from further combat. This defeatism spreads until the losing side's armed forces fall apart. For this reason, few wars or battles are fought to the death. Some groups have such a high degree of conviction that they will continue until all are dead or incapacitated.

The 1979–89 Afghan war showed how a tradition of warlike behavior plus multiple loyalties (tribe, ethnic group, nation) can produce an extremely high degree of conviction. This conviction was the main reason the Afghans have never been subdued. Being the planet's poorest nation did not substantially diminish this intense conviction in the face of the world's largest army. Less frequently, personal gain and a thirst for adventure propel people into combat. Patriotism plus a dash of adventure have been a traditional lure to get young men to volunteer in the early stages of a war. The adventure rapidly dissipates when the survivors straggle back with tales of how it really is. The bloody horrors of war are not going to prompt many to enlist, so duty and adventure are stressed during recruitment and training. Once under fire, most soldiers fight well enough because it seems a reasonable thing to do in order to survive.

Magic bullets. Many politicians and military leaders are misled by the performance of weapons. Troop leadership and motivation are slippery subjects. Buying the latest high-tech instruments of death and destruction appears as a more certain way to obtain combat power. This is not the way the world really works. The best weapons available in the hands of poorly led, ill-trained, and unmotivated troops will lead to defeat. This is historical experience. The arms merchants' sales brochures will not mention these unpleasant facts. Weapon performance is more capable of measurement in peacetime than motivation, leadership, and competence.

Throughout history, peacetime armies have tended to rely more on technical superiority than on the more slippery factors. Many examples exist. The Soviet army in 1941 was one of the most lavishly equipped in history. Poorly led and trained, and not very well motivated, the Soviets melted before the onslaught of the Germans. The Wehrmacht was not only outnumbered but also had inferior weapons. Another example was the fighting between Israel and Syria in 1982. The Syrians took a beating. Yet Israelis insist that if each side used the other's weapons, the outcome would have been the same. Past experience shows that this is probably true. The most recent example was the Gulf War of 1991. Despite many years of recent combat experience and lavish amounts of weapons and equipment, the Iraqis were overrun by the better-trained and better-led American troops. Yet much of the media coverage of the war emphasized the technology. With more wealth and technology available today than ever before, there is still a tendency to rely on gadgets as an expression of combat power. The preference for hardware over human values in magnificently equipped armies manned by the incompetent and led by people who believe their own press releases is all too common. The historical record tells a quite different story. Again and again, ill-trained troops get their hands on high-tech weapons and make a mess of it. Most of the wars in the Middle East had numerous examples of this. Even the industrialized nations have their shaky moments with their wonder weapons. It's difficult to keep all these wonder weapons in perspective. If you don't, unexpected losses and unpredictable performance will focus your attention.

Money still works. If you pay enough, and your training and leadership appears high (and the quality of the opposition low), you can get some pretty good troops. Mercenaries are still quite common. Some do it as much for adventure as for money, but for most it's a living. The majority of today's mercenaries are government employees. Over 100,000 Cubans have served in Africa as paid representatives of Soviet interests during the 1980s. North Korea, Pakistan, Nepal, Britain, etc., export mercenaries under government contract. Several other nations like Israel, the United States, Russia, and Ukraine do it unofficially. With the end of the Cold War, several consulting companies were formed that provided military advice (and services) to nations in need of it. One can make a case that anyone who volunteers for military service is a mercenary. The dividing line appears to be whose interests you are defending. If you are bearing arms for your own government, you are not a mercenary. If you do it for someone else's, you are. Perhaps the true dividing line is whether or not you are getting shot at. Few of today's mercenaries take up their work with the idea that the job will be fatal. Mercenaries have a bad reputation because they are essentially guns for hire. Whoever hires them tends to use the mercenaries in an abusive manner. They are folks with guns doing the dirty work for people with money. Money still motivates.

Theory and Practice

In modern warfare, the vast majority of troops are never in combat. Even as long ago as World War II, no more than 25 percent of those who served in the U.S. Army ever came under enemy fire of any sort. Today, troops in combat units comprise less than 10 percent of Army strength. The infantry, which takes most of the punishment, accounts for less than half of all "combat" troops. The Air Force and Navy expose even fewer of their personnel to the dangers of combat. In the Russian army, the infantry accounts for less than 20 percent of total manpower. For every infantryman, there is another soldier who gets shot at but is still at less risk than the infantry. Although there is a lot more firepower today, the troops are spread out more. This is a trend that has been going on for the last few centuries. As weapons increase in lethality, the troops take more energetic measures to avoid injury. In theory, the rear-area troops have always been liable to air or long-range artillery attack, and yet they have managed to avoid injury. The use of nuclear weapons can change all that, but in the meantime, wearing a uniform is not as dangerous as it used to be.

With a small fraction of uniformed personnel now assigned to fighting, it becomes more difficult to motivate the combat troops. There is a feeling of unfairness when one is thrust into danger while so many others serve in essentially civilian jobs. This corrosive attitude tends to grow as the combat lengthens and the casualties increase. The classic approach to this problem is to shower the combat troops, and their surviving families, with material and spiritual attention. Cash and praise go a long way toward stiffening the embattled troops' resolve. When these measures are not taken, your combat power fades away. Many nations realize this only when it is too late. A recent example of this can be found in Iraq, where substantial payments were made to the survivors of troops killed in combat during the 1980–88 war with Iran. Combat is an activity for which populations rapidly lose their enthusiasm. U.S. commanders in the Persian Gulf were told during the summer of 1990 that keeping U.S. casualties low was a very high priority. As a result, operations likely to result in high casualties were avoided, which was why there were no amphibious or airborne assaults. One comment heard from several senior officers in the wake of the U.S. Gulf War victory was that no one wanted to be in charge in a future war where more than 200 Americans were killed. No one relished having to explain to Congress why this was so, and why the Gulf War was an exceptional situation that could not be expected to occur in future wars.

The Future

The trend is toward increasingly violent combat that is more debilitating. The faster tempo and increased firepower of modern warfare increase demoralization and combat fatigue. World War I experience with chemical warfare and large-scale artillery barrages demonstrated that the troops on the receiving end of this punishment can quickly be shocked into a state of apathy. Current weapons can generate sufficient firepower more easily and quickly, to do in days or hours what weeks of punishment in World War I required. Nuclear weapons are also expected to have a devastating effect on the morale and motivation of survivors. Sustaining mental health looms as an increasingly crucial task for leaders at all levels. Warfare in the eighties (Afghanistan, Iraq, Lebanon, the Falklands, and the Gulf War) all revealed higher rates of combat fatigue. This problem is exacerbated by the increasing presence of portable radios among the troops. Friendly and enemy news broadcasts make it more difficult for commanders to "control" troop morale. Psychological warfare against enemy morale and motivation has had scant success in the past. But the psywar crowd keeps trying and is getting better. A new form of demoralization is looming, and the first example of it was demonstrated during the 1991 Gulf War, where the Iraqi army was completely demoralized by air bombardment, psywar, and an overwhelming ground offensive. A similar campaign was used against the more resolute Taliban troops during the 2001 Afghan war, with similar results.

The increasing dependence on electronic sensors finds larger number of troops staring at computer terminals. While this is sometimes akin to playing a video game, the results can often be fatal for the player. The troops know this, and their nervous faith in their instruments' reliability creates a new form of stress. Expect to see more combat fatigue among the silicon warriors. The only exception to this is those troops, particularly in the West, who spent many youthful hours playing electronic arcade games. It seems that this experience makes them very facile dealing with the intimidating arrays of screens and buttons found in modern military equipment.

Of more interest to military commanders is the capability of film and video to portray the horrors of war realistically. The pervasive presence of the media makes it important for the government to control information and ensure that the bad news is kept from damaging morale. Most people don't want to fight in the first place and are easily discouraged when confronted with the realities of war. Too much reality, too fast, turns the most stout-hearted troops, and their families, into reluctant warriors. Again, the 1991 Gulf War revealed how seriously the U.S. military considered this problem, and how strenuously they dealt with it.

Peacetime armies tend to lose sight of the need for unit cohesion. Some nations are more successful at maintaining effective unit organization and cohesion in peacetime than others. It is always a problem, so you should expect some surprises when troops go into combat for the first time.

13
Leadership

Good leadership is the glue that keeps a military organization together despite the stresses of combat. Effective military leadership is a fragile thing. It tends to shrivel up and disappear in peacetime. Incompetent wartime military leaders are often highly regarded peacetime commanders. This has been a common pattern throughout history, and for good reason. You can prepare for war, but you can't actually practice the real thing. This places a premium on leaders who can prepare seemingly adequate military forces under peacetime conditions. A lot of their efforts will go toward convincing their superiors that all their efforts and expenditures will have the desired effect when the shooting starts.

Fighting a war, it turns out, requires a quite different mindset than preparing for one. Another problem of military leaders, especially in peacetime, is their tendency to prefer hardware over less tangible items like training and creating effective troops. Hardware you can see and feel. The troops? The goal is often to have the troops smartly turned out. Never mind that effective armies often look like a bunch of bandits. Perfectly aligned and attired formations of soldiers are easier to comprehend than their ability to inflict devastation upon the enemy.

Some nations avoid these peacetime traps to a greater degree than others. A country with a long and systematically preserved military tradition develops better wartime leaders. These military traditions are usually preserved with wars each generation to ensure that memories do not grow dim. The habits and customs of war are bizarre to a nation at peace.

The armed forces must maintain these attitudes blindly between wars. They can do this only after establishing generation after generation of soldiers who will accept certain practices blindly and accurately. This is military tradition. It is sniggered at in peacetime but saves lives in battle. Not all nations have such traditions. Germany has a military tradition, even though it has not

295

won a war in over a century. A military tradition is not about winning wars, but fighting them efficiently. Political leaders start wars and set the stage for eventual victory or defeat. Soldiers fight the battles as best they can under the conditions laid down by the politicians. Other nations with military traditions are Britain, France, Russia, and Japan. The United States has a military tradition for its Navy and Marines, but less so for its Air Force and especially its Army. This underwent a profound change between the end of the Vietnam War (1975) and the late 1980s. The U.S. Army and Air Force radically reformed the way it prepared its leaders and troops for combat. The results were vividly demonstrated in the "hundred hour" war of 1991.

In peacetime, air forces and navies do much the same tasks as they would in wartime. Just moving all their machines around comes very close to wartime conditions. Armies attempt the same thing, but it is too expensive to move large masses of troops around in peacetime. Armies are normally less ready for war than navies and air forces. Human nature being what it is, most leaders, military or otherwise, seek the easy way out. Unless feedback corrects ineffective procedures, bad habits become standards. Flying and navigating the oceans are unforgiving exercises; mistakes are painfully apparent. Pilots and sailors tend to get buried with their mistakes. As a result, navy and air-force leaders are forced to get to know their subordinates' strengths and weaknesses. Armies are larger and more expensive, and there is a great deal of pressure to keep costs down. Army leaders have to rock the boat to smoke out officers who may be ineffective in wartime. Making a commotion is dangerous in any large organization, so the incompetents tend to remain. A leader who either knows from experience or intuition that a subordinate will be ineffective in combat cannot normally take any action. The victim of this dismissal can insist that no grounds exist for the charge. Unless commanders are supported by a widely accepted military tradition, they will be forced to retain a large number of ineffective combat unit commanders. This is the factor that makes some armed forces more effective than another of the same size and composition.

Even experienced and tradition-minded armies find 50 percent or more of the leaders ineffective in wartime. Many will get themselves killed or captured. Unfortunately, the same fate will befall the troops in their charge. How quickly these inadequate leaders can be replaced once the shooting starts is a key ingredient for ultimate success in a war. Meaningful reform of military leadership is no easy task. It can be carried out only by a truly exceptional leader or after a traumatic national defeat. It hardly ever occurs in a nation that has won its previous wars. A rare exception was the reform of the Russian (Soviet) navy under Admiral Sergei Gorshkov. But, then, one can make a case for the Russian navy having "lost" most of its battles during World War II. Although Russia defeated Germany, the Soviets diligently copied many German techniques and weapons after that war. They knew that, man for man, the Germans outfought them.

Scientific Leadership

Leadership is a nebulous quality. While science has conquered many irksome aspects of human frailty, attempts to develop a "scientific" approach to leadership have been difficult. Russia has provided one of the more fascinating attempts with this form of leadership development. Before the 1917 revolution, Russian armies were not much worse than any others. A significant defect was that the highest commands were given to Russian nobles without regard to merit. Other nations did this, but they managed to screen their candidates more carefully. Russian troops, whose training, equipment, and leadership were fairly good, were often misused. After the revolution, three major changes were made. First, officers were appointed on the basis of merit. Second, a scientific approach was embraced for all training and leadership. Third, technically advanced weapons and techniques were sought. All of this affected leadership profoundly. Initiative, resourcefulness, and imagination in combat were to be replaced with scientific planning and precision. During World War II, it was modified by a very large dose of combat experience. Combat experience is highly perishable. The doctrine of scientific leadership was made of more durable stuff. Toward the end of the Soviet period (the 1980s), the Soviet armed forces had become similar to their pre–World War II predecessor. The "Red Army" looked splendidly equipped and scientifically led, but neither the splendid equipment nor the scientific doctrine and leadership have been tested thoroughly. Whenever their armed-forces doctrine had been tested, as during the Afghanistan or Arab-Israeli wars, the Russian approach has been found wanting. Even the noncombat experience of Czechoslovakia in 1968 exposed glaring leadership and control problems.

The Russians have an advantage in that if their training works, their troops will perform their duties according to set procedures. This will give commanders a degree of control and knowledge of who is doing what, even if what the troops are doing is ineffective. Russian officer training emphasizes knowing the "correct" procedure and keeping your wits about you long enough to carry out your orders. To assist this process, every Soviet unit commander had a deputy representing the Communist Party. This fellow also went to officer training school but has selected a decidedly different specialty. The political officer was responsible for the ideological purity of the troops and reported to the party, not his unit commander. This "*zampolit*" recruited informers among the troops and used these agents to keep an eye on everyone and everything. If the unit did not perform well, both the military commander and the political officer were in big trouble. The political officer typically covered his ass by sending in a lot of reports to the party. If things got hairy, he could at least say he had warned the party authorities. In practice, the political officer and unit commander normally worked well together. Both had the same goals of military effectiveness. However, if there was any dissidence among the troops, or any incident that smacked of "anti-party" attitudes, the harsh hand of party discipline came down hard and fast. In this case, military effectiveness took a back seat to ideological purity. The military commander constantly had to look over his shoulder at his *zampolit*. This was not a very efficient system, and this was demonstrated frequently. During World War II, the political officers lost some of their power and got it all back as soon as the Germans were defeated. Variations on the *zampolit* system are common in the armies of dictatorships. Interestingly, the Russian army reintroduced the *zampolit* (under a different name) in 2001. The new *zampolit* was more of a morale officer and ombudsman. It will take a while to discover if a nonpolitical *zampolit* will work.

Western armies often place too much responsibility on the individual leaders and less on the system. This is fine if the leaders are up to the demands. But the only substitute for combat experience is some form of system. The Germans were good at developing both system and leadership. The German army entered World War II with a tactical doctrine based upon a careful analysis of their World War I experience. This doctrine was put into a manual that was regarded as a bible by combat officers. The procedures found in *Tante Friede* ("Aunt Friede," the nickname for the manual) got officers through enough combat to give them experience. At that point they could use their resourcefulness and imagination to stay one jump ahead of the enemy. This German approach was at once purposeful and pragmatic. It helped the slow learner to survive and allowed the talented combat officer to achieve great success.

Operating Within the Cycle

Combat is generally a series of intentional or accidental ambushes. Self-preservation and the obvious appeal of hitting the other fellow when he can't fight back make ambush the most sought-after situation. To pull this off, you must practice another skill: operating within the other guy's cycle. A person's or unit's "cycle" is nothing more than its limitations in reacting to events. In sports, athletes outperform less skillful opponents by moving or reacting first. A superior boxer, as an example of maneuver warfare, doesn't just parry his opponent's punch; he gets in one of his own. A superior fighter operates within his opponent's ability to respond. Skillful soldiers operate the same way. Even if a defender seems to have every advantage, a more skillful attack can uncover and exploit the defender's weaknesses. An attacker's superior ability to move, conceal himself, and use his weapons can negate a defender's advantages and enable the attack to succeed with minimal losses. Leadership makes this work. But it takes a particular kind of leader, one that not every nation can produce. Such leaders must know the techniques of their craft, whether it be air force, army, or navy. These leaders must know their troops well and be actively involved in their training and well-being. Last, good leaders must lead. This often involves getting out front where it is quite dangerous. One indicator of a well-led army is that officers have a higher casualty rate than their troops. History has demonstrated through the ages that any troops can be turned into competent soldiers if they have competent officers. Leadership is always the key.

Push-Button Leadership

Until about a century ago, leaders had to command through shouting, messengers, or signal flags. They still got the job done. Today, leaders are often helpless without radios, telephones, and other electronic gadgets. Leaders can now command far beyond what they can see. Extreme examples were seen during the Vietnam war, when platoon leaders in the bush sometimes got tactical advice direct from the White House. Micromanagement was rarely that extreme, but it was pervasive. Senior commanders tend to want more control and information. Only exceptional leaders can resist this temptation. During World War II, the Germans went out of their way to keep senior commanders from running small-level operations they could not see. The Soviets and Japanese didn't have sufficient communications equipment. The other Western armies did start a trend that eventually turned the American president into a platoon commander. This problem is now recognized by all armies. Everyone assumes at least a lip-service attitude toward a solution. However, there is a positive side. The information flows both ways. Commanders of larger units can get a more accurate picture of how their entire organization is doing. The hundreds of reports that move up the chain of command help to dissipate the fog of war.

Computers are increasingly used to sort out this data quickly. This effort is called "digitalization," and it basically means connecting all the tanks, warplanes, artillery, and infantry as if they were in an office computer network. Making this work has been a major American military goal for most of the 1990s. In Kosovo (1999), there were times when it was possible to pull it off. It isn't easy, but when it worked, it was great. A recon aircraft points a heat-sensing camera at enemy territory; the picture is sent, via satellite, back to the United States, where targets are found by powerful computers. The target location is sent back, via satellite, to a U.S. bomber in the vicinity, which then enters the location of the target into a GPS-guided bomb and releases the now-enlightened bomb that promptly hits the target. All in minutes. The same thing can be done when some infantryman on the ground sees a choice target. A bomber, artillery, or tank fire can be called in within minutes. Digitalization wasn't universal during the Kosovo campaign, but it was used enough to make everyone believers. Even more of it was used in Afghanistan two years later, with even more impressive results. Oddly enough, digitalization is helping the lower-level commanders and troops avoid micromanagement. Digitalization speeds up operations so much that there's literally no time for more senior commanders to interfere.

Since the 1960s, there have been efforts to provide "artificial intelligence" programs to help the commander make effective decisions with these increasing masses of information. Some items, like artillery, logistical planning, and intelligence analysis are ideally suited to this approach.

If the electronic tools are not working, the effects on leadership can be devastating. This is why we have electronic warfare (EW). Communications are the primary target of EW. Without fresh supplies of data, the computers no longer have much to do. Exclusive reliance on electronic tools, without adequate backup systems and procedures, can prove fatal in wartime. Western armies have tried to solve this problem with more technology, while Russian-style armies go back to simpler manual methods for backups.

Facing up to such problems and developing effective solutions is another characteristic of superior leadership. Something as simple as using EW frequently during exercises can give the troops invaluable experience in coping with these problems. Attention to this has been spotty. One of the more embarrassing aspects of a major future war would be the general inability to cope with the loss of communication because of electronic warfare.

Creating Leaders

There are only a few basic approaches to selecting and training military leaders:

The gentleman officer is the oldest approach. Get an overeducated fellow with a lust for blood and adventure, and give him a pretty uniform and some authority. The United States inherited this terrible system from the British during the Revolution and still uses it. This is sometimes called "Burgoyne's revenge," after the remarkably inept British general "Gentleman Johnny Burgoyne." Note that Britain's long combat experience produced customs that negated many of the bad effects of this system. For example, British NCOs tend to be superb. The officers are expected, if nothing else, to provide a good example for the troops. If this means little more than standing up, leading the attack, and being quickly killed, the officer has done his duty. Unfortunately, not all nations that adopt this system have good NCOs, or inept officers who will get out in front. The gentleman-officer approach, still widely used in Third World nations, generally leads to a credibility gap between the troops and the leaders appointed to lead them.

The aspirant is a more effective system. This is a "trial by experience" method of selection and promotion. It can be traced back to the Romans (2,000 years ago), and earlier. This really works best during a war, although it has advantages even in peacetime. Potential officers are selected from the troops and systematically put into higher and higher positions of responsibility. The theory is that a man who can't lead a squad isn't going to do any better with a platoon, company, battalion, or army. Germany and Israel, an odd pair, both use this system. In peacetime. the officer candidate is also given a technical and scholarly education, if he isn't already a university graduate. Education is considered a nice touch, but the cut is made ruthlessly at each level of command. At worst, you will end up with good small-unit commanders. Troops and subordinate leaders respond well to this system, as they know that their leaders have been where they are and know what it's like. Most nations fall back on this system in wartime to a certain extent by turning many capable NCOs into officers ("battlefield commissions").

Trial by examination. This is a pervasive curse of educated cultures. Academics are obsessed by the thought that you can evaluate a person's abilities through written examination. It is true that people who excel at examinations are often bright, but what has that got to do with leadership? Particularly leadership in combat? Very little. The examination process does select leaders who at least have book knowledge of their profession. Russia uses this method extensively, as do, to a lesser extent, other industrialized nations. Its major drawback is that it tends to depend on the examination process to rate qualities that are not easily evaluated by written exercises. In particular, promotions are often dependent on examination performance. This system is usually accompanied by an officer-rating system, where each year commanders rate their subordinates. While this spotlights the really outstanding people, it really does nothing for the vast majority. This path of least resistance becomes a fatal flaw when the shooting starts.

Trial by fire. In wartime, this is often the system that just naturally emerges. In the hazardous atmosphere of combat, only the competent survive. This is a new system in peacetime, however, and it was pioneered by the United States. The American version arose from the proliferation of electronic substitutes for weapons and the ancient (but rarely used) technique of training against people operating like potential enemies. The Air Force and the Navy were the first to introduce this system during the 1970s. The Navy's Top Gun school for training carrier pilots was adopted by the Air Force. The Navy used similar technology to train its submarine and surface-ship crews. In the early 1980s, the Army applied the use of electronic scoring and a realistic opposing force to train units. All of these techniques were initially used simply to train the troops more effectively and to make them more capable of dealing with the often quite different techniques potential enemies might use. But after Vietnam, the U.S. Army also took a hard look at its use of the gentleman-officer system and made some key changes. The principal one was a result of the use of more realistic combat training. The use of electronic scoring of weapons "fired" led to the evaluation of officers on their performance under these realistic conditions. Many officers were found wanting, and the presence of such a screening device profoundly changed the attitudes of the officers and their troops. Since battlefield competence could now be measured more accurately in peacetime than ever before, the officers adopted a much more professional attitude toward their jobs. At base, the U.S. system was still the "gentleman officer," but now the gentlemen were much more effective combat leaders, as was vividly demonstrated during the 1991 Gulf War.

Variations. Each nation selects its military leaders on the basis of its military traditions, experience, and perceived needs. Nations that have been defeated are prone to change their systems. Similarly, nations that have not suffered a traumatic defeat, or have not fought a war for a long time, will not change. Resistance to change often occurs after a dramatic victory, resting on one's laurels, as it were. This is how obviously inefficient systems have persisted. It is unlikely that change will occur any other way. Vietnam was the "defeat" that spurred reform in the U.S. military, and the Gulf War looms as the "victory" that may cause a lapse into bad habits.

At the end of the book we have a chart that gives a quality value for each nation's armed forces. This is an indicator of leadership quality. It shows who is ahead in this area and who needs improvement. A common problem in many nations is the ability to attract good candidates. It is easier to create superior leaders if your raw material is superior to begin with. This happens only if the military attracts superior candidates. Social attitudes toward the military profession in peacetime vary from nation to nation. Most societies view the military profession with some disdain. At the very least, several other professions that engender more respect and career prospects will attract much of the talent the military needs to be effective. After all, the military absorbs considerable sums of money in return for an intangible, and often debatable, degree of national security. There is no way, short of a war, for the military to prove that it is doing its job adequately.

The Zero Approach

"Zero tolerance" has become the military mantra in the United States for dealing with embarrassing publicity. But by taking a "no mistakes allowed" approach, much damage has been done to combat readiness and troop morale.

Getting ready for combat means taking chances with people and making mistakes. You can't do that anymore. It wasn't always that way. In fact, it's only in the last century that the military has gradually come to operate in a glass bowl. All this media attention has created a lot of embarrassment for the troops. Men who prepare themselves for combat do some strange things. For thousands of years, this odd behavior was ignored.

The generals noticed the growth of mass media and the increasing attention the military was getting. In the 1920s, when radio came into use, Douglas MacArthur was appointed the Army's first media liaison officer. MacArthur was an inspired choice for the job, as he had a talent for publicity and sufficient ambition to make the most of it. And the military did well with the media up until the late 1960s, when public dissatisfaction with the progress of the Vietnam War showed the brass that media scrutiny could also be very painful. Moreover, the electronic media turned out to be even more casual with the truth than its print colleagues. Facts were not allowed to get in the way of a good story, and since TV news moved faster than newspapers, there was even less time to double check things. We had entered the era of urban legends: plausible-sounding events that, while widely believed and repeated, were revealed as false when examined closely. A lot of unflattering urban legends came out of the Vietnam era. The media was no longer content to leave the military alone. The troops were now fair game, and all those odd customs and practices were great television.

The military was also changing from within, reacting to cultural changes. Early in the century, the military went high-tech with expensive and complicated warships and equally complex new weapons for the Army. By 1920, air power was a major force. Recruiting standards went up. Being a good warrior was no longer enough for most jobs; you had to have some education. It wasn't until World War II that the old-style soldiers (dutiful but a little dim) disappeared. One nasty side effect of this change was the segregation of the Navy in 1914. Since its beginning, the Navy had been integrated. But in the late nineteenth century, the southern states regained their self-rule and imposed segregation to maintain whites in power. Service in the new high-tech Navy became attractive to more southerners. Naturally, it would not do to have white southern lads serving alongside blacks, so pressure was applied and the Navy was segregated. Integration did not return until the 1950s.

Women in the military became an issue after Vietnam, when slogans replaced common sense. For thousands of years, women had served among the mass of civilians who followed the army to take care of the camp, tend to the wounded, and otherwise keep the troops alive when they weren't fighting. This fell out of fashion in the last two centuries as armies became more professional and a largely men-only operation. That began to change a century ago, when World War I and a manpower shortage put women into uniform for the first time. No longer civilian camp followers, women now did the increasing number of military jobs that did not require a lot of muscle and murderous intent.

For the last thirty years, it has become fashionable to believe that soldiers are just another bunch of civil servants and that the troops should behave like civilians. For the last century, more and more people in uniform were doing civilian-type jobs, so it seemed reasonable to expect civilian-type behavior. But there were still a lot of trained killers in the ranks, men (and a few women) who had gone through the ancient drills that turn an ordinary person into someone who will murder on command. These lads were always difficult to control when they weren't in combat.

But it got worse as the late twentieth century brought with it a lot of sensitivities. Gender, sexual preference, and ethnicity were the big taboos when it came to loose talk and physical harassment. The generals knew they had a problem with all these new demands, so they decided to cop out and insist on zero tolerance. Anyone who got out of line was severely punished: one strike and you're out. This got the brass off the hook, but it changed the atmosphere in the ranks. Millions of hours a year were now devoted to sensitivity training. The troops were made to understand that any misbehavior would get you in big trouble, perhaps even booted out of the service. The new atmosphere did discourage a lot of young men from joining and encouraged many more to use the new easy-out option (tell your commander that you are homosexual, even if you aren't; most let out of the service this way are not). Career officers and NCOs under pressure to keep people in uniform and out of trouble had only one option: cover up transgressions. Zero tolerance soon became a game. If someone got out of line and it made it into the media, than you hung him out to dry. But otherwise, you played the game and pretended zero tolerance was working. Training, morale, leadership development, retention, and a lot of other things took a back seat to playing the game. No one in politics or the media wants to look at what's really happening in the ranks, for that would be an admission of failure. It was a truly zero approach.

Marketing the Product

To obtain additional funds from unenthusiastic taxpayers, the military tends to downplay its abilities relative to its potential enemies. The average citizen wonders where all the money is going when the armed forces always protest that they are not up to doing their job without seemingly endless additional funds. The situation is different in nations bordered by obviously belligerent and historically hostile forces. Here the average citizen regards the military in a different light. Service in the military is seen as a high calling, a true public service that can attract superior manpower. In a situation like this, the military gains further credibility because it possesses superior officers. This is especially true in nations that fill the ranks by universal conscription. Israel, Switzerland, and

Germany are examples of this type. Germany has a long tradition of threatened borders and a need for strong and effective military forces. Even the traumas of World War I and II have not shaken this tradition.

Another method of attracting superior talent is by having less competition from the civilian economy. Less developed nations lack enough suitable jobs for young, talented, ambitious, and educated youngsters. The result is a highly professional, often well led, although usually poorly equipped, military. This is not the case if the military is simply a police force for the party in power. In this case, these bright young lads become the leaders of heavily armed cops. India, China, and even Russia have superior candidates for their officer openings because of a lack of opportunity in the civilian sector. As China loosened up its economic controls in the 1980s, it had to demobilize over a million soldiers to save money for development and modernization, and to avoid a labor shortage. In this way they got rid of a lot of deadwood that had accumulated during over 20 years of little military, but considerable political, activity in the armed forces. The other extreme is the United States and Western nations. Except in countries where the military has a modicum of respect, recruiting the best leadership talent is an uphill struggle.

The Obvious Effects of Superior Leadership

Consider the numerous examples of the impact of excellent leadership. World War II revealed many. In 1950, the American counteroffensive against North Korea was a brilliant illustration. Shortly thereafter the Chinese provided another example when they moved into Korea. The Arab-Israeli wars are a continuous chain of combat successes caused by superior leadership. Most of these events were the result of Israeli leadership. But in 1973, the Egyptian commanders outdid the Israelis in the opening stages of that war. Superior leadership need not be of earthshaking dimensions in order to be effective. As long as one side's leaders are demonstrably better than the other's, speedy victory will usually result. All other things being equal, if a war breaks out and does not come to a rapid conclusion, you can be fairly certain that neither side has a marked leadership advantage. If one side is larger than the other, you can assume that the smaller force, by avoiding rapid defeat, has superior leaders.

In peacetime, the effects of superior leadership are more difficult to detect. Success does not manifest itself until the improvements are put to the test of combat. However, some examples are so extraordinary in their results that they spotlight superior peacetime leadership. Admiral Hyman G. Rickover's role in the development of American nuclear submarines is one example. Admiral Sergei Gorshkov was a counterpart in the Soviet navy. The Army and Air Force officers who reformed the U.S. military after Vietnam have yet to get the recognition they deserve. Many other peacetime leaders exist who almost single-handedly introduced reforms or the development of radically effective new weapons or equipment. Unfortunately, it is more difficult to determine before-hand who the effective future combat leaders are. And on that issue, the potential outcomes of these wars become murky.

The Troops

Although the old truism, "There are no bad troops, only bad officers," still applies, there are significant differences in the intrinsic quality of troops. Let's start with the basic distribution of skill and intelligence in any population. Tests have shown that troops drawn from the more intelligent 20 percent of the population can perform tasks about twice as efficiently as those in the lower 20 percent. This applies particularly to such things as hitting another tank with a missile or gun. A cross-section of tests on infantry skills yields the same results. There are also very real cultural differences. The Ghurka soldiers from Nepal have served as highly valued mercenary infantry for several centuries. Many other cultures are noted for their skill and enthusiasm for combat. There is another problem found in mercenary troops that applies to many national armies. In the former Soviet Union, for example, nearly half the population was not fluent in Russian, and recruits had to be first taught a sparse "military" vocabulary before they could be trained in military skills. Russia, today, still has a substantial minority of recruits who do not speak Russian and has had to continue the old Soviet practice. Age also plays a role, with men in their 20s much more efficient than teenage soldiers. An effective officer must be aware of the nature of his troops and the proven remedies for whatever shortcomings these recruits may have. Military history is littered with unsuccessful officers who lacked insight and forethought. It's not enough to lead; you have to know where you're coming from and where you're going.

Low-Sweat, High-Casualty Training

Turning civilians into soldiers has always been a tricky process. But as we enter the twenty-first century, it's gotten even more difficult.

For thousands of years, experienced combat troops have known that "the more you sweat in peace, the less you bleed in war." But basic training, that initial two or three months of intense instruction that tries to turn a civilian into something resembling a soldier, is falling apart in the U.S. military. This is particularly sad in light of the American experience with "boot camp." During World War II, the U.S. Army surveyed the troops to see what they thought about their training, leadership, and a host of other items. The surveys were published after the war in a two-volume work called *The American Soldier* (Stouffer, et al.). One of the more surprising things to come out of these surveys was the feeling among combat troops that their training wasn't tough enough. World War II "basic" was generally quite intense, more severe than anything recruits experienced in the last 50 years. But actual combat quickly revealed that even more intensity in that training would have been a big, often lifesaving, help.

Why has basic training gotten less effective since those surveys were taken? For the same reason it is so difficult to explain what a "warrior" is and what it takes to turn citizens into efficient killers. Combat is an experience far from everyday life. It's very difficult to explain it to those who haven't been there. But a growing problem is the changing composition of the military, with less than 10 percent of the recruits headed for exposure to combat. A combination of ignorance and nonchalance creates an attitude that considers overkill the rigors of effective basic training. Many of the kids complain, and in peacetime the parents are less likely to see the need for all the stress and danger of realistic training. They, too, complain to politicians (usually a member of Congress), who will contact the Pentagon and demand an explanation. The brass, not willing to offend someone who votes on the military budget and approves their promotions, will too often take the easy way out and tell the training NCOs to cool it.

Another problem is that the men who conduct the training, specially selected NCOs, are not always able or even allowed to explain to Congress, or the public, what they are doing and why they are doing it. The NCOs have a particular interest in training the recruits to a high standard, for duty as basic-training instructor is a temporary one. Eventually these NCOs go back to units that have to make use of troops who went through basic training. If it's a combat unit, the NCO instructor's own life is at stake, for badly trained recruits will make mistakes in combat that will get themselves, and their NCOs, killed. But to most civilians, all the running around and shouting "kill" by the recruits is, at the very least, distasteful and, to an increasing number of voters, not really necessary.

With the officers putting a brave face on it, and the Pentagon not in the least interested in measuring what effect bad training is having on combat readiness, the issue will stay buried until the next war. The troops that then come out of combat complaining about the inadequacy of their training will get some attention. But with the return of peace will come a return to business as usual. The cycle will begin again: some recruits will complain, the media will do a story or two about the needless stress and brutality of basic training, and the standards will be cut down again.

How bad has it gotten? Let's take the stress angle. This is what aggravates most recruits, even though it's supposed to. The primary purpose of basic training is to prepare troops for the stress of a combat situation. You learn to keep your wits about you in a chaotic situation by having NCOs create nonlethal situations that mimic the chaos and pandemonium of combat. This includes physical exhaustion and being forced to react quickly and automatically to certain situations, like getting shot at or being fired on by artillery. Well, you can't do that with live ammunition in peacetime, but the military has found relatively safe ways to recreate it. And all the time, your NCOs are shouting orders at you and correcting your mistakes. In combat, your mistakes are usually fatal, with no opportunity for your NCOs to point out your errors and advise you on the correct procedures.

In the last few decades, yelling at recruits, except in the Marines, has become a no-no. If the weather is too hot, too cold, or too wet, then training is canceled that day. If a recruit seems stressed out, officers (rarely NCOs) will intervene to ease up the tempo of training. The current feeling is that the recruits should feel comfortable as they go through their training. The officers in charge of recruit training have gone for this low-stress approach in a big way, for they get unwanted attention from politicians if they do not, and nothing bad happens to them if they turn out troops unready for war.

The combat units know better and try and make up for the deficiencies of basic training. After basic training, soldiers get specialized training. Combat troops get, in effect, another few months of basic. But this advanced training is supposed to concentrate on perfecting their combat skills, not teach the basics of discipline and dealing with stress. The infantry, armor, and artillery troops passed from advanced training on to combat units sacrifice their training in practical skills for remedial training on how a soldier is supposed to react in combat.

Another important purpose of basic training is to teach discipline and the ability to respond quickly and effectively to orders from your NCOs and officers. The emphasis on not "stressing the recruit" means that you find that you are getting a lot of surly, undisciplined wimps. Even noncombat units suffer from this, for even support troops are called on to work crazy hours or suddenly move themselves and all their equipment thousands of miles on short notice. Without discipline this becomes difficult, and often the units are unable to do their job adequately. In any situation short of a major war, you can hide these problems, and that's what happens with increasing frequency. Welcome to the low-stress twenty-first century.

The Lessons of Vietnam

As we enter the twenty-first century, we face more small, complex wars, rather than larger, straightforward ones. With that in mind, it's a good idea to review one of the most complex wars of the twenty-first century. The lessons of the Vietnam war were many, but the most important insight is that we have gone on to ignore all of them. Are you shocked? Read the list and get depressed.

Don't get involved in civil wars. That's an old historical lesson no one should forget. But now we have gotten into Civil War Central with troops stationed all over the Balkans, and many Americans urging that troops be sent to African civil wars as well.

Don't micromanage the troops. This got a lot of Americans killed in Vietnam, where rapid global communications made it possible for the president to direct operations personally. Now we have even better spy satellites that send information straight to the White House. Commanders on the scene who complain about it get bad-mouthed.

Let the military run the military. No more. Congress issues more detailed instructions than ever on how the military must (not should) recruit, train, and discipline its troops. The military calls it social engineering; Congress calls it pandering for votes. Officers and NCOs are leaving in numbers so large that even the normally comatose generals and admirals have to take notice.

Don't get in a war you don't intend to win. That one was never popular with politicians. As long as they had good polls behind them, they never met a war they didn't like. If the voters changed their minds, so would the politicians. This sort of thing leaves a bad aftertaste among the voters, but they have short memories. And the troops hate it, for it means they are risking their lives so someone way up the food chain can improve his chances for reelection.

Incrementalism doesn't work. This is not exactly true. Applying military pressure in stages didn't work in Vietnam because the Communists were willing to accept all the pain we could apply. The North Vietnamese had the backing of Russia and China to prevent us from really doing a number on them. In the past, "gunboat diplomacy" has worked to change a government's mind. But it's a dangerous game to play. Guess wrong and you either look like a fool (as in Somalia) or get sucked into a war you don't want (Vietnam). Incrementalism is especially popular among politicians and diplomats who see soldiers' lives as something used to buy a temporary political advantage with.

Telling the truth. The U.S. government would never admit exactly what its prospects were in Vietnam, especially when they were mixed or bad. It was the lies, as much as the dead GIs, that turned the voters against the war effort. The same thing happened in Somalia, and a similar situation is brewing in the Balkans.

Ignoring history. Taking a sober look at history would have kept us out of Vietnam. But politics is often the triumph of political ambitions over historical facts. It is still happening. We never seem to learn.

See what is really there. The lies were bad enough, but it had an equally unpleasant side effect in distorting history, or at least the popular versions of events. For example, U.S. troops were never defeated in Vietnam. The Communist troops were thoroughly cowed by American battlefield prowess, and after 1968 they basically retreated to the bush to wait us out. American troops left Vietnam in 1972, not 1975 as many current news stories have it, and the troops left because Congress and the president ordered them out. In 1972, the North Vietnamese tried to conquer South Vietnam with conventional forces and were defeated by South Vietnamese troops and American airpower. In 1975, Congress had cut off most support for South Vietnam, and the third North Vietnamese invasion of the south succeeded. A similar outcome was seen in Somalia in 1993, where 18 U.S. troops were killed after they were set upon by a much larger Somali force (which lost some 500 dead). The U.S. troops wanted to go back the next day and finish the job, and the Somalis were thoroughly cowed (not an easy thing to do to the combative Somalis). But overnight, the U.S. media declared the Somali defeat, a U.S. defeat and that was that.

As has often been said, those who fail to learn from history are doomed to repeat it. The war on terrorism was a wake-up call. It was an unambiguous attack on America, and it focused leadership on lessons of experience in a manner not seen since World War II. Will this focus last?

Rank and Organization

Worldwide, military organizations tend to use the same patterns and rank structure. Ranks are divided into three groups; troops, noncommissioned officers, and commissioned officers. The "ordinary" soldiers have ranks for recruits and one or two ranks for trained soldiers. Terms in English-speaking countries for these lowest ranking troops are: private, soldier, marine, seaman, and airman. Noncommissioned officers are the traditional professional, long-term soldiers with sufficient experience and talent to lead or supervise soldiers. British-derived terms are sergeant and petty officer (navy).

Several grades of NCO ranks exist, corresponding to the size of the unit. NCOs command units from fire team (4–5 men) to platoon size. At the platoon level, NCOs sometimes share command with the lowest rank of commissioned officer.

Commissioned officers are so called because they are "commissioned" by their government to lead the combat forces. Three levels of officers exist:

Company grade (lieutenants and captains in the army/air force; ensigns and lieutenants in the navy). These are the apprentice officers and rarely command more than a company or a very small ship.

Field grade (majors and colonels in the army/air force; commanders and captains in the navy). Field-grade officers command battalions, regiments, and brigades, as well as ships of all sizes.

Flag officers (generals in the army/air force; admirals in the navy).

Staff officers serve in staffs of units one level higher than they would normally command. More officers serve in staff than in command positions. This is because each unit of battalion size and larger has but one commander but four or more staff officers. Each unit from company size up also has one or more "assistant commanders" who help the commander out and take his place if he becomes a casualty. These assistants are customarily one rank lower than the commander. Significant variations can be found, particularly in the organization of staffs. Nearly all nations organize their staffs along these functional areas:

Personnel. Keeping track of the troops, and maintaining performance records for officers (and often NCOs) to determine who should be promoted and when. Dictatorships often use the "personnel" staff officer as the local spy, to keep an eye on officer and troop loyalty.

Intelligence. Collects and analyzes information about the enemy. This is a cushy job in peacetime, but a real career-killer when the shooting starts and you have to perform against a hostile and secretive enemy.

Operations. Planned and supervised operations of the unit. The head of this section was often also the "chief of staff" and was the first among equals among the staff section commanders. Good performance in this job was generally a prerequisite for promotion to command of the unit.

Logistics. Taking care of supply and maintenance of equipment. This is another job that is often much more difficult in wartime than in peacetime.

Other. Most common is a section dealing with civilian affairs in enemy territory. Some nations also have a separate "political" section.

Several nations provide a separate set of ranks for "technical experts" to recognize technically expert troops who do not perform supervisory functions. Most of the time, this is done by expanding the number of NCOs to provide the needed monetary and social incentives. Only those NCOs occupying leadership jobs have the traditional authority and rank of NCOs. The specialists have the same pay scales as the NCOs but sometimes are given different titles. For many years the U.S. Army used a parallel rank structure for enlisted troops. Instead of a lot more NCOs, you had troops with the rank of Specialist 4, 5, 6, etc. (the numbers representing pay grade). This caused problems with the older troops in the senior grades, to the point that in the early 1980s, all grades but Specialist 4 were eliminated. For the older and more experienced technical people, use was made of four grades of warrant officer. This rank was given all the privileges of officers but, in theory, none of the leadership responsibility. The "warrant" approach is quite common as the need for uniformed technicians increases. This has been another case of making people something that is neither fish nor fowl. Many nations use warrant officers and then eliminate them, and then bring them back again. Russia's inability to develop effective NCOs caused them to introduce their version of warrant officers in the 1970s. They were unable to attract a large number of candidates, partially because of resistance from regular officers.

Camp Followers in Uniform

Finally, after thousands of years, we got around to putting the camp followers in uniform. This is another of those remarkable, and largely unnoticed, twentieth-century military developments.

Camp followers usually are thought of as loose women following an army to service the troops. There was always some of that—still is—but historically, camp followers have largely been male, and mainly there to do the housekeeping and keep alive the troops in the field.

Battles have always been relatively rare, but the health hazards of camping out, with thousands of men and horses crowded together, were constant and abundant. The troops knew this, and until the last few centuries, most soldiers were volunteers of one sort or another, and few generals could get their lads to rough it without a lot of camp followers to keep everyone in good health.

There were usually more camp followers than troops, with the ratio of helpers to fighters as high as 10:1. There was a lot for camp followers to do. Pack animals had to be cared for, tents pitched, water carried, wood chopped, food bought or stolen from the locals and cooked. Then everything had to be packed up for the next march. During battles, the camp followers stayed behind in the camp, often fortifying it and using a few weapons and their bare hands to defend it against any enemy troops who got that far. After the battles, camp followers tended to the injured, buried the dead, and plundered the enemy corpses.

While it was much more efficient to have the troops do their own housekeeping in the field, few armies were disciplined enough to pull this off. The more successful armies did, like the ancient Romans, who traveled light. When a Roman army of 10,000 showed up, there were some 8,000 fighters with it. Most other armies could produce only a few thousand warriors. Since most armies lived off the land, and this often limited the size of the army, the force that hauled along the fewest camp followers had a substantial military advantage.

This lesson eventually was relearned, and camp followers began to thin out in most Western armies. A century ago, support troops amounted to less than 15 percent of an army. But in the last century a lot more equipment has been added. Not just things like trucks, trains, transport aircraft, and cargo ships that civilians could be hired to run, but weapons and other gear close to the front that needed soldiers to take care of them. Now the camp followers comprise about 85 percent of the troops. Yet everyone wears the same uniform and gets the same pay. Combat troops get a small bonus when they are in a combat zone, but that's about it. Combat officers still get most of the senior positions, but that is starting to change because of the sheer number of noncombat officers versus the warrior types.

This change has been going on for several generations, and, more and more, the generals think less like fighters and more like bureaucrats. In the past, whenever bureaucrats have been appointed to run an army, disaster arrived along with the next war. Watch for it.

Theory and Practice

Peacetime soldiers lack practical experience with combat activities. Most troops have not actually used many combat techniques, or have not used them in cooperation with other combat units. The knowledge of these procedures and the ability to use them determine who will prevail in a war. Peacetime leadership comes down to whether or not leaders can maintain a knowledge of efficient combat activities and effectively pass this knowledge on to their troops. The patterns of a combat officer's daily routine differ considerably in peacetime and wartime. Wartime conditions are hellish and not fondly remembered or re-created in peacetime. Peacetime habits tend toward bureaucratic routine and avoiding unpleasantness. Officers that push their troops toward more rigorous, and inevitably dangerous, training activities are often tolerated and accepted by the troops. Such officers can, however, get in trouble with the civilians and the press. In democracies, more training injuries can attract unpleasant attention from the press and elected officials.

Dictatorships are often in worse shape in wartime because officers are chosen first (in peacetime) on the basis of their political reliability. Such individuals have shown themselves more comfortable behind a desk than thrashing about in the bush with a bunch of lowlife enlisted scum. Some nations rise above the tendency to be unprepared for combat. They do this by following military "traditions" blindly and/or having a good supply of clear-headed and persistent officers who never shut up about the importance of keeping the troops in shape for combat. But these groups are the minority. Military leaders tend to be bureaucrats in uniform.

Another problem with military leadership is that there tends to be a relationship between the ratio of leaders to troops and the effectiveness of those leaders. It is easier to create additional officers than it is to ensure that those you have are up to their jobs. This is one area where quantity does not compensate for quality. Various reasons are put forward for this officer explosion. One is that more complex technology requires more officers who tend to be better educated. This, however, clouds the issue of what a military officer is. Originally, officers were government officials who performed a dangerous job—they led soldiers in combat. That description today fits less than 10 percent of officers. While all officers are thought of as soldiers, only a small percentage are. Some armies solve this problem by creating new classes of officials, who are paid more and given officer-like privileges, but are not considered officers. In most armies, there is little obvious distinction between combat and noncombat officers. The net result of all this is to diminish the stature of the real combat leaders, the ones who actually direct the fighting. This weakens the armed forces in order to give the noncombat officers a vicarious thrill.

Normally, it is nearly impossible to give leaders of combat units realistic training during peacetime. In the past this was overcome only during the 1800s when the Germans introduced detailed war games. These games required time and diligence to use and were only as good as the historical experience that was built into them. Such games could not easily represent new developments in weapons, equipment, and other factors. Few officers had the devotion necessary to make these games work. In the 1980s, the United States began using a new training system that used nonlethal lasers to represent real weapons. All participating troops and vehicles have sensors so that hits can be recorded. The entire battle area is wired with sensors so that all the action can be recorded and reviewed later. At first, only direct-fire weapons were wired into the system. But now mines and some forms of artillery are incorporated. At the U.S. National Training Center (NTC), U.S. battalions go up against a U.S. version of a Russian infantry regiment. The "Russian" unit is quite good, as it gets a lot of practice. This unit is said to be the best Russian infantry regiment in the world. The American units get very realistic training, as can be seen from the similarity of the results with what is encountered during combat. The good news is that this is a source of combat experience without massive loss of life. The bad news is that each U.S. combat battalion can get only two weeks of this training every two years. This program has been expanded, especially after the demonstrated success of the program's training effect in the Gulf War. No other nation has anything quite like it, although many are trying to set up their own versions. If history is any guide, those nations with a predilection for routine drills will prove debilitating if they ever encountered American units possessed of realistic training. This is precisely what happened in the Persian Gulf. These same training practices are applied in the U.S. Air Force and Navy.

During the Vietnam War, both the Air Force and naval combat pilots discovered how inadequate their peacetime training had been. The Top Gun training programs begun in the late 1960s have been continued and expanded. The Navy has used similar training for their ship crews, although they have been unable to provide realistic training for the most dangerous, unpredictable, and chaotic of their combat operations: damage control.

The Future

During peacetime, armed forces endure a constant struggle between the "warrior" and "manager" mentality, and it's getting worse. Peacetime soldiers have always grumbled about "political generals" and officers more concerned with their careers than their ability to succeed in combat. This debate has taken on new meaning as armed forces become more mechanized and automated. An increasing proportion of officers will never lead troops in combat. Their jobs, even in wartime, consist of keeping a lot of machines operational. That group of hard-charging and ruthless characters known as "warrior officers" becomes increasingly smaller. When it comes to a shouting contest over policy, numbers still count. Although combat officers are usually given priority when it comes to promotions to general and admiral, there is increasing pressure to give the technician officers more of the goodies. We are already seeing problems with more senior commanders being very timid and tentative commanding combat units. This was seen in the 1991 Gulf War (where the U.S. ground-forces commander was roundly criticized for timidity), in 1993 in Somalia (where senior commanders underestimated both the opposition as well as the ferocity of U.S. troops), and in 2001 in Afghanistan (where it took a while before the senior commanders figured out what American combat troops could and could not do).

14

Intelligence

Obtaining timely and accurate information about your opponent, and preventing him from doing the same, is what military intelligence is all about. Three distinct layers of intelligence exist, each with its own characteristic needs and methods.

Strategic intelligence. This covers everything the enemy is capable of doing. The sheer mass of information available at this level must be simplified and generalized for the senior officials who must use it. Information obtained at other levels is passed on to be analyzed for strategic implications. Satellites and large computers have made strategic intelligence less a matter of cosmic guesswork. Strategic intelligence must be updated monthly, although computers enable more frequent updates.

Operational intelligence. This level goes into more detail as it covers smaller areas: a continent like Europe, or the Pacific Ocean. It is often further divided by activity: land, naval, air operations, economic, political, etc. Commanders of armies and fleets use operational intelligence. The means of gathering this information are the same as for the strategic level. The data are studied and analyzed in greater detail, as users at this level are dealing in more specific operations. Hence the use of the term "operational." Data must be updated weekly, daily, or more frequently, depending on whether a war is going on. The strategic-level people keep in touch with the operational-level crew to let them know when a strategic development affects the lower level.

Tactical intelligence. Also known as battlefield intelligence. This is very detailed and usually needed immediately. Updates are required at least a few times a day to be useful. Units down to battalion, or major warships, assign people to collect and analyze data. The analyzed data are passed on as quickly as possible to the operational- and strategic-level people. In turn, the other levels pass down the implications of their analysis on each tactical situation. The increased use of computers and more capable sensors allows tactical intelligence to be collected and used in real time. In other words, a radar not only detects objects but uses its analysis capabilities to determine what has been spotted and what it may be up to.

Electronic sensors collect the majority of information, and computers play a large role in analyzing what information is obtained. The only place where people still do most of the work is in ground combat. The infantry must still patrol. No one has come up with a way of automating this bloody exercise. Reconnaissance resources are always limited. It takes time to get a good picture of what the other fellow is up to. During battles, or when a lot of combat units are moving, it is very difficult to get a detailed picture of the enemy situation. As a rule of thumb, when everyone settles down, you can reveal 10–20 percent (or more) of the enemy's situation per day. A week or so of this leaves you with a good idea of the enemy's strength, dispositions, and capabilities. This assumes the two sides have equal information-gathering ability. If one antagonist has inferior intelligence-gathering capabilities, he will be in the dark longer, perhaps indefinitely. A nation with superior counterintelligence abilities, like Russia, can conceal its situation longer. This is a necessary skill for the Russians, as their intelligence-gathering capabilities are not up to Western levels.

The West has taken a long-standing skill at intelligence gathering and made it even more formidable through the use of technology. Satellites, electronic sensors, high-resolution cameras, and powerful computers give the West a considerable edge. This advantage is not always decisive. The pursuit of technology often overlooks the insights of a human analyst. It is possible to become overly dependent on technology. This is more likely when you consider that intelligence work does not have a terribly high status within the military. While some very bright people are attracted to this kind of work, they are not ordinarily the ones who become generals in great numbers. The combat arms are where the action is promotion-wise. Some armies habitually send their marginal officers into intelligence work. In Russia, the analysis of intelligence data is considered something good only "for women and lieutenants." The effects of this policy are not usually felt until the shooting starts.

Recent Developments

Things have become considerably more complex since the end of World War II (1945), more complicated than people realize. At the beginning of this century, intelligence work was much as it had been for thousands of years. Spies, diplomats, and diligent trivia seekers collected strategic intelligence, often of dubious value. The same crew collected operational-level intelligence, although combat units often contributed. Tactical intelligence was normally as fresh and accurate as the enemy fire coming in your direction. Intelligence work began to change during World War I (1914–18). Aircraft reconnaissance was introduced on a wide scale and provided a good look at enemy territories. You were no longer dependent on groups of hard-riding horsemen to find out what was going on in the enemy rear area. Radio also came into general use. This brought forth electronic intelligence, otherwise known as eavesdropping. Shortly thereafter, the cryptographers were called in to devise codes for radio messages and the means to break the enemy's codes. World War II generally refined World War I developments. Air photography and photoanalysis became more effective. The big breakthrough came on the allied side as many German and Japanese codes were broken continually throughout the war. We still live in the shadow of this achievement.

The Data Explosion

In the past, intelligence analysts could never get enough information. This is no longer the case. Electronic collection provides an avalanche of data. The problem now is separating useful information from the noise. This glut of intelligence comes from a variety of distinct sources.

Electronic reconnaissance. Originally this was just listening in on enemy radio transmissions. Currently, anything that is transmitted electronically can be plucked from the ether for later examination. This includes some emissions people aren't aware of, such as things like infrared (heat) images and disturbances in the magnetic field. This last item is created whenever a large metal object moves around. Sound is also becoming a popular transmission to monitor, especially when it travels through the earth or water. The sensors to pick up all this information are found at all levels. Infantrymen have sensors for detecting sound and electronic emissions. Aircraft carry just about every sensor imaginable, as do satellites. Helicopters 25 kilometers behind the front, hovering at 1,000 meters, can monitor transmissions hundreds of kilometers away. Any transmitter broadcasting continuously for more than 30 seconds (and often a lot less) can be located to within one or two kilometers (or much less). More powerful computers are making these locating devices even more accurate.

Photo reconnaissance. More precise locations of any object can be obtained by photo reconnaissance. Satellites and aircraft do most of this work. Photographs taken from a U.S. satellite 128 kilometers up can show objects as small as one foot in diameter. They can distinguish between civilian clothes and uniforms.

The cameras are no longer just cameras; sensors would be a more apt term. Traditional photographs are still taken. Other images are also taken showing patterns of heat, radiation, magnetic fields, and any other items that imaginative scientists can dream up. All of these sensors are quite accurate. These other images get around the problems cameras have, such as darkness, clouds, and camouflage on the ground.

Spies, informants, and prisoners. "Human intelligence" is still potentially the most valuable. However, people are more difficult to deal with and interpret than photography and electronic data. It is easier to favor the more "precise" information. But the photos and sensor data, as tangible as they are, can also be misleading. A sufficient amount of human intelligence can determine what is likely to be true and what is not. A lot of information from human informants (spies) can clarify all the stuff the satellites and other sensors pick up. During peacetime you don't get many prisoners of war (POWs), a copious source of human intelligence. With POWs, you can also cross-check their stories to find out who is telling the truth. Spies and informants in foreign countries often provide data that is difficult to verify. Spies are expensive to train and support, particularly in peacetime. Informants in the enemy camp are erratic. In peacetime, many of the military plans you attempt to uncover are just that, plans. You may never know if they were real, or would even work. The same problem applies to enemy weapons and military units. Worst of all, without human intelligence, there is less appreciation of what is going on behind the photo and sensor images. The United States, because of its lead in photo and electronic sensors, tends to slight the use of spies and informants. It's easier to peruse masses of sensor data that won't contradict whatever you are looking for. Those nations with less sensor capability must use human sources more heavily. Given a choice, most nations would opt for more sensors. However, slighting the human element provides the risk that the image seen is not the image that is there.

Technical intelligence. Most nations have similar weapons; at least appearances indicate equivalence. The reality is quite different, but this is not known until you can examine the other fellow's stuff as carefully as your own. In wartime, you expect that a lot of everyone's material will be captured and examined. In peacetime, the situation is somewhat different. Several ways exist to gather technical intelligence on forces you are not at war with. For the very wealthy, there are satellite photos. But these are limited in their detail and rarely show you the inner workings of tanks, aircraft, and ships. Spies can be useful, especially in the West, where enough cash will often obtain technical manuals. Better than documentation is the equipment itself. This is still the favored method. Money usually changes hands, and the gadget is quickly smuggled out of the country. Because of the more open nature of Western societies, it is relatively easy for considerable data to be collected by subscribing to technical journals, buying books, and attending trade shows. While diplomats openly collect printed material, foreign intelligence agents approach technical specialists with offers to pick up some fast money for a little photocopying or the loan of some technical manuals for a few hours. More elaborate operations strive to prey upon ethnic loyalty or simply an eagerness to talk about techie subjects. In this way, China has obtained much technical intelligence about American weapons.

Analysis

The cutting edge of intelligence work is no longer the collection of information, but the sorting out of all that data and making some sense of it. In other words, analysis. This task is further complicated by the ever-present problem of figuring out what the enemy intends to do. Moreover, people do not think alike, and people from different cultures even less so. Analysis is not easy. In fact, it's nearly impossible. Success is how much better you do it than analysts in opposing nations. It is relatively easy to count rifles, tanks, ships, or missiles. It is more difficult to answer questions like:

- What is a particular piece of equipment really capable of?
- What does the enemy believe his equipment is capable of?
- What is the enemy equipment capable of in relation to your own equipment? For example, what can the Chinese Type 90 tank really accomplish on the battlefield, and what do the Chinese believe this tank can do? More important, what can this tank do versus Western models like the U.S. M-1? And then you must ask yourself the big question: what do they intend to do with all this equipment? For example, Iran purchased several thousand Russian armored vehicles in the early 1990s. Does this mean they think they can successfully overrun Iraq, or the Gulf states? And if they tried it, how successful would they be? And that's not all. Suppose the Iranian leadership changed its military plans for defending Iran, or attacking Iraq. What could it reasonably expect to do? All of these questions must be applied across the full spectrum of military equipment, troop capabilities, and anything else that has a bearing on the subject. Lots of ground to cover, and many opportunities to get it wrong.
- What should we report back to our own troops, and when? This is the major problem with the United States. There is so much data coming in from so many sources, and the analysis bureaucracy is so large, that a disproportionately small amount of analysis gets back to the troops who need it. And when the data does arrive, it is often too late.

Recent examples of insufficient analysis abound:

- During the Vietnam War, U. S. pilots discovered that the air-combat techniques they had developed since the Korean War 15 years earlier were not effective. Although the United States had a considerable amount of intelligence on Soviet aircraft, tactics, and pilot training, American pilots were going to war trained to fight American pilots in American aircraft. Intelligence had not gotten across the point that the Soviets, who supplied and trained the North Vietnamese air force, used markedly different aircraft and tactics. It took several years before American pilots could be retrained and achieve decisive success. And it's easy to fall back in this old bad habit.
- During the 1973 Arab-Israeli war, the Israeli air force ignored intelligence data on the upgrading of Arab air-defense systems. In particular, Israeli commanders thought they could counter new radar-controlled cannon and missiles with pilot skill. This was considered cheaper than buying expensive electronic countermeasures (ECM) equipment from the Americans. Heavy aircraft losses taught them a hard lesson. The information was not lacking; the proper analysis was.
- Ground forces also have their problems. During the Soviet invasion of Afghanistan in 1980, the initial analysis was that they had pulled off a masterful land operation. Soon afterward, reports from inside Afghanistan indicated that the Soviets had grossly misinterpreted their intelligence data on the Afghans. Overoptimism, a common problem with intelligence analysis, had caused the Soviets to go charging into numerous combat situations where they found themselves more disadvantaged than their analysts had predicted.
- During the 1991 Gulf War, U.S. battlefield commanders were open in their criticism of the vast U.S. intelligence bureaucracies and the inability of these bureaucracies to deliver useful information in a timely manner. "Muscle-bound" is probably the most succinct way to describe the U.S. intelligence organizations. Too much of a good thing can have unfavorable results.

Every war reveals examples of faulty analysis or intelligence gathering. Some mistakes are understandable. Too many mistakes can threaten the success of the operation and the survival of the nation that undertakes it.

One of the more frequent reasons for bad analysis is the multiplicity of intelligence agencies in many nations. This makes it difficult to determine which of the many, and often contradictory, analyses is correct. It's often not just a matter of different analysts coming to different conclusions. Each intelligence group represents a different interest. Often each branch of the armed forces, foreign office, national intelligence group, and other organizations has its own institutional requirements when gathering and interpreting information. One of the more extreme examples is the United States. Each branch of the armed forces has its own intelligence group, as does the Department of Defense. On top of that, the Secretary of Defense has his own personal group of analysts. In addition, there is the CIA, the State Department, the National Reconnaissance Office, and many more. Who's where on the playing field? It depends on which team you belong to and whose game you are in.

GOOD ANALYSIS IS
ONLY HALF THE JOB

The mass of annual data—billions of words plus pictures—collected by a major nation's intelligence agencies is too enormous for any individual to handle. Even the summaries are millions of words. The problem is compounded by the dynamics of secrecy; much information cannot even be looked at by all analysts available. The reason analysts exist is to somehow make sense out of all this information. The analyst's client, the decision maker, is typically not involved in intelligence work. Normally this person is a political leader, senior civil servant, or military commander. An analyst's job consists of more than simply going through masses of information and deriving conclusions. First, he must find the data. This is a never-ending process. Analysts are forever saying things like, "Hey, I didn't know that." It is the nature of the analysis process to turn over stones and find unexpected items crawling out. This makes the analyst product tentative, always subject to revision and reissue. This disturbs decision makers. What antagonizes them even more are analyst conclusions that conflict with policy makers' view of the world. The analyst must take this situation into account. A good intelligence analyst makes many enemies. A good analyst has the misfortune to spot new military developments before others do. This is especially vexing in peacetime, where there is no clear-cut way to prove yourself right, or wrong. A good analyst survives in such a situation by becoming very persuasive. The analysts must also be able to defend their conclusions effectively. To achieve all the above, a good analyst does the job in three phases:

Phase one is accurately determining what the client (politician or military) wants and finding the raw data.

Phase two is doing the analysis, including smoking out the client's biases and preconceived ideas.

Phase three is following up the analysis with effective rebuttals of client objections. There is always the possibility that the client will find valid flaws in the analysis. A good analyst must be capable of dealing effectively with these, also.

A competent analyst is part detective, part evaluator, part diplomat, and part politician. The analyst is up for election every time the work goes out the door.

The Same, but Different and a Lot Cheaper

Before the CIA, there was Britain's MI6. Britain has been playing the espionage game long before the United States even existed. When the CIA came along after World War II, it was based on the wartime OSS (Office of Strategic Services) and the need to have a central organization to sort out the intelligence from all American intel operations and give the president one report.

But the legacy of the OSS was one of having agents in foreign countries and running active operations to gain information and weaken enemy capabilities. So in the decades after World War II, this led to interference in foreign nations, overthrowing governments seen as harmful to U.S. interests, and working with a lot of unsavory people. By the 1970s, many of these operations were seen as embarrassing, and restrictions were put on this sort of thing. The British MI6 suffered no such restrictions, mainly because MI6 was smaller, not given to large-scale adventures the CIA was fond of, and, perhaps most important, had much longer experience in dealing with espionage in foreign nations.

MI6 is less than one-tenth the size of the CIA (in manpower) and has a budget that's even smaller. But the CIA is by no means 10 times as effective as MI6. For all its size and resources, the CIA cannot, or often will not, do things that MI6 will. Part of this has to do with MI6's greater experience and need to make do with less. But a lot of it has to do with different styles of operation. Both organizations are in the overseas espionage business, but both go about their business in quite different ways, and with often quite different results.

A large part of the difference can be traced to the fact that MI6 has always had a healthier relationship with its diplomats. CIA agents operating overseas often operate out of the local U.S. embassy. Their cover is a diplomatic passport indicating they work for the State Department. But from the beginning, the diplomats were hostile to this sort of thing (British diplomats were not). So CIA people were forced to use diplomatic passports indicating they were part of the "Foreign Service Reserve" instead of just "Foreign Service." For those in the know, and that means just about everyone, it was easy to find out who the CIA guys were.

MI6 has a degree of legal cover for its operations that the CIA could only envy. Under the Intelligence Services Act of 1994, MI6 officers have immunity from prosecution for crimes committed outside Great Britain. The Criminal Justice Bill of 1998 makes it illegal for any organization in Great Britain to conspire to commit offenses abroad, but Crown agents have immunity. Which means, in effect, that yes, Her Majesty's Secret Intelligence Service really is licensed to kill.

Through most of the 1990s, and up to September 11, 2001, MI6's efforts (agents and money) were assigned: Russia, 15 percent; the Middle East, 15 percent; China and Hong Kong, 5 percent; Argentina, 4 percent; terrorism, 10 percent; the spread of nuclear, chemical, and biological weapons, 10 percent; the Balkans (mainly what used to be Yugoslavia), 10 percent; southern Africa, 5 percent; narcotics trafficking, 5 percent; and money laundering, 5 percent. The rest went to various special projects. Since September 11, the allocation has shifted, with more effort going into fighting terrorism and money laundering.

Compared to the CIA, with over 20,000 people, MI6 is tiny, with about 2,400 personnel. But with this small force, MI6 maintains 51 foreign stations. MI6 divides the world into six geographic regions, each run by a controller. While some of the smaller stations have only one or two people, a large one has a station chief, a deputy station chief, two or three case officers to handle locals working for MI6 (as informants or spies), three or four clerical workers, a special clerk to handle classified files, plus specialists to handle communications and ciphers (secret codes). Unlike American practice, MI6 will sometimes establish headquarters outside the embassy.

Another advantage of MI6 is that they have a number of SAS commandos trained to work with MI6 who are always available for any MI6 needs. This commando organization is called Increment and is used for assassinations, sabotage, or other dangerous jobs (like arresting war criminals in the Balkans). In addition, every station chief has a direct line to SAS headquarters and a good working relationship with the commandos.

Another advantage of being small is that most of the key MI6 people know one another. It's easier to put together special teams without a lot of time being consumed as people get used to one another. MI6 also tends to have a good reputation with foreign intelligence services, in part because it is not seen as a huge bureaucracy.

MI6 has been ahead of the CIA in other ways. Recruiting a lot of women was pioneered by MI6, and, as they suspected, the women often had an easier time going undetected overseas than their male counterparts. MI6 was also quick to use its "license to kill." Usually this was applied to low-level thugs and troublemakers. But at least two attempts were made to get Muammar Qaddafi, the erratic dictator of Libya.

When the Cold War ended, MI6 turned its considerable skills to collecting commercial intelligence, often from NATO allies. MI6 was discreet, although some operations were revealed. Such information is turned over to British corporations or the government, depending on who could do the most with it.

MI6 is also noted for its skill at getting people into and out of unfriendly countries. This came from decades of practice operating inside the Soviet Union and Eastern Europe. The CIA often calls on MI6 for help in rescuing people stuck in hostile environments. In return, the CIA shares its copious information collected with a fleet of spy satellites and eavesdropping aircraft.

Since September 11, 2001, MI6 has shifted a lot of its resources to antiterrorism activity. You never hear about MI6, but when you hear about "British SAS commandos" operating some place like Afghanistan, you can be sure that MI6 is involved as well.

Theory and Practice

Often, all that stands between war and peace in times of crises is an intelligence officer's analysis of what the other fellow is really up to. It is easy to forget in peacetime how crucial good intelligence is during wartime. In a pattern ongoing over many centuries, intelligence work is not seen as a fast-track assignment and does not attract the best people. Thus, the reputation of peacetime intelligence people is so low that this carefully crafted analysis often has little impact on the decision maker. Analysts are often seen as similar to economists, always saying, "On the other hand." Decision makers under the gun don't care what's on the other hand; they are simply desperate to know where they stand relative to the other fellow. This dismal state of affairs arises from the tendency of government officials to believe what they want to believe. In peacetime, there is little to divert them from this course.

Ongoing efforts are made by the intelligence community to probe the future systematically. Gaming and simulation are used, with varying degrees of success, to forecast difficult situations in time for solutions to be devised. These techniques are useful in technical areas. Wind tunnels are used to test aircraft designs. Computer simulations check out electronic equipment designs. Flying simulators help train pilots and later teach them new skills. When it comes to actual warfare, and the political conditions that bring it about, most nations, their governments and armed forces, play another game. What passes for war gaming is often a predetermined confirmation of policies already decided upon. Although this attitude is not always present, it is pervasive enough to poison nearly all the military uses of modeling and gaming. What happens is that this form of research has very little credibility. Partially, this is human nature. Unlike wind-tunnel tests, you rarely get a chance to see if the results of a war game will reproduce themselves on the battlefield. But mostly, it is a self-inflicted wound. Fortunately, gaming and simulation are even more widely used outside the intelligence community, particularly in the United States. The availability of different groups gaming the same future has led to some realistic consensus on what the future holds, and this knowledge gets to the commanders, even if it doesn't come from the intelligence crowd.

Wars also have a way of revealing faults in even the best-prepared and -equipped intelligence organizations. The 1991 Gulf War was no exception. Numerous details of the Iraqi nuclear weapons program were unknown or vastly underestimated. On the battlefield, U.S. intelligence found itself muscle-bound in some respects and underequipped in others. There were so many strategic intelligence organizations, and so much capability to collect information, that the intel bureaucracies back in Washington were unable to sort out and forward useful information to the Gulf in time to be useful. There was also a major underestimate of how much air reconnaissance would be needed to support the air campaign. Without timely "Battle Damage Assessment" (BDA), targets that needed more attention didn't get it, while targets that had been destroyed the first time around got revisited. The ground troops were a little better off, mainly because the JSTARS aircraft (an AWACS for ground forces) was far enough along in its R&D to be sent in quickly for its first battlefield use. These problems are not new; they happen in every war. But the U.S. Air Force never seems to learn.

After going back and forth several times in the Pentagon, by late 2001, there was finally agreement on how effective the 1999 air campaign against the Serb army in Kosovo was. Survey teams confirmed that only 52 armored vehicles and artillery were destroyed. Some of this had to do with weather. Of 6,766 sorties planned, 56 percent were aborted because of bad weather. Of those sorties that were carried out, a third were not as effective as they could have been because of weather. Because of this, less than half the targets selected to be hit from the air were attacked. Still, as the 78-day campaign went on, the Air Force thought it was hurting the Serbs. Initial assessments, at the end of the bombing, estimated that 880 Serb armored vehicles and artillery were destroyed. That's some 80 percent of what we thought the Serbs had in Kosovo. In September, after journalists began to notice how few destroyed Serb vehicles were to be seen in Kosovo, NATO lowered the estimate to 635. The following year, after Kosovo had been thoroughly searched, it was realized that only 14 tanks, 18 APCs, and 20 artillery pieces had been destroyed.

During the 1991 Gulf War, some A-10 pilots commented that operating in the desert was a lot easier than other places they had served in, especially South Korea and Germany. Finding anything in the hills and forests of those areas was a lot more difficult. This seemed to prove that point. But the Gulf War was also embarrassing for the "death from above" crowd. During the 44-day Gulf War air campaign, 1,028 Iraqi armored vehicles and artillery were destroyed. Before the ground war began, the Air Force insisted it had destroyed several times that. But after the four-day air war, a survey of the wrecked Iraqi vehicles showed that, in four days, ground troops had destroyed 3,117 Iraqi armored vehicles and artillery. Unlike the Serbs, the Iraqis didn't have hills and forests to hide in. But, as ground troops have shown again and again over the last 60 years, they quickly become very good at hiding from air attacks. The coalition air forces sent 46,000 sorties against Iraqi ground forces. That's 45 sorties for every Iraqi vehicle destroyed. That's only 23 Iraqi vehicles destroyed a day. It wasn't a wasted effort, for the constant air attacks demoralized the Iraqis and made the job of the coalition ground forces easier. But in decades past, the same result could have been achieved, at less cost, by heavy artillery.

But that would not have worked as well in Kosovo, for the hills and forests provide ample opportunities to avoid getting hurt. Areas with forests also tend to have more overcast weather. In Kosovo, 56 percent of the 6,766 sorties planned were aborted because of bad weather. And a third of those sorties that did go forward ran into clouds or fog that interfered with finding and hitting their targets. So in Kosovo, we have one Serb vehicle shot for every 72 sorties. And with the nasty weather, you can't just pile on more sorties like you can in the more hospitable desert. The Air Force would like to take some comfort in the improved accuracy of its weapons, but it is handicapped by the current policy of not losing an aircraft at any cost. Ground targets had to be attacked from three miles up. During World War II, you could expect to nail an enemy combat vehicle for every few sorties. But back then, warplanes went in low and exposed themselves to enemy fire. Many aircraft were lost, but the enemy ground forces were hurt, and their vehicle movements often shut down (at least during the day). Better weapons don't always work out if you are forced to use inferior tactics.

The Future

Computers and other electronic aids are transforming intelligence work. For the past 40 years, increasing masses of information were collected electronically, but the means to analyze this flood of data lagged way behind. Microcomputers have been infiltrating intelligence work since the 1980s. As these machines become more powerful, they enabled individual analysts to process enormous amounts of data effectively. More so than with other branches of the military, individual initiative is more critical in modern intelligence work in order to use limited resources to ferret useful information out of the masses of data collected. The right details are not always selected for closer scrutiny. Larger and more powerful computers have long been applied to this problem at the highest levels, but the real work gets done further down.

The United States has developed a joint Army/Air Force intelligence collection and analysis system for divisions and brigades. This system takes advantage of the power and portability of microcomputers. Digitized maps, a growing number of sensors, and better communications make this system possible. Another capability for field units is immediate access to data collected by satellites and other high-flying sensors. The images, and other data, are collected and processed in minutes. This provides a tremendous advantage in combat, where in the past it has taken hours or days to get this information to the field commanders. While some are dubious of it working, the same criticisms were made when similarly "advanced" systems were introduced during World Wars I and II. New technology is not always perfect, but it is usually better. Eventually. In this case, parts of this system were available in the Gulf War; most was not. Missing parts were truly missed.

Signal processing is maturing more rapidly and acquiring the capability to efficiently find the right needle in the information haystack. This is another offshoot of the rapid increase in computing power. Unfortunately, programs must still be written to tell the computers what to do. The lack of efficient software is still one of the most significant choke points for automated intelligence work. This becomes more crucial as advances in technology make it more difficult to find what you are looking for. An example is decoys representing tanks and aircraft on the ground designed to respond correctly to the several different sensors carried by recon aircraft and satellites. You've got to figure out what pattern of signals to look for in order to separate the decoys from the real thing. Deception is becoming more a war of computers. It has even spawned MASINT (measurement and signature intelligence).

The failure to detect the terrorist operations leading to the September 11, 2001, attacks on New York and Washington caused intelligence agencies to rethink the attitude toward spies and agents. This often messy and tricky use of people to seek out information personally had been gradually replaced by satellites and computers since the 1970s. This proved to be an overly optimistic belief in the power of technology. How far back the pendulum will swing toward the ancient art of spying is hard to say, but there will be more people out in the field double-checking what the machines have picked up.

15

The Primary Law of Warfare: Murphy's

"Anything that can go wrong, will go wrong. And at the worst possible moment." Engineers love this one and refer to it as Murphy's Law. Soldiers have good reason to add to this O'Niel's Law: "Murphy was an optimist." Warfare is, by its very nature, a chaotic and unpredictable undertaking. Combat and the endless preparations for it are fraught with unanticipated problems. This becomes acute during the opening stages of a conflict, when all the differences in weapons characteristics, tactics, doctrine, and quality become concrete. Once the war settles down to a steady grind of mutual destruction, it is possible to get a fix on many of the interactions. More precise planning is then possible. Before that occurs, key factors are largely unknown.

Infantrymen have always been the most frequent victims of Murphy's Law and, as one would expect, gradually codified their collective observations in a list of "Murphy's Laws of Combat." I've seen variations of this list in different infantry units, as well as in several foreign armies. Bad news travels fast. Below is a composite of several of these lists. They are a telling testimony to the vagaries of ground combat.

Murphy's Laws of Combat

You are not Superman.

Suppressive fire won't.

If it's stupid, but works, it's not stupid.

Don't look conspicuous. It draws fire.

Never draw fire. It makes everyone around you nervous.

When in doubt, empty the magazine.

Never share a foxhole with anyone braver than you.

Always keep in mind that your weapon was made by the lowest bidder.

If your attack is going well, it's an ambush.

If you can't remember . . . the claymore is pointed at you. (The claymore is a flat mine that is set up and pointed at the enemy, unless you set it up the wrong way.)

All five-second grenade fuses are three seconds.

Try to look unimportant. The enemy may be low on ammo.

If you are forward of your position, the artillery will be short.

The enemy diversion you're ignoring is the main attack.

The easy way is always mined.

The important things are always simple.

The simple things are always hard.

When you have secured an area, don't forget to tell the enemy.

Incoming fire has the right of way.

No combat-ready unit has ever passed inspection.

No inspection-ready unit has ever passed combat.

Teamwork is essential. It gives the enemy other people to shoot at.

If the enemy is in range, so are you.

Friendly fire isn't.

Anything you can do can get you shot . . . including doing nothing.

Make it too tough for the enemy to get in . . . and you can't get out.

Tracers work both ways.

The only thing more accurate than incoming enemy fire is incoming friendly fire.

Radios will fail as soon as you need something desperately.

When both sides are convinced they are about to lose . . . they are both right.

Professionals are predictable, but the world is full of amateurs.

All-weather close support doesn't work in bad weather.

The bursting radius of a grenade is always one foot greater than your jumping range.

The only terrain that is truly controlled is the terrain upon which you're standing.

The law of the bayonet says the man with the bullet wins.

REMF (rear-echelon motherfuckers, or noncombat troops) is everywhere.

The best tank killer is another tank. Therefore, tanks are always fighting each other . . . and have no time to help the infantry.

Precision bombing is normally accurate within plus/minus one mile.

Cluster bombs from B-52s and C-130s are very, very accurate. They always hit the ground.

Murphy was an 11 Bush (11B is the U.S. Army job code for basic rifleman).

Perfect plans aren't.

The easy way generally gets you killed.

The side with the fanciest uniforms loses.

Armored vehicles are bullet magnets, a moving foxhole that attracts attention.

If you are short of everything except enemy, you're in combat.

No plan survives the first few seconds of combat.

Ammo is cheap; your life isn't.

It's easier to expend material in combat than to fill out the forms for Graves Registration.

If you can't see the enemy, they still may be able to see you.

Final protective fire doesn't.

You can win without fighting, but it's a lot tougher to do. And the enemy may not cooperate.

Weapon Effectiveness

High-tech weapons provide numerous examples of things that not only don't work, but often don't even let you know they don't work. A recent example was the U.S. Navy's S-3 antisubmarine aircraft. Introduced in the mid-1970s to operate from carriers, it had a new electronics system to control the data coming from the sonobuoys it dropped. The rough carrier landings jarred the delicate equipment to the extent that the operators often did not get the information the sonobuoys were broadcasting. For some years, it was not realized that this was happening. Only when several highly experienced operators began to suspect a malfunction and complained was the situation carefully looked into. It took quite a while to get things working right. At least one hopes the system was fixed.

The only weapons you can really depend on to perform as expected are those that were used in the last war. Even improved, as opposed to radically new, weapons are suspect. Another example occurred just before World War II when the U.S. Navy introduced a new torpedo. One of the improvements in this model was that it exploded under the target ship instead of hitting it. Testing demonstrated this. This improved the chances of destroying the ship. Soon after the war began, reports about dud torpedoes came back from subs in the Pacific. The naval-weapons development people did not believe it and resisted change for a year. Finally more tests were performed, and it was found that the temperature of the water influenced the operation of the torpedo. The water temperature in the Pacific was different, just different enough to make the torpedo fail. Peacetime testing had not revealed this. There were many other examples during World War II. Every nation had problems with this, some more than others. In 1987 Britain deployed a new class of destroyer. While testing the new ship, it was discovered that unanticipated engine noises made the sonar nearly useless. The Soviets had similar problems on many of their ships and in many cases never really eliminated this flaw. During the 1973 Arab-Israeli war, the U.S. TOW antitank missile often became unstable when fired across the Suez Canal. The TOW missile was controlled through a thin wire between the missile and the operator's guidance system. Electrical signals went through the wire, keeping it on target. The canal was full of salt water, which had different electrical properties than fresh water. This problem had not been detected during testing and was soon fixed. In the meantime, Israeli troops became quite wary of the TOW.

Also during the 1973 war, it was discovered that the hydraulic fluid used in the M-60 tank was too readily ignited when the tank was hit. Minor, or at least nonfatal, damage was turned into a major problem. The fluid thought to be safe was soon replaced by a less flammable type. Speaking of hydraulic fluid, Russian tanks use alcohol. If the troops lack anything to drink, they have been known to consume this fluid. The Russians still have problems with this, in that sometimes tanks are made inoperable due to fluid consumed by the troops.

Even more bizarre examples can be found. At the start of World War I in 1914, there were two types of artillery shells. One was high explosive. The other, more expensive to build and theoretically more effective, was shrapnel. This type was like a shotgun shell; it exploded in the air and sprayed the ground below with metal balls. Tests had shown that these balls would penetrate wood boards set up to represent troops. Because of the expense, less than half the shells used were shrapnel. In the 1930s a group of American technicians were setting up some shells for a test, and the shell exploded prematurely, peppering some of the people with the "lethal" metal balls. They all survived. Further investigation revealed that human skin, muscle, and bone were far more resistant to the metal balls than wood boards. Combat surgeons, when questioned, remembered that they had never seen a penetration wound caused by shrapnel balls. There has never been much official note made of this very humane weapon.

Other weapons lethal more in appearance than reality are bayonets and sabers. U.S. Civil War medical records (of dead and wounded) noted that less than 1 percent of all wounds were caused by from these weapons. Sabers were dropped from most arsenals 60 years ago. Recently, armies have designed bayonets better suited for cutting wood and wire than enemy soldiers. This could also have been deduced from American Civil War experience, where officers noted that bayonet attacks rarely resulted in anyone being stabbed by a bayonet.

High-technology weapons are the most common types to suffer multiple flaws. The numerous MiG-21 fighters suffered a number of serious shortcomings that were only discovered when a large number of users could be interviewed by Western intelligence analysts. The most serious flaws in this aircraft occurred during the violent maneuvering that accompanied combat. The gunsight was easily thrown out of alignment. This gave the pilot false information as to what his guns might hit. In effect, the cannon became useless. Add to this the crude nature of the MiG-21's air-to-air missiles, and you had a relatively harmless fighter. Except to the pilot. The other problem had to do with the fuel tanks. When more than half the fuel was gone and the aircraft was violently maneuvered, fuel stopped going into the engine and the aircraft lost power. Very embarrassing. Things have not changed a lot in the aircraft industry. In 1987 there were published reports in the Soviet Union about continuing design and quality control problems with the new AN-28 light transport. This corroborates the reports of recurring crashes and groundings of MiG-23/27 aircraft. Western aircraft also have these problems, but not to the same extent. Part of the problem is the quality of the ground crews. In the West they are largely volunteers, with technicians having many years' experience.

Like the United States, the Russians also have their problems with tanks. Their T-62 model had a host of problems, some minor and some serious. One of the more vexing ones was its tendency to throw the tracks off the road wheels when the vehicle was violently maneuvered. This would not happen frequently in training but would be a common occurrence during combat. A Czech civilian technician eventually came up with a simple modification that eliminated the problem. Meanwhile, the T-62 was replaced earlier than usual. The remaining vehicles still have a bad reputation among their users. In most cases, the simplicity and robustness of Russian weapons appeal to the Third World. However, this low-tech approach can backfire. Iraq, like many buyers of Soviet tanks, found that they could make tank ammunition themselves. The simple construction of Soviet tank guns allowed this. However, tank ammunition is a key component of a tank. You can't cut corners in its manufacture. The Iraqis did, and their use of low-grade materials in their T-72 tank gun ammunition resulted in shells that bounced off U.S. M-1 tanks even at point-blank range.

Superior Western technology is not immune to embarrassing flaws. There was the case of the harmless ballistic missile. During the early 1960s, the warhead of the U.S. Polaris missile would not detonate. The error was not detected for a while. When it was, the problem proved immune to numerous solutions. Meanwhile, the missiles might as well have carried rocks in their warheads. Most of the embarrassing failures of weapons in combat are a result of poor testing. Antitank missiles that cost $10,000 and antiaircraft missiles that cost $2,000,000 make extensive live-fire training risky for the budget. Equally frightening, from a fiscal point of view, is destruction testing of increasingly expensive vehicles. This involves firing enemy weapons, or something close, at your stuff to see how robust your vehicles are under combat conditions. As a practical matter, this destruction testing is rarely done, particularly with the expensive systems like air- craft. Instead, some parts of the vehicles are shot at. This helps, but it does not expose those embarrassing vulnerabilities that show up when the shooting starts. Lack of adequate testing goes against the ancient combat wisdom, "The more you sweat in peace, the less you bleed in war." One bright spot in this situation is that many weapons developed in peacetime are "overbuilt." This accounts for a lot of the high cost of weapons. But this makes them more flexible when facing uncer- tain wartime conditions. Weapons developed and built in wartime can zero in on precisely what they know they have to do. But it's nice to have halfway decent weapons for those first few battles of a war.

A particularly persistent problem with weapons' effectiveness has to do with air power; in particular, the unending problem of solving the BDA prob- lem. BDA stands for Bomb Damage Assessment, the procedure whereby the Air Force tries to figure out how much damage it did to the enemy after apply- ing bombers and fighters. BDA doesn't work too well. It never has. Things always look different from the air, especially when the people on the ground are trying real hard to blur your view.

For nearly a century. air forces have struggled to figure out BDA. Every time they thought they had a new gizmo or technique to do the job, they found out, after the war, that the bad guys had foxed them again. This has been a source of much embarrassment to the air force generals. After World War II, a period of enormous bombing campaigns, it was found that the Germans and Japanese were devilishly clever at deceiving the bombers and the recon aircraft that came by later to check on the damage. Much ink, and black coffee, were spilled in efforts to come up with solutions. All failed.

During the Korean War, the Chinese and North Koreans demonstrated that a million troops with shovels, and the cover of night, could hide targets, or, if the targets were hit anyway, hide the true extent of the damage. For example, bridges that appeared from the air to have been dropped into a river by bombs were actually partially rebuilt and only used at night.

One advantage of Korea was that much of the land was free of trees. Not so in Vietnam, where jungle or forest covered most of the landscape. The Communist troops used this cover, and their shovels, to hide. New electronic devices were thought to clarify the situation, but no one was sure. The only BDA approach that worked for certain was to send small patrols deep into enemy territory by helicopter. Once on the ground, these LRRPs (Long Range Reconnaissance Patrols) poked around until they found targets to hit, or to what extent previous ones had been. LRRPs were expensive, though, with casualty rates of over 100 percent (many LRRP troopers were wounded more than once.) Twenty years after the war ended, many Communist Vietnamese were writing openly about their experiences, and Americans were able to return as tourists, and even talk to the Communist troops they had fought. What emerged was not encouraging, as usual, for the BDA specialists.

Then came the 1991 Gulf War. Same story, even though there were much more accurate bombs and even more snazzy electronic devices for seeing at night and through clouds. The usual sitting-duck targets (headquarters, barracks, airfields, etc.) were attacked and obviously destroyed. But the Iraqis, while thrown out of Kuwait, were not beaten from the air. In fact, when American troops examined destroyed Iraqi armored vehicles, they found out that only 10 percent had been destroyed from the air. Before the ground war began, the Air Force announced that 50 percent of Iraqi armored vehicles had been destroyed. The Iraqis had cooperated by figuring out what a "destroyed" tank looked like from the air and arranged to make their undamaged vehicles appear destroyed from the air.

The Gulf War also highlighted another aspect of BDA: how much damage is needed to achieve a military goal. During the war, it was announced that once air power had destroyed 50 percent of the Iraqi armored vehicles, the ground troops could go in and mop up. It turned out that the 50 percent value was made up, as well. The question was originally raised when the U.S. staff officers were planning the air campaign and trying to come up with some way to know when they should send the ground troops in. Someone said "50 percent of Iraqi armor destroyed," and everyone picked up on it. What is scary is that this same 50 percent value is again being used in the Balkans air campaign, although in this case the magical event is supposed to be the collapse of the Serbian armed forces. Let's hope someone got the Serbs to agree beforehand. Apparently not.

Once NATO troops (KFOR) got into Kosovo, it was obvious that much less damage was done to the Serb troops than NATO claimed (5,000 dead and 10,000 wounded). On leaving Kosovo, the Serbs announced their losses during the 11-week air campaign as 169 dead and 299 wounded. Those numbers were never contradicted. No one ever said BDA was going to be easy, but no one should put too much faith in the current state of the art, either. And it's amazing how incapable the Air Force has been in solving the problem.

Another problem with perfecting weapons in peacetime is unimaginative and unenergetic leaders. Efficiently re-creating the chaos of combat is the stage director's art, and military leaders are not selected for their theatrical abilities. Those armies that have more successfully gone from peacetime theory to wartime practice have done so on the backs of effective training exercises. Each nation's doctrine and standard operating procedures also play significant roles in combat readiness. Weapons and equipment are used as little as possible to preserve them for war. No armed force is immune to this idea. But it's also a historical fact that the troops do well in war in direct proportion to how long and hard they have trained with their equipment. The dangers of waiting until the shooting starts before discovering the weapons and troops are not up to it is a lesson that is never really learned.

Tactical Principles

The same weapons are often used quite differently by nations. This creates problems in cooperating with allies and recognizing different tactics of opponents. Chauvinism, inertia, and sundry other factors lead armies to view potential enemies as clones of themselves. The results are interesting history and ugly battlefield incidents. In the opening stages of World War I, the French were so obsessed with retaking their two lost provinces on the lower Rhine River that they paid little attention to the Germans marching through Belgium. The French nearly lost Paris, and the war, as a result. On a tactical level, all combatants misunderstood the impact of machine guns and rapid-fire artillery. The French, in particular, thought that energetic and persistent attacks could overcome anything. They were wrong, and hundreds of thousands of French soldiers died in futile attacks before the end of 1914. World War I was full of technicians unwilling to perceive the differences between their own tactics and those of their opponents. The Germans were the first to pick up on these differences and exploit them. This brought them close to victory again in 1918, even though they were outnumbered.

World War II was equally embarrassing in its repetition of many of the perception errors of World War I. The Germans had developed a new set of tactics, blitzkrieg, based on motorized units led by armored vehicles. Germany's opponents had the same, and in some cases superior, equipment. German tactics were developed from the writings of British theorists, so there was no secrecy involved. Even though German doctrine was widely known, it came as a nasty shock when confronted in practice. Granted, German success was largely due to superior training and leadership. Yet without these dynamic tactics, and their enemies' lack of the same, Germany's early success would not have been nearly as complete.

After World War II, tactical blindness continued unabated. In Korea, Chinese infantry tactics smothered enemy units unaccustomed to opponents running up and down hills without benefit of abundant supply lines. The American forces quickly adapted to this, but not before many friendly troops were lost in the confusion. The 1973 Arab-Israeli war held surprises for all parties. Israel did not anticipate Egypt blasting its way across the Suez Canal and just digging in. Israeli disdain for Egyptian tactical competence led to one very embarrassing incident in which a well-prepared Egyptian defense destroyed an Israeli armored brigade. In Syria, another illuminating example unfolded. Syrian armored units, well drilled in Soviet tactics, found themselves defeated by a moving ambush. Outnumbered Israeli tanks refused to stand and be overrun. Leapfrogging backward, Israeli tanks destroyed the advancing Syrian divisions piecemeal. The Soviet Union immediately reconsidered its tactics, and Israel designed a tank with a larger ammunition capacity and better protection. This included development of reactive armor. The Soviets obtained some of this when the Syrians captured some Israeli tanks in the 1982 war. Manufacturing a crude version of their own, Russia now looks to reactive armor as a partial solution to the Israeli leapfrog ambush tactics. Since reactive armor does little to deflect tank shells, they still have not overcome the tactical embarrassment of Syria. The Soviets were similarly surprised at the one-sided air battle over southern Lebanon in 1982 between Israeli and Syrian aircraft. In one battle, the Syrians lost dozens of aircraft and the Israelis none. This operation was carefully analyzed by the Soviets, and, according to the articles published in their military journals, they were more intent on finding excuses than reasons. They did little to change the weapons, equipment, and training of their air force. This reaction is not uncommon. Tactical myopia is frighteningly persistent.

Lurching Forward

Solving problems in the military is further hampered by the contending "unions." Between and within each branch of the armed forces, sundry factions battle over limited resources. The U.S. Navy has five major career groups: surface ships, the Marines, aviation, submarines, and strategic missiles. The U.S. Defense Department is probably the worst example of office politics. The U.S. defense budget contains over 5,000 separate line items and over 1,500 different programs. Each has an interest group of contractors and military personnel pulling for it. To confuse the issue totally, over 100 different accounting systems are used in the U.S. military. Comparisons are difficult, cooperation is rare, duplication is rampant, and delays are interminable. It's a Darwinian system where the political performance counts for more than combat capability. Pragmatic military men soon adopt the attitude that they'll attempt to get what they think they'll need. Get what they can. Do what they can with what they've got. Hope they've guessed right.

How does one analyze the experience of the past and predict how new techniques will work in the future? Over the past 60 years a debate has gone on between the historians and the technocrats. Before World War II, history, not science, was more frequently invoked to settle disputes over what direction to take in military planning. The avalanche of new gadgets produced during

World War II gave the technocrats the edge after 1945. Since then, experience has shown that warfare is ill-suited to effective analysis with current scientific tools. At the same time, history-minded planners got a bad reputation from their frequent resistance to, and ignorance about, new technology. In the last 10 years, the historians have made a comeback, and the technical types have come round to accepting a hybrid modeling process using historical experience. Ironically, Russia has always stayed with historical analysis, even though they worship science in military affairs. European armies are also less mesmerized by technology, although the United States has forced its technology approach on its allies whenever it has had the chance. The study and analysis of historical experience has returned to favor. A synergy is growing between historical experience and rapidly changing technology. Although planning still lurches forward into the unknown, it is less frequently lurching forward from the unknown. The results of this synergy could be seen in the number of times U.S. military planners were right on the money during the 1991 Gulf War.

Theory and Practice

The most effective work on re-creating combat conditions under peacetime conditions has been done in the West. This began in the 1960s with increasingly realistic aircraft simulators. Work on these devices began with the commercial market, to train airline pilots at less cost. Air combat is more complex, and it wasn't until the late 1970s that fighter pilots had realistic simulators. The U.S. Navy has kept pace with the Air Force, training in the development of realistic training simulators for their ship crews. By the early 1980s, the U.S. Army had developed the first realistic ground-combat training system. Not a simulator, exactly, it worked by fitting troops and equipment with sensors that could detect lasers fired from mechanisms attached to infantry and vehicle weapons. For the first time in history, ground troops could exercise under something approximating combat conditions. This has had a significant effect on improving combat skills. Other Western nations also adopted the aircraft and naval simulators. Lacking the technology, Soviet forces were stuck with less effective simulators and significantly lower skill levels. This was one reason why Russian officers demanded a professional, volunteer army even while the Soviet Union was collapsing.

Western forces, notably the United States, have also maintained their use of dissimilar forces training. In other words, their opponents in the simulators and training exercises operate as likely opponents would: the opposing force uses Russian weapons and tactics. The Soviets paid less attention to this type of training. The net result of all of this is that Western forces are better prepared to fight than their potential Soviet-equipped and -trained opponents. In Soviet military circles there was extensive debate during the 1980s on how to overcome this, but they were never able to get far in solving the problem. This bodes ill for all those Third World nations that use Russian equipment and doctrine. As Iraq painfully discovered, the American troops were better prepared to fight Russian-equipped armies than the other way around.

While great strides have been made with training, serious problems persist with equipment performance and reliability. The British had considerable first-hand experience with damage control in modern warships during the 1982 Falklands campaign. But five years later, the U.S. Navy had an embarrassing experience when the *Stark* was hit by an Exocet missile in the Persian Gulf. What is unnerving is that this type of situation constantly repeats itself. Before new systems enter combat, all manner of studies and estimates are made about what they need and what they can do. This is usually off the mark somewhat; that's only human. But sometimes the performance estimates are way off. And even in wartime, remedial action often comes too slowly or inaccurately. Peacetime situations, like those that led to the Stark's problems, are typically worse.

The Future

"Battle management" is one of the latest military buzzwords. For decades, the Soviets were working on "cybernetic" combat control systems. Their theory was that if information could be passed efficiently enough between troops and commanders, decisions could be made more easily with the help of an optimal solution suggested by a computer. This would have the effect of making your troops more lethal while lowering your losses. The Western approach is basically the same. All of this battle management depends on two technical items: effective communications and efficient computers to sort out all the data quickly. Because of the energetic efforts to jam communications, and the relative inexperience in developing computerized "expert systems," there is a lot of uncertainty on how effective these systems would be. Historically, getting the hang of effective combat leadership is a skill largely acquired on the battlefield. Extensive changing of the rules during peacetime creates more chaos in the initial battles.

Digitalization is the future. Connecting all the tanks, warplanes, artillery, and infantry as if they were in an office computer network has been a military goal for most of the 1990s. In Kosovo, there were times when it was possible to pull it off. It isn't easy, but when it worked, it was great. A recon aircraft points a heat-sensing camera at enemy territory, and the picture is sent, via satellite, back to the United States, where targets are found by powerful computers. The target location is sent back, via satellite, to a U.S. bomber in the vicinity, which then enters the location of the target into a GPS-guided bomb and releases the now-enlightened bomb, which promptly hits the target. All in minutes. The same thing can be done when some infantryman on the ground sees a choice target. A bomber, artillery, or tank fire can be called in within minutes. Digitalization wasn't universal during the Kosovo campaign, but it was used enough to make everyone believers.

Electronic warfare is more important than we thought it was. After the Gulf War, the Air Force agreed to get rid of its highly capable EF-111 electronic warfare aircraft and pay to use the Navy's equally capable EA-6 aircraft. It saved money, but in Kosovo it was discovered that the need to provide maximum security for aircraft meant that you needed more electronic warfare aircraft than were available. One reason the F-22 budget was cut recently was to provide money for more desperately needed electronic-warfare planes.

Smarter targeting. Limited wars mean you have limits on how much violence you can use. Late twentieth-century wars are also conducted in the glare of global mass media. You have to look your best while you are killing people and breaking things. This means targets have to be selected with the media and local politics in mind. If you are bombing a nation where you have a faction that favors you, then you have to be careful that bombs do not hit your friends down there. So you don't bomb neighborhoods full of people who hate the local government. Go after the secret police headquarters, and the mansions of corrupt politicians. It was easier in the old days; you just bombed whatever might aid the war effort. But today the war effort includes press conferences, so you bomb the enemy media early on.

Drones are good. Finally. Having been around for several decades, and used successfully by nations like Israel, the United States finally gets behind UAVs (the buzzword for unpiloted aircraft). Part of this has to do with the new mania for zero casualties. Lose a drone, and none of your people are hurt. It was also discovered that you could send a drone in low with a laser-target designator and have a manned aircraft higher up drop bombs. Even through the clouds, that drone's laser would guide to the target.

Better BDA. Bomb Damage Assessment (BDA) has, for most of this century, been an afterthought. You got into the enemy territory you had bombed and discovered that, oops, you had not hit all the targets you thought you had. How could this happen? Simple: the fellows on the ground had a tremendous incentive to not get hit, and to make those damn pilots think they did hit something so they won't come back and bomb you again. After Kosovo, everyone is either denying the Serbs were so clever, or promising the BDA will be better next time. Déjà vu all over again.

However, as more distance separates the major armed forces from their last sizable battles, the opportunities increase for more things to go wrong. The very success of Western forces in the Gulf War puts them under a lot of pressure to not misinterpret the factors contributing to their victory. This effect is compounded by the vast changes in technology. If there is another major war between large, modernized armed forces, there will be a lot of sorting out to do. A lot of needless deaths will occur before everyone gets a good idea of how things are supposed to work.

16
Who Wins

Nobody wins, but this is often forgotten. Wars are easy to start, expensive to continue, and difficult to stop. Wars often begin when someone feels that victory is assured. The fighting continues largely because of national and personal pride. Wars end when one or both sides are devastated, demoralized, or, rarely, suddenly enlightened by the absurdity of it all.

Starting Wars

Armed forces are almost always raised for defense. But once you have all this armed strength, there is the temptation to use it. A large dollop of military force encourages nations to be more aggressive in their dealings with others. Military and diplomatic adventures become more common. This causes some wars to start by accident, the result of playing with fire. At other times, the situation becomes quite depraved, with nations doing the "grab what we can and sue for peace" drill. The illusion of military power is not easily given up because of a few battlefield setbacks. Political leaders have followers who are killed and injured in these defeats and demand revenge. Even though leaders know how bad the situation often is, they preach optimism. Otherwise they could be replaced by less defeatist politicians. Wars acquire a life of their own and just keep going. They are a triumph of hope over experience. Defenders are extremely resilient. Defeat rarely settles anything except the certainty of another round of fighting.

Attitudes are different on the battlefield. For one thing, it's difficult to tell who's winning. This is especially true during combat in this century. Previously, battles rarely lasted more than a day. Larger twentieth-century armies faced each other continually, engaging in a lower-level but endless violence that now passes for combat. Results of this carnage are reported by publicity professionals. The endless stream of press releases gives the impression that no one ever losses a battle. Back on the battlefield, if one side really got the worst of it, the troops would decide who won, and the losers would move smartly to the rear, perhaps overrunning their publicity people in the process. Even so, it was usually possible for noncombatants to maintain a reasonable belief in continuing victory. Without knowledge of the big picture, a local disaster could be explained away as an exception to the favorable prospects everywhere else. What soldiers see as victory or defeat varies with where the troops are and what they are doing. Perceptions also vary greatly with one's rank and situation.

Perceptions of Victory in the Foxhole

Troops in modern combat often find themselves in situations where they are forced to fight for survival. Heroism is not always a voluntary act: "A hero is a coward that got cornered." Individuals and small groups fight to survive. More frequently, they avoid fighting to survive. Fire teams, squads, and aircraft crews require a combination of discipline, effective leadership, fear of reprisal, self-delusion, and peer pressure to generate an effective fighting attitude. Ship crews operate in a more controlled situation, where training and technical skill are decisive. These are the conditions that enable one side to prevail. Soldiers recognize that the war will not end until one side or the other can no longer put up any resistance. Individual soldiers know little of the war's progress beyond their immediate vicinity. Combat troops attempt to survive from one day to the next. When there is combat, a soldier's objectives become even more immediate. The troops that do the fighting operate in a very small battlefield. The more dangerous the activity, the more each minor part of that activity becomes an occasion for victory or defeat. Crossing an area possibly covered by enemy fire, sticking your head around a corner, firing a weapon, calculating where the enemy is, and a multitude of other actions constitute the hundreds of little battles the soldier fights. In combat, a participant's concept of victory is very short range. There isn't much choice.

Victory in the Middle

Combat leaders who are not in the middle of the fighting themselves, or command troops they can't see and supervise, have a different perspective. Commanders of platoons, companies, battalions, ships, or aircraft squadrons are primarily concerned with the contributions of their unit to the success of a larger operation. The commander views the unit's contribution to an operation as more important than the survival of any individual. This seemingly callous attitude is one aspect of military operations that is distasteful, but necessary. The unavoidable death and destruction of warfare makes for an impersonal attitude in commanders. To grieve for each death or mutilation would quickly make leaders ineffective. A successful combat commander is a strange bird, and normally difficult to spot in peacetime. While individual soldiers consider survival a victory, unit leaders consider success a group activity that often crushes men beneath it.

Historians play down what middle-level commanders do with their time. Studying the brief moments makes for more exciting reading. Correct moves in combat are more clear in hindsight. During the battle, the usual chaos is made worse by inept, unreliable, or incompetent subordinates. Issuing orders for the obvious solution to a combat situation is a futile exercise if those orders cannot effectively be carried out. A common problem is commanders of platoons and companies not knowing their troops very well. A ship captain cannot succeed if he is ignorant of who his sailors are and what they can do. Air forces come to grief when pilots do not develop a bond with their fellow pilots and ground crews. Commanders of aircraft units succeed or fail in proportion to how well they know their aircraft and their pilots' capabilities. Ignorance of the capability of one's troops and equipment can be overlooked in peacetime but becomes painfully apparent during the stress of combat. Commanders at this level are truly middlemen. They are not privy to all the highest-level decisions, nor do they participate in the daily routine of the fighting troops. Yet these officers are directly responsible for carrying out the nation's military policy. Commanders at this level fight a two-front war. They fight the enemy, if somewhat abstractly. They also fight their peers and superiors for scarce resources. Rarely do these commanders have to face the enemy personally. They do regularly confront their own subordinates. If they cannot motivate these subordinate leaders to perform well, they cannot defeat the enemy.

Winning at the Top

At the moment, not many generals and admirals exist who have been in combat as generals and admirals. Many saw action as junior officers, which is some help if war comes. But the number of serving officers with combat experience as generals is, at any time, less than 1 percent of those available. This is a serious problem that is usually overlooked. It cannot be overlooked when a war starts, as a majority of the peacetime generals are found wanting when commanding troops in battle. This has been the experience throughout history. Generals and admirals have fairly substantial egos. The system encourages them. A person in this situation tends to believe he knows what he's doing.

Who's going to contradict him? Certainly not some civilian who happens to be the head of state. Competent military leaders at the senior levels prefer to avoid wars. They know the history of people in their position. They also prefer to retire with their honor and reputation intact. They know well the risks of war and that history is unkind to losers. Effective leaders are aware of their limitations. They also know that it is easier to defend than to attack. Let some other miscalculating egomaniac start something. High military command is inescapably a political activity. Generals learn along the way the importance of good public relations. The generals, strong-willed men with considerable self-confidence, must constantly contend with their military and civilian peers for limited resources. This does not make them venal or any less public-spirited. It does make for a lively exchange of views on what is really needed for defense. Senior commanders fight a war in the shadows, where goals and methods are often lost in a fog of political decision making. In peacetime they are directed to plan and prepare for a number of potential wars. Sometimes the war they have to fight is one of these, often it is not.

In wartime, generals have a difficult time staying in touch with the results of their orders. Their concept of victory is often more political than military. The general's concept of winning is far removed from that of the soldier in combat. Sometimes a general maintains the good will of his troops, sometimes not. The more successful ones do, but no general can succeed if he cannot generate enthusiasm from his subordinate commanders.

Nationalism and War

America has generally been reluctant to get involved in wars. This has been so for several reasons:

America is a nation descended from draft dodgers. Most migrants to America are from nations where war, or the threat of war, made emigration a promising option. So off they went to America, and they brought their distaste for military affairs with them. This is the source of the isolationism still prominent in America.

As a democracy, America has a hard time making the decisions necessary to get a country into a war. It took German U-boats killing U.S. citizens to get America into World War I (at the very end of the war) and Pearl Harbor to bring the United States into World War II (after every one else had been at it for a year or two). Korea and Vietnam caused such a political ruckus that presidents now think twice about sending off the troops, even for minor events like Grenada and Panama. The Gulf War required a formidable public-relations effort on the part of the government, and there was a lot of pressure on the generals to win and win big.

America has less to go to war about than most nations. Protected by two vast oceans and bereft of any significant military threats in their part of the world, few Americans see anything worth fighting for. The Persian Gulf with its oil was one of the few exceptions. Attacks on major U.S. allies such as Japan, Korea, or Europe would also qualify. The terrorist attacks on New York City in September 2001 also did the trick.

Vietnam provided most Americans with a vivid lesson of what happens when the troops are sent to fight a war without most of the population behind them. While one can get the population excited at the beginning of just about any war, if things go badly and there is not a very compelling reason to continue fighting, the population quickly losses enthusiasm. Even during World War II, popular enthusiasm was beginning to decrease in 1945. One reason for dropping the A-bombs on Japan was that the government did not want to risk the huge casualties an invasion of Japan might have entailed.

This need for popular enthusiasm cuts both ways. During the 1991 Gulf War, the Iraqi people, and most of the Iraqi troops, were not enthusiastic about invading an Arab neighbor. Months of sitting in the desert, weeks of U.S. bombing, and a few days of ground fighting were all it took for the vast majority of Iraqi troops to throw their hands up and surrender.

It's much easier to get into a war than it is to keep the troops, and the people, at it.

Winning in the News

Secrecy is a goal governments pursue at all times. During a war, secrecy is a veritable article of faith. The temptation to manipulate the news during a war is frequently overwhelming. The farther away from the slaughter, the more optimism replaces reality. Reality is often nonexistent at the highest decision-making levels. This is especially true when you are losing a war. News of what is happening at the fighting front comes down from on high. Some of the most fantastic fiction ever written appears in a nation's media the day before surrender. Correspondents at the front see only a small portion of what is going on, even if they are allowed to wander around. Optimism can easily prevail over an unpleasant reality, especially as "defeatist" journalists are typically quickly replaced. War is such a discouraging process that media manipulation is often the margin of victory. Populations are making many sacrifices, and without encouragement, defeat will soon appear preferable to continued fighting. A common example occurs when the winning side calls upon the loser to surrender, sometimes on favorable terms. A government recognizes that its war effort will not survive long after negotiations are announced. Thus news of a possible settlement or negotiations is kept secret or disguised. Since Vietnam, governments have come to realize how powerful an effect on public opinion TV coverage can have. The Iraqis certainly recognized this in 1990–91. TV journalists will probably never again have as much of a free hand as they had during the 1960s, and this was borne out in Grenada, Panama, and the Persian Gulf. The proliferation of radios has made it more difficult for governments to hide completely the true nature of the war's progress. Enemy broadcasts can be jammed or the truth can be mangled by your own media, but enough of the truth always gets through. Despite the energetic, and generally successful, efforts of the United States to keep a lid on the media during the Gulf War, the public still had access to accurate information about what was going on. Military security was kept intact, the reporters were ticked off, and the public was not left in the dark. Managing the news may have become more difficult, but it has become no less important.

Journalists were upset that they were not allowed free access to American military operations in the Afghanistan war. Some of the older reporters remember the freewheeling days of the Vietnam War, when journalists could go anywhere they wanted. This was because Vietnam was not, technically, a war. Anyone could buy a airline ticket to South Vietnam and do whatever they wanted. During the Gulf War, journalists were upset at the restrictions put on them. What few journalists remember is that in America's wars during the last centuries, restrictions were the norm. The armed forces have long been leery about journalists inadvertently leaking important information to the enemy. This was first seen in the 1860s, during the American Civil War. After getting burned during the Spanish-American War (1898, and its aftermath in the Philippines Rebellion) and World War I (1917–18), a mutually agreeable system was developed for World War II. War reporters were put into uniform. No, they were not part of the military. Their newspapers and radio stations still paid them. But the war reporters were fed and housed as if they were officers and were subject to military law. Press officers accompanied them and saw that their stories went to the military censors before being transmitted back home. There were no damaging leaks. In the Korean War, the reporters were asked to censor themselves. But this didn't always work, and many journalists asked for military censors to check their work to make sure they did not release anything that could hurt the troops. While many journalists are not aware of this bit of history, most senior military commanders are. And they have acted accordingly.

Winning After Winning

One generally unrecognized aspect of military affairs that got some exposure in the 1991 Gulf War was the civil affairs troops. This military specialty is a twentieth-century development that came of age during World War II. The civil affairs units deal with civilians in the combat zone and take over government functions in areas recently conquered, or liberated. During World War II, major population areas were rapidly occupied by allied troops. Naturally, the existing governmental institutions were either destroyed or severely damaged in the process. All those leaderless civilians, many of them refugees or injured, had to be dealt with before they got in the way of the military operations. The civil affairs troops were created to do this. Basically, the civil affairs units were trained to take over the government in battle-torn areas and quickly restore order and relief for the battered civilian population. The civil affairs troops proved to be a key element in a lasting victory. In the immediate aftermath of war, a lot can go wrong, and the population generally blames the winners. Between World War II and the Gulf War, U.S. civil affairs units managed to restore economic and social order rapidly in the fought-over areas. The civilians did not forget, and this memory has contributed to the lasting peace since World War II.

Theory and Practice

The psychological distance between troops and generals reached a peak during World War I. During that war, especially between 1915 and 1918, most generals were unaware of how wretched a time the troops were having in the trenches. Since then, generals have attempted to eliminate this distance, if only because of the unrest and rebellion the World War I situation brought about in 1917. Not every commander has a knack for keeping his wits about him under fire. Since 1918, combat has become more spread out, although this has largely been overcome by commanders' use of helicopters to get up to the front. Reconnaissance aircraft and satellites can now send back detailed television pictures in real time. Commanders who avail themselves of opportunities to get up front and see things firsthand also expose themselves to somewhat more danger. Future wars will see long-range rockets and aircraft looking for headquarters to obliterate. This will ensure that life in the rear is not nearly as secure as it once was. Long-range weapons and the more diffuse nature of the battlefield has increased the degree of constant insecurity all troops must endure. The absence of a well-defined front line makes everyone more nervous. Current wars still have a "front" but tend to be more fluid and densely populated by helicopters and robotic weapons. Weapons may have limitless possibilities, but the troops don't. Exhausted and reluctant soldiers slow things down to a more tolerable pace.

Nuclear and chemical weapons were not enthusiastically received by combat troops. These weapons are not directed against the enemy so much as they are unleashed on the enemy. Such indiscriminate destruction causes uncertainty in an already ambiguous effort. As the implications of this have sunk in, there has been a move away from using nuclear and chemical weapons. These munitions will never disappear, but the owners are increasingly less disposed to use them, lest they be used against them in turn.

The Future

Micromanagement and media management are the future trends that will determine who thinks he is winning. Micromanagement, most notable when the chief of state directs the actions of a platoon, first became possible during the Vietnam War. This meddlesome custom was most noticeable in the United States, where the technology and lack of military tradition combined to make presidents into platoon leaders. Most other major nations know enough to leave battlefield leadership to the commanders on the scene. In light of the Vietnam experience, the United States also backed away from micromanagement. However, current and future communications capabilities make the temptation real, and a severe case of anxiety at the highest levels can now be sated by picking up the phone and calling the fighting troops directly. These same communications capabilities also serve the useful purpose of giving battlefield commanders more control. The current generation of U.S. recon satellites has the capability of showing moving and still pictures in real time. Woe be to any platoon commander who screws up on camera. As the technology becomes cheaper and more reliable, micromanagement will spread, or at least the temptation. During the 1991 Gulf War, U.S. commanders, many the victims of micromanagement while junior officers in Vietnam, refrained from returning the favor. This attitude continued in the 2001 Afghanistan war. But the temptation remains. Even guerrilla units are often equipped with portable radios, and guerrilla commanders can sometimes be overheard trying to micromanage their subordinates.

Innovations in training have improved the attitudes toward who can win, and to what degree, on the battlefield. The American "wired battlefield," where troops, weapons, and equipment carry sensors that allow for "hits" and "damage," quickly drive home how easily one can become a statistic on the battlefield. Some commanders, however, have still not fully accepted the fact that when something is lost on the battlefield, it is gone and it isn't coming back. The tendency during training is to resurrect casualties quickly and reintroduce them as "replacements." Real combat doesn't work that way, and if you don't learn to cope with the losses in peacetime, you'll have to learn the hard way, on the battlefield.

The art and science of promoting one's beliefs and ideas through the media continues to grow in power and effectiveness. In warfare, these media campaigns increasingly decide whether or not there will be a war and, if there is one, how long it will last. The "will to fight" can be sold like cornflakes, and increasingly it is, and very effectively at that. You can look forward to this year's wars being promoted as effectively as the latest consumer products.

17

What Armed Forces Do in Peacetime

Most soldiers spend their entire careers without seeing combat. Even if there is a major war, most people in the military do not have a combat job. In other words, for most people in uniform, their job is little different than a civilian occupation. There is a lot of work in the military that has no exact counterpart in the civilian world. And military people will often pull more overtime, have to salute their superiors, and be subject to a more rigid code of conduct than civilians. The American military is also unique in that it moves its people around the world every few years. In most nations, troops are assigned to a unit and rarely leave one location for their entire career. On the positive side, military jobs are generally more secure, being a form of civil service.

Combat and combat-support troops will spend a lot of their time running about the countryside practicing violence. All troops will devote most of their time to maintaining equipment and learning new skills. Noncombat troops follow a workday routine little different from that of civilians. Less wealthy armies will put the troops to work on nonmilitary tasks: public works, farming, and the like.

The Daily Routine

Unmarried troops customarily live in barracks. Depending on the nation's wealth, these range from crudely heated barns with no plumbing to Western college-style accommodations. Married troops, usually NCOs and officers, live with their families in government housing or private homes near the military base. Troops serving overseas often do so without families. In this case, the officer and NCO barracks are more plush than troop accommodations.

Quality of housing varies with rank, as one would expect. Some navies have additional housing ashore for unmarried sailors; a few put the troops up in ships even when they are in port. The day normally begins at an early hour, five to six A.M. There is at least one assembly of each company-size unit each day where announcements are made or a head count taken. Some units do this several times a day. The daily routine is set by a long-established schedule. Meals, taken in large dining halls, are usually at fixed times. The increasing 24/7 approach to warfare now has many dining halls open around the clock.

Sailors at sea run a different routine, customarily one of four hours of work ("on watch") followed by eight hours to themselves. Often much of their personal time is usurped for other vital activities. When a ship is practicing for combat, they are lucky to get four hours' sleep a day. Western armies tend to require five or six eight-hour workdays a week. Workdays are generally nine to five (or 8:00 A.M.–4:00 P.M.).

The regular schedule is often disrupted by "alerts" and field exercises, primarily in combat units. Here the entire unit must quickly turn out as if for combat. Some noncombat units will also go on field exercises or otherwise work longer hours in support of the combat troops. The alerts merely test a unit's ability to be ready for combat on short notice. Field exercises range from a day to a week, or more. This is as close as peacetime units get to combat conditions. Night training also disrupts the regular routine. Perhaps once a year, entire divisions might operate in the field as they would in wartime. This is very expensive; thus, there is a temptation to avoid it or to cut corners. One of the advantages of the six months U.S. forces were in the desert before the 1991 Gulf War ground offensive was the opportunity for the divisions to practice together under wartime conditions. Armed forces in less wealthy nations do fewer field exercises and send their ships to sea and fly their aircraft less frequently. All these activities are expensive. Armies in less wealthy nations will often send the troops out to help with economic emergencies. Helping with the harvest, tending vegetable gardens, or helping to repair the damage wrought by natural disasters is common. This last task is performed by nearly every nation's troops. Poor nations tend to have more devastating natural calamities and thus rely on troops more.

Armed-forces routines vary from nation to nation. Western nations are the most easygoing. The Russian system, often adopted by Third World nations, is severe and regimented. When you are in a Russian-style army, there's no mistaking where you are. The attitude is that less educated (often illiterate) troops require more supervision.

Keeping Score

Armed forces exist to make war, yet they cannot do this in peacetime. This presents a problem in evaluating a force's capabilities in peacetime. The problem is an ancient one. The enduring solution, inspection, is almost as old as organized combat itself. The Inspector General system is only a few hundred years old and is currently used by most armed forces. A separate bureaucracy, the Inspector General (IG), conducts regular and surprise inspections on all units. The IG inspection is generally an annual affair, and the careers of commanders rise or fall based on their unit's performance. In between these annual horrors, daily, weekly, and monthly inspections of varying severity occur. Inspections don't just evaluate the completeness and readiness of unit personnel, weapons, and equipment, but also attempt to assess potential unit combat performance. Inspections are also held during field exercises. Units are rated on how well they perform battlefield tasks. Some of the mundane matters examined are how quickly a unit can move from one location to another, how well they camouflage their vehicles, and whether field fortifications are prepared adequately. Hundreds of skills and procedures must be checked.

The IG system does not always work at peak efficiency for two reasons. First, the items to be checked are part of an ever-changing list. Part of this is to be expected; new equipment and tactics require new inspection criteria. It takes a while before an efficient inspection procedure is found for new items. This begets the second problem: the urge to cheat. Inspectors tend to set standards that the troops and their limited budget cannot meet consistently. Because everyone's promotions depend on looking good, there is an irresistible urge to fudge a bit. Actually, there tends to be a lot of hanky-panky. The only incentive to be honest is a potential advantage in combat. But battle may never come while peacetime promotions are right around the corner for the creative scorekeeper.

Characteristics of Peacetime Armed Forces

All peacetime armed forces share certain key characteristics. What is interesting about these traits is that they are now widely known outside the uniformed services.

Short memories. Armed forces tend to remember no more of their past than their oldest members. History presents an endless cycle of armies sinking into peacetime routine that prepares them less for war than for the establishment of another bureaucracy. War comes and the bureaucracy is transformed into a fighting organization through a bloody and expensive process. The war ends and the combat veterans, as long as they remain, maintain a sense of what must be done. The veterans age and depart, and the cycle begins again. There is also a generation gap in many armed forces, especially those that depend on conscription. Conscript armies generally consist of only 15–30 percent long-term professionals. Volunteer armies comprise 40–70 percent personnel who stay beyond their initial three-to-six-year term. New recruits will be 18–21 years old. The average of the long-term professionals (lifers) will be 10–15 years older than that. Volunteer forces will narrow that gap quite a bit and create a greater sense of shared values. This is an important, but frequently underestimated, advantage.

Fear of flying. Several things that ought to be done in peacetime are avoided for various reasons. Exercises using live ammunition provide more realistic training, but they do cause more casualties. This is often unpalatable in peacetime. Russian-style armies do a lot of live-fire work, but they are less subject to adverse public opinion, and the casualties are not reported in the press.

Draftees versus regulars. Conscription is preferable if you must have (or simply want to have) a large armed force. This has several advantages. It is cheaper, as you don't have to pay salaries competitive with the civilian job market. It exposes all classes of society to military service, and each other. This doesn't work if the wealthy are allowed to buy their way out. High-performance standards are nice in theory but difficult to maintain in practice. You need a strong tradition concerning what warfare is all about and the ability to attract top people as officers.

Quality versus quantity. Even the wealthiest nations are torn between buying more equipment and investing in, maintaining, and using what they already have. The size of the armed forces and their actual combat power are not the same thing. However, size is more visible than power. Buy more tanks, put more men in uniform. These you can see and count. Training is expensive, especially firing those expensive weapons frequently. The results cannot be seen in peacetime, although this type of expenditure pays off in combat. Nations tend to have a lot of troops and equipment that are not being used together. Training on the cheap makes it easier to get killed when the shooting starts.

Who is the enemy? Without a war to settle the arguments, solutions to doctrine and equipment design debates must be found elsewhere. Often there is no elsewhere, and the debates wander aimlessly. Equipment design and doctrine development also wander, to everyone's detriment. It's not entirely the intelligence agency's fault for not coming up with a convincing evaluation of what the enemy forces are all about. The military is an instrument of the political process and must periodically change course in response to political trends. The military budget is often a political football, largely because there is no way of shutting down the legislators with unequivocal information on what the potential opponents are up to. All of this is an ancient problem. Some nations deal with it more effectively than others. The United States is not one of them, and the Soviet Union was not much better.

Paper bullets and ticket punching. The paper bullets of peacetime administrative combat tend to make cowards of officers who would more bravely face the metal variety. Death in battle provides recognition for valiant service; dismissal during a bureaucratic dispute is rather more ignominious and just as fatal to one's career. It's a case of the pen, indeed, being mightier than the sword. Making waves is not the key to peacetime promotion; getting the right assignments and not rocking the boat is. This is similar to combat, where some jobs are deemed more important than others. Unlike combat, values placed on choice peacetime assignments are often more political than practical. In combat, what doesn't work becomes painfully evident rather quickly. In peacetime, combat effectiveness is something more talked about than acted upon. If you want to get ahead, go along. The warrior mentality is usually out of place, and often out of a job, as well.

National Differences

Over 100 nations have significant armed forces. Until quite recently, there were only three general models for running these combat organizations: Soviet, Western, and Third World. The Soviet style was characterized by the use of conscription, few real NCOs, and an officer class that held it all together. Other habits included the reluctance to use equipment. Soviet doctrine insisted on having the maximum amount of weapons and equipment available for combat. Because of the enormous turnover in troops, nearly 40 percent each year, most training time was devoted to basics. Crude simulators were used more than actual equipment. Discipline was strict and amenities few. Except for the privileged officers, service was boring and physically demanding. Low morale, theft, abuse of recruits, and alcoholism were major problems. Much of the stealing went to purchase vodka. The dedication of the officers and strict discipline enabled Soviet forces to get moving in short order. However, spotty training and strict adherence to drills and regulations created a rather wooden battlefield manner. Ironically, these were the patterns that had persisted in the Russian armed forces for centuries. Communism had had little effect on it, except to make it worse. After the Cold War ended, the Russians realized that their system was fine for wartime, but otherwise, volunteers, a lot more training, and good NCOs (that is, "the Western style") was the way to go. Reforms in that direction are underway, although a minuscule defense budget (about $10 billion a year) makes for slow going.

Western-style armies are characterized by more volunteers, competent

NCOs, and extensive use of equipment in peacetime. Conscription is still used by many nations but is going out of style and being replaced with use of volunteers. Western nations also go for more technology and wider use of it. Western doctrine is also less bloody-minded, trying to minimize friendly casualties.

Third World nations fall into two broad groups, those with a long military tradition and those without. Nations like China and India have had organized armed forces far longer than Western nations and have maintained many useful military traditions (and a few bad ones, like corruption). Another key element among Third World nations is wealth. A few oil-rich nations can afford all the high-tech weapons they desire. Most Third World nations have to get along with what little they can afford. Those nations with a military tradition can attract qualified recruits and turn them into excellent soldiers. The more technical services, the air forces and navies, suffer somewhat because their nations cannot afford the expense of using aircraft and ships enough to give their crews experience.

The Bad Drive Out the Good

People join the military because of patriotism, adventure, a desire to render public service, careerism, a need to accomplish something. People of vastly differing abilities join. Too many of the best, especially the "warriors," leave in peacetime. The "warrior" and the "manager" are two distinct types. The warrior tends to be uncompromising, always striving for unambiguous results. A warrior searching for trial by combat leaves the peacetime military for the "real" world. Battles conducted with balance sheets and market shares are unambiguous indicators. Those left behind are the ones who pay more attention to career than combat. The end result of this careerism is a decline in the quality of leadership.

When the real conflict comes, the pinstripe soldiers often return, many from reserve units. Fortunately, many with uncommon determination and patience remain in the military. Their critical leadership staves off defeat until the nation's strength can be militarized. The pool of good combat leadership in the active military varies for each service and nation. Navies and air forces retain more warriors in peacetime. Flying and working a warship are essentially the same in peace or war. Sailors and pilots can test many of their wartime skills without a war.

Some nations give greater status to the military than others. If a country takes its military very seriously, then the military has an easier time attracting high-quality leaders. Also, political considerations carry less weight than professional military judgment under these conditions.

Theory and Practice

Most soldiers are young males, frequently teenagers. They are generally away
from their families for the first time. When not being shouted or shot at, these
guys tend to horniness and boredom. Playing with weapons is exciting, chasing
the local women is looked upon as both fun and exciting. Venereal disease is a
common affliction of soldiers and often accounts for the majority of noncombat casualties. When women are not available, the troops will go after alcohol
or drugs, or each other. Managing armed teenagers recently liberated from
parental supervision has never been easy. During the twentieth century, with its
largely more indulged and aware adolescents, the control problem got worse.
Armies that can afford it try to use as few teenagers as possible in peacetime.
In wartime it's a different story, because you're either working them round the
clock or getting them killed off before they can cause too much trouble.
However, armed forces are at peace most of the time. Those that still depend on
conscripts therefore have serious problems. The Soviets essentially turned their
military bases into prison camps, with very low pay, constant activity, and negligible access to the outside world. Still, their troops managed to get alcohol,
either from vehicle systems or by secretly trading equipment to civilians for it.
In one glaring example, a Soviet tank crew in Czechsolvakia got lost on a field
exercise, stumbled across a country inn, and traded their tank to the inn keeper
for all the vodka they could drink and carry. The drunken troops were found,
and the innkeeper caught, before he was able to cut the tank up for scrap and
parts.

   The successful approach to these problems is to develop good NCOs and
officers and keep the troops busy. This combination is rarely achieved. Combat
troops in particular are hard to handle. The noncombat forces generally skim
off the brightest and most able recruits, leaving the infantry with a higher proportion of problem cases. The noncombat troops also have more useful and
interesting work to do than infantry without a war to fight. Volunteer forces
handle this problem by filling the combat ranks with a lot of people who want
to be there. The Soviets handled this problem by putting all real and potential
troublemakers in labor battalions. Six days a week of manual labor takes the
mischief out of most youngsters. Unfortunately for the Soviets, they had the
most manpower-intensive armed forces in the world and not enough need for
labor battalions to take care of all the slackers. The personnel problems in the
Soviet armed forces constantly went from bad to worse and eventually contributed to the collapse of the Soviet Union. Even before the Soviet Union disintegrated, officers were writing articles in the military press advocating an all-volunteer force. This movement became a flood once the Cold War ended.

   The desertion of 74 Russians from one company in the summer of 2001
caused a stir in Russia. The incident spotlighted the unique problems Russia

has in trying to reform its armed forces. The Russians who deserted were all Slavs (the population of Russia is 74 percent Slav, nearly all of them Russian). The young lads were fleeing the bullying of older Dagestani soldiers in their company. About 7 percent of the troops in the Russian armed forces are from the Caucasus, about half of them from Dagestan. These guys make good soldiers. They drink and smoke a lot less than the Slavs, are in good physical shape, and are quick and eager to obey their officers. For this reason, Caucasian recruits get promoted fast. The officers find them reliable and don't much care how their Caucasian NCOs get things done.

The problem with bullying goes back to the disastrous war with Japan in 1904–5. Up until then, a small number of the male population was conscripted for 25 years. If they survived that, they were given a grant of land, much respect back in their village, and other perks. These men also had ample opportunity to become NCOs. But after huge losses and defeat by the Japanese in 1905, the government went over to the West European form of conscription (nearly all young men taken for 2–3 years). While at first there were lots of good NCOs from the old "25-year men" group, World War I destroyed those guys, and in the chaos of defeat and civil war, the idea of a professional NCO corps got lost. Instead, the Soviets decided just to have more officers. This was a mistake. Lower-ranking NCOs live with the troops; officers never do. This means that officers are never with the troops 24 hours a day. Left to their own devices, the troops established their own pecking order in the barracks. The new guys were bullied, abused, and made to do all the dirty work by conscripts who had been in service a year or more. This was made possible by several additional quirks of the Russian system. A new bunch of conscripts was brought in every six months, unlike other nations where new men are called up every day and sent to special centers for several months of training. When such European and American recruits finally get to their unit, they already have learned a lot about military life and are not so green. But in Russia, most new conscripts were sent right to their unit, where they received their training. This means a company of 120 Russian soldiers would, every six months, see two dozen of the most senior guys leave (usually after a raucous celebration) and two dozen civilians brought in. While officers would supervise and train these new recruits during the day, at night and on weekends, the soldiers who had been in six months or longer used the new guys as servants or objects of nasty abuse.

The degree of abuse varies. In some units, the tradition is one of mild abuse. But other units, especially when you have non-Russian senior soldiers (especially from the Caucasus) and a lot of Slav Russian recruits, things can get very unpleasant. The Caucasians dislike Russians more than the other way around. Caucasian young men also tend to be tougher and more aggressive than their Slav counterparts. Moreover, Caucasians see military service as a necessary rite of passage to adulthood. To most Slavs, it's something to be avoided if at all possible. For decades there has been a rule to never put more than five Caucasians in a company (of a hundred or so troops). Experience showed that all it took was half a dozen tough Caucasians to take control of a company. The Caucasians would cut a deal with the tough Slavs to dominate everyone else. Often the domination was little more than getting someone else to do your barracks chores and run errands. But sometimes it descended to robbery and sadism. With the end of the Soviet Union, there was a higher proportion of Caucasians in the population and, gradually, the "five Caucasians" rule faded away. This made renewed attempts to eliminate bullying more difficult. Many senior officers, especially those who have spent time with European and American military units, have urged that the Western system be adopted. Few disagree with this, but that would cost a lot of money. The army doesn't have the cash and will have to live with the bullying in the meantime.

The few Western nations that still rely on the draft cope by keeping the period of service short, between 12 and 24 months, and paying close attention to troop morale. The nations with volunteer forces have the age-old tool for troop control: do the job or become unemployed. This works wonders to stimulate performance in peacetime. Volunteer forces are not without their problems. Long-term troops mean wives and families. This tends to divide the attention of the troops, even though their primary loyalty is, in theory, to the armed forces. In practice there is an above-average divorce rate and a lot of alcoholism. It's not generosity that causes volunteer forces to offer retirement after 20 years. Although many troops stay beyond 20, this practice does serve as a safety valve. Navies have particular problems with the long periods of sea duty. Especially in Western navies, sailors can be away for up to a year at a time. The situation is worst in the American Navy. This is especially difficult with the ballistic-missile subs and their crews of highly skilled technicians. Serious problems are encountered trying to keep these people in the service. The original idea was to have two crews per sub, but even with that you still have six-month cruises to contend with. This, however, is nothing compared to the Soviet (and now Russian) problems with radiation poisoning and naval bases in Arctic areas. Moreover, Russia must use some conscripts and generally less-skilled crews for their nuclear ships.

The Future

One major trend is reducing the size of armed forces in order to make them more professional and combat-capable. Another growing trend is the use of troops for nonmilitary tasks. As one would suspect, few nations follow both of these trends at once. The Chinese, in an effort to modernize their armed forces and economy, discharged over a million troops in the early 1980s and several hundred thousand more in the early 1990s. The Soviets began a similar excision in 1990, and this was carried further after the demise of the Soviet Union. Also, despite their drive toward professionalism and combat capability,

Russian and Chinese troops also spend much of their time on nonmilitary tasks like tending vegetable gardens and helping out civilian industries.

A problem common in nations with bustling economies is a shortage of people willing to put up with military service unless suitable financial inducements are made. Weapons and equipment cost is growing even faster. When the cuts must be made, it tends to be people. While there may be more troops worldwide because of all the low-cost light infantry running around in less affluent nations, the industrialized powers are headed toward fewer people in uniform. Indeed, another variation on this trend is the tendency to use civilians for skilled technical posts. Even large warships tend to go to sea with several dozen civilian technicians performing jobs no uniformed personnel can be trained and/or retained for. Another tendency is that the farther we get from the last major war, the more unreal peacetime conditions in the military become. As civilian living standards increase, troops expect better living conditions during military service, and in combat. This is raising the cost of war, and troop morale, throughout the world.

PART FIVE

SPECIAL WEAPONS

Modern technology has created entire new classes of weapons. Most of these high-tech wonders never see combat before they are "improved" and replaced with new models. These new devices are potentially the most decisive contrivances ever sent into combat. Some are thought too lethal to be unleashed. Only time will tell.

18

The Electronic Battlefield and Information Warfare

Communications, and the control of information, are the glue that holds armed forces together. It is what turns a potential mob into an organized fighting force. During the U.S. Civil War (1861–65), electronic communications first came into wide military use. Initially, only the telegraph was used. But this allowed forces hundreds of miles apart to communicate almost instantly. In some cases, wire was strung throughout a battle area so that a commander could instantly receive reports and issue orders instead of relying on messengers. Fifty years later, World War I saw smaller units and some aircraft using wireless telegraph. Less than 20 years after that, during World War II, infantry units were carrying their own wireless telephones (radios). Most aircraft and tanks had radios. Today, more than a third of all soldiers operate some sort of electronic device. In some cases, like the U.S. Army, it's nearly 100 percent. Not all the devices are radios; some are sensors. And some are computers.

Information Warfare

The enormous growth of electronic devices in the last century has led to the emergence of a new flavor of combat: information warfare. This new form of combat is difficult to describe accurately, as it still means different things to different people. To military communications people, it means keeping the many military networks (both intranet and wireless) safe from enemy interference. At the same time, the military hackers strive to figure out ways to crash or listen in on enemy networks. To the psychological-warfare crew, it means getting a favorable spin on information about an ongoing war. Information war means all of these things, as well as the traditional arts of deception.

Indeed, the classic forms of deception are still the basic tools of information war. These include such time-honored techniques as:

Concealment. This is similar to camouflage, except that all you do is move your forces behind a natural obstacle. Concealment is the most ancient form of deception, first used by hunters sneaking up on their next meal or a human foe. Armies have long marched all, or part, of their forces behind a hill or into a forest where the enemy could not see them. Sailors have long known the advantage of heading into a fog bank to escape pursuing ships. Aircraft use the same trick. Modern sensors like radar have rendered fog or clouds less useful for concealment, although aircraft have discovered that flying close to the ground keeps you below what most radars can see. Ground forces still make good use of what nature has provided. There is also strategic concealment, hiding the direction of one's movements on a grand scale or hiding other useful information from the enemy; and political concealment, hiding one's political objectives. Not telling newspapers "the facts" is a form of concealment, eminently valuable on the strategic and political level. Hackers often conceal their movements through the Web by hiding among millions of anonymous users and the sheer mass of information moving across the net.

Camouflage. Nearly as ancient a technique as concealment, camouflage is creating your own concealment. Humans probably figured out camouflage by observing how animals use camouflage to hide themselves from enemies or prey. In fact, there are few wild animals that do not have camouflage built in. Arctic foxes, for example, have a dark, dull coat in the warm season. This makes it difficult for prey, or enemies, to detect them in underbrush or out in the open. But in the winter, when there is snow everywhere, the Arctic fox grows a white coat. For soldiers, good camouflage means being able to hide your movements better than the enemy hides his own. While ambushing the enemy is good, being able to move around undetected is even better, and more difficult to accomplish. When warfare and armies developed several thousand years ago, camouflage became much less a central part of combat. When armies became more the norm in warfare, camouflage became more difficult, and less frequently used. An army, by definition, is a large group of warriors acting together. Such a large group cannot easily sneak around as a dozen or so raiders would. The concept of a "battle," of large groups of men lining up and going at each other, caused camouflage to be used infrequently. The golden age of camouflage arrived early in the twentieth century. Armies had become huge. Armies began to dig in, and the "front line" became hundreds of miles of trenches. Under these circumstances, being so close to the enemy and vast amounts of hostile firepower, camouflage became much more popular among the troops and, eventually, the army leaders themselves. But technology caught up with camouflage in the twentieth century. First came aircraft, which were initially used primarily for scouting. Camouflage that hid you from someone on the ground was usually ineffective when enemy aircraft flew over. Not only that, but camouflage now became a life-saving measure for troops normally out of sight of the enemy. Through the middle of the twentieth century, troops developed efficient techniques to hide themselves from aerial observation. The most ancient camouflage techniques are still very effective. These involve covering the troops, or their positions, with foliage most of the year, or with white cloth when there's snow. The use of winter camouflage is a recent development because winter warfare did not become common until this century. Whatever the season, the principal function of camouflage is to make your troops invisible to the enemy. This invisibility is sometimes achieved, but usually the invisibility is not complete, and result is that the enemy is never sure exactly what you have and precisely where it is. The use of infrared (heat) sensors has made it possible to tell quickly what is live vegetation and what has been cut down for camouflage. Infrared can also see through foliage and detect the warm bodies of troops, and the heat from engines and recently fired weapons. Other sensors can detect large masses of metal (tanks and trucks). But as things stand now and in the foreseeable future, camouflage is still very effective against troops who do not have the latest sensors. Even against high-tech armies, camouflage will hide you a lot of the time, and this can still be an advantage. In electronic warfare, camouflage is anything that makes information look like something other than what it is.

False and planted information. This form of deception became popular once writing was invented and written orders and reports became common tools for generals to communicate with. Before that, putting false footprints or other information where the enemy would find it was useful and popular. Bits of clothing or broken weapons from another tribe, left in the right place, could cause the enemy scouts to think this other tribe was marching with your troops. But for a long time, this form of deception has taken the form of letting the enemy get their hands on information that will hurt him and help you, if he won't know that he's being taken for a fool. This often involves some espionage (double agents and the like) as well as understanding your opponent better than he understands you. The problem with false and planted information is that you are never sure the enemy will fall for it. If your opponent sees through the deception, he can use that as a weapon. Like most forms of deception, this one can cut both ways and only works in the hands of a skillful and resolute general. This form of deception is particularly popular in electronic warfare and has been very popular when one is manipulating the media.

Ruses. These are displays that use enemy equipment and procedures to deceive, to make the enemy think he is seeing his own troops when in fact he is facing enemy troops. From a distance, all troops tend to look alike. It is only in the details of how they hold their weapons or move across the battlefield that you can sometimes tell who is who. Thus an army a thousand years ago might deceive the enemy by having the troops carry their weapons as did the enemy (for example, with spears pointing skyward, rather than at an angle) and move like the enemy (in a V-shaped formation rather than a straight column). By the time the enemy discovers the deception, it may be too late for him. These techniques include "false colors" (enemy flags and uniforms) that also make the enemy think he is seeing his own troops when, in fact, they are enemy forces. The effectiveness of this deception can be seen in the centuries-old custom of immediately executing enemy troops found trying to pass as your troops. In this century, ruses have extended to electronic deceptions. Pilots have been known to switch to enemy frequencies and deliver misleading orders in the enemy's language. Sometimes this works; often the accent gives the ruse away. Of course, simply breaking in on the enemy frequency is a ruse, and just giving a wordless cry of pain can be discomforting and distracting to the enemy (who now thinks one of his fellow pilots is in trouble). Electronic warfare makes heavy use of ruses, such as having your ships or aircraft transmit signals indicating they are enemy vehicles. Hackers use ruses to gain entry to computers they are not supposed to be in. The most obvious ruse is using a password you are not supposed to have.

Displays. This is doing whatever it takes to make the enemy see what isn't there. You are not trying to hide your presence; you're simply attempting to make it appear other than what it really is. One of the oldest ploys is to have a few horses drag branches behind them to create a lot of dust so that a distant enemy thinks it is a larger cavalry force than you actually have. Variations on this can still be used today, but not as frequently because of binoculars and aircraft. Lighting many campfires where there are no troops is also an ancient display technique, and one that still has uses today in guerrilla warfare. More modern examples of displays are fake artillery (painted logs still work), dummy aircraft and armored vehicles (often inflatable), and a lot of radio traffic (to represent units that don't exist, or units that do exist being stronger than they actually are). If effectively used, displays can give you more military power than you actually have. If your display is convincing, the enemy will assign some of his forces to keep an eye on your conjured-up troops. This leaves your opponent with a smaller force for your real units to deal with. In this century, with modern technology making it easier to create effective displays, such practices have made a difference in many battles. Electronic warfare early on discovered the usefulness of displays. You can transmit a lot of signals so that a few ships or aircraft appear to be a lot more. Ground units can do this as well, and this technique has been widely used in the past 60 years. Hackers now have to be wary of "Honeypots," Internet computers dressed up to be valuable places to break into, but that are actually traps meant to snare interlopers.

Demonstrations. These are, literally, demonstrations of your military power, in an attempt to confuse the enemy about exactly what you are going to do with it. Making such moves with your forces attempts to imply imminent action but does not follow through. In ancient times, this often involved moving your troops back and forth where the enemy could see it. The foe would then have to consider where you were going to attack and might be encouraged to shift his own forces about. Today, demonstrations often mean sending a naval force near a hostile coast or an armored unit down a road where it is likely to be spotted by enemy recon aircraft or satellites. Any time armed forces move, the military situation is changing and the other side has to rethink its plans. Cleverly orchestrated demonstrations can drive the enemy to distraction, and often to make a fatal mistake. In media warfare, "demonstrations" are issuing a lot of press releases and holding press conferences to make it look like you are going zig, when you actually mean to zag. Putting the right spin on things, so to speak.

Feints. These are similar to a demonstration, but instead of just showing your forces off, you actually make an attack, or, rather, a "feint." Such an attack is meant to make the enemy believe that this feint is the main attack when in actuality it is done to distract the enemy while your real main assault occurs elsewhere. Since modern attacks go on for days, and involve several waves of troops, a feint would normally last only a day and involve far fewer troops than the main effort. But for that day, and perhaps a little longer, the enemy could be deceived into believing that the attack at hand was the major assault they were expecting. If this deception was successful, the enemy would reorganize his forces to face your feint. This would leave the area where the real main attack was coming rather less well protected. Thus, your big attack would have a better chance of succeeding because of a well-delivered feint. Again, this is a popular technique in media and network warfare. Both of these types of combat mainly use a lot of words or electronic signals. It's easy to generate a lot of heat to hide behind and deceive with.

Lies. The commonest form of deception (in war and peace) is flat-out lying. In wartime, this is usually done to good effect when communicating with the enemy. This is something that has been going on as long as there has been war. When there was no actual fighting going on, it is common for officers from both sides to "parley." These talks often include a demand for the other side for to surrender. These conversations are often full of imaginative fibs, and the side that can lie most effectively under these circumstances often gains an advantage. Diplomats tend to stay in touch even as their armed countrymen are slaughtering each other on the battlefield. So there's still opportunity for lying your way to victory, even if this job has now been taken from the soldiers and turned over to professional liars.

Insight. Deception is largely a mental game. While camouflage, for example, involves a lot of hard work, its effect is dependent on the enemy believing they are not seeing what is there. Between opposing generals, and to a lesser extent opposing troops, it's a battle of wits. If one general understands the other better, that provides a huge advantage for some effective deception. The classic example is one general knowing what deceptions his opponent is prone to fall for. This is all sort of like a chess game, where this form of deception is widely practiced. While it's easier to describe a lot of more tangible deception techniques, all of these depend on how the commanders involved use psychology. The most common cause of a deception failing is that the putative victim simply doesn't fall for it. The examples of deceptions, ruses, and the like in this book describe many instances of tricks that worked or didn't work because of the mental abilities of one or both commanders.

A lot has happened, and a lot has changed, since the battlefield was first electrified in the 1860s. The concept of information war has been building since the nineteenth century. The idea of using the classic forms of deception along with mass media and manipulating communications networks eventually became recognized, in the 1990s, as information war. It's nothing new, but it is different in scope and detail from any past forms of deception.

The Impact of Mass Media

War isn't what it used to be before radio and television. Because of instant media, public opinion guides military decisions far more than in the past.

Now, it's not just the generals and political leaders who get information quickly. Anyone watching the 24-hour news networks is nearly as well informed. In fact, the brass have found it useful to keep an eye on TV since civilian camera crews often dig out useful information before anyone in uniform can.

Commercial radio broadcasting did not appear until the 1920s. When World War II came along, radio news was a big business, and while live broadcasts from the combat zone were not possible, you could do it from major cities. And that was pretty impressive, especially since London was being bombed while some of those broadcasts went out.

When television came along after World War II, you got to see film flown in from combat zones. By the 1980s it was possible to send video from the battlefield to millions of homes via portable satellite transmitters. This changed warfare dramatically. Voters could see the horrors of war in real time and demand that something be done. They saw their troops being hurt. It was one thing to see a casualty list in a newspaper, as had been the case from the American civil war on; it was another to see dead or captured American soldiers, often in real time, on a television screen.

The impact of this instant information was felt first during the Vietnam War. The images of all that suffering were, understandably, disturbing to the folks back home. Americans never were eager to get involved in war in the first place, especially when America had not been directly threatened. Our Communist opponents quickly grasped the possibilities here and made the most of them. The result was a loss of public support for the war effort and eventual withdrawal of American troops. Potential foes of the United States noted this impact of media on America's war-making ability.

Saddam Hussein used the media as a major military weapon during the 1991 Gulf War. Knowing how quickly the American public would see video of any battlefield action, he tried to arrange for enough American casualties so that a public uproar in the United States would cause an American withdrawal.

Saddam got plenty of media play before the American attack began in January 1991. But he was outsmarted, and the attack on the Iraqis resulted in minimal American casualties: fewer than 300 deaths, unprecedented for an operation involving half a million troops. This had an unexpected side effect: the American public promptly decided this was a new development in warfare, and that all future American military operations should have equally low casualties.

This posed a problem. The Iraq operation had taken place under unique conditions that, in the past, had also resulted in low casualties. Ever since World War II, if you fought in the desert and had control of the air, you were likely to win the battle with very few casualties. The British won similar victories against the Italians under similar conditions in 1941.

But 24-hour television news networks did not cover those battles. In 1941, the generals explained how they won and why, and the newspapers reported that. In 1991, there were hundreds of experts (some real, some just glib). Since "all the news all the time" television demanded dramatic statements, the concept that bloodless warfare was at hand was jumped on big time. No amount of sober statements from military experts could contradict this misleading bit of analysis.

Somalis, Serbs, North Koreans, and many other hostile powers have adopted the new information-warfare tactics. They work. A battle between American rangers and Somali militiamen in 1993 resulted in 100 U.S. casualties and more than 1,500 Somali losses. The Rangers wanted to go back in and follow up their victory. But the next day they, and the Somalis, saw that the

American news media had declared it an American defeat because there were more than a few U.S. casualties.

The public desire to wage war with minimal losses has yet to come up against a truly desperate situation like World War II, Korea, or Vietnam. Against much weaker opponents, the American armed forces can pick and choose how they wish to fight. But there will be situations where those options are not available, and the way to victory will require heavy losses.

The Afghanistan war saw the United States make masterful use of information war, both on the battlefield and around the world. U.S. losses were kept low, as were civilian casualties. Enemy troops were induced to surrender via heavy use of information war, and some unsteady allies were kept on our side using information-war techniques.

In the century since mankind learned to broadcast information long distances, electronic communication has gone from being a military tool to being a military weapon. And this evolution isn't over yet.

What makes information warfare such a scary concept is that there are so many unknowns. This has led to disagreement on exactly what information war is and how to go about it. One could say that information warfare is whatever you do to preserve the integrity of your own information systems from exploitation, corruption, or destruction, while at the same time exploiting, corrupting, or destroying an enemy's information systems and in the process achieving an information advantage if it comes to armed combat. Well, that's the Pentagon's take on information war. You don't have to use force as a follow-up to information war.

Cyberwar

Cyberwar is another concept that's still in the process of being invented. Cyberwar is the use of all available electronic and computer tools to shut down the enemy's electronics and communications, and to keep your own going. No holds barred, anything goes. A lot of what can be done in this area is speculative, partly because new equipment is constantly appearing on the scene, and partly because it's only recently that military planners began looking at this angle as a new form of warfare. Earlier, elements of cyberwar were found here and there, as opportunities presented themselves. But cyberwarriors see themselves ensconced in combat information centers (CICs) filled with video displays and skilled technicians feeding commanders the latest data on who's (and what's) on and who's off the screen. This is actually the over-50-year-old story of radar and sonar operators playing with their equipment to nail the enemy. It's just writ larger, with a lot more gear tied together electronically and run from the same place. The U.S. Navy introduced the use of the CIC over 50 years ago. And it just kept growing and being adopted by the other services.

Ironically, it was the junior troops who dragged the armed forces into the personal computer age. In the late 1970s, junior enlisted troops and officers bought their own personal computers and saw opportunities to automate a lot of the administrative tasks they had to deal with, things like maintenance schedules in tank battalions and aircraft carriers, and nuclear weapons inventories (three late 1970s examples I personally came across in Europe). The senior officers noticed this, and thus there was little opposition from the brass to adopting personal computers on a wide scale in the 1980s. The troops had already shown how useful computers could be. When the Internet and the World Wide Web became widely used in the early 1990s, the military was already working on "networking" their ships, aircraft, and tanks. This would make it possible to pass target information and data on where friendly and enemy forces are. The easy-to-use technology of the Word Wide Web seemed an ideal solution. But there was a catch. The Internet and its World Wide Web component were created by thousands of independent programmers. The software was often created as "freeware" (to be given away) and continually updated by eager volunteers. When you change software a lot, you make some mistakes. The mistakes that are missed are the ones that don't affect operation, but rather compromise security. These trap doors and loopholes are the cause of most network break-ins. The other major security hole was the inside job, or a stolen password.

Recent attacks on major Internet sites remind military commanders of the dark side of their increasing use of the net. Several major distributed denials of service (DDOS) attacks in 2000 were seen as vandalism, for none of the attacked sites were penetrated, but merely overloaded and shut down by a flood of bogus "visitors." Yet for many military sites, DDOS attacks can have serious implications. The military is becoming increasingly dependent, and increasingly efficient, by using the Internet for communications. In the civilian world, this is also happening. In fact, B2B (business-to-business) intranet operations are larger than the more visible Internet shopping by consumers. If there were another war like the 1991 Persian Gulf conflict, the enemy could cripple logistics and maintenance operations (crucial to air operations and getting the troops to the battlefield) by making heavy and repeated DDOS attacks on military and defense Web sites used to deal with supplying and moving the troops.

But it gets worse. The February 2000 DDOS attacks were made possible by two different hacking tools. The more obvious one was the sending of millions of bogus requests to the target site. This is done using programs like Trinoo, which was created (by Russian hackers) and released on the net in the fall of 1999. Since then, Trinoo (and similar programs) have resulted in over 300 DDOS attacks a day. None of these were at major sites, where they would attract mass media attention. The big sites are designed to handle a large number of requests, so one computer using Trinoo to shut down another site would not work. This brings us to the second, and more ominous, aspect of the major attacks. Whoever launched these attacks did so by taking over dozens of other net computers. This is done by cracking into those machines and installing the DDOS software and a timer so that all the penetrated computers will begin the attack at the same time.

How does one break into so many computers? It's not easy, but it's possible with the right tools, a little skill, and the fact that a large percentage of the net computers (the "servers" that hold the Web sites) are not properly maintained. This is the Internet's biggest weakness and vulnerability. The Internet was designed to be flexible so that it could survive a nuclear war, and with this flexibility came a lot of ways for a malicious user to get into other servers and do whatever he wants. The engineers who work on the net software constantly look for these loopholes and plug them. But the people who take care of the servers, the sysadmins (system administrators), vary greatly in capability, competence, and time available for their duties. As a result, at any given time, many of the net servers are not equipped with the latest software. Hackers have long had tools (freely available on the net) to search automatically for vulnerable servers. Using these tools to invade servers has become an avid pastime among some teenagers. The "script kiddies" (who take the tools and follow the simple instructions for their use) are a nuisance. But some of these kids get older, more skilled, and more malicious.

Some of these malicious hackers also acquire radical political ideas. This is a dangerous combination. While more common in Europe, politically motivated hackers exist wherever there is a large community of Web users. As far back as the 1980s, the KAOS Computer Club in West Germany was hired by the KGB to carry out espionage for the Soviet Union. The KAOS members were caught and prosecuted. But the Russians, especially after the Soviet Union disintegrated, realized that they had a lot of computer-savvy people, and many of them took to the Internet enthusiastically. Same thing in the other Eastern European nations, as well as China and places like Iraq and Iran. When the Internet became a major factor in the industrialized nations, and the U.S. military, potential enemies of the United States realized that they might have an equalizer in the form of Internet warfare.

But to wage this kind of war, you need troops. Currently, there are over 50,000 script kiddies (of all ages) out there, and the number keeps increasing. Any nation with net users can turn many of their users into script kiddies without too much trouble. But these folks are not capable of doing serious damage. There are about a thousand really capable net engineers out there who can penetrate most vulnerable systems. Not many of these are malicious, and about 10 percent of them work for outfits like the CIA and FBI. There are also some 5,000–10,000 experienced net users and administrators who could be drafted into offensive, or defensive, net-efforts. There is a larger pool of over 100,000 net enthusiasts and people in the software business would could also be recruited and trained for net warfare. Most of these net-savvy people are

Americans, but thousands reside in nations that might some day be at war with the United States. And a few percent, the ones we have to worry about right now, have some real or imagined grudge that leads them to go to war on the net all by themselves. It is members of this group that probably launched the recent attacks. And they have done a public service by doing so. For Internet users now have a little more incentive to beef up their defenses. But as with any war, no matter how strong your defenses, there are always vulnerabilities.

Fortunately, unlike conventional warfare, the net-war troops get to practice their skills even when the bullets aren't flying. If you tried to get into Yahoo, Amazon.com, or another large site recently and were unable to, you were caught in an infowar skirmish. But some time in the future, such attacks will cause more than inconvenience.

Military Targets

Trying to hack into someone else's computer network has become a major indoor sport. Naturally, hacking some nets gains you more points than others. The biggest score is the U.S. military. The Department of Defense runs some 10,000 different networks using 1.5 million PCs. Most of these nets are linked to the Internet, providing access for malicious hackers worldwide. Some 2,000 of the Pentagon's nets are critical, controlling essential functions like command and control, logistics, nuclear weapons, research, and intelligence.

In 1999, the Pentagon detected some 22,000 attempts to hack into their systems. Most of these were amateurs, often teenage script kiddies employing easy-to-use tools widely available on the Web. In 2000, there were about 10 percent more attempted hacks. About 3 percent of these attempts caused some Web pages or local nets to be shut down for a short time. About 1 percent of the hacks actually got into a site, but none were able to get into classified databases or take control of critical functions. Or at least no such hacks were detected. Hacking activity continued to increase in 2001.

What worries Pentagon computer security experts is the number of professionals who are trying to get in. Even during the 1980s, long before the Internet and the World Wide Web became widely available, Soviet intelligence agencies were hiring hackers to get into Pentagon networks. Some of these attempts succeeded, or at least they got in and were later found out. A professional hacker wants to get in, take information, and not be caught. Classified information stolen that way is a lot more valuable than when your hack is detected after you get it. Some of the recent successful hacks were traced back to military organizations in China and Russia. Both countries deny that they were trying to hack the Pentagon.

It was the military that created the Internet, but it did not use it in a big way until civilians got access in the early 1990s and the World Wide Web appeared in the mid-1990s. No one expected the Web to have such a enormous impact on how people communicated. Soldiers as well as civilians eagerly took advantage of the many opportunities presented by the Web. Faced with all the clamor for military Web use from their own troops, the generals gave in and began using the Web everywhere, even on the battlefield. Very quickly, however, everyone was reminded how easy it was to hack into other people's Web sites and the computer servers they ran on. But hacking wasn't the only problem.

In early 2000, a Pentagon task force took a close look at 800 major military Web sites. They found 1,300 instances where sensitive or even classified information was available. Shortly thereafter, most U.S. military Web sites were shut down for "reorganization." When these sites came back on-line, there were a lot more restrictions on who could see what. Either you needed a military account (ending in the designation ".mil") or a password to get to the good stuff. Less visible were the frantic changes made to try to keep the hackers at bay.

Beefing up network defenses called for recruiting more computer-savvy soldiers (which gets easier as more kids grow up with PCs) and establishing special teams of military and civilian contractor network experts to probe military sites, find weaknesses, and fix those problems.

At the same time, the Pentagon went on the offensive. The most sensitive sites were given the most attention, something that was not always done in the past. To cut down on the amateur attacks that succeeded, traps were set up. False files, labeled to appear top secret, were placed on servers' hard disks. These files were decoys to entice intruders to stick around long enough for the hackers to be traced and caught. A few well-publicized prosecutions discouraged many casual hackers. The professionals are another matter. These hackers are careful and skillful. They will hack into a site and just look around to find traps, and see how security is set up. The professional hackers will then come back and do some real damage. It's not just stolen files that are a worry, but the planting of programs that can be set off later, as in during wartime, to trash the network and its files or send operational data to the enemy. These pros have made forays into American military sites, and the ones that were traceable were traced back to hackers in China and Russia. But that was spying, something America does to foreign military and government Web sites (but denies, of course).

No one has pulled off a major network attack yet, but the potential is there. Because the United States has more PCs and networks than any other nation, it appears to be the most vulnerable to such an offensive. But most of the work on network security is being done in the U.S. No one knows how likely Web warfare is, but no one believes it is impossible. Someone will eventually become the victim of a "Pearl Harbor" attack delivered by hackers. Until that time, everyone is eligible for this dubious honor.

America's Great Cyberwar Weakness

A major problem the armed forces has had since networks became military equipment is the difficulty keeping net-savvy troops in uniform. Those soldiers with computer experience are leaving in droves. Part of this is because of better economic opportunities in the civilian economy. But another critical reason is the workload these cyberwarriors are burdened with. As the armed forces install more networks, they encounter more problems and more exposure to hacking. The basic problem is that the best defense against hackers is well-trained systems administrators (sysadmins) to keep the software up-to-date and secure. Most net penetrations are the result of software that was poorly installed or not updated with the latest patches and protections.

But a more pressing reason for the cyberwarriors not sticking around is the strain of moving these troops around as new crises crop up. The military uses networks everywhere and is working on equipping the combat infantry and armored vehicles with them. When the troops were sent to places like Bosnia during the 1990s, nets were set up (linked worldwide with portable satellite dishes). There were problems with this in Bosnia, and a lot of cyberwarriors found themselves back in Bosnia, often more than once. Network and computer problems in relatively quiet places like Korea and the Persian Gulf also create a demand for specialists to be sent there. The Afghanistan war created a new emergency demand, in faraway places, for network experts. This is not an ideal lifestyle for most people, especially married soldiers. And most soldiers today are married. Troops often have to chose between their military careers and their marriages. The marriages usually win. The demand for good sysadmins made young soldiers trained in these skills a hot item on the civilian market. The military had a hard time getting these troops to reenlist. The military had a hard time just training enough sysadmins, and often military servers and nets were run by anyone in the vicinity who admitted they "knew something about PCs."

Several new approaches were taken to solve the sysadmin shortage. Providing better centralized support for military Web sites made it easier for the overwhelmed (and very young) military sysadmin to get help. The military also began using its own teams of hackers to attack its own sites and networks periodically to see how secure they were. The weak sites got more attention. It wasn't a perfect solution, but it was better than the earlier anarchy.

Most young soldiers who get computer experience in the military promptly leave for better-paying jobs outside, no matter what their workload. But this is not a new problem for the military. The Army and Marines see their highly trained infantry leave after a few years, and pilots are nearly as quick to depart. So the military has a large training establishment. The military has gotten used to training a lot of new geeks.

But there are never enough sysadmins to go around as the military constantly expands their inventory of networks. Hiring much more expensive civilian contractors, often former cyberwarriors, helps somewhat. But Congress does not like the much higher price the civilians charge. It's possible for another nation (like China) to assemble a large number of cyberwarriors and overwhelm the undermanned ranks of American network operators. The current hope is that a sufficient number of patriotic and skillful civilian network experts could be recruited and put into action quickly enough (days or weeks) to prevent a major network defeat.

Information War and Good Intentions

The military is not the only practitioner of information war. Civilians use it as well, and often the victim is the military. For example, in 1997 a treaty to ban land mines was signed by most of the world's nations. Attempts to ban weapons have never been very successful, but treaties to "ban" chemical weapons, nuclear weapons, and land mines will at least discourage their use. And that is a good thing. What was unique about the campaign to ban land mines was the skillful use of misinformation, lies, and rewriting of history to get the treaty signed.

The basic premise of the anti-mine movement was that mines have no military usefulness and are used primarily against innocent civilians. Wrong on all counts. Explosive mines are a twentieth-century development of ancient snares and traps used by hunters and soldiers for thousands of years.

It wasn't until World War II that the technology was developed to make possible mass production of cheap and deadly mines. At the end of the twentieth century, any nation or group with access to explosives and simple metalforming equipment could make land mines cheaply and quickly. A toy factory can do it, if it has the explosives. Mines were used so widely during World War II not because the generals were a bunch of sadists, but because the skillful use of mines reduced their own casualties and could mean the difference between victory and defeat.

But after World War II, land mines found a new use. The many guerrilla wars that have been waged during the last half-century introduced land mines as a political weapon. Most of the mines used against civilians were intended to terrorize the civilians into supporting the guerrillas or not supporting the government. This was not brought out during the anti-mine crusade because it did not fit the mind-set of the crusaders, who sought to pin the blame on the nations providing most of the mines. Ironically, the chief supplier of mines, particularly in Cambodia where the civilian population suffered horribly from them, was China. And it is China that refuses to have anything to do with an anti-mine treaty. Most of the nations that signed the treaty either have not used or are not likely to use mines in wartime. But the nations that supply most of the mines, and the terrorist and political groups that use them to cause most of the civilian casualties, have not signed the treaty, nor do they show any inclination to do so.

What the crusaders did make much of was their assertion that there were over 100 million mines in use and that over 25,000 people were injured each year by mines. The anti-mine enthusiasts made up both numbers. Later examination found that there was no basis for their statistics.

It just goes to show that you can't believe everything you read. For example, it was asserted that there were 35 million Russian mines left behind in Afghanistan. This number withstood all scrutiny until mine clearers on the spot began to develop their own statistics (it being a matter of life and death for them) and came up with an estimate of 600,000 mines. The most absurd aspect of all this is that the vast majority of the mines in question were sold or installed by people who do not, and probably never will, release any accurate figures. So you have to estimate, and if you are a political advocacy organization, you estimate in your favor.

The best thing to come out of the treaty is putting more attention, and money, into clearing mines in poor countries. Massive numbers of mines have been cleared before. Europe, the most extensively mined area in history during World War II, was, right after the war, cleared of most mines within a few years. Same with Korea. Any twentieth-century war leaves a lot of buried explosives. World War II–era bombs are still being dug out of the major cities of Europe.

But on the negative side, the nations that did sign the treaty will, when they send their soldiers into some future war, lose more of those troops for want of land mines. Oh, the mines will be produced quickly once the reports get back from the front, but many of their citizens in uniform will die needlessly in the meantime.

The anti-mine activists knowingly used information warfare to achieve their goals, and their example has encouraged others to do the same. If you have a cause that is generally considered worthy and are willing to lie, cheat, and deceive to achieve your goal, information war is the way to go.

Command, Control, Communications, and Intelligence (C³I)

Warfare is a complicated business, and the introduction of electronics didn't simplify things much. In the decades since World War II, there evolved a concept known as C³I (Command, Control, Communication, Intelligence). This implied that if a commander had sufficient quantities of communications and intelligence fed to him electronically, he could communicate with his subordinate units electronically and control them with heretofore unknown efficiency. The theory has not held up well in practice through most of the twentieth century. Indeed, it has not been attempted in a war with both sides using a lot of the latest electronic gear. The 1973 Arab-Israeli war and the 1991 Gulf War came pretty close, and things got gummed up pretty badly in the first week or so. Jamming and using everything at once under combat conditions introduced unanticipated traumas to the undertaking. Undismayed, commanders have redoubled their efforts to make C³I work. This is little different than attempts in the past to make new technologies work in wartime. Success comes eventually. It did in the Gulf War, as Iraqi jamming had limited effect and U.S. C³I capabilities finally delivered the degree of control generals have sought for centuries.

The original use of military electronic communications was nothing more than adaptation of existing civilian telegraph resources. The military had made no effort to prepare "militarized" systems beforehand. World War I was also largely an improvise-as-you-go situation. Going into World War II there were more custom military systems, especially for the control of artillery and aircraft. Both these systems required considerable debugging and refining before they became practical on the battlefield.

The latest systems have three major problems:

- They are complex and in a constant state of flux as new features are added and existing ones are repaired.
- The commanders and staffs who will use these systems don't have experience with them, particularly under the chaotic and uncertain conditions of combat. Many portions of these systems will be randomly destroyed in combat. Unanticipated technical problems will crop up. The results of all these problems, and their solutions, will not be known until the battle is fought.
- There is the false security one obtains from seeing the situation neatly displayed on a computer terminal. The real world is not that neat, and the users will have to learn how to relate the electronic version of the battle with what is really happening.

Commanders had good reason to be nervous about what would happen when they tried to run a war with all these C³I goodies. This happened in the

1991 Gulf War when the U.S. JSTARS aircraft gave commanders the last link in the electronic chain of control that had been building for over a century. For the first time in history, the commanders could see units moving, in real time, across an area hundreds of square miles in size. The catch was that the images on the computer screen didn't positively identify whose units they were. There were some anxious moments as U.S. and British divisions almost collided with guns blazing. This has happened before, but some frantic radio conversations sorted out who was who and prevented a repetition of a common twentieth-century friendly-fire incident. The next major war will see wider use of this technology, and the danger that the next opponent will have an electronic means to muddy the picture once more.

Realizing this, the United States armed forces spent most of the 1990s working on the problem. Their solution was called "digitalization." The emergence of the World Wide Web in the mid-1990s had something to do with this. The whole idea is sort of a battlefield intranet. But it's also another attempt to make information technology work better on the battlefield. The use of "digitalization" on the battlefield means putting computer displays in most combat and command vehicles. Information is shown about where friendly and enemy troops are, as well as the position of things like minefields and obstacles. As the computer displays fill up with symbols, the troops tend to believe they know where everything is and concentrate on running a fast break on the enemy. In theory, this is good. The digitalization gives the user an information advantage. While the enemy is still trying to figure out who is where, the digital force knows where everyone is and is executing a crushing attack. In reality, not all the information on the displays is accurate or up-to-date, and this has led to some embarrassing friendly-fire accidents. Not to mention wandering into minefields or roadblocks no one managed to get into the digital database. This can be characterized as growing pains with the new technology. But it also points out that the digitalization technology works best, if it works at all, only with trained and disciplined troops. Most of today's troops grew up with video games. One thing that characterizes these games is the widespread use of unambiguous information. What you see is what you have to deal with. On the battlefield, things aren't so clear-cut. In fact, dealing with ambiguous information is one of those skills required for survival in combat. So the Nintendo generation must lose some bad habits before it can take full advantage of battlefield digitalization.

This has already been seen during the first full field tests of digitalization with ground troops. These tests put a "digitalized" brigade against a well-trained but non-digitalized unit. It turned out that there was a learning curve. Commanders had to learn to deal with sometimes false information. Troops had to learn to react quickly to opportunities presented by the increased situational awareness of this battlefield intranet. After some practice, commanders figured out how to develop a backup plan quickly if that wonderful opportunity they saw on their monitor turned out to be false. The troops got used to moving quickly to attack unseen (by eye) opponents detected by a UAV or other sensor.

As predicted, combat became a lot more hectic. But it worked. As tired as the digital troops might get, it was worse for their opponents. The non-digitalized troops became more cautious as they soon learned that any contact with the enemy could rapidly turn into a desperate battle against a foe that knew more about what was where and who was doing what.

The war in Afghanistan was the first chance to try out digitalization on a battlefield. UAVs were used extensively. The Predator UAV was particularly useful. Able to fly above a battlefield for 12 or more hours, it transferred information to nearby warplanes or ground troops, and the enemy below was left wondering (if it survived) where all this grief was coming from. The armed Predator was used as well. Carrying a pair of 100-pound Hellfire missiles, it could attack targets immediately without waiting for bombers to show up. The Special Forces troops carried radios, navigation equipment, and special computers to control air and ground forces. If the Special Forces guys found a good target, the target was often attacked before the enemy even knew someone had spotted them. The Special Forces teams could also be directed to an area where enemy activity was suspected. Often it was not clear if the activity on the ground was civilians or enemy troops. But the Special Forces teams could get a close look and make the call to attack or not. This kept the civilian casualties way down, for in the past, warplanes in a combat zone would often err on the side of prudence and attack any suspicious-looking activity on the ground (which might sometimes be friendly troops).

This was information war on the battlefield. The side that isn't wired for it will be at a big disadvantage.

Electronic Warfare

Shortly after the first military messages went over the wire, other soldiers saw ways to use this dependence to their advantage. Electronic warfare was initially crude. Cutting the telegraph wire or listening in were effective. Later attempts were made to send false messages. During World War I codes were used, and regularly broken. Radio direction finders were used, and microphones were planted on the battlefield to detect enemy activity. Dummy radio traffic was used to deceive enemy intelligence analysts.

By the end of World War II, electronic warfare had become a major factor in combat planning. Major offensives were not planned without drawing up a communications deception plan. It wasn't enough to declare radio silence; the enemy would know something was up. Dummy radio traffic was established. Enemy radars and navigation devices were jammed or deceived. Since World War II, electronic warfare has matured into a decisive weapon. Tests have shown that units become aimless and unresponsive when hit with effective jamming, artillery, electronic-warfare-controlled radio-direction finding, and electronic deception. Oddly enough, none of the major armed forces have yet had an opportunity to use current electronic-warfare techniques on one another. These imposing systems have been used on minor countries with devastating effect. U.S. aircraft over Vietnam, and Israel in the Middle East wars, were extensive and devastating examples. In 1991, the Iraqis were able to use some of their EW equipment, but not enough to have any critical impact. Peacetime application of EW to field exercises has often been catastrophic in its effectiveness. When both sides can use electronic warfare on each other at full blast, it is expected that the effect will be similar to chemical or nuclear weapons. Not so much in terms of direct casualties, of course. But the confusion and disorientation is expected to be massive. Given the various good reasons for not using chemical or nuclear weapons in a major power war, electronic warfare may well be the most overwhelming new entry to the battlefield of the future.

Russia always took electronic warfare seriously. In theory they were less dependent than Western forces on continuous radio communication. Soviet ground forces' doctrine was to point their combat divisions in a certain direction and turn them loose. They were expected to keep going until they reached their objectives or burned out in the attempt. The Soviets continued to place great emphasis on nonelectronic communications like flares, flags, and messengers. They also favored field telephones when in static positions. Their air force and naval units were arguably more dependent on radio than Western counterparts. Moreover, throughout the Soviet armed forces there was a tradition of not doing anything untoward without detailed instructions from the high command. Soviet units practiced operating without radio in field exercises. However, their own military writers criticized these same field exercises for being stage-managed and not representative of an actual battlefield. In the future, the greatest danger from Russian-built and -exported EW gear and doctrine is their use by Third World nations against Western forces. Many of these less wealthy forces customarily use more nonelectronic communication. They are simply not as dependent on electronic tools as we are. The Soviet Union may be gone, but their EW legacy will be with us for some time to come.

While all armed forces may find their dependence on electronic equipment threatened by electronic warfare, there are also electronic solutions. Again, computers come into play. One of the more common solutions to jamming is the use of computer-controlled frequency hopping. This has the transmitter constantly switch frequencies at high speed. As it is very difficult to jam all frequencies, a frequency hopper will generally get the message delivered.

The problem with defending against electronic warfare is that the solutions are implemented on paper and frequently never get any further. Russia turned out a lot of crude EW equipment. Most Western EW gear stays in the laboratory. Only in the air and at sea is Western EW equipment getting into the field in quantity. A future major ground war could be very interesting. Even ground wars against Third World armies will be fraught with unforeseen consequences if the bad guys are using Russian jamming gear.

Components of Electronic Warfare

Electronic warfare is not a simple matter. It consists of several distinct activities. Each of these is quite complex in itself, and understanding some of this complexity gives you an idea of how vast a subject electronic warfare is.

ESM (ELECTRONIC SURVEILLANCE MEASURES)

Just keeping track of the enemy's electronic devices has become a major operation, especially since no one knows exactly how everyone's electronic equipment will interact until there is a sustained period of use. Such use does not occur in peacetime, when the EW equipment is used infrequently for training and testing. All electronic equipment has a unique electronic signature. Even equipment that is not broadcasting will appear a certain way to various sensors like radar or sonar. Thus, a critical peacetime function is to determine what these signatures are. For this reason, navies and air forces devote a significant amount of their time tracking other nations' capabilities. As a counter to ESM, equipment is disguised where possible. Signals can be varied in some circumstances. For equipment that is detected by shape and composition, like aircraft and ships, their shape and substance can be designed to minimize detection. This is the essence of the stealth technology that the United States is applying to a number of vehicles, especially aircraft. Small ships, aircraft, helicopters, and vehicles loaded with sensors do most of the collecting. Low-flying satellites are useful for catching signals deep inside a nation's territory. UAV aircraft are used also, plus robotic sensors that are left on the ground or sea bottom.

Collection involves more than sensors. Recording devices, foreign-language interpreters, and signal-processing equipment also come into play. Computers are increasingly crucial in sifting through the ocean of data swept up. Huge libraries of signals are collected, analyzed, and boiled down to manageable amounts of data that friendly troops and weapons can use. ESM has been so successful that one entire class of sensors, active sensors, has become endangered. Active sensors detect things by broadcasting a signal. When this signal bounces off something, the sensor detects the bounce-back and knows something is out there. This is the basis of radar, which broadcasts microwaves, and sonar, which broadcasts sound. Because of the signal being broadcast, a passive sensor can detect it. Passive sensors just listen. Because active sensor signals must reach an object in sufficient force to bounce something back, a vehicle carrying a passive sensor will detect a vehicle carrying an active sensor first. This is what happens when you use a radar detector in your car to detect police speed-trap radars. You usually have time to slow down before your illegal speed is detected by the police radar. As users of these devices well know, there is constant competition to come up with better radars and countermeasures. Passive sensors are the hot item in research and development these days, and for obvious reasons. Passive sensors are nearly impossible to detect. Passive sensors can also pick a wide variety of signals. Infrared sensors can detect heat, including something as faint as body heat or the hot skin of an approaching jet aircraft. How seriously do nations take this? The Chinese were harassing our EP-3 ESM aircraft because they knew that American ESM collection in peacetime could hurt them quite a bit in wartime. Early in the Cold War, the Russians shot down, or shot at, dozens of American recon and ESM aircraft and ships.

Photography is also an increasingly effective passive sensor. Using a TV camera–type device to capture images and heat, and applying a lot of computer-processing muscle, these sensors can see at night, through fog and smoke. Satellites and aircraft are major users of these image sensors. As image sensors get smaller, they are found more in ground vehicles. Modern Western tanks use such devices.

Sonar is not the only form of sound sensor. Indeed, the earliest application of this technology was as sound ranging, which detected the range of distant artillery by counting the seconds between the flash of the gun firing and when the sound reached you. Sound travels though the air at a fairly standard rate (the "speed of sound"). This century-old technique has been coupled with signal processing to create passive sensors for ground troops. In the same circumstance, often within the same unit, seismic sensors are also used. These sensors listen to sound transmitted through the earth by approaching vehicles. Sound and seismic sensors are often packaged together with a radio transmitter and dropped behind enemy lines. They can be delivered by aircraft, artillery, shell, or by hand. There they wait for some activity. When something is detected, a short, high-intensity burst of compressed data is radioed back. This method of transmission is used in order to avoid enemy detection of the sensor. These sensors are frequently designed to resemble local vegetation. Sometimes these sensors are easier to find. During the Vietnam War, an early form of this sensor was designed to resemble a bamboo plant. The ones that were not used in Vietnam were shipped to Germany. These were eventually replaced before we could find out if Soviet troops would recognize bamboo plants as out of place in a pine forest.

In the last 10 years, these sensors have been combined more frequently with weapons. Naval mines have been using these techniques for over 50 years. Now miniaturized electronics have enabled land mines to have their own sensors. Vehicles, especially heavy ones like tanks, make a lot of noise. Some mines currently available can detect when a tank is moving over it and fire an small armor-

AN/PVS-5 night vision goggles

piercing charge through the thin bottom armor of the vehicle. Other systems actually fire a mortar-like projectile that in turn detects an armored vehicle and fires a projectile through the thinner top armor. Where previously you would use several tons of mines to destroy one tank, you now need only several hundred pounds' worth. This is a twentyfold increase in efficiency. Although the new mines are 10 times as expensive, weight is the critical factor on the battlefield. You can't carry a lot onto the battlefield; every pound counts.

Passive sensors are becoming the dominant form. They are limited in their range compared to active sensors. But they have the invaluable advantage of concealing their presence from the enemy. Sensor projects in the West are capitalizing on technological advantages in electronics and computers to give passive sensors greater range. Moreover, computer-controlled weapons can be radically changed more quickly by reprogramming the instructions. Change will come even faster on the current and future battlefield.

ECM (ELECTRONIC COUNTERMEASURES)

Electronic weapons begat electronic defenses. This wide range of techniques deceive or disrupt electronic devices. Jamming is one of the more obvious forms of ECM. This consists of broadcasting a loud signal on the same frequency the enemy is using for communications, or whatever. More sophisticated jamming makes the enemy equipment appear defective or makes it show erroneous data. Chaff jamming is done with a cloud of metallic strips. This makes radar think the chaff cloud is the target. Flares do the same for heat-seeking (infrared) sensors. Electronic noisemakers draw missiles with passive sensors that hone in on active sensors.

ECCM (ELECTRONIC COUNTER-COUNTERMEASURES)

These are various techniques for dealing with ECM. One of the unsophisticated forms is simply to crank up the transmitter and burn through the enemy jamming. A more practical variation is burst transmission: the message is compressed and transmitted in a very powerful but brief burst of energy. Automated frequency hopping has become a standard high-tech solution to jamming and signal homing. Two radios with the same built-in computer rapidly switch frequencies as they transmit and receive. Computer software can also be used to reconstruct any portions of the messages that do get jammed. To jam a frequency hopper requires jamming a large number of frequencies. This takes a lot of equipment and power, two things in short supply on the battlefield. Another straightforward form of ECCM is to give missiles more than one type of homing system. It's expensive, but some missiles have radar, radar-homing, and heat-seeking devices. Of course, all three can be jammed.

SIGNAL PROCESSING

This has become a large and crucial component of electronic warfare. Signal processing is a ten-dollar word for a computer doing what humans have been doing for many years. For example, a photo interpreter recognizes patterns representing certain types of enemy fortifications or installations. Thousands of years ago, scouts learned to recognize whose army a horse belonged to by the shape of the tracks left behind. You can still do this with tanks by examining the thread marks they make in the ground. And so on. You get the idea. When computers came along, it was possible to let machines keep track of the patterns. In addition, more complex patterns could be identified and remembered. The sounds made by ships or the signals broadcast by radars all are as unique as fingerprints. And computers now take care of identifying fingerprints, as well as thumb and palm prints and even retina (eye) patterns, for security systems. As the computers get smaller, it is possible to do signal processing where previously there wasn't sufficient space, like the guidance systems of missiles or the fire-control mechanism of tanks and ships.

The first dramatic use of computer signal processing was in passive sonar. The ocean is a noisy place, further confused by layers of water with different temperatures, which makes sound bounce around and become distorted. Sorting out the sound of a submarine from the mackerel gossip and merchant ships was first accomplished by signal processing. Vast libraries of sounds are kept in the computers' memories, and updated periodically, so that individual ships can be identified, as well as their course and speed. Similar libraries for aircraft and ground combat allow the identification of signals quickly and accurately. The air force uses signal processing to identify radar and radio signals and enable aircraft to avoid antiaircraft weapons and interceptors. Targets can also be found more easily, as well as areas covered by friendly radars. Ground units use signal processing for air defense and intelligence gathering.

A variation on signal processing is traffic analysis, the study of past patterns of enemy messages and sensor use. For different operations, like preparations for attack or defense, different patterns are watched for.

One final aspect of signal processing is that the substantial advantage of Western nations' lead over other nations in computer technology makes this weapon largely a Western one.

EDM (ELECTRONIC DECEPTION MEASURES)

These are an assortment of techniques to deceive the enemy. Transmitters can be set up solely to divert the enemy's attention or simulate the presence of one of your units. Simulated message traffic can indicate a unit is going to attack, when it is really going to move elsewhere. The oldest deception technique is sending messages in code. This field, cryptography, is almost entirely dependent on electronic devices. Computers devise the codes and attempt to break them. Sensors continually monitor enemy codes looking for new variations to be broken. Simpler, cheaper, and often more effective methods exist based on how long you broadcast. The more modern radars are accurate enough to stay on for a few seconds and then use that "snapshot" for up to a minute or more before turning on again. These short bursts of radar usage can be powerful enough to overcome most jamming. This is another example of how simplicity is often the most effective solution.

Offensive Electronic Warfare

When a force is attacking, electronic warfare provides a number of critical functions:

Target acquisition. Sensors, ESM, and signal processing aid the attempt to identify the activity, strength, and position of enemy units. From this list, critical targets are selected for attack.

Disruption of C³ (command, control, and communications). Jamming of enemy communications, sending of false messages, and destruction of enemy communications equipment prevent your opponent from opposing your attack effectively.

Deception. EDM deceives the enemy about your real intentions before you lower the boom.

Defensive Electronic Warfare

In electronic warfare, defense is far more important than offense. Because everyone is so dependent on radios and sensors, disruption of these devices can be dev-

IAN/TPQ-36 Firefinder radar

astating. Fortunately, EW does not disrupt radio and sensor use continually. Jamming equipment is expensive and attracts a lot of unwanted attention when it is used. Antiradiation missiles have an easy time homing in on jammers that broadcast continually. Jammers are generally used when a crucial operation is underway, primarily offensives. Defenders have several remedies available.

Alternative communications. Alternatives to radios are available: messengers, field and regular telephones, flares, etc. All of these are either slower or less flexible than radio. To plan for their use you must be prepared to adjust your operations accordingly. Alternative sensors are also less powerful. These include more lookouts, trip flares, minefields, and so on. The important thing is to be prepared for the loss of normal radio and sensor capability. Being caught by surprise is the worst possible situation for the defender.

Communications discipline. Because ESM is the one electronic warfare activity carried out continually, it is the one you must fear the most. If your troops get into the habit of using radio and sensors in the same predictable way all the time, your opponent will soon know about it. The enemy will be able to pinpoint your key installations and units and hit or jam them effectively in the opening stages of an attack.

ESM. Electronic surveillance is critical because if you do it right, you will know what your opponent is up to. Not being surprised is more than half of an effective electronic defense.

Equipment hardening. Nuclear explosions release a pulse of electromagnetic energy (EMP, or electromagnetic pulse) that will disable or destroy electronic equipment. A one-megaton nuclear explosion high in the atmosphere will disable electronic components thousands of kilometers away. There are now available nonnuclear explosive devices that deliver an EMP pulse over a much shorter distance (a few kilometers), but with the same lethal effects to electronics. Some of this equipment can be used again in minutes or hours; others will be permanently crippled. Closer explosions will destroy more equipment. Most of this can be avoided by shielding and/or redesigning solid-state equipment to resist this surge of energy. Such measures increase the cost of equipment 5 percent or so. This hardening is becoming a common practice.

Only a few nations have access to all the above tools. Less technically endowed nations compensate with several clever strategies:

Barrage jamming. Lacking the sophisticated jamming Western nations are capable of producing, many countries opt for barrage jamming of many frequencies. They can build lots of simple jammers and generators to power them. They also put a lot more radio direction-location equipment into the field.

Concealed equipment. Many potential enemies are closed societies with a mania for secrecy and deception. Countries like this kept some new equipment from their own troops, the idea being that their troops could learn to use it quickly enough and the enemy would be in the dark longer. This approach has been used successfully many times in the last century. You can be assured that not all the electronic-warfare equipment of many nations is known to their potential opponents.

Redundant systems. Many nations' ships, aircraft, and ground units often appeared to have more equipment than Western counterparts. They did, and it was partly because they couldn't maintain their equipment as well as Western troops, and also because this gave them more options in combat. If one system was defeated by Western countermeasures, perhaps a different one would do the trick. Crude, but effective.

Spies. Traditionally more inclined to use spies than the United States, many nations find that a handicap in the fancy electronic-espionage department can be made up with more human agents.

To counter many of these practices, the better-equipped nations still have more flexible equipment. Computer-controlled EW gear can be quickly reconfigured. Western forces increasingly capitalize on this.

Theory and Practice

Remember that for all its apparent efficiency, electronic-equipment performance is a now-and-again thing. Anyone who has experienced the occasionally unstable performance of radio, PC, and TV equipment has experienced this. Any electronic gear that sends signals through the atmosphere must contend with natural interference. As a result, equipment specifications are misleadingly deceptive. A radar with a quoted range of 100 kilometers will not spot every target every time at that range. More detailed equipment specs will show that at 100 kilometers, targets of a certain (usually large) size can be spotted 90 percent of the time and at 50 kilometers 99 percent of the time. In practice, spotting probability may be under 10 percent at 100 kilometers and only 50 percent at 50 kilometers. This is the idea behind stealth technology: not to make something *invisible* to radar, simply harder to detect. Since detection must be continuous to be useful, a target that blinks on and off upon the radar screen is less likely to be tracked and hit by a missile. The electronic battlefield is one of probabilities, not certainties. Victory will go to the side that can best cope when the gadgets don't perform according to the spec sheet. But as electronic equipment gets cheaper, it becomes possible to equip things like bombs with backup systems. Smart bombs that use GPS satellite signals often have a backup system using older technology made more affordable by cheaper microelectronics. The bombs and missiles even have their own diagnostic computers on board that will constantly test the system for flaws, and report them to pilots or technicians when something goes wrong. So more powerful electronic equipment can also become more reliable.

But electronic-warfare worries have largely been replaced by the unknown terrors of information warfare. Electronic warfare has been around for about a century, and people have gotten used to it. What we call information warfare has been around a lot longer than that, except for one element, the Internet. The Internet is new (at least as a worldwide monster of a network), and you can do a lot more with it than you can do with a telephone. Actually, people are fearful of the bad guys doing dastardly things with not just the Internet, but with several other networks. One of these networks, the international telephone network, is actually much larger than the Internet. While the Internet runs on telephone lines as it goes the last few miles to homes and offices, beyond that the Internet often travels on separate electronic networks. There are also many other separate and critical networks in operation, most of recent vintage. The CIA has its own private Internet (looks and operates like the Internet but is not connected in any way to *the* Internet), and other government and business organizations are looking to go the same way. The problem with this is that bad stuff tends to sneak in, anyway. The whole point of Internet technology is a standard for moving information around. But the separate nets do eliminate a lot of the trash from malicious users. For the military, reducing the problem is possible, but eliminating it is impossible (or not worth the cost).

The major problem with information war is that it is so new and there are so many unknowns. The major unknown is that there have not yet been any major military campaigns featuring the all-out use of information-war weapons. There have been some skirmishes. In April 2001, Chinese hackers began a popular movement to deface U.S. Web sites in protest to an American patrol plane's collision with a Chinese fighter. The Chinese didn't do so well, defacing, at most, 300 sites while American hackers, in retaliation, defaced over 900 Chinese sites. Unbowed, Chinese hackers apparently were responsible for unleashing the Code Red worm, which brought down over 300,000 (mostly American) Web sites. Code Red was traced back to a university in China. China openly proclaims its belief that cyberwar is one area in which it can achieve world-class capability and meet America on even terms. Many net attacks on U.S. targets have been traced back to Chinese locations, often Chinese government servers.

Another example of Chinese cyberwar prowess has been seen in Internet battles between Chinese and Taiwanese hackers over the last few years. The dispute between China and Taiwan over Taiwan's independence has been fought most viciously on the Internet. The action has largely been minor stuff, trashing each other's Web sites and the like. But there have been indications of more potent action. The most damaging Internet attacks require a lot of preparation, and this usually involves quietly sneaking into the computers of potential victims to scout out defenses and sometimes leave programs for later use. There are a lot of Chinese cyberwarriors sneaking around the Internet these days.

Aside from the unknowns of information war, there is also the problem that most cyberweapons have a short shelf life. Information-war weapons depend on software flaws that are constantly being discovered and fixed. But this is where China has an edge, for as the number of skilled Chinese software engineers and hackers increases, so does the ability of China to discover, and exploit, Internet flaws more rapidly than anyone else.

Worst of all, China has made no secret of favoring this kind of low-cost approach to warfare. While salaries must be paid to some of China's cyberwarriors who staff the cyberwar headquarters, much of the work is done by patriotic volunteers among the ranks of China's growing number of software engineers and programmers. The eagerness of these cyberwarriors has been seen in the skirmishes with the Taiwanese, where volunteers jumped right in to defend the motherland. The only bright spot in all this is the Taiwanese, who are well aware of their position on the front lines of the looming cyberwar.

Thus, most of the activity in the information-war area takes place in the shadows. Everyone has to develop new weapons and new defenses as the software that propels the Internet, or electronic-warfare equipment, constantly changes. It's hard to practice for information war when you're not sure what weapons the enemy has. The opening rounds of any future information war will be full of surprises. If you are really ready, most of the surprises will be pleasant ones.

The Future

Weapons will get smarter and smarter as electronics get cheaper. An example is the JDAM guided bomb that got its first workout in the Afghanistan war. Guided by GPS satellite signals, the JDAM kit costs only $18,000. And most of that is the mechanical stuff that powers and controls the fins that direct the plain old high-explosive bomb to within 30 meters of the location the GPS has been programmed with. The GPS electronics costs less than a hundred dollars.

This is but one of the many opportunities the continuing development of microcomputers has introduced in weapons design and fabrication. To appreciate the scope of these developments, consider the costs of computing power over the last few decades. One standard measurement of computing power is

MIPS (million instructions per second that a computer can perform). In the mid-1970s, the most powerful mainframe computers available could generate 1 MIPS. At that time, a few thousand instructions per second powered the most advanced missiles, and less than a MIPS was used to perform signal processing for advanced radar and sonar systems (at a cost of over $1 million). By the early 1990s, the largest mainframe computers possessed hundreds of MIPS at a cost of $50,000 per MIPS. Minicomputers and workstations generated under 100 MIPS at a cost of $1,000 per MIPS. Microcomputers put out over 20 MIPS at a cost of under $500 per MIPS. By 2001, the cost per MIPS had fallen to under $10 and was still falling. As the cost of computing goes down, micro-processors show up in more weapons and equipment. Radios, bombs, vehicles, binoculars, and cooking stoves all have their own computers. The American military has subsidized research into even faster microcomputers for immediate use in new and existing sensors and weapons. Now a tremendous amount of calculation can be performed quickly and cheaply. By itself, this is an important capability. It is made even more revolutionary by the ability of troops and civilian contractors to develop new software (instructions) quickly and easily for the microcomputer-powered machines. In the vanguard is the American military, which has purchased hundreds of thousands of the latest civilian microcomputers and spread them around liberally. Just as American and Canadian troops had an advantage in World War II because most could drive vehicles, a similar edge is now held because so many U.S. troops can use and/or program microcomputers. This process has been going on since the late 1970s, when troops bought the first microcomputers with their own money and automated their military duties. The military in the West has taken advantage of this situation by short-circuiting its own procurement system. Civilian microcomputers have shielding and shockproofing added to them, producing computers at one-fourth the cost and five years earlier than equipment developed expressly for the military. In some cases, they were able to replace military equipment that was much less powerful and cost 10 times as much as the militarized civilian equipment.

All this additional computer power works even more effectively when you take advantage of that fact that computers can be reprogrammed. Computer programs are not easily created, but in a pinch they can be gotten together faster than anything that requires bending metal. Increasingly, computers and their programs are driving other electronic equipment. The Western lead in computer technology appears as a decisive advantage in the full spectrum of electronic equipment. A current example is ECM systems that store the characteristics of enemy radars and then can recognize and jam them quickly. You don't have to reprogram these devices; simply update the data files that identify enemy electronic equipment. Radars and sonars are benefiting the most from cheaper and more powerful computers. This is because the key problem with radars has not been sending the signal out, but correctly interpreting the fainter signal that bounces back from the target. Much of the Western stealth technology is still based on the weakness of the (often Russian) radar technology. It is possible to build radars that can spot stealth aircraft, but you must have powerful enough computers to interpret the signals correctly, and transmit the right signals in the first place. This computer power also makes over-the-horizon radars practical for ships and mobile antiaircraft units. The United States is pushing many new electronic items for the troops. While many seem off-the-wall, there is a solid track record of success over the last few decades. Indeed, it's gotten to the point where a major headache for supply officers is keeping the troops supplied with batteries.

19

The War in Space

The upper reaches of Earth's atmosphere will be a battlefield in any future war. The reasons are the same as in the past; everyone wants reconnaissance. Space has been used for surveillance since the 1960s. Space war will occur when there is a war involving the nations that use space. More nations are capable of this, even Third World nations. In addition, there will be more at stake. Space is used not just for reconnaissance; it has also become a crucial link for communications. A growing space-based capability is the potential for attacking missiles as they take off and arc toward their targets thousands of kilometers away. Called Star Wars or SDI (Strategic Defense Initiative), this system also threatens other nations' satellites and their ability to launch new ones. At the end of the Cold War, in the early 1990s, there were about 1,500 satellites in orbit, of which nearly 400 are still functioning. Some 40 percent are Russian, 40 percent American, and the remainder largely belong to other Western nations. Nearly 50 percent of these birds were military. A decade later there were over 600 operational satellites up there, and far fewer of them Russian.

Satellite launchings declined in 1999 and 2000, falling 25 percent in 1999 and 15 percent in 2000. The cause of the decline, which will last until 2003–4, was the large number of launches in the 1990s (70–100 a year). Launches will pick up when the new generation of low-orbit communications satellites starts arriving. Satellites have been getting smaller, to the point where two or more can be put up in one launcher. There is also a surplus of launch capacity because so many nations got into the business during the 1990s. The U.S. Space Control Center tracks nearly 9,000 man-made objects, softball-size and larger, orbiting Earth. About 7 percent of these objects are operational satellites, 15 percent are rocket bodies, and the remainder are fragments and inactive satellites. Satellites are expensive. Not just the satellites themselves, which cost anywhere from $100 million to $700 million, but also launching them. This can cost anywhere between $50 million and $500 million.

Military satellites are increasingly the minority in space. At the same time, many more of the civilian satellites perform the same functions (reconnaissance and communications) as military ones. The space battlefield extends 150–36,000 kilometers above the Earth's surface. The upper limit of conventional aircraft is about 36 kilometers. Although air forces would prefer human pilots taking care of things, it's cheaper to put unmanned satellites up. A war in space will be largely a robot war, a truly automated battlefield.

Military Uses of Space

While an increasing number of civilian satellites are put up, most of the money still goes into military birds. These cover a number of specifically military uses.

PHOTO RECONNAISSANCE

This is perhaps the most important military use of space. These satellites use cameras as well as infrared and passive electronic sensors. Electronic data is transmitted to ground stations for further processing and analysis. High-resolution camera photographs are sent back in canisters. Western technology increasingly uses digital photographs, of the same high resolution, that can be transmitted back. The U.S. technology can distinguish objects less than a foot in diameter. These satellites are of low altitude and short endurance because they must carry fuel for maneuvering and, in many cases, film. U.S. models have always been on the cutting edge of this technology. The KH series (for Key Hole) began in 1961 with primitive KH-1s and -4s. These took pictures and sent the film back in canisters. Comparable Soviet models had to bring the entire satellite back. The next generation, KH-5s and -6s, lifted off in 1963. These birds were able to transmit some of their pictures back. This was a major advance, as it allowed satellites to remain useful for more than a few weeks. The major limitation now became fuel, which allowed the KH "birds" to maneuver over the area to be searched.

The next generation, KH-7 and -8, went up in 1966 and were notable for their wider variety of sensors. Infrared sensors could detect heat, making it more difficult to conceal things. Multispectral scanning could detect different materials and gave satellite data another dimension, as well as making deception more difficult. More capable cameras were also carried, producing photographs that identified objects two or three inches small. This allowed detailed technical analysis of troop units in the bases and on maneuvers, airfields, missile sites, warships, ports and potential landing beaches, bridges, roads, railways, and terrain in general. The next jump in resolution, to an inch or less, allowed detailed analysis of supply dumps, rockets and artillery, aircraft, headquarters, nuclear weapons, and vehicles.

All of this was not without problems. High-resolution photos still had to come back in canisters. The KH-8s were still used into the late 1980s, partially because they were relatively lightweight (at under four tons). The next generation, the KH-9, was a major advance. First launched in 1971, these birds were large, nearly 15 tons. Their nickname was Big Bird. This larger size was needed to support larger sensors. The KH-9 was meant for wide-area surveillance. Although it could detect items only 12 inches small, it could take pictures of thousands of square miles in minutes. This resolution allowed precise identification of all classes of objects, although not detailed analysis. It also allowed technical intelligence on transportation networks and urban areas. These photos still had to come down in canisters. Data from the other sensors could be transmitted. With the KH-9, you could keep an eye on continents, and even do it at night. This required larger sensors and a lot of fuel. The KH-9 was a thirsty bird, as it had to use fuel frequently to change orbits. Initially, KH-9s lasted 52 days, but this was increased to nine months by the early 1980s.

Through the 1970s, the United States depended on the KH-8 for close-in photo work and the KH-9 for covering larger areas. In 1977, the fifth generation dawned with the launch of the KH-11. This was a major breakthrough, as canisters were no longer needed and resolution was such that objects a few inches in size could be identified from over a hundred miles up. The KH-11 telescopic cameras operated like a high-resolution TV camera. Images were captured continuously and transmitted to Earth stations. Computers were used to finish the process and produce photos identical to those taken by a conventional camera. You could even have motion pictures, as well as indications of heat and the nature of the various items. KH-11 often could tell what kind of metal an object on the ground was made of. This did not come cheap; these birds cost over $400 million each and lasted three or four years, depending on fuel usage. Moreover, you needed two of them up at the same time in order to guarantee coverage and save the birds from having to change orbit too frequently. The next generation, the KH-12, was supposed to have been launched in 1987. Because of the Space Shuttle problems, only a belated KH-11 was launched in October 1987. The KH-12 has several advantages over the KH-11. Along with improvements in ground data-processing equipment, the KH-12 could send back data in real time. You could watch events on a large, high-resolution screen as they were happening. This would also allow military headquarters and other users to get their satellite information directly, without going through a CIA or NRO (National Reconnaissance Office) processing center. Data from the more esoteric sensors would still have to be studied by the specialists elsewhere. The KH-12 was expected to make users even more enthusiastic about satellite reconnaissance. Such enthusiasm may be needed when shrinking defense budgets force decisions between birds in the sky and weapons in hand.

Normally, the number and types of satellites available for use are a military secret. But during the 1991 Gulf War, a lot more information got out for one reason or another. The U.S. satellites available in early 1991 comprised the following:

KH-11 series reconnaissance satellite. There were three KH-11 satellites in orbit. These were launched December 1984, October 1987, and November 1988. There were also four advanced KH-11s (also called KH-12s). These were launched August 1989, February 1990, June 1990, and November 1990. These advanced models had the standard KH-11 equipment but were also capable of photographing objects at night using an infrared scanner, plus a sensor package capable of detecting some materials used in camouflage. The December 1984 KH-11 was apparently no longer fully operational in early 1991 because of lack of fuel or multiple system breakdowns. One of the advanced KH-11s apparently failed in orbit, although no one would confirm it. This left five KH-11s available for observing the Gulf by early 1991. The KH-11 birds move about in orbit and can observe an area for about two hours while passing over. The detailed photos are transmitted via relay satellites to a ground station in Maryland and then retransmitted or further analyzed. These images could be shown within minutes to U.S. analysts and commanders in Saudi Arabia but often were not. The analysts in the United States usually hung on to the data for further analysis and then forwarded their report to the Gulf.

One Lacrosse radar satellite (launched December 1988) can see through clouds and other atmospheric obstructions. This satellite can detect items buried up to 10 feet underground to pinpoint missiles and other equipment hidden in trenches and bunkers. It is available only a few hours a day.

Two Mentor SIGINT (signal intelligence) satellites (launched January 1985 and November 1989) sat in fixed orbit and eavesdropped on Iraqi transmissions (communications, radars, etc). This supported photo recon by giving an indication something was down there because of the electronic emissions from a well-hidden enemy facility.

One Vortex SIGINT satellite (launched May 1989) is like the Mentor but more specialized.

The Defense Support Program satellites (exact number is classified, but an advanced model was launched November 1990 to increase Scud missile launch coverage) used a large infrared telescope to locate the hot plumes of Scud missile launches, providing warning to target areas. It was able to give only a few minutes' warning, but that was enough, and a good example of real-time satellite recon.

GPS (Global Positioning Satellite) System. This provides precise location information (to within 25 meters or less) via a handheld satellite signal receiver. Not all 24 satellites were in orbit when war began, but there were enough up there to give coverage over most of the Gulf except for a few hours in the late afternoon. While not a recon satellite system, the GPS proved crucial in supporting ground-based recon in the desert.

The Soviets were always at a major disadvantage in the recon satellite area. They were at least two generations behind the United States. However, they had one large advantage in that they have had more birds in the air and a large stockpile of ready-to-go launchers. The Soviets could get a new bird in orbit with a few days' notice. In America it takes at least a few weeks, and usually a few months, to do an unscheduled launch. The Soviets did at least one launch a week and kept stockpiles of satellites and launchers in readiness for emergencies. In wartime, with satellites being shot down, the Soviets hoped their birds would be the only ones left in orbit—at least until they ran out of fuel and film.

Because of the expense of U.S. birds—over $500 million for the KH-12 and $100 million for many of the smaller ones—fewer of them are used. American satellites last longer than Russian ones, so the failure of one of them is more of a problem. If there is trouble getting replacements into orbit, the situation becomes acute. This is what happened to the United States in 1987. The Shuttle *Challenger* disaster in 1986, plus the loss of an expendable launcher several months later, left the United States with only one aging KH-11, with dwindling fuel and limited mobility, to supply all its high-quality photo reconnaissance. This situation began when the United States decided to use the shuttle for all recon satellite launches. This policy was later reversed, with Titan 4 expendable boosters also being used.

The new KH-12 birds are nearly twice as heavy (18 tons) as the KH-11. The KH-12 is heavier largely because of its large fuel load (seven tons). This bird is designed to be refueled in orbit by a space shuttle tanker mission (usually "classified shuttle missions"). In addition to refueling, shuttles can also perform repairs by replacing the largely modular components. In this way, the KH-12 can be kept up indefinitely, or at least a lot longer than previous classes of satellites.

The KH-13 hasn't gotten off the drawing board yet, mainly because of the cost. The KH-13 is basically an unmanned space station built to provide antimissile defense support. This means detailed coverage must be continuous. If ballistic missile defense ever gets off the ground, the KH-13 probably will, also. Otherwise, a system of four KH-12s, serviced and upgraded by shuttle flights, may be up there for quite a while. There are still some older KH-11s up there that are still functional.

The KH-12 points out an important facet of satellites: they don't wear out, but dry up. Fuel is needed to position the birds over targets. Because of the low orbits, fuel is also needed to make frequent adjustments to an orbit that is constantly slipping closer to a fiery plunge through the atmosphere. With a larger fuel supply, satellites can move to new locations quickly. This is very useful for the bird's more discriminating sensors. Russian satellites took a different development course. Unable to match U.S. technology, more attention was paid to signal collection and radar observation. There were several reasons for this, all of them typical of Russian pragmatism. Aside from their inability to match American capabilities in photo reconnaissance, there was the fact that in the more open U.S. society, it was easier to send people over with cameras to take pictures from the ground or commercial aircraft. Russian photo recon birds were used primarily for emergency photo work. Their photo satellites rarely stayed up for more than a few weeks before returning with their photos. Before the Soviet Union collapsed in 1991, they were beginning to use birds approaching the KH-11 in capability, but they still have reliability problems. The "Soviet" satellites could stay up 6–8 months. Russia inherited the Soviet Union's satellite program and promptly cut it back because of the enormous expense. The Russians still have satellites up there, just not as many. In fact, Russia now sometimes goes months without a single spy satellite in orbit.

While Russia fades as a builder and user of spy satellites, other nations move in. China put up its first digital camera spy satellite in late 1999. This bird, the ZY-2, is roughly equivalent to the early KH-11s of the late 1970s. France, Japan, Israel, and India began putting up recon satellites, and several other nations are working on it.

COMMUNICATIONS

Satellites are excellent relay stations for ground communications. They are cheaper than equivalent facilities on the ground and are more flexible and relatively immune to interference. Increasingly, the military uses commercial communications satellites.

OCEAN RECONNAISSANCE

Radar and other sensors track surface ships. Strategic radar satellites cover large areas by radar. Smaller birds use electronic sensors. The Russians put up a number of radar satellites powered by a special, short-life nuclear reactor. These birds were heavy, weighing between 10–20 tons. These satellites broke apart once they wore out so that the radioactive components were vaporized on reentry. Soviet naval recon satellites gave the location of most Western task forces every four days. The Soviets planned to put up more capable birds so that they could bring this down to every three days. These birds required a lot of power, also from a small nuclear reactor. Lasting about three months, their constant replacement contributed to the 100 or so satellites a year that the Soviets launched. Soviet ocean-recon birds worked in pairs, one with radar and another listening for just electronic emissions. The Soviets used a more powerful radar than Western models, getting better coverage. But this came at a cost that helped bankrupt the Soviet Union. None of these big Russian birds are operational anymore. In the 1990s, the new Russian government was quite eager to sell this nuclear-reactor technology to the United States at a very attractive price.

In the summer of 2000, the U.S. Air Force secretly launched the fourth Lacrosse radar imaging satellite from Vandenberg Air Force Base. This was the fourth Lacrosse, the second of the new, advanced type. The first pair were launched in 1988 and 1991; the third was launched in 1997 but was soon brought down in a controlled crash into the ocean. The 2000 launch replaced the 1991 bird. The new Lacrosse satellites operate at an altitude of 425 miles and weigh 15 tons. The cost of one new Lacrosse and its Titan 4B booster is over $1 billion.

ELECTRONIC INTELLIGENCE

These birds fly in very low Earth orbit and pick up transmissions. Called "ferrets," they carry a variety of sensors. The Soviets launched about six a year, the United States half that number. Russia currently launches one very rarely and is apparently holding those birds they have for any future emergency.

Ferrets are small and often piggyback with a larger satellite when launched into space.

EARLY WARNING

These reconnaissance satellites are specially designed to detect missile launches. They also collect information on missile performance during tests. They use infrared sensors to spot the missiles' rockets on takeoff. Electronic sensors pick up test missiles' transmissions of data. The Soviet Union launched about four a year. American versions have virtually unlimited endurance, but one or two new ones containing improved sensors and other equipment are launched each year.

NAVIGATION

These satellites maintain stable, fixed orbits in order to give reliable position data to vehicles on Earth with a receiver. America has spent years installing a system of 24 GPS satellites. It costs over $600 million a year just to maintain them. The Soviet Union had a similar GLONASS system, which Russia is still trying to get operational. These systems are needed for highly accurate missiles, which correct their position using the satellite transmissions.

WEATHER SURVEILLANCE

These satellites' image and heat sensors plot weather movements. The United States has four in orbit and must launch one or two a year to keep them operational. Russia also has four in orbit and must launch two or three a year to maintain that number. These are for civilian use, but a few special military weather satellites are up there also.

SCIENTIFIC

These conduct a wide range of experiments for civilian and military research. Several are launched each year. Many are not announced. One with some military use is the Vela, which can detect the characteristic double flash of an atmospheric nuclear explosion.

ANTISATELLITE

These destroy other satellites. The Soviet Union was suspected of having several in orbit, but they never came clean, and Russia is unlikely to support these efforts further. They have had mixed success testing these. The Soviet versions were basically space mines that move close to their victim and explode. A more pragmatic and effective approach has been developed by the United States. Here, a high-altitude fighter carries a special missile and releases it. This has proved a very inexpensive way to hit low-altitude reconnaissance satellites, just the kind you would want to destroy in wartime.

FOBS (FRACTIONAL ORBITING BOMBARDMENT SATELLITE)

They carry reentry vehicles similar to the warheads of ballistic missiles. By launching their warheads in orbit, they gain the element of surprise that ICBMs find difficult to achieve. These are illegal, and probably unwanted because of the risk of accidental launch of warheads. They could be put up with existing technology.

BATTLE STATIONS

Very large manned or unmanned satellites carrying a wide variety of sensors, communications gear, power supplies, and weapons. Such systems are an essential component of Star Wars antimissile defense systems. None has been built yet, but there is lots of planning activity.

Getting into Orbit

Getting a workable satellite into orbit requires three things:

- Sufficient thrust to overcome the Earth's gravity and get the satellite high enough so gravity is very weak.
- Accurate control to place the satellite in a proper orbit.
- Effective communications with, and control of, the satellite so that it can perform its tasks.

In the late 1950s, the first satellites had little beyond minimum thrust and imperfect control when achieving precarious orbits. Through the 1960s, thrust increased enormously, allowing larger satellites to be sent up. Control became more precise, allowing for more efficient orbits. Expense is now a greater limitation than technology. The cost of putting a satellite up varies from $500–$10,000 a pound. The primary purpose of the U.S. Space Shuttle was to bring this cost down. This did not happen, primarily because the American space program became obsessed with high technology to the point where it was costing it 10 times more per pound than the Soviets to put a satellite into orbit. The cheaper Soviet launches were partially a result of more launches. Soviet technology was of a lower standard and their satellites did not last as long, so they had to launch more of them. The Soviets launched 8–10 times as many satellites each year as the United States but had only 10–15 percent more birds in orbit at any one time. Thus, they achieved economies of scale in mass-producing vehicles, which were often, basically, ICBM rockets modified for satellite launching. The biggest Soviet cost advantage was that they stayed with a basic design of low-potency fuels and simple motors. The Soviet launchers were less reliable, but this could be attributed to the lower reliability of Soviet technology in general. However, even taking into account the cost of lost satellites from less reliable launchers, the Soviet system still cost less than one-fifth as much as the U.S. approach. One justification of the more reliable U.S. high-tech rockets is the need for more safety in launching manned missions. This did not stop the Soviets from pursuing a more ambitious manned spaceflight program. Moreover, this ignored the fact that space missions can be executed more cheaply and safely using robots. It's easier to get money for manned spaceflight than for robotic missions. Post–Cold War budget cutbacks may force the United States and Russia to give the robots more opportunities.

Improvements in technology have made satellites more capable on a pound-for-pound basis. This is crucial, as the cost of putting them up there has not come down in the West. Costs of over $5,000 a pound for low-Earth orbits (LEO) and twice or more of that for high orbits (GTO, geosynchronous transit orbit) make lighter satellites very valuable. The higher (36,000-kilometer) orbits are for the stationary satellites used for communications. The lower orbits are not stationary and tend to degrade over time, until the satellite plows into the thicker atmosphere and burns up from the friction. Nations like China and Russia offer much lower launch costs ($50–100 million), but their lower reliability drives up insurance costs. But this, at worst, will double the cost of a cheap Chinese or Russian launch. This still makes it the best price available. What keeps the more expensive Western launch providers in business is the military satellites, and circumstances where, even with insurance, you can't afford the time (years, in some cases) to build another bird.

Limits of Satellite Endurance

If placed in a stable orbit, a satellite can stay up indefinitely. But a number of other factors limit a satellite's useful life besides how long it can maintain its orbit:

Stability of orbit. Satellites stay up longer in higher orbits. Coming in closer brings the satellite in contact with more of the Earth's atmosphere, which extends over a hundred kilometers out. That far out it is pretty thin, but not so sparse that a fast-moving satellite will not be influenced. Not all launches are perfect, and sometimes the satellite is positioned in a less than optimum orbit.

Endurance of maneuvering system. Although most satellites have some propulsion capability, it is intended for minor adjustments, not repairing a bad orbit. These small rockets are to turn the satellite around to catch more sunlight, or to position another instrument. In some satellites, such as those used for electronic reconnaissance, a substantial amount of fuel is carried so the orbit can be adjusted. When this maneuvering fuel is gone, the satellite loses a lot of its capability. Low-orbit satellites often move lower and burn up. Larger satellites take up over five tons of fuel with them.

Power supply. Power is needed to transmit data back to Earth. Other equipment can have varying power loads, ranging from low for some sensors to high for powerful radars. The power source is typically a combination of solar panels to batteries. Batteries are needed for those times when the satellite is in the Earth's shadow. Russia uses a special nuclear reactor, not the same type used in power plants, that generates a lot of energy in a few months and then runs down. If the satellite has low power requirements, solar panels can keep it going for hundreds of years.

Expendability. Pre–KH-11 U.S. recon satellites used film cameras and sent the film back to earth in canisters. When the film was gone, the satellite was no longer useful. KH-11 and later models took electronic pictures. All Soviet photo satellites had to return to Earth for film to be recovered.

Fatigue. Any complex electromechanical device will eventually have one or more parts wear out and fail. Although built with many redundant systems, satellites operate in a harsh environment. Constant use, extremes of heat and cold, plus the occasional damage from a piece of high-speed dust will wear them down. Extensive self-test equipment allows ground controllers to repair some damage, or work around it. One of the advantages of the space shuttle is its ability to help repair satellites, or recover them for overhaul on the ground.

Obsolescence. Technological improvements are relentless. A satellite built to last for 10 years might find itself so outclassed by new models that it might not be worth using anymore. Again, this is where the space shuttle comes into play, being capable of bringing down older satellites for rebuilding.

Vulnerability

Destroying satellites in wartime is a high-priority task. It would make enemy surveillance, communications, and navigation more difficult. Various methods exist to accomplish this destruction:

Destroy the ground stations. This is the simplest method, but it becomes more difficult as the stations multiply. The saucer-shaped send/receive antennae are becoming cheaper and more numerous. However, a few of these stations also contain extensive computers, retransmission, and satellite-control facilities. If this equipment is destroyed, the satellites they support become less useful.

Destroy satellite launch bases. Few of these exist. The United States and Russia have two major bases each, which account for the vast majority of launches. For example, the first launch of the Russian Energia rocket so damaged the launch site that it was nearly two years before repairs were made and another could be sent up. A few minor launch bases are available. The United States and Russia developed ways to launch small satellites using military ballistic missiles. These could even be launched from submarines.

Prevent additional launches. Star Wars–type weapons have the capability to destroy satellites as they are being launched. This was worrisome to the Soviets, who had to launch three or four satellites to each one sent up by the United States to achieve the same effect.

Jam, blind, or otherwise disable enemy satellites. Electronic jammers on the ground, in aircraft, or in other satellites can do this. Blinding visual sensors with high-powered lasers is possible. A low-flying satellite can receive temporary or long-term damage from lasers. The electromagnetic pulse from a nuclear explosion will also disable satellites that are not hardened against this. Reducing a satellite's effectiveness is the next-best thing to destroying it.

Destroying the satellite itself. This is no easy task, as it currently involves sending up a "killer" satellite to attack another. It is also dangerous: attacking satellites may be easily considered an act of war, given their strategic importance. The Soviets had their space-mine satellites, which had to come up close to their victims and then destroy both in a large explosion. The advantage of this approach is that you can use a nuclear warhead. This will not only guarantee the destruction of the nearby enemy satellite, but will disable any other satellites within a few hundred kilometers (depending on the size of the nuke). The primary system available in the West is ASAT, a satellite-homing missile that is launched from a high-flying fighter against low-orbit recon satellites. This system is cheap, fast, and difficult for the defender to detect. However, this leaves mid-range satellites safe for the moment. The only current way to get at the communications satellites in their 36,000-kilometer orbits is to send out a nuclear-bomb satellite to their vicinity. You don't have to get real close, just near enough for the powerful electromagnetic pulse to scramble the satellite's innards. Unfortunately, only a few positions exist for these satellites to orbit; thus, such an explosion might get one of your birds, also. In addition, no one has tried to send a killer satellite out this far, with or without a nuke. Moreover, a future enemy may see an advantage in leaving Western navigation satellites up, as many of their ships, aircraft, and missiles can use Western satellite signals. Also keep in mind that satellites are small objects in a large space. Only the high communications satellites stay in one place. Those in orbit usually have some capability to shift orbits. Tracking your own and others' satellites has become a big business.

American capabilities are extensive and include the ability to make detailed films of satellites in action, including detailed examination of what space shuttle or satellite crews do when outside their vehicles. U.S. capabilities are such that a baseball-size object can be detected nearly 40,000 kilometers out. The West has more mobile satellites and a greater capability of tracking them. In addition, there are the little-discussed efforts to employ electronic warfare in space. Satellites are controlled by ground stations via radio link. If these control messages can be jammed or mimicked, the satellite in question will be neutralized or destroyed. Who is ahead in this area will not be revealed until hostilities begin. To tip your hand earlier allows the enemy to develop countermeasures. The opening of major hostilities will reveal very strange events in the orbital arena.

Satellite Defense

Aside from small size and the ability to shift position somewhat, there are several other ways to increase a satellite's survivability:

Components can be shielded from the electromagnetic pulse of a nuclear weapon. Some hardening is also possible as a defense against laser attack.

Defensive missiles can be carried to home in on a killer satellite's tracking radar. Large and important satellites could be equipped with radar and missiles against killer satellites that use passive sensors for homing.

Satellites can be equipped with more fuel so that they can move about more. Antisatellite warfare will probably come to resemble a high-speed chess game played on a very large and spherical surface.

The foremost defensive advantage the Soviets had was a higher rate of launches, about a hundred a year. This gave them about 150 useful satellites in orbit. The higher launch rate gave the Soviets a better capability to replace war losses quickly, assuming their launch facilities were not damaged or that Star Wars did not become operational. They were also thought to be looking into using land-based ICBMs as emergency launch vehicles. The United States investigated the same technique, although with an emphasis on using submarine-launched ICBMs. Neither nation went very far with this idea, mainly because of the cost of developing satellites for the different shape of combat-missile warheads. The testing expense also would have been high. With the demise of the Soviet Union, no one now has that kind of fast satellite-replacement capability.

The least talked-about defensive technique is deception. Most satellites' purposes can be easily identified. Land-based U.S. cameras can count the rivets on low-flying satellites. Many satellites collect electronic intelligence on other birds. Satellites that broadcast data Earthward often disguise these transmissions by routing them through another satellite. Existing models often have additional capabilities added without changing the external appearance of the satellite. Typically, a photo recon bird is given electronic easedropping capabilities. Radar and photo-recon capabilities are difficult to hide, as they require large mirrors or radar receivers. All is not what it appears to be in the heavens.

Theory and Practice

Satellites are notoriously unreliable and unpredictable beasts. Despite all the money and skill poured into them, they have to be used carefully to prevent catastrophic failure. This situation is understandable when you realize what these birds have to go through. First of all, they carry extremely delicate instruments into one of the harshest environments known to man. The trip itself is a trauma, rising from the Earth on a pillar of flame, accelerating quickly to several times the speed of sound. When the satellite launcher has done its job, the bird is in a vacuum, exposed to temperature differences ranging from very cold to very hot, depending on which part of the satellite is facing the sun.

Once in orbit, the satellite systems must perform precision maneuvers with exacting instruments. Systems are built with double and triple redundancy. You cannot test the satellite in its operating environment but must simulate it as best you can on the ground. Elaborate procedures are worked out to reconfigure how a bird can maintain some form of functionality as components fail. The space shuttle is a partial solution to this, but it will take time. Existing satellites must be brought down for repairs. Newer satellites are designed for modular replacement while in orbit, as well as in-flight refueling. All of this increases the cost of the birds. The maintenance trips are not cheap, either. Each major satellite launch costs over $300 million, and a shuttle mission costs over $500 million. Cost was one area where the Soviets came out ahead. Their low technical capabilities forced them to stick with simple, and cheaper, boosters. The United States gambled that their high-tech approach would eventually be cheaper. It was wrong, and the United States ended up paying six times more to get a pound of anything into orbit. Currently, it costs Russia between $500 and $1,000 per pound and the United States between $4,000 and $8,000 per pound to get into low orbit. A further complication of satellite operations is that there are over 40,000 manmade objects in orbit. These are just the ones the size of a pea or larger. Moving at over 5,000 meters a second, even these tiny objects can wreck a critical satellite component. Right now, a large satellite has to be in orbit 10 years to get hit, with the chance of destruction being nearly 1 percent. But as more litter is left in orbit, the odds of a collision increase. Hardening to provide protection will raise cost and weight still more.

New satellites always perform better on paper than in orbit. The big problem with photo and infrared reconnaissance is atmospheric cover, which cloaks much of the Earth's surface at frequent and unpredictable intervals. The 1982 Falklands war, for example, was shielded from satellite viewing most of the time by fog and cloud cover. More exotic sensors can penetrate this cover to some degree, but the fact remains that a satellite overhead does not always guarantee a picture. Experiments have already been conducted to blind or deceive satellite sensors with lasers, or something as mundane as a gigantic smoke screen. The new KH-12 birds are intended to operate as a four-satellite system, providing continuous coverage over the entire planet. With spares and maintenance flights, that's $1 billion a year of satellites. In addition, you need radar satellites and lower-flying electronic birds, and higher communications satellites. Then there is the cost of ground processing and support equipment, as well as research and development. The total cost comes to some $30 billion a year. And you are still not guaranteed to get a picture of what you want when you need it. You pays your money and takes your chances.

The Future

Chinese, European, and Third World satellite launch capabilities will continue to grow. Even more capable Western satellites will be launched. China is also becoming a major player in space. Their first recon satellite was launched in 1975, returning film capsules after a few weeks. A shortage of launchers prevented sending up more than one bird a year. In the next year or so, the Chinese plan to put up a recon bird that can broadcast images back to Earth while staying in orbit for months or years. Other nations, such as Japan, will develop a lesser launch capacity. The problems with the Space Shuttle program are causing a major revision in U.S. satellite launch organization. In the late 1980s and early 1990s, demobilized Titan II ICBMs provided over a dozen launch vehicles. A larger model of the Titan series, the Titan IV, provides dozens of additional launchers for use well into the twenty-first century.

Major improvements are slowly coming from the major satellite launching nations. These improvements are in several areas:

Increased satellite maneuverability by carrying more fuel, or refuel capability.

More accurate navigation satellites enable air and ground units to locate themselves more accurately. This is the GPS system, which was completed in the mid-1990s and is being upgraded as new satellites are sent up. The current GPS system provides 10–30-meter accuracy, but upgrades are planned that will do even better than that.

Better satellite self-defense through the use of onboard protection and self-defense weapons. This is a likely post–Cold War victim, until a hostile nation starts launching antisatellite systems.

Better attack systems to disable enemy satellites. This is another post–Cold War victim, although the United States may press for this to stave off "orbital terrorism."

Improved resistance to jamming and more powerful transmitters are also high-priority items. This is a possible victim of budget cuts.

Better satellite repair and replacement capability. This is a major reason for the U.S. Space Shuttle. This capability is actually used, although many of the missions are classified.

More secure ground-control facilities, which are currently one of the more vulnerable portions of satellite systems. This is less likely in the post–Cold War world, but smaller, cheaper, and more capable ground stations have arrived, anyway. Progress on the civilian side of the satellite business has had a lot to do with this.

More relay satellites, making it easier to transmit data to and from birds no matter where they are in orbit.

Mini-satellites to replace birds knocked out in combat. Numerous small satellites also have an advantage in that the enemy needs one or two orbits to detect a new satellite. While a satellite is undetected, it can observe activities that would normally be hidden from orbital observation. These smaller satellites perform only one or two of the functions of the standard, much larger, systems. These mini-birds would weigh under a ton (or as little as a 100 pounds) and be launchable by ICBMs or missiles carried by high-flying bombers. Such satellites can also be put up in groups of two or more in current commercial launch vehicles. This concept is still being pursued after the Cold War because it provides some peaceful use for a lot of ICBMs tagged for demobilization. But the "minisats" are arriving, again, because they make sense for many commercial users.

Satellite Launch Vehicles

Designation is the name of the vehicle. These are the most common vehicles. Many were originally designed as ICBMs. The U.S. Space Shuttle is supposed to replace all other U.S. and Western vehicles. This seems unlikely in light of its reliability and cost problems.

Designation	Satellite lift		Launch weight (tons)	Stages	User	Cost (mil)
	LEO (tons)	GTO				
Delta III	4.2	3	330	3	U.S.	$55
Titan IV	23.5	6.3	1,050	3	U.S.	$300
Long March CZ2E	5	3.7	502	2	China	$50
Space Shuttle	24	2	2,250	2	U.S.	$550
Soyuz	7.5	1.1	310	3	Russia	$30
Soyuz-U	7.7		341	4	Russia	$20

Satellite lift, low, high is the amount of weight in tons each vehicle can put into LEO (low earth orbit, 150–1,000 kilometers) or GTO (geosynchronous transfer orbit, 36,000 kilometers). The latter is the orbit in which the satellite stays over one spot on Earth and can cover about half the planet.

Launch weight (tons) is the total weight of the vehicle with payload. Most of the weight consists of fuel.

Stages is the number of sections the vehicle is divided into. Most of the fuel is burned during the first few kilometers of climbing. Rather than drag huge, empty fuel tanks into orbit, vehicles are separated into different sections, or "stages." Each consists of a motor and fuel tanks. The final stage, containing the payload, comprises less than 10 percent of the total vehicle weight.

User is the nation that manufactures and uses the spacecraft. Many nations are building launchers, including India, Israel, Japan, and a European association.

Cost is the approximate cost of sending this launcher up, in millions of dollars.

Satellites

Type is the function of the satellite. See this chapter for details.

Typical weight (tons) is the weight of most satellites of each type. Most could be larger if there were a cheap enough way to get them into orbit. Inflation will have its way with satellite weights, as it does with everything else.

Typical orbit (kilometers) is the height at which each type normally operates. Most orbits are not circular but elliptical. The work is usually done at the lower phase of the orbit.

Type	Typical weight (tons)	Typical orbit (km)	Typical endurance (days)
Navigation	0.3	1,000	2,400
Communications	1	36,000	Unlimited
Ferret	0.3	200	100
Surveillance	12	12	200
Weather	0.7	800	100,000
Early warning	1	36,000	1,000

NOTE: A Ferret is a low-altitude recon satellite.

Typical endurance (days) is the typical useful life of the satellite. Endurance is largely a function of supplies and other expendable items. Often the spent satellite is sent toward Earth, where it burns up while reentering the atmosphere. This is to prevent useless objects from clogging up valuable orbital space.

20

Chemical, Biological, and Nuclear Weapons

These are the weapons no one wants to use. In fact, the major military powers have outlawed chemical and biological weapons. Yet most major nations can create them on short notice, and many minor nations (Iraq, North Korea, Iran, and so on) build chemical and biological weapons despite the international bans. These weapons are unpredictable and cause disorder among the user's troops as well. Warfare is unpredictable enough; none of the practitioners want any more confusion. In 1997, most nations possessing chemical weapons signed the Chemical Weapons Convention. This agreement calls for 20 percent of each nation's chemical weapons to be destroyed by 2002, and for all the weapons to be destroyed by the end of the decade. Money and the difficulty of destroying these weapons is slowing down the process, but no one is backing away from the commitment.

The Specter of Nuclear Escalation

The chief reason for avoiding the use of CBN (chemical, biological, and nuclear weapons, sometimes called NBC) is the possibility of escalation to a worldwide nuclear holocaust. Escalation is easily accomplished with CBN weapons because they are all wide-area weapons. The effect of their use is not only unpredictable, but also takes a larger toll among local civilians than the troops. Soldiers are trained to deal with these horrors; civilians are not. Large civilian losses put nations in a position where they want to make retribution.

This is especially true in places like Asia, where an increasing quantity of the world's CBN weapons are available. While the threat of a NATO/Warsaw Pact chemical and nuclear war in Europe is gone, the weapons still exist. A global nuclear holocaust is less of a threat, but the potential still exists.

The current concept behind using CBN is to do so only when you are on the ropes militarily and have no other option. If it comes down to a choice between CBN and defeat, you choose CBN. This is where it starts to get complicated. Many Third World nations have, or soon will have, one or more CBN weapons, and many of these nations have shown little hesitation to use them. Western nations have shown themselves reluctant to reply in kind, preferring to threaten severe retribution with conventional weapons. However, if Western forces found themselves in danger of defeat or severe damage because of another nation's use of chemical or nuclear warfare, the option of using chemical or nuclear weapons first, or in retaliation, is a real possibility. The basic problem is that no one wants to lose a war, yet no one wants to get rid of their chemical weapons. These weapons are increasingly seen as "the poor man's nuclear weapons." Chemical weapons are relatively easy to make and use. And smaller nations have been doing just that for the past 40 years.

Chemical and nuclear weapons have been used before. The extensive past experience with chemical weapons offers mixed signals on what might happen in the future. Modern chemical weapons were first used in 1915. Development work on these weapons quickly made them more lethal. By 1917, 15 percent of British casualties were caused by chemical weapons. Moreover, chemical weapons tended to be less fatal than conventional arms like artillery and machine guns. While 30 percent of conventional weapon casualties were fatal, only half as many chemical casualties died.

For fear of retaliation in kind, chemical weapons were not used during World War II. There were a few isolated cases, but always against an opponent who could not respond with chemicals. The same pattern has persisted to the present. Even during the 1991 Gulf War, Iraq refrained from using its chemical weapons against coalition forces that had them and their implied threat to use them in retaliation.

After World War I, the effectiveness of chemical weapons was increased. The Germans developed nerve gas during the 1930s. Here was a weapon of mass destruction, at least against dense, unprotected populations. Nerve gases killed within minutes and could enter the body through the skin or inhalation. Only minute quantities of nerve gas were needed to be effective, much less than with previous poison gases. Although only the Germans had large quantities of nerve gas during World War II, they never used them because they feared the allies had these easily manufactured nerve agents, also. German nerve gas was developed from research done in the United States and Russia on insect killers. This was one of the earliest "balance of terror" situations. Nerve gas would cause such massive casualties in urban areas that the

Germans refrained from using it for fear that the allies would do the same, especially after the allied bombing of German cities got in gear. They assumed that the allies were following the same logic about nonuse. This was a situation remarkably similar to current attitudes toward nuclear weapons. Moreover, the World War II situation involved one of the more bloody-minded dictators of recent memory, Adolf Hitler.

Here is a historical precedent for restraint with a weapon similar to nuclear weapons. Does this historical lesson still apply? Available evidence is mixed. After all, Hitler himself was gassed during World War I, while no current world leaders have experienced nuclear war. The Soviets equipped their troops with chemical weapons on a lavish scale. They published procedures for the extensive and immediate use of these weapons. They trained their troops, and their allies, accordingly. However, Soviet chemical doctrine underwent a gradual softening during the 1980s. They eventually adopted a doctrine in which they would use chemical weapons, if they used them at all, largely against rear-area targets only. They had recognized that using chemical weapons in the midst of the fast-moving combat units would be counterproductive. But their backing away from chemical weapons was also recognition that Western armies were increasingly capable of retaliating in kind. The Soviets recognized that chemical weapons, if they do nothing else, slow things down. As they expected Soviet troops to be doing most of the moving, chemical weapons would have been a net disadvantage. After 30 years of threatening and posturing with chemical weapons, both Soviet and Western armies in the 1980s began pulling back from any chance of using these horrors in combat. Meanwhile, Third World nations like Iraq were demonstrating that desperate nations could still resort to chemical weapons.

Despite all the nonuse of chemical weapons, their mere existence has had a serious effect on military operations. Troops are still equipped with protective gear and often lug this equipment with them into combat. Beyond the physical burden of taking the chemical-protection stuff into combat, the troops have yet another battlefield terror to worry about. These worries are not trivial, as all battles have mental-stress casualties. These stress losses are frequently a major portion of combat losses.

The Nuclear Battlefield

Nuclear weapons are easy to use on the battlefield. Put simply, they are tremendous multipliers of the firepower in existing weapons. A single 100-pound nuclear artillery shell more than equals the destructive effect of at least 8,000 conventional shells. This saves 350 tons of conventional shells, plus the wear and tear on the guns, time, transportation, etc. Beyond equaling the blast effects of conventional shells, nuclear explosives also produce radiation.

Armies try to manufacture nuclear weapons that release a minimum amount of radiation. These "clean" weapons are not developed for humanitarian reasons, but because the radiation lingers and attacks friend and foe indiscriminately. For this reason, the major producers of nuclear artillery shells, America and Russia, have removed them from use.

It doesn't take too many small nuclear weapons to make a difference on the battlefield. The mathematics of this mutual slaughter are straightforward. It only takes two or three nuclear weapons per enemy battalion to assure destruction. A combat division averages about a dozen combat battalions. Smaller nations would likely have only a few nuclear weapons and would be disposed to use them to greater effect against enemy cities. Each nuclear weapon used would kill several thousand civilians even if it missed an enemy city and simply landed on a nearby densely populated area. What eventually made tactical nukes unpopular with the generals was the realization that their use almost guaranteed that, were enough available, they would quickly spread beyond the fighting front.

For example, most nuclear weapons are delivered by aircraft or missile. Therefore, a primary target of each side is the airfields of nuclear bomb–carrying aircraft and wherever you think the missile launchers might be. As all these nuclear bombs and missiles rain down, it won't take too much paranoia to make one believe that the other side is going a little too far, and maybe we should up the ante a little bit. Before long, the number of targets being hit grows to the point where the local nuclear war is causing destruction about equal to a general one. Partially in response to the ease of escalation, nuclear-bomb designers came up with some new twists to the traditional mushroom-shaped cloud. These "designer nukes" have less blast and long-term radioactivity and more emphasis on short-term radioactive effects. The best example is the neutron bomb, which has been around on paper for 30 years. The effect of these weapons is mainly short-term radioactivity, with much less blast effect. Other designer nukes could focus their short-term radioactivity to hit an even smaller area. These weapons only make sense if everyone uses them. Newly minted nuclear powers don't have the technology to immediately (or even eventually) equip their nuclear arsenal with designer nukes. The only positive aspect of this is that, if the industrialized nuclear powers find they have to meet a first use of nukes with their own nuclear weapons, they can at least do it with relatively "clean" nukes. Scant satisfaction, that.

The Chemical Battlefield

Like nuclear weapons, chemical warheads multiply the firepower of conventional artillery and air power. Moreover, chemical weapons are generally used only against troops and, in any event, are less lethal than nuclear weapons.

Chemical weapons can be designed to have immediate effects, and then dissipate. Or, by changing the formula slightly, the effects can linger for hours, days, weeks, or even decades. Troops can more easily protect themselves from chemicals than from nukes. If properly equipped, well-trained, and given warning, these preparations can reduce the effect of a large-scale chemical attack to less than 2 percent losses per day. On the other extreme, casualties can range between 70–90 percent, with a quarter of these being fatal. This is also a war of materiel. Protective equipment must be replaced frequently as it becomes contaminated. Gas masks require new filters, protective garments must be replaced, and antidotes and protective ointments must be replenished. The troops have every incentive to use this equipment, and there is a lot to use as different items are needed for protection against different chemicals.

Prolonged injury from chemical weapons is a very unpleasant way to die. Like nuclear weapons, chemicals are best used against targets far from your own troops. Enemy airfields are a favorite target. Other choice targets are supply dumps and rear-area combat support facilities. When front-line units are hit with chemicals, it is often over a several-day period. This wears down the troops as they continually struggle to avoid injury from the toxic chemicals. Chemical weapons can be used defensively. This was done in 1917–18, when large areas were sprayed with chemicals to prevent enemy troops from moving through rapidly. This is still considered a viable tactic for chemical weapons today. Indeed, the primary effect of chemical weapons seems to be slowing down operations on the battlefield. The protective clothing is cumbersome. In warm weather, this clothing also becomes unbearably hot if the wearer moves about too quickly or too much. Specially equipped vehicles also offer some protection. But under the stress of combat use, these chemical-proof systems can be expected to leak a bit. Troop morale would be devastated if chemical casualties began to occur in supposedly secure vehicles. Because the troops know there is a defense against chemical weapons, they will attempt to protect themselves. No matter how well trained and disciplined, troops will slow down in a chemical environment. During the initial use of chemical weapons, operations will be slow because of unfamiliarity. This slowdown in operations is one of the least talked about, yet most arresting, effects of chemical weapons use.

Nerve gas has long been touted as the most common chemical weapon to be used. It hasn't been used that much because, in practice, it is tricky to manufacture in truly effective forms, difficult to store and deliver, and often not as effective as predicted. Still, nerve gas is something to be very wary of. Despite masks and special suits, there is still a chance of getting a touch of this nasty stuff. When this happens, there is a minute or so to apply the antidote. This consists of sticking a syringe into a large muscle; the thigh is preferred. If you inject this stuff when you are not ill from nerve agent, you get sick from the antidote. Perhaps in recognition of all these problems, armies would prefer to stay out of contaminated areas as much as possible.

When attacking, only nonpersistent chemicals are used on defending troops. Chemical monitoring teams travel with all units to give maximum warning about entering an unanticipated contaminated area. These "dirty" areas must be crossed as quickly as possible. If a unit assembly area is hit with chemical weapons, the area is evacuated as quickly as possible. It comes down to this: when chemicals are in the area, you either move on or stay in place and slow down a lot. You also start losing people and enthusiasm real quick.

Actual holdings of chemical weapons are still well-kept secrets. Western forces, mainly the United States, held some 40,000 tons of the stuff through the end of the Cold War. At least 16 nations currently possess chemical weapons, including several in the Middle East. Not all the chemical agents are loaded into artillery shells or bombs, because once loaded, the shells and bombs will become subject to leakage and degradation. The stock immediately available to troops was probably no more than a few thousand shells, plus a smaller number of bombs and still fewer warheads for missiles. It would take a month or more to load the remaining stocks into weapons. Until the early 1990s, about half of all U.S. chemicals were stored in Europe. These have largely been withdrawn and destroyed. The Russians have withdrawn all the Soviet chemical weapons from Eastern Europe and are working on destroying them, as well as much of what was stored in the former Soviet territories.

Western armed forces were slow to realize the seriousness of the Soviet chemical warfare capability. It was only during the 1980s that Western forces became serious about preparing their troops for the strong likelihood of chemical warfare. Western intelligence forces have labored mightily to avoid surprise attacks. But there's no escaping the shock that troops will get when they encounter chemical weapons on the battlefield for the first time. Prepared troops hit with an artillery, chemical-shell barrage of chemical and nonchemical shells would suffer 10–30 percent casualties, one-quarter of them fatal. Anyone with overhead cover would suffer half the casualty rate. If the troops are fatigued and off guard, the rate would rise to between 40–50 percent. If the troops are untrained, 80 percent could be killed or permanently out of action, while 20 percent would be temporarily incapacitated. This rate would also apply to civilians, of which there might be over 100 per square kilometer in European areas. Surprise can also be achieved away from the fighting line. Aircraft and helicopters can spray lines of gas many kilometers long. If the wind is blowing the right way, a wall of gas rolls over the unsuspecting troops. Although the gas alarms will go off, a 10 kilometers-per-hour wind can catch more than half the troops before they can put on their masks and protective clothing. Time-delay chemical bombs and mines can be dropped near enemy positions. Set to go off at night, they can have devastating effects.

Despite all the exotic methods developed for using chemical weapons in the last 60 years, the actual methods used in combat have been more prosaic. The largest use of chemical weapons recently was during the 1980–88 Iran-

Iraq war. Iraq used chemical weapons, and the favorite method of delivery was via artillery shell or canisters dropped from aircraft or helicopters. Not very exotic, but effective enough. The threat that Iraq might use chemicals again in the 1991 Gulf War was very real. Again, the threat of retaliation in kind worked its magic. But the threat of retaliation cannot guarantee a chemical-free battlefield every time.

Casualties: Physical and Mental

The chief characteristic of the chemical/nuclear battlefield is the increased number of wounded casualties. During the long wars of this century, there have been 20 or more non-battle casualties for each man killed or wounded in combat. Chemical and nuclear weapons will increase the number of both combat and noncombat casualties. Calculating the effect of nuclear and/or chemical weapons in a future war is part of the peacetime planners' art. World War I losses were 10–15 percent when troops advanced into a gassed enemy position. Under these conditions, the defender's losses exceeded 60 percent, thus justifying the attacker's losses to chemical weapons.

Soviet planners, who expected widespread use of chemical weapons, envisioned daily loss rates of 20 percent under chemical-warfare conditions. After five days of such operations, they assumed that a unit, now reduced to one-third of its original strength, would have to be withdrawn and replaced.

The most terrifying effect of nuclear weapons is radiation. While the blast effects of nuclear weapons are formidable, they are at least somewhat familiar to anyone who has experienced shellfire. Radiation has long-term effects. It's common knowledge that radiation, if not taken in large enough doses to be immediately fatal, will do you in within hours, days, weeks, or months. Beyond that, the long-term effects can be sterility, birth defects, cancer, and general unpleasantness. Radioactivity is odorless, tasteless, and colorless.

The effects of chemical weapons are less insidious. Nerve gas has its immediate effects and then either kills you or wears off, although some long-term damage is suspected. While there is quite a lot known about nuclear weapons' effects on humans because of their actual use during World War II, there is little comparable data on the effects of nerve gas. Other chemical agents take effect immediately and also have long-term effects. Blister gases leave wounds and scars; blindness and damaged lungs are common. Blood agents damage internal organs such as the kidneys and the liver. The constant danger of injury from chemicals has greatly increased the potential for stress casualties, otherwise known as combat fatigue. Consider the symptoms of radiation and some chemical sickness: listlessness, upset stomach, headaches, fatigue. These same symptoms can also result from stress. What could be more stressful than the knowledge that you might accidentally, and unknowingly, pass through a contaminated zone? Regular doses of tranquilizers have been seriously considered as a means of calming everyone's nerves.

The fighting on a chemical and/or nuclear battlefield may quickly evolve into an exhausted stalemate or a series of duels between the scattered survivors. Historical experience reveals that survivors of high-attrition combat either give up completely or fight only to survive. It will be difficult to carry on a war if the soldiers are either immobilized by shock or ready to fight only in self-defense.

The Radiation Problem

Radiation is not as great a problem as most people think. To understand this, you must consider the role radiation plays in our lives under normal conditions. Radiation is a natural occurrence. We are all exposed, on the average, to 160 mrem per year. An mrem (milliroentgen equivalent to man) is a standard measure for radiation absorbed by humans. This exposure causes the following annual health problems per 100 million population: 4,100 fatal cancers; 2,500 nonfatal cancers; 4,600 genetic defects (not all of which are obvious). For every additional mrem per person per year, the above rates will increase .67 percent (75 cancers and genetic defects per 100 million population). About a fifth of the average natural radiation (30 mrem) is received from the sun, which is an ongoing thermonuclear explosion. About 25 mrem come from proximity to building materials, stone being the most radioactive. Living inside a stone building will add 50 mrem a year. The things we eat and drink add another 40 mrem. The remaining 65 mrem come from such manmade sources as X-rays and medical treatments (50 mrem), air travel (1 mrem per 1,500 miles), watching TV (1 mrem if you watch 6.67 hours a day; the average American watches some 2,600 hours a year), fallout from previous atmospheric nuclear-weapons tests (4 mrem), and the remainder from various consumer products. Spending all your time next to a nuclear power plant adds 5 mrem, less than 1 mrem if you live 2 kilometers away and zero mrem if you are 8 or more kilometers distant. If a nuclear power plant does blow, like Chernobyl, you get doses similar to those received from nuclear weapons.

During the 1980s, another major cause of radiation was discovered: radon. This is a gas produced from the natural breakdown of uranium in the earth. The gas seeps into houses and concentrates to the point where it gives the inhabitants an average of 200 mrem per year. The problem with radon is that its concentration varies from one area to another. In a few places, inhabitants of well-insulated houses sitting atop large uranium deposits can receive more than the safety limit of 5,000 mrem per year. The key factor here is modern, well-insulated housing, which allows the radon to accumulate. People living in more primitive shelter have little to fear from radon gas.

Nuclear weapons are noted for longer-lasting radioactivity as well as instant blast and heat damage. The unit of radiation for nuclear weapons is the rad, which is equal, for our purposes, to 1,000 mrem. Radiation kills over time. If enough radiation is received in a short period, it can kill immediately or within days, weeks, or months, depending on the dose. Six hundred or more rads can kill within hours and disable immediately; 500–600 rads are always fatal, often within days. About 50 percent will die with 200–500 rads. At levels of 100–200 rads, 5 percent will die, although long-term effects (cancer) become a major factor. A 50-rad dose will induce nearly 2 percent early deaths from cancer and genetic defects.

These high levels of radiation exist very briefly, only seconds in some cases. In the area closest to a ground-level explosion, which is preferred for destroying missile silos, there will be hot spots of intense, longer-lasting radiation. One year after the explosion of a one-megaton bomb on the surface, the 100-rad zone will be a circular area of 46 square kilometers (7.6 kilometers in diameter). Nearly 4 percent of the population in that area will die prematurely. Many others will suffer radiation sickness. This area should be a forbidden zone, even though it will be teeming with vegetation and small animals. The point of highest radiation in this zone will be the explosion crater, 360 meters wide and 120 meters deep. The next zone has an average of 50 rads and covers 67 square kilometers (9 kilometers in diameter). There will not be as much radiation sickness, but 2 percent of inhabitants will die early. The 10-rad zone covers 300 square kilometers (20 kilometers in diameter.) This could be lived in, although there would be three or four early deaths per 1,000 population. Within a few years, even the crater will be under the 10-rad level. You can also forget about giant spiders and two-headed mutants. Insects are far more resistant to radiation than mammals. Mutations are generally either fatal or unnoticeable. Natural radiation has been responsible for more mutation than any nuclear war could ever produce.

Navy and Air Force

Naval forces have fewer problems with chemical weapons. Seawater quickly absorbs chemicals, and there is usually more wind at sea to blow the stuff away, and ships can more easily wash themselves down. Also, when you fight ships, you want to destroy them, not just their crews. Air forces have a more complex problem. At higher altitudes, pilots have little to fear from chemicals. However, they are at risk when they fly close to the ground. Low-level flight is very common, either on strike missions or simply to evade detection. Ultimately, all aircraft have to land, and their bases may have been gassed. Ground crews have a more difficult time of it. Their work is strenuous and must often be done quickly to get aircraft refueled and rearmed for another mission. Working inside masks and protective clothing makes you tire more easily. Fatigued ground crews are also more likely to make errors, which can be fatal for the pilots later on. The ground crews will wear out more quickly, and in some cases aircraft won't get into the air because of it. Another problem that will plague the air force pilots and ground crews is the marginal effects of nerve gas. In diluted concentrations, nerve gas still has an effect, typically blurred vision or disorientation. These symptoms can be quite fatal for a pilot, and potentially dangerous for ground crews handling fuel and munitions. Of the three services, air forces will quite likely have the worst time of it with chemical warfare.

The effects of nuclear weapons on naval targets and airfields are much the same as on army targets. In addition, it has been widely believed that nuclear weapons may be used more freely at sea. As the saying goes, "Nukes don't leave holes in the water." Neither do dead fish prompt escalation in the same way that dead civilians do. Despite this, there is a growing reluctance to use nuclear weapons at sea. New antisubmarine weapons don't have nuclear warheads. It has been recognized that even nuclear weapons used at sea can trigger a general holocaust. Several thousand tactical nuclear weapons are still at sea, down from over 6,000 at the end of the Cold War. These were, and are, largely with the U.S. and Russian fleets.

Biological Warfare

Biological warfare is nothing new. For thousands of years, spreading disease throughout the enemy's army was considered a practical tactic. Even in the last century, disease killed more soldiers than battle in wartime. Disease has always been so endemic in Russian forces that as recently as World War I, it was said to be more dangerous to shake a Russian soldier's hand than to be shot at by him.

For all the work that has been done on biological weapons in this century, few have tried to use them. Oddly enough, it is the Japanese who are responsible for the only two biological warfare campaigns in the twentieth century. After World War II, the United States discovered the extensive biological and chemical work done by the Japanese in China during World War II. The most gruesome operations involved the development and use of biological weapons against the Chinese. These devices were created in Manchuria by a special unit given the innocuous name "Unit 731." In addition to developing a (bubonic) plague bomb, Unit 731 conducted sundry forms of "medical research" on Chinese and Western prisoners. The plague bomb never really worked. The basic idea was to spread the plague (the medieval "Black Death") in Chinese-held territory. The first field experiments were conducted in 1940. No discernible effect was noted. The weapon itself was an aircraft bomb containing plague-infected fleas instead of explosives. In 1942, the fleas were released

near the front to halt the advance of Chinese troops. Again, there was particular
impact on the Chinese. This may have been due to the fact that the plague was
endemic in China and that there were plenty of other diseases going around at
the same time. Moreover, the fleas could not survive long without a host (usually rodents). Even attempts to spread the plague by releasing flea-infested rats
had no effect. The 3,000 members of Unit 731 and its four subunits did manage
to kill several thousand people with their medical experiments. These included
"experimental surgery" and equally grim procedures performed in the name of
"medical research." Perhaps the only practical effect of Unit 731 was letting
prisoners, and captives held for interrogation, know that if they didn't cooperate they would be sent to Unit 731 for "processing." The word got around
China during the war that the unit existed and that being sent there was worse
than any of the more mundane atrocities the Japanese committed on their victims. Fifty years later, a Japanese religious cult, Aum Shinrikyo, tried again,
with even less success then Unit 731.

It appears that the balance of terror is at work here, also. To use biological
warfare, you first invent a new disease, usually a variant of an existing one that
will spread rapidly and be fatal or very debilitating. Then you immunize your own
troops. However, because these diseases cannot easily be controlled, you may
have to immunize your entire population. Therefore, this approach is viewed with
some circumspection. Another approach is to develop a fatal disease that will not
spread from each victim: you can only catch it from the powder or spray dispersed
from the bomb or artillery shell. However, none of these appears to be much more
flexible or fatal than the various nerve gases around. What makes biological warfare so frightful is that no one has actually tried it on a large scale. And there is a
primordial memory in all soldiers of the depredations of disease among their
ancient (and not-so-ancient) comrades. Biological weapons are currently noted
mostly for their terror effect.

If biological weapons are such a terror, why haven't terrorists used them?
There are two reasons. First, most biological weapons are difficult to use. With
many of them, there is always a chance that the weapon will backfire and kill your
own people. While many terrorists are suicidal, few of their leaders are. Second,
biological weapons are difficult to make. The ones that are easier to use are even
more difficult to manufacture, and apparently only the Russians have those. Since
we have a pretty good idea of what the Russians have (after the Soviet Union fell,
people talked), and the Russians need economic assistance from the West, the
"designer bugs" are unlikely to get loose. The designer bugs are things like
anthrax strains that are more lethal and easier to set loose. This is the basic thrust
of designer bugs: existing diseases genetically (or otherwise) altered to make
them deadlier, sturdier, and more easily spread around.

But there is one biological agent that does fit the bill without modification. It's smallpox, the most formidable killer of the twentieth century. This disease killed some 400 million people in the last 100 years but was wiped out in

1980. Officially, only two samples remained, one held by the United States, the other by Russia.

But since the Soviet Union fell in 1991, information about their biological weapons program has been leaking out. One report tells of several million doses of smallpox being manufactured and still stored in Russia. Or so the rumor goes. Smallpox is a very contagious disease that kills some 30 percent of its victims. Most Americans were vaccinated against smallpox, at least until smallpox disappeared in the United States and vaccination stopped in 1972. Most of those vaccinated earlier have lost their immunity, meaning some 90 percent of the U.S. population is now vulnerable. One dose of smallpox could infect several hundred people before all those infected were quarantined and treated. The United States has a stockpile of 40 million doses of smallpox vaccine, but most doctors and nurses no longer know how to recognize or treat the disease. Moreover, an outbreak of the disease would take its toll on medical personnel before the disease was identified and precautions taken.

One interesting piece of information is missing about the Russian situation. How many doses of vaccine do the Russians have? And could they distribute it, given the current sad state of their medical system? It's unlikely that the Russians would use smallpox on anyone, even if they did have vaccine stockpiled. Although the Russians officially deny all of their forbidden (by treaty) biological weapons research, if the stuff exists, so do terrorists with millions of dollars for bribes. The real worry is terrorists getting their hands on a few dozen doses of smallpox virus.

The Russians have been pretty good about guarding their Cold War arsenal of nuclear, chemical, and biological weapons. This is even more true since the Russians have been battling rebellious Muslim Chechens. Because of that, Russia is now a potential target of Islamic terrorists. However, the economic situation in Russia is dire, and some Muslim terrorist organizations have access to a lot of money. A few million-dollar bribes in poverty-stricken Russia could set the pox lose. While America has supplied millions of dollars, and hundreds of technical experts, to help Russia destroy unneeded nuclear, chemical, and biological weapons, many remain. It only takes a few Russian technicians or security personnel to weaken and take the money. While smuggling bulky nuclear or chemical weapons is difficult, a few dozen doses of smallpox can be taken out in someone's pockets.

There have been many attempts to use biological weapons. Until quite recently, they have been unsuccessful. Between 1900 and the summer of 2001, there were 262 attempts to use bioweapons worldwide. With the exception of a few Japanese biowarfare attacks on the Chinese in World War II, 60 percent of these biological attacks were by terrorists, and 40 percent were purely criminal (extortion, attempted murder, etc.). However, 66 percent of these 262 attacks were hoaxes, 21 were threats that never came off, and only 13 percent real. Of these actual attacks, 24 percent were in the United States and resulted in no fatalities. But the 76 percent that occurred outside the United States did kill 77 people. The Japanese Aum Shinrikyo cult made 20 attacks between April 1990 and July 1995. Half the attacks were with biological weapons (botulinum toxin and anthrax), but these only killed eight people. Most of the rest of the attacks used VX and sarin nerve gas. Most of these attacks caused only a handful of injuries. But one sarin attack, with gas released in five subway cars, killed 12 people and sent over 5,000 to the hospital (but only a fifth of these had noticeable nerve-gas injuries).

The Aum Shinrikyo members included many skilled engineers and scientists, graduates of Japan's best universities. Aum Shinrikyo also had plenty of money (over $300 million). Recognizing the shortcomings of their biological and chemical weapons, Aum Shinrikyo was getting into molecular engineering when the organization was broken up by the police in 1996. Had Aum Shinrikyo been able to keep at it for a few more years, they might have been able to develop far more deadly "designer bugs" that, so far, have been produced only in American and Russian military labs.

Many other terrorist organizations have tried to develop and use biological weapons. During World War I, a pro-German doctor in Washington created a supply of anthrax and glanders. He then used pro-German dock workers to use these two agents to infect animals being shipped to Europe for the war against Germany. This effort was not terribly successful, but it did have an effect and shows how one man, with the proper knowledge and resources, can create and employ biological weapons.

But there is a major problem: biological weapons are difficult to distribute. Yes, it's true that you can hold a quart bottle that could contain enough of some toxin to kill millions. But that's only if you can deliver to each of these people the minute amount of toxin that will kill them. This has proven to be more complex and intractable a problem than terrorists or government scientists initially realized. Moreover, the biological agents tend to be greatly weakened (or destroyed) by exposure to sun, wind, or moisture. In other words, you need some very specific weather conditions for a biological weapon to spread, and the conditions you need are rare, or subject to change unexpectedly. This is what the Aum Shinrikyo kept running into during their many unsuccessful biological-weapons attacks. Even releasing biological weapons inside a building's air-conditioning system can run afoul of air filters and the like.

Perhaps the most discouraging aspect of terrorist use of biological and chemical weapons is that your attacks are often ignored. This was the Aum Shinrikyo experience, where many of their carefully prepared and carried-out attacks were ignored, even when they caused some injuries. Locals would comment, "Must have been something in the air," or, "It's the weather," in the wake of the attacks. Not the stuff to be picked up by the media, even if one or two bodies were hauled away. This is the ultimate disappointment for a terrorist, not to be noticed by the media.

Aware of this problem, terrorists have been looking for solutions. The most obvious one is to obtain military-grade biological and chemical weapons. Easier said than done, as little of this stuff is made anymore, and existing stocks are being destroyed. Moreover, most of the terrorists looking for this material are Islamic radicals who have vowed to destroy the nations that made and still possess a lot of it. This makes it very difficult for terrorists to bribe Russian or American officials to part with any of these weapons or the technology to make them. Faced with this, terrorists are trying to duplicate the government technology that has produced more lethal (and easier-to-distribute) biological and chemical weapons. Aum Shinrikyo was trying to do this by obtaining the needed expensive lab equipment when the group was broken up in 1996. Only five years later, we have new technologies using genetic engineering that can produce even more lethal biological or chemical weapons. Moreover, the technology for genetic engineering (which promises cures for cancer and many other afflictions) is getting cheaper and easier to use. So there is a future out there that is rapidly approaching. And this future features terrorists working in labs, not furtively planting explosives or hijacking aircraft.

In September 2001, there was another biowarfare attack, this time using anthrax spores sent through the mail. As a weapon, the anthrax was remarkably ineffective. There's good reason for this. For thousands of years, anthrax was known as a livestock pest, regularly killing animals that grazed on land infested with anthrax spores (the animals breathed in the spores as they pulled up grass and released the spores from the soil). Humans could get infected as well, usually by getting spores on a cut. This skin (cutaneous) form of anthrax was fatal in up to 20 percent of the victims, depending on how potent the anthrax strain was and how many spores got into the sore. People who worked with sheep's wool also got cutaneous anthrax, as did those working with the hides of animals that grazed in areas containing anthrax. In the 1970s, imported wool from an anthrax area, improperly cleaned, infected a number of Americans. Anthrax is a bacteria, and some people and animals can fight off infections and even develop an immunity.

Anthrax has long been pitched as an effective biowarfare weapon. Britain developed a military form of anthrax during World War II. At the time, it was seen as an effective weapon because the Germans didn't have antibiotics (only the allies had this then-new medication that easily cured anthrax infections). Since then, work has continued on anthrax, developing more potent strains (so less of it was needed to kill) and making anthrax resistant to antibiotics (difficult to do, although current genetic engineering techniques make this easier if you have the qualified scientists and engineers). The major problem with anthrax is delivering it. The spores, in their natural form, don't travel well in the air. "Militarizing" anthrax consists of processing the spores so they don't clump together and thus can more easily float away in a breeze. But sunlight and heat can kill the spores, and even if they float through the air, they can disperse so that anyone breathing them in will not get a fatal dose (10,000–50,000 spores). Thus there exists the need for militarized anthrax to be grown from more powerful strains.

Naturally occurring anthrax (which exists in most parts of the world) varies in its potency. Wealthier nations, like the United States, give animals in anthrax-ridden areas a vaccine that protects them. There have long been vaccines for humans as well, to protect farmers and veterinarians. Agricultural researchers have collected many strains of anthrax, and the more potent ones are kept and cultured to provide material to test new vaccines. But even the most potent militarized anthrax isn't that powerful. We know this from a military anthrax accident in 1979. A Russian biological warfare plant outside the city of Sverdlovsk accidentally released some militarized anthrax. Some 5,000 people were infected. But there were only 70 deaths. What was particularly discouraging to Russian military bioweapon scientists was that only one of the dead was of military age, and he was already ill from other ailments. All of those who died from the anthrax were old, and usually sick. All the victims had weakened immune systems. Many had lung ailments. The Russians initially denied that there was an accident and did not treat the locals for anthrax. Later they said the deaths were caused by people eating meat infected with anthrax (a common way for people to die from it). It was only after the Soviet Union fell apart that Western researchers were able to get into the area and interview survivors and discover that people with normal immune systems were able to fight off an anthrax infection.

The 2001 anthrax attacks in the United States used a form of natural anthrax. There were six deaths. More will die and get ill, but not from anthrax. Millions of people are taking powerful antibiotics, just in case they were infected. This massive use of antibiotics will cause other bacteria to become resistant to antibiotics, and the resulting "super bugs" will kill a lot of people (a trend that has been noted over the last decade or so). The problem with anthrax as a weapon is that you have to use it in secret and get a lot of people to breathe in the spores. While the less lethal cutaneous form announces itself with a ugly sore (which can then be treated with antibiotics), the pulmonary (breathed-in) form announces itself with flu-like symptoms a few days after the infection. By then it is too late, and death occurs in almost all untreated cases. With prompt treatment, the death rate is still nearly 50 percent. But if you know you have breathed it in (and a test can confirm this), you can be treated with antibiotics. So far, anthrax has not really made the jump from livestock pest to biological-warfare weapon.

Another use of biological warfare is strategic warfare. New plant diseases can be inflicted on the enemy's cropland. Herds of domestic animals can be decimated by diseases that work only on a particular species. Whatever the possibilities, no one seems eager to unleash biological warfare. There appear to be too many risks with this potentially uncontrollable form of combat, even though biological weapons theoretically can be developed that will attack only crops or animals used in specific regions..

Strategic Nuclear Weapons

Strategic nuclear weapons, delivered by long-range missiles, are instruments of mass destruction. They are a much-feared, never-before-used weapon. No one knows how leaders will react when confronted with actually using them. Even with restrained employment, the destruction will be enormous. Military planners have, from the late 1970s into the 1980s, seriously looked into the mechanics of fighting and winning a nuclear war. But it was eventually realized that nuclear wars were unlikely to have any recognizable winners. Since the mid-1980s to the present, most nations have united to reduce the number of nuclear weapons on the planet.

Proliferation

It used to be that the nuclear war everyone feared was one between superpowers and involving thousands of warheads. With the end of the Cold War and the collapse of one of the world's two superpowers, major nuclear war has become less likely. Today, the next use of nuclear missiles is expected to occur between two smaller nations. At the height of the Cold War, over 50,000 nuclear warheads were in the hands of the United States, Russia, Britain, France, China, India, Pakistan, Israel, and South Africa. The two superpowers had 95 percent of them, and the United States had the majority of these. While the end of the Cold War brought about a welcome cutback in the number of weapons (to about 15,000 by the turn of the century), many will remain ready for use. The great fear is that more smaller and less stable nations will obtain these weapons. By the turn of the century, Pakistan and India had openly admitted to possessing nuclear weapons, and North Korea and Iran were known to be working hard to do the same.

Reliability

Figuring out how to build a nuclear weapon, and a missile to deliver it with, is a very complex undertaking. Even after decades of experience building such devices, there are still serious reliability problems. Reliability varies from missile to missile. Like complex machinery everywhere, missiles will work only some of the time. Consider satellite launchers, which are coddled far more than combat missiles. The U.S. success rate is over 90 percent. The Soviet (and later

Russian) success rate was closer to 75 percent (and this has since improved a bit). The success rate of satellites functioning as designed after surviving the launch process is somewhat better. No one wants to admit it, but combat missiles will probably perform less well than satellite launchers. In addition, several other problems with combat missiles must be dealt with:

Navigation. Several factors can degrade the accuracy of missile-guidance systems. The most prominent one is called bias. This arises from most missile tests being from east to west or west to east. In combat, most of the missiles will be going north, over the Pole. This makes a big difference, as vagaries in gravity, magnetic fields, and weather are quite dissimilar going over the Pole. Although guidance specialists insist these problems have been solved, we'll never know until many missiles go flying over the North Pole. As that would be considered an act of war, we are at an impasse on this problem. Then again, it may be something of a nonproblem. The effect of bias would be to degrade the accuracy of the warheads. The CEP (circular error probable) may increase by hundreds or thousands of meters. This will only diminish the accuracy of missiles attempting to destroy other missiles in their armored, underground silos.

No one admits to any desire to achieve such a capability. An attempt is moot because the missiles from invulnerable submarines would survive to destroy everyone's industry and population. When you are city bashing, such inaccuracies mean little. However, whenever people talk about first-strike capability and silo busting, remind them of bias and reliability in general. The Soviets were always worried that Western technology would do them in once more. American engineers have developed terminal homing devices that allow a ballistic-missile warhead to make fine adjustments as it hustles Earthward. This generally involves an image-processing capability, a technology more highly developed in the West. The same sort of thing is used in cruise missiles. Another approach is a warhead navigation system that can take positional information from navigation satellites (GPS). This assumes that these satellites have not yet been destroyed.

Fratricide. This is what happens when the explosion of one nuclear weapon causes problems for other warheads that are still burning through the atmosphere toward their targets. Nukes going for urban areas explode in the atmosphere. They suck up a lot of dirt and debris, blasting it all upward some 20,000 meters. Warheads going after silos explode near the ground, throwing even more crap skyward. Any warhead following the first one into the same target area gets a blast of radiation and, worst of all, lots of more substantial garbage thrown into its path. Zipping along at thousands of meters per second, little grains of sand can destroy or disrupt incoming warheads.

Reliability. This is taken for granted. This is easy to do, as these weapons are rarely tested and have never been used in action. Ballistic missiles consist of several complex systems, each of which must function individually and with the other systems. The simplest system is that of the rocket motors. Most are solid fuel, which is actually a slow-burning explosive. Manufacturing these solid fuels is an exacting process, one very few nations are very adept at. However, the process is not perfect. Like flashbulbs, you can't test solid-fuel rockets. You can poke and probe them and double-check them. Ultimately you play the percentages and hope your numbers are high enough. The Soviets were still using liquid-fuel motors in many of its ICBMs right up until the collapse of the USSR. Nations trying to join the ICBM club, like North Korea or Iraq, will probably start with missiles driven by liquid-fuel engines. As these liquid-fuel motors are mechanical devices, there is a heavy maintenance load and even higher probability of system failure.

Holding the rocket motor, and everything else, is the rocket structure. This is the shell into which all components are fitted. This is quite a complex piece of work, as missiles consist of two or three stages. That is, you actually have two or three rockets piled on top of each other. The first section, or stage, is the largest and contains a large rocket motor. The second stage is another motor, and the third stage is the warhead, guidance system, and smaller rocket. Thus, there is not one structure but three. Modern missiles use MIRVed (Multiple Independent Reentry Vehicle) warheads. This is a final stage now renamed a "bus" that releases warheads like passengers getting off at different times. This requires another mechanical device linked to the guidance system to ensure that the warheads are let go at the proper time. Another time-critical event is the separation of a lower stage during flight. This is done with explosive bolts. Should one or more of these fail, the entire missile is lost.

The entire process is intolerant to any failure. There is much that can go wrong and ample opportunity for failure to occur. The rocket motor and missile structure are simple items compared to the guidance system and warheads. The guidance system is a particularly complex piece of electromechanical precision. It is responsible for guiding the missile and its warheads over a course of up to 10,000 kilometers and hitting within 100–2,000 meters of the target. Not only are these systems subject to frequent failure, they are also at the mercy of their computer programs. Undiscovered errors on these programs have previously caused many embarrassing breakdowns. Frequently, flaws in the system are not discovered until after months or years of supposedly combat-ready deployment. The warheads are subject to many of the same ills experienced by the guidance system. A nuclear weapon is not a simple device. Basically, it is a bit of radioactive material surrounded by high explosives and other elements needed to produce the desired explosive effect. Extraordinary measures are taken to ensure that these weapons do not go off except when intended. These safety devices are complex and numerous. Should any one of them fail, the weapon will not go off.

Readiness. As complex as these missiles are, they have one more obstacle to overcome before they have a chance to complete their mission. Years of inactivity are spent buried within underground silos or aboard submarines. The dozens of major electronic and mechanical systems are constantly monitored. Periodically, a missile is taken out of service for repairs or maintenance. Overshadowing all this effort is the realization that there has never been a mass attack with these weapons. What the exact readiness level will be is unknown. One can only estimate from related equipment. The closest parallel is combat aircraft. Readiness levels here vary between 50–90 percent. This is the result of decades of testing and preparation. Alas, missiles just don't get used that much. Currently a few percent of all missiles are test-fired each year. But the testing is not pure; it cannot be. The guidance systems have to be reprogrammed to hit a location in a testing area, not an enemy target. Moreover, the missiles are often moved from their silos to a special test silo. There is lots of opportunity to cook the books in this sort of testing. The peacetime military environment being what it is, the tests do not always reveal the problems they are meant to seek out. Military history is replete with large organizations that spent decades preparing for battles in which their initial performance was deplorable. Strategic rockets seem quite capable of falling into this trap.

The more recent members of the nuclear ICBM club (including China) have been able to build only a few missiles. These can be watched from space, and activity necessary to ready them for firing noted. Nations like India and Pakistan have less mature missile technology and will rely on delivering their nukes via aircraft. This is not the preferred way to do it, as the bomber can be shot down. Even then, there is still a high probability that the weapon won't go off. It takes a long time to work out how to produce reliable nuclear weapons.

Joining the ICBM Club

With Russia no longer pointing its ICBMs at the United States, we have to worry about several smaller nations that would like to. This list includes North Korea, Iran, Iraq, Libya, Pakistan, and India. The first four nations that had them (Russia, the United States, Britain, and France) spent hundreds of billions of dollars to build their ICBMs. All four nations had enormous technical resources to throw at the problem. Future members of the ICBM club will join like China did, using a lot of borrowed and off-the-shelf technology. The Chinese experience is instructive.

China's DF (Dong Feng, or "East Wind") series of ballistic missiles are not numerous. Although China has been developing ballistic-missile technology for over four decades, they have not built a lot of them. Instead, they have put most of their resources into improving accuracy and reliability. This effort has been complemented by an energetic satellite-launcher program. These missiles are actually older technology, but by offering reliable and cheaper launch services, the Chinese have managed to bring in foreign money, and technology, to their entire missile program. Because American satellite companies have used Chinese launch services, much valuable missile technology was obtained. This caused a scandal in the United States during the late 1990s as the extent of illegal technology transfers was revealed. The Chinese obtained the technology using many different approaches. Faced with the loss of valuable satellites, but unwilling to forego cheap Chinese launch rates, American companies helped the Chinese. This assistance was exploited to obtain technical information useful for the military missiles. Chinese agents also scoured the United States, Japan, and Western Europe for additional technology, exploiting the good will of overseas Chinese as well. This last angle often appeared innocent, with the scientists from "the old country" entertaining the Chinese immigrants and talking about events back home. These conversations often resulted in inadvertent disclosures of secret technology. All this is nothing new, as China's ballistic missile program began when U.S. Air Force colonel, Qian Xuesen, went back to China in 1955, along with four other Chinese-American missile scientists, and began work on Chinese missiles. Qian had come to America in 1935 to study and graduated from MIT and Caltech. He was long suspected of being a Chinese spy and eventually lost his security clearance before returning to China.

The chaos of the Cultural Revolution stopped most missile development from the mid-1960s to the late 1970s. It wasn't until the 1980s that China got four ICBMs operational. Before that, it had several dozen shorter-range missiles that could keep the Russians at bay.

By 2000, the Chinese had six missiles in their DF series. The 20 DF-5s have a range of 12,000 kilometers. Keep in mind that Chinese missiles follow the curve of the Earth and are fired over the Arctic. With that approach, Los Angeles is 10,600 kilometers away and Washington, D.C., 11,700 kilometers away. There are 40 older DF-3s (range of 2,800 kilometers) and 20–25 DF-4s (range of 4,700 kilometers).

China is increasing its stock of shorter-range missiles (DF-15 and DF-11). These are the weapons most likely to be used in a war with Taiwan. The DF-15 (exported as the M-9) has a range of 600 kilometers, the DF-11 (M-11) 480 kilometers. Currently, China has 300–400 DF-11 and DF-15 missiles and is likely to have 650 of these missiles by 2005. Taiwan currently has Patriot missiles that might be able to shoot down half the DF-11/15s fired at them. Even if China got a few hundred of these missiles on target, the damage would not be devastating. The DF-15 carries an 1,100-pound warhead, the DF-11 a 1,760-pound warhead. China would likely use conventional explosives in these warheads. They could do damage, but no more than aircraft bombs. Indeed, the missiles are less accurate than most aircraft bombing systems. But while Taiwan stands a good chance of stopping nearly all Chinese bombers, at least half of the missiles will get through. Most of these missiles are stationed on the coast opposite Taiwan. China is improving the guidance systems of the DF-

11/15, making them more accurate, and better able to avoid getting shot down. Chinese scientists make no secret of where they are getting the technology from this: they are getting it from the United States. These improved missiles could be decisive in a war with Taiwan.

China is also preparing a new generation of missiles for deployment before 2010. They all feature solid-fuel propulsion, greater reliability and accuracy, and multiple warheads. The 1,700-kilometer range DF-21 is actually a land-based version of a missile carried on nuclear subs (China has only one such boat, carrying a dozen missiles). The DF-21 will replace the DF-3. In a similar fashion, the 8,000-kilometer DF-31 is the land-based version of the new submarine missile. The DF-31 will replace the DF-4. About 10 years down the road, the 12,000-kilometer range DF-41 will replace the DF-5.

When the Chinese protest U.S. efforts at building ballistic-missile defenses, what they are really saying is, "Don't force us to build more of these new missiles in order to overwhelm your defenses." Unlike the United States and the Soviet Union, which both had over 10,000 nuclear warheads aimed at each other at the end of the Cold War, the Chinese prefer to build just enough to make their point. Most of China's longest-range missiles are aimed at American targets. Even some of the shorter-range ones target U.S. bases in the Pacific.

While the rest of China's armed forces are still rather low-tech, China's missiles are not. And China is willing to sell the missiles and the technology to other nations. China obtained much of its initial missile technology from Russia and now is passing it on (for a price) to other ICBM wannabes. This is how North Korea, Iraq, and Iran got their start in the ICBM business.

Russia has been selling Scud missiles for decades. They sold them to just about anyone. The Scuds use a liquid-fuel system, While this is less efficient than the technologically more advanced solid-fuel systems, it is easier to scale up a solid-fuel missile into an ICBM-class vehicle. This is what China, North Korea, Iran, and Iraq have done. Tinkering with Scuds is an excellent way to learn how to build ICBMs. The biggest obstacle is the guidance system. But even this is becoming easier with the growing abundance of electronic technology and engineers available. There's also GPS, which can also be used to help guide long-range missiles. China got its first ICBMs operational about 10 years ago. We can expect more nations to do the same before 2010.

Political Distortions

Initially, users were grateful to see the missiles lift off and go in the general direction of the target. Success begat excess, and before long the strategy of the first strike appeared. This notion sprang from the theoretical accuracy of multiple warheads launched from MIRV missiles. With more than one warhead coming from each missile, it was theoretically possible to launch enough warheads to destroy all the enemy missiles in their silos. Enemy missiles left at sea in their submarines would presumably submit to some equally devastating technological breakthrough. These tantalizing technological possibilities put the missile people in an embarrassing position during the 1970s and 1980s. To admit that their weapons were not capable of such feats was not politically prudent. A vicious cycle developed as each side suspected the other of superior technological capabilities. Lacking any means to prove the other fellow actually had these capabilities, the claims became more outrageous and expensive to counter. More pressure was put on the commanders of the missile forces.

In the Soviet Union, where the spirit and practice of the Potemkin village, a motion picture–like false front, survived for many years, the national mania for secrecy only made the validation problem worse. The possibilities were endless, as was the expense. Even more dangerous was, and still is, a national leader believing the illusions and attempting to use them. The arms race turned into an illusions race. Various missile, bomber, nuclear-weapon, and Star Wars gaps appeared and eventually melted away. All of these gaps turned out to exist in the imagination, not reality. This did not, until the collapse of the Soviet Union in 1991, give any of the participants pause. The untried weapon continued to proliferate, unfettered by reality. What was real was that enough of these weapons would work well enough essentially to wreck most of the economies and societies on the planet if there is a nuclear war. How such a nuclear war would occur was open to vivid speculation. No one wants to use nuclear weapons because nearly every world leader recognizes the no-win aspect of a nuclear war. A nuclear war could start by accident. A missile could be fired by a submarine commander even though he was not authorized to do so. A technical failure could cause a missile to launch and attack its targets.

Last, and least likely, a national leader could deliberately order the missiles launched. It is always least likely that a national leader would launch a major war. Yet this has happened twice in this century. In 1914, it was an overconfident leader of Russia forcing his will on the Austrians, and an overconfident Austrian expecting German support to make the Russians back down. In 1939, it was an overconfident German leader invading Poland, with the cooperation of the Soviets. What was different between 1945 and 1991 was that only two major powers existed; all other industrialized nations were secondary military powers.

For nearly half a century, only the Soviet Union and the United States could start a world war and could also stop nearly any war they wanted terminated. Smaller nations are already obtaining nuclear weapons. It's almost inevitable that some of these weapons will eventually be used. What will happen then? It all depends on who uses the nukes, and for what purpose.

Ballistic Missile Defense

For over four decades, hundreds of billions of dollars have been spent on developing weapons to stop nuclear missiles. In the past, these efforts faltered when it was realized that such a system would make the enemy more trigger-happy. This was during the Cold War, and it took the United States a while to realize that to the paranoid Soviet Union, American missile defenses were an offensive weapon. By Soviet logic, we were building missile defenses so we could nuke Russia without fear of retaliation. In the 1970s, both sides agreed to refrain from working on missile defenses. This calmed down the Russians, who had been making noises about "launching a first strike" before the American missile defenses went into service. But in the 1980s, the United States began work on an even more ambitious missile defense system: "Star Wars." This turned out to be a clever move. Doing research and development on missile defense was not against the treaty, but actually putting the system into operation was. The Cold War ended before the United States got its Star Wars system working, so we never found out how the Russians would have reacted. The ambitious and expensive new technology proposed for Star Wars played a part in the collapse of the Soviet Union. The Russians later admitted that the prospect of trying to match the Star Wars effort demoralized the Soviet leadership.

The Soviet Union evaporated in the early 1990s, but many of its nuclear missiles did not. More ominously, everyone noted that Iran, Iraq, and North Korea were working on long-range missiles and nuclear weapons. This is where the doomsday math comes in.

The justification for keeping the missile defense efforts going through the 1990s and into the twenty-first century is the possibility that eventually Iran, Iraq, North Korea, or some other hostile nation will get their hands on nuclear weapons and long-range missiles to carry them to North America. At the end of the Cold War, there were some 40,000 nuclear weapons, about half that number deliverable by aircraft or long-range missile. Some 10,000 of these warheads were aimed at the United States. Today there are about 15,000 nuclear weapons on the planet. Some 7,000 belong to the United States, and these are in pretty good shape. Russia still has some 6,000 nukes, but far fewer of them are in any condition to be used. This is where we must consider a dirty little secret of the Cold War. Many of the nuclear missiles were not expected actually to work under wartime conditions. The reasons are many, having to do with the design of the electronics and quality of the maintenance. One reason the Soviet Union had 10,000 warheads aimed at us was that even if most of the missiles failed, there would still be enough to vaporize us.

Ten years later, Russia can still get about 1,000 warheads on target, out of the 6,000 they still possess. China has a few hundred warheads and maybe a dozen missiles capable of reaching western North America. No other potential foe has missiles that can reach the United States. But if you are planning a missile-defense system, you have to plan for what will be out there 10 years in the future. This is where the debate gets interesting.

A missile-defense system that can stop a few incoming missiles will cost over a $100 billion. Probably closer to $200 billion. This means spending a fraction of 1 percent of annual GNP on this project. Nations like Iran, Iraq, and North Korea can develop a nuclear-equipped ICBM if they are willing to spend enough money. A few percent of GNP over 5–10 years will do it. What are the chances of that happening? Well, let's consider other things that are going on in these nations. Iran has a growing reform movement. Iranians are tired of all the fundamentalist rhetoric and religious rule and want some prosperity. It's unlikely that Iran will reverse its current trend and put a lot of money into building nukes and ICBMs. Possible, but not very likely. Iraq has the money, and a police state to keep people in line while money is spent to produce ICBMs. But Iraq first has to get rid of the UN blockade. Then Iraq has to worry about Israel. Middle East politics cannot be ignored, and Israel is Iraq's principal foe. If Iraq gets close to having a nuclear missile, Israel will attack. Israel did this in 1982, destroying a reactor that was a key component of Iraq's nuclear-weapons program. The chances of Iraq keeping it all together until it has an ICBM that can reach America are slim indeed. And then there is North Korea. The country is broke, and the situation is getting worse by the day. In 10 years it's more likely that North Korea will have been absorbed by South Korea. While it's true that the north has starved to death over a million of its citizens to support its massive army and ICBM program, it's also true that such heroic efforts have failed in the past. The prospect of an individual like Osama bin Laden building an ICBM only happens in movies.

Beyond the practical problems of mobilizing resources to build nukes and an ICBM, there is also the retaliation factor. Launch a nuke at the United States and our satellites will immediately identify the launch site. If a lot of Americans are killed, the "remember Pearl Harbor" reflex will take over, and the launching nation will disappear in a radioactive cloud. You have a chance of covering tracks when committing a terrorist act. But an incoming ICBM leaves tracks that lead right back to the attacker. Think of the retaliation as doomsday math.

But there are always tyrants who aren't very good at this kind of math. Saddam Hussein has amply demonstrated this when he attacked his larger neighbor, Iran, in 1980. After barely surviving that war, he attacked Kuwait, a friend of the United States, in 1990. That didn't work out so well, either. You also have an unstable leadership in North Korea. Religious fundamentalists still control most of the military forces in Iran. Iran is also trying to build nukes and long-range missiles. And these three nations led by unstable maniacs are not the first of their kind. Adolf Hitler was simply one of the more powerful, and well known, of these people. There have been many more in the past; we can expect to see more in the future.

This is apparently what accounts for the continued acceptance by American voters of work on ballistic-missile defense. The idea is apparently not that these defenses will be perfect, but that if they stop one missile, they will be worth the cost. When New York City totaled up the damages of the September 11 attack on two of its tallest buildings, it came to $83 billion. A nuclear attack would have cost a lot more.

Stopping ICBMs is not impossible, just difficult and expensive. Citing the pathetic performance of antiaircraft missiles misses an important point. Most of the surface-to-air missiles fired over the last four decades have been Russian. And these missiles have usually been fired at American aircraft. Less capable Russian SAMs trying to hit higher-tech American aircraft has been a dismal exercise. But when you look at the smaller number of American-made SAMs fired at Russian-made aircraft, the hit rate goes way up (more than 10 times). So no matter how daunting the task of building anti-ICBM systems, their political popularity and technical inevitability will continue to outvote the technical and fiscal pessimists.

Theory and Practice

This area of warfare is far more theory than practice. Indeed, the practical experience has been so scanty and discouraging that most armies have been gradually edging further and further away from using chemical, biological, or nuclear weapons. After many years of studying the use of CBN and practicing and simulating it in exercises, professional soldiers seem reluctant to unleash weapons that appear ever more capable of upsetting their carefully honed visions of what war should be. As soldiers practice defending against ever more capable nuclear and chemical weapons, they realize that they would have little time or energy for anything else. They have come to fear, in effect, that nuclear and chemical theory would become practice. Soldiers are traditionalists—they would rather practice their craft with the familiar.

Military professionals who have worked with biological and chemical weapons are also quick to point out that these things are not nearly as lethal or easy to use as the media makes out. But chemical and biological weapons are excellent for creating widespread terror, even if the body count doesn't match up.

But the threat remains and becomes more acute as more nations obtain genetic-engineering technology. The objective here is to develop biological weapons that will be devastating but won't spread back to your own country. This is not easy to do and so far is only theoretical. In the meantime, the possibility of terrorists getting their hands on this sort of thing is becoming more worrisome. And this is not theoretical. The one terrorist group that has actually used biological weapons and nerve gas, Aum Shinrikyo, was intent on causing devastation on a global scale to achieve their twisted religious ends.

The Future

Smaller nations have increasingly fixated on the idea that if they had a weapon of mass destruction, they would have more leverage dealing with larger nations and unpleasant neighbors. The technology needed to build these weapons (chemical, biological, or nuclear) is becoming cheaper and easier to operate. Want to make nerve gas? The raw materials will cost you less than $200. The skills necessary to make sarin are learned by most college-level chemistry or chemical engineering majors. Want to make weaponized anthrax? You can find anthrax in the wild (you'll have to travel to the American Midwest or overseas), and processing it is easy enough for someone with a degree in biology. Nuclear weapons require more engineers and money, but the technology is no big secret.

Will many smaller nations, and terrorist organizations, create these weapons (many already have), and use them (fewer have so far)? No one knows, and fewer people want to find out.

Tactical Nuclear Weapons' Effects on Ground Forces

Type of target. Down the left side of the chart are listed various situations troops may find themselves in when a nuclear weapon goes off nearby.

Troops in the open. It is assumed that most troops in the field will be in this situation when a nuclear weapon detonates. Because most of a nuclear weapon's energy goes into creating blast and heat (or flash), it is more successful if it surprises troops outside shelter or vehicles. The flash/heat travels at the speed of light and is nearly instantaneous. It burns exposed skin and blinds those looking at it. Flash will be diminished by clouds or fog. Clothing will also absorb a lot of flash damage. Bad weather will not only provide more protection with clouds and fog, but more troops will be inside some form of shelter and wearing more clothing. This can reduce flash casualties by more than half. Under most conditions, the majority of injuries will be from flash. In addition, there will be blast injuries. Blast travels at the speed of sound, about 325 meters a second. Nuclear-weapon blast arrives as a high-speed wind. For each weapon size shown on the chart, the wind is about 130 kilometers per hour at the maximum distance, and about 380 kilometers per hour at half that distance. A hurricane generates winds of 120–200 kilometers per hour, a tornado up to 480 kilometers per hour. The flying objects tossed about by these winds cause additional losses, although troops have a few seconds to seek shelter. Troops at the greatest risk are those away from the fighting, where at least half may be in the open during daytime.

		Meters from point of explosion where 50 percent of people in the area will be hurt						
Type of target		1	10	20	100	200	500	1,000
		Numbers above indicate yield of weapon in kilotons.						
Troops in the open		1,000	2,154	2,714	4,642	5,848	7,937	10,000
	Sq. km →	3	15	23	68	107	198	314
Troops protected in open earthworks		700	1,508	1,900	3,249	4,094	5,556	7,000
	Sq km →	1.54	7	11	33	53	97	154
Non-armored vehicles and aircraft on ground		600	1,293	1,629	2,785	3,509	4,762	6,000
	Sq. km →	1.13	5	8	24	39	71	113
Armored vehicles		450	969	1,221	2,089	2,632	3,572	4,500
	Sq. km →	0.64	3	5	14	22	40	64
Heavy structures of concrete, etc.		200	431	543	928	1,170	1,587	2,000
	Sq km →	0.13	0.58	0.93	3	4	8	13

Troops protected in open earthworks represents troops in foxholes, trenches, vehicles, and other light structures that shield them from much of the flash and blast. There would still be significant losses from fire and falling debris.

Non-armored vehicles and aircraft on ground would have enough components damaged to be unusable. The primary cause of damage will be blast. Winds of over 400 kilometers per hour (240 MPH) will do terrible things to trucks and parked aircraft.

Armored vehicles are generally too heavy to be severely damaged by high winds. Antennae, searchlights, and other protrusions can be damaged. Heat will also damage nonmetallic items like fire-control and sighting gear. At the ranges shown, radiation will kill or injure crew members inside vehicles. Any crew outside the vehicle at the ranges shown will certainly be lost. Crews spend 85 percent of their time outside their vehicles. Without trained crews, the armored vehicles are useless.

Heavy structures of concrete, etc. This represents substantial commercial buildings as well as military bunkers. Personnel inside will be protected from most radiation effects.

Weapon size is represented across the top of the chart in equivalent kilotons (thousand tons) of TNT explosive. The common sizes for tactical nuclear weapons are from 1–1,000 kilotons, with the preferred range under 100 kilotons. Larger ones (over 1,000) are used in strategic missiles, although these systems are also tending toward the 100–500 kiloton range. (Note that 14-kiloton weapons were dropped on Japan in 1945.) The effects of the weapon are shown by the two numbers within the chart. The top figure is the distance from the explosion at which 50 percent of troops or vehicles will become casualties. One-third of the casualties will be fatal immediately. Another third may be fatal eventually without adequate treatment. Casualties may increase a further 50 percent if radioactive fallout is not avoided or decontamination does not take place. The range of effect is measured from the explosion. An airburst is assumed. The height of the airburst varies with the size of the weapon. The only reason for using a ground burst is to increase radioactivity or to ensure destruction of hard targets.

Tactical nukes want to avoid radioactivity as much as possible. The second figure for each type of target is the area covered (in square kilometers) by the effects of various weapons under the conditions shown. This is convenient when comparing effects that depend on the density of troops or equipment in the area.

Tactical Nuclear Weapons' Effects on Ships

Sink or permanently disable indicates sufficient damage to either sink the ship outright or disable it to the extent that repairs at sea are impossible. Immediate radiation casualties at this range will also be high, putting up to 50 percent of the crew out of action. This is also the range for damage to modern submarines from an underwater explosion of a nuclear weapon. Older subs would be damaged or destroyed even at these ranges, perhaps 25-percent longer.

Temporarily disable mobility indicates sufficient damage to the ship's power plant to impair or completely shut it down. On aircraft carriers, any aircraft on the flight deck would be destroyed. Landing and takeoff operations would probably be impossible for at least a few hours. Many aircraft in the air would have to find an alternative landing field, as most U.S. carrier aircraft are launched on the assumption that they will land within two hours. Repairs on ship power systems could take from hours to days. Meanwhile, these ships would be more vulnerable to additional enemy attacks. This range is also the extreme range that underwater nuclear explosions can cause any damage to modern nuclear submarines. Older, nonnuclear, subs could still be hurt at 25 percent longer ranges. Surface ships could also receive some damage from underwater nuclear explosions within this range.

Type of effect on ship		Range of effect in meters			
		20 kiloton	200 kiloton	2,000 kiloton	20,000 kiloton
Sink or permanently disable		800	1,724	3,714	8,001
	Sq. km →	2	9	43	201
Temporarily disable mobility		1,500	3,232	6,962	15,000
	Sq. km →	7	33	152	707
Temporarily disable sensors and Weapons		2,000	4,309	9,284	20,001
	Sq. km →	13	58	271	1,257

Temporarily disable sensors and weapons. Physical damage to antennae and viewing devices as well as light deck structures, especially missile launchers, would be significant. Within this range, any aircraft in the way would also suffer severe, often fatal, damage. Ships without sufficient onboard repair capability would have permanent damage. The electromagnetic pulse of the explosion would also extend for hundreds of kilometers. This would be very dangerous to aircraft in the air within the range of the pulse. Submerged submarines would be unaffected by underwater nuclear explosions at this range.

Across the top of the chart is shown the weapon size (in kilotons). Naval nuclear weapons tend to be larger than land versions. The 2,000-kiloton weapon would be found only in strategic missiles, which may be used at sea if satellite surveillance becomes efficient enough. The 20,000-kiloton weapon exists in small quantities but is likely to disappear during post–Cold War disarmament. However, such weapons can be produced again by any nation so inclined.

The effects. The top figure gives the range of that effect. The bottom figure is the area covered in square kilometers. An average task force of 8–12 ships would occupy an area up to 1,000 square kilometers. A merchant convoy of 30–50 ships, plus 8 or more escorts, would cover the same area. The more important ships occupy the center of such an area.

Number of Losses Assuming Indicated Densities

This chart shows the losses in troops, vehicles, or structures, depending on the nuclear weapon's size and posture of the target. Across the top of the chart are the various sizes of nuclear weapons and below each is number of personnel, vehicles, or structures that would be injured depending on their situation.

Density per square kilometer is the assumed density of personnel for calculating casualties. The targets are assumed to be battalion size, the basic combat unit in all armies. Each contains from 400–1,000 men, and the battalions would be distributed throughout their assigned areas. A battalion normally deploys in an area covering 5–12 square kilometers. Some battalion deployment areas overlap others, to a minor extent. Support units also frequently occupy the same area. The chart shows only losses from single battalions. There is some "empty" space between battalions, occupied only by any civilians who have not fled the area. Smaller nuclear weapons are more effective, as larger ones waste much of their effect on areas not occupied by combat troops. These larger weapons will injure one-half to one-third the number shown on the chart because of the "empty space" they will hit.

	Density per Square Km	1	10	20	100	200	500	1,000
		Numbers below represent the losses in each category as shown in the first column.						
		Number above indicates yield of weapon in kilotons.						
Troops in the open	35	55	255	405	1,185	1,881	3,465	5,500
Troops protected in open earthworks	35	27	125	199	581	922	1,698	2,695
Non-armored vehicles and aircraft	5	3	13	21	61	97	178	283
Armored vehicles	5	2	7	12	34	54	100	159
Heavy structures of concrete, etc.	20	0	1	2	7	11	20	31
Civilian losses	250	193	894	1,418	4,147	6,583	12,127	19,250
Dwellings rendered uninhabitable	85	262	1,215	1,929	5,640	8,953	16,492	26,180
Civilians made homeless		770	3,573	5,671	16,583	26,323	48,488	76,969
Distance at which housing is rendered uninhabitable (in meters from bomb)		1,400	3,016	3,800	6,498	8,187	11,112	14,000

Troops in the open. Normally, half the troops are outside, and half are under cover in open earthworks or some other shelter. If the weather is bad, or it is night, more are under cover. The more troops are in the open, the more will get hit.

Non-armored vehicles. Density is for an entire division area. These are largely trucks.

Armored vehicles density is for a combat battalion (average).

Heavy structures density is of a heavily urbanized area.

Civilian losses density is for Germany. Belgium and the Netherlands have a higher density. The rest of Europe has about half the density of Germany. Civilian casualties will vary considerably throughout a country. The heavily built-up areas have densities of over 5,000 people per square kilometer, which is typical for cities and urban areas worldwide. Even agricultural areas will have densities of over 400. Nonagricultural rural areas will have densities of less than 100, all the way down to 10. If "dirty" nuclear weapons are used, eventual casualties will be more than doubled due to delayed radiation effects. The magnitude of civilian casualties will overwhelm medical facilities, and otherwise nonfatal injuries will kill. Fifty percent of all casualties will be fatal under these conditions. Many of the civilians will have fled the combat area, or will have attempted to do so. However, they have to go somewhere. Because nuclear weapons will be used largely against rear-area targets, the density of civilians may be greater in these areas because of refugees. It will be difficult for civilians to stay away from military targets, as the troops will be widely dispersed to lessen the effects of nuclear weapons.

Dwellings rendered uninhabitable. Given the density of population, this is the number of dwellings rendered uninhabitable by each size weapon.

Civilians made homeless is the average number of civilians whose residence is no longer livable. Up to a point, these civilians can be accommodated in other homes. The average dwelling in Europe has four or five rooms with less than one inhabitant per room. Other parts of the world typically average two or more people per room and fewer rooms per dwelling. Each dwelling lost is a significant loss for the inhabitants.

Distance at which housing is rendered uninhabitable (in meters from bomb) is heavy damage. It includes broken windows, minor fires, roof-tile damage, and the like. Without repairs, this housing is only marginally habitable. Still, it's better than staying outside.

Density of Troops, Vehicles, and Weapons on the Battlefield

This chart shows the average density of troops and vehicles in units of the United States Army (or armies of other Western nations) and Russian/Third World–style armies.

Unit designation represents the most common units of both armies. The U.S. corps and the Russian army are roughly equivalent in combat power and manpower. The U.S. corps contains two divisions, an armored cavalry regiment, and support units. The Russian army contains four divisions and support units. The figures for both armies are averages for combat, combat support, and supply units. Each division contains 12–16 battalions.

Local civilians gives the average density of civilians, dwellings, and vehicles located in the combat unit deployment area.

Area is the area in which the combat units are dispersed, in square kilometers. Generally, this is an irregular area roughly resembling a rectangle. The corps/army occupies an area 50 by 50 kilometers, divisions 25 by 24 or 20 by 17. The battalion area is 3 by 4 kilometers. These are averages; they are often half as large when a unit is attacking.

Troops total is the total number of troops assigned to that unit. The divisions usually are in contact with the enemy and thus occupy most of the forward portion of the corps/army area. The empty space at the front line is covered by

Unit designation	Area (sq km)	Troops total	Armored vehicles total	Trucks total	Troops per km	Armored vehicles per km	Trucks per km
U.S. corps	3,000	55,000	0	10,000	18	0	3
Russian army	3,000	61,000	0	9,000	20	0	3
U.S. division	600	20,000	0	3,500	33	0	6
Russian division	350	14,000	0	1,500	40	0	4
U.S. battalion team	12	900	60	10	75	5	1
Russian battalion team	10	600	50	2	60	5	0
Local Civilians	All				250 Civilians	85 Dwellings	90 Cars and trucks

corps/army reconnaissance troops. The corps/army rear area has the lowest concentration of troops.

Armored vehicles total is the total number of armored vehicles in the unit. This includes tanks, IVF's, and self-propelled artillery.

Trucks total is the total number of non-armored vehicles in the unit. This includes aircraft.

Troops per km is the average number of troops per square kilometer in the unit's area.

Armored vehicles per km is the average number of armored vehicles per square kilometer in the unit's area.

Trucks per km is the average number of non-armored vehicles per square kilometer in the unit's area.

Chemical Weapons

Gas name is the common name of the chemical agent. It is derived from its effects on troops:

- *Tear gas* is commonly used by police and military forces. It has been produced in many variants; other names are CS, CN, etc. Because of its generally nonlethal nature, tear gas has been accepted as not being a chemical agent in the common sense of the word. In other words, tear gas is widely used. However, it can be lethal. Some of the more powerful variants induce severe coughing, involuntary defecation, and vomiting. These effects can render a victim quite helpless. Tear gas is also used in a powder form to serve as a persistent harassing agent on the battlefield.
- *Vomiting gas is a super tear gas.* Also known as Adamsite, it was a favorite with the Soviets. Like tear gas, it is ideal for clearing out enemy troops, or anyone else, in built-up areas, caves, and fortifications. While tear gas will often cause vomiting, this stuff will practically guarantee it.
- *Blister gas* was a Soviet development, an improvement on World War I mustard gas. Also known as phosgene oxime, it acts more quickly than mustard gas and completely destroys skin tissue. Very ugly stuff.
- *Mustard gas* is an updated version of the harassment agent used extensively during World War I. It is really a liquid spray, not a gas. It takes a while to act, but once it gets going, it leaves ugly blisters. Many victims still carry scars, not to mention blindness and lung injuries, from this

Gas name	Code name	Physical effect	Used to	Persistence (hours)	Inhaled agents		Skin contact agents		Can it be smelled?	Tons to cover (sq km)
					Time to take effect (minutes)	Minimum dosage level	Time to take effect (minutes)	Minimum dosage level		
Tear	CS	Irritation, tears, nausea	Harass	0.5	1	1,157	NA	NA	Yes	NA
Vomiting	DM	Headache, cough, nausea	Harass	0.5	1	4,080	NA	NA	No	NA
Blister	CX	Severe skin blisters	Harass	36–1,300	NA	NA	100	5	No	NA
Mustard	HD	Severe skin blisters	Harass	36–1,300	NA	NA	300	6	Yes	10
Choking	CG	Cough, suffocation	Kill	0.1	600	89	NA	NA	Yes	NA
Blood	AC	Convulsions, suffocation	Kill	0.1	8	139	NA	NA	Yes	NA
Nerve	GD	Convulsions, suffocation	Kill	.2–50	8	2	8	143	No	1.0
Nerve	VX	Convulsions, suffocation	Kill	1–2,700	6	1	6	28	No	0.3

gas. Used by Iraq in the 1980s Persian Gulf war, some of it was said to be a powder that burned deeply into the skin. Very nasty stuff.

- *Choking gas* is one of the first modern chemical agents. It is also known as phosgene. It caused 80 percent of the gas fatalities during World War I. It is still available, mainly because it's so easy to manufacture.
- *Blood gas* also had its origins in World War I. It was valued for its ability to act quickly by causing suffocation. This made it the ideal surprise agent. The original was called cyanogen chloride (CK). Modern versions are prussic acid and hydrogen cyanide. Even the names have a grotesque ring to them. This one was another favorite of the Soviets.
- *Nerve gas* was first developed during the 1930s as a variation of an insecticide. It has gone through many reformulations and is known by a variety of names: tabun (GA), sarin (GB), soman (GD), CMPF (GP), VR-55, VX, etc. It comes in persistent and nonpersistent forms and can be used in lethal and harassing concentrations. Perhaps the most widely stockpiled agent, it would probably be the most widely used. It shuts down the body's nervous system, causing suffocation, etc. Light doses cause blindness or blurred vision, severe headaches, and disorientation. The Germans used a nerve gas in their extermination camps. Very ugly.

Code name is the two-letter U.S. Army code name.

Physical effect on victims. Most chemical agents are fairly simple elements that primarily irritate tissues, like the skin and eyes. Any that get into the lungs have a more pronounced effect. The only chemical agents that go beyond these simplistic effects are blood and nerve gases. Blood gases interfere with the absorption of oxygen by the blood in the lungs. This causes a form of suffocation. Nerve gases interfere with the transmission of messages in the body's nervous system. All these agents are potentially fatal. The fatal ones will not kill in smaller doses. This phenomenon exacerbates any hypochondriac tendencies among victims. Sickness in general tends to be higher among troops in the field. Fewer than 5 percent of the casualties in an army are the direct result of combat; the remainder come from a variety of accidents and common illnesses. Chemical agents and their ability to make troops slightly ill will combine with the troops' fear of gas fatalities to produce some very nervous and unwell soldiers.

Used to indicates whether the chemical agent is intended primarily for harassment or killing. Harassment agents are popular because they can be used more aggressively without endangering your own troops. A harassment agent that is nonpersistent (see next column) can be used without fear of causing significant injury to your own troops. This makes an ideal weapon for use at the front, where friendly troops are nearby. Harassment agents are customarily fired on

Trident II (D-5) Fleet Ballistic Missile

troops about to be attacked by your own troops. In the short term, this forces the defenders to put on their protective gear. This makes them less effective. Sometimes harassment agents are fired at defending troops over a period of days. This can substantially wear down the enemy's willingness to fight. Harassment agents are also used to create large areas that are difficult for the enemy to pass through. Lethal chemical agents are principally used on enemy targets far to the rear, where your own troops are unlikely to be affected. Dead and wounded soldiers do have an impact on the survivors' morale and willingness to go on. Consider, for example, the effect on a soldier's fighting spirit after he has been gassed once, or more than once. A harassment agent is not used just to be humane; it is an attempt to discourage troops from fighting by forcing them to wear cumbersome protective gear and by inflicting painful injuries. Surviving an encounter with chemical injuries can be more damaging to an army than fatalities. The victims, instead of being buried with their pain and horror, live to tell others about it.

Persistence (hours) is the length of time the chemical agents remain effective after they are released. The least persistent form of chemical is gas or vapor. Like common smoke, this quickly dissipates in the atmosphere. Depending on the concentration of the chemical, wind speed, and humidity, the potency of the agent may disappear in minutes. Other factors affect chemical persistence. Persistent agents will last longer in vegetation. Porous soil will retain them longer. Nonporous soil allows water or wind to carry the chemicals away quickly. Sunlight causes most agents to degrade quickly, with nerve-gas effectiveness diminished by more than 60 percent. Temperature also affects chemicals, in two ways. Cold decreases the speed of dispersal, which keeps the chemicals in a smaller area and in higher concentrations. A high-temperature gradient—cold air near the ground and warm air just above it—holds the chemical agents to the ground, which makes inhalation less likely. Moisture washes the agents away. A bad side effect is the contamination of any nearby water supplies until the agent is diluted enough to become ineffective. With gas, it's one damn thing after another.

Wind both aids and hinders the gases. It dilutes them to an impotent level more quickly. A 20-kilometer-per-hour wind reduces area coverage over a 4-kilometer-per-hour wind by more than 60 percent. Wind also creates a downwind hazard. Depending on the time of day and wind speed, nerve agents can cause nonfatal injuries 120 kilometers away. A high wind, at any time of day, can carry effective concentrations of nerve agents up to 75 kilometers. On a sunny day, with winds of under 10 kilometers per hour, the agent will travel no farther than 1 kilometer. At dawn, dusk, or on a heavily overcast day, the range will be 10 kilometers. The worst conditions are a calm night. Even with only a 4–5-kilometer-per-hour wind, the nerve agents will travel from 45–120 kilometers. Any troops in the path of these agents will be manning sensors, on guard duty, asleep, or driving. The damage caused by impaired vision, dizziness, and other nonfatal effects could be considerable, especially with drivers having accidents. Gases tend to flow along the contour of the ground, collecting in low areas. One bright young officer on a training exercise set off some tear-gas grenades on the high ground overlooking an "enemy" headquarters. As the cloud charged down the hill, the lieutenant and his troops advanced behind it to mop up. Altogether, the above climate factors decrease by more than 90 percent the area effectively covered by chemical agents. For example, in most cases a 155mm artillery chemical shell would spread a lethal dose (to 50 percent of unprotected troops) of nerve gas over a 13-meter radius from the shell burst. Winds faster than 38 kilometers per hour disperse the chemical so quickly that you have to be four meters from the shell burst to get a fatal dose. With a 28-kilometer-per-hour wind, it's only six meters. With a sunny day and a 4-kilometer-per-hour breeze, the distance is 7.5 meters. In subzero temperatures, this would go up to eight meters. The best conditions for chemicals are cold, windless evenings in terrain with porous soil and lush vegetation (northern Russia in the summer). The worst conditions are hot, windy daylight in an area with nonporous soil, little foliage, and lots of rain (the Persian Gulf coast during the rainy season). Persistent agents work best in winter, except for the fact that potential victims are bundled up. Mustard gas will last up to eight weeks in the winter, seven days during the summer, and only two days during a rainy period. VX, a liquid, persistent nerve agent, will last 16 weeks in winter, three weeks in summer, but only 12 hours in the rain.

Inhaled time to take effect is the shortest average time for the agents to take effect through inhalation, in minutes. This assumes a sufficient concentration. The quickest agents are those that work on the nervous or respiratory systems. Nerve gas is by far the fastest, at least in theory. If inhaled, its effect can be within seconds. Even exposure to nerve agents through the skin often takes effect in minutes. Blood gases act quickly to block the absorption of oxygen by the body, producing the equivalent of suffocation. Tear gases act upon the sensitive eye tissues, and to a lesser extent on the skin. Blister and mustard gases can be inhaled. In less lethal doses, which will be quite common, agents will take longer to have an effect. Normally, the gases will continue to diminish and dissipate, and their effects will not get worse.

Minimum dosage level is the relative amount of agent, in milligrams, that must be present in a cubic meter of atmosphere, during a one-minute period, to kill 50 percent of unprotected personnel. Multiply by 36 to get the actual lethal dose.

Skin contact time to take effect is the shortest average time for the agent to take effect through skin contact, in minutes. For mustard and blister gases, this is the time required to cause blindness. The eyes are the most sensitive external part of the body; mustard and blister gases attack the eyes first. The substance can enter the eyes if a soldier gets some of the agent on his hands and then rubs his eyes. Over 10 times more of the chemical agent is required to blister the skin. To inflict fatal casualties, 50 times as much is required.

Minimum dosage level is the minimum amount required to have the desired effect on 50 percent of unprotected personnel. A higher dosage is required for skin transmission than inhalation. The skin is designed to repel foreign substances; the lungs are constructed to absorb things quickly. A mask cannot provide sufficient protection because so many agents can enter through the skin. Many agents need not even be fatal in order to put a soldier out of action. Nonfatal doses of nerve gas, either inhaled or absorbed through the skin, have a very debilitating and demoralizing effect. Nonfatal doses of blister agents are equally unpleasant.

Can it be smelled? This is an important consideration. If the agent cannot be smelled, its presence will be announced either by scarce and sometimes unreliable "chemical warning instruments" or by troops becoming casualties. Gases that can be smelled can also often be seen. However, many of the more modern agents are odorless and invisible. This makes detection instruments all the more important. These devices usually detect agents in sublethal doses or even before they are concentrated enough to do much damage at all. This gives troops a chance to put on protective equipment or stay away from the contaminated areas.

Tons to cover sq. km indicates the tonnage of the chemical agents required to cover a square kilometer. The method of delivery is spraying the agent from aircraft. This is not only the most effective method of delivering chemical agents, but likely to be the most widely used one in the opening stages of a future war. Spraying is likely to be favored because of the emphasis on surprise and the use of aircraft to deliver chemicals. A typical fighter-bomber aircraft can spray four tons of GD over a six-kilometer frontage in less than a minute's flying time. One kilometer downwind, this six-kilometer wall of gas will cause 50 percent fatalities. Five kilometers downwind (in open terrain, with a light wind, etc.), unwarned but gas-trained and -equipped troops will likely suffer 20 percent fatalities and 70 percent nonfatal casualties. GD nerve gas is a vapor and travels with the wind. VX is a "drizzle" agent. Its large droplets will not travel far before hitting the ground and staying there. An aircraft laying down a line of VX two kilometers wide and 130 kilometers long will kill 50 percent of any unprepared troops entering this nerve-gas zone. Why bother with anything but nerve gas? The main problem is decontamination. Nerve agents are potent, persistent, and unable to tell friend from foe. Protective clothing and masks cause a significant loss of efficiency. For example, voice communication and vision are reduced 25–50 percent when masks are worn. When the temperature rises above 60 degrees, troops cannot be active for more than a few hours without risk of heat prostration. Prolonged wearing of full protective gear causes additional problems, as it is difficult to sleep, eat, or drink. The only way out of this mess is to decontaminate. Even leaving the contaminated area will do you no good, as you take the gas along. Decontamination of nerve agents means washing everything down with a lot of water, or a lot less of a special decontamination solution. Even when you use the special solution, 320 pounds of liquid are required to clean up one vehicle. Other methods, faster and using less liquid, are available but are not 100 percent effective. What will happen to troop morale and effectiveness if casualties are caused by chemical agents on previously "decontaminated" vehicles?

Strategic Weapons

Weapon is the designation. For former Soviet weapons (now Russian), the NATO designations are used. Often a missile is modified over the years, resulting in

Weapon	Missiles deployed	War-heads	Total warheads	CEP (meter)	Range (km)	Warhead yield (kt)	Year deployed
U.S. Totals	1,326		8,448				
Russia Totals	1,131		4,944				

United States

Land-based
Minuteman IIIB	500	3	1,500	220	12,800	335	1980
B-1B	91	8	728	90	14,000	200	1986
B-52H	57	8	456	90	12,000	200	1959
B-2A	20	8	160	90	10,000	200	1959
DF-31 (China)	6	3	18	300	12,000	90	1979
Peacekeeper	50	10	500	100	11,000	350	1986
DF-5 (China)	24	1	24	300	12,000	3,000	1981
Total	748		3,386				

Submarine-based
Poseidon C3	160	10	1,600	450	4,600	40	1971
MSBS M-4 (Fr)	32	6	192	600	4,000	150	1985
MSBS M-45 (Fr)	32	6	192	600	6,000	150	1985
Trident II D5 (UK)	56	8	448	120	12,000	400	1989
Trident C4	192	8	1,536	450	7,400	100	1979
JI-1 (China)	12	1	12	2,000	2,500	1,000	1984
JI-2 (China)	16	3	48	300	2,500	90	2002
Trident II D5	240	8	1,920	120	12,000	400	1989
Total	740		5,948				

Russia

Land-based
SS-19 Mod 3	140	6	840	300	10,000	550	1982
SS-18 Mod 4	180	10	1,800	250	11,000	500	1982
Tu-95	72	2	144	200	8,000	500	1955
Tu-160	15	4	60	200	7,000	0	1989
SS-25	360	1	360	300	10,000	700	1986
SS-27	24	1	24	200	10,500	550	1998
SS-24	36	10	360	250	10,000	100	1988
Total	827		3,588				

Submarine-based
SS-N-18	112	3	336	1,100	7,200	500	1978
SS-N-6			0	1,300	2,500	500	1974
SS-N-8	12	1	12	1,000	7,700	750	1973
SS-N-23	96	4	384	900	8,300	200	1985
SS-N-24 (SLCM)	24	1	24	200	2,400	200	1992
SS-N-20	60	10	600	1,000	9,000	100	1981
Total	304		1,356				

variants with very different capabilities. Weapons listed for bombers are gravity bombs; they are simply dropped. Other nations with known delivery systems are also listed.

Missiles deployed is the number of missiles ready for use in underground concrete silos, on board submarines and aircraft, or otherwise deployed for action.

Warheads is the number of warheads per missile.

CEP (Circular Error Probable) is the measure of a missile's accuracy. The CEP is measured in meters from the intended point of warhead impact. This circle represents the area into which 50 percent of the warheads with that CEP will fall. Farther out, the circle eventually covers an area in which more than 99 percent of the warheads will fall. The CEP represents a convenient midpoint for measurement. If you are attacking industrial or population targets, CEPs of 1,000 or 2,000 meters are no big deal. For example, over 30 warheads are thought to be targeted at the New York City metropolitan area. More than half will hit close enough to their targets. The rest of the warheads are going to do substantial unintended and unpredictable damage to suburban communities and the local fish population. When hitting hardened targets, like command centers and missile silos, accuracy and small CEPs become crucial. There is a limit to how small CEPs can go just using the missile-guidance system: a CEP of 150 meters for land-based missiles and 400 for submarine-launched missiles. To get smaller CEPs, you need some form of terminal guidance in the warhead, either radar or pattern recognition. Some American cruise missiles already have this capability. Finally, keep in mind that many CEP figures have to be taken with a grain of salt. It is often prudent to add a few hundred meters to CEPs.

Range is the maximum range of the missile. There is also a minimum range of up to a few hundred kilometers for any missile.

Warhead yield is the destructive power of nuclear weapons expressed in terms of kilotons (thousand tons) of conventional high-explosive TNT.

Year deployed is the year in which the missile was first available for use. A new type of missile is built for several years, and then its assembly line is taken over by a newer model. The older missiles stay in service for many years after the last one is built. Like any complex piece of equipment, a missile can be made to last forever by replacing worn parts. Although the missile is used only once, it is alive while sitting around waiting. The guidance system is always active whenever the missile is available for use. The electro-hydraulic systems that work the mechanical controls—fins, flaps, and air brakes—must be exercised periodically. This exercise will eventually fatigue them, as will guidance system wear

XM-93 Fox chemical monitoring system

out from constant use. The fuel, even if solid, deteriorates over time. The warhead components, especially the electronic ones, also degrade over time. Russian warheads have to be rebuilt every 10–15 years, while Western warheads are replaced every 10–20 years as improved components become available. The longer a missile sits around waiting, the lower its reliability and serviceability rates.

Other Factors

Nothing is perfect. A certain number of missiles will be out of service for repairs or maintenance. Once launched, some missiles and/or warheads will not perform as planned. Even the best-built and -maintained missiles suffer from this. For example: the Minuteman III could have 100 warheads available, but only 90 percent would be serviceable, and only 80 percent of the remainder would perform reliably, resulting in only 72 warheads reaching their targets. Russian and now Chinese missiles tend to have lower service rates and greater reliability problems.

Equivalent megatons (EMT) was a popular yardstick used during the Cold War. This compared the destructive effects of nuclear weapons on all targets except hardened ones, namely underground missile silos. The formula is the number of weapons times yield of each in megatons, to the two-thirds power. Thus, a 9-megaton weapon is equal to 4.34 EMT, a 1-megaton weapon is equal to 1 EMT, a 170-kiloton weapon is equal to .31 EMT, and a 40-kiloton weapon is equal to .12 EMT. EMT expresses the fact that larger explosions are less efficient than smaller ones. The effects of a 1-megaton weapon are as follows. If detonated as an airburst at 2,000 meters up, nearly every building within 7 kilometers of the explosion will be destroyed or damaged beyond repair. Virtually everyone within this area will be killed or severely injured, without hope of medical aid. How large an area is this 14-kilometer-diameter zone? Pick a ground zero, the point on the ground directly under the blast. Drive about 6.5 minutes in any direction at 40 MPH. Or walk for an hour and a half. That's 7 kilometers, or a total area of 154 square kilometers. Population densities go from 3,000–4,000 people in "sprawl"-type cities to over 100,000 (New York City) per square kilometer. A single EMT would put any area back into the Stone Age.

A popular item during the Cold War, when the huge American and Soviet ICBM arsenals made people think seriously about blasting enemy missiles in their silos, was the "K factor." This was the warhead's silo attack—ICBMs versus silos—value. To destroy an enemy missile silo, the attacking warhead must explode as closely as possible. The K factor is derived using this formula: K = weapons yield (to the two-thirds power) divided by CEP (to the second power). Accuracy is far more important than yield in this area. This was why accuracy (CEP) was such an important factor during the Cold War arms race. The objective was to build missiles that were able to disable a missile silo with 97 percent probability. Thus, a 100-psi (pounds per square inch) silo requires 20 K; 300 requires 45; 1,000 requires 108; 3,000 requires 200. In response to more accurate missiles, each side built more hardened silos. Hardening these silos to withstand greater explosive force was expensive. Building a 3,000-psi silo costs over $20 million. Just hardening a bare-bones 100-psi silo to 1,000 psi costs over $3 million. Unfortunately, it became cheaper to make attacking missiles more accurate, so the trend moved away from silos. Mobile land-based missiles were deployed by the Soviet Union but demobilized in the early 1990s. The United States placed more warhead power in its submarine-launched ICBMs.

Missile-Construction Techniques

The basic principles of ballistic-missile construction were developed and tested over 60 years ago. The first practical application was the German V-2 rocket, during World War II. Technology has become more refined, but not radically different. A rocket must attain speeds of 6,000–7,000 meters per second to escape Earth's gravity. This is achieved by stacking a series of rockets on top of each other. The first rocket, or "stage," comprises more than 75 percent of the total vehicle weight. Once in the upper atmosphere, this stage is dropped, and a second stage (15–20 percent of vehicle weight) puts the warhead into an orbit that will take it 10,000 kilometers or more to its target. The third stage is the unpowered warhead, typically less than 3 percent of vehicle weight. The warhead is equipped with a thermal shield to prevent burn-up on plunging through the Earth's atmosphere at speeds in excess of 13,000 meters per second.

The first rocket motors used liquid fuel. This was a reliability nightmare; plus, you had to go through a several-hour fueling process just prior to launch. The big breakthrough was solid-fuel rockets. The United States was the first to develop and perfect these items.

Meanwhile, the Soviet Union came up with a less reliable and more manageable low-tech approach with storable liquid fuel. Many Soviet (now Russian) rockets still use storable liquid fuel. The liquid is not as stable as solid fuel, and there's still all that damn plumbing. Solid fuel has additional benefits: smaller rockets and more stages.

The U.S. approach also developed smaller warheads, although 15–20 percent heavier in relation to total missile weight than liquid-fuel rockets.

Along with more efficient warheads and guidance systems, the United States was able to build missiles one-fifth the weight of their Soviet counterparts, but with equal range, greater accuracy, and equivalent destructive power. No less critical was the lower cost of these solid-fuel systems. Higher manufacturing and maintenance costs led the Soviets to spend three times as much per missile. Their earliest missiles for submarines (SS-N-4 and SS-N-5) were liquid-fueled. Their first attempt at solid fuel for land-based missiles was the SS-13, which they never were able to get working right. They chopped it down to a two-stage, shorter-range system, the SS-20. Everyone still uses liquid-fuel rockets, as they are still the best method for lifting very heavy loads into space. For this reason, the large number of oversize, liquid-fuel Soviet rockets used for strategic combat gave them an additional source of satellite lift.

Aircraft, Tactical Missiles, and Artillery

At the end of the Cold War, Russia and the United States had thousands of artillery pieces that could fire nuclear shells. These have all since been retired, along with most short-range nuclear missiles. The principal means of delivering nuclear and chemical weapons is now either aircraft or short-range missiles. These missiles are also called Theater Ballistic Missiles. There are actually dozens of different types. But most of them are variations on missiles like the Scud and tend to have a range of about 500 kilometers. Below are the longer-range missiles, the ones most often used to deliver nuclear weapons.

Theater Ballistic Missiles

These are the missiles that smaller nations, with or without nuclear weapons, use to threaten not just their neighbors, but their entire region. The main source of the missile technology was Russia. Actually, you can blame it on the Germans. After World War II, the Russians grabbed a bunch of German rocket scientists, some V-2 rockets, and the result was their extensive missile program. But one of their early products, the Scud, was exported in large numbers. The Scud was literally the "son of V-2" and was simple enough that you could tinker with it and make modifications. This was how the Chinese and North Koreans got into the missile-development business. Iran and Iraq also modified Scuds (usually something as simple as making the missile longer, so it could carry more fuel and go farther) during their 1980s war.

Conceptually, there's nothing terribly complicated about building long-range missiles. What is difficult is the precise engineering required for the guidance system and tricky things like multiple stages. You also have to spend a lot of time and effort figuring out how to build larger rocket engines and the rugged controls that take instructions from the guidance system. Iran and Pakistan have skipped ahead in the missile race by purchasing No Dong missiles (and technical assistance on how to build them) from North Korea. China has also sold missile technology to Iran and North Korea. India got help from Russia, although India's biggest asset is a larger industrial base and a lot of skilled scientists and engineers.

Missile	Country	Range (km)	In use
DF-3A	China	3,000	80
DF-3A	Saudi Arabia	2,500	50
DF-21	China	1,800	60
DF-4	China	4,700	25
No Dong	North Korea	1,200	12
Taepo Dong 1	North Korea	2,000	2
Agni II	India	1,250	0
Jericho 2	Israel	1,200	10
Ghauri	Pakistan	1,200	2
Shahab 3	Iran	1,200	3

To build really long-range missiles, you must master the technology for multiple stages. Most of the above missiles have two stages. Once you get to three stages, you can launch satellites or intercontinental missiles. Indeed, several nations with ICBM capability "test" their missiles by launching satellites. Herein lies the problem with ICBMs: any nations with sufficient money and determination can produce them. We see this with North Korea and India. Or you can buy the technology, as did Pakistan, Iran, and Saudi Arabia (which only uses conventional warheads). But a nuclear ballistic missile is still more complicated, requiring a lot of specialized engineering to get the nuke to work after being launched and hurtled through the higher reaches of the atmosphere to its target. This technology is not something you can get off the shelf. It is generally highly classified. This is good, for it means it takes a lot of time and effort for nations like North Korea or Iran to reinvent a lot of this stuff. But this is also why most nations get upset when countries like China sell ICBM technology to potentially troublesome states.

Many nations that build nuclear weapons arrange to deliver them by aircraft. Even nations with ICBMs still retain the capability to drop nuclear bombs (or launch short-range missiles) from aircraft. Most fighter aircraft can carry at least a ton of bombs, and most newly developed nuclear weapons can be engineered down to that weight pretty quickly. But aircraft can be shot down; missiles cannot. If you can build reliable long-range missiles to deliver your nuclear weapons, your neighbors will notice. And probably do whatever it takes to develop their own nuclear-tipped missiles.

21

Operations Other
Than War (OOTW)

The military has long recognized a gray area between peace and war. In this region exist things like:

Showing the flag. This is mainly a Navy and Air Force thing. Want to remind someone that America has military power that might be used if things got nasty? Send ships and aircraft to the vicinity of the nation in need of a reminder.

Gunboat diplomacy. This is showing the flag with a bang. A century ago, it meant having a battleship move close to a port city belonging to someone who has done us wrong, and having the battleship fire some shells into a few government buildings or military installations. Today we let cruise missiles do the same thing. A variation on this is the constant combat air patrols over Iraq. This is not popular with the pilots, as it is pretty boring and repetitive duty.

Training and advising foreign troops. This is good way to improve the military power of an ally, or someone you want to be your friend.

Dealing with guerrilla warfare. This goes beyond training and advising foreign troops and includes supplying additional equipment and weapons and some U.S. troops to operate the stuff. This is how we got into the Vietnam War, but that was the exception.

Relief operations. The military has a lot of ships, air transports, helicopters, and young guys ready to go off quickly to distant places to do stuff. It's also great public relations to have U.S. troops going in to help victims of some natural or man-made disaster. This is expected within the United States, and appreciated overseas.

Fighting terrorists. The war on terrorism and the war in Afghanistan is what this is all about. But the troops also contribute information-collecting equipment (UAVs, aircraft, satellites), transportation, and security for the full-time anti-terrorism troops (police, FBI, CIA, diplomats).

Peacekeeping operations. This is sending troops to an unruly area to encourage the locals to keep cool.

Assisting police operations (drugs and border control). Whenever the police (including the Coast Guard, who actually are sea-going cops in peacetime) are overwhelmed, the troops are called out to help.

Military support of civil authorities. Helping with riot control, labor disputes that imperil public safety (police, postal workers, firemen, etc. on strike), and whatever else requires a lot of organized and disciplined people.

All of these chores have existed for centuries. But toward the end of the twentieth century, the military noticed that·they were spending a lot of time on operations other than war (OOTW), and, you know, maybe it would be a good idea to study the matter some more and find ways to be better prepared for this sort of thing.

With the end of the Cold War, OOTW became even more important, as it was now less likely that the troops would be involved in a major war. Not all the troops were enthusiastic about OOTW. But many soldiers wanted to spend their time getting ready for a real war, where lots of training can be the difference between surviving combat or not. But most troops didn't care, for the majority of people in uniform would be doing the same thing in a shooting war or an OOTW. Indeed, only a small percentage of the soldiers, namely the ones in combat units, were on the short end of this OOTW deal. In the American Army, combat troops comprise less than 10 percent of the force. These guys (they are mostly guys) are the ones who will have to stop their combat training so they can go man roadblocks, deal with unruly foreign civilians, or escort relief supplies through bandit country. Actually, that last one has some appeal, for there could be a firefight or two. What really burns the combat guys is that they get the worst jobs in the OOTW department. Everyone else—the supply folks, intel pukes, pilots, and technicians—will be doing what they were trained to do. Only the grunts get screwed. But then, the grunts are kind of used to that.

Using the combat troops for OOTW does indeed decrease their readiness for combat duty. Typically, a combat unit assigned to a six-month peacekeeping stint will spend six months training for the quite different peacekeeping duties. After they come back from the peacekeeping job, they will have another six months of training before they are ready for combat once more. So each tour of peacekeeping takes a combat unit out of "ready for combat" status for 18 months.

There are two proposed solutions for this. One is to have special peacekeeping units. These would be trained and equipped for nothing but that duty. This is impractical because such units would spend most of their time overseas, separated from their families and doing a noxious job. The other solution, to use more reserve troops, is being used more often. But this is not popular with the reservists, who get pulled away from their civilian jobs for a year at a time. Eventually, this makes it harder to get people to join the reserve units.

The other OOTW chores are less of a problem, for they are of shorter duration and are often similar to a unit's regular combat duties.

What Causes Peacekeeping Situations

The causes of OOTW are many, but one of the more prominent ones these days is religious conflict. Most of these spats are between Christians and Muslims. And this unpleasantness is best described as a worldwide Green Line.

During the Lebanese civil war of 1975–90, Christians and Muslims fought bitterly over political, cultural, and ultimately religious differences. The capital, Beirut, was divided into Christian and Muslim sections by the Green Line. The name came from the fact that in this rubble-filled no-man's-land, only grass and weeds survived. There have been a lot more green lines since then. Few realized it at the time, but this war was but the first of many between Christians and Muslims in the twentieth and twenty-first centuries.

Many of the earliest Muslim converts were Christians. And many of the peoples Muslim armies unsuccessfully sought to conquer were Christian. But as a political force, Islam was in decline for several centuries until the 1970s. Then things changed and continue to change. Islam was again on the march, and few have noticed how many places it was turning into religious war with Christians and other non-Muslims.

In Asia we have a green line between India and Pakistan. Inside India, many Muslim communities remain, and feelings aren't always neighborly. Indonesia and the Philippines suffer growing strife between Muslims and non-Muslims. Malaysia has more fanatical Muslims persecuting more laid-back ones. China has a large Muslim community that generates an increasing amount of violence. Russia and America have formed a curious partnership to deal with Islamic-based terrorism coming out of Afghanistan. And in Chechnya, Russia faces Islamic-inspired violence all alone.

Africa has a rather dusty green line south of the semiarid Sahel region. Many African nations are split by increasingly sensitive religious differences. The Muslims are in the north, Christians and animists in the south. Nigeria, Chad, and Sudan are among the more violent hot spots at the moment. Although when the Muslim Somalis stop fighting each other, they will return to raiding their Christian and animist neighbors to the south.

The Middle East still contains many non-Muslims. None have their own country, except for Israel. But Egypt contains five million Copts, native Christians who did not convert to Islam. Similar small Christian communities exist throughout the Middle East, and growing hostility from Muslim neighbors causes many to migrate, or get killed. Muslims have also turned their righteous wrath on dissident Muslim sects. The Druzes and Alawites are considered by many Muslims as pagans pretending to be Muslims. Similarly, the Shiites of Iran and neighboring areas are considered less orthodox not just for their admitted differences, but because many adherents openly practice customs of the pre-Islamic Zoroastrian religion. These differences are less frequently overlooked today. To survive, the many Druzes have allied themselves with Israel, and most of the current Syrian leadership comprises Alawites.

Even Europe has a green line. The Muslims in the Balkans (Albanians and Bosnians) have been a constant source of strife for the last decade. Muslim migrants in Europe face even more persecution because of all those green lines, and this makes it easier for radical groups to recruit and carry out their crusade against Christians.

But the green lines are about more than religion. A lot of it is politics. One of the reasons Islam ran out of steam centuries ago was that the Muslim areas never embraced democracy. Until the twentieth century, most Muslims lived in colonies or totalitarian kingdoms. The colonies are gone, but democracy has had a hard time taking hold. The dictatorships are still there. And the people are restless. Radical Islam arose as an alternative to all the other forms of government that never seemed to work. In theory, establishing "Islamic republics" would solve all problems. People could vote, but only Muslims in good standing could be candidates for office. A committee of Muslim holy men would have veto power over political decisions. Islamic law would be used. It was simple, and it makes sense to a lot of Muslims in nations ruled by thugs and thieves.

Islamic republics don't seem to work. The only one that has been established (not counting others that say they are, but aren't) is in Iran. The major problems were twofold. First, the radicals had too much power. Second, radical religious types are no fun, and you can't argue with them because they are on a mission from God. Most people tire of this in short order. To speed this disillusionment, many of the once poor and now powerful religious leaders became corrupt. This eventually sends your popularity ratings straight to hell.

It will take a generation or so for everyone in the Muslim world to figure out where all this is going. This is already happening in Iran, where moderates are getting stronger every day and everyone is trying to avoid a civil war. While the radicals are a minority, they are a determined bunch.

Radicals throughout the Muslim world continue to take advantage of dissatisfaction among the people and recruit terrorists and supporters. To help this process along, they invoke the ancient grudges popular among many Muslims. Most of these legends involve Christians beating on Muslims. To most radicals, it makes sense to get people agitated at far-away foreigners rather than some strongman nearby.

Most radicals lack the skills, money, or ability to carry their struggle to far-off places. So most of the agitation takes place among Muslim populations. Any violent attitudes generated are easily directed at available non-Muslims. Thus we have all those green lines. But the more violence you have along those green lines, the more really fanatical fighters are developed. These are the people who are willing to travel to foreign lands and deal with nonbelievers, and kill them for the cause. We call it terrorism; the fanatics call it doing what has to be done. All because of religious wars in far-off places. When it comes to terrorism, the world is a very small place.

All this religious antagonism has spawned a lot of terrorism. And the terrorists are often found in unruly places. U.S. troops have already spent a lot of time chasing down terrorists as part of peacekeeping operations in the Balkans. And then there was Afghanistan. There's a lot more OOTW opportunities along the green line.

Why Peacekeeping Is Popular, and Unpopular, with the Troops

Peacekeeping is an increasingly popular use for American troops. Unlike a similar enthusiasm early in the twentieth century, today's version is destroying America's military power. During the first three decades of the twentieth century, the U.S. Marines were sent into disorderly foreign nations so frequently that this became their main job. In the late twentieth century, intervention became fashionable again. The numbers tell the tale. From 1956 to 1992, U.S. troops were sent into foreign nations 51 times. About 1.4 interventions a year. Since 1992, we have also gone in 51 times, about 6.5 times a year. That's a nearly fivefold increase. A third of American armed forces are currently tied up supporting various peacekeeping missions, even more if you include those in the half-century-old Korean "police action." But so often are U.S. troops called on, usually at the behest of the United Nations, that you now have the American Army referred to as "UN troops."

But this is not quite true. Most of the real UN peacekeeping troops are from anywhere but the United States. Less affluent nations are eager to offer troops for

UN service, as the UN pays these soldiers more than they make in their own countries. Contributing troops to peacekeeping operations looks good and pays well. The UN shakes down the wealthier nations to provide the money. Most American peacekeepers are tied up in NATO-sponsored operations in the Balkans. U.S. troops are also stationed, for one reason or another, in 55 nations.

Since the end of the Cold War in 1990, America's armed forces have faced more changes than at any other time in its history: radically new weapons; a new, and uncertain, array of potential foes; new demands for peacekeeping missions; worst of all, a lack of strong leadership. During the 1990s, America spent over $25 billion on peacekeeping. That was about 1 percent of the defense budget, but it was also a time when the armed forces were being reduced by a third. There was a lot of bureaucratic pushing and shoving over which projects would get cut. Politicians didn't want bases closed, as that annoyed local voters. It was the same with expensive weapons projects, for the contracts were spread around to as many congressional districts as possible. Even within the armed forces, there were many officers who saw these Cold War–era projects as still important, important enough to push just about anything else out of the way. This ongoing budget brawl has had some predictable effects. Training got cut. There was less money for keeping equipment maintained and up-to-date. Promotions slowed down. People got scared and insecure. The more able officers began to bail out as careerism and caution got in the way of innovation and bold leadership. No one wants to take any chances when the budget is shrinking and no one is sure of what, or who, will get cut next. Right after the Berlin Wall came down in 1989, many of the fast-track officers were talking about their resumes and what kind of opportunities there were outside the military. The brass began to notice the lower quality of leadership. This became more of an issue once Bill Clinton became president and the military was ordered to become more sensitive to cultural, gender, and sexual differences. If that wasn't bad enough, the policy of "zero tolerance" came along with all the other mandates. So supervision was increased. Avoiding any political incorrectness became a higher priority. NCOs, who for centuries had been left to manage the troops, now increasingly found themselves being closely supervised by an officer. Colonels and generals kept a close eye on captains and lieutenants. CYA (cover your ass), not boldness and initiative, were now the guiding rule for a successful military career.

With lower-quality leaders, you had lower-quality troops. And the word soon got out that the armed forces were not what they once were, and it became harder to get any troops at all. This became an important issue as peacekeeping became the major mission. While fighting a war requires a lot of skill, peacekeeping requires more. This soon became apparent, as did the post–Gulf War demand that there be no casualties. When things heated up in Somalia during 1994, there were a dozen American generals in the area, every one of them anxious to avoid any "problems." Eighteen American soldiers got killed anyway, but this did not dampen politicians' enthusiasm for peacekeeping, it just made everyone more determined to do it without getting any Americans killed. We can see how this works in the Balkans. American troops spend about 60 percent of their time peacekeeping, and 40 percent providing security for themselves. But the British troops spend only 14 percent of their time in self-defense and get a lot more done in the peacekeeping department. American troops, much to their chagrin, are increasingly seen as a bunch of wussies by the other NATO contingents they work with (especially the Russians). Good at giving impressive briefings and building themselves luxurious accommodations, but of dubious worth when the chips are down.

Ninety years ago the U.S. Marines took another approach to peacekeeping. Officers, NCOs, and men were told to keep the peace, and they did. There was no micromanagement, nor fear of taking losses if that was required to do the job. Actually, the Marines are still that way. This makes politicians leery of using Marines in peacekeeping operations. "Too aggressive" is the excuse most often given. Then again, there may be something to all that. Decades of Marine peacekeeping in Central America and the Caribbean did keep things quiet but didn't change any of the nations involved. The current American policy is to pull out if things get too hot. Hard to do that with Marines, as they will quell any unrest quicker than the folks back in Washington can issue a "cease and desist" order.

Many Army officers, feeling themselves in a no-win situation, have suggested that brigades of specially trained military police be organized just for peacekeeping missions. But to do that would admit that the concept of using combat troops for peacekeeping is a mistake. That is politically unacceptable. Illusions are much easier to sell. Welcome to the twenty-first century.

It Gets Ugly, and Then They Leave

One of the many military reforms of the 1990s was the quadrennial review. Once every four years, the Pentagon has to come right out and say what it is preparing to do, and how it plans to do it. The president and Congress can modify these plans, but once all the arguing dies down, everyone knows what the troops will be ready to do over the next four years. Since the mid-1990s, the military has been ready, on paper, to fight two wars (Korea and the Persian Gulf, most likely) at once and win. This is a fantasy, of course, but one that must be maintained. The entire defense budget is held together by the many "requirements" for the two-war doctrine. Meanwhile, everyone is scrambling to reorganize for the wars that are happening right now: that is, peacekeeping and policing. The forces, training, and leadership needed for the "two wars" and the peacekeeping are very different. So the question is, Can the armed forces be in two places at once? Can the weapons and training needed for wars be used for peacekeeping? Ask the Pentagon about this and you get a well-crafted mutter. That's another way of saying, "no, but we'd rather not dwell on it." It gets pretty ugly.

Peacekeeping operations are expensive. About a third of our forces are currently tied up in various police missions. Much of the money for peace-keeping comes out of the training budget. But with all this peacekeeping, there's not much time to train anyway. The troops hate this sort of thing. All their training is directed toward breaking things and killing people. The troops are taught to shoot first and to keep shooting until the enemy succumbs. Peacekeeping is a cross between permanent guard duty and taking abuse from ungrateful foreigners. In peacetime, guard duty is often given out as a punish-ment. But an even more severe punishment is sending combat troops to do riot control. Having rocks thrown at you while you stand there with an unloaded weapon does a real number on morale. It hasn't taken long for the bad actors to realize that they can throw rocks and bottles at our troops without getting fired on. In response to this abuse, the Pentagon is passing out "nonlethal weapons" (rubber bullets, tear gas, sticky foam, dazzler lights, and the like) so that our lads have a sporting chance. But the soldiers did not enlist to play games with foul-tempered foreigners, but to kill them, take the fight out of them, and go home. Endless peacekeeping duty feels like punishment, which it often is. As a result, the volunteer armed forces are short of people. It's actually worse than that, for to keep numbers from falling through the basement, recruiting, train-ing, and discipline standards have been lowered.

But it gets worse. American peacekeepers in the Balkans are, in effect, under house arrest. They can go outside their compound only when on duty, usually guard duty or patrolling (which is basically guard duty where you get to move around a bit more). From time to time they have to confront rioters, people who throw things at them. Or go on a raid to find illegal weapons, which often ends up like a mini-riot. Back in their well-appointed barracks (no expense was spared to build permanent housing for what was supposed to be a temporary assignment), you can't get a drink, and celibacy, while not manda-tory, is certainly encouraged.

The Air Force situation is the same, but somewhat different. Pilots like the fact that they are getting a lot of flying time, but most of it is flying in circles. Air patrols over the Balkans and Iraq get old fast. The pilots and their ground crews don't live under restrictions quite as bad as the GIs, but they do spend a lot of time away from home. Too much time, according to the many Air Force personnel departing the service. The Navy and the Marines are largely doing what they would do in wartime, steaming around far-off hostile shores. But you don't take your family with you on these six-month deployments, and you don't get much shore leave, either. Sailors with technical skills are finding out that they can quit the Navy, get higher pay, go home each night, and even afford to buy their own boat if they still yearn for a little salt water from time to time. But not six months at a time off the coast of China, Arabia, or the Balkans.

Rules of Engagement

Peacetime soldiering is much less tolerant of mistakes than that of wartime. This fear of error has produced the justly maligned, feared, and ever-expanding "Rules of Engagement." Or ROE for short. Now, ROEs are not unknown in wartime, but there they are meant as general guidelines that the troops can modify as the situation dictates. It's quite different in peacetime. Strict adherence to peacetime ROEs have also been quite fatal for the troops involved.

The main purpose of peacetime ROEs is to avoid any diplomatically embarrassing incidents. Since most peacetime soldiering involves some sort of peacekeeping, the ROEs are set up to prevent the troops from harming local civilians, even if it's a matter of self-defense. This became an issue when a Marine barracks was blown up in Beirut in 1983 and nearly 250 Marines were killed. This was the result of ROEs that violated seven standard security procedures all units in a combat zone are supposed to use. Had the Marines followed their own security rules, the tragedy would almost certainly have been avoided. Consider what was ignored. First, the troops were all living in one location. Standard procedure is to disperse people as much as possible when in a combat zone. There was also no inner security in the form of a truck-proof barrier. Nor were the inner-zone guards allowed to load their weapons. In addition, there was no outer-zone security; the outer-zone posts were manned by Lebanese troops, with no Marines present even as "observers." Moreover, there was no long-range monitoring of the outer zone by troops with binoculars. And intelligence processing was deficient, for information on the planned truck bombing was available but had not been passed on to the Marines. Finally, the commander of the Marines was at the end of a long and complex chain of command. It was not entirely clear who was in charge. Actually, the State Department was calling the shots. Which was ironic, as before World War II, the Marines were sent into so many nations for diplomatic reasons that they were called "State Department troops." But those were different times. Mass media now magnifies, and often distorts, any violent incidents that involve U.S. troops overseas. Armchair generals and eager pundits looking for a newsworthy angle are quick to jump on "trigger happy" American soldiers. Beirut in the 1980s was a wild place, with numerous heavily armed militias shooting at one another and anyone else that got in their way. Left to their own devices, the Marines would have had little trouble defending themselves. But with most of their self-defense tactics forbidden by the ROE, the terrorists got in.

Despite all the money being thrown at the military in the 1980s, nothing was learned from the Beirut tragedy. This became obvious to the military, if not to the media, when American troops poured into Saudi Arabia in 1990. Many noncombat units had overlooked weapons training, even those outfits that could expect to run into armed Iraqis during a fluid desert battle. So as units were ordered to the Middle East, remedial weapons training was ordered, lest there be the risk of embarrassing news stories about untrained U.S. troops. However, once the troops got to Saudi Arabia, they found that while they had weapons, the ammunition was locked up and tightly guarded, often in out-of-the-way storage areas. In fact, many of the first U.S. troops on the scene did not have any ammunition for their rifles. When they finally did, they were told not to break the seals on the ammo boxes unless orders came from on high. All this obsession with keeping the troops away from live ammunition had two effects. First, it hurt morale. The troops considered themselves well-trained professionals, yet here they were being treated as a bunch of irresponsible louts. Second, there were several alerts that Iraqi commandos were operating in the area. It was a good thing the Iraqis never tried anything so bold, for they would have found most U.S. troops (except for a few armed guards, who could not actually load their weapons without orders) armed but without ready access to ammunition.

Even during combat, troops were often ordered to unload all weapons, with officers going around to verify that the unit was "clean." An accident could prevent someone from getting promoted to general. So precautions had to be taken. Only when in close proximity with the enemy were the troops allowed to proceed with loaded weapons. Of course, the enemy doesn't always cooperate and sometimes shows up when you don't expect him. We were lucky this didn't happen in the Gulf War.

In the Balkans, U.S. troops are confined to their bases when not on duty. No alcohol or off-duty contact with locals is allowed. American soldiers are ridiculed by other peacekeeping troops because of these "safety measures" and the larger proportion of time U.S. troops spend on self-defense. These ROEs were not only making American peacekeepers less effective but depressing their morale and familiarity with the locals, as well.

The ROEs showed up again when the U.S. destroyer *Cole* steamed into the Yemeni harbor of Aden to refuel. Armed guards were posted around the ship in case any terrorists showed up. But their rifles were unloaded, and the guards were ordered not to load and fire unless fired on first. Very sporting, unless you happen to be the sailor trying to load your weapon while being fired on.

Learning from experience, the ROEs were loosened up quite a bit during the Afghanistan war. But that was a real war, not just peacekeeping. When the troops shift from fighting to peacekeeping, you can expect the ROEs to be there, as ugly and dangerous as ever.

The Rogues' Gallery

But terrorists are not the most common problem troops encounter during OOTW operations. The troops are far more likely to run into warlords, bandits, gangsters, and rebels.

Right now, there are several dozen nations suffering through civil wars, rebellions, and general unrest. There is much enthusiasm for sending in peacekeeping troops and police to calm things down. What is forgotten is that we are not dealing with wars, in most cases, but heavily armed gangsters. Oh, you could say that most wars are about money or real estate. Japan wanted China and Germany wanted *Lebensraum* ("living room") in World War II. But the current crop of patriotic mobsters are rather more crass than Tojo or Hitler. Moreover, many of the current wars are taking place in areas where there was never much government (central or otherwise) in the generally accepted sense. Africa is torn apart by tribal loyalties, which count for more than national unity when the chips are down. Places like the Balkans and Chechnya have historically been finely divided into a patchwork of clans, causes, and criminal gangs who never got along well with one another.

Entering the twenty-first century, we still have a lot of medieval politics being practiced in many parts of the world. Mostly, there are warlords. This is nothing more than an enterprising individual who has managed to raise an army of his own. It doesn't have to be a really big army, just large enough to defeat, or frighten away, anyone else's army in the area. Thus equipped, the warlord goes into business, for a warlord is essentially a businessman who turns heavily armed muscle into money. If you have the only army in the neighborhood, your word is law and your needs are promptly attended to. It's no wonder so many people want to become warlords. This technique is thousands of years old, and it still works. Modern warlords are clever fellows and, like their ancient predecessors, dream up new scams to suit current conditions. They now know how to work the media, humanitarian aid organizations, clueless peacekeepers, and whatever passes for central government in their part of the world. Warlords often have other warlords as competition, and this can produce a Wild West atmosphere. Somalia, Afghanistan, and Chechnya are current examples of warlords at work. Afghanistan has lived with warlords for thousands of years. Same situation in Somalia, except there is no one likely to get the warlords organized and bring peace to the land. Chechnya has the Russian army trying to crush the warlords. The Russians have done this before over the past two centuries. But the warlords always come back, eventually.

Even if you manage to disband the warlord armies, you find that former "soldiers" were often little more than bandits and gangsters. Warlords can't be too choosy when putting their army together. The ranks are filled with whatever riffraff can be found and controlled with the promise of loot, fear, and freedom from prosecution. Many national armies use the same recruiting practices. After the Soviet Union fell, it was discovered that the Soviet secret police (KGB) used criminal gangs for dirty work. With the KGB gone, the "Russian mafia" flourished, now that they didn't have the KGB to provide some degree of control. Other national armies are little more than gangsters pretending to be soldiers. It's also quite common for rebel organizations to turn into criminal gangs after the local despot or foreign invaders are gone. Thus, the Italian mafia had its origins in a patriotic movement fighting French (and other) invaders of Sicily and southern Italy. The same thing happened to the Irish Republican Army, which, like many rebel groups, used robbery, extortion, and other scams to finance their rebellion. South American and Asian rebel movements are fond of kidnapping these days.

So what is a peacekeeper to do when dealing with rebels whose regular gig is drug smuggling, or opposition political parties whose idea of fundraising is extortion and prostitution? How do you settle a civil war when the primary beef is who gets to control the diamond mines? Thus far, the attitude has been to downplay the criminal element and make whatever deals can be made to quiet things down so the peacekeepers can depart with their reputations intact. That rarely works, as peacekeepers worldwide are discovering the hard way. The UN has tried to deal with this angle by bringing in policemen. But effective policing depends on knowing the people you are policing. This is hard to do if you don't speak the language. And the UN has had a hard time getting cops from member nations for duty in troubled areas. Moreover, many nations are reluctant to send their best policemen on what many consider a fool's errand. So an inadequate number of second-rate cops are sent to police people who speak a different language, have different customs, and have more firepower than anything the foreign constable ever had to face back home.

Another solution is to disband the corrupt local cops (assuming there are any local police left at all) and train a new force in kinder, gentler, and more effective policing methods. This has proven difficult. War-torn areas usually have a tradition of corrupt policemen that is hard to stamp out. The new recruits often forget their training once they hit the streets. If anything, they learn how to play the game of pretending to be straight while shaking down everyone in sight. New cops don't mean clean cops.

What has worked in the past, but is not as acceptable today, is the old colonial method. Basically, you take over the local government completely. You bring in your own people for long tours of duty (5–10 years or more) so they can learn the local language and customs. The outsiders run things and carefully groom junior civil servants and police and never let them slip back into the bad old ways. After a generation or so of this, you have cleaned things up and can go home. It's expensive as hell, though, and one reason the European countries eventually wised up and dumped their colonies. But it works, if you can afford it.

But there are some things even the cops have a hard time dealing with. We're talking about kids with guns. Lots of kids with really big and nasty guns.

NGOs (nongovernmental organizations) have rediscovered the ancient practice of children in armies. The NGOs have started a campaign to expose this despicable practice and put a stop to it. The UN passed a resolution in 2000 forbidding anyone under 18 from serving in the military. So far, 79 nations have signed the treaty, but only six have ratified it. The guesstimate of 300,000 children serving with armies is, for once, probably low. For a number of reasons, both historical and technical, the head count for kids in armies is probably higher now than it has ever been in the past. And children serving with armies has a long, long past.

For thousands of years, kids went off to war. The younger ones as servants, to help around the camp. The older ones, as they got bigger, worked their way into the fighting line. About all that anyone in Western nations knows of this is the medieval tradition of children serving as pages and squires, and ultimately becoming knights. That was for the children of the nobility. Commoner kids also had opportunities to become professional warriors if they survived to adolescence and avoided death from the ill treatment they faced while living with callous soldiers and the rigors of living rough while the army was on campaign.

The twentieth century changed all that. With smaller rifles and automatic weapons, younger kids could be armed and sent off to fight at an earlier age. As in the past, many young boys were fascinated with weapons and violence. "Running off to join the army" was around long before "running off to join the circus." There has never been a shortage of volunteers. Starting in the 1940s, kid-size military weapons (the Russian SKS rifles and 9mm machine pistols) began to appear in large quantities. After World War II, the Russian AK-47 showed up and became the weapon of choice for child soldiers everywhere. With the end of the Cold War, and the collapse of Communist governments, millions of AK-47s suddenly appeared on world markets. At first, the AK-47s were so cheap that they were practically given away ("buy a rocket launcher and we'll throw in a free AK-47 . . ."). Whereas in the past, kids had to make themselves useful, and show they had a minimum of smarts and initiative, before getting a weapon, the flood of AK-47s made it possible to arm the children much earlier in their military career (within hours or days, rather than weeks or months). The hordes of adolescents wielding AK-47s gave new meaning to the term "wild child." And these kiddie gunsels are more dangerous than the adults. Teenagers are difficult to discipline under any conditions. But when the young man has an automatic weapon, youthful petulance takes on a new meaning.

Until lighter-weight weapons came along, the kids in the military were lightly armed (maybe with a knife) and generally responsive to a smack upside the head. Once they got their guns, discipline became more harsh. One vivid example of this showed up in the 1963 movie *Mondo Cane* ("It's a Dog's World"). This Italian "shockumentary" showed odd behavior from all parts of the world. It was all real; nothing was staged. In one scene, filmed in the camp of some African guerrillas, a 10-year-old kid is saying something to an adult that is apparently not appreciated. The adult pulls out a pistol and shoots the kid in the chest. The body flies back into the bush; all that can be seen is the kid's shoes. A lesson, no doubt, to the other kids in the camp to show some respect to their elders.

In better-organized armies, children served as drummer boys until about a century ago. In some navies, kids can still serve as cabin boys, a tradition that goes back many centuries. When children like these are serving in an organized military unit, they have a degree of protection. At least they cannot be executed out of hand. The UN got into a snit with the United States and Britain, which have long allowed 17-year-olds (and even younger boys in Britain) to join up with parental permission. The UN didn't make much progress against the long-standing recruiting practices of America and Britain. But the real target was guerrillas and irregulars who are waging war in a medieval fashion. That means these paramilitary units are living off the land. This has always meant stealing people as well as food and valuables. But guerrilla movements have always appealed to kids, mainly because of the ideological and revenge aspects. Guerrillas know their attacks on the government will usually bring retaliation against the local civilians. Every time a father is killed by the soldiers, the older sons (and sometimes the daughters) feel compelled to seek revenge. In many parts of the world, the "blood feud" tradition is strong, and there are few impediments to a kid joining the local guerrillas to avenge his kin. In these circumstances it's almost impossible for a fourteen-year-old not to volunteer. The UN/NGO campaign plays this down, if they play it at all. Instead, the incidents of guerrillas forcibly conscripting kids for military service is put out front. This may make for better PR, but ignoring local customs makes eliminating underage soldiering a lot more difficult.

Even if the guerrillas and bandits (sometimes it's difficult to tell the difference) were convinced to stop taking kids, it's much more difficult to stop the kids from joining. Revenge, adventure, altruism, and the thrill of wielding the power that comes from holding a gun will bring in the underage recruits for a long time to come. And peacekeepers are going to have to deal with it.

Tribal Tribulations

It's bad enough when you have kids with guns out there. But you also have tribes of kids with guns. It's not considered politically correct to talk about tribes anymore. Instead these distinct cultural organizations are referred to as "ethnic groups" (which they often are) or "clans" (which are subsections of tribes). But much of the world's populations still owe their primary allegiance to tribal organizations. Africa, South America, and parts of Asia are largely tribal areas. Europe still has a few. But the Scots clans are largely just social organizations, although in Eastern Europe you can still find functioning clans.

Over the past few thousand years, tribes evolved (by more powerful tribes conquering weaker ones) into kingdoms, and then, with the addition of robust economies and a lot of bureaucrats, nations. So you tend to find tribes in less affluent parts of the world. The majority of our planet's population is poor. But a third of the world's population is in China and India, two places where the strong tribes long ago conquered all the weaker ones. Africa, Southeast Asia, and the Pacific islands still have a lot of unconquered tribes.

Tribes tend to fight a lot. Most tribes are agrarian, and there are always disputes over land and crime. Tribes don't have the strong legal systems of kingdoms and nations, so justice is seen as a personal chore. Within tribes, there is usually a system of tribal elders who arbitrate these disputes. But when the disputes are between tribes, arbitration is difficult, usually impossible. Violence and endless blood feuds result.

Africa has the largest number of active tribes on the planet, over 500 major ones at last count. The nations of Africa are artificial creations, put together by European colonial powers in the late nineteenth century. In the 1950s and 1960s, most of these colonies were given their freedom. These new nations still had their tribes, plus poverty and weak legal systems. The colonial powers enforced peace, often with guns, but also with thousands of bureaucrats imported from Europe. After independence, most of these bureaucrats went home. The tribal animosities began to emerge very quickly after independence. Most of these nations soon found themselves run by military dictators. It was ugly, but it kept the peace. However, unlike the colonial bureaucrats, the locals were far more corrupt, often because they were intent on taking care of their tribe at the expense of everyone else. The corruption ruined the economies, as well as making most of the population increasingly angry with the poverty and injustice. When democracy got its chance again in the late 1990s, it was because Africans realized that, alone in the world, their economies had been steadily shrinking through the 1980s. The end of the Cold War also eliminated the ability to play off the superpowers against each another, thus eliminating another source of income. They needed change, but democracy alone was not enough.

With the generals replaced by politicians, tribal violence is on the rise again. A good case in point is Nigeria, Africa's most populous nation. Nigeria has some 250 "ethnic groups" (most organized as tribes around shared customs, language, and culture) in a population of 122 million. Precolonial tribal warfare is returning. In the past, the various kingdoms that existed before the colonial period had ethnic minorities who were oppressed, and they have not forgotten. It's fashionable to blame all this on the European colonial governments, but the one sub-Saharan nation that was not colonized, Ethiopia, also experiences frequent civil war and rebellion because of its dozen or so different ethnic groups. No one has yet come up with a quick solution for this problem. Historically, the only thing that works is gradual absorption of many of the smaller groups into the larger ones. This has been going on more rapidly in the last few centuries, making it easier for many stable nations to form. Africans want to hold on to their colonial-era borders, even if it means a constant threat of unrest. This is preferable to the precolonial tribal warfare. But how do you keep the tribes from fighting?

Admitting there is a problem is the first step, and most African nations are doing that. They are stressing the need for national unity. But with corrupt police and civil servants, plus rampant poverty, too many people still have to fall back on the tribe for economic and judicial relief. History provides little comfort. Everywhere else, tribes only faded away after centuries of increasing prosperity and the development of honest and efficient government. Put more simply, the central government had to compete with the tribal organization to provide better living standards and legal systems. This works, it was working during the colonial period. But it only works long term if the locals themselves provide the judges, police, politicians, and bureaucrats.

Meanwhile, the tribal violence increases. Between late June and early July, 2001, several hundred Nigerians died, and over 100,000 fled their homes because of tribal violence in one region alone. In the last decade, millions have died from tribal violence in Africa. Guns won't solve the problem. In fact, the end of the Cold War has brought millions of cheap AK-47s to Africa. This has increased the death toll, as assault rifles can kill a lot more people than the traditional spears and bows. Indeed, previously only the bravest tribal warriors went to war, because it was up close and personal. You had to be tough, experienced, and brave. With AK-47s, any kid can become a badass, blasting away from a distance. Where in the past women and children were generally spared, now they are the first victims of the AK-47-armed teenagers.

Money alone won't solve the problem of tribal violence; honest government will. But you can't easily buy that. The locals have to put aside centuries of custom to make government work. That won't happen fast, and when it does, it will take a long time to eliminate the tribal loyalties. Any time you send peacekeepers into an area populated by tribes, there will be tribal violence to deal with.

Balkan Nightmares

In 1999, conflict over the Yugoslav province of Kosovo led to a real war, followed by continuing OOTW. Kosovo has been a war waiting to happen for most of the last century.

The population of 1.7 million is about 90 percent Albanian. Kosovo's southern border is with Albania. Six hundred years ago, Kosovo was a battlefield between the Serbian kingdom and the advancing Turks. The Serbs lost, and the Turks kept going until they were stopped on the Austrian frontier. In the last century, the Serbian population of Kosovo became the minority and the Turks were thrown out of the Balkans. Subsequently the locals fought four wars with one another, with the last one still going on.

The Balkans have been pacified in the past, but we tend to ignore the methods used to accomplish this. Some 2,500 years ago, King Philip of

Macedon and his son Alexander the Great made their reputations by bringing a semblance of peace to the Balkans. They did it via massacre, hostage taking, strategic marriages, and bribery. Five hundred years later, the Romans inherited the area and spent several centuries keeping the peace with the same methods. Before the Turks took over, the locals fought one another and the Serbs established their rule over the area, and maintained it the same way.

The Turks carried on the ancient, bloody-minded approach, with the addition of a religious angle. If any of the local Christians became Muslim, they got a break on taxes and dibs on government jobs. Working for the Turks was mostly collecting taxes and keeping the peace. It's no wonder the Bosnians and Albanians (Balkan Muslims) found themselves unloved by their neighbors. During World War II, the Germans took advantage of this by recruiting several SS divisions from the Bosnians and Albanians and turning them loose on the locals to keep the peace. It was an ancient tradition, and it worked—for a while. The Germans, of course, lost the war.

Before World War II ended, the anti-German Balkan partisans liberated themselves. The fighting in the Balkans killed more Yugoslavs and Albanians than Germans, and the killing continued after World War II as scores were settled and the Communist government made it clear that peace would return, using the same techniques that previous rulers had used for thousands of years.

The peace held for nearly 50 years—awkward as it was—until the death of Tito, the World War II partisan leader who forced the many ethnic groups to behave. Within five years, the old antagonisms resurfaced, and another ethnic conflict was underway. NATO nations, led by the United States, brokered a cease-fire in late 1995 and then sent several NATO divisions to keep the peace. But the locals were quite open about considering the agreement a breathing space for everyone to rest and rearm for the next round of fighting. As long as NATO nations are willing to spend billions of dollars a year to keep their troops there, peace will prevail.

Which brings us back to Kosovo. The peacekeepers in Kosovo face armed local Albanians fighting for an independent Kosovo, and Serbs fighting to keep Kosovo part of Yugoslavia. The peacekeeping goes on and on. It could get ugly and is unlikely to be resolved. The intentions are good, but the prospects are not. Peacekeeping is a case of "no good deed goes unpunished."

Making Money Talk

Faced with the unpleasant prospects of OOTW, the wealthier nations have come up with (or revived) less painful solutions.

Bribes have long been an important part of warfare. Why fight when you can bribe the enemy general to surrender or, better yet, join your side? But this approach has never been all that well regarded in the West. Other parts of the world have been more pragmatic, and less bloody-minded. Chinese military history is full of battles and wars won not with fighting, but with a few well-placed bribes. In the West, the best practitioners of the wartime bribe were the Byzantines (the eastern remnant of the Roman empire that existed for a thousand years after the city of Rome fell to the barbarians in the fifth century). There was, unfortunately, a lot of religious, cultural, and military ill will between western Europe and the Byzantine empire (the Balkans and Anatolia). To this day, there is a lot of public revulsion toward the use of bribes to deal with military situations. We call that sort of thing "Byzantine diplomacy" and still consider the Byzantines and their ways rather unsavory. All because of some ancient animosities between priests and politicians.

But this attitude toward Byzantine ways is changing. America found that a more effective way to run down international terrorists was to offer multimillion-dollar rewards. This often came down to bribing the bodyguards or government that was sheltering the fugitive terrorist. And while we don't like to admit it, most of our foreign aid over the last half century has been seen on the receiving end as a bribe. The 1995 Dayton Agreement that ended (or, according to the locals, suspended) the war in Bosnia was basically a bribe. Billions of dollars a year in "aid payments" and other benefits were involved. Many European military and political leaders pointed out that this arrangement, including NATO troops to police the peace, would have to go on for decades. But all acknowledged that money was cheaper than blood. Victory in Afghanistan during the 2001 campaign was made easier because $70 million in cash was given out to encourage enemy troops to switch sides, or friendly commanders to stay friendly.

Using a bribe is not always easy. Sometimes the issues that drive the fighting don't easily lend themselves to a cash solution. Early in the Vietnam War, American president Lyndon B. Johnson offered the North Vietnamese a large amount of cash aid if they would stop trying to take over South Vietnam. The Communist North Vietnamese refused this. But the potential was always there. However, the possibility of a bribe working decreases considerably once the shooting starts. If America had approached the North Vietnamese in the late 1950s with a cash solution, it may well have worked. At the very least, it would have gotten a more serious reception. Brokering these deals is not easy. Again, a close study of Chinese history shows that the application of a bribe was usually surrounded by complex and intense negotiations. There is never an easy solution to situations likely to turn into a war. Diplomats on the scene are often not up to the task. For many statesmen, war is the easy way out, at least in the short run. In the long run, a war is a losing proposition for all concerned. There are no winners, only varying degrees of loss.

In early 1999, the Kosovo insurrection against their Serb rulers intensified. TV images of Kosovar refugees fleeing the fighting caused public opinion in Europe and America to call for something to be done. The solution most mentioned was bombing the Serbs, who had refused to allow foreign troops to occupy Kosovo to stop the fighting. No one mentioned a bribe. But it came to that. Bombing the Serbs wasn't working. Eventually, a large sum of money paid to Russia caused that nation to withdraw openly its support for the Serbs. Lacking a major ally, and being offered better terms (no independence for Kosovo), the Serbs caved. Money is cheaper than blood.

Making Do with Mercenaries

And then there are mercenaries as a better way to deal with OOTW.

The economic, social, and political chaos in many parts of the world has produced one benefit, a new type of mercenary. For thousands of years, organized groups of soldiers have hired themselves out to whoever will pay the going rate. As nations became better organized and armed in the past century, the use of mercenaries declined. But going into the 1990s, there was a mercenary revival. The big difference today is that the mercenaries not only offer well-armed, -trained, and -led soldiers, but also all the combat-support services that made national armies so powerful that mercenaries nearly disappeared. Mercenaries showed up as corporations like Sandline International; Executive Outcomes, Ltd.; Globe Risk; and MPRI (Military Professional Resources, Inc.). These organizations specialized in noncombat services like training, procurement, maintenance, public relations, and political consulting. Africa, the region with the greatest amount of need, has some 90 mercenary organizations in action. Most are mainly beefed-up security firms, providing protection to mining companies and other commercial operations. Some provide mercenaries and gun running for rebel movements or factions in a civil war.

MPRI is one of the more notable of these new mercenary outfits. Formed in 1987 and chartered, unofficially, by the United States, MPRI deals largely with clients approved by the American government and provides services that might be politically embarrassing if done by the U.S. government itself. MPRI's staff is largely former members of the U.S. military. MPRI has worked in Croatia, Colombia, Bosnia, Sweden, Taiwan, Macedonia, Saudi Arabia, Kuwait, and Africa. An example of how this works is the contract MPRI had with Croatia in the second half of the 1990s. Although the civil war in Yugoslavia ended in 1995, Croatia still had problems with large numbers of Serbs who had lived in northern Croatia for centuries and were demonstrating separatist tendencies. MPRI provided training in logistics, communications, and weapons use that enabled the Croats to run the Serbs out of northern Croatia in a very quick and efficient campaign. The Croats insist that they did it all by themselves, but they had a lot of good advice, and they paid MPRI for it.

In 1997, Sierra Leone's elected president, Ahmad Tejan Kabbah, was overthrown by his army. But he hired Sandline International, a British mercenary firm, which organized an armed force that put him back into power. Some mercenary outfits specialize in air transport to difficult areas, whether it be crude airfields in the bush or places where they can expect to get fired on while delivering the goods. Other companies clear land mines, deal with kidnappers, or arrange peaceful relations with guerrilla movements or well-organized bandits. In regions beset by armed groups, some mercenary organizations simply provide sufficient firepower to keep the unfriendly locals under control.

Many of the current mercenaries are hired guns in the classic sense. Russian and East European veterans of disbanded Communist armies have hired themselves out to anyone, for anything. These lads show up in Africa a lot, often with a large array of Russian-designed weapons. These include helicopter gunships, jet aircraft, and large transports. Called "white devils" by the locals, these largely Slavic mercenaries are backed by gun-running operations back home. There are enormous quantities of Cold War–era weapons available in Eastern Europe, and several organizations (most only vaguely legal) have appeared to ship this stuff anywhere, to anyone at any time, for a price.

But the future is in outfits like MPRI. Operating legally, and serving only legitimate (more or less) governments, the new twenty-first-century mercenaries provide support that lasts. Instead of just bringing in troops to do the dirty work, the idea now is to show the clients how to do it themselves. And there is much to do. Many nations today have, in theory, the resources (in men and money) to form their own armed forces. But military matters are now more complicated than just giving a lot of young men guns and paying them regularly. There are complicated logistics and maintenance issues for the more powerful, and more complex, weapons. You need experienced people to train your troops how to use, and fight with, the weapons. In a world driven by instant news, governments have to know how to play the press for maximum diplomatic and military advantage. Governments also need advice on how best to handle international organizations like the UN and IMF, not to mention the hundreds of NGOs that rush to disaster areas. These mercenaries now arrive in suits as well as battle dress.

Video Killed the Riot Squad

One of the more perverse aspects of OOTW in the twenty-first century is the effect the electronic media has on how the troops operate. There was a time, before television and the Internet, when riot control was a lot easier. Most rioters were amateurs, and troops, regular police, or special riot police generally had little trouble dispersing a mob. A few lines of club-wielding cops, some tear gas, maybe a water cannon, and it was all over. But then TV came along, and potential rioters began to get educated. Seeing what they were up against beforehand, radicalized students began to use their talents to develop new techniques that would trip up the riot police. Unofficial manuals on "how to riot and win" were prepared in many nations and passed around. With the Internet, these documents are widely available. This led to an arms race between rioters and riot police.

Over the last 30 years, this has escalated to the point where riot control is a full-time job in many nations. France has 15,000 riot police in 63 units around the country. These lads are called out about three times a month for one major demonstration or another. But there are riots and there are riots. Most of the action in France is political protests or sports-related mayhem. There are semi-pro rioters who travel around from one event to another, and these are the lads (the vast majority are men) who provide the riot police with the most trouble. These guys will often come equipped with helmets, gas masks, gasoline bombs, rocks, slingshots, and violent intent. The police call them agitators, and the term is pretty accurate.

Normally, the riot police want to deal with a violent situation by using as little force as possible. Politicians don't like to turn on the TV and see riot police injure citizens. But the agitators know that if they can lay enough hurt on the riot police, they will provoke a charge on the crowd. This will create great photo opportunities and encourage some in the crowd to join in the violence.

The best-equipped riot police are well equipped. Typically each man will have a riot helmet with neck protector and visor (with a fluid seal to prevent noxious stuff from dripping onto the face). The helmet often contains a radio (receive-only for most of the troops). They wear waterproof, flame-resistant overalls or uniforms, to provide protection from gasoline bombs. They have padded high-wrist riot gloves to give some protection from thrown objects or clubs wielded by rioters. They wear high-leg combat boots with steel toe caps and anti-stab soles (as protection from sharp objects on the ground). They usually carry gas masks, as well. Over the uniform are worn shin, knee, forearm, elbow, and groin protectors. Flak jackets are often worn for additional protection. They carry transparent, shatterproof shields. Most riot police will be armed with a riot baton (a thin three-foot club reinforced with metal). Plastic handcuffs, pepper spray, a high-intensity flashlight, and smoke and stun grenades are also carried by most troops. Some are armed with shotguns firing rubber bullets. Others have tear-gas guns. Some snipers will be armed with rifles, if it is suspected that there will be firearms in the crowd. Armored vehicles with water cannon and searchlights are also found in some countries.

The tactics used are several thousand years old. Basically, it's several lines of riot police advancing shoulder to shoulder to force back the crowd. They use a special step, bringing the right foot down hard, and then making another noise by dragging the left foot a bit. The sound is unnerving. Some riot police add another ancient sound effect by rhythmically banging their batons on their shields before they begin marching. When troops are used for this sort of formation, they sometimes advance with fixed bayonets. The sight of a wall of soldiers advancing with bayonets on the end of their rifles, plus the thud and scrape of their boots, must cause the crowd to flee. If not, the troops will rarely use their bayonets on unarmed civilians. Thus, the switch to batons. Clubbing civilians is rather more acceptable than sticking them with bayonets.

An increasingly frequent problem arises when the crowd will not flee. Over the last few decades, many agitators have equipped themselves for fighting. The hard-core rioters will throw rocks and gasoline bombs to try to break the police line. If they can do that, then some will go in with their own wooden batons or iron bars and fight it out with the police. It often gets worse, when men with guns move among the unarmed civilians (especially women and children) and then open up when they are so close they can't miss. This is a particularly popular tactic with Somalis. In one case, two dozen UN peacekeepers died as a result of this sort of thing. Palestinians sometimes use this approach, as well. But the Palestinian gunmen have to be careful, as the Israelis know what's coming and have snipers ready to take out armed men in the crowd, and Israeli riot police use rubber, plastic, and real bullets freely if it appears there might be a firefight.

The solution to this is to develop a nonlethal weapon that will disperse a crowd before they get within a hundred meters of the riot police. Beyond a hundred meters, gunmen in a crowd have a hard time getting a good shot at the distant riot police. Only the United States has such a device (a directed-energy "searchlight" that causes a burning sensation in the skin of rioters) to deal with this, and they refused to sell it to Israel. So the Israelis are developing their own device that produces a similar effect.

Rioters, especially those driven by political or religious beliefs, are quick to adapt to new weapons, equipment, and techniques used by riot police. This has produced something of an arms race as governments put more effort into developing more novel and (hopefully) effective "nonlethal weapons." But we should all remember that for thousands of years, no new weapon has been around too long before someone came up with a way to counter it. Television and the Internet have speeded up that process, leaving the riot police still using the ancient "get there first with the most" tactic, and battle tactics that have changed little since the Bible was written.

The Growing Terrorism Threat

We should keep in mind that terrorists and terrorism are nothing new. Terrorism has been around for thousands of years. Today, however, it is different. It's more organized. It has to be. Unlike the past, police are plentiful. But still the bombs go off.

It was after World War II that terrorism as we know it showed up, a new form of international terrorism unlike anything seen before. Modern terrorism is most likely to succeed if there are well-educated and well-trained terrorists who are backed by a network of safe houses and special services such as forged identities, intelligence, transportation, weapons, and safe contacts overseas. Funds are needed to pay the terrorists, for they often have families dependent on them. Modern terrorism is run like a business, which is the key to whatever success it has.

The principal backer of modern terrorism was the Soviet Union. It wasn't until after the Soviet Union collapsed that it became widely known just how much money and effort the Communists poured into producing professional terrorists.

But money and training facilities are not enough. Eager volunteers are required for the extremely dangerous missions. Since terrorism is the only practical form of warfare for vastly outnumbered factions, volunteers must be inspired to step forward. The Soviets developed effective techniques for producing volunteers, then indoctrinating and training them. The Soviet support for international terrorism was just another Cold War tactic for them.

Meanwhile, most of the world's terrorists did their work at home and were rarely heard about abroad. Terrorism is based on illusions. Despite the tens of thousands of terrorists trained and equipped over the last three decades, only a small percentage ever get into action. Yet each successful terrorist mission has the desired effect of making many people terrified at the prospect of further atrocities.

In reality, international terrorism is very difficult to pull off. Dozens of operations are planned, then aborted as too risky, for each one that comes off. The nations targeted for this terrorism react strongly to the attacks, so strongly that it is now standard for most terrorist acts to go unclaimed by any traceable organization. Even nations that rather openly support terrorist organizations, such as Iran, Lebanon, Syria, and Afghanistan, publicly deny any such support.

The most effective way to deal with international terrorists is to destroy their training bases and make their movement more difficult. This is why America went to war in Afghanistan. Bases are hard to get at; it is easier to foil the movements of the terrorists. False passports can be detected; satellites can use cameras and eavesdropping equipment to detect terrorist movements and plans. Good intelligence and police work in the target countries is the most common way of stopping and catching terrorists.

From a public-relations angle, antiterrorism measures are a hard sell. Target countries cannot show what they are doing lest the terrorists see what to avoid as they sneak in and set up their operations. Even the police work can backfire when you make the wrong moves with an immigrant population (usually Muslims these days) that might provide some support to terrorists.

The terrorists don't have an easy time of it, doing what they do, and the potential victims are not helpless. But the war against terrorism takes place largely in the shadows, where a lot of murky business is taken care of. What you see about it in the news is only a tiny portion of the business being transacted. Putting soldiers into the middle of this makes them nervous. This is police work. But sometimes you need more manpower, as when you have identified terrorists in an area that needs a lot of people to search quickly before the bad guys get away.

And then there are those most fearsome terrorists who use suicide to accomplish their mission.

Ever wonder how suicide bombers are recruited? There's a method to this madness, and the methods have been around for centuries. The oldest recorded suicide terrorist organization existed a thousand years ago. A radical Islamic sect, it was established in the eleventh century in modern day Iran. Hassan Sabbah, the founder, was the son of a noble family. He had a grudge and genius for organization and persuasion. Using religion, sex, and drugs (a formidable combination), he persuaded capable young men to become assassins. But these killers, unlike your average medieval hit man, were not bothered about getting killed in the act. And this made the "ashishin" (from "users of hashish") not just killers, but highly effective terrorists. The sect maintained a number of mountain fortresses, and over the two centuries it existed, it came to control considerable territory in Iran and Syria. Terror was its main weapon, for its assassins were known to be virtually unstoppable. Finally, in the thirteenth century, Mongol and Arab armies went after the "assassins," destroyed their castles, and killed their leaders. The sect continued as a religious organization but gave up the use of assassination and terror. Some 150,000 sect members still live in the Middle East, where the methods of the medieval suicide terrorists continue to be practiced by other groups.

Recruiting suicide terrorists is difficult, but obviously not impossible, if you set up an organization devoted to it. First, you need a cause to attract and motivate recruits. Suicide terrorists don't pop up just anywhere. You need a group of people, preferably poverty-stricken and feeling oppressed by neighbors. Thus, we find suicide terrorists in the Middle East, Sri Lanka, and Chechnya. Religion is not essential. The Tamil terrorists in Sri Lanka don't use it, and the Chechens don't use it as much as their Muslim allies would like. But oppression and a well-run organization to channel the resentment is essential. In Israel and Afghanistan (Osama bin Laden's organization), religious students are recruited. The suicide terrorists must be volunteers, but there is a certain amount of brainwashing going on to persuade the prospect that getting oneself killed for the cause is a worthwhile effort. Some of the attractions are material. The family of the terrorist is rewarded with money and public praise after the attack. This is important, as it makes future recruiting easy, at least among the poor young lads who have few economic prospects. Poverty, resentment, religious and nationalistic zeal, and even bitterness over a relative killed by the enemy all are used to recruit, motivate, and train suicide terrorists successfully.

In Chechnya, suicide terrorists are relatively new. The Chechens received several million dollars in 2000 to finance a suicide-bomber unit (the Shahid—

suicide attacker—battalion). The Iranian-backed Hezbollah provided advice on how to set up and run the operation. There were a few differences from the usual Islamic suicide bombers. Chechens are not as religious, so other angles had to be exploited. Locals who had lost a limb or an eye proved to be a good source of recruits. As with Hezbollah, people with mental problems are also usable, as long as their disability does not make them incapable of learning how to handle the explosives and follow instructions. Widows or unmarried women who have lost their parents are another source of recruits. In Chechen culture, such women face bleak prospects. People who have been condemned to death by religious courts are given the option of being a suicide bomber to atone for their crime and provide some cash for their families. Another source of volunteers are men who have lost many family members to Russian troops and are keenly aware of the Chechen tradition of revenge. The region is cursed with many blood feuds, and the Shahid battalion offers are a pretty certain way for anyone to settle a blood debt against the Russians. As an added inducement for all volunteers, the rebels provide cash payments ($500–$1,000) and promises to take care of surviving family members. There are also some volunteers from Arab countries, but these are more expensive. These payments eat up a lot of cash, as does the expense of setting up training camps and providing support and equipment. False documents have to be obtained to get the suicide bombers through Russian checkpoints. Vehicles have to be provided for car and truck bombs. There is also the staff of the training camp, and other specialists to guide the bombers to their targets and scout them beforehand. Even with all this preparation, there is sometimes a shortage of volunteers. The Russians suspect that in some cases, non-suicide bombers, especially people who aren't too bright, are given escape routes that do not work and bombs with timers that go off prematurely.

Historically, there are only two ways to eliminate suicide terrorists. One is the "Mongol method" (kill most of the population from which the terrorists are recruited); the other is to address the grievances that generate the suicidal volunteers. That isn't easy, as there are usually grievances and resentment on both sides. In the twenty-first century, a third method has been found, but it involves a lot of troops and technology. Israel doesn't get enough credit for the dents it has made in the suicide terror operations directed against them. The Israelis have stopped a lot of suicide attacks, but most of these actions cannot be mentioned without exposing intelligence sources. The most visible aspect of the Israeli method is the use of a lot of military manpower. It's more OOTW.

22

Special Operations:
Commandos,
Paratroopers, Marines,
and Special Forces

Special Operations troops are elite forces, small units of men selected and trained for the most difficult operations. They are an ancient practice. It's long been known that a few well-trained, well-led, and skillful troops can use a carefully planned attack to enormous effect. The oldest example was over 3,000 years ago, when a handful of Greeks hidden in a wooden horse left outside the gates of Troy led to the city's falling. The Trojans, seeing that the Greek army had given up their siege and sailed away, thought the wooden horse was a way of acknowledging the Trojan victory. So the Trojans hauled the horse into the city, held a great celebration, and, when everyone was sleeping that off, the Greek troops hidden in the horse quickly killed the few guards still awake, opened the city gates, and let in the returned Greek army. This was a classic commando operation. Had any of the Greeks in the horse made a noise or moved around and given away their presence, it would have been all over. Once out of the horse, the Greeks had to move quickly to open the city gates, killing any Trojan guards before an alarm could be given.

Today, the elite forces come in three flavors. First, there are the traditional commandos. The United States has Delta Force, Britain has the SAS, the Russians have their Spetsnaz, the Germans have GSG-9, and so on.

Next come the large elite units. These used to be called "guard" units, as many of them were the elite units that guarded the king. The U.S. Marine

Corps transformed itself into such an elite force as a way to avoid being disbanded. U.S. Army airborne divisions serve a similar elite-combat function as the Marines and were formed early in World War II after the successful use of German paratroopers was noted.

The third category is a uniquely American one: the Special Forces. These fellows are a combination of commando and secret agent. First formed in the 1950s, they were meant to work with friendly (or potentially friendly) civilians in enemy territory. The Special Forces were first intended to operate in Eastern Europe, where unpopular Communist governments were expected to be a source of people willing to fight. This was to happen if the Soviet Union went to war with NATO. This never happened, but there was Vietnam. South Vietnam was full of anti-Communists, and the Special Forces did quite well among the tribal peoples of central Vietnam. But beyond that, there weren't a lot of similar situations. Yet there were a lot of opportunities to provide military training in foreign countries, and it was found that the Special Forces were very good at this. It wasn't just that the Special Forces guys were knowledgeable soldiers and good instructors. Most important, the Special Forces were trained to try real hard to relate to foreigners, and the foreign troops they trained really appreciated that. But the Special Forces are, first of all, elite infantry. When the war in Afghanistan broke out in 2001, the Special Forces were the first to go in, and they performed very well indeed.

The need for commandos was seen early in World War II, and six battalions of Army Rangers were formed, as well as additional battalions of Marine raiders, Navy underwater demolition teams, and units like Merrill's Marauders in the Far East. The Germans formed their Brandenburg regiment, and the British basically wrote the book on commando operations while forming several different commando units (SAS, Special Air Service; SBS, Special Boat Squadron; Long Range Desert Patrol; Popski's Private Army; and so on).

After World War II, the U.S. commando units were disbanded. Part of the reason for this was that the American commando units were too large and expensive to maintain in peacetime. The Rangers were trained, as much as possible, to SAS standards. This was very expensive. The British were able to maintain a smaller (less than a battalion) size SAS/SBS unit. They also used their commandos to support overseas espionage and intelligence operations.

But when the Korean War broke out, commanders in Korea quickly scrounged up veterans of the Ranger battalions and formed new Ranger companies for those special chores that required highly skilled troops. Since then, the United States has organized more Special Operations troops. This was helped by the experience in Vietnam, where Special Forces troops provided manpower to staff the first LRRP (Long Range Reconnaissance Patrol) units. In the meantime, the Navy had seen its World War II underwater demolition teams evolve into SEAL (Sea Air Land) commandos. The Air Force also got into the game with an elite force trained to rescue downed pilots in enemy ter-

LCAC (Landing Craft Air Cushion)

ritory and to parachute into hot spots to provide target spotting for warplanes overhead.

In response to increasing terrorist activity worldwide, the U.S. Army formed the 1st Special Forces Operational Detachment–Delta (SFOD-D) in 1977. Less well known is another unit formed about the same time: the Naval Special Warfare Development Group. SFOD-D came to be known as Delta Force and was basically an American version of the British SAS. The founder of Delta Force, Colonel Charles Beckwith, had served with SAS (on an exchange program) in the early 1960s and long wanted to establish something like SAS in the United States.

Unlike the SAS, which is constantly involved in operations that the British manage to keep secret (or at least out of the mass media), Delta has had few opportunities to strut its stuff. Its first combat operation was in 1983 (Grenada), followed by Panama in 1989. Delta saw a lot of action during the Gulf War, and several Delta troopers were decorated for their work in Somalia in 1993. When the war in Afghanistan got underway, Delta Force was in the thick of it once more.

The United States has long maintained a huge force of elite infantry. Since the fall of the Soviet Union in 1991, the United States has the world's largest force of this type. This includes an airborne division, an air mobile division, and two divisions of Marines. Actually, American generals eventually discovered what the British have long known: that an all-volunteer force produces an overall level of excellence that approaches that of the traditional elite units. This was seen during the 1991 Gulf War, where all American ground units operated with a level of efficiency that startled even American brass. This despite the sometimes inept opposition by the Iraqi foe. Even the fairly good elite Iraqi units were quickly chopped up by American infantry and armor units. Military analysts in Moscow recognized what was going on in the Kuwait desert. Ever since the Soviet Union fell apart, Russian military reformers have been working to convince the politicians that an all-volunteer force was the only way to go. Indeed, the trend is against conscription, with more and more nations dropping it and going for volunteer armed forces.

The concept of volunteering for commando-type units is essential, for this type of service requires troops to train with an intensity that few people will tolerate. What made the non-commando units so effective by the end of the twentieth century was the fact that so few people in the military were combat troops. There just aren't that many people in any society who have the physical, intellectual, and mental talents to be exceptional warriors. As the proportion of noncombat troops began to outnumber the fighters in the course of the twentieth century, it became possible for the combat units to have a higher proportion of people who wanted to be there and were good at that sort of thing. Higher levels of health and education have also helped, for today's warriors have to handle a lot of technology, and they need robust health to endure the grueling, 24/7 pace of combat operations.

While this selectivity has produced superior "regular" combat units, it has produced some spectacular commando outfits. And the reason for all this excellence is the same for both regular and elite units. It comes down to careful selection of the volunteers, constant and effective training, and good leadership.

What makes the commando units the best is that they get a better deal in selection, training, and leadership. They are also allowed to select their own equipment. The quirky gadget master Q in the James Bond films is based on fact. During World War II, the first commandos began the tradition of getting the right tools for the job, especially if the armed forces didn't have what they needed. This tradition continues.

Another advantage commandos have is that they generally have more time to plan their operations carefully. This usually ensures that they can surprise their opponent, and surprise is always the most powerful weapon a military force can have.

The United States has the largest force of commandos in the world. Some 46,000 troops are assigned to the American Special Operations Command (SOCOM). Only about a quarter of these men (they are largely men) are "operators" (troops that go out armed, into harm's way). The rest of the SOCOM personnel provide support. Most of this has to do with transportation and firepower support. There are also a lot of Q types supplying special equipment, and communications geeks who ensure that the operators stay in touch wherever they are. The SOCOM also contains civil affairs units (to deal with foreign civilians when the shooting has stopped) and psychological warfare (propaganda and information war) units. The cutting edge of SOCOM is a Ranger regiment (three battalions), seven Special Forces groups (21 battalions) and Delta Force (a small battalion), and eight SEAL teams (equaling a small battalion). The Air Force provides a lot of specialized aircraft, but they have a few hundred commando-grade troops who can get on the ground and do really useful stuff.

Each of the Special Forces groups specializes in a particular part of the world, learning languages and customs unique to that area. Each group is shown below with its area of specialization in parentheses:

- 1st Special Forces group (East Asia and the Pacific).
- 3rd Special Forces group (Caribbean and West Africa).
- 5th Special Forces group (Middle East and South Asia).
- 7th Special Forces group (Latin America).
- 10th Special Forces group (Europe).
- 19th Special Forces group (a National Guard unit that covers the same territory as the 1st and 5th Special Forces groups).
- 20th Special Forces Group (a National Guard unit that covers the same territory as the 7th Special Forces group).

A Special Forces group contains three Special Forces battalions and a small headquarters unit. A Special Forces battalion has four companies (three operational and one support) plus a C detachment that serves as battalion headquarters. An operational company has six ODAs (Operational Detachment Alpha, otherwise known as "A Teams") and a "B Team" that serves as company headquarters. Each A Team has twelve men. The total strength of a Special Forces company is 83 men. The total strength of a Special Forces group is about 1,200 troops.

The Special Forces troops have lots of support. These units include the 112th Signal Battalion and the 528th Support Battalion. In addition, there is the U.S. Army Civil Affairs and PSYOPS Command (containing the 2nd, 4th, 5th, and 7th Psychological Operations Groups), the 96th Civil Affairs Battalion, 351st Civil Affairs Command, 352st Civil Affairs Command, and the 353rd Civil Affairs Command. Most important of all is the 160th Special Operations Aviation Regiment (three helicopter battalions). In a sense, the 75th Ranger Regiment (three battalions) is also a support unit for the Special Forces, ready to provide more muscle for special operations. The Special Forces recruits heavily from the Ranger Regiment.

The Navy SEALS are organized into 120-man teams. There are, as of 2002, eight teams. They are allocated, like everything else in the Navy, either to the Atlantic Fleet or the Pacific Fleet. Each SEAL team gets special training in a particular part of the world. This "area of specialization" is shown in parentheses below.

The Pacific Fleet's SEAL teams are controlled by Naval Special Warfare Group One, which operates out of San Diego, California. Assigned are: SEAL Team One (Southeast Asia), SEAL Team Three (Southwest Asia), SEAL Team Five (Northern Pacific), SEAL Team Seven (no specialization announced).

The Atlantic Fleet's SEAL teams are controlled by Naval Special Warfare Group Two, which operates out of Little Creek, Virginia. Assigned are: SEAL Team Two (Europe), SEAL Team Four (Central and South America), SEAL Team Eight (Caribbean, Africa, and the Mediterranean), SEAL Team Ten (no specialization announced).

A third to half of all SEALs are normally deployed overseas or on American warships.

JSOC (Joint Special Operations Command) is the principal commando counter-terrorism unit, containing Delta Force and SEAL Team Six. There are about three hundred elite commandos in JSOC, and a lot of support troops. While well trained, JSOC has not had much success since it was first formed in the early 1980s.

Finally, below is a short list of "Special Operations Forces truths" that is found posted wherever commandos operate:

- Humans are more important than hardware.
- Quality is better than quantity.
- Special Operations Forces cannot be mass-produced.
- Competent Special Operations Forces cannot be created after emergencies occur.

That says it all.

Inventing the Marines

A navy exists to settle disputes between nations. As these disputes escalate toward more extensive forms of warfare, ships are not sufficient to force a decision. The final arbiter of armed conflicts is the infantry. The ultimate form of naval warfare is landing infantry on your opponent's territory. The current term for this is "power projection." Until this century, power projection meant landing army troops. During the 1920s and 1930s, the U.S. Marines developed theories and equipment for a new form of amphibious warfare. This was what we think of as amphibious warfare today: specialized troops storming ashore in the face of stiff opposition. After this, amphibious warfare would never be the same. During World War II, the United States rewrote the book by raising a specialized army-size amphibious force, the U.S. Marine Corps. The Marines provided training for the U.S. Army, which eventually performed more amphibious operations and itself invented many key amphibious techniques. After World War II, the U.S. Marines retained its relatively large size and, more important, maintained its specialized skills as amphibious troops. Like most other maritime powers, the United States always had a Marine Corps.

The U.S. Marine Corps always attracted innovative and determined officers, and it was these leaders who created the "can do" spirit and dedication to professionalism that allowed the U.S. Navy's Marines to turn into one of the largest "commando class" fighting forces in the world.

Marines were originally organized as shipboard close-combat specialists at a time when ship crews still boarded each other to decide naval battles. When landing parties of infantry were infrequently needed, they were largely sailors led by marines. During the last hundred years, most navies used their marines as on-board police, gun crews, and, occasionally, landing parties. World War II brought forth the capability to move hundreds of thousands of heavily armed troops long distances quickly by sea and land them on an enemy shore. The current U.S. Marine Corps basically invented itself during the 1930s (when they invented modern amphibious warfare techniques) and World War II. The first Marine division was not organized until 1942. By the end of World War II, there were six American Marine divisions.

Currently, over half the world's officially designated marines are American. Only the U.S. Marine Corps maintains its own air force as well as a fleet of specialized amphibious ships and equipment. Although all the ships and aircraft, as well as the Marine Corps itself, are nominally under U.S. Navy control, the U.S. Marine Corps manages to maintain an individual identity.

The marines concentrated on being very good at some key tasks:

Raiding. These are commando-type operations. The British Royal Marines excel at this and have largely written the book of how to do it. Such employment requires troops with above-average combat skills and high training levels. Although all marine forces are highly trained and somewhat elite, when used in raiding they must be even more so. Raids often involve parachuting or descending from helicopters. The United States has even modified some of its older nuclear ballistic missile subs as high-speed transports for raiding parties.

Spearheading amphibious operations for army troops. This is something like a raid, except you don't always have to fight your way out. If the job is done right, the non-marine troops coming ashore behind you will bail you out. Marines are often called upon to make the initial beachhead on an enemy-held shore. Functioning like assault troops, they use a variety of special skills and equipment so that the army troops can get ashore with a minimum of trouble. At that point, the marines can be withdrawn. Often they have to stick around. After all, marines are very capable infantry. While the marines practice coming in over the beach, they prefer to go in via helicopter. This goes back to the pre–World War II method of landing marines were there was no opposition. The head-on amphibious assault techniques the marines pioneered in the 1930s were developed because armies had gotten so big (or because some Pacific islands were so small) that all landing areas were covered. Once the marines got their helicopters, they had a lot more landing options.

Getting there first with the most. Often military action is needed and regular ground forces are either not available or cannot get there fast enough. The marines are often trained, equipped, and used as a rapid-intervention force. They are basically light infantry. Although normally moved by ship, they can, and sometimes are, put into aircraft. During the 1982 Falklands war, the first British ground forces on the scene were marines. The U.S. Marine Corps has a long list of areas they train to move into during an emergency. These include Europe, Japan, Korea, the Persian Gulf, Iceland, and several others.

The last amphibious assault against a defended shore was in 1950, when U.S. Marines invaded at Inchon, Korea. This was arguably the most difficult amphibious operation of all time, and there hasn't been another amphibious assault since. Noting that, the U.S. Marines have again transformed themselves, depending more on helicopters for moving inland from their ships. While the traditional Marine divisions still exist, U.S. Marines are organized for action in miniature armies (MEUs, or Marine Expeditionary Units) of some 2,000 men. Basically, an MEU is a Marine infantry battalion with enough support units to allow it to operate by itself in enemy territory. The MEUs spend a lot of time at sea, in small aircraft carriers that carry helicopters and vertical takeoff bombers (AV-8s).

Two distinct types of amphibious capability exist: long range and local. Only the United States has any significant long-range amphibious capability. All the other major amphibious forces are equipped for local operations. One reason for the long-range U.S. capability is that most of the potential invasion sites are outside the Western Hemisphere. At the moment, no nation is ready to launch the multi-division type of amphibious invasion that we traditionally think of as an amphibious operation. The reason for the lack of this capability is simple: such large operations are needed only during a major war. Only the United States has sufficient amphibious shipping to lift an entire division, and these specialized ships are spread all over the world. At the moment, amphibious forces are most useful for their ability to put a few thousand Marines swiftly ashore in some hot spot. America, Britain, China, and France are very keen on this. Other significant amphibious powers merely want the capability to land troops quickly either somewhere down their own coast or on a hostile neighbor's. Although ground forces can be moved farther and faster by aircraft, amphibious shipping maintains a considerable cost advantage. It's cheaper to float than to fly. Besides, with amphibious ships you don't have to find the naval equivalent of an airfield. Keep in mind, though, that amphibious shipping cannot land on any coast. Some shore areas are too rough for landing. Some areas are better than others. That less than 20 percent of most shorelines lend themselves to amphibious landings is a major reason why the U.S. Marines are provided with a dozen helicopter carriers by the U.S. Navy. More so than other military operations, amphibious assaults are very susceptible to things going wrong, with the worst possible results. Speed is imperative, both in planning and execution. It is likely that Marines will have to undertake operations with fewer amphibious ships than they would like. Ships are always being lost or kept in other operations longer than expected. A Marine's greatest asset is an ability to improvise. It is not enough to possess uncommon courage in the face of the enemy. Equally important is the ability to make do in the face of your own side's shortcomings. Things will go wrong, often very wrong. The U.S. Marine Corps is accustomed to taking heavy losses, heavier than those of normal combat, in order to compensate for the uncertainties of amphibious operations. While it's easier to avoid, or improvise around, the mistakes in the first place, there is often neither the time nor the opportunity.

Natural-Born Killers

The U.S. Marines have a macho reputation, and they like it that way. One member of the Clinton administration described the Marines as "extremists." Privately, many Marines took that as an unintended compliment. Potential recruits see the Marines the same way: a bunch of tough, lethal, disciplined troops with impressive uniforms. And since most of the potential recruits for any branch of the military are teenagers, the Marines have a natural appeal. If you need any convincing, just take note of the kinds of music and movies teenagers like, and the fact that the Marines have the least trouble meeting their recruiting goals. Further proof can be found by attending the recruiting presentations regularly held in many high schools. Each of the services gets up and makes their pitch. The Army, Air Force, and Navy rattle off all the goodies they offer, like travel to foreign countries, money for college, career training. Many of the students nod off. Then the Marine sergeant gets up and shows a short video of tough-looking teenage Marines storming beaches, jumping out of armored vehicles and helicopters, and generally behaving like natural-born killers. The sergeant then tells the kids that the Marines can only promise them challenges. Not everyone can be a Marine, and he only wants to recruit those who are up to it. The students are fully awake through all this, and the Marines generally end up with more recruits than anyone else. The other NCOs mutter about how they would do better if they had a better-looking uniform.

The Marines have another advantage. Just about all Marines have combat jobs. The Navy provides all the support troops. It's as if the Army Rangers or paratroopers had their own recruiters. Their pitch would be very similar to the Marines' and would get similar results. That idea has been tossed around in the other services, but no one has taken the plunge yet. Yet it's an old idea. For thousands of years, individual military units went out looking for recruits. The idea of one recruiting organization for everyone is relatively new. In the past, each regiment or ship had its own small recruiting staff, and the new guys were generally taken from the same area. This was a big help for unit cohesion, which is today called "team building." Commanders have known for thousands of years that in the thick of combat, the principal motivation is men fighting for each other, for their friends and "teammates." Military and civilian organizations strive to build this unit cohesion. Few military organizations, or companies, pull it off. Except for the Marines.

What the Marines have done is part showbiz and part common sense. Everyone notices the snappy dress uniforms and military bearing of Marines. There's also that cocky attitude. And career Marines are expected to scowl at the camera when official photos are taken. All that is the showbiz. The common-sense angle is the Marines' emphasis, in their training and indoctrination, on their main job: ground combat. Get ready for that and you get fewer Marines killed when you get into a fight. Even though the Navy supplies many of the support functions, many Marines are not in combat jobs. Yet it's a tradition that "every Marine is a rifleman." Noncombat Marines spend part of each year going through infantry drills. The older NCOs repeat the stories of how, in the past, Marine cooks and clerks were thrown into the line when the situation got desperate. And the Marines relish a desperate situation. They have favorite maxims like, "There's no such thing as being surrounded, but there are times when you can attack in any direction."

But soldiering has changed for most of the other troops in the world. It's fashionable to play down grim and costly ground combat in favor of precision weapons and push-button warfare. For this reason, the Marines are seen as a bunch of roughneck throwbacks. Yet even today, in any of the two dozen wars being fought around the world, the troops who are the most successful are the ones that operate most like the Marines. What the Marines are may not be fashionable, but when you have to get close to the enemy, what they do works.

Paratroopers

Parachutes have been around for over two centuries but were only perfected during World War I (1914–18). Toward the end of that war, the allies were forming the first parachute units and were planning to use them against Germany if the war went into 1919. The war ended, and the idea was put aside. During the 1930s, interest in paratroopers revived, and the Germans formed the first parachute units to see combat. Russia, Britain, and the United States noted the success of the paratroopers and followed suit. It was noted, during the war, that dropping paratroopers behind enemy lines, while effective in weakening the enemy, tended to cause enormous casualties among the paratroopers. After World War II, paratroopers came to be seen as elite infantry who, while trained to jump out of airplanes into combat, were more useful as a giant SWAT team. When there was a military emergency somewhere, you could always depend on the paratroopers to go in and do whatever could be done. In addition to their parachute training, the paratroopers were given a lot of infantry training. Paratroopers were carefully selected and well led. Well, most of the time. In many nations, paratroopers were selected mainly for their political reliability. These guys ended up as paratroopers in name only. The wealthier nations tended to maintain a brigade or two of paratroopers and used them for emergencies overseas. Paratroopers are expensive to maintain and get chewed up pretty quickly when fighting mechanized forces. When selected, trained, and led correctly, paratroopers are excellent elite troops. Not quite as good as your classic commandos, but good enough for a lot of jobs commandos are called on to do.

Commandos

Most nations have some kind of commando unit, usually 100 or so specially selected and trained troops. Often, the British or American commando units (SAS/SBS, Special Forces) are called in to conduct training. As a general rule, the larger the nation's armed forces, the more likely they are to maintain a useful commando force. This is because the commandos are usually recruited from people already in the military. Leaders for commando units are selected from those who have served in the commandos. The smaller commando forces in most nations tend to vary quite a bit in quality, depending on how good the current leadership is. Larger nations have a larger pool of troops to select from and thus are able to maintain quality in their commandos. But in many smaller nations, the local commandos are, at best, a SWAT team with fancier uniforms.

The Organization of a Marine Amphibious Force

Through the 1980s, the U.S. Marines developed a modular organization for amphibious operations. The traditional Marine division is basically an administrative organization in peacetime. In wartime, the division headquarters controls a division or two's worth of units, depending on what got to the battlefield. The typical combat unit in peacetime is a brigade, and the brigade will often land and fight as a brigade unless there is sufficient time to bring in enough units to form a division. Such was the case in the 1991 Gulf War, where there was sufficient time to organize two Marine divisions.

The following description refers to a division-size "amphibious force," one of many organizations that the Marines are prepared to use in wartime. The 60–65 ship American MAF (Marine amphibious force) consists of an 18,000-man Marine division and a Marine air wing (MAW). A MAW (17,000 men) has 159 aircraft (including F-18s, AV-8s, EA-6s, A-6s, and KC-130s), 156 helicopters (including CH-46s, CH-53s, UH-1s, and AH-1s), one SAM battalion, and 75 Stinger teams. Most of the MAW can operate from carriers, initially, but will shift to land operation as soon as a field is captured or prepared. There are some variations depending on where each of the four Marine divisions is expected to fight. Some have more or fewer tanks and other equipment. All of the ships are "combat loaded." That is, men and equipment (especially equipment) are spread among many ships so that the loss of one vessel will not result in the loss of all of a particular unit, like an engineer battalion. All equipment goes into the ships so that it may be quickly unloaded in the order needed. The total is some 50,000 men, over 300 armored vehicles, over 250 aircraft, and 1.2 million tons of shipping for one division-size amphibious force.

The Future

The future is supposed to be predicted by the past, and it usually is. But this really only works if you go back a long time, instead of looking at just the last war. With the outstanding work done by commandos and special forces in Afghanistan, the pundits will start talking about another revolution in warfare and the declining need for large-infantry units. This will play into the U.S. Air Force's view of future warfare. The Air Force believes that most future wars will be fought like Afghanistan. To some extent, they are right. A revolution has taken place. GPS and new communications gear allow a few guys on the ground to bring down very accurate bombing on nearby enemy ground forces. And the Air Force view of the future is also accurate in that a lot of the "little wars" we may get involved in will have lots of local guys providing friendly infantry. But it's the exceptions that can kill you. There are still potential foes (Iraq, North Korea, China) out there whom we will have to take on by ourselves. So the concept of a few hundred Special Forces on the ground and a few hundred warplanes in the air only works sometimes. It's another form of warfare, the new form of warfare.

We must also go back to our World War II experience with commandos and reflect on those times where the commandos had bad luck, often combined with bad planning, that led to very high casualties. These disasters are why commandos and elite forces were cut back so severely after World War II.

The U.S. Army reads the same tea leaves as the Air Force and comes up with a slightly different version of the future. With all that accurate bombing available, infantry and armor units can now slice and dice large enemy ground forces much more quickly. To make this work, the ground troops have to be highly trained and bright enough to handle all the new weapons and gear coming into use. Commandos are still useful behind enemy lines, but the heavy lifting still requires infantry and armor divisions.

The Air Force feels that their anti-armor cluster bombs can take care of any large enemy formations, and that all the Army has to do is get some lightly armed troops (like paratroopers) over to the trouble spot real quick. The Army is a little nervous about this, as taking down hundreds of hostile tanks with these new bombs has never been tried. The first attempt could be a little embarrassing (for the Air Force) and fatal (for the paratroopers). But "could be" is not the same as "probably." Weapons testing has gotten a lot better in the last few decades. Still, warriors are always a little nervous about going into action with radically new weapons. It's kind of personal, because if the new stuff doesn't work, the grunts get killed.

Based on their success in Afghanistan, the concept of Special Forces (soldiers capable of training and leading soldiers from many different nations), previously an American monopoly, will get picked up by other nations. The trouble is, few other nations can really make the Special Forces idea work. America is a nation of immigrants from all over the world, and the rest of the world knows it. Americans are seen as something of an everyman bunch, not just a specific ethnic group. But some European nations, like Britain and France, have a long history of working with many ethnic groups and may decide that some Special Forces–type troops are in order. Same thing with a nation like India, which is actually quite multiethnic, with 19 major languages and over a hundred minor ones. Of course, this will end up with American Special Forces being called on for yet another overseas training mission: to train newly formed Special Forces units in other nations.

PART SIX

WARFARE BY THE NUMBERS

Behind every infantryman, pilot, or sailor we find many more troops moving supplies, pushing paper, and operating computers. These days, there are often ten or more support troops for every fighter. The warriors and the clerks have a symbiotic relationship. You can't wage war unless both groups do their jobs well. The numbers war demonstrates how important calculation has always been in warfare.

23
Logistics

If the troops have no ammunition, they can't do much damage to their opponents. Without food and medical supplies, your soldiers will melt away without ever fighting a battle. Without spare parts and fuel for their vehicles and equipment, this gear quickly becomes inoperable. The task of supplying ammunition, food, fuel, spares, and other items to the troops is called "logistics." It's not a very glamorous task and is often neglected. Such lack of dedication normally leads to disasters. It's an ancient military maxim that "amateurs study strategy and tactics, professionals study logistics."

Grim Numbers

Problems with logistics are quite common in military history. These disasters occur not just because commanders ignore logistical matters. Astute opponents remain very aware of logistics and go out of their way to protect their own and disrupt their opponent's supply arrangements. Much of the military effort in the Vietnam War was directed at disrupting North Vietnamese supply efforts. The results of the largest bombing campaign in history were mixed, although the bombing did cause the North Vietnamese and Vietcong enormous casualties and considerable trouble. A similar campaign against Chinese forces in Korea (1950–53) met with equal lack of success. The same thing happened in the campaign against German forces in Italy during 1943–44. The problem was primarily that the supply requirements of military forces are relatively small in comparison to the ability to transport material. It is rarely possible to stop all supply movement. What does get through is usually enough to keep the fighting going.

Consider the following situation. A double-line railroad can, under wartime conditions, move at least 50 or more trains (400 tons each) a day.

That's 20,000 tons a day. A two-lane, hard-surface road can handle at least as much traffic, although at greater expense. Trains are cheaper to operate than trucks. A dirt road can handle half as much traffic and requires even more expense (more trucks, more breakdowns, etc.). With no roads at all, you have to create some kind of road, and these are generally no better than a single dirt road, and often much worse.

A non-mechanized army requires only 15–30 pounds of supply per man per day. Every 1,000 tons of supply keeps 100,000 men in combat for a day. If one rail line or road enters an area occupied by 100,000 troops, it must be cut for over 95 percent of the time to have any effect. And it must be cut for a sustained period, because military forces stockpile supplies when they have a chance. Even if you get supply below the minimum levels, combat capability won't be reduced until over one-third of the requirement is denied. Once that level is reached, for every percentage point of supply denied, 1 percent of the unit's combat power is lost. Even when completely cut off from supply, the average unit still retains one-third of its combat power.

The typical non-mechanized army these days is often guerrillas or some other kind of irregulars. These guys can live off the local civilians, either by collecting a "revolutionary tax" at gunpoint or because the locals agree with the rebels.

Mechanized units have more vehicles and weapons and require over 10 times as much supply per man. Unit mobility in mechanized units is the first thing to go when supply is shut off, because of the weight of fuel required to keep things going. Such units have to choose between staying in place or moving and abandoning some vehicles.

Units without supplies can still fight, but at greater cost in casualties. As the Chinese in Korea and the North Vietnamese in Vietnam demonstrated, it is possible to take more casualties in lieu of using ammunition and still stand off a better-supplied force. In Korea it was found that with twice the manpower taking twice the casualties, the Chinese were able to match better-armed and better-supplied UN units. Lack of food and medical supplies gradually wears down the troops.

The key point is that the adverse affects of reduced or no supply are gradual. Troops can continue to operate under these conditions for weeks or months. How is this so? Call it the "use what you got" rule of supply. When troops are well supplied, they are profligate. When times are lean, so are expenditures. Necessity is the mother of efficient supply use. When supplies dry up for any reason, expedient methods are found to get by with less. History is full of examples.

Logistics can become very expensive when your opponent deliberately attacks your supply forces. Supplies and their transport are destroyed, to be replaced at no small cost. This exercise becomes a battle of wealth and materiel. A single sortie by a fighter-bomber can cost $500,000. A truck is about $50,000–100,000, plus the cost of its cargo. A train and its cargo will cost tens of millions of dollars and up. Bridges, tunnels, and railroad yards are equally expensive. To replace these items is also costly in time. While portions of the transportation network are being rebuilt, additional expense is incurred in detouring around blown bridges or tunnels. Because most of this damage is outside the combat area, civilian resources can be used for the repairs. This makes it difficult to destroy transportation paraphernalia and keep it destroyed. Worse yet, the defender soon learns the advantages of camouflage and deception, making it difficult for the attacker to find out if a line has been cut, is still cut, or has been repaired.

There are two situations where logistics becomes the overwhelming factor: wilderness (deserts, jungles, mountains, etc.) and small islands. The 1991 Gulf War showed what dire straits an army (the Iraqis) is in if caught in the desert without supply. The same thing happened in the Arab-Israeli wars in the Sinai desert, and during World War II in the North African desert. The perils of having troops on an isolated island was vividly demonstrated during World War II in the Pacific. While the islands that U.S. Army and Marine infantry assaulted were costly, many more enemy-occupied islands were simply bypassed, with many of the enemy troops starving to death before the war ended. Even the islands attacked were not as stoutly defended as they could have been because the U.S. blockade had prevented a lot of troops and materiel from reaching the islands before the U.S. assault.

It's easier to move troops than to move the supplies needed to keep the troops fighting effectively. If you want to determine who is going to win a future war, examine the supply situation first.

The Modern Major General's Dilemma

Anyone who has been involved with moving household goods several hundred or thousand miles has an inkling of what soldiers are up against. Few of us have any logistical experience beyond getting the groceries from the supermarket to the kitchen. Contemporary soldiers deal with numbers that quickly grow to immense proportions. Each trooper needs six pounds of food daily, plus 20 pounds of water. The water often has to be delivered, and not just taken from a nearby lake. The food weight includes packaging, which is somewhat more copious than the wrappings found in your local fast-food outlet. Such basic necessities are the least of the supply officer's worries.

In typical operations, over 60 percent of the weight of supplies moved is fuel. The next largest category, ammunition, takes up some 20 percent of the weight transported. This is in sharp contrast to the World War II supply needs.

The German army, somewhat of a cross between the largely motorized Western armies and the generally unmotorized Soviet army, required an average of 28 pounds per day per man. Some 40 percent was ammunition, 38 percent fuel (one-quarter being fodder for horses), and the remainder rations and spares, etc. American units required 55 pounds per man per day. About half was ammo and 36 percent fuel. Current U.S. divisions require between 100–500 pounds per man per day, depending on the type of operation. Fuel and ammo still comprise over three-quarters of the requirements. Air Force logistics requirements have increased along the same lines as the Army. Navy requirements have grown little. Smaller crews (automation), less fuel (nuclear power), and less ammo (more missiles) are the cause.

Although modern armed forces are burning more fuel and firing more ammo, this does not mean an equal increase in combat performance. All that extra fuel is needed to move heavier and more numerous vehicles around. Many of the armored vehicles are for transports, not combat. Ammunition does not represent combat power, but its ability to destroy enemy combat forces. More capable ammunition has been countered by better-protected troops and vehicles. Thus the vast increase of ammunition weight available since World War II is not meaningful unless you are fighting a World War II–type force. One of the major differences between World War II weapons and current ones is that the logistics people have to move over five times more materiel to support the current arms.

Rules of Thumb

The easiest way to comprehend logistical calculations is to start with the large numbers and work your way down into the detail. Taking the American situation today, every soldier operating outside the United States needs 100 pounds of supply per day. Each sailor needs four to six times that amount, and each airman up to 1,000 pounds a day. Troops on land can be cut down to under 50 pounds a day if they are not doing anything. Sailors at sea require 300 pounds each just to keep the ships operational. When supply is moved by sea or rail, the fuel required is not a significant factor. To move a ton of material 100 kilometers by train uses 14 ounces of fuel. A large ship uses about half that. When material is moved by truck or air, it's a different story. By truck, 1 percent of the weight moved will be consumed as fuel for each 100 kilometers traveled. By air, the cost will be from 2–5 percent, depending on the type of aircraft. Large commercial cargo jets are the most efficient. Helicopters are notorious fuel hogs and can consume 10 percent of their cargo weight for each 100 kilometers traveled. This is often much more, as helicopters often return empty from battlefield supply missions. Smaller helicopters, like the numerous UH-60s, can use up a ton of fuel to move two tons of supplies 200 kilometers.

Moving supply by animal, including humans, will have the same fuel cost as aircraft because of the food required. A recent innovation is the portable fuel pipeline, quickly laid alongside existing roads. It is twice as efficient as trucks, but more vulnerable to attack. A lot of supply will be in transit at any given time. You always encounter problems with keeping things moving, and some types of operations require larger amounts of logistical support. To cope with these conditions, forces strive to keep reserves, 30–90 days' worth of supply on hand in locations around the combat area. For land operations, this would amount to 10 tons of supplies for each man in the area. For an army of 250,000 men, this will be a fairly large quantity of supply to store and keep track of, about 2.5 million tons. The half million coalition troops massed for the liberation of Kuwait in 1991 piled up over 7 million tons of supply to support their efforts. The dimensions of the problem are becoming clearer.

The 2001 war in Afghanistan presented a worst case. The campaign was fought in a landlocked nation. The United States was able to operate from some bases in Pakistan, Uzbekistan, and Tajikistan. Only Pakistan had a seacoast. Afghanistan was roughly 700 kilometers north to south and 700 kilometers east to west. Pakistan would not allow Americans to bring a lot of ground troops or warplanes into the country. So all that could be operated out of Pakistani air bases were helicopters and support aircraft (although warplanes were allowed to land for emergencies and carrier-aircraft refueling). To the north of Afghanistan was Uzbekistan and Tajikistan, each with a rickety railroad connection to Russia. In effect, everything had to be flown in. Several hundred Special Forces troops were put in on the ground, but they required helicopter support from the northern nations, or Pakistan. Some Army helicopters were flown off a U.S. carrier off the Pakistani coast. But all the helicopters were operating at their maximum range (or close to it). Each UH-60, the standard transport helicopter, took off with about a ton of fuel on board but could only go about 240 kilometers before it had to return. AH-64 helicopter gunships could only go about 200 kilometers. The specially modified commando helicopters (most operated from the carrier) had much longer range, particularly since they could refuel in the air. But everything was constrained by supplies. Without fuel, the helicopters could not cover all of Afghanistan, and until bases were established inside Afghanistan, U.S. helicopters could not cover the entire country. The campaign in Afghanistan was an extreme case of how restricted military operations can be because of logistics.

Running the Store

Modern military commanders don't get to practice fighting, but they do get a lot of practice at logistics. Even in peacetime, large quantities of war materiel must be moved. Valuable experience is thus gained for the more massive demands of wartime. Peacetime logistics officers are primarily concerned with maintaining war-reserve stocks and the regular flow of spare parts, fuel, and food. War-reserve stocks are stockpiles of supply that, it is hoped, will get units through the first 30 or more days of combat. These stocks are absolutely essential for a unit's wartime effectiveness. Immediate resupply from the civilian economy is unlikely, and these reserves are all the combat units will have initially. The war-reserve stocks include everything needed: ammunition, fuel, food, spares, and supplies of every description. A three- to five-day supply of all items is carried by each division at all times. Air Force and naval units have similar reserves. The remainder is stockpiled in the rear areas, away from the expected battle areas. "Getting into the enemy's rear" and destroying these supplies often means that the enemy is soon going hungry, immobile, and fighting with empty weapons.

The placement of war-reserve stocks is critical. Ammunition is preferably stored in bunkers. This affords some protection from enemy attack and decreases the possibility of one exploding bunker igniting another. These bunkers have to be located where they are unlikely to be overrun quickly by an advancing enemy. Bunkers must also be placed close to roads, rail lines, and perhaps water access. These bunkers witness a fair amount of activity as munitions are moved in and out.

Ammunition, as well as fuel, is perishable. Fuel cannot be stored for more than a year. Fuel and munitions must be rotated regularly. This is no problem with fuel, as vehicles use it constantly. Munitions are another problem. Peacetime use for training is much less than wartime use. At peacetime rates of use, munitions would last for decades. Unfortunately, munitions eventually begin to deteriorate and become unreliable. The explosives and propellants in munitions will begin to degrade after several years. This is a vexing problem. Nations take two different approaches to the problem. NATO nations tend not to maintain large stocks of munitions. They also use a lot more in peacetime and keep their stocks current. On the downside, these nations often have less than 30 days of munitions available for combat. The other approach, followed by many Third World nations and Russia, keeps munitions until they are obviously useless. This produces a lot of munitions that do not work in combat. An example was the large number of Argentinean bombs that did not explode during the 1982 Falklands Islands war. The Soviet Union maintained large stocks, up to 90 days' worth, in some categories. However, their munitions were frequently unreliable due to their age. Even the new stuff suffered from above-average manufacturing defects. Overall, this degraded the effectiveness of Soviet munitions up to 50 percent. With the demise of the Soviet Union, many of these older ammunition stocks were destroyed, so the successor states have less, but marginally more reliable, munitions on hand.

Another growing problem is spare parts, and replacements for lost equipment. Weapons, equipment, and munitions have all become more complex.

Armies now have more technicians than infantrymen. All this to keep all this complex gear functioning. This is a difficult task even in peacetime. This process is complicated by the design of military equipment. To make repair possible using hastily trained repairmen, military gear tends to be modular. Entire assemblies are taken out and replaced, even if only a single component of the assembly is defective. It is often possible to repair assemblies if skilled technicians are available. Otherwise, it is sent back to the factory, if possible, and a working one brought forward. The cost of spares to keep an F-15 going in combat is over $300,000 a day if assemblies are used. If the technicians can make more detailed repairs themselves, the cost is reduced over 70 percent. The weight of these spare parts is not great, just their value. We are talking about a lot of electronics and precision components. Complications proliferate with these millions of different parts. Each component in an aircraft comes under different types of stress, depending on what the aircraft does. Different types of missions wear out different components at different rates. Not knowing exactly how the aircraft will be used in wartime, peacetime planners have to make educated guesses as to how many of what spares to stock. There really is no easy way around this. Aircraft usage depends a lot on how the enemy operates, and one can only make estimates about this. Not only is there likely to be the wrong mix of spares, there will also be too few of them. Money is always short in military budgets. When push comes to shove, more effort is put into producing weapons, and less emphasis is placed on spares procurement. One might say this is another reason why professional soldiers wish to avoid war. If widespread combat occurred, complex weapons systems would quickly, too quickly, run out of spares. This would not shut them all down. Some aircraft, for example, can still fly and fight with a number of complex systems inoperative. The aircraft is less capable and more at risk, but it is still out there swinging. In addition, some aircraft can be cannibalized for parts to keep others going. The net result is that low spares inventories means weapons work less well and are destroyed sooner in combat. Spare parts are as essential as fuel and ammunition to keep a modern armed force functioning.

Some forms of supply can be obtained locally. Food, water, and fuel are commonly foraged. Unlike the good old days when the troops were instructed to grab whatever wasn't nailed down, living off the local population must be conducted in an organized manner for the best results. Planning for this foraging is done in peacetime and often practiced as well. A strong local economy is a vital wartime asset. American forces in Europe obtain many needed items locally in peacetime and expect to continue if war comes. An example of how this worked occurred during the Korean War (1950–53), where Japan was able to produce many items UN forces needed. Indeed, this business gave Japan a start on the way to reconstruction from the economic devastation of World War II. During the 1991 Gulf War, much of what the troops needed was obtained locally. Ironically, because of a shortage of refinery capacity, oil-rich Saudi

Arabia had to import millions of tons of refined petroleum products to support
the coalition forces. But even in this case, the abundance of oil-shipping facilities in the area was a big help.

The increasing use of computers has made the logistics planner's task somewhat more manageable. Yet the very complexity of modern logistic arrangements
has made them more vulnerable to disruption. There has been only one experience in maintaining such technically sophisticated armies in a major war, the
1991 Gulf War. The experience served as a wake-up call for the generally blasé
attitude toward logistics in peacetime. Not only do logistics planners face
unprecedented problems, they also have to fight the ever-present general attitude
that the supply situation will somehow take care of itself. It won't.

Us Versus Them

The Soviets developed a different attitude toward logistics, one that they
passed on to many of their Third World clients and one that these generally
poor nations would have been forced to adopt even without Soviet advisers.
This system doesn't worry as much about spare parts. This system treats everything as expendable, including large units like divisions. If it breaks, bring up
another. As Lenin put it, "Quantity has a quality all its own." Obviously, we
have here at least two different styles in logistics. Western nations in general,
and the United States in particular, prefer high quality in their equipment,
troops, and combat units. A constant stream of replacements, spares, and other
essentials keep the combat units constantly in action. In the Soviet-type armed
forces, the priorities are munitions, fuel, and little else. As equipment is disabled it is allowed to fall by the wayside, to be picked over and repaired if possible by technical units that follow the fighting. Especially during combat,
logistics is stripped down to the basics. Food, sleep, and maintenance can wait.
The Soviet approach was, and is, pragmatic. They could not keep track of huge
parts inventories or move massive tonnages of different supplies as efficiently
as Western nations. To overcome these problems, Soviet units were to begin
combat operations loaded with several days' worth of fuel and munitions. Food
and other "nonessential" items might never reach the troops. Soldiers were
encouraged, by hunger if nothing else, to live off the land. Units were to
advance for a few days or a week and then halt to rest and resupply. Western
units attempt to maintain continuous operations.

Whichever supply method is used, supplies are maintained at several different levels. The lowest level is the munitions carried with the weapon. This is
commonly called a "unit of fire." An infantryman carries with him up to 300
rounds of assault-rifle ammunition. An artillery piece carries 50–100 or more
rounds depending on caliber. A tank carries 40 or more rounds for its main gun,
about a ton of all munitions, and up to a ton of fuel. Artillery units carry several

tons of munitions with each gun. The next higher unit, usually a division, will carry additional units of fire. At army and theater level, a dozen or more units of fire are held, typically immobile in supply dumps. Now you know where that term came from: they dump the stuff anywhere in the expectation that it will be moved and used shortly. A Soviet division tried to carry into battle five units of fire (1,000 tons each) and three or four refills for its vehicles' fuel tanks (1,000 tons each). U.S. and Western divisions are larger. U.S. divisional fuel refills and units of fire weigh about 1,100 tons each. Western divisions carry fewer of each, closer to two of fuel and three of munitions. Western units expect supply to keep moving; the Soviets were more pessimistic, or pragmatic.

Soviet and Western supply-delivery systems differed in who was responsible for moving supplies. In Soviet practice, senior units were responsible for moving supplies forward to their subordinate units. In Western units it works both ways, primarily because there is more transport and because subordinate units have more leeway in how they operate. The Soviet system was more straightforward and pragmatic; it was also more easily disrupted and prone to collapse. The Western system requires a lot more on-the-spot decision making. It is a more flexible system and more likely to survive a fluid battlefield. This was demonstrated during the 1991 Gulf War. Even before that, Soviet officers were agitating for adopting a more "Western" style of warfare. After the Soviet empire collapsed later in 1991, this movement went into high gear. While the current successor states to the Soviet Union still possess very "Soviet" armed forces, many of the officers in charge look to Desert Storm as an example of how it should be done.

On one point, both Western- and Soviet-style armies were converging: the overriding dependence on firepower. Soviet armies always used a lot of firepower, but largely in fixed situations. For example, Soviet armies were legendary for their prodigious artillery preparations. Fewer opportunities are expected for this use of artillery. Everyone is expected to move around a lot, and artillery preparations will be have to be delivered hastily before the opportunity passes. Unstable battlefields and unpredictable supply deliveries will be the norm. The future is a logistical nightmare.

Looting and pillaging will become more common. Soviet planners always kept an eye on civilian fuel storage areas. Whether planned or not, troops will grab whatever they require in times of need. In the best of times, arming a man still seems to change his concepts of property rights. Iraqi troops in Kuwait gave a rather vivid demonstration of this in 1990.

Fists of Iron, Feet of Clay

Failures in the logistical system are quickly recognized. The absence of food or fuel are noticed even if no one is shooting at you. Logistics people are aware of this and expend considerable effort in contingency planning. Although planning is ordinarily done around logistical constraints, the logistics planners are never aware of all the new twists in overall military plans. Worse, you never know exactly what your potential opponent has in mind for your logistical efforts. If your own people decide to pursue a new tactic for using artillery and, perhaps, order the armored vehicles not to move around as much, this is going to change supply demands. The supply people will be informed of these changes, but no one knows exactly how this will impact ammo and fuel expenditure on the battlefield. Despite its dour reputation, keeping the supplies moving can be very exciting.

An intelligent and perceptive commander will always attempt to deny his opponent supply while preventing the enemy from doing the same. Most combat sorties are flown against enemy supply lines and dumps. If one side gains air superiority for any length of time, his opponent can generally forget about victory. With an enemy air force overhead, supplies are constantly being hunted down and delayed or destroyed. As in the past, it is possible to hide your supplies and their transports completely from enemy air power. Some supply will always get through. That is sufficient if you are a guerrilla force fighting a regular army. If you are a mechanized army, these troublesome air attacks can be fatal. This was first seen in the summer of 1944. Allied airpower shut down all rail and most road movement within several hundred miles of the D-Day invasion beaches at Normandy. The Germans fought at a severe handicap. This is just as well; it took the allies over a month to break through the German resistance. A motorized and heavily armed army is in worse shape today. The aircraft have better sensors, can fly in any weather, and carry more lethal warloads. Although antiaircraft weapons are also more powerful and numerous, the aircraft still have the advantage of choosing where they will go and when. Enormous quantities of supply are required to maintain a combat division. It takes over 200 tons of fuel to move a division 100 kilometers. A single U.S. M-1A1 tank battalion in the 1991 Gulf War could consume nearly 500 tons of supply (mostly fuel and water) in 24 hours of constant movement and fighting. Worse, it takes five tons of conventional artillery to inflict one casualty on the enemy. Not having the degree of supply you are used to creates a cascade of unwelcome events. Well, they are unwelcome to some. Lack of supply slows down the tempo of combat and results in fewer casualties. Lack of mobility prevents units from getting to the fighting, or avoiding being bypassed. Combat units often begin abandoning vehicles and equipment in order to move some of their strength. This abandonment diminishes combat power, if not immediately then eventually. Support vehicles, such as repair and supply resources, will be needed soon. Lacking this support, combat vehicles will be lost where they could normally be saved. The impact of poor supply is more acutely felt when attacking. A defender can more effectively stretch diminished resources. A shovel needs no fuel or spare parts. Mechanized combat divisions, with all their high-tech weapons, are very fragile units. When their constant and copious supply of fuel, munitions, and spares are interrupted, they are revealed to have fists of iron but feet of clay.

Air Force and Navy Logistics

Air forces, including naval air forces, concentrate on one thing: generating sorties. A sortie is one flight by one aircraft on some kind of mission. Hundreds of man-hours and 10–20 tons of supplies are needed to launch one sortie. The cost is over half a million dollars if it is a combat mission. For each ground combat division in a battle area, there would be about 100 combat aircraft. In the first few days of an operation, each aircraft could fly about three sorties. Three hundred sorties equals about 4,000 tons of supplies, over twice the daily rate for a division. Fortunately, air bases are not as mobile as combat divisions and are typically at least 50–100 kilometers away from the fighting. An air unit's primary problem is just getting the supply to the aircraft. At sea, the major consumer of supply is the aircraft carrier. A large carrier carries sufficient supplies to support about 1,000 sorties. With about 80 aircraft, most of these sorties will be flown by support aircraft, or combat aircraft on patrol missions. Like land-based combat aircraft, their naval counterparts will consume the same prodigious amounts of material on strike missions. A carrier task force can easily consume 5,000 tons of supply a day while at sea. A non-carrier task force will need less than a third that amount. Navies prefer to keep their supply mobile, with dozens of tankers and dry cargo ships chasing after or accompanying the task forces. These combat support naval ships are constantly at risk from enemy submarines. Even at sea, the people who move supplies are eagerly sought targets. Wartime demands require that civilian merchant ships be pressed into service to supply the fleet. Navy technicians and some special equipment is required to perform at-sea resupply. Sometimes, naval personnel are put aboard merchant ships to make them capable of at-sea replenishment. More often, merchant ships move supplies to forward naval bases, where the specialized naval supply ships pick them up for transport into the combat zone.

Few nations have any at-sea replenishment capability at all, and none have the ability to supply so many ships so far from their home port as the United States.

Theory and Practice

The magnitude of unrepairable breakdowns of high-tech equipment in wartime will be shocking only to those who ignored the trends. The Western nations have similar problems, but at least they see them coming and are better equipped to overcome the shortages. During the 1990 buildup for the Gulf War, U.S. forces quickly discovered which items had not been stocked in sufficient quantity in peacetime to support a wartime level of operations. A strong and resourceful market economy back in the United States made it possible to manufacture (sometimes after quickly designing the item first) the needed parts and equipment.

More so than in past wars, supply movements will face greater danger than ever before. Missiles and a more fluid battlefield will eliminate the relative reliability of past supply movements. Western nations have a more serious problem in their reluctance to stockpile spares and munitions for the opening stages of a war. The combat-unit commanders plan to use thousands of tons of munitions per day in the opening battles. Many smaller Western nations have stocks to last less than a week at this rate. Nations like the United States aren't much better off.

One of the recurring problems of the last century has been commanders underestimating supply requirements during the early stages of a war. America had the problem during Korea and Vietnam and even in the 1991 Gulf War. The Soviet Union was similarly caught short in Afghanistan. The wisdom gained in these wars proved to have a short shelf life. Face it, logistics is not the sort of thing that gets the attention of commanders and their budgets in peacetime. It is too easy to ignore it or simply study the problem to death without undertaking a solution.

Another problem unique to the United States is the level of additional goodies peacetime planners add to what is "required" for troops overseas. The Army is the biggest offender in this area because Army troops do not normally train at moving large units overseas, for extended periods. The Navy is constantly overseas, and their Marines regularly land units up to brigade strength over distant shores. Fortunately, most potential wars involving the United States require small numbers of troops. American planners, however, live in fear of being asked to move several divisions quickly to a distant battlefield, and keeping them there for months under combat conditions. This happened in 1990–91. What prevented a logistical disaster was a six-month period of no enemy activity to allow for a supply buildup and the construction of a supply system. The Army general in charge of logistics was promoted during the operation. He received this honor because he was able to improvise solutions for many of the logistical nightmares U.S. forces brought with them to the Gulf. Some of these improvisations were directly a result of civilian technology that Western nations have in abundance. For example, it was discovered that it was taking too long (several weeks) to get parts requests back to the United States using the normal "system." So, a laptop computer and satellite communications link were rigged together, and a parts clerk was able to sit in the desert and get parts requests transmitted to America, and get confirmations on availability sent back to the desert, in less than an hour. You need that kind of resourcefulness, and resources, to avoid logistical disasters in modern wars.

The 2001 war in Afghanistan taught American commanders a valuable lesson in the limitations imposed by logistics. After the lavishly supplied 1991 Gulf War, operating in Afghanistan was the other side of the coin. Anyone who wasn't a believer in logistics before Afghanistan was a believer after.

The Future

Commercial methods of handling and moving materials have made tremendous advances during the last few decades, even if many of these developments were not adopted by the military. The 1991 Gulf War saw an extensive adoption of commercial materiel-handling techniques and equipment. Modern weapons are built to fire a lot more ammunition in a shorter time than in the past. Current armored fighting vehicles are faster and more agile than equipment 30 or 40 years ago. Logistics vehicle mobility has not improved as rapidly. Slowly, some nations are producing resupply vehicles that can keep up with the fast-moving armored fighting vehicles. The biggest question mark is whether enough of these vehicles will be available during a major operation. During the Gulf War, sufficient heavy-lift vehicles had to be begged, borrowed, leased, and in a few cases stolen to meet the troops' needs. The United States did, in the 1980s, begin to build specialized cross-country military transports. Several thousand of these 10-ton, cross-country HEMTTs (Heavy Expanded Mobility Tactical Trucks) trucks were available in the Gulf, and they were a vital part of the success of the campaign. The U.S. also had about a thousand HET (Heavy Equipment Transporter) tank transporters available. More of both classes of vehicles are being built.

On the positive side, the increasing use of private automobiles provides enormous stocks of gasoline for military vehicles that do not require special fuel. This was a valuable asset in Saudi Arabia, as it would be in major industrial areas like Europe. But in too many potential hot spots, there's not much of anything to sustain a major mechanized force. In most parts of the world, all the logistician will find are headaches and aggravation.

Divisional Daily Supply Requirements

This chart shows divisional supply requirements for each day of operations. For logistics purposes, we have four types of operations: offense, defense, pursuit, and reserve. Reality is not as neat as this chart. Offensive operations will generally use all the supply they can get. Defensive operations try to adapt their supply needs to the intensity of their attackers' efforts. Sometimes a unit will use enormous quantities of supply on the defense if the materiel is available and the position must be held. At other times the defender will be parsimonious with supplies while sacrificing men and ground instead. A pursuit is similar to simply moving around a lot. Reserve is sitting in one place, sometimes in contact with the enemy, using as little supply as possible. The last category is the average of all the above operations, in a mixture typical of future combat. This is the average amount of supplies given an assumed mix of the different types of operations. Troops don't spend all their time doing any of the four types of combat, but a mix. The supply norms for U.S.-type divisions were estimated from each nation's policies. Divisions can easily consume three or four times more ammunition in a day. Often this is the case. For planning purposes, norms are established so that operations can be planned without exceeding available supplies.

Supply type is the class of supply. The official NATO terms for the various classes of supply are: Class 1, Food; Class 2/7/9, Individual equipment/medical/spares; Class 3, Fuel; Class 4, Barrier and construction material; Class 5, Ammunition.

Ammo is munitions, primarily artillery ammunition.

Fuel is all types of fuel, for vehicles, aircraft, and power generators. Usage is highest in pursuit operations because every vehicle is moving. In combat operations, combat vehicles do most of their moving as they maneuver about the battlefield. In reserve operations, most movement is by noncombat support vehicles.

Food includes canned and other long-shelf-life combat rations, as well as fresh provisions for units in stable situations.

Spares is all the spare parts to keep equipment going and the troops in good health. It also includes medical supplies, normal replacements for clothing and equipment, and so on.

Tons is the number of tons of supply for each class and type of operation.

% shows the percentage of each class of supply for each type of operation.

Lbs./man is the pounds per man of supply for each type of operation. Armies other than those of the United States have similar supply norms. Other Western armies use, if anything, somewhat higher norms than the United States, especially for ammunition. Armies using Russian equipment generally use somewhat lower norms. Less wealthy nations also use lower norms. Norms will always be modified by the quantities of men, weapons, and equipment in divisions, as well as the tempo of operations.

It is still possible to fight a low-budget war. It depends on whom you are fighting and where. An ill-armed and ill-equipped opponent requires less

Supply type	U.S. armor division (tons)		U.S. infantry division (tons)	
Offense				
Ammo	2,300	64%	2,500	66%
Fuel	1,133	31%	1,210	32%
Food	40	1%	51	1%
Spares	137	4%	55	1%
Total	3,610	100%	3,816	100%
lbs./man	481		525	
Defense				
Ammo	3,000	81%	3,500	82%
Fuel	616	17%	671	16%
Food	41	1%	49	1%
Spares	40	1%	50	1%
Total	3,697	100%	4,270	100%
lbs./man	493		587	
Pursuit				
Ammo	400	17%	410	21%
Fuel	1,914	80%	1,496	75%
Food	42	2%	50	3%
Spares	46	2%	44	2%
Total	2,402	100%	2,000	100%
lbs./man	320		275	
Reserve				
Ammo	390	41%	438	46%
Fuel	484	50%	440	47%
Food	41	4%	48	5%
Spares	44	5%	20	2%
Total	959	100%	946	100%
lbs./man	128		130	
Average				
Ammo	1,135	65%	1,309	68%
Fuel	467	27%	461	24%
Food	73	4%	79	4%
Spares	74	4%	65	3%
	1,749	100%	1,914	100%
	233		263	

ammunition to fight. More fuel may be required for running around a lot, as in anti-guerrilla actions. Modern armies fighting guerrillas also use a lot of munitions trying to keep the little buggers out of mischief.

M-939A2 five-ton tactical truck

Ground-Transport Characteristics

This is easy. There are a few rules of thumb for military transport. The most important one is the amount of fuel used by trucks to travel a hundred kilometers, as a percentage of their load. It's between .5 and 1 percent of that load. Most military trucks are basically four-wheel-drive versions of civilian models or simply civilian trucks with a drab paint job. The carrying capacity of military trucks is generally between 3 and 10 tons. The smaller vehicles, like the Jeep and Hummer, consume between 1.2 percent (Hummer) and 4 percent (some types of Jeep). But these smaller vehicles have a much smaller carrying capacity (.4–.5 tons for Jeeps and 1.1 tons for the Hummer).

Armored vehicles are a different matter. To move these beasts a hundred kilometers it takes 5–15 pounds of fuel per ton of vehicle weight. At the lower end you have lighter armored vehicles using low-power engines and wheels. At the high end you have very heavy tanks (like the U.S. M-1) using a gas-turbine engine.

Supply Requirements for Aircraft

Aircraft logistics is complicated by the spares situation and unused munitions. High-performance aircraft literally burn up many of their components.

Engines are the biggest item. These must be replaced every few hundred or few thousand hours, depending on the aircraft and the amount of stressful maneuvering. The weight of a new engine won't add that much to each sortie, but the expense will be noticeable. On the bright side, many aircraft return from missions with expensive weapons they did not have to use. This is common with interceptors; they don't always have to fire all the missiles they carry. Bombers no longer jettison their loads if targets cannot be found. The down side of this is that you have a lot of aircraft landing with live ordnance dangling from them. This adds a little more excitement to landing accidents.

Aircraft	Tons carried Fuel	Warload	Avg. sortie per day	Tons/100 sorties	Tons/100 aircraft	Percent of supply warload	Warload /100 aircraft
Russian land-based							
MiG-21	2.1	1.5	1	360	360	42%	150
MiG-23	4.7	1.5	1	620	620	24%	150
MiG-27	4.7	4.5	1	920	920	49%	450
MiG-25	15.1	2	0.5	1,710	855	12%	100
MiG-29	4	4.5	2	850	1,700	53%	900
Su-17	3.3	4.5	1	780	780	58%	450
Su-24	24	4.5	1	2,850	2,850	16%	450
Su-25	3.5	6.5	2	1,000	2,000	65%	1,300
Su-27	5	2	2	700	1,400	29%	400
Tu-22M	13.4	8	1	2,140	2,140	37%	800
Mi-8	2	4	4	600	2,400	67%	1,600
Mi-24	1.5	1.7	4	320	1,280	53%	680
Western land-based							
F-4	5.7	7.2	2	1,290	2,580	56%	1,440
F-16	3.2	6.9	3	1,010	3,030	68%	2,070
F-15	6.1	7.2	3	1,330	3,990	54%	2,160
A-10	6.1	7.2	5	1,330	6,650	54%	3,600
Mirage III	2.7	1.5	2	420	840	36%	300
F-104	2.8	3.4	1	620	620	55%	340
Harrier	3.5	3.6	5	710	3,550	51%	1,800
Tornado	5.2	7.2	2	1,240	2,480	58%	1,440
Alpha	1.5	2.2	3	370	1,110	59%	660
F-6	1.8	0.5	1	230	230	22%	50
F-111	15.4	10	1	2,540	2,540	39%	1,000
UH-1	1	2	5	300	1,500	67%	1,000
AH-1S	1	0.5	4	150	600	33%	200
UH-60	2	3	5	500	2,500	60%	1,500
AH-64	7	1.7	4	870	3,480	20%	680
U.S. carrier aircraft							
F-14	7.5	6.5	2	1,400	2,800	46%	1,300
A-7	4.5	6.8	3	1,130	3,390	60%	2,040
A-6	7.2	8.1	3	1,530	4,590	53%	2,430
F-18	5.1	7.7	3	1,280	3,840	60%	2,310

Aircraft is the aircraft designation, although more than one variant of an aircraft often exists. These variants sometimes differ significantly in characteristics. An average is used here.

Fuel is the average tonnage of fuel used on one sortie.

Warload is the average load of disposable weapons carried on one sortie. It is assumed that some of the air-to-air missiles will be brought back unused. Unused bombs are sometimes dropped to avoid landing accidents.

Average sorties per day can vary quite a lot depending on the situation and the skill of the ground crews. Number used here is the average.

Tons/100 sorties is the total tonnage of supply required for 100 sorties. This includes an allowance for maintenance supplies and supply needed to maintain personnel.

Tons/100 aircraft is the total tonnage of supply for 100 aircraft of each type per day if they are flying the average number of sorties per day.

Percent of supply warload is the percentage of the total supply requirements that is disposable weapons (bombs, bullets, missiles, etc.). You can see significant differences in carrying capacity, particularly between Western and Soviet aircraft.

Warload/100 aircraft is the warload carried by 100 aircraft of each type per day if they are flying the average number of sorties per day.

24
Attrition

Combat does not destroy armed forces; it merely hastens the process. The real killer is day-to-day wear and tear. Armies die by inches, not yards. Attrition is people and their equipment wearing out. Even in peacetime, up to 2 percent of combat aircraft can be lost to accidents and deterioration each year. In wartime, up to 50 percent of aircraft will be lost each year to noncombat wear and tear. Rarely more than 90 percent of armored vehicles will be in running condition at any one time. Those vehicles that are running will likely break down after going less than 500 kilometers. More important, people wear out, too. Without enough people to tend them, the machines wear out even faster.

What Really Destroys Armies

Annually, disease and noncombat injuries often cause far more loss than the dangers of combat. Most major wars go on for years. Battles are relatively infrequent. As long as the troops are living in primitive field conditions, they are more prone to disease and injury. The annual loss rates in the wars of this century, expressed in terms of average daily losses per 100,000 men, bear this out. Battle losses, killed and wounded but not prisoners, varied from a low of six per day in World War II theaters such as North Africa to over 200 Germans a day on the Soviet front. Soviet casualties were sometimes double the German rate. World War I had battles where the rate exceeded several thousand per day. Nuclear war could easily exceed even these horrendous rates.

The World War I casualty rates, and the numerous mutinies they eventually caused, were not forgotten. The butchery of World War I made an impression, and the casualty rates were consistently lower in World War II. Since World War II, still more efforts have been made to protect the troops. Armored

517

vehicles and protective gear have become more commonplace. Daily loss rates of 40 per 100,000, similar to the Western allies of World War II, can be expected in the future in a war between equally matched armies. Nuclear or chemical weapons may push this up, but high loss rates in a short time may also cause disintegration of military units. This is likely because these wide-area weapons are intended for use against combat support and supply units. The combat forces cannot advance with empty weapons and stomachs.

Non-battle casualties, primarily from disease and especially in tropical and winter conditions, regularly reach 200–500 men per day per 100,000 strength. Malaria alone can cause nearly 200 casualties a day. Another constant menace in populated areas is venereal disease, which can render ineffective as many as 40 men per day. Injuries often exceed battle losses. The troops tend to get careless in the combat zone. Vehicle and weapons accidents were so common in the past that they often reached 20 men per day per 100,000 troops.

The Forms of Combat Losses

Losses as a direct result of combat—the effects of enemy weapons as opposed to indirect effects such as trench foot, malaria, or pneumonia contracted from sleeping in a wet trench—fall into four categories:

Fatal. The victim is dead.

Wounded. The victim is injured, but not fatally, and has a good chance of returning to combat.

Mental. The victim suffers a mental breakdown from the stresses of combat.

Absence. The victim is captured or deserts.

FATAL/WOUNDED RATIOS

The rate and lethality of combat casualties vary with such factors as the amount of enemy artillery fire versus machine-gun fire. Artillery will cause more, but less lethal, casualties than bullets. Closed terrain like forests and towns allow proportionately more bullet wounds by reducing the effects of artillery. Fast-moving operations prevent treatment of wounded troops; many more die or take longer to recover. Better-prepared and better-led troops avoid casualties. Armored vehicles, fortifications, and protective clothing all reduce casualties and their severity. Finally, the availability and efficiency of medical care make a difference. Leaving out the absent prisoners and deserters and assuming the usual heavy use of fragmentation weapons (shells and bombs), historical experience suggests there will be one fatality for every three wounded troops. About 80 percent of these casualties will be caused by fragments. About 12 percent of these wounds will occur in the head (43 percent immediately fatal), 16 percent in the chest (25 percent fatal), 11 percent in the abdomen (17 percent fatal), and 22 percent in arms and legs (5 percent fatal). In the past, 20 percent of all wounds were multiple and over half of those combinations were fatal. Modern lightweight plastic armor in the form of Kevlar cloth or rigid plate will reduce fatalities and injuries up to 25 percent. This material does cause heat buildup in warm weather, sometimes leading to heat-exhaustion injuries. If it is used selectively for troops in exposed situations, its beneficial aspects are retained without injurious side effects. Although the jackets cost over $500, the savings in troops, not to mention the morale boost, are well worth it. In addition to the armored jackets, improved helmets, boots, and protective curtains for vehicle interiors are available. Many of these items were first widely used during World War II by U.S. bomber crews. The U.S. Army is now the leading proponent of these protective measures, followed by other Western nations and, lately, even some Third World nations.

MENTAL CASUALTIES

Combat is an extremely stressful activity that causes a number of nervous breakdowns and related disabilities. These disabling maladies are commonly called combat fatigue. The rate of breakdown is highest in poorly trained and badly led armed forces. During World War II, the U.S. Army had three combat fatigue cases for every two troops wounded in combat. For every 100 men killed, 125 were discharged from service because of mental breakdown. The average combat-fatigue victim was out of action half as long as men who were physically wounded. The German army, in contrast, had only 13 combat fatigue cases for every 100 wounded. This was primarily a result of better training and leadership. Other armies fell somewhere in between these extremes. A contemporary war may well produce higher levels of combat fatigue because of the higher intensity of fighting and lower levels of training and experience. The Germans did better handling combat fatigue in World War II because they carefully studied their World War I experience and planned accordingly.

PRISONERS AND DESERTERS

Losses are not always due to death and injury. Soldiers are taken prisoner, and others decide to pursue more peaceful endeavors and desert. The number of prisoners and deserters varies considerably depending on how badly you are losing. Even a victorious force lists a few percent of its total losses as MIA (missing in action). About 50 percent of MIAs are KIA (killed in action) or badly wounded and dead before they can be identified. Many of the rest turn out to be deserters (who sometimes surface years later) or prisoners (who die in captivity). In the U.S. Army, it has sometimes happened that men who were killed in combat were reported as missing by friends so that the dead man's family could continue to receive his pay. Eventually, MIAs are declared dead, their pay stopped, and death benefits paid.

Deserters will often come forward after the war and throw themselves on the mercy of the courts. In wartime, desertion is punishable by death or a long prison sentence. Waiting for the war to end thus improves a deserter's chances of getting away with it. Most deserters are actually combat-fatigue cases who simply broke and ran for it. A substantial minority of deserters are criminals who calculate their prospects are better by leaving their units and continuing their black-market or other criminal activities out of uniform.

Historically, many men who surrender are not captured alive by the enemy. Up to 50 percent of those surrendering do not survive the process. They are either killed on the spot or die in captivity. Troops in combat quickly learn this, which explains why surrender is not more common. When survivable surrenders do occur, they tend to be in large numbers or by negotiation.

WASTING AWAY

It's not unusual for armies to waste away to nothing without ever having come in contact with the enemy. Historically, natural causes have killed or disabled far more soldiers than combat. Many wars are won by the side best able to maintain the health of their troops. Perceptive military commanders have long recognized the substantial assistance of General Winter, Colonel Mud, and the carnage wrought by pestilence, poor climate, thirst, and starvation. An armed force may be an impressive sight. Yet people have to live. They must eat, sleep, and escape the elements. Disease and injury are ever present. Adequate medical care prevents minor afflictions from becoming major ones. More important is public sanitation. Many diseases thrive in careless accumulations of human waste. Public sanitation, even within an army on the move, eliminates the cause of most disease. For example, from 1900–1940 in the United States, the average life expectancy of males increased 12 years (a 31 percent increase) as a result of improved sanitation. Since 1940, the introduction of many wonder drugs and medical procedures have lifted life expectancy another nine years (a 15 percent increase). During World War II, sanitation was so bad in the Japanese army, and disease so widespread, that infantry battalions in tropical areas would lose over 10 percent of their strength per month just to disease and privation.

The American Army's history of disease deaths is illustrative. In 1846

(Mexican-American War), 10 percent of troops died from disease. In the 1860s (Civil War), 7.2 percent. In 1918 (World War I), 1.3 percent. In the 1940s (World War II), .6 percent. Although the deaths due to disease have declined markedly, the incidence of disease has not. Historical experience with noncombat losses demonstrates that armies are never far from a disaster of uncontrolled disease. The 1991 Gulf War was unique in that for the first time this century, an American army suffered more noncombat than combat casualties. This was an aberration because of the overwhelming combat power brought to bear on the enemy. Most battles are more evenly matched and not fought in as disease-ridden an area as the Persian Gulf.

Useful Combat Life

Warfare produces many bizarre situations. For example, a dead soldier is less of a loss than a wounded one. While a dead soldier is no longer useful, neither is a wounded one, and a wounded trooper requires the attention of others and is not always returned to action. Some armies actually do follow this cold-blooded policy, either officially or due to circumstances, of killing the badly wounded. A "shoot the wounded" policy soon demoralizes troops to the point where they will desert or violently resist their leaders. Some armies enforce such bloody-minded systems with ruthless efficiency. In the Soviet army, a division had a hospital with only 60 beds. Medical facilities throughout the division were slight. Wounded men were to make their way to the rear as best they could. Those who couldn't generally perished. Draconian methods were used to ensure acceptance to this system. As Josef Stalin put it, "It takes a very brave man to not be a hero in the Red Army."

Commanders must still take into account the mathematics of combat casualties. Combat wears a man down and out, particularly infantry fighting. Experience has shown that the average soldier can be effective for about 200 days of combat. After that, you generally have a case of combat fatigue—someone dangerous to himself and those around them. At that point, these veterans are best removed to noncombat jobs or civilian occupations. Let us assume that this will provide another 400 days of useful service. If a soldier is killed after 100 days of combat, the armed forces lose 500 days of service. During World War II, 65 percent of all incidents of lost time in the U.S. Army were from noncombat injuries. These resulted in very few deaths. Still, each case put a soldier out of action for 10 days. The average combat injury put a soldier out of action for 100 days. Twenty percent of combat injuries resulted in death. For each day a soldier is out of action due to wounds or disease, one or more additional soldiers are assigned to taking care of him. For this reason, nonfatal casualties comprise two-thirds of the days lost due to injury or illness. Therefore, taking 100 injured soldiers we have the following pattern of lost days:

- *Combat deaths*—1. 500 days lost or 21 percent of total days lost for injuries. This is only 13 percent of days lost if time of medical personnel is included.
- *Combat wounded*—4. 400 days lost or 17 percent of days lost, although 22 percent if medical personnel time is included.
- *Noncombat deaths* (mostly accidents)—1. Same as combat deaths.
- *Noncombat illness and injuries*—94. 940 days lost or 41 percent of time lost; some 52 percent if medical personnel time is included.

Chemical and nuclear casualties (nonfatal) tend to be more severe than the usual noncombat "illness," but not as devastating as combat wounds from shot and shell. Perhaps only 50 days are lost per chemical/nuclear casualty. With medical personnel time added, this comes to over 100 days lost per incident. Since each soldier may be wounded by chemical agents several times, the total time lost approaches that of a combat death. Moreover, chemical and nuclear injuries are expected to have a severe psychological effect, probably resulting in higher combat-fatigue losses. This is another reason why commanders are reluctant to use these weapons. They risk losing control of their troops.

The Rate of Return

Depending on the quality of training and leadership, the rate of troops returning to duty after combat injury will vary. During World War II, the German army achieved an 80 percent return rate, while the U.S. Army returned 64 percent. The higher German rate was partially the result of returning slightly disabled troops to less physically demanding duty, and partially attributable to better administration. Generally, 60 percent of the combat wounded who eventually recover return to duty within three months, 85 percent within six months, and over 95 percent within a year. Fifty percent of the noncombat casualties return within a month, 85 percent within three months, and nearly all by six months.

Since World War II, the United States has pioneered rapid evacuation of wounded troops, usually by helicopter. This is a major advantage, as the treatment a wounded soldier receives within an hour of being wounded often determines survival or how rapid eventual recovery will be. The high quality of U.S. medical care has saved many troops who previously would have died. The return-to-duty rate has not gone up because of this.

Naval and Air Casualties

Navies and air forces suffer far fewer casualties, in absolute and relative terms, than armies. Exceptions to this are not uncommon. Aircraft crews and submarine personnel take a pounding, often proportionately worse than the infantry. But there are a lot more infantry getting shot at. In a large-scale war, when naval and air bases are attacked, the naval and air force personnel casualty rate can be expected to be one quarter to one half the army's rate.

Most naval casualties are suffered at sea. About a third of the deaths are from noncombat injuries. Combat deaths generally equal combat injuries. This is because ships suffer catastrophic damage—being blown up or sinking quickly and killing or injuring nearly all the crew. Modern ships are heavily armed and unarmored, which makes them prime candidates for massive losses from smoke and fire.

During World War II, the loss rate—dead, wounded, and captured—for long-range bombers averaged nearly four men per aircraft lost, and one aircraft was lost for every 100 sorties (66 sorties for bombers, 145 sorties for fighters). Altogether, 40,000 aircraft were lost during the three-year strategic bombing campaign in Europe. Current aircraft fly one or two sorties a day and would probably last less than three months in constant combat unless they were on the side that quickly obtained air superiority. This has been the case with American warplanes over the last two decades, and this has kept American warplane losses very low. But the losses for American opponents have been correspondingly huge. Most modern aircraft have a crew of one, which results in a much lower rate of air-crew losses. Modern aircraft are also more reliable, lowering noncombat losses and increasing chances of surviving battle damage. Air bases are likely to take a greater pounding now than in past wars, largely because of more capable aircraft, weapons, and ballistic missiles.

Theory and Practice

Casualties in wartime are taken for granted and accepted. What to do about them is less clear. Casualties have several effects. The victim feels it first, and longest. But the victim's companions also get hit with a bit of stress and dismay. The unit suffering casualties undergoes instant reorganization, whether it is ready or not. Some armed forces cope with the psychological problems accompanying losses better than others. Combat units rarely have the number of troops they are supposed to have. Noncombat losses and administrative requirements will keep between 3–10 percent of a unit's strength unavailable at any time. Combat losses simply increase the organizational disruption. During the opening stages of a major and protracted war, not all attempts to cope with these losses will be successful. Aside from the problems of anticipating what equipment and types of troops will be lost and in what quantities, you have better and worse ways to send the replacements in. Generally, it is more effective to pull battered units out of combat, rest them, introduce new men and equipment, and put the revived unit through some training. The temptation is strong to keep units in action and feed in the replacements. This rarely gives good results but is often done, anyway.

Firepower has increased since World War II, even without taking nuclear weapons into account. Armies have equipped themselves with more potent weapons in nearly every category. For example:

Infantry weapons. At the end of World War II, the Germans began to arm their infantry with the SG-44, which the Soviets copied as the AK-47. The United States responded with the M-16 (first proposed in the 1930s). It has long been noted that a machine gun generates firepower equal to ten or more rifle-armed troops. Now nearly every soldier has a machine gun, albeit a lightweight one. Still, infantry firepower has more than tripled since 1945.

Artillery. The bigger-is-better concept applies to artillery, increasing size development. The average artillery shell in World War II weighed about 33 pounds (105mm); today it is close to 100 pounds (155mm). Armies plan on firing more shells per day per gun, something on the order of three to five times more weight of shell per day. The design of artillery munitions has changed. Shells are now two to three times more lethal for those nations that can afford these ICMs (Improved Conventional Munitions). Improved fire control, and the use of rockets, provides the most devastating artillery ever available. The introduction of ICM with robotic submunitions will make artillery even more lethal.

Armored vehicles. Armies have a lot more of them. In 1945, the average Western division had about ten AFVs (armored fighting vehicles) per thousand troops. Today, we find nearly one hundred AFVs per thousand troops in the armies of industrialized nations. The quality of AFVs available to different armies also varies much more. The United States and other Western nations have very capable tanks like the M-1, while many Third World nations have T-55s and T-72s, which are far outclassed by the M-1-type vehicles.

Air power. This never has been a significant source of injury to combat troops, although it is the scourge of support units behind the fighting line. The introduction of the helicopter produced an air weapon that caused the combat troops a lot of grief. Air forces have also produced special fixed-wing aircraft for support of front-line troops. Until the 1980s, helicopters provided the majority of the air power for use against combat troops. But during the 1980s, fighter-bombers received much more accurate bombing systems, enabling them literally to take out one target with one bomb more than half the time. AFVs in particular have more to worry about from air weapons than ever before.

Electronics. Most new weapons depend on electronic controls and sensors for their efficient operation. This increases the accuracy of weapons, even though electronic warfare is more common. However, the electronic warfare is largely directed against communications, not weapons sensors and controls.

Chemical and nuclear weapons. Considerable inhibitions exist against using these weapons, especially against someone who can return the favor. If they are used, all previous norms for casualty rates go out the window. Losses would be four, five, or more times the rates with conventional weapons. This is very true if nuclear weapons are used. Chemical weapons, based on past experience, would increase casualties but may well slow operations to a crawl.

Considering these developments, what is to prevent casualty rates from doubling, tripling, or worse? Several other defensive measures are now available. Many troops have flak jackets and better helmets. This provides good protection against artillery fragments and some bullets. In addition, nearly every combat soldier rides in an armored vehicle. Recent experience has shown that more armored vehicles have not reduced the casualty rate appreciably, although vehicle losses are increasing enormously. What may decrease losses in a major war is the peculiar relationship between personnel and AFV losses. For all their apparent robustness, AFVs are more fragile than troops. Experience shows that the percentage of AFV losses will be 4–10 times personnel casualties. If troops suffer 5 percent losses, the units' AFV losses would be 20–50 percent. Many of the AFV losses are not combat-related but are the result of breakdowns. AFV casualties can usually be repaired quickly, over 10 times as fast as wounded troops are returned. If the troops continue fighting without their disabled AFVs, their losses will increase. This will have a more debilitating effect on the staying power of assaults than most commanders would like to admit. Once troops have tasted the security of armored vehicles, they are less enthusiastic about advancing on foot.

Navies have paralleled the increasing lethality of ground-force weapons. Most naval firepower now comes from missiles, which may be carried by ships of all sizes, and submarines. Those navies with aircraft carriers have increased their firepower through more capable aircraft and more lethal aircraft weapons and sensors.

The Future

Current weapons are more lethal, making it possible to increase historical daily loss rates by a factor of two or more for as long as the expensive munitions hold out. The other side of this is that an army that achieves surprise and attacks with overwhelming force can reduce its own casualties to historical lows. This is what the coalition forces did in the Gulf War and why they achieved a historically low loss rate among their own troops. This has been the trend among industrialized nations. For example, in the 1860s, during the American Civil War, 1 in every 16 soldiers died in battle. A century later, 1 in every 184 soldiers died in Vietnam. In the 1991 Gulf War, one in every 3,300 was killed in combat. Losses were even lower during the 2001 Afghanistan war. Noncombat deaths have been reduced enormously. For nonindustrialized nations, losses are still similar to those in the American Civil War.

After the ammo is gone, things settle down quite a bit, and this still happens quite a lot in wars we generally don't hear much about. The greater mobility of modern armies is also likely to expose more troops to combat, particularly support units that are not as adept at it. Traditionally, a 2 percent daily casualty rate for a 15,000-man division translated into a 10–20 percent rate for the 1,000–2,000 troops actually in contact with the enemy. Better sensors and ICM, plus breakthroughs by the more numerous armored vehicles, can easily increase the daily losses.

Armed forces are better prepared to take care of and prevent noncombat casualties than ever before. Not so mental fatigue, which is likely to be a lot more common during increasingly hyperactive combat. The Germans, during World War II, developed pragmatic techniques for treating combat fatigue that were widely adopted by other nations. During the Korean War, and until the last few years of Vietnam, American troops had combat-fatigue losses at less than a quarter of the World War II rate. However, Israel had increasing levels of combat fatigue in the 1973 and 1982 wars, and again during the 2000–2001 civil disorder with the Palestinians. In 1982 their rate was similar to the U.S. experience of World War II. Part of the 1982 experience can be attributed to the unpopularity of the Lebanon invasion. The same thing happened when combat troops were sent to put down Arab riots in 1987–88. Any future wars featuring increased firepower, lower public support, and sustained combat can be expected to produce above-average combat-fatigue losses.

Equipment attrition can be expected to be higher in future wars. This arises from a combination of new, un-battle-tested equipment made of high-tech, low-reliability components.

Basic Daily Loss Rate

This chart shows the basic daily personnel-loss rates of modern armies, as well as the factors that will increase or decrease these rates. Each factor can increase or decrease casualties, depending on the situation. The examples following these notes explain this phenomenon:

Attacker is the basic daily combat loss rate (3 percent of personnel) for the attacking division-size force. This is a daily loss rate derived from historical experience since 1940. It includes losses from all combat-related sources—dead, wounded, combat fatigue, prisoners, desertion, etc.

Defender is the basic daily loss rate (1.5 percent) for the defending force.

Max effect, maximizing effect, is the most that a particular factor can increase casualties.

Min effect, minimizing effect, is the most that a particular factor can decrease casualties.

Cumulative max/min effect. The cumulative maximum effect for each factor for both attackers and defenders. This shows extent of growth or decline of casualties if all factors are going for or against you.

Size of force takes into account the fact that larger forces devote a smaller proportion of their total manpower to combat troops. Minimum-size force here is a regiment/brigade task force of 3,000–5,000 men, which has double the loss rate. Maximum-size force would be an army of up to 250,000 men, which halves the loss rate. This is another example of the inefficiency of large organizations.

Posture indicates the type of operation the unit is engaged in. Normal attack or defense posture is a 1. Various degrees of retreat cut the basic daily loss rate by up to 70 percent (.3). A retreat, in most cases, is trading space for casualties. These movements can be tricky; if mishandled, the enemy will catch the defenders in the open and inflict even greater losses. Some forms of attack can modify losses. A well-prepared and -executed attack will be easier on the attacker and harder on the defender than a hasty advance in the direction of entrenched defenders.

Modified by the following factors	Max effect	Min effect	Attacker cumulative Max effect	Min effect	Defender cumulative Max effect	Min effect
Size of force	200%	50%	2.0%	0.50%	6.0%	1.50%
Posture	100%	30%	2.0%	0.15%	6.0%	0.45%
Force ratio	160%	70%	3.2%	0.11%	9.6%	0.32%
Time of day	100%	50%	3.2%	0.05%	9.6%	0.16%
Main effort	150%	70%	4.8%	0.04%	14.4%	0.11%
Supply	200%	100%	9.6%	0.04%	28.8%	0.11%

Force ratio. All other things being equal, 10,000 troops of one army are equal in combat power to 10,000 troops of another army. The force ratio, the ratio of one side's troops to another, increases the basic daily loss rate for the side with the smaller force and decreases the loss rate for the larger side. At a 3+:1 ratio, the larger attacking force's loss rate is decreased 30 percent (.7). At a 1:7+ ratio, the smaller attacking force's basic daily loss rate is increased 60 percent (1.6). At 1:1 there is no effect. Examples: a 3+:1 ratio would be a force of 30,000 (or more) versus a force of 10,000. A 1:7+ ratio would be a force of 1,000 versus a force of 7,000 or more. But all things are not equal. It is rare for troops of two different armies to have equal combat value. Before force ratios can be calculated, a unit's combat power must be calculated. This is described in the Factors Modifying Unit Combat Power chart (page 819).

Time of day has not always been an important consideration. In more civilized times, battles almost always took place during the day. Fighting at night is safer, however, and cuts your daily loss rate in half. The reasons are quite simple: you can't shoot accurately at what you cannot see. If you are getting the worst of it, you can more easily hide.

Main effort indicates the intensity of combat. This is usually dictated by the attacker. If the attacker increases the level of activity, the defender must respond. This increased level of activity is typically more artillery fire and keeping up the patrol and assault action around the clock. For this the attacker increases its basic daily loss rate 50 percent. The defender has its basic daily loss rate increased 20 percent. Withdrawal actions increase the basic daily loss rate 30–50 percent.

Supply represents adequate, or degrees of inadequate, materiel. If one side is lacking supplies of ammunition, fuel, food, etc., they will suffer more casualties as they substitute people for materiel.

Examples and Worst Cases

The chart demonstrates that there is a wide range of possible daily casualty rates. All of these combinations of attacker and defender rates have some basis in reality, no matter how bizarre some may appear. Take the extreme case of a 4,000-man force, lacking supplies, making a main-effort attack in daylight against a 100,000-man force that then proceeds to retreat. The attacker would suffer losses of 9.6 percent a day (384 men), the defender .31 percent (310 men). A plausible rationale for this action would be a smaller force trying to pin down a larger force to prevent it from moving off to a more important battle. It happens all the time. A more common situation has the larger, well-supplied force making a main-effort attack against the smaller one in daylight. The unsupplied defender does the wise thing and withdraws. In this case, the attacker's daily loss rate would be .53 percent (530 men) and the defender's 4.5 percent (180 men). If the defender stood his ground, his daily loss rate would go up to 19 percent (760 men). Normally, a 4,000-man force outnumbered 25:1 would not last long. In terms of actual casualties, though, the above figures are historically accurate. It is also historically accurate that the 4,000-man defending force would soon be run right off the battlefield. Naturally, you can only run so far before there is nowhere else to hide. Other possibilities include being surrounded. Being deprived of supply and attacked on all sides further increases your casualties. A week of this and there is little left of the defender. Often, the attacker will simply leave a detachment of 5,000 men to surround the smaller defender and move on with the main force. Other factors can enter into the equation. If the smaller force is defending a mountain pass or other constricted area, the larger force cannot bring all of its combat superiority to bear. A 4,000-man guerrilla force is even more difficult to bring to battle. All this demonstrates that there is more to warfare than simple attrition.

A Multitude of Exceptions

Some armies are more prone to attrition than others. Some wars are, likewise, more prone to higher casualties. Such an unfortunate matchup occurred during World War I. Some armies consistently produced attrition rates three and four times the above rates. No one during World War I had less than double those rates. It is feared that the next big war will again see the basic rates doubled, even without chemical or nuclear weapons. This assumes that everyone does not run out of these highly destructive, and expensive, munitions.

Armies that put a premium on skill and/or technology in place of masses of troops tend to use the basic attrition rates. Nations without the skill or technology go with rates two or three times the basic rate. The Japanese, Chinese, North Vietnamese, Koreans (North and South), and Soviets all experienced doubled rates the last time they fought major wars. The armies of the industrialized nations are more sparing in their use of manpower. During World War II, even though the Germans lost millions of troops, the losses were according to the basic rates. The Soviets lost at twice the rate. Of course, the Soviets won the war. But so did Britain and the United States. The Japanese, who had a somewhat callous attitude toward casualties, also lost. There is no gainsaying that the road to victory, or defeat, is paved with dead bodies.

The Afghan Way of War

The world was reminded in 2001 that there is a more ancient way to fight. Americans were perplexed as they watched Afghans fight in a manner quite unfamiliar to people brought up the Western way of war. The Afghans wage war in their own unique way, and it is quite different from what we normally think of as war. First, it is important to remember that Afghanistan is largely a warrior society, especially among the majority of the population living out in the countryside. An Afghan goes to war not as a soldier, but as a warrior. As such, the Afghan warrior places more importance on honor and showing off than following orders and "accomplishing the mission." American troops carefully plan their operations and everyone follows their orders. Afghans will do what strikes their fancy and pay more attention to perceived slights than getting the job done.

Afghans have a feudal sort of military organization. All the lads going off to war from a village, neighborhood, or valley will follow the most charismatic and most battle-experienced of their group. This guy will be the leader. Not an officer in our sense, but, well, the leader. Very democratic, but the leader might not know a lot about tactics or other military matters. These local groups, rarely more than a few dozen strong, will band together with similar-size groups from their region under an even more famous and charismatic leader. This gets you a group of a few hundred fighters and an organization roughly comparable to what we call an infantry battalion. At this point, money becomes important. Whoever leads several of these battalions is usually wealthy, or is an exceptional battlefield commander who is backed by people with money. Someone has to pay for the food, trucks, ammunition, and whatever else a popular commander can scrounge up (like medical supplies, artillery, tanks, helicopters, housing, and even cash). Several battalions give what is called an "army" (we would call it an infantry brigade), and the leader is often called a warlord by Western reporters.

The warlord's troops do not understand the concept of a Western army's discipline and ranks. In a Western army, any officer can order any soldier to do something. In an Afghan army, a soldier obeys only those leaders he knows. An Afghan warlord cannot be ordered to take part in an operation but must be convinced via a war council. And even his assent does not always translate into consistent performance on the battlefield. Lacking the discipline of a Western army, an Afghan leader has to be very careful when it comes to casualties among his troops. This accounts for the unique way in which Afghans fight battles. Traditionally, Afghan warfare has been more about making an impressive show than getting right down to a hack fest and a lot of dead bodies. A warrior society won't last long if the warriors are too eager to get killed. These days, a loud and impressive display of firepower, but not a lot of casualties, best represents your typical Afghan battle. When someone does lose and gets

taken prisoner, he is often set free in a later exchange of prisoners. Afghan warfare can get very nasty. If the defender strongly resists, and inflicts a lot of
casualties, the attacker will often massacre a lot of local civilians, especially if
they belong to a different ethnic group.

The 1996–2001 war between the Taliban and Northern Alliance largely
consisted of the more powerful Taliban trying to run the Northern Alliance
troops out of Afghanistan (or getting them to switch sides). Each spring, the
Taliban would begin gathering troops for a summer offensive. A dozen or more
Taliban brigades (often over 20,000 troops) would head north to clean out
another Northern Alliance–held region. Meanwhile, both the Taliban and
Northern Alliance depended on local men with guns to hold the passes to their
valleys or the high ground overlooking the roads the enemy trucks had to travel
to get to the local village. Most of the "troops" the Taliban and Northern
Alliance claimed were the men who stayed home. But some of these guys did
go off and join the "field army" for a few weeks or months. These were the
lads in the trucks rolling off to attack, or help defend, some piece of real estate.

Real military power in Afghanistan comes from how many armed men you
can put into trucks and move to other areas to attack or defend. Some artillery
and a few tanks are also useful, but ammunition for these big guns is scarce, so
the big stuff is largely for morale effect. Afghan campaigns are chess games,
where each side shifts its truck columns around to counter enemy moves.

Geography and climate have a lot to do with how battles are fought. Most
of central Afghanistan is mountainous, with many fertile valleys. When there is
only one pass into a valley, you can fortify that and hold off a larger force.
When winter comes, unsuccessful attackers usually have to go home. Trucks
have a hard time bringing food to the troops when the snows start, and in the
cold weather you also need heavier clothing and fuel to keep warm. Those
defending their valley grow their own food and can bring in small stuff like
additional ammunition over mountain trails. Why doesn't the attacker use
those mountain trails to get into the valley? Because the locals know the trails
better and can guard them with a few men.

Which brings us to another aspect of Afghan warfare: keeping the casualties
down. An Afghan commander can see his troops leave for home real quick if too
many of them get killed or injured in combat. Most Afghan battles result in very
few casualties. When one side sees that it is outclassed and likely to be defeated,
it just takes off in the night. If the defender is protecting his valley or town, he will
start negotiating a surrender. Actually, surrender is too strong a word. The preferred move is to switch sides. This is why some areas were "Taliban territory"
but not "Taliban controlled." The surrender options came down to becoming a
Taliban ally (without Taliban troops occupying your area) or part of Taliban-
controlled Afghanistan (with the religious police and all the other stuff).

When up against professional soldiers, the Afghans don't change their
style. They will get their women and children out of the way and then go after

the soldiers. The Afghans won't attack unless they stand a good chance of success. They will flee from more powerful units. Instead, they will attack supply trucks and smaller patrols. If you want to fight the Afghans and win, you have to find them first. But don't expect them to stand still and duke it out with a more powerful opponent. If professionals realize they are fighting warriors, and not regular soldiers, the Afghans can be beat. Otherwise, you are playing into the Afghans' strengths, and you will lose.

Unmodified Historical Casualty Rate

This chart gives the United States' casualty experience in World War II. It demonstrates the rapidity with which combat units melt away due to normal casualties. The figures are for infantry, tank, or reconnaissance battalions: combat units of 500–1,000 men. These units comprise 50 percent of a division's strength but incur 80–90 percent of the division's casualties. This means that these rates are at least 20 percent higher than those of a regiment (3,200 men) and 50 percent higher than those of a division (15,000 men). From this you can deduce that there is a lot of inactivity in battle for divisions to attain the overall average 2 percent per day loss rate. American troops have not fought battles like this since Vietnam. Since that time, weaponry and tactics have changed considerably. Most important, the American people have become much less tolerant to these kind of casualties. But if the stakes were high enough, that could change. Losses like this only occur if both sides are evenly matched in terms of combat power. This has not happened since Vietnam, and even there the U.S. forces had a substantial edge.

Type of action names the types of combat activities that would produce the different rates of loss.

Meeting is a meeting engagement. Both sides are marching, on foot or in vehicles, when they encounter each other. The side that takes the initiative and becomes the attacker suffers proportionately less than in other types of engagements. These actions are rather confused affairs with less artillery and more infantry and tank firepower used.

Attack of position (day 1) is the first day of a normal attack, that is, an attack in which the defender is prepared. This first day is generally the day of heaviest fighting. The attacker knows that a quick decision is preferable and the defenders are fresh. The defender wants to prolong the fight, as this will allow time for defender reinforcements.

	Combat battalion daily losses		
Type of action	Attacker	Defender	Ratio
Meeting Engagement	7.5%	4.9%	1.5
Attack of position (day 1)	11.5%	6.1%	1.9
Attack of position (day 2+)	6.1%	3.5%	1.7
Attack fortifications (day 1)	18.7%	9.8%	1.9
Attack fortifications (day 2+)	9.8%	5.2%	1.9
Pursuit (ambushes, etc.)	4.3%	3.2%	1.3
Inactive (patrols, etc.)	2.6%	2.6%	1.0

Attack of position (day 2+) represents subsequent days of fighting if the first day's push fails to decide the issue. This is attrition fighting, which favors the defense.

Attack fortifications (day 1) is similar to the position attack, but the defender is better prepared and the attacker is making a more substantial effort.

Attack fortifications (day 2+). Grinding into enemy fortifications is even more expensive, and risky, than going after normal defensive positions. Prepared fortifications are often prepared in great depth. Multiple lines of fortifications over a depth of several kilometers are not unusual.

Pursuit is combat between a rapidly advancing attacker and a defender attempting to delay this pursuit. Ample opportunities are available for defenders to prepare ambushes. The attacker has such a high degree of initiative that the defender is not able to take full advantage of the attacker's often reckless movements.

Inactive is opposing forces in contact, not actively fighting, but aggressively maintaining their positions. There is still a lot of artillery and small-arms activity from time to time. Patrolling also takes a heavy toll as both sides attempt to keep tabs on each other.

Attacker and defender indicate the daily loss rates, as a percentage of current personnel strength, for the attacking and defending force, respectively. The units involved are the combat battalions doing the fighting.

Ratio is the ratio of attacker to defender losses. The attacker often loses more men. This ratio shows that the attacker is better off in some types of actions than in others.

Factors Modifying Unit Combat Power

This chart shows how various factors can lower the combat power of an army unit. The adjusted combat values show that units of equal size and equipment are not equal. A unit's basic combat power resides in the destructive power of its weapons and the ability of the weapons' users to apply that firepower efficiently. Various formulas exist for calculating the raw combat power of a weapon. Adding the human element is a bit more complex and more of a moving target. For one overall calculation of combat power, see the charts in this chapter showing casualty rates by branch.

There is nothing fundamentally complex about calculating basic combat power. Most nations have the same standards of organization and levels of equipment.

The most powerful individual army weapons today are tanks and artillery. Assigning each tank a value of, say, 40–100 and each artillery piece a value of 20–50, a rough combat power for a unit can rapidly be calculated. To put these values in perspective, an infantry squad with its assault rifles, machine guns, and other weapons would have a value of 1. If this squad had an armored personnel carrier or IFV, the vehicle itself would have a value of 5–40+, depending on the weapons carried. An antitank missile system would have a value of 8–25. Calculating precise capabilities of weapons is an inexact science. A precise calculation would be irrelevant anyway, as the basic combat value of a unit is a small fraction of its eventual combat value. Many other factors modify the

Factor		Cumulative effect	
	Minimizing	Worst	Average
Natural elements			
Terrain	50%	50%	75%
Climate	80%	40%	68%
Command elements			
Air superiority	90%	36%	64%
Leadership	60%	22%	51%
Posture	60%	13%	41%
Surprise	60%	8%	33%
Supply	50%	4%	25%
Training	30%	1%	16%
Command, control, and commo	30%	0.35%	10%
Morale	20%	0.07%	6%

Percentages show portion of unit's original
combat value remaining after factors applied.

basic values, and the mastery of these modifiers are the keys to success in combat. Note that the techniques of calculating combat values of units and the effects of modifiers were derived from the experience of designing historical simulations (war games) of military operations. The techniques are valid only because they could constantly be tested using the known outcome of the historical events being simulated.

Natural elements are the elements over which man has no control. The effects of natural factors on combat performance will generally persist only as long as the natural element is present.

Terrain is the effect of geography. Some terrains are more difficult to fight in than others. Terrain becomes difficult by creating three conditions favorable for the defender. Mobility is reduced by rough terrain (mountains, hills, riverbanks) as well as by soft ground (swamps, sand dunes) and numerous obstructions (forests, built-up areas). The range of weapons is cut by obstructions, particularly by forests, underbrush, hills, and buildings. Observation is cut by obstructions that allow the defender to conceal himself more easily and to prepare the classic ambush combat troops fear so much. Terrain can cause these losses of attacker effectiveness: mountains, 25–50 percent; swamps, 20–40 percent; hilly terrain, 0–20 percent; flat terrain (soft ground and sand make it worse), 0–20 percent; built-up areas, 10–20 percent. Each type may also contain forests, which tend to aid the defender.

Weather. Here we are talking about fog, temperature, winds, and the like. Weather affects performance in three ways (in order of performance). Rain, snow, and excessive humidity cut mobility and the efficiency of weapons and troops. Fog, clouds, and mist obstruct observation. Fog aids the attacker by masking his troops from enemy weapons. Many nations have sensors that can overcome this problem, if the troops have them and the gadgets are in working order. However, what you can't see you can't shoot at, and this allows the attacker to get closer before being fired upon. Extremes in hot and cold temperatures have adverse effects on troops and machines, as will high winds.

Command elements are the human factors. These are more important, because human factors persist where natural factors come and go. The first two factors in this category (leadership and training) are more controllable than the remaining "battlefield" factors.

Air superiority is the impact of air control and the ability to go after the enemy with aircraft. For the side without air superiority, mobility is impaired as units move and operate more cautiously to avoid air strikes. For the side with air

superiority, operations proceed more smoothly as a result of superior reconnaissance, inferior enemy air recon, and relative freedom from air strikes.

Leadership is defined here as the quality of the unit commanders. Good leadership, given enough time, can train troops properly. On short notice, good leadership gets the most out of poorly motivated or badly trained soldiers. Good unit
leaders often overcome the debilitating effects of an inefficient high command.
Good leadership and good training often go together. Cases of well-trained troops
and poor leaders are not unknown and result in good troops being poorly used.

Posture is the nature of the unit's activity when the combat takes place. Other
things being equal, it is easier to defend than to attack. The stronger the defensive posture, the more it will decrease the attacker's combat power. The weak-
est defensive posture is a retreat, either just to escape or to delay the attacker's
advance. Then, in ascending order, are hasty, prepared, and fortified defense.
The attacker has a similar set of postures. If a force deployed for attack is suddenly forced to defend by the approach of a larger force, they will be at a disadvantage. Troops assume different formations for attack and defense.

Surprise is another often underrated factor. Surprise comes in various degrees. It
increases the effectiveness of the attacker's weapons and mobility while decreas-
ing the defender's. Basically, the force with the advantage of surprise gets to beat
on their opponent for some time without reprisal. Usually, it is the attacker that
has the surprise advantage, although on occasion the defender has it.

Supply—the lack of it—stops a successful army from doing anything.
Normally this is not a critical factor, as many commanders do pay attention to
logistics. At least they avoid reasonable risks for fear of supply problems. The
effects of supply problems are typically sporadic, as they can arise from chaos
in the supply system, as well as from shortages.

Training is the extent to which troops are taught to use their weapons and
equipment effectively. Not until this combination of men and machines is put
into combat is the training quality conclusively revealed.

Command, control, and commo (C³) is the commander's ability to control his
army effectively. If control is lost, the ability to respond to enemy action and
coordinate one's own forces is also lost. Blitzkrieg warfare is aimed at destroying the enemy's C^3, rather than undertaking the more formidable task of
destroying the army itself.

Morale is often underrated. This is the state of mind of the troops, their attitudes toward their prospects of success, and confidence in their side's abilities.

Large relative differences in morale have a devastating effect on combat performance. Morale is modified by leadership, training, situation, politics, weather, and numerous other factors, probably including the phases of the moon.

Minimizing effect is the maximum minimizing effect or deflation of the unit's base combat power. The basic combat value of a unit is multiplied by these deflators to determine the actual combat value. For example, if a unit had a basic value of 400 and it was operating in the worst possible terrain conditions (a deflator of .5), then the unit's actual combat value would be 200. As the other factors are applied, this value can decline still further.

Cumulative effect is the percentage of the unit's original strength remaining after the factor has affected it. With each factor, the worst case is given to show the extremes to which a unit's theoretical strength can be reduced. The average effect is also given.

Calculating Who Is Winning

The above values allow you to calculate the effective combat power of each side in a conflict. These values are used on the basic daily loss rate chart to determine casualties. We know how many people are likely to be injured. But who will win? Defeat goes to the side that quits first. This means that some wars are bloodier than others. The elusive "resolve" often determines the victor.

For a rough-and-ready rule for who will win, consider the "force ratio," that of the stronger force to the weaker one. Assume two forces each contain 10,000 men, 200 tanks, 300 IFVs, 50 artillery pieces, etc. Assume each one's basic combat value is 30,000. Let us make the following assumptions about the effect of various factors on the attacking force:

- *Natural factors.* No loss of effectiveness.
- *Command elements.* Losses of 20 percent (deflator of .8). Brings actual combat value to 24,000 (.8 x 30,000).

Let us make the following assumptions about the effect of various factors on the defending force:

- *Natural factors.* No loss of effectiveness.
- *Command elements.* Less well-trained and -led (with deflators of .7 and .8 creates a deflator of .56) brings the basic value down to 16,800 (.56 x 30,000). Morale is not as high (.8 x 16,800 = 13,440). They do not have air superiority (.9 x 13,440 = 12,096). They are surprised (.6 x 12,096 =

7,258). This gives the attacker a force ratio of over 3:1 (24,000:7,258, or 3.3:1). After a few days of fighting, both sides have lost about 5 percent of their strength. The ratio of forces is now 22,800:6,895, or 3.3:1. The attacker has disrupted the defender's supplies (.7 x 6,895 = 4,826) and gotten into the defender's rear area and disrupted his command and control (.5 x 4,826 = 2,413). The ratio is now 22,800:2,413, or 9.4:1. There is little chance of recovery from such an unfavorable ratio. History has shown that as the force ratio approaches 10:1, another factor becomes important: the breakpoint. At a certain point in a battle, the side facing a large deficiency in force ratio simply falls apart. The exact point at which a unit collapses depends on a combination of casualties, leadership, unit disintegration, and troop training. Well-trained and -led units can continue resistance until they are almost wiped out. Less well-endowed units will collapse after less than 10 percent of them have been injured. Eventually, all defending units see the handwriting on the wall. Bloody-minded commanders will infrequently attempt fighting to the last man. The troops have a different agenda. Even if the entire unit does not give up, parts of it will. This makes the force ratio worse for the weaker side. That's how battles normally proceed. This description could very well have been the debacle in Russia during 1941, or the Sinai campaigns of 1967 and 1973. Or it could be somewhere else tomorrow. Before you rush off to calculate World War III, keep in mind that these calculations are most accurate in hindsight. Do the calculations to recreate Desert Storm to see how mismatched the forces were in that battle. There is also a lot of variability in battles not yet fought. This is sometimes called luck, chance, or the "fortunes of war." Don't underestimate it.

On the Ocean and in the Air

Most of the above factors also apply to naval and air forces. Weather is the same. Terrain has some interesting similarities; water is not all the same. Read Chapters 9 and 10 for more detail on the differing composition of water. Operating near land favors the defender. Small patrol boats armed with cruise missiles can be quite effective. In areas with hot climates, another aspect of naval "terrain" becomes evident. A zone up to 100 feet thick, where the hot air meets the cooler water, creates a space where long-range radar doesn't work too well. In effect, low-flying cruise missiles become difficult to detect. Coastal submarines also benefit from heat effects when underwater. Many layers of different-temperature water confound sonar. Shoals and reefs provide additional hiding places. In addition, we have the familiar sight of storms churning the sea into awesome shapes. Yes, there is terrain at sea.

In the air, we find basically three flavors of terrain; high, medium, and low altitude. The high altitudes, over 10,000 meters, have thin air, which harms engine performance and the maneuverability of aircraft not built for operating under those conditions. The low altitudes, less than 1,000 meters, have a thicker atmosphere. When on the deck (100 meters or less), debris can be sucked into the engine. Birds can hit the canopy and injure the pilot. These are the minor risks of operating close to the ground. The most serious problem is sheer fatigue. More concentration is required when operating at 100 meters altitude and moving along at 200 or more meters a second. In the middle altitudes there are still problems. Clouds are more common, and these not only provide concealment and the opportunity for collision, but often confound heat-seeking missiles. All the other factors apply.

Supply effects are immediate for aircraft. If you run out of fuel, you hit the ground. Not a lot of ammunition is carried, perhaps four missiles and 20 seconds' worth of cannon shells. Bomb loads are heavier, although the average is only a few tons. More important for air force logistics is the amount of supplies getting to the air bases. Most bases are surrounded by dozens of supply dumps containing thousands of tons of fuel, munitions, spares, and other supplies. That's why these complexes are called air bases instead of airfields. Aircraft carriers are more restricted, carrying supplies for less than a thousand sorties, depending on how many strike sorties are flown. Strike missions use up more fuel than patrols. Naval supply is limited by carrying capacity. Many smaller ships must be refueled once a week. There are rarely sufficient munitions on board for more than a few full-scale battles. Most smaller warships (especially those of Soviet design) carry no reloads for many of their weapons.

Attrition is similar to the land situation. Air losses are calculated in losses per 1,000 sorties. A loss of more than 2 percent (20 per 1,000) is dangerous to unit integrity and morale. Aircraft may fly more than one sortie per day. See the chart on aircraft attrition (page 543).

Naval losses tend to be more catastrophic, partially because you have fewer "vehicles." Unlike ships in the last major naval war (1939–45), most modern ships are not armored. Peacetime accidents and limited combat experience indicate that wartime losses are likely to be higher than in the past. Training, especially in damage control, becomes a critical factor. Training, leadership, morale, C^3 are all areas in which Western navies have a comfortable, but not invincible, lead over potential opponents.

Noncombat Casualties

Average (constant) is the percentage of a unit's strength that will be out of action due to noncombat injuries at any one time. This is an average of operations in all climates and conditions. Disease, including venereal, and accidents are the cause.

Eighty-five percent of those affected will return to duty after an average ten day absence, compared to 100 days for combat casualties. Medical services will devote over 35 percent of their efforts to treating noncombat injuries. As long as medical services function, there will be daily, cumulative losses of only 15 percent of those afflicted. Because the average time in hospital is 10 days, only 200 men out of 100,000 need get sick to represent a 2-percent daily loss. Thus some 15 percent (30 men) will not return to service. This represents a permanent daily loss rate of 30 men per 100,000, or .03 percent.

Climate can modify the loss rate considerably. Temperate climates can reduce the loss rate. Deserts, jungles, severe cold, and other unhealthy environments will cause more disease and injury. Tropical rain forests are possibly the worst. Any area is a bad climate if disease conditions are harmful to the troops operating in it. For example, troops from tropical areas would suffer somewhat in temperate areas. Any troops going from their own "disease pool" to an area of unaccustomed diseases will suffer. Troops from industrialized nations going to out of the way parts of the world will encounter diseases they are unfamiliar with and more susceptible to.

Living conditions represents the level of sanitation and general living conditions. Living in tents is more injurious to health than living under more substantial cover. Sleeping on the ground is not healthy. Lack of regular, nutritious meals and clean, dry clothing can eventually become critical.

Level of medical care is the crucial factor. Without medical services, minor afflictions become major ones. Even in temperate zones, lack of medical services, particularly public sanitation, will rapidly increase the rate of losses.

Multiplier is the multiplier effect of climate, living conditions and level of medical care on the average noncombat casualty rate. At the extreme end, all the troops will be afflicted with disease severe enough to require hospitalization. Under such conditions, few, if any, will receive medical attention. This occurred during the Korean War, especially among Chinese troops, who had a lax attitude toward battlefield medical care. The Germans, during their first winter in Russia, were similarly unprepared and suffered accordingly.

Permanent losses (daily) is the percentage of disease and injury that results in permanent loss. These losses include death and permanent incapacity for military service. When these losses are high, many troops will simply become ineffective. Without good leadership and training, units will disintegrate or cease to function.

Permanent losses per 100,000 (daily) is the number of noncombat dead, or permanently incapacitated, per day for a force of 100,000 troops.

			Permanent losses		
	Multiplier	Daily sick rate	Daily	Daily losses per 100,000	Monthly losses per 100,000
Average (constant)		2.0%	0.03%	30	915
Variable factors increasing losses					
Climate	1.5	3.0%	0.045%	45	1,373
Living conditions	1.5	4.5%	0.068%	68	2,059
Medical care level	2	9.0%	.14%	135	4,118

Permanent losses per 100,000 (monthly) is the number of dead, or permanently incapacitated, for a force of 100,000 over a period of a month. These complications show that without effective measures to control noncombat casualties, an army will disappear without ever seeing the enemy.

Navies and Air Forces

Navies and air forces are more dependent on weapons and equipment readiness than armies. Air forces often suffer up to 2-percent aircraft losses per year in peacetime. These losses are a result of training accidents and just plain accidents. Western air forces have lower loss rates, while Third World– and Soviet-style air forces have higher, often considerably higher, rates. Western rates are lower because the aircraft are better maintained and the pilots are more experienced, flying from 200–500 hours a year. Western pilots also have access to realistic aircraft simulators. Soviet aircraft are more accident-prone because of design defects. Peacetime personnel losses are lower in air forces because these troops work out of fixed installations and spend little time under field conditions. In wartime, air bases are created rapidly in many godforsaken parts of the world. Despite their fixed nature, air-force personnel suffer noncombat losses just like the combat troops while the base is being built. If the established base can eliminate unhealthy conditions, noncombat losses will decline accordingly.

Navies also suffer from peacetime attrition. Normally, 15–25 percent of a fleet's ships are in port for various degrees of repair and maintenance. At sea, they suffer a loss rate approaching 1 percent a year, depending on skill and intensity of use. Disease is a lesser danger because of the controlled environment on ships. Injuries from accidents are somewhat higher because of cramped conditions and constant working with heavy, complex, and often dangerous equipment.

National Differences

Some armies are more efficient, or callous, than others in dealing with noncombat casualties. During World War II, 89 percent of German hospital admissions were noncombat casualties, while in the U.S. Army the figure was 96 percent. Precise data for the Soviet and Japanese armed forces are lacking, but available information indicates that noncombat admissions were closer to 60 percent. The Soviets and Japanese suffered more frequent and overwhelming casualties and had fewer hospital beds available. Both nations' armed forces also had lower standards of public sanitation and disease control. It is quite likely that over 90 percent of hospital admissions were for combat casualties. Post–World War II practices did not change a great deal in the Soviet army. A Soviet combat division had only 60 hospital beds, clearly insufficient to care for peacetime injuries and disease. Even support from higher units would not enable the Soviets to do more than simply attempt to care for combat casualties. This is another example of how wealth can enable an armed force to literally buy lives for money.

Air Combat Attrition

Period/theater is the time frame in which the air combat took place and the area in which the fighting took place. The years 1939–45 include all air operations in Europe; 1942 was the beginning of the large-scale bombing offensive in Europe; 1943–44 was the height of the bomber offensive; 1945 was the height of fighter-bomber operations; 1950–51 was the Korean War; 1966–68 were three critical years of the air war in Vietnam; 1971 was the India-Pakistan war; 1973 was the Arab-Israeli war; 1982 was the Falklands and Lebanon wars; 1986–87 was the Afghan war after the Afghans got surface-to-air missiles; 1987 was also the Iran-Iraq war; 1991 was the Gulf War. The loss rate to enemy action during the 2001 Afghanistan war was essentially zero.

Loss rate per 100,000 sorties is the number of aircraft lost for each 100,000 sorties (one aircraft flying one mission).

Nation (attacker) is the nationality of the air force that was doing the attacking and incurred the losses. *Allied* means Britain and the United States.

Aircraft type is the type of aircraft that took the losses. *All* means all types. *Bombers* are primarily four-engine bombers (B-17, B-24). *FtrBmbrs* are fighter-bombers (P-47, Typhoon, F-4, etc.) appropriate to the period. "A-4" is an American light bomber used by Israel. *F-1* is the Mirage F-1 fighter-bomber, as well as other types used by Iraq.

Period/theater	Loss rate per 100,000 sorties	Nation (attacker)	Aircraft type	Defender loss caused by enemy
1939–45/Germany	900	Allied	All	All
1942/Germany	200	Allied	Bombers	Flak
1943–44/Germany	400	Allied	Bombers	Flak
1945/Germany	650	Allied	FtrBmbrs	Flak
1950–51/China–N. Korea	440	U.S.	All	Aircraft
1966/N. Vietnam	350	U.S.	All	All
1967/N. Vietnam	300	U.S.	All	All
1968/N. Vietnam	150	U.S.	All	All
1971/Pakistan	1,250	India	All	Aircraft
1971/India	1,700	Pakistan	All	Aircraft
1973/Egypt-Syria	800	Israel	All	80% flak
1973/Egypt-Syria	1,200	Israel	A-4	Flak
1982/Syria	10	Israel	All	Flak
1985/Afghanistan	100	Russia	All	Flak
1987/Afghanistan	200	Russia	All	Flak, Stinger SAM
1986/Iran	100	Iraq	F-1	Flak, SAM
1991/Iraq	40	Allies	All	Flak, SAM
1999/Kosovo	5	NATO	All	Flak, SAM

Defender weapon is the type of enemy weapon that caused the loss. *All* is aircraft and antiaircraft artillery (flak). *80% flak* means that 80 percent of aircraft losses were caused by enemy antiaircraft weapons and 20 percent by enemy aircraft.

Changes Through History

The majority of aircraft combat losses in World War II were caused by other aircraft. As the German air force became weaker, its flak effectiveness increased. More resources were devoted to flak in the last year of the war, and a higher proportion of allied aircraft was brought down by flak. This still resulted in relatively lower allied aircraft losses, as flak could be avoided more easily than enemy fighters. After World War II, the attrition rate continued to decline. In Korea, there was less flak than in World War II. Political considerations prevented the air war from escalating too far. Communist pilots were greatly overmatched by veteran U.S. pilots. This was not a high-intensity war. In Vietnam, the attrition rate declined still further. The flak defenses, however, were the heaviest ever deployed. U.S. forces responded by mounting massive flak-suppression operations, thereby lowering aircraft losses to flak. This was not a representative situation, as it was a war between unequal opponents. The

North Vietnamese were in no position to force the issue. U.S. air operations had none of the time pressure experienced during World War II. This was an unusual war in the air.

The war between India and Pakistan was frighteningly intense. The air forces were more evenly matched. The war was fought with Korean War vintage aircraft. It was also fought with great vigor and skill by evenly matched pilots. The loss rate was disturbing. In the 1973 Arab-Israeli war, the Israelis had a substantial edge. The Egyptians made the best of a bad situation and built up their ground-based air defense. Unlike the Americans in Vietnam, the Israelis discounted this development. Once the war began, Israel did not have time to eliminate systematically the formidable Arab flak defenses and ran up large losses. The air battles in the Falklands and Lebanon again showed that well-trained pilots and thoughtfully designed aircraft and weapons will swamp less-prepared opposition. The success of Afghan irregulars with portable surface-to-air missiles bodes ill for air forces operating over large concentrations of these weapons. The decades of preparation to take on the massive Soviet air defenses in Central Europe paid off for the largely NATO air units in the 1991 Gulf War. Iraq's largely Soviet-supplied air defense system was handily shut down by coalition air forces, and new lows in attacker air-loss rates were achieved. The lesson was repeated even more convincingly in Kosovo and Serbia in 1999.

In most periods, however, noncombat losses equaled or exceeded combat losses. Landing accidents are most common, and as recently as Vietnam and Afghanistan (in the 1980s), accidents and equipment failure have accounted for 2–3 percent losses per month. Most observers concentrate on combat losses without doing a little arithmetic to discover that a lot of aircraft were going into the combat zone, avoiding enemy fire, and never coming out again. The Gulf War was an exception, primarily because of the high training levels of the pilots and ground crews, as well as the first combat use of the AWACS control aircraft. This led to the unprecedented absence of any air-to-air collisions, a common wartime occurrence in airspace swarming with combat aircraft. This performance was repeated in the 2001 Afghanistan war.

Casualty Rates by Branch

Armies are divided into "branches": infantry, armor, artillery, and support.

Infantry is the branch with the most casualties, usually 50–80 percent. Infantry divisions with no tanks and minimal artillery suffer the most infantry casualties. Industrialized nations provide even their infantry divisions with 100–200 tanks and over a hundred artillery pieces. Infantry includes reconnaissance troops. Contemporary divisions consist of less than 25–50 percent infantry, often closer to one-third. As recently as World War II, infantry comprised nearly two-thirds of personnel in most divisions.

Armor is the branch with the most firepower per man. Armor combat strength declines rapidly because the heavy combat vehicles tend to break down easily. In combat divisions today, armor troops comprise 5–30 percent of manpower. Depending on the type of division, armor troops will suffer 10–30 percent of the casualties.

Artillery is the combat branch that inflicts the most casualties and receives the least. As the armor and infantry waste away in combat, artillery becomes the principal provider of combat power. In combat divisions today, armor troops comprise 10–25 percent of manpower and suffer 5–10 percent of the casualties.

The remaining manpower includes the support troops that may come under fire but do not regularly confront the enemy in combat. These troops comprise 25–35 percent of division manpower and suffer 1–3 percent of the casualties.

For the most part, these soldiers are found in battalions composed exclusively of troops of that branch. In some armies, artillery is often assigned to infantry units. Most armies equip their infantry units with mortars. Mortars, because of their short range and limited ammunition supplies, are considered infantry weapons.

If a division is reported to have taken 10 percent casualties, you can safely assume that the infantry has lost 20–25 percent of its strength. Tank units will generally lose strength in proportion to divisional losses (if the division has 10 percent casualties, so do the tank battalions). One new element in modern combat divisions (especially American ones) is an aviation brigade, with about 80 helicopters. This puts about 200 crewmen at risk. The risk isn't as much as you might think. During the Vietnam War, American helicopters flew 36 million sorties between 1966–71. Helicopters could fly a dozen or more sorties a day. The most commonly used choppers were the UH-1 and AH-1 (just now being phased out of U.S. service, but still widely used around the world). On average, every 100,000 sorties saw 13 helicopters crash. But 55 percent of these were not combat-related. For every 100 helicopters lost in combat, 145 crew and passengers were killed. For every 100 choppers lost for noncombat reasons, 89 people died. Helicopter crashes were more likely to have survivors because the choppers were usually operating close to the ground and capable of slowing down their impact even with the engine shut down ("autorotation" of the rotor). Helicopters (the UH-60 and AH-64) are more resistant to damage and crew injury than their Vietnam-era counterparts.

Combat Power and Patterns of Combat Losses

The Soviets put most of their efforts into providing many tanks, a trend that proved mistaken. Seventy-two percent of the combat power of a full-strength

Soviet tank division came from its tank forces. Although this seems high, the lowest value is 52 percent, for a U.S. infantry division. This is a crucial factor in modern warfare. Heavy combat vehicles, tanks, and IFVs break down more quickly than the troops. After a division has taken 30 percent personnel casualties, tank forces suffer more in lost combat power. At that point, divisions have lost 42–50 percent of their combat strength. Armor branch forces will have lost over 60 percent. The infantry suffer even greater damage at the 30 percent divisional casualty level. The division is left with a lot of tanks needing repairs, some infantry, some usable armored vehicles, and a relatively large amount of artillery.

Some strange things happen after combat has converted a division to this new, smaller format. One day of heavy combat or several days of lighter action against a determined opponent can result in losses as high as 10 percent. At this point, the heavier loss rates in infantry and armor branches begin to show. At 30 percent loss levels, divisions show serious signs of disintegration. This is the optimal time to take a division out of battle and rebuild its combat branches. Combat beyond this point will practically wipe out a division's combat power. It is anticipated that in a future war, divisions will routinely be pushed beyond the 30 percent level if they fight someone with similar weapons and quality of leadership. Experience has shown that once a division loses 50 percent of its strength through ground combat, there is little left but support troops. In most cases, support troops will then be serving, without enthusiasm, as infantry. Most tanks, although not all crews, will be out of action. Only the artillery will be largely intact. Without infantry to protect them, the artillery will soon be overrun and lost. Continuing to fight beyond the 50 percent level quickly results in the complete destruction of the division. Because the support troops are less effective as infantry, they will be destroyed more quickly. Their skills as technicians are generally more difficult to replace than those of infantry and tank crews. With no one to protect the division's support equipment, the division ceases to exist. Russian-type armies are armies of extremes. Their infantry divisions are built to take enormous losses and still retain remnants of all their combat arms. Their tank divisions, in similar situations, are quickly reduced to some artillery, with tank crews and support troops serving as infantry. The more highly trained support troops do not serve in divisions but are retained in nondivisional units.

Combat divisions are resilient, if they are not hit with too much combat power in too short a time. Most of their casualties return to duty within a month. Losses average 2 percent a day when facing a combative opponent. The lesson here is that after two weeks of heavy combat, a division should be withdrawn for up to a month so that the lightly wounded can be returned, replacements can be integrated into their units, and vehicles repaired. You then have a unit of the same strength as before, but with a lot more practical experience. Warfare rarely allows for such efficient use of a division. Units often are kept under fire for extended periods and are not given sufficient time to recover. Warfare is a debilitating process.

A recent example of the above was in the 1991 Gulf War. The Iraqi divisions were isolated in the desert and blasted with accurate air and artillery fire for six weeks. Without access to replacements or regular supply, most of these divisions lost their combat power, their cohesion, and, in many cases, their will to fight. Coalition ground forces advanced against little organized resistance, and that advance quickly turned into a pursuit. Coalition troops never had to face sustained combat, so effective was the preliminary bombardment by air and artillery firepower.

25

Victory Goes to the Bigger Battalions

The Cost of War

Peace is cheaper than war, but often not by much. People don't complain as much about the cost of war while the shooting is going on. When things settle down, taxpayers become more boisterous, as well they should. Peace is a more common condition than war. The cost of maintaining armed forces for the next war is often more expensive than the war itself. Yet as much as people complain about the expense, victory almost always goes to the bigger battalions. Those battalions are built during peacetime. To put it another way, victory is a property of the wealthy. Battles may be won by a David, but the Goliaths win the wars.

The wealthier nations tend to be conscious of their material advantages and are quick to arm themselves in self-defense. By 1945, the United States was maintaining 12 million troops at an average annual cost of over $40,000 per soldier. Over 40 years later, four million were still directly involved in military affairs at nearly double the cost per individual. (Unless otherwise noted, all prices and costs are given in 2002 dollars.) After 1985, annual defense spending in the United States began to decline again, but not by a great deal. Aside from the debatable cost effectiveness of this expensive situation, there is some doubt as to whether the United States could afford another war of the magnitude of World War II. Since 1945, per capita income, adjusted for inflation, has increased over four times. The wealth is there; what might not be available is the time to hammer all those goodies into weapons.

Can We Afford Peace?

Peace can be more destructive to a nation's economy than a war. The high human costs and economic costs limit the duration of wars. Peace lasts longer and eventually costs more. Currently (2001–02), the nations of the world are spending some $800 billion a year on armed forces. This is more than was spent during the peak year of World War II (1944). About half of that is spent by NATO nations (with the United States accounting for two-thirds of that). At the height of the Cold War, the world was spending $1.2 trillion a year, with NATO accounting for half of that. The Soviet Union and its allies accounted for about a third of the global defense spending. You can see why they called it a Cold War. There might not have been much fighting, but there was plenty of spending on armed forces.

During this Cold War era, the rest of the world accounted for less than 20 percent of the world's arms spending. The spending patterns have changed quite a bit. NATO is still the big spender, but spending by the former Soviet Union (and its former allies) has dropped some 80 percent. NATO spending is down some 25 percent. But America still spends about the same (there was a 30-percent dip during the 1990s, but the defense budget has since grown back toward peak Cold War levels). Spending in the Middle East is down some 30 percent. But elsewhere it is up. South Asia (mainly India and Pakistan) is up some 50 percent. East Asia (mainly China) is up some 30 percent. In Latin America, spending is up some 60 percent.

Defense spending accounts for about 4 percent of global GNP (gross national product). This is down from 6.7 percent at the end of the Cold War. The percentage varies from nation to nation. The NATO nations, on average, spend 2.2 percent, but most are lower than that. This is because the United States spends 3 percent of GNP on defense. The Russian percentage is nearly 5 percent, which is a third of the percentage spent during the Cold War. This high rate of spending, over several decades, was a major reason for the economic collapse of the Soviet Union. The people also got tired of the lackadaisical dictatorship the Communist leadership provided. South Asia has increased its spending rate from a Cold War average of 4.2 percent to a current 5.3 percent. In East Asia, the rate has declined (even though actual money spent has gone up) from 6.4 percent to 3.3 percent. This is because of the dramatic growth of the Chinese economy over the last 20 years. But China is still spending only about $18 billion a year on defense. The Chinese military threat is mainly bark, for the Chinese have yet to invest in a really effective bite.

A major war will generally consume 30–50 percent of GNP for as long as the war lasts. One year of a major war then equals 3–30 years of the Cold War (depending on which nation you look at). From an economic point of view, World War II was refought over five times during the Cold War (1945–91). But defense spending since 1945 was different than spending in the previous century. For one thing, there was more to spend. We tend to forget that industrialization, and all the wealth it creates, is relatively recent. Britain went through it first, in the early 1800s. Then came the United States and most of Europe in the late 1800s. Russia didn't really get started until the 1920s. Japan was also a late starter, getting into gear only in the 1950s. But something happened after 1945 that severely limited the economic strength of the two economic superpowers, the United States and the Soviet Union. Both of these nations began putting enormous portions of their capital funds into military spending.

Without getting too far into economic theory, let us explain this by comparing national economies to an apartment house. Both are similar. A national economy provides all that is needed to sustain the population. The apartment house provides shelter for people. The apartment house lasts a long time, if properly maintained. This maintenance is largely a rebuilding process that eventually results in most major components of the building being replaced as these items wear out or are supplanted by more efficient components. If these repairs and modifications are not made, the building becomes less efficient, or even uninhabitable. The money for these expenses come from rents. If the apartment-house owners hire a security guard, this will not bankrupt the building. But if they hire a dozen guards and neglect routine maintenance, the building will eventually fall apart. Moreover, tenants will move out, while new ones will be reluctant to move in, and rent income will fall.

This is what happened with the United States and Russia. As of 1980, the United States was spending 20 percent of its new capital (money used to replace worn-out factories, farm equipment, and things like roads and other infrastructure) for defense. Japan was spending 3.5 percent. Germany was spending 16 percent, France 21 percent, and Britain 24 percent. Russia was spending over 40 percent. The nations that can spend more on rebuilding and replacing their factories and other productive assets are more competitive in world markets. To get back to our hypothetical apartment house, people will obviously be attracted to the higher quality and lower rents of the Japanese apartments. During the Cold War, if you wanted security, you could go live in the well-guarded Soviet apartment bunker. You had to be careful, though, as the plumbing didn't work very well, and the elevators rarely ran.

Japan has other advantages, primarily the tendency of its people to save more of their income. These savings can be invested in still more productive assets. Generally, a nation can spend its production on capital goods (to produce more), maintenance (of people and their tools), and consumption (second homes, larger cars and homes, vacations, generally having a good time). Defense falls into the consumption category because it neither produces anything nor maintains productive assets.

We live in an uneasy and violent world. History shows that you have to defend yourself. But armed forces become counterproductive if their maintenance destroys the economy they are there to protect. This has military implications. Military security requires that you be able to build adequate weapons, or obtain them from a reliable ally who can. The Soviet Union was unable to keep up with Western military technology and compensated with larger quantities of weapons and equipment. Those nations that regularly spend more than 10 percent of their GNP on defense are not noted for economic vigor and stability. Among these high spenders are Iraq, Kuwait, Saudi Arabia, Eritrea, Angola, and North Korea. Many nations used to spend more than 10 percent, but it eventually caught up with them and they were forced to scale back defense spending. Low-spending nations like Japan and most industrialized nations live in the protection of high spenders like the United States. Think of this as a form of foreign aid, not to mention a great deal of trust and lack of paranoia.

The high Soviet military spending at the expense of civil-sector capital investment only began in the 1960s. At that time, Russia's economy was still booming from the post–World War II reconstruction programs. The leadership decided to divert capital funds to the military even though this change could not be sustained indefinitely. Eventually the national economy would decline from lack of new factories and production equipment. At this point, there was less capital available for everyone, including the military. By the 1980s, this process had caused massive damage to the civilian economy, and even the military was feeling the effects. The only benefit from this Soviet economic policy was a military buildup and a larger military establishment that was, in effect, temporary. Such a buildup could not be sustained into the 1990s. By the late 1980s, it became obvious that if the civilian economy was not revived, military spending would go down, and down. On top of the capital-spending problem was the intrinsic inefficiency of the Communist-style command economy. Together, these two forces—excessive military spending and a command economy—brought on the collapse of the Soviet Union.

The Soviet armed forces did not disappear in late 1991, but as they were parceled out among the successor states, particularly Russia and the Commonwealth of Independent States, the Byzantine Soviet military budget system collapsed. In the wake of the changeover, former Soviet officials admitted that they had no clear idea how much was spent on the military, much less where it came from. The new states emerging out of the Soviet Union grabbed all the funds they could in a scramble to reform their reeling economies. Most of the former Soviet military immediately found themselves with uncertain funding. Factories that had long produced items for the military discovered that their customers could no longer pay. As a result, the industrial side of the Soviet military-industrial complex began to shift away from weapons work to civilian production, which could be sold to customers who could pay. As was the Soviet custom, many of these military-oriented industrial centers were self-contained communities that took care of far more than providing jobs and producing military equipment. These "collectives" also controlled the local civilian economy and government. In the economic chaos following the Soviet Union collapse, these collectives, in effect, were separated from the military. A harsher situation faced the military units themselves, which also operated as "collectives." Most military organizations tried to associate themselves with some government entity that could collect taxes and support the troops and their families. As about a third of the Soviet military were long-term professional troops, these people had nowhere to go if they left the military. Many of the conscript troops went home (with or without permission), and an increasing number of new conscripts chose not to show up for service. By the end of the 1990s, the former Soviet military had lost its morale, many of its conscripts, most of its cohesion, and over 80 percent of its funding. By 2000, the U.S. Army was actually larger than the Russian army and had a budget larger than the entire Russian armed forces. The successor states of the Soviet Union were even less capable of supporting this military-industrial complex, causing the Soviet military to go from the world's largest to one barely in the top five within the space of a few years. The result is a vivid example of what excessive military spending can do to a nation.

What do nations get for their defense dollar? Often one never really finds out. Wars are not that frequent, and the results are not always conclusive. The German army, for example, has lost every war it has fought for over 100 years, and is still highly regarded. Russia has won most of its wars during the same period and is held in lower regard. Quality will prevail only up to a point. In most cases, the economically stronger nation, the "bigger battalions," will prevail. The remainder of this chapter will cover what money can buy when you want to make war.

Top Ten U.S. Defense Budgets

You can tell a lot more about military affairs by looking at the budget. Checking the news and history books doesn't show you nearly as much. So let's look at the 10 biggest defense budgets since 1940.

Annual defense spending in America is now running about $275 billion. Since 1940, we've spent nearly $20 trillion on defense. The smallest annual budget in this period was 1948, when we spent only $90 billion. The largest was 1945: $768 billion.

Year Defense Budget, in Billions of Year-2000 Dollars

1.	1945: 768	6.	1988: 415
2.	1944: 724	7.	1989: 409
3.	1943: 595	8.	1990: 398
4.	1986: 418	9.	1946: 393
5.	1987: 417	10.	1968: 393

Not surprising that the three largest budgets were during World War II. This was an even bigger effort than it appears to be, for the population was much smaller than today (135 million then, 270 million now). And the GDP was smaller still. At the start of World War II, the GDP was $1.4 trillion; in 1945 it was $2 trillion. Today, it's close to $9 trillion. World War II was a major national effort, with nearly 40 percent of GDP going for defense by the end of the war. It never came close to that again for the rest of the century. But we were still spending a lot more on defense in the 50 years after World War II. Even the smallest postwar budget, the $90 billion spent in 1948, was some four times larger, as a percent of GDP, than before World War II. The largest chunk of GDP for defense after 1945 was 13 percent in 1953 ($317 billion), at the end of the Korean war. For the rest of the 1950s, defense spending consumed about 9 percent of GDP. Even at the height of the Vietnam War in 1968, defense spending was only 9.2 percent of GDP. A growing economy made it easier to handle the growing military spending.

But after Vietnam, it wasn't the money that bothered the voters, but the 57,000 Americans who were killed in that war. So the defense budget shrank big time, going from $393 billion in 1968 to $263 billion in 1976. OK, it was $286 billion the year before we got sucked into Vietnam, but military gear was getting more expensive. However, government spending did not decline, for another war was declared, the "war on poverty." The federal budget was $871 billion in 1968, and nearly $1.1 trillion in 1976. Spending on welfare quadrupled in the 10 years after 1965. Urban renewal doubled. But that was not all. The politicians decided that it was best to have something for everyone, especially those who voted (the poor tended not to). More money went to hospitals, education, and Social Security. Something for everyone, except the troops.

Everything changed when it became common knowledge that the Soviet Union had started an arms race in the mid-1960s. This was part of a deal between the generals and some politicians to get rid of Nikita Khrushchev. Poor Nikita had the misfortune to try and cut back on military spending and put the money into building up the economy. Khrushchev was a true believer in the ability of Communism to deliver the good life, but he could count and knew this wasn't going to happen as long as the military was absorbing so much of the Soviet Union's wealth. Fellow politicians saw their opportunity, agreed to a massive increase in defense spending, and Nikita was history. President Dwight D. Eisenhower had warned America about the power of the military-industrial complex; too bad the Russians weren't paying attention.

By the late 1970s, the alarming growth of the Soviet military brought forth a demand that America respond. We did, thus five of the biggest defense budgets since World War II were those between 1986 and 1990. Then the Cold War ended. We had spent the Russians into the ground. Turns out Khrushchev was right. The Soviet economy could not grow without defense spending getting cut. And as the Russians increased military budgets instead, the Soviet economy just slid down and down. It was a mess.

The Soviets were devoting up to 30 percent of their GDP to defense. The Russians weren't sure, as accurate accounting practices were seen to be counterrevolutionary. Meanwhile, America was having its own economic problems. Fighting a war in Vietnam and against poverty simultaneously actually brought "war spending" to World War II levels. At the same time, Japan was becoming a formidable industrial power and exporting much of its production to America. Germany was recovering from the devastation of World War II and also flooding America with high-quality goods. Steel, ships, automobiles, and consumer electronics industries in the United States were feeling the heat. The stock market, always the canary in the coal mine, sensed this first and headed south for most of the 1970s.

American management and workers, in moves that shocked the Japanese, Germans, and many local pundits, reorganized themselves and got the economy going again. Right about that time, the Russian arms buildup became an issue. The result was a string of huge defense budgets. The Russians soon folded, mainly because their economy had already been trashed by 20 years of unbearable military spending. Top-ten lists don't have to be funny to be useful.

Why Does Everything Cost So Much?

Weapons have always been expensive; they have also tended to become more complex and less reliable over time. This has become more of a problem as new weapons come into being before the previous generation can be fully mastered. The first weapons were rocks. A rock is quite simple. It can also be quite cheap. No doubt the first weapon-cost overrun occurred when the chiseling of special war rocks took longer than anticipated. Military hardware tends to get more complex and expensive as users continually strive for that extra edge in performance. In life-and-death combat situations, every advantage counts. Consider, for example, radar in a Cold War–era fighter aircraft. Basic radar with a 30-kilometer range that can track air targets would cost about $210,000. By raising the price to $450,000, we obtain a 40-kilometer range, better accuracy, some resistance to countermeasures, and the ability to guide missiles to a target. For $600,000, we get some more range (70 kilometers), so perhaps the enemy has a hard time shooting back. Raise the price to $1,000,000 and we add accurate ground tracking, which allows the aircraft to fly close to the ground safely in bad weather. This would also include a data link to ground stations for better coordination and navigation. For nearly $2 million, we get a 180-kilometer range, better resistance countermeasures, and more bells and whistles in general. As things become more expensive and complex, they become less reliable. Reliability is a quality that is often overlooked, particularly as combat conditions involve previously unencountered stresses and less stringent maintenance.

Studies have shown the following statistical relationships between electronic component cost and MTBF (mean time between failure). A radar set might have hundreds or thousands of such components. Most of them are rather inexpensive and reliable. A few are quite expensive, critical, and more prone to failure. A component costing less than $1,000 fails, on average, once every 1,500 hours. Unless another component can pick up the slack, the entire system fails or is degraded in performance. A $5,000 component fails every 250 hours. A $10,000 component fails every 120 hours. More theoretical $100,000 components fail every 12 hours, and an unlikely million-dollar component fails before it gets warmed up. Using duplicates of more failure-prone components increases reliability but at greater cost, weight, and size. Most modern combat aircraft have electronics systems that fail, on the average, every 10 hours or less. It is difficult to predict exactly when the electronics will go, forcing you to be ready for failure at the worst possible moment. Repairs can take hours to minutes, depending on the design of the system.

Extremely expensive items like the Space Shuttle flight control systems use five identical computers, as protection against failure or accident. At least one Space Shuttle launch was held up because one of these computers failed checkout. High-performance aircraft often have triplicates of key systems. In wartime, these aircraft can go into action with one or two of these systems inoperable. This increases the risk of losing the aircraft or inability to complete the mission. This is considered a normal wartime risk. Examples of past weapons that became more complex and less reliable are numerous. When spears replaced rocks, there were new problems with warped shafts and loose stone spearheads. Then came swords, where impure metals caused brittleness and failure during the stresses of combat. Bows were prone to broken strings and warped arrows. The age of gunpowder brought forth very delicate trigger mechanisms, defective powder, wet powder, and impure metal in barrels. This was a portent of what was to come. Very reliable rifles took over two centuries to come along. Early machine guns were very vulnerable to mechanical breakdown. Aircraft, electronics, and guided missiles merely compounded these earlier problems.

If complexity is held constant, cost will decline and reliability will increase. In the last 50 years, technological advances and military requirements have replaced weapons before they could obtain these cost and reliability advantages. The average weapons system (tank, aircraft, missile, etc.) becomes obsolete in 10 years or less. In the United States it takes an average of eight years to bring a new system from idea to troop use. New weapons must be produced constantly to keep up with those of your opponents. American project managers at the end of the Cold War had an average tenure of 30 months, causing a lack of development continuity. Other Western nations have similar, although less severe, problems here. However, the United States is still leading the technology parade. Where American technology stumbles, all nations that follow tend to do likewise. New weapons often reach the troops shortly before they become obsolete and typically never see use in combat. Many systems produced in the last 40 years saw little or no combat.

The common pattern is to replace systems that have not yet worked out all their bugs with even more problem-prone and equally untried weapons. A common pattern is to modify extensively major systems to the extent that they become essentially new systems. Take the U.S. M-60 tank. The initial M-60A1 was a refinement of a late World War II heavy tank. The M60A1 cost $1,200,000, including $62,000 for the fire-control system. The M-60A3 came out 10 years later in 1973. It cost $1,450,000, including $312,000 for the fire-control system. In the early 1980s there was the M-1 tank, costing $2 million including a $745,000 fire-control system. These costs do not include development or operating costs, which normally triple the ultimate cost.

The M-60A3 was a greater improvement over the M-60A1 than the "all new" M-1 was over the M-60A3. Different versions of the same weapon often differ more from each other than from the next new model of that type. Soviet weapons development policy tended to follow gradual improvements, even though new models are identified as new systems. The Soviets would have called the M-60A3 the M-65. This Soviet identification policy often alarmed many in the West for no good reason beyond ignorance of the other side's slightly different way of naming new vehicles.

Escalating costs are a very intractable problem. While it may be technically possible to calculate accurately the cost of a new weapon system, political pressures and human nature conspire to prevent it. No one who is supposed to know the cost of a new system will admit to ignorance. An initial cost is conjured up and then modified by political considerations. This is of little consequence, as the price will invariably rise. Indeed, any American project will cost, on the average, twice the original estimate. The original estimated cost implies a threshold of intolerance, a price that, if exceeded, will result in project cancellation. The threshold is a natural reaction if a handful of new programs obliterates all other projects. The formula for this threshold, based on past experience, is:

$$10^{10}/(\text{number of units to be produced})^{1.2}$$

In plain English, this means that if there is to be only one item, it can cost $12 billion. Two items can cost no more than $5.2 billion each; 10 items can each cost $757 million each; 100 items, $48 million each; 1,000 items, $3 million each; 10,000 items, $190,000 each; 100,000, $12,000 each, 1 million items, $757 each. The averages were made from dozens of weapon systems and were based on 2002 dollars. This phenomenon has another insidious aspect. Costs rose toward the limit even if there is no other reason. A more expensive tank tends to have more expensive components (driver's seat. heater. paint job, etc.) than a less expensive tank. There is no reason for these components to be more expensive other than that a more expensive system attracts higher prices for inherently cheap components.

As unit prices of weapons increase, there is a tendency to test less. Tests often require weapons to be destroyed. Expensive weapons require expensive testing. Expensive weapons tend to be less reliable and require more testing. As absurd as this might appear, it is common to cut corners on testing of expensive systems in order to reduce the howls of anguish over high cost. If the weapons infrequently see combat, and avoid the ultimate test, this is taken into account. It's a dirty little secret that is no secret.

The so-called more effective weapons tend to be less effective. For example, antiaircraft cannon have been around for over 80 years, but the missile has been used in combat only during the past five decades. Extensive combat experience has shown that cheaper cannon systems account for a higher proportion of aircraft damage than more expensive missile systems. So why continue to build missile systems? Partially because they are possible. They also force aircraft to fly lower, where cannon are more effective. And as history and the 1991 Gulf War demonstrated, the new weapons eventually get some age on them and become effective. New weapons also force design changes on existing weapons systems. Some helicopters have been made very resistant to light cannon, but not as much to light missiles. Now most helicopters are equipped with a number of missile-warning and antimissile systems. Also, once a new weapon appears, it acquires a life of its own. New systems are rarely killed until newer and usually more expensive systems appear. Missiles are currently in danger of being replaced by "death ray" systems using lasers or charged particle beams. Another $12 billion, please. The longer a project takes, the more expensive it becomes. The more expensive a project becomes, the more complex it becomes. Greater complexity breeds still more complexity. It is often a violent process to get a weapon system away from the development people and into the hands of the troops.

The Peace Dividend

When the Cold War ended so suddenly, the nearly half-century-long arms race it spawned led to some rather bizarre consequences. As President Eisenhower warned in the late 1950s, as the arms race was just getting started, the "military-industrial complex" was going to be a growing problem in the future. This became blatantly obvious when, as the Cold War came to an abrupt conclusion, weapons manufacturers pleaded successfully that defense production could not be drastically cut because unemployment would result. That wasn't convincing enough, as Congress began hacking away at the defense budget. So the defense contractors pled that if the cuts went too far, we would lose the "technology base" needed to build things like billion-dollar aircraft and $2 billion submarines. The military-industrial community had long stressed these economic angles and now, as they were the only arguments they had, they played it off the politicians to good effect. Weapons production and the maintenance of large armed forces now became a form of public works. President Eisenhower, who had spent most of his adult life as an army officer, was certainly on to something and can be faulted only for not being able to impress on the American public just how unyielding the Cold War defense budget, and its benefactors, would be to an outbreak of peace.

While the Cold War defense budgets did prove invulnerable to sharp cuts, they are not invulnerable. The Cold War ended as the United States was in the midst of a recession, a presidential election, and several politically embarrassing scandals in Congress. The legislators were reluctant to take the heat for any lost jobs resulting from defense cuts. This was a knee-jerk reaction, as defense cuts benefit the economy in the medium and long term. Defense spending ties up a lot of vital human and economic resources while producing little of economic value. While it does cost something to convert that defense spending to civilian use, the resulting economic activity produces more jobs and greater overall economic benefits. Defense spending tends to use more highly educated workers and produce things in an economically wasteful manner. There is always a shortage of highly educated workers in the civilian economy, and the ones released from defense work are quickly absorbed into non-defense work. The market-driven, highly competitive economy of the civilian sector also makes for much more effective use of capital than does defense production. The dot-com boom of the late 1990s not only absorbed any unemployed defense engineers and technicians, but actually caused an acute talent shortage for the defense companies. Then, as if on cue, along came the war on terrorism. America was at war again, and the call went out for more equipment, technology, and weapons. Defense budgets will rise faster now. The peace dividend never really amounted to much, and now it's gone for good.

What Kind of Post–Cold War Military Will We End Up With?

When the Cold War ended, the Soviet armed forces, formerly the largest (and arguably the most powerful) in the world, went into a decade-long collapse. The Soviet Union split into nine new nations, with Russia being the largest. With the economy in free fall, the Russian defense budget quickly shrank to a fraction of its former size. Military spending in Russia dipped, by the mid-1990s, to about 20 percent of its 1980s peak. But manpower only shrank from 5.2 million to a million today. The Russians were spending most of their energies looking after the economic needs of the troops and destroying most of their nuclear weapons, and trying to keep the rest in working order. This last item, the great nuclear disarmament of the 1990s, came about for three reasons:

- The series of disarmament treaties signed by the United States and the USSR in the late 1980s and right up to the collapse of the Soviet Union in the summer of 1991.
- The inability to, and unwillingness to, support all those nuclear weapons because of the economic cost. This was acknowledged by most Soviet leaders up until the 1991 collapse, but after the Communists were out of power, it became an article of faith. With the Cold War over, there was no need for all those nukes.
- The Western nations made it known that they would be far more generous to the successor states of the Soviet Union if a lot of the Soviet nukes were destroyed. It was not hard to sell this idea to the former Soviets, as they didn't want to pay for the upkeep of all those weapons, and they certainly wanted to encourage generosity in the West.

Even the U.S. military publicly recognized that the formidable military force they and their allies had been preparing to fight since the 1950s had suddenly become but a shadow of its former self. Through most of the 1990s, the biggest danger the former Red Army posed was to itself. Discipline broke down as pay and food were often in short supply. Officers and troops selling weapons and equipment became a major problem. As the twenty-first century dawned, Russia was trying to move toward an all-volunteer force. Units were disbanded so that there were some outfits that could be trained to retain some military effectiveness. Making this work will take until the end of the decade. Meanwhile, the mighty Red Army is no longer much of a threat to anyone.

In the West, the military did not collapse. Moreover, a large contingent of the NATO forces that had long confronted the Red Army in central Europe managed to show off their superior skills by making short work of the Soviet-equipped Iraqi army. But without a Red Army to fight, the Western military now had to face a much more formidable foe: its own citizens and taxpayers. Throughout the Cold War, most Western taxpayers put up with the large defense budgets needed to support armed opposition to the Red Army. With the red menace defanged, the Western generals and admirals had a difficult time maintaining the force levels they have become accustomed to for several decades. While the former Soviets had little choice but to cut their military strength, the Western nations can still pay their bills. Nevertheless, the cuts were underway within a year of the Soviet Union's collapse. The major holdout was the United States, where the military budget had become a form of political patronage, and it was the politicians who were having a difficult time with cutting the military budget.

In the United States, it was thought that post–Cold War cuts would result in a smaller but still professional and effective armed forces. This would have been in sharp contrast to the bits and pieces of military power the Soviet successor states were able to cobble together. The officers of the former Soviet military make no secret of their desire to emulate the Western armed forces. This means fewer conscripts, more quality in training and equipment, and discarding their 80-year-old Communist military tradition. The Third World nations that used the Soviet military as their model are equally dismayed with what they ended up with, and many of these nations are also looking to the West for a more effective military model. But the Western nations have a significant advantage in their use of professional troops. A Western-type armed forces requires easy access to a highly industrialized economy and a well-educated pool of recruits. Only the Western nations have both of these elements. The images of Western troops quickly devastating the Russian-style Iraqi army in 1991 will long haunt Third World military leaders. While the image may not be entirely accurate, it will influence military thinking in all nations for the rest of the decade.

But the result was not exactly what American military leaders were hoping for. In 1991, when the Gulf War ended, America had the most powerful armed forces on the planet. But the Cold War was over, the Persian Gulf was quiet, and a lot of the troops were no longer needed. So through the 1990s, the armed forces lost a third of its people. Reasonable enough. But only about a fifth of the bases were shut down. It took billions to keep the unneeded bases open, but to Congress these bases represented votes back home, and to be associated with closing one was political suicide. Billions more were spent on weapons and equipment the troops didn't need or want. While training costs billions for fuel, spare parts, and ammunition, these goods are not as noticeable politically as building new weapons. Those factories are easy to identify and quickly become a political football if they are threatened with closure.

But what did the troops need? They needed time and money to train. Most don't get the time because so many of our forces are overseas performing peace-keeping, antiterrorism, or showing-the-flag missions. Many units are under-strength because of this and a scarcity of new recruits. Everyone in Washington agrees that "readiness" (being trained to fight) is important. But maintaining politically important bases and purchasing projects has higher priority.

What this means is that when the troops do have to fight, they take more casualties and more time getting the job done. Until the Gulf War, U.S. troops always went into their first battles unprepared. The generals and admirals noted the big difference in performance, and casualties, in the Gulf War. There, for the first time in our history, we were ready for the first battle. Despite all the attention given the high-tech gadgets, the professionals know that training—lots of it, and quality training at that—was what made the difference. But now the politicians are playing games with the defense budget, and this compounds several other problems unique to the post–Cold War period.

After the Soviet Union disappeared, so did the urgent need for a lot of well-trained troops. This gave all concerned an excuse to tolerate the sharp decline in readiness. But the booming economy also created another problem. The all-volunteer armed forces have to compete with civilian employers for recruits. When the economy is good, recruiting is bad. The Army gets fewer guys willing to enter the combat arms. The Air Force loses more pilots to airlines. The Navy not only has a hard time getting new sailors, but loses more of its best technicians to better pay, and to avoiding six-month cruises to the Persian Gulf.

But the people the services do have would be a lot more effective if billions were spent on training. Not spending that money also hurts morale. The troops know how important the training is, for they will pay the price if they have to go into combat without it. To turn the screw a little more, there is also less money for maintaining the bases that are still open. Troop housing goes without repairs, as do the roads and everything else.

Readiness is like the weather: everyone talks about it, but no one does anything about it. Unlike the weather, you can do something about readiness, but no one in charge will. The readiness problem will remain a major problem for the foreseeable future.

Anatomy of an Arms Race

The Cold War was hot in one area: the development and production of weapons. Now that the Cold War is over, and before another one begins, it would be instructive to take a closer look at what happened last time around.

Weapon-development projects are typically begun in response to a perceived rather than actual threat. Because it takes nearly 10 years to develop a new weapon, work must begin before the enemy version appears. Most of the really new weapons came from the West, because this is where most new technology came from. To keep up, the Soviets often applied Western technology to weapons before Western nations did. This meant that the Soviet systems were typically less reliable and capable than Western versions. Although combat experience constantly demonstrated this, Western nations often responded to Soviet developments and touched off still another round of development.

The result was a large number of weapon systems begun and precious few canceled. After its first year of existence, an American system had a 4 percent chance of cancellation each year right up until it went into production. This has been the experience during the past 40 years. Soviet systems experienced even less chance of cancellation. Ineptly implemented or no longer needed Soviet systems went into limited production, anyway. These turkeys then either faded away or were converted to other uses. A good example was the U.S. B-70 bomber. This was an early 1960s project, a replacement for the B-52, which would be 10 years old and "obsolete" in the late 1960s. ICBMs seemed a better investment, and the B-70, which showed every sign of being hideously expensive, was canceled. The Soviets, in the meantime, began developing an aircraft to counter the B-70, the MiG-25 Foxbat. The MiG-25 was not canceled and was available in 1970. Without a fast, high-flying bomber to intercept, the MiG-25 didn't have much to do. It could fly fast and high, although not very far. It was a cranky aircraft without carrying capacity, not very maneuverable, and feared by its pilots. It was specialized for one job, going after fast, high-flying bombers, and this job no longer existed. Initially the MiG-25 was turned into a camera-carrying reconnaissance plane. Operating alone, it could fly high and fast into an area, take photos, and get out with less risk of interception. The MiG-25 eventually evolved into the MiG-31, an interceptor that depended on look-down radar and new air-to-air missiles. In the West, the MiG-25 was viewed with alarm. Here was this huge, fast, ominous-looking plane. Something had to be done. No one mentioned that something had already been done when the B-70 was canceled. It was ignored that the MiG-25 had only one useful mission left, and that was to frighten Western governments into countering the MiG-25's mythical capabilities. The result was a number of very capable and expensive Western aircraft and missile systems.

The Soviets, and now the Chinese, not unmindful of their technological and financial disadvantages versus America, compensated in several ways:

The Soviets copied Western technology extensively. Although Soviet industry was often incapable of duplicating Western technology, it came close enough by producing a large number of less sophisticated weapons that cleverly worked around what it couldn't duplicate. China has taken this one step further, allowing free enterprise to create factories that can reproduce American high-tech equipment.

The Soviets did not leap from one technological breakthrough to another. They allowed their systems to evolve gradually. Seemingly new systems would eventually be revealed as progressive upgrades of the previous model. Their tanks and aircraft were noted for this approach. The Chinese follow the Russians in this respect but go one step further by buying the best military technology the Russians have and then copying as much as they can.

The Soviets often mass-produced weapon designs that were not technologically advanced and were simply not made by Western armed forces anymore or in large quantities. This enabled them to achieve some capability in areas where they were technically inferior. Depth-charge throwers and many types of missiles were examples. The Chinese still do this, if only because they have so much old equipment and cannot yet afford to replace the old stuff with new models. But as the Chinese economy grows, so will the quantity of new weapons.

Soviet commanders accepted a higher discrepancy between actual and theoretical performance than Western nations. This outburst of pragmatism came from their realization that their systems tended to be perfected in use, often carrying uncorrected defects through their entire lifetimes, were produced to lower industrial standards, and had less capable operators. The Chinese are moving away from this as they try to get more Western-quality weapons.

Soviet doctrine called for heavy use of the particularly Soviet quality known as quantity. This became more difficult as they tried to match Western technology and unit cost escalated. Western nations had the same problems with high technology, but the ratio of Soviet to Western systems did not change appreciably. The effort to keep up in the technology race was killing the Soviet economy and eventually forced them to rethink their approach to defense spending. The Chinese have long believed in this and can be said to have invented this angle.

Soviet planning was long term. It dealt in 10-, 20-, and over-20-year planning cycles. As alien as this is to Westerners, it was a necessary practice in the Soviet Union. The entire Soviet economy was centrally planned and required long lead times to accomplish complex tasks. This planning was not detailed. The tank-building plan would assume a new version of their main battle tank every five or six years. The required manpower and resources would be set aside for that task. What exactly the tank would be like was left up to the designers. If this did not leave enough engine-building capacity to expand automobile production, then the planners knew that they wouldn't get the additional cars. Military production came first, but within the planned limits. Resources were made available for opportunistic projects. The reactive armor added to Soviet tanks in the mid-1980s was an example. Again, China is way ahead of the Russians with this approach. China plans for the long haul, and at the moment they see themselves being back on top in a few decades.

The United States responded to the arms race by doing what it had always done best: developing new technology and spending a lot of money. As in the past, this approach worked. It was not a cheap victory, the financial cost of the Cold War being greater than all other U.S. wars combined. China is not engaging in an arms race, though. It is upgrading its armed forces slowly as its free market allows for it. We can only hope that economic growth in China will bring with it a less warlike attitude.

The United States:
The High Cost of Being First

When the United States put a man on the moon in the 1960s, a very expensive myth was born: with sufficient funds, any technological feat could be accomplished. Weapons development turned out to be different. The budgets are smaller, public support often nonexistent, the problems less well defined, and the tasks often more difficult than staging a lunar press conference. The resulting weapons often do not perform as expected and cost more than anticipated. They cost more than the budget can sustain, so fewer are produced and/or corners are cut in the design. Making fewer systems or reducing performance is compounded by not providing sufficient spare parts for wartime use. This is a flaw that will not be appreciated fully until the shooting starts. The spare-parts shortage was present in the 1991 Gulf War and would have gotten really ugly if the fighting had lasted more than a few weeks.

All of this gives new technology a bad name and makes it difficult for deserving projects to get funds. The escalation of claims causes bigger lies to be told in a vicious circle that makes it difficult for anyone to speak honestly. Being first is very expensive, and not just in terms of money. The system changes considerably when a war breaks out, because you now have a means of determining what works and what doesn't. Much of the indecisiveness and overbuilding of weapons stops. Because new weapons are needed quickly, less time is available to spend money. Because more of each type is built, the unit cost comes down. Typically, if you are building a new tank and planned to produce 10,000 for peacetime use, producing three times as many during a war reduces unit cost 20 percent just for lower development expense. This is because development cost typically represents 30 percent of the total. During wartime, as little as a year is needed for development, thus cutting the development bill by more than half. Costs are reduced further because feedback from the combat troops produces a simpler and more effective design. This produces a weapon that does more of what you need to do and has less gold plating to provide for endless contingencies. Overall, wartime weapons cost less than half as much as peacetime systems. Peril is an excellent motivator. There is no such motivation in peacetime. The most recent example of lower weapons-development cost occurred during the brief 1991 Gulf War. Shortly after the air phase of the war began, it was discovered that the Iraqis had bunkers so deeply buried that no current bomb could get to them. A new weapon was needed, and the 19-foot-long, 4,700-pound GBU-28 was developed, tested, and delivered in six weeks at a cost of $335,000 each. Of the thirty delivered, two were actually used (two others were used in testing). During testing, the GBU-28 penetrated over 100 feet into the earth during one test and 22 feet of concrete in another. Two more bombs were used for testing after the war. The other 24 remained in the Air Force inventory, eventually being used in the Afghanistan war 10 years later. The cost was kept low because discarded barrels from Army eight-inch guns were used as the bomb body. A specially hardened front end was attached, and the bomb was filled with 650 pounds of explosive. Normally, producing such a new weapon takes at least two years. During the Afghanistan war, a similar program to link B-2 bombers with reconnaissance UAVs via satellite links was implemented in a few weeks. This involved a jury-rigged satellite antenna on the B-2 and a laptop computer for the weapons officer. Crude, but cheap and effective. A peacetime project for this capability was also underway (it would work from the displays already present for the weapons officer). But the capability was needed right away. In another year or so the peacetime version will show up.

All nations suffer to a certain extent from the inefficiencies of peacetime procurement. But the United States has developed a particularly insidious and expensive host of problems. For starters, the American military has lost control of weapons procurement. The legislature has seized effective control because of the vast funds that can be channeled into their constituencies when defense funds are handed out. The military cannot be too rough with the legislators; otherwise, they may find their budgets cut. The legislative control over defense budgets also prevents long production runs, as the quantity of weapons to be produced is largely at the whim of political requirements. These requirements change every year. During the Korean War, the habit of developing weapons in a hurry was institutionalized. This meant building the production facilities before the design of the system was finished. These crash projects were useful in wartime, but in peacetime there is no incentive to finish them quickly. The expense of changing the production facilities was added to the normal expense of redesigning the weapons. The high costs associated with doing everything at once continues for years, further driving up the costs. This made defense business uncertain and discouraged competition. Lack of competition reduced the need to be efficient. Wartime style "cost plus" (profit fee) does not, in the long run, encourage efficient production. The oldest and least efficient production facilities are to be found in defense plants. Worse yet, the military personnel that supervise the projects are not procurement professionals. Other nations make procurement a career path. In the United States, an officer slips into procurement for a few years and then goes on to something else or retires (and often ends up working for a defense supplier). It gets worse. The U.S. defense procurement bureaucracy has grown to the point where dozens of committees and individual officials must pass on, make suggestions about, and generally impede the progress of new systems. The net result is U.S. weapons costing several times more than they should. Often, needed weapons do not survive the process, and the required systems never get built.

Paying for the Next War

Despite wartime economies of scale, the cost of fighting a war today will be substantially higher than peacetime operations. This is largely due to the high cost of ammunition. Currently, a ton of conventional ammunition costs about $10,000. A ton of missile munitions costs over $700,000. ICMs (Improved Conventional Munitions) cost at least 10 times more than old-fashioned bombs and shells. The high cost of ICMs and missiles represents two things. One is the greater development cost. Second, their greater complexity requires a more elaborate manufacturing process. Under wartime conditions, economies of scale and expediency could reduce the cost by five or more times. Still, the price of an average ton of munitions would still be $30,000 and up. With U.S. divisions consuming at least 1,000 tons a day, the bill would be over $20 million per division per day for just munitions. Intensive combat can up the daily munitions expenditure to 5,000 tons. Fuel, at $500 a ton, would be only $500,000. Fuel would represent as much weight as munitions. Replacing lost and damaged equipment, assuming 2-percent daily losses, plus food, spare parts, wages, and anything else, brings the daily bill to over $70 million a day. The eight U.S. divisions that found themselves fighting during the 1991 Gulf War, in only three days of combat, used up several billion dollars worth of resources. The Air Force, at several hundred thousand dollars per sortie, cost over $44 billion during the seven weeks of active air operations. Transportation and naval expenses are included.

The six months of operations in the Persian Gulf cost over $70 billion. That included seven weeks of air combat, three days of ground combat, and six months of getting ready. The cost was over 20 percent of the annual defense budget. If there had been more combat, the costs would have escalated sharply. One month of heavy ground combat can easily cost over $100 billion for this same eight-division force.

While the Gulf War was a major operation, it fell far short of the kind of operations the U.S. has been getting ready for since the 1950s. The United States has considerable economic resources and was, and still is, ready to mobilize most of it for a major war. Consider the overall situation for a major war. The U.S. economy, if mobilized for war, could increase its GDP by perhaps a third. Half of this could be devoted to military needs. A ground force of 30 divisions, each in combat for 120 days, would cost over $300 billion. Over $100 billion would be required to operate 3,600 aircraft for 120 days. Air operations have always been more expensive than ground operations. A hundred aircraft are generally considered to cost about the same as a division. Looking at it this way, twice the resources are devoted to aircraft, despite the fact that an air force unit of 100 aircraft requires one third the manpower of an army division. Air power is more expensive, but less costly in human life, at least for the user. Taken in this context, the Gulf War saw Air Force resources exceeding ground forces by over 50 percent. While you'll always need ground forces to go in and finish a war, the Gulf War demonstrated that, if you have the material and financial resources, you can do most of the work with air forces.

A navy of over 300 combat ships and 1,400 aircraft in combat would consume over $300 billion in 120 days. Over 60 percent of this would be for aircraft operations (both land- and carrier-based). With the Soviet navy rapidly losing its former capabilities, there is no major opponent for the U.S. Navy. Thus, the 300-combat-ship operation is less likely to occur. But a naval effort of half that size remains a possibility. Combat would not likely be continuous, or even intense, but we could still see a cost of over $1 billion a day to keep the ships out there, ready for anything.

If operations were carried out at the above levels, the direct cost would be over $600 billion for four months of operations. Only about 10 percent of this is for replacement of destroyed equipment. The majority would be for munitions. Guided missiles and other so-called smart munitions would account for most of the ammunition cost. With no major opponents left on the planet, such enormous expenditures will not be needed. Iraq was one of the few nations that possessed large quantities of armored vehicles, which are the primary target of all those expensive, high-tech munitions. The cost of the Gulf War is the likely model for wars the United States and its Western allies will face in the next decade.

In addition, there will be no additional expense of building more ships, aircraft, and weapons to replace stuff lost in combat, or for new divisions. There will also be less expense for aiding allies, replacing lost satellites, caring for the wounded, and compensating for any damage done to domestic facilities and populations. The tempo of a future war will still be dictated by the ability to produce these expensive and complex munitions as well as the high-technology weapons that use them. But unlike the Cold War era, all you have to do is have a stockpile handy for the next "little war."

Throughout the 1990s, and into the twenty-first century, we saw the pattern of less expensive little wars and peacekeeping operations. The Afghanistan war will cost a lot more in humanitarian aid after the fighting (tens of billions of dollars) than the combat operations themselves (probably less than $10 billion).

Getting Ready for the Next War

The U.S. munitions budget was about $14 billion a year at the end of the Cold War. Stockpiles represented under $120 billion worth of munitions at current prices. It was understood, but rarely acknowledged too loudly, that this would not last long in a major war. If you ended up blowing off nearly $120 billion worth of munitions a month for three or four months, only a fraction would come off the shelf. The rest has to be manufactured, but only after you build the factories and train the workers. This means increasing manufacturing capacity severalfold. Manufacturing managers and engineers are very resourceful people, but a first-year increase in munitions production would most likely create less than a quarter of the requirements for a major war. Something has to give. What happens is that either one side wins very quickly, or the war settles down to a staring contest while the factories come on-line. If peace has not broken out yet, a war of attrition ensues. This is not based on speculation, but observation. World War I followed this pattern, as did our own Civil War, the first of the modern industrial wars. World War II was a different story, as it began in fits and starts. Moreover, the major combatants started mobilizing several years before they came to blows. Throughout both wars, battles often ground to a halt when both sides ran out of munitions or fuel. The same pattern appeared during the 1973 Arab-Israeli war. If the 1991 Gulf War had gone on for another month or so, the United States would have run out of several types of high-tech munitions. This surprises some people. It shouldn't.

Most nations perceive the solution to this problem to be the quick victory. This is another myth regularly worshiped by military planners. While possible, a short war is unlikely against most foes. The Iraqis cooperated by letting themselves be embargoed and then leaving their army out in the desert.

Vietnam was a more likely case, where weapons of mass destruction were avoided and a war of attrition ensued against an elusive and resilient foe. Vietnams will be avoided by the United States and other nations for another generation or two, at least until that sorry affair becomes a dim memory.

It should also not be forgotten that a major war, while unlikely, is still a possibility. Mobilizing for a major war would take several years. If we entered a major war tomorrow there would be a severe munitions shortage within a month or two. This is not as disastrous as it sounds. At the moment, there's no one on the planet with a large pile of munitions. Running low on ammo means that we will have to take longer to do whatever we want to do. An inconvenience more than a disaster.

You need several years to create the tools and train the staff to produce large quantities of munitions, weapons, and military equipment. Training the troops also takes longer than in the past, especially the larger number of technicians. Industrial mobilization for war has been a serious problem for the past century and has been getting worse. The problem tends to solve itself if the combatants cannot. The root cause is the difficulty in maintaining large peacetime stocks of munitions. Not only is ammunition expensive, it doesn't last long in storage. The stuff may look OK in the warehouse, but let's face it, progressive deterioration soon sets in. The rot is not apparent until you use it. It's one of the dirty little secrets of military life. When you use old ammunition, a lot of it lands with a thud, not a bang.

Meanwhile, we have a lot of little wars. Gold-plated little wars are even more expensive than less-than-total total wars. Here the natural temptation to use weapons that are safer to users, and more expensive ones, will be difficult to resist. Vietnam was such a war, and expensive munitions were just starting to get really expensive. Warfare has never been cheap, Vietnam showed that it can only get more expensive, and the 1991 Gulf War proved it.

The Price of Things to Come

Several cost trends have been inexorably progressing through this century. Aircraft costs, for example, have been increasing four times every 10 years for the past 90 years. During the past 40 years, this disease has spread to land and naval weapons. Currently combat aircraft cost from $500 a pound (cheap MiG-29s) to $1,600 a pound (top-of-the-line F-22). Armored vehicles cost $5–$25 a pound, and warships $50–$100. These three items also cost two to four times their acquisition cost for operations and maintenance over their 10–20-year peacetime life. Missiles cost 3–10 times more than aircraft on a per-pound basis. Satellites cost over $10,000 a pound to build and over $3,000 a pound to put into orbit. The chief culprit is electronics. Promising a lot, and sometimes delivering it, electronics tend to become so complex that mere humans cannot easily ensure their reliability. During World War II, combat aircraft had less than a hundred pounds of electronic gear. Today, a ton, 2,200 pounds, is the norm in Western aircraft and rising rapidly. In the last 20 years, tank fire-control systems have gone from 6 percent (M-60A1) of total vehicle cost to nearly 40 percent (M-1). As one calculation pointed out, if the trends of the last 80 years persist, by the middle of the next century the entire defense budget of the United States will be spent on one combat aircraft. Something has to give. The end of the Cold War has provided something of an escape hatch. With less money to spend, there will be more incentive to spend it more effectively.

Let us also examine the relationship between cost and effectiveness. Compare a modern carrier task force with one of World War II vintage.

Task Force 58, in 1944, cost $720 million and had 112 ships, over 40,000 men, and nearly 1,000 aircraft. These aircraft could deliver 400 tons of ordnance. A modern task force of 9 ships, 90 aircraft, and nearly 9,000 men costs $17 billion. Its aircraft carry the same amount of ordnance. The aircraft cost twice as much and require less than 10 percent as many air crew. The modern aircraft can fly more frequently and have fewer accidents. A hundred fewer ships are needed to support this air capability. Task Force 58 costs much more after adjusting for inflation and other costs. It required nearly five times more manpower. Cost have increased, but potential capability has increased faster. More important, far fewer men are needed to man the weapons. When the cost of training and maintaining manpower is added, the modern task force is actually cheaper. The only drawback to all this is that unit costs are increasing far faster than the ability of national economies. Modern warfare is becoming something other than World War II with faster aircraft and fewer ships.

The future is already here: fewer weapons were being purchased even before the Cold War ended. The Soviet Union, and to a lesser extent the United States, crippled their economies with huge arms expenditures. Japan, spending one percent of its GNP on arms, compared with over six percent in the United States, used the difference to build up industries producing a wide range of industrial and consumer goods. Soviet industry was so far behind it was hardly in the race anymore by the end of the Cold War. An arms race is a luxury few can afford, and even then not for long. An arms race contains the seeds of its own destruction, either through a war or the stagnation of the economy supporting it. The lost economic growth that pays for the arms race eventually catches up with you. Arms races exist only when there is a lot of wealth and weapons to spend it on. These conditions have been prevalent more in the past century than at any other time in history. Fear and paranoia produce these spasms of excessive arms spending. It's a hard habit to break. In addition to the diversion of resources from the economy, arms building produces one-third fewer jobs than do non-arms spending. The result of all this spending is often of dubious value. There is always the tendency to seek technological solutions to problems that are the result of ill-trained personnel and poor leadership.

The primary objective of peacetime arms expenditures often appears to be just spending money. Those nations that can break out of this cycle will be not only better defended but considerably wealthier. The ultimate cost of excessive military spending was political unrest rather than nuclear war. This happened in the Soviet Union first, where the ill effects of arms spending reached crisis proportions. High military spending also caused political unrest in the United States and Western Europe. One way or the other, the cost of war is felt even in times of peace.

Theory and Practice

The Soviets stockpiled two to three times more munitions than their Western opponents. Unfortunately for them, a lot of this stuff was so old and ill cared for that it proved as dangerous to its users as to their opponents. This created a major ecological disaster along the former East German border. That was where the Soviets kept a lot of their best stuff. Some of the smaller NATO nations kept dangerously skimpy ammo stockpiles, giving them only a week's supply in some categories if ever there were a war. These two extremes pretty well define the approach of most nations to paying for wars not yet fought.

The end of the Cold War has left the world awash in cheap arms. These weapons may not go to fuel another world war, but they have nourished many small wars. Century-old conflicts between farmers and herders in Africa are now wiping out entire tribes because cheap, Cold War surplus AK-47s have replaced spears and bows. Afghanistan has enough AK-47s to arm every adult male, and enough left over to equip most of the women. As an aside to this, it should be noted that there are still a lot of leftover weapons in Afghanistan from World War I and World War II. Arms races may end, but they leave behind a lethal legacy.

The Future

The industrialized nations are running out of soldiers and taxes. In a familiar pattern, rising living standards have led to lower birth rates. The pinch is felt most in the armed forces, where large numbers of increasingly scarce young males are needed. The money shortage is caused by increasing competition with more recently industrialized nations. The classic example is Japan capturing markets from the United States and Europe. This competition forces the heavily militarized Americans and Europeans to cut back on defense spending in order to make their industries more competitive. Military power begins with economic power. Lose your productivity and the armed forces shrink accordingly. The armed forces must get by with fewer people and less money. Those nations that don't adapt to this situation will see their combat power and economic strength suffer. The Cold War ended just in time for the industrialized nations of NATO. By 2000, most European nations had downsized their armed forces to the point where they could get rid of conscription.

China has demobilized over a million troops in order to pay for more high-tech weapons, and the Soviets announced a similar solution before the 1991 collapse. The future holds a hard decision between guns or butter. Many nations are learning to compromise. Older systems are rebuilt and updated instead of being replaced with new weapons. Big-ticket items, particularly strategic nuclear weapons systems, no longer have the blank-check authority of the past. Disarmament was caused by fiscal exhaustion as well as fear. The Soviets had an additional problem with its centrally planned economy slipping further into terminal stagnation. All the planned (socialist) economies have encountered this stagnation problem. While the end of the Cold War has lifted the economic burden of the arms race from the West, it has left still left standing a curious change in these enormous "postindustrial" economies. This is a change that has yet to be tested during a major war, but may still be: a postindustrial economy that employs a lot more people providing services and fewer actually producing goods. A major war in the future would reveal some curious insights into postindustrial economies. Going into World War II and through the 1950s, the United States was a manufacturing economy: primarily goods, but also substantial construction and raw materials. But in the 1980s, America has lost nearly a third of this manufacturing capacity. More economic effort goes into services. It is difficult to find a place in a war economy for bankers, insurance agents, and lawyers. Perhaps we can use them to improve the quality of the infantry. Some of the new economic activity is transferable to military uses. The hundreds of thousands of additional computer specialists and medical specialists can have an impact. This will create a military effort unlike any currently envisioned.

As a historical example, consider World War II. In 1940 and 1941 there were plans to build a lot of large warships. But shipbuilding takes time. Building more plants to produce "heavy metal" goods also takes time. What the United States did have was a lot of skilled workers and light metal-fabricating capability. So America built a lot of aircraft, which could be manufactured quickly and put right into action. The massive effort to build the atomic bomb was also an application of abundant scientific resources. Mobilizing for another world war today would find even more emphasis on building what could be put together quickly and to the best effect. This would again mean more aircraft and light combat vehicles, and simplified missiles and electronic weapons. A future war would test the theory that Western engineers could rapidly retool their appliance production for some kind of effective weapons. Russia already has an enormous heavy-metals industry with which they build lots of armored vehicles. World War III, or any war of the 1991 Persian Gulf war class, if it happened and lasted long, would be a curious contrast in styles and substance. High-tech versus heavy metal. Place your bets.

This is nothing new. For centuries, nations have fluctuated between smaller, professional armies and larger forces filled with a lot of amateurs. In the past, the key factor in the decision to have a mass army was how much danger the nation was in and how many weapons the nation could afford. We are entering the "Small Army Zone." Some time in the future, something will happen that will put a lot of people in uniform again. But for the moment, small is seen as good.

Cost of War

There are many kinds of wars, and not all of them cost the same. The 1999 bombing campaign against Kosovo cost some $4 billion. The 1991 Gulf War was the last large war the U.S. has fought. It lasted six months and cost about $75 billion (in current dollars). But that war has not ended, and the military forces we have kept there since 1991 are costing some $800 million a year. The last long war, Vietnam (1965–72), cost some $800 billion ($100 billion a year). World War II cost $2.7 trillion ($540 billion a year). These costs include costs of caring for veterans of those wars. All three of these wars were also different in more ways than their cost.

Even peacekeeping operations can cost several billion dollars a year. Putting a brigade (about 4,000 troops) into the Balkans for peacekeeping costs about $1 billion a year. Add all the support troops and you have, in a place like Bosnia, an annual cost of $2 billion. More remote places with more warlike natives can drive that cost up 50 or 100 percent. Even the operations against Iraq to enforce the embargo cost about $1 billion a year (and cost a total of $7 billion through the 1990s). Even the brief Haiti operation cost $1 billion, and the two years of operations in Somalia cost $1.5 billion.

Since you already have the troops, ships, and warplanes, you might ask, what are the extra costs of peacekeeping? Two things normally comprise the largest expense in combat (aside from people getting killed or injured): ammunition and replacement. For example, if an armored division is in combat for 30 days, the largest single expense will be about $2 billion worth of munitions. But the second-largest expense will be $730 million to replace worn-out or destroyed equipment. That $730 million figure is for a low-casualty type of war. It doesn't make any difference if there are no troops hurt at all; if you have to boogie around the battlefield shooting a people for a month, you are going to do a lot of damage to your own equipment. Even if you lose only 200 troops after a month (this would actually be a lower casualty rate than the Gulf War), your equipment replacement bill would be nearly $400 million. In peacekeeping operations, you don't use much ammo at all, and the replacement costs are pretty low. But you do have two other major costs: construction and transportation. For peacekeeping you end up building bases to house the troops and their equipment. This gets pretty expensive. In Kosovo, it cost $70,000 per soldier to build rather nice basing facilities. It costs $10,000 per soldier to maintain the bases. The transportation cost is initially large as you move all the heavy weapons and equipment to the area of operations. After that, you just have to move the troops every six months or a year (depending on how long the tour of duty is).

So even a little war, like the 2001 operation in Afghanistan, is expensive because of the cost of ammunition and moving people and stuff around. Even though there were only about a hundred sorties a day, each of them cost between half a million and $1 million. Most of the expense was in the munitions, but there were also considerable expenses for fuel, spare parts, and additional maintenance. Since the 1991 Gulf War, smart (and more expensive) bombs have become the more common weapon, mainly because you can use them at high altitude (safe from enemy antiaircraft fire).

Getting the troops to the battlefield is always expensive. It costs $100,000 a day to charter a large transport (which costs over $100 million to build). It takes eight of these ships to move an armored division, the kind of unit you want if there's going to be some serious ground fighting. If the battlefield is halfway around the world, as they often are, it's going to take you about 20 days to get there. Well, let's see, eight ships times 20 days times $100,000 a day. That comes to $16 million. Then you have to move the troops: that's another couple of million. You also have to pay for getting the division from its base in, say, Texas, to the port. That's another million or so. Just getting the division there costs some $20 million. It actually can be more expensive if the ships have to steam into a war zone, as this will require additional payments for insurance and danger pay for the crews.

Moving stuff to a combat zone in a hurry is limited by the number of heavy transports. The largest fleet belongs to the U.S. Air Force. But this is only about 350 aircraft (C-4s, C-141s, and C-17s). There's another 500 medium-weight (and -range) C-130s. Fighting a FedEx war (flying everything in) can be done. Much of the action in the Afghanistan war of 2001 was by air freight. But you are severely restricted. Using 160 of the heavy transports, you can bring in about 1,500 tons of stuff (bombs, weapons, food) a day. Using the medium transports, you can get in another few hundred tons from local sources (the Persian Gulf, Europe). The C-5s cost $6,000 an hour to run, the C-17s $5,000 an hour, and the C-141s $3,500. Running these big birds the usual 10 hours a day week after week gives you an air-transport bill of $240 million a month for air freight. The Air Force will also charter civilian transport, but this will cost the Air Force more than twice as much as the military transports. The problem with air freight is you can't bring in a lot of stuff. For example, during the Afghanistan campaign, the 1,500 tons (actually, it was more, because a lot of stuff could come from Europe instead of North America) was pretty much taken up supporting commando operations in Uzbekistan and Tajikistan and getting spare parts, some bombs, and special electronics to the heavy bombers operating on Diego Garcia. The Navy proved once again that if you want to move serious quantities of supplies, you have to do it by sea. Although American carriers travel with enough fuel and bombs on board to launch a few hundred bombing sorties (depending on how far away the targets are) per carrier, the Navy can, given a week or so, get tankers (with jet fuel) and freighters (with bombs and spares) out there to keep the sorties coming.

Lots of money won't solve the air-freight problem, either. There are a limited number of air transports and a limited number of places they can land. Even the move toward smart bombs has not changed this, for the average bomber takes off carrying more tonnage of fuel than smart bombs. The expensive air freight is becoming more useful, despite its cost, but it will be a long time before it will seriously threaten the need for sea transport.

As we enter the twenty-first century, warfare is dominated more and more by air power. The reasons are many. Airpower is more flexible. During the Afghanistan war, B-2s regularly flew missions from the American Midwest to Afghanistan. This is still pretty expensive (lots of in-flight refueling on an aircraft that needs a lot of expensive maintenance). But this is the future. The Afghanistan war also saw the first use of the Global Hawk long-range recon drone (UAV). This UAV can fly, controlled only by its internal software, from the United States to a place like Afghanistan, fly recon for several hours, and then fly back to America. But in practice, Global Hawk was stationed as close to Afghanistan as possible so it could spend more hours keeping an eye on potential targets. UAVs are cheaper (by over 40 percent) than manned aircraft and can stay in the air a lot longer. In Afghanistan, Predator UAVs carried Hellfire missiles and were very successful with them.

But overall, the increasing use of air power drives up the cost of air power, and not just for the Air Force. Half the cost of an aircraft carrier is the aircraft carried on it. The most expensive item of equipment in a U.S. armored division is not the tanks, but the 140–150 helicopters. Aircraft use more expensive munitions than ground troops or warships. Aircraft use more fuel and require much more expensive maintenance. The most expensive category of weapons bought by the U.S. armed forces is aircraft.

The American way of war changed fundamentally late in the twenty-first century. Americans have always been very sensitive about soldiers getting killed in war. The futile fighting in Korea and Vietnam, with over 80,000 American dead, further increased this reluctance to lose U.S. troops in combat. As bombing became more accurate, and aircraft safer, dropping smart bombs from high altitudes (outside the range of most antiaircraft weapons) became the preferred form of combat. There has also been more willingness to use greenback diplomacy (bribes, rewards, or threats to cut off aid). Another popular direction is combat robots of all types (for land and naval warfare, as well as the current UAVs). Robotic weapons used to be more expensive than those operated by soldiers, but this is no longer the case. The electronics revolution of the late twentieth century has reached the point where it's becoming cheaper to send in the droids.

Cost of Raising a Division

The basic unit of land combat is the division. They are expensive creatures. The costs shown here covers only hardware, weapons, and equipment. The cost of recruiting and training personnel equals a third to half the personnel cost. In addition, there is the cost of housing a division in peacetime, which equals at least half the hardware cost. Personnel and housing about double the hardware cost. Support facilities for maintenance and training, plus specialized units for combat support and noncombat units for medical, supply, and transportation units, also add to the final cost of a division, which can be up to three times the hardware cost shown. Training time to obtain qualified staff varies from a few months for the simplest jobs to years for the more technical ones. Time spent in schools and other training programs can amount to several "division man-years" (the number of people in the division times 2,000 hours). These trainees must be paid and maintained. Their instructors are an additional expense. Even

Item	Quantity	Avg. unit cost	Total cost	% of total
		U.S. mechanized infantry		
APCs	727	$1,100	$799,700	13.1%
Tanks	290	$4,500	$1,305,000	21.4%
Munitions, tons, 30 days	34,050	$60	$2,043,000	33.5%
Aircraft	143	$6,000	$858,000	14.1%
Misc. equipment and supplies			$180,000	3.0%
Trucks	3,500	$100	$350,000	5.7%
Communications and EW Equipment			$140,000	2.3%
Air defense weapons	108	$800	$86,400	1.4%
Field artillery	143	$900	$128,700	2.1%
ATGM	660	$150	$99,000	1.6%
Personal equipment	16,600	$3	$49,800	0.8%
Infantry weapons	24,000	$1	$24,000	0.4%
Fuel Stocks (30-day supply)	8,184	$1	$8,184	0.1%
Food Stocks (30-day supply)	2,184	$9	$19,656	0.3%
Total (millions of dollars)			$6,091	100%

Summaries

Combat vehicles			$2,962,700	49%
Other weapons			$338,100	6%
Other equipment			$719,800	12%
Supplies			$2,070,840	34%

on-the-job training can be costly, as you must divert trained people from their normal duties so that they can instruct the new troops. Training adds to equipment cost as equipment is worn out by the trainees and must be replaced. Equipment without qualified personnel to operate it is useless. To operate a division's equipment requires 12,000–16,000 men. Some 20 percent are the cadre—the officers, reserves, and noncommissioned officers (NCOs). These troops require years of experience and six months to a year of training. Most of them, NCOs and lower-grade officers, can be created in a year or two. Senior officers (majors, colonels, and up) usually need 5–10 years as senior officers to be most effective. Competent civilian managers can often fill in with only a year or two of training and experience. The quality of the cadre determines the quality of the remaining troops in the division. About half the division's troops can be trained to an adequate degree of competence in six months. These troops handle fairly basic tasks that people of average skill and intelligence can handle. These are the combat troops and "common" technicians. Any skill that can be learned in a few months falls into this category. Another 30 percent, the specialist technicians, requires a year or more of training and experience. These specialists can often be obtained directly from the civilian economy. Armed forces must constantly cope with an inadequate supply of cadre and specialists. A specialist shortage can be covered with a number of expensive but reliable alternatives. The most common is using more equipment. Without sufficient repair personnel, or enough experienced operators, you go through a lot more equipment. This leads to one of the more insidious peacetime practices, pretending that everything is all right. A fresh coat of paint often stands in for good maintenance. The cadre problem is the most critical because there is no easy way to overcome it. Careful selection of leaders and adequate training programs are a good first step. Unfortunately, few nations are very successful in either selection or training of leaders.

Item is the main equipment category.

Quantity is the quantity of that item found in the division. Division types shown are U.S. mechanized infantry-division and Soviet motor-rifle division (a common unit organization that will survive the demise of the Soviet Union for a decade or more).

Avg. unit cost is the average unit cost of each item of equipment in thousands of 2002 dollars. Only new equipment is considered. Where the range of item types within a category is too great to be meaningful, no number appears in this column.

Total cost is the total cost of all items in that category.

% of total is each item's percentage of the total cost of the division.

Summaries show general categories of the division's equipment.

Combat vehicles comprise the largest single expense for most modern armies. Until recently, tanks represented the bulk of this category. With the development of the IFV (infantry fighting vehicle), the armored vehicles for the infantry are looming larger in the equation. IFVs are becoming tanks in their own right. Compared with many tanks of 40–50 years ago, modern IFVs have equal or superior firepower. Aircraft assigned directly to the division have become a major factor. More capable drone aircraft accelerate this trend. Current armies devote about half their divisional equipment budget to combat vehicles. This ratio is not likely to increase.

Other weapons consist primarily of artillery, particularly antitank and antiaircraft artillery. This includes missiles, whose cost is rapidly overwhelming conventional artillery.

Other equipment is a rapidly growing category, as it includes many electronic items.

Supplies are often overlooked items. Thirty-day stock for the early stage of a war is the accepted standard, although many armies skimp. Such frugality is fatal if a war breaks out. Another potentially serious problem is improper storage and maintenance of these supplies. All these items are perishable and must be rotated. Fuel is the most perishable of all and is generally the best cared for. Ammunition must be fired off regularly and replaced. This is becoming expensive as the cost of missiles and ICMs escalates. Often these munitions are rebuilt to incorporate new developments. Storage is another problem, since there is a temptation not to disperse these supplies in protected areas in order to save money. Supply dumps are no secret from the enemy and make ideal targets for aircraft, artillery, and missiles.

PART SEVEN

MOVING THE GOODS

One of the more momentous revolutions in warfare during the past century
has been the greater capacity to move things. You can't have a world war
unless you can quickly move combat forces around the globe.

PART SEVEN

MOVING THE GOODS

26

The Navy:
The Tonnage War

In the last three centuries, some nations have found it possible to increase their wealth and military power through the use of extensive naval trade. These nations became known as the oceanic powers. Britain was the first major modern example; Japan and the United States are the latest. Those nations capable of achieving great wealth without naval trade are known as continental powers. First France, then Germany, followed by the Soviet Union. Now China and Russia are the principal continental powers. When oceanic powers come into conflict with continental powers, the battle comes down to the land-based nation attempting to disrupt the naval trade of the oceanic nation. For over 80 years, the submarine has been the chief means of assaulting naval trade. Guess who still has the world's largest submarine fleet.

The navy is responsible for mobilizing and protecting the civilian merchant fleets in wartime. These merchant ships are needed for moving and maintaining air and ground forces, supplying the navy, and providing the nation's industries with raw materials.

The Tonnage Numbers

Most of the world's merchant shipping, over two-thirds, is devoted to moving raw materials in bulk. Over 40 percent of these materials are petroleum. About 30 percent of available shipping can be used to move military supplies and equipment, in addition to tankers taken over to move military fuel. Shipping available for military equipment and supplies equals over 100 million gross register tons (GRT). To simplify a bit, one gross register ton equals one metric

581

ton of dry military cargo. Want to move a ground combat division? You'll need 250,000 GRT. Keep it supplied for a month? Another 30,000–50,000 GRT, depending on how intense operations are. What about nondivisional troops? Ten GRT per man to get them there. Figure 40,000 nondivisional troops per division, including Air Force. That's 400,000 GRT. One GRT per man per month for support, another 40,000 GRT. In summary, getting one new division overseas will require 650,000 GRT initially and up to 100,000 GRT a month for support, most of which is tankers. Air Force units require much less shipping but consume more fuel and munitions during combat. Naval operations are also consumers of enormous resources. Assume one GRT for every two or three displacement tons of combat ships. This will vary, especially with the carriers, according to the intensity of operations and the distance from bases.

To lessen this burden, and save shipping time, the United States has prepositioned the equipment for three divisions in Germany, with smaller stockpiles in Diego Garcia (Indian Ocean) and Guam (Pacific Ocean). Only the troops have to be flown over to make the divisions fully functional. These troops leave 500,000 GRT of divisional equipment behind. This material, and that of up to nine other divisions, can be whipped into shape and shipped within 90 days. Other equipment, and a lot of supply, must be shipped quickly to replace losses and keep the battle going. With the end of the Cold War, the European stockpiles future is in doubt. Also doubtful are the plans to send massive reinforcements to Europe. By the mid-1990s, the decades-old plans for reinforcements were no longer possible because of cuts in the defense budgets.

Getting Organized

The Navy is responsible for mobilizing, supervising, and safeguarding these movements. Until the end of the Cold War, it was expected that such movements would be made via the stormy North Atlantic and through a gauntlet of Soviet subs. The post–Cold War world poses different problems, the primary ones being the quick movement of troops and supplies. However, lest we forget, it's important to keep in mind the worst-case situation. Twice in this century, merchant ships have had to fight their way across a submarine-infested Atlantic Ocean. It could happen again. The next time, it could involve running transports past Chinese subs.

From the Navy's point of view, the biggest problem is lack of control. Although the merchant-shipping fleets are vast, they are not normally under any central control. Over 60 percent of the world's merchant fleet is under the control of companies in eight Western nations. Companies using flags of economic and legal convenience (Liberia, Panama, etc.) control over 25 percent of all shipping. These flags of convenience are largely owned and controlled by U.S. and British companies and often have crews partially composed of U.S.

and British citizens. This control does little for the ability to muster these vessels quickly into military service. Let us examine the problems of mobilizing merchant shipping fleets in a military emergency.

Assembling crews. Aside from possible problems with unions or noncitizen crews, there is the very basic problem of convincing merchant seamen to serve in a war zone. As losses to enemy action increase, it becomes more difficult to man the ships. It is especially difficult to do so in the winter, when a dunk in the frigid North Atlantic is certain death. The shortest shipping routes from North America to Asia go through the North Pacific. Each time a ship goes down, about 25 percent of the crew dies, varying with the severity of the weather and the volatility of the cargoes. The government can offer inducements such as danger pay and conscription. The best inducement is the ability to protect the ships from enemy attack. All these measures will take a while. Meanwhile, some of the ships may not move, lacking crews. Modern merchant seaman are primarily technicians; unskilled substitutes will not work.

Mobilizing merchant ships. The bulk of the world's shipping travels a few routes. Two thirds of the total shipping activity moves between North America, Europe, and the Persian Gulf. Add Japan and Australia and you cover 80 percent of the shipping movements. Less than three percent of these ships are needed immediately to support a worst-case situation, a major nonnuclear war in Europe. Certain ships are already under contract to switch over to military service in war time. However, these ships, as well as most others, are engaged in normal shipping activities and are thus scattered all over the world. The quickest way to get ships is to grab whatever is close by. This disrupts commercial schedules and requires some quick work on the part of governments. Another complication is that few ships are suitable for moving combat vehicles. Most merchant ships are designed to carry liquids, bulk raw materials, or containers. Moreover, many of the tankers are equipped to load and unload at only a few specialized terminals, thus limiting their flexibility. The RoRo (roll on/roll off) ships are needed to carry tanks and other military vehicles most efficiently. Many of these ships are also equipped with loading ramps that can be used only at certain port facilities. How successfully the initial muddle phase is passed will determine how quickly the reinforcing units arrive in the war zone.

Forming convoys. This procedure is practiced only during wartime. Forming convoys is like any other technical operation; make mistakes and you pay for it. The basic cost is a lot of ships waiting around for the convoy to proceed. A considerable amount of coordination has to take place between the military planners, the war-materiel producers, and the convoy control staff. Based on World War II experience, a convoy schedule would be established. Every few days so many thousand GRT would go east or west. Coastal feeder convoys would leave ports up and down the coast for transoceanic convoy assembly points. So that the scarce and valuable escorts' time would not be wasted, ships that don't make it to the assembly point would have to wait for the next convoy. All this discipline and coordination is not unknown to modern shipping operations. Since World War II, ships have become more conscious that time is money.

Moving convoys. The Navy cannot afford the expense of much practice with civilian merchant shipping. Some exercises are held to give escorts practice. The biggest problem will be getting civilian shipmasters to conform to the discipline of convoy operations. Steaming in formation and staying calm under combat stress are qualities not usually expected of civilian skippers and crews. Nothing quite prepares one for carrying on while merchant and combat ships explode about you. Mistakes will be made, unnecessary losses will be taken, and eventually hard experience will be won.

Time and Space Variables

In order to organize merchant shipping on a war footing, reallocations will have to be made, quickly. The warship escorts are normally in or near their home ports. Most of the merchant ships are scattered over the worldwide trade routes. It will be an interesting exercise as ships are brought in to the ports from which military units are to embark. It would take a week or two for the military equipment to be moved by rail from their bases to the ports. How efficiently this is handled will not be known until it actually has to happen. There is very little practice for this sort of thing in peacetime. These exercises are expensive and time-consuming. One nation that has practiced this extensively, the United States, was able to move divisions expeditiously to the Persian Gulf in 1990. No other nation has as much experience as the United States in these kind of moves, and such experience evaporates quickly if the training isn't constantly repeated.

Once convoy operations are underway, the chief variable will be the distances to be traveled and the time urgency of getting the movement done. Steaming at 20 knots (36 kilometers per hour), merchant shipping can move 800 kilometers per day. In wartime there will be a certain amount of going to and fro to avoid suspected enemy submarines, merchant shipping, or land-based air or surface ships. Forming into and operating as convoys will lose more travel time. Figure on making some 500 kilometer-per-day headway. Without the threat of enemy action, and using the fastest available commercial shipping, daily headway can be more than doubled.

From the East Coast of the United States to Europe, you must travel 5,500 kilometers. That's 12 days of convoy travel. Depending on the condition of the ports on each end, a few days are needed for loading and unloading. A group of ships and their escorts could make one round trip a month. In the Pacific, it's 8,800 kilometers from the West Coast of the United States to Korea. That's 18 days at sea or two round trips every three months.

Going to the Persian Gulf while being unable to use the Suez Canal requires a 21,600-kilometer trip from the East Coast of the United States and around South Africa. That's a 44-day journey, or three and a half round trips each year. If the seas are swept free of enemy ships and loading and unloading at each end is optimal, these transit times can be cut by more than half. A common premise is that 90 percent of the tonnage going to a major overseas war will have to go by sea and the rest by air. This could require as many as 6,000 ships, about 72 million GRT, over a period of six months. At the same time, there will be several times more shipping going each way to support nonmilitary activity, primarily support of the economies on both sides of the ocean.

Theory and Practice

The basic problem is that there is no shortage of merchant shipping worldwide. There are currently (2001) some 27,000 large merchant ships out there, about two-thirds of them cargo, the rest tankers. A major U.S. military operation only needs a few percent of those ships. The problem is getting the ships you need quickly enough to move the troops and supplies.

Since the 1970s, plans had been made for getting a lot of stuff to the Persian Gulf in a hurry. During the 1980s, special ships were bought and legal and financial arrangements made to get control of merchant ships to take cargo into a combat zone. During the Gulf War, some 20 percent of the cargo arrived in foreign-flag ships. These ships served when called upon, and the already-enacted legislation allowing the U.S. government to requisition foreign flag (but U.S.-owned) ships did not have to be used. These efforts paid off. Without all this behind-the-scenes work, the ground forces would had taken months more to get there, and the aircraft would have had fewer bombs to drop and less fuel and spare parts to get them into the air. The war wouldn't had been such a world-class and low-casualty effort without the behind-the-scenes logistical planning and preparations.

To support the war effort, the Allies moved seven million tons of material to Saudi Arabia. Most came by sea from U.S. ports, while 900,000 tons from U.S. armed-forces stocks in Europe. This was largely stocks of the U.S. 7th Army Corps stationed there since World War II. Throughout the air war, each combat sortie used up over 10 tons of fuel, munitions, and spare parts (in that order). That's nearly 200,000 tons a day when you include the supplies to support the 130,000 Air Force personnel. The ground forces had 30 days of supplies stockpiled for an offensive that, fortunately, was over in a few days.

Fuel turned out to be the major item of supply to be moved. Over 5 million tons of fuel was used, and, while much of it was procured locally, a lot had to be shipped in. Before Desert Shield and Desert Storm were over, more than 200 merchant ships were used to move all the ground and air units to the Persian Gulf. Nearly 500 shiploads of material were offloaded in Saudi ports. This included over seven billion tons of cargo, a third of which was fuel. Although Saudi Arabia is awash in oil, it did not have refineries to produce all the fuels combat units needed. Worse yet, in January half of Saudi Arabia's refining capacity was knocked out by a fire.

By August 15, over 30,000 Marines had been flown into Saudi Arabia, and, after a week's steaming from the tiny island of Diego Garcia 2,500 miles to the south, 10 MPS (Maritime Prepositioning Ships) arrived in Saudi ports and the Marines unloaded their equipment, which included trucks, tanks, artillery, and supplies. All this equipment had been stored for years in the air-conditioned holds of the MPS ships. Checked regularly, and thoroughly gone over every 30 months, it was in working order because the Marines made the effort to make sure it was always ready.

The first heavy Army division to arrive had to come from North America, over 15,000 kilometers away. For this purpose, the Navy had purchased eight high-speed cargo ships during the 1980s. These civilian ships were capable of steaming at high speed and could carry heavy vehicles (like tanks). The first of these ships arrived at a U.S. port on August 11 and arrived in Saudi Arabia on August 27 with its load of trucks and armored vehicles for the troops of the 24th Infantry division, which had already been flown over. Seven of these fast cargo ships could move one Army tank or mechanized division (which are organized almost identically) every 31 days. And this they did, including side trips to Europe to get the U.S. 7th Army Corps and to replace most of the M-1 tanks previously delivered to Saudi Arabia with the more powerful M-1A1.

The United States maintains 40 large cargo ships that hold equipment and supplies for the Army, Navy, and Air Force. These ships are stationed near potential hot spots, ready to support any military operations. Navies have long used this technique, and the U.S. Navy perfected the system of floating supply dumps during World War II. ServRons (Service Squadrons with hundreds of transports carrying fuel, food, ammo, and much more) kept fleets at sea for six months or more at a time. After the war, we had plenty of bases, and ServRons went out of style. But in the late 1970s, the Persian Gulf began to get ugly, and a little quick math showed that we would not be able to get troops and supplies there quickly enough to put out fires. So work began on reviving the ServRons, but with a new twist. With the end of the Cold War and a growing number of potential hot spots in out-of-the-way places, the Persian Gulf was no longer the only problem area. For the slow learners, there was the 1990–91 Gulf War, where the transportation and supply problems were vivid and scary in the days and weeks after Iraq invaded Kuwait.

So for the last 20 years, a fleet of large transports was put together. The Marines use 16 ships organized into three groups stationed in the Atlantic, Pacific, and Indian Oceans. Each group of ships carries the equipment for a

Marine brigade and enough supplies to keep it going for 30 days. All you have to do is fly the Marines in, land the equipment, and you have a Marine brigade ready to fight. The process takes less than a week.

The Army has weapons and equipment for seven brigades stored around the world, most of them on land. Three are in Europe, two in the Persian Gulf, one in Korea, and one afloat in the Indian Ocean. Most of the Army's 14 ships carry equipment for setting up ports and supplies for supporting troops and providing peacekeeping services. The Air Force, Navy, and Department of Defense each have three ships carrying fuel to support their operations in distant areas. The Navy group includes a hospital ship.

With all these prepositioning ships, you can get a brigade of heavily armed troops, and another brigade of lightly armed paratroopers, to an out-of-the-way hot spot within a week. OK, what does that do for the cause of world peace or American interests? As it turns out, not a lot. Mainly because the hot spots most in need of Marines or paratroopers are the same ones that have no impact on world affairs or American interests. For decades, the Marines have had several battalions afloat at all times. These have been used mainly to help evacuate American embassies and local Americans when things get particularly ugly overseas. This has been the most frequent use of American troops overseas. The paratroopers have been flown off to emergencies less frequently. The Army's seven prepositioned brigades are largely in places left over from the Cold War (three brigades in Europe, one in Korea). The two in the Persian Gulf are a leftover of the 1991 Gulf War. The one floating around the Indian Ocean could go to Africa or Indonesia, but there is little enthusiasm back home for such adventures.

A war, rather than peacekeeping or dealing with a small squabble, requires heavy (armored and mechanized) divisions. These have to be moved by ship, and one major new development in sea movement since World War II is the high-speed (twice as fast as regular transports) RoRo (roll on/roll off) ships. The United States has eight of these high-speed RoRos, enough to carry an armored division. The roll-on/roll-off angle is important, as it speeds up loading and unloading the ships considerably. It takes a day for military vehicles to drive ("roll") onto the ships, and less than a day to roll off. That's less than half the time required with a regular transport. The eight fast RoRo ships carry as much as over a thousand C-5 or C-17 heavy air transports. The military would like to buy more fast RoRos. But over $8 billion was spent on new transport ships in the last 20 years. New, fast RoRos cost over $100 million each. Finding the money for something as unsexy as fast RoRos is difficult. If there's a major war, the current fleet will be adequate, not just to move the troops, but also to carry the enormous amount of supplies (over 100 pounds per soldier per day) to keep the troops in action. The 1991 Gulf War required the movement of seven million tons of stuff to supply half a million troops for six months.

Politics decides whether U.S. troops are used overseas, and politics can change. You can't quickly change your ability to move troops quickly. If you have to get a lot of firepower to a distant trouble spot, bombers don't always provide sufficient intimidation. Shiploads of tanks and troops deliver a more powerful message. In a world prone to random violence, ships that wait provide a quiet measure of security.

The Future

The U.S. armed forces are trying to develop high-speed transports, but so far this has only led to fast ships (up to 90 kilometers an hour) that can't carry much (up to 5,000 tons). However, ships like this might have other uses. In 2001, the U.S. Army and Navy paid $20 million to charter a 317-foot wave-piercing catamaran for two years. Called the HSV-1, the vessel is being evaluated as a high-speed naval transport. The HSV-1 can carry 450 tons of cargo plus 325 troops (or 570 tons of cargo). It can do this at a speed of 63 kilometers an hour in heavy seas for 2,000 kilometers in heavy seas (sea state 3). This is a 31-hour voyage. The vessel can also launch and recover helicopters in small boats in rough seas. The HSV-1 can carry armored vehicles (IFVs and smaller). Such a ship could quickly move ground forces and supplies in crisis situations where time was critical and airlift was not available in sufficient quantities (or have access to nearby airbases).

Merchant ships are not likely to get any faster, so increasing reliance will be placed on transport aircraft, amphibious ships, and prepositioning of heavy equipment in order to get combat forces to distant areas quickly. Each of these three options have serious limitations. When push comes to shove, extensive merchant-ship movements are needed to carry the day for any war lasting more than a month. It still takes time to get these movements organized. The United States maintains a special staff that keeps an eye on the world situation and what ships are available for a sudden deployment of forces from North America. Without this organization, the six months available to mass coalition forces in Saudi Arabia during the 1990–91 war would not have been enough.

Prepositioning equipment paid off in the 1991 Gulf War, but you can't preposition equipment everywhere. Amphibious shipping carries a limited number of troops (about a division's worth) and are typically scattered all over the globe. Transport aircraft are in limited supply and require landing facilities at the other end. U.S. transport aircraft can deliver about one infantry division (with most of its heavy equipment) in a few weeks.

Future wars will depend on all of the above to maximize chances of success. But for anything less than a very small military operation, lots of merchant ships will have to be found, loaded with troops and supplies, and sent chugging off to the distant battlefield. Any operation that needs more than a division of troops for more than a few weeks will have to fall back on this old standby.

27

The Air Force:
Air Freight

Speed—getting there first with the most—is a valuable military advantage. Air-force transport units exist to deliver this advantage. Technical advances in the last 60 years have made air transportation only about twice as expensive, over long distances, as land movement. This is not a very extravagant expense by military standards. The primary limitation to air transport is the lack of aircraft and the weight and size of military equipment.

Will Air Freight Work?

Peacekeeping is a bit like fighting forest fires. If you can pile on the fire before it has a chance to spread, it's a lot easier to put out. Fires, like unrest in far-off places, spread unexpectedly. Getting there fast may not be fast enough unless you use the air-freight approach. In 2000, the U.S. Army decided that 96 hours is fast enough, at least to get a medium brigade of nearly 4,000 troops and their wheeled armored vehicles anywhere in the world. Makes sense. Crises in places like Sierra Leone, Rwanda, and Somalia would have turned out different with the timely arrival of an American brigade. But not so crises in places like Korea, Taiwan, the Balkans, or the Persian Gulf. These areas contain large numbers of more heavily armed bad guys. Not to worry, for the new plan also calls for a full division to be on the spot within 120 hours.

As with most plans, there are a lot of troublesome details. For example, the current medium brigade has over 300 LAVs (light armored vehicles, all with wheels), plus other equipment, weighing 10,504 tons. The newest transport aircraft, the C-17, can carry six LAVs each. So you need over 50 C-17s just to carry the armored vehicles. By 2005 we are supposed to have 120 C-17s; right now we have barely enough to move the medium-brigade LAVs. There are plenty of older transports available, like the C-141 and C-5, that can also do the job. But that's not the problem. According to Air Force planning guidelines, getting the brigade to a far-off spot will take at least 106 hours. OK, close enough for PR purposes. But there are more problems. When you look at the potential difficulties with airfield capacity and refueling the transports along the way, the transit time goes to at least 126 hours. We are getting into serious trouble. And it gets worse still. By the time all the problems of refueling, airport capacity, maintenance, and the like are taken into account, it takes over 150 hours to get a brigade to the Middle East. Going to someplace closer like the Balkans or Africa doesn't help much. Both of those places have a real shortage of airfields and ground facilities. This was demonstrated during the 1999 Kosovo war, where there was only one decent airport in Albania and too many people (UN, U.S., NATO allies, air organizations) were trying to use it simultaneously. At one point, French and American troops were on the brink of fighting each other over whose aircraft would land when.

To get a division (three brigades) over there in 120 hours, you need three times as many aircraft. At that point, you are using most of the transports available, and this will cause problems with the Air Force. When there's a crisis overseas, the Air Force wants to get its warplanes there fast. While the combat aircraft can fly to Korea or the Middle East by themselves, they require a lot of aerial refueling along the way. And there's a lot of ground-support equipment that requires the services of many Air Force transports. But we have only 126 C-5s, 40 C-17s, and 158 C-141s. That's barely enough to move two brigades, to say nothing of all the Air Force stuff and anything else you want to get into the area in a hurry.

What to do? Well, the Marines already have a solution, which is to have battalions and brigades of Marines on ships off potential hot spots. The amphibious ships have helicopters that can carry the Marines quite a ways inland, thus covering over 80 percent of the world's potential hotspots. The Marines, and the Army, also keep ships or warehouses full of weapons and equipment. Just fly in the troops and you are ready to roll. The Army can also fly paratroopers to any part of the world, but these guys would be light infantry once they hit the ground, without any armored vehicles. While an American airborne battalion or two will do wonders for local unrest, the troops require a lot of support. In many parts of the world, if they don't get clean water and medical support right away, the battalion will start melting away from sickness. And putting paratroopers down in some out-of-the-way place also requires several dozen communications troops and their gear so everyone, including the airplanes bringing supplies, can keep in touch.

The air-freight approach is being oversold, but that's normal Pentagon practice. The medium brigade allows more GIs to be flown into some far-off

C-17 Globemaster III

mess on short notice. But not 96 hours, and not with enough firepower to deal with a well-armed and determined foe. But this might still work if a messy situation needs rapid attention, like the 1994 massacres in Rwanda. In areas where there is likely to be more resistance, like the Middle East or Korea, there are already heavily armed allies available, not to mention American reinforcements close enough to be flown in by the larger fleet of shorter range C-130 transports.

But for those FedEx situations, you can simply order the troops off before all the political arrangements, here and over there, have been made. This usually takes a few days, and if things don't work out, you can turn the transports around before they land. It might work. This is what happened when we went into Haiti in 1993. The paratroopers were in the air while the politicians here and in Haiti were still negotiating.

There's a lot more to air freight than catchy slogans.

Mechanics of Air Transport

The major military nations have large fleets of specialized cargo aircraft. The United States now has the largest military air-transport capability on the planet. Most nations have also made arrangements to militarize their civilian transport fleets in the event of war. How much capacity is available? The U.S. military air transport fleet could lift over 40,000 tons 5,000 kilometers in one flight.

The world's airlines have a total fleet of about 18,000 aircraft serving nearly 10,000 airports. Currently, over 30 million tons of freight are transported by air each year. But a lot of this is moved by passenger jets and short-range freighters. For military purposes, only some 800 of the largest aircraft (like the 747) configured as freighters are really useful. These large aircraft cost $100–$220 million each, about the same as a large sea transport. The only civilian aircraft capable of moving large amounts of military-type cargo is the 747-400F. This aircraft can carry 21,347 cubic feet of cargo on its main deck, with a cargo weight of 120 tons for a distance of 8,000 kilometers. Unfortunately, there are only about a hundred of these 747s in service, and they can't refuel in the air. No military operation could get more than a fraction (maybe 20 percent) of this fleet chartered for military use. This would increase the capacity of the U.S. military fleet by about 30 percent.

Military equipment, even the smaller IFVs, can be carried only by large cargo aircraft. The air transports would also carry ammunition, fuel, and other supplies for two or three days' combat. Aircraft carrying capacity is restricted by size ("cube," or cubic feet) as well as weight. Thus the movement of commonly used but large and lightweight military equipment wastes capacity. Therefore, it will take about 60 C-141 or C-5 aircraft to move a U.S. mech infantry battalion's 2,500 tons of vehicles. Civilian aircraft can be used to move most of the remaining men and supplies. Only three wide-bodied passenger aircraft would be required to move the battalion's 900 men, including their personal equipment, weapons, and supplies in the aircraft's cargo containers. Nearly 100 military and civilian aircraft would be required to move this one mechanized infantry battalion complete with weapons and equipment. You could not move more than five battalions at a time because only about 300 aircraft are available that can carry the armored personnel carriers. Forget about tanks; only the C-5 can carry them, and only one at a time. A tank battalion has 58 tanks; the U.S. Air Force has about that many C-5s ready to fly at any one time.

The basic problem is that despite all this lift capacity, it isn't enough to get a lot of armed might to some far-off battlefield rapidly. To address this problem the U.S. Army has organized medium brigades, which use wheeled armed vehicles instead of tracked ones. But even this unit is too much for the limited air transport resources. Moving a wheeled brigade combat team requires 62 C-5s and 81 C-17s and can do the job in approximately 88 hours (or a little less if air-to-air refueling is used).

If you are content to carry only nonmotorized infantry, the carrying capacity increases quite a bit. War can be waged without tanks, particularly when defending. Antitank missiles (ATGM) weigh, at most, 50 pounds each; mortars can fit into a cargo container. Except in primitive areas, you can commandeer local trucks. Thus a light infantry battalion of 900 men armed with 18 120mm mortars, 90 tons of mortar ammo, 60 ATGM launchers and 1,000 missiles, 50 tons of mines plus the usual armament of machine guns, rifles, grenades, sensors, and other supplies will require only 20 wide-bodied civilian aircraft.

Lift-Capacity Restrictions

These theoretical lift capacities are misleading for several reasons. First, what you can lift is dependent on how far you are going. With an average cruising speed of 500–800 kilometers per hour, a 5,000-kilometer "hop" would take seven hours. Landing, unloading, refueling, and reloading take another hour or two. Round trip flight time: 14 hours. And that's without any but the most routine and perfunctory maintenance. The following typical distances, in hours, of flying time (at 800 kilometers per hour) do not include refueling stops every 6–10 hours for aircraft that cannot refuel in the air:

From Washington, D.C., to Berlin, 8.5 hours; to Cairo, 12; to Istanbul, 10.5; to London, 7.5; to Madrid, 7.5; to Teheran, 13; to the Persian Gulf, 12; to South Africa, 16.

From San Francisco to New Delhi, 15.5 hours; to Hawaii, 5; to Hong Kong, 14; to Tokyo, 10.5; to Peking, 12; to Singapore, 17; to Saigon, 16.

From Moscow to Berlin, 2 hours; to Tokyo, 9.5; to Teheran, 3; to Nairobi, 8; to South Africa, 12.5; to Peking, 7.5.

It takes seven hours, and 84 tons of fuel, to get across the North Atlantic. Lift capacity also depends on refueling opportunities. U.S. military aircraft can refuel in the air; Soviet aircraft cannot. No civilian aircraft can refuel in the air. A Boeing 747 wide-body jet burns 12 tons of fuel per hour of flight. There has to be fuel at both ends of the trip, as well as a stock of spares, technicians, and maintenance facilities. There aren't many airfields capable of handling large transports. These large fields make good targets for enemy aircraft, missiles, and ground forces. Europe has about 50 that can support long-range aircraft, but most of the refueling and maintenance capacity is concentrated in 30. Losing an airfield is bad enough; when the maintenance and refueling facilities are gone, you are worse off because these items are harder to replace.

The Soviet Union developed a different air-mobility concept that has since turned into a lucrative air-transport business for moving stuff into remote and primitive airfields. Russia has airfields at no less than 1,000-kilometer intervals along the entire border of the former Soviet Union, except in the Arctic north. Soviet aircraft often can operate from unpaved fields and with less ground equipment. For example, many Soviet-era aircraft can be refueled without fuel pumps. This takes longer but eliminates another piece of ground equipment. Soviet aircraft often travel with a larger crew containing both flight and maintenance personnel. These aircraft have a lower readiness level for sustained operations, but they can operate under more primitive conditions than Western aircraft. Within Russia one finds many primitive areas that can be reached only by air and must be serviced by aircraft of this type. For these reasons, Russian aircraft are favored by many Third World nations possessing largely primitive support facilities. Russia continues to produce and sell some of these Soviet designs.

Helicopters are often used for transport. They can land just about anywhere but have low carrying capacity (usually under three tons) and short ranges (typically under 500 kilometers). The entire U.S. helicopter fleet of over 8,000 aircraft could lift about 7,000 tons of weapons and equipment at one time. In function, helicopters have more in common with trucks and IFVs than they do with aircraft. Helicopters generally fly within the combat zone, and their bases are also located there. Unlike transport aircraft, they are often armed. Most helicopters perform primarily as combat systems or in direct support of combat units. Not all aircraft are available at all times. As many as 20 percent will be out of service for maintenance. This figure will be higher for most Third World armed forces.

With sufficient flight and ground crews, an aircraft can theoretically be kept going 24 hours a day for a month. After a 12-hour maintenance check, it can go up for another month. Every 3,000–4,000 hours the aircraft must be pulled out of service for several hundred hours of overhaul. As a practical matter, such a tempo of operations would soon exhaust available maintenance personnel. Soviet-type aircraft also require maintenance and overhaul more frequently, often 3–5 times more often, than Western machines. A more practical use pattern is 10–12 hours of operations a day, with occasional surges of longer activity and breaks for the 4,000-hour overhauls. This can go on until the 20,000–30,000 hour flight lifetime of an aircraft is reached.

Military transports are built somewhat differently than civilian transports and thus have dissimilar operating characteristics. Civil transports are built to operate continually from well-equipped commercial airports. They are also built to carry passengers, plus cargo in containers. Some aircraft are freighters; others are convertible from freighter to passenger service. Military transports are built to operate more spasmodically, from crude air fields. Their layout is for loading vehicles and a secondary mission of carrying passengers. Keeping commercial airports intact will pay large dividends in a future war, as it will allow civil transports to carry a lot of the load and preserve the military transports for those missions only they can perform. A major advantage in the Gulf War was the availability of first-class commercial airports in Saudi Arabia. Without these facilities, the amount of people and cargo landed would have been much less.

Aircraft maintenance is a massive undertaking, requiring extensive facilities, skilled technicians, and large stocks of spares. More recent aircraft designs are notable for their lower maintenance requirements. All transport aircraft have instruments that continually monitor all systems whenever the aircraft is operating. Before takeoff, crew and maintenance personnel run through checklists of items to be monitored. Every 50 or 60 flight hours, the maintenance personnel spend several hours going over the aircraft more thoroughly. Marginal items are fixed before they become critical. Every 300–600 flight hours, an overnight check is performed, requiring about 100 man-hours. Expendable items are often replaced and some major items are partially disassembled. Sometimes more serious conditions are discovered, and more extensive maintenance is performed. This is also one of those times when some upgrades and equipment modifications are performed.

After 3,000–4,000 hours the aircraft disappears into the hangar for several days. Most major components are disassembled, and many items are replaced. This is when major maintenance and upgrades take place; items such as new interiors, paint jobs, or electronics are installed. It is at this point that many aircraft have their engines replaced. The removed engines are then rebuilt for installation in another aircraft.

The average civilian aircraft flies 3,000–4,000 hours a year and has a useful life of 20 or more years. This level of activity requires six different air crews working the aircraft in shifts. Because aircraft are so well taken care of, and practically rebuilt over their lifetime, many are still performing reliably after 40 years of service. A classic example is the 1930s-era DC-3. This twin-engine transport is still the backbone of many small Third World airlines. With good maintenance, this aircraft can continue flying for another few decades. Many 30-year-old, four-engine 707s are still flying. Of the 9,000 commercial jets built since 1959, over half are still in use. Fewer than 400 have been lost to accidents. The loss rate per 100,000 flight hours has been less than .3. This is about one-tenth the loss rate of combat aircraft in peacetime. Commercial aircraft are worked hard and are maintained with equal diligence. Military aircraft are equally durable. Forty-year-old B-52s and 30-year-old F-4s are common. The biggest danger to military aircraft is the rigors of practicing for combat. Military transports are not used as intensively as their civilian counterparts. Military transports often fly less than 1,000 hours a year, most of it just for training. While civil transports require an average of seven mechanics to keep then going, lower military usage allows for half the number of mechanics to keep the aircraft operational.

CRAF (Civilian Reserve Air Fleet)

In America, the Air Force and Army are working hard to develop forces and plans for quick intervention in overseas hot spots. It's often pointed out that there are not enough military air transports to support all these schemes. Congress is reluctant to fund something as unexciting as additional transport aircraft. But there is another reason to be hesitant. Some 70 percent of the current missions flown by 800 U.S. military transports are operated by reserve crews. Same with the ground crews and other support people. All these pilots and technicians are "borrowed" from commercial airlines. In addition, some 600 commercial aircraft (and their crews) belong to CRAF (Civil Reserve Air Fleet). In a wartime emergency, the CRAF aircraft are mobilized for military use (in peacetime, the airlines are paid a fee for making these transports available).

The United States has long had formal (fiscal and legal) arrangements to take over the use of civilian airliners in wartime. The size of CRAF fluctuates, but is currently about 600 aircraft. Some 80 percent of these are large, long-range aircraft (B-747, A-310, B-757, B-767, L-1011, MD-11, DC-10). The military tries to sign up as many freighters as possible, so half the large aircraft are of the freighter type (most civilian airliners, as one would expect, are the passenger types). The short-range CRAF aircraft are mostly passenger jets, with only about a dozen freighters. These would generally be used within the United States. The long-range aircraft would move troops and equipment overseas to civilian airports. There, they would often be moved to the combat zone using C-130s.

Another problem with reservists flying military transports is that many of these flights are with empty aircraft. The reserve pilots have to fly a certain number of hours a year in the military transports to maintain their skills. Military transports are different than civilian airliners in many ways, and if you don't practice you will not be ready for an emergency. The many "empty flights" are kept quiet, as this is periodically pounced upon by the media as another example of "Pentagon waste." This in turn gets Congress upset, which makes it still harder to get money for still more transports. But the fact is that the only way America can maintain such a large military air transport fleet is because of the huge American civil aviation fleet.

Theory and Practice

During the 1990–91 Gulf War, the military air transport got a thorough workout. Over 15,000 flights were made by military and civilian aircraft. These delivered nearly 600,000 troops. By March 25, 1991, over 590,000 tons of cargo had been shipped in by air. Within Saudi Arabia, short-range transports (mainly C-130s) made over 7,000 flights carrying troops and equipment. Some 65 percent of the personnel and 20 percent of the cargo came in by commercial airliners. Getting the troops out after the war saw commercial airliners moving 85 percent of the personnel and 45 percent of the cargo. At its peak, 110 commercial aircraft were being used for Gulf operations. Because of the tempo of operations, with aircraft in use over 15 hours a day, four crews were required for each aircraft, and often this was not enough.

Several hundred civilian transport pilots were also Air Force reserve pilots.

Scheduling gets tricky once these lads are called up. The several months of peak activity during the 1990–91 Gulf operations were handled by shuffling people around a lot and getting permission to have pilots sometimes fly more hours per month than normally allowed.

After the Gulf War, the Pentagon determined that it needed sufficient military force to fight two Gulf War–size conflicts simultaneously. This idea was eventually discarded once it sunk in that the American military had a hard time supporting just the Gulf War effort. After that war, the armed forces were cut by a third. It was also discovered that there was not enough air transport to support two wars, which needed 54–67-million-ton-miles per day of airlift. This exceeded the available capability, even with the planned purchase of new aircraft. The Army suggested that civilian 747 cargo planes could make up the difference. But this was dismissed because Civil Reserve aircraft are unable to operate from anything but first-class airfields and can't refuel in the air.

The Future

The V-22 Osprey, an aircraft that combines the best characteristics of a helicopter and a fixed-wing transport, was due for wide use in the early 1990s for short-range tactical transportation. Design problems delayed this until the first decade of the twenty-first century. Even before the Cold War abruptly ended, the V-22 was in trouble because of its cost. After 1991, the V-22 became a political issue, with the Congress wanting it for the patronage its manufacturing jobs created and the Pentagon not wanting it because they felt there were other items that were more needed in the age of rapidly shrinking defense budgets.

America is in the process of introducing the C-17, a replacement for the C-141. While the C-17 is a very capable aircraft, it is expensive, and the Air Force would rather invest in warplanes than transports. Faced with increased demand for air transports, the Air Force proposed that airlines buy the C-17 for commercial use. The approach would reduce the price the Air Force pays for its C-17s (due to larger production runs) and would create a Civil Reserve fleet far more useful for military needs. Current commercial cargo planes available for military use cannot refuel in the air and don't really have large enough capacity for critical military equipment (like armored vehicles). Under the Air Force proposal, an airline would buy 50–60 BC-17s (the civilian version of the C-17), and the government would guarantee them cargo-carrying contracts. As an additional option, the government would buy the planes back if the deal didn't work out. In addition, the government might subsidize the purchase price, as the C-17 (at $150 million each) is about 50 percent more expensive than roughly comparable civilian transports. This idea actually has a long history. Centuries ago, kings would provide subsidies to ship and horse owners so that in wartime more ships and horses would be available for military use. In the nineteenth century, governments worked out similar deals with railroads so that in wartime the armed forces had access to ample railroad capacity. In the twentieth century it was common for armies to mobilize civilian trucks for military use in emergencies. Currently, 150 C-17s are to be built. The Air Force would like to have more like 200. The basic problem is that the aging C-141s have to be replaced, and the original plan was to build 134 C-17s for that purpose. This does not increase carrying capacity much at all; it just maintains it by replacing older aircraft with new ones.

Strategic Military Airlift

This chart shows the strategic military transport aircraft available to the major military powers. Only the United States has a significant fleet of strategic transport aircraft. The Russian (formerly Soviet) strategic transport aircraft fleet is closely integrated with the national airline Aeroflot. However, Aeroflot was taken apart, to a large extent, after the breakup of the Soviet Union, and many of its aircraft are now owned and operated by the non-Russian successor states of the Soviet Union. The U.S. Air Force fleet could be called the world's largest airline, at least in terms of lift capacity. Not included are the twin-engine tactical transports that equip most other nations' air-transport fleets. Most of these lift five tons or less. Few nations have more than 20 or 30 of them. These are transports designed for combat-zone movement of men, equipment, and supply. This is short-range work, 1,000 kilometers or less.

Passengers are the number of seats installed and available for troops. These seats are usually temporary, easily removed or folded into the wall to make room for cargo.

Aircraft characteristics	C-5	C-141B	C-130	C-17
Passengers	345	168	220	102
Cargo (tons)	120	41	34	59
Average range (km)	4,800	6,400	4,600	5,200
Empty weight (tons)	151	66	33	117
Max takeoff weight (tons)	349	156	79	258
Max fuel load (tons)	130	72	30	62
Minimum airfield length (m)	2,600	1,000	1,100	1,000
In-flight refueling?	Yes	Yes	No	Yes
In service 2002	126	130	526	80

Average tons per man for division types: U.S. light infantry, 1.2; U.S. mech infantry, 1.8; Airborne, .4

Cargo (tons) is the average cargo load that can be carried. Containers are often used, although military transports are primarily designed to accommodate military vehicles. The largest military transport aircraft can even move tanks (C-5, C-17), although rarely more than two at a time. It is far more efficient to carry lighter military vehicles like trucks, IFVs, guided missile launchers, artillery, etc. Pallets of ammunition are another favorite cargo. Most of these aircraft have large doors in the rear that can be opened in-flight. Their cargoes can be landed with parachutes.

Average range (kilometers) is the average range with a full cargo load. An empty aircraft with a full load of fuel can go 20–60 percent beyond its full-load range. An important difference between civil and military transports is that civil aircraft operate one-way trips; they refuel at their destination. Military transports normally drop or land their cargo and then return without refueling. Typically, their only refueling opportunity along the way is in-flight with a tanker.

Empty weight (tons) is aircraft weight without fuel or payload. A glance at the potential fuel capacity, possible cargo capacity, and maximum takeoff weight shows the trade-offs that have to be made. Military transports must be able to move very heavy loads for short distances or lighter loads over long hauls. They carry extra weight in their structure to support the heavy loads, and this heavier structure makes them less efficient than comparable, and lighter, civil transports.

Max takeoff weight (tons) is the maximum takeoff weight of the aircraft. This indicates the aircraft's size. The C-5 (347 tons), for example, is 245 feet long, 65 feet high, with a wingspan of 223 feet. The C-141B (155 tons) is 168 feet long, 39 feet high, with a wingspan of 160 feet. The C-17A (265 tons) is 174 feet long, 55 feet high, with a wingspan of 165 feet. The C-130 (79 tons) is 98 feet long, 38 feet high, and has a span of 133 feet.

Max fuel load (tons) demonstrates that the primary cargo of military transport aircraft is fuel. Large quantities can be carried without sacrificing space by putting almost all fuel in the wings. A major problem in wartime is getting these large quantities of fuel where it is needed when it is needed.

Minimum airfield length (meters) is the minimum size airstrip needed for takeoff. Takeoff always requires a longer airfield than landing. Taking off with maximum load requires 30–40 percent more space than that in the chart. To get off the ground in the shortest possible space, the aircraft will have to go half-loaded.

In-flight refueling? This indicates whether or not the aircraft can refuel in flight. The tankers transfer more of their own fuel than the additional fuel they carry in their cargo spaces. The KC-135, a militarized 707, normally carries 73 tons of fuel, plus another 15 tons as cargo. The aircraft can draw upon all fuel carried for its own engines, Depending on how far the aircraft has to travel, it can transfer up to 90 percent of its total fuel load. The larger KC-10 normally carries 108 tons, plus another 53 tons as cargo. Of this 161 tons, some 90 tons are available for transfer. The most efficient use of tankers is to allow aircraft to take off with maximum weapons or cargo load, but not maximum fuel load. Once airborne, the fuel tanks can be filled to the point that the aircraft can still fly but would actually be too heavy to take off. Tankers can also meet aircraft returning from a mission and refuel those that are short of fuel. This is often the case with aircraft that have had to use high-speed, high-fuel consumption maneuvers in combat. Cargo aircraft can be refueled on long flights so they won't have to land and refuel. Sometimes there is no place to land, and in-flight refueling is the only option. The quantity of fuel that large aircraft carry is shown on this chart and on the similar one for civilian transports. By far the worst offender is the B-52, which carries 141 tons of fuel. For this reason, two tankers are typically assigned to each B-52. Smaller combat aircraft are at the other extreme. Fuel load for the F-4 is 6 tons; for the F-16, 3 tons; for the F-15, 5 tons; for the F-18, 5 tons; for the A-6, 7 tons; and for the F-14, 7 tons. To accommodate the larger number of combat aircraft that can be refueled by one tanker, the KC-10 may be equipped to refuel three aircraft at once.

This chart gives the average characteristics of each type of aircraft. More so than military aircraft, civilian aircraft are built in many variations. Averages are perfectly suitable if you are dealing with large numbers of aircraft.

Passengers are the number of seats installed for peacetime operations. Given enough time, more seats could be put in with a less luxurious standard. Yes, fellow air travelers, it can get worse.

Aircraft characteristics	757	767	A-300	747	L-1011	DC-10
Passengers	180	211	220	350	220	260
Cargo (tons)	20	34	34	75	38	46
Average range (km)	4,400	5,200	4,600	9,000	9,000	6,000
Empty weight (tons)	59	74	78	177	110	120
Max fuel load (tons)	33	48	44	150	73	112
Max takeoff weight (tons)	108	136	150	370	210	252
Max load capacity (tons)	80	114	111	278	144	197
Practical load (tons)	49	62	72	193	100	132
With full fuel (tons)	16	14	28	43	27	20

Flight distances (km)   New York to Paris, 5,798; Montreal to Ireland, 4,600; London to Rome, 1,420; Rome to Cairo, 2,120; Cairo to Teheran, 2,000; Moscow to Berlin, 1,650; Moscow to Baghdad, 2,600; Montreaal to Iceland, 3,800; Iceland to London, 2,000; Moscow to Beijing, 5,900; California to Hawaii, 3,900; Hawaii to Tokyo, 6,200; Tokyo to Beijing, 2,100; New York to Cairo, 9,100

Cargo (tons) is the average cargo load that can be carried in their cargo spaces, in containers. Modern aircraft are weight, not space, limited.

Average range (kilometers) is the average range with a full passenger load. An empty aircraft with a full load of fuel can go 20–60 percent farther. Commercial aircraft must maintain fuel reserves to allow for landing at another airport in case of foul weather or heavy traffic. These reserves can add up to 1,000 kilometers to an aircraft's range.

Empty weight (tons) is aircraft weight without fuel or payload. A glance at the potential passenger load (at 300 pounds each), fuel capacity, possible cargo capacity, and maximum takeoff weight reveals that everything won't go into the air at once. This is intentional when the plane is designed; tradeoffs must be made during aircraft operations.

Max fuel load (tons) demonstrates that the primary cargo of commercial aircraft is fuel. Most of this fuel is carried within the wings, leaving other space for crew and cargo.

Max takeoff weight (tons) is the maximum takeoff weight of the aircraft. It indicates the aircraft's size. The 747 (370 tons), for example, is 232 feet long and 63 feet high with a wingspan of 196 feet. We are dealing with very large machines.

Max load capacity (tons) is the weight of everything you can get onto the aircraft. It includes passengers, cargo, and fuel. Because of takeoff weight limits, you can't take it all. This number gives a good indication of the aircraft's capacity and flexibility.

Practical load (tons) is what you can get off the ground as cargo and fuel. This is the maximum takeoff weight less the weight of the empty aircraft. This is an indicator of the aircraft's actual lift capacity.

With full fuel (tons) is the practical load when carrying a full fuel load. It indicates the long-distance carrying capacity of the aircraft.

Flight distances give point-to-point flying distances in kilometers. What this points out is that with sufficient airfields along the way, it is possible to cover long distances with short-range aircraft or with long-range aircraft carrying heavier loads. For this reason, Iceland is very important to the United States and Western Europe. Hawaii is important to the United States.

PART EIGHT

TOOLS OF THE TRADE

With over a hundred million active and reserve troops under arms, nearly $1 trillion a year in military spending, and tens of thousands of tanks, aircraft, ships, and other major items of equipment, we must summarize.

28

The Weapons
of the World

Throughout the book you have seen numbers indicating weapons capability. The numbers by themselves don't mean a whole lot. At best, analytical and subjective evaluations of weapons will tell you what they can, or simply might, do. This chapter will briefly discuss the general effectiveness of weapons. More important, one must consider why weapons often do not work. Of even greater interest and importance is the frequency with which weapons do not function as the users think they are functioning.

Untried Technology

Weapons are often conceived, designed, manufactured, and used in a triumph of hope over experience. This was less true in the past, when weapon designs persisted for hundreds of years. When weapons were around for centuries, their capabilities became well known. Changes were minor and generally made small improvements in performance. All this has changed in the past century. Weapons rarely work as intended the first time they are used. History is full of examples. The first machine guns overlooked the fact that the barrel would soon overheat from use. In time, ways were found to deal with this, but not fast enough for the troops using them first in combat. The first bayonets were attached to the musket by plugging them into the barrel. Fine in theory, but troops would forget to take them out before firing their weapons. The results were disastrous, and the design was soon changed. The use of bayonets revealed a more subtle form of misperception. For all their fearsome reputation, few casualties are caused by bayonets. When longer-range rifles were introduced in the 1850s, bayonets were used even less. Yet bayonets are issued and troops are trained in their use to this day. Slowly, leaders learned that bayonets were less a weapon than a morale-building device and battlefield tool. For most of this century, the bayonet was actually a hazard to its users. In hand-to-hand fighting, troops tend to use their rifles as clubs. With a bayonet attached and swung like a club, the bayonet has a tendency to cut the user. This is what the troops reported, at least the survivors.

Often the misperceptions are expensive. The modern battleship, heavily armored, with many large guns and a price tag to match, was built in large quantities. Some 170 were built between 1906–1945 at a cost of $220 billion in 2002 dollars. These were supposed to be the primary naval weapon, yet most never saw action against another battleship. Battleships were rarely exposed to combat; they were literally too expensive to lose. Although 55 were sunk, only five were sunk by other battleships. Some 17 percent of the losses were accidents, usually by an explosion while in port. Aircraft got 44 percent. Submarines, torpedo boat, and other ships got 10 percent. Torpedoes accounted for 38 percent, generally delivered by an aircraft. Originally designed to secure control of the oceans, they spent most of their time fearfully hiding out in port. Cheaper weapons—aircraft, submarines, and mines—made the high seas too dangerous for the big ships. During World War II, the aircraft carrier decisively demonstrated the ineffectiveness of battleships as the premier warship. Before this lesson was learned, a record was set for how much was spent on a weapon for so little return in battlefield effectiveness.

The battleship fiasco was bad, but electronics set the stage for truly monumental high costs and low benefits. Electronics have become the major component of aircraft, ships, and, increasingly, land weapons. Electronics, because of their expense and complexity, are tested less thoroughly than cheaper weapons. Rapid developments in electronics make weapons using them obsolete more quickly. Entire classes of weapons are developed, built, and retired without ever seeing combat. Unlike battleships, you cannot replace most electronics-based weapons with something simpler and cheaper. This creates a ruinously expensive competition that no one can afford to drop out of. While the expense strains budgets, the uncertain effectiveness of these weapons confronts commanders with unprecedented problems. Not knowing with any certainty how their electronic weapons, or those of their opponents, will perform, battlefield leaders have a more difficult time planning for combat. The nature of the uncertainty is complicated by the extent and nature of countermeasures used. This is a problem that will only get worse. The more flexible soldiers will prevail, but only after a lot of headaches and frustration. Testing weapons successfully has become the most important battleground for armed forces. War is a sometime event; peacetime conditions are more the norm. The urgency of effective testing is slowly becoming accepted. America has taken the lead in this area, mandating greater use of simulators and testing of weapons against facsimiles of anticipated opponents' systems. Taking testing to its logical solution and using large quantities of weapons during tests is still horrendously expensive. The lessons of sweating more in peacetime so as to bleed less on the battlefield is a lesson not yet fully accepted.

World War II Versus Today

When we think of a future war between the major powers, we still think of World War II. World War II was the last war between major nations and the last war involving large-scale air, land, and naval forces. However, World War II is less and less likely as a benchmark for future conflict because of the increasing accumulation of changes in the nearly 60 years that have passed since that last large-scale war. Although massive wars in the Third World still appear remarkably like World War II battles, the major powers have not unleashed their heavily refurbished arsenals on one another during that period. With this in mind, we can still compare today's armed forces to the last "big war."

INFANTRY WEAPONS

These have changed little since World War II, except for a lot more automatic weapons being used. Nearly every infantryman now has an automatic weapon, a policy the Germans were implementing at the end of World War II. Since most troops have been equipped with automatic weapons, they have become more likely to use their weapons. This has created problems with uncontrolled use of weapons and, at times, ammunition supply problems. Mortars, grenades, and machine guns are basically the same, with many incremental improvements. The only radically new items have been electronic. These are primarily sensors, especially radars and night scopes, plus navigation and communications gear. The new sensors are not widely used and are used primarily in prepared defenses. The new communications equipment is also not widely used. But for U.S. and other Western armies that do have GPS and jam-resistant radios, the average infantryman on patrol or otherwise on his own has seen electronics become a major factor in making battlefield life easier.

Antitank weaponry has seen a major jump in performance and has moved away from being an infantry weapon. The World War II rocket launchers are still with us, although improved in performance. Tanks have developed thicker skins, and this gave rise to the antitank guided missile. Some of these weapons were not portable at all but required a vehicle to carry them. Those that were portable were only marginally so. Meanwhile, tanks became better protected. Not just thicker armor, but better armor, like composite ("Chobham") and add-on armor (spaced or reactive). More important for the infantry are the changes in tank tactics. To make themselves less vulnerable to nuclear weapons and other wide-area munitions, tanks now operate spread out, with distances up to 100 meters separating them. Moreover, tanks have learned that they must operate in close cooperation with infantry. In other words, the situations where infantry faces tanks alone would be the exception. Moreover, most portable antitank weapons the infantry possesses are, like their World War II counterparts, best used against the sides or rear of tanks. The rear shot, in particular, gives the infantry a good chance of evening the odds. Because tank crews can see little from inside their vehicles, a rear shot is not impossibly difficult to arrange in a confused situation. The newest generation of portable antitank weapons detonates above the tank, penetrating the thinner top armor. These are more complex missiles, all lethal to all tanks.

In line with the changes in antitank warfare, there has also been a wholesale mechanization of infantry since World War II. While the troops spend most of their time outside their armored vehicles, their IFVs are always handy, along with the heavier weapons they carry. These vehicles now have small turrets holding automatic cannons. In effect, these vehicles often function like light tanks. Many are heavier than most tanks used in the early days of World War II. Experience so far has shown that the infantry is still most effective when outside their armored vehicles. The modern battlefield is crowded with a lot more armored vehicles. The only place you find infantry operating alone is in terrain unsuitable for armored vehicles.

TANKS

During World War II, there were frequent instances where one side had a tank model possessing frontal armor that was invulnerable to the other side's antitank weapons, at least for a while. This can still happen, as was the case in the 1991 Gulf War. The invulnerability of U.S. tanks in the Gulf was largely a result of the Iraqis using homemade tank shells against the latest U.S. armor design. Moreover, the fighting in the desert made it more difficult for the defending Iraqi tanks to get shots at the thinner side or rear armor of U.S. tanks. Generally, however, the little ditty "What you can see you hit and what you hit you kill" succinctly sums up the situation in tank warfare, at least for tanks and their large guns. The unarmored antitank weapons used by the infantry are the first to fall short when a new defensive measure is introduced for tanks.

Aside from being more vulnerable, tanks have more company. Far more tanks are available today than during World War II, in addition to an even larger number of lighter armored vehicles. In some respects this is helpful. All these additional armored vehicles "draw fire," as armored vehicles always have. Thus, individual armored vehicles don't stand out as much today as they did during World War II. Alas, all those heavy, tracked vehicles tear up the battlefield to such an extent that everyone has a hard time getting around. Since World War II, tanks have become twice as heavy and not quite twice as fast, agile, or reliable. Modern tanks contain far more electronics and have smaller crews. The latest generation of tanks has shown an uncommon ability to flit around the battlefield. American combat-training devices, the ones that use lasers to score hits, have provided realistic training that, in turn, has revealed that these new tanks can operate remarkably more efficiently in combat. These same vehicles have mature and well-tested fire-control devices that are far more effective than anything available in the past. These new training devices, combined with the new tanks, produced amazing results on the battlefield during the 1991 Gulf War.

ARTILLERY

More artillery is self-propelled. The average caliber is now closer to 155mm than 105mm. Improved transportation allows greater tonnages of munitions to be fired, and fired farther. The munitions themselves have become two, three, or more times as effective thanks to ICM (Improved Conventional Munitions). Because of the cost of the modern stuff, many armies still have essentially World War II–era guns firing World War II–style munitions. Such nations are at a great disadvantage against modern artillery, particularly because of the more efficient artillery-spotting radars and computer-controlled fire. The rich guys have some very deadly stuff. The Iraqis discovered this in 1991. The Iraqis also discovered how effective modern artillery rockets could be, with the U.S. MLRS being the artillery weapon the Iraqis feared the most.

THE AIR FORCE

Dramatic changes have taken place since World War II. Modern aircraft fly over three times faster, over 50 percent higher, and carry over three times more munitions. Range and reliability have increased, and the most common air-to-air weapon is now the missile. For all this, air combat has changed little. Because of physical restrictions, combat usually takes place at speeds only about 50 percent greater than World War II. Bombing still takes place at slow speeds, primarily because the pilots can't see much if they go any faster. Electronic-bombing and air-combat aids have helped but have not proven a perfect solution to the complications of air warfare. Despite the repeated promises that electronics will make it all better, pragmatic pilots retain their cannon and skills at close-in fighting. Munitions, particularly bombs, have become over 10 times as effective as their World War II predecessors. It also takes far fewer people to do the work. A World War II four-engine bomber, the B-17, weighed 25 tons and carried 7 tons of bombs and a crew of 11. A 25-ton F-15E fighter carries over 11 tons of bombs and a crew of two. The replacement for the B-17, the 45-year-old B-52, can carry over 25 tons of bombs. Moreover, modern smart bombs are so accurate that an F-15 can take out 10 times as many targets per sortie as the B-17. Far fewer aircraft are available today, and they take five times longer to build (at wartime rates). The F-15, for example, takes 18 months to build in peacetime. In wartime, that might be brought down to three months, but no one has tried it, so no one really knows.

THE NAVY

In World War I, navies put most of their money into battleships, although submarines did most of the fighting. During World War II, aircraft carriers got most of the attention, although it was submarines that shut down the Japanese economy and came close to doing the same to Britain's. If a major war started tomorrow, aircraft carriers would still be the most prominent symbol of naval power, along with their numerous escorts. But today the biggest threat is from nuclear-powered submarines. However, submarines have serious problems. For one thing, they don't communicate too well when submerged. And most of the time they are under water. Although subs are equipped with missiles that can attack land and naval targets at long ranges, they carry fewer munitions than surface ships. Basically, a nuclear submarine functions best as a lone operator, stalking prey in its own killing zone. A nuclear sub has a difficult time telling if the ship it is going after is enemy or friendly. You don't direct the operations of submarines; you unleash them to sweep an area clear of any ships or subs. Think of a nuclear submarine as a mobile naval mine with a well-trained and intelligent crew. All of this is even more troublesome because nuclear subs have no wartime experience. A British nuclear sub's sinking of an Argentinean cruiser in 1982 is all the combat experience these boats have. Under wartime conditions, changes will be made in the face of the unexpected. This is as it has always been, and nuclear submariners and sailors in general feel a bit uneasy over it. Meanwhile, carriers, with increasingly capable aircraft and smart bombs, ensure that naval aviation remains the most useful part of the fleet.

The other dramatic change in navies since World War II has been the enormous growth of electronics in every area of naval operations. The computer operators and technicians are the naval warriors of today. Seamanship has been playing a declining role in naval operations for over a century. This trend continues. Electronics can tell ships how to avoid nasty weather but still does not provide a cure for seasickness when the ocean reminds sailors whose backyard they are playing in.

AMPHIBIOUS OPERATIONS

It's comforting to see that some things don't change. Aside from improved amphibious shipping and landing craft, the only new development has been helicopters. The Marines also have whatever new weapons and equipment their land-based brethren have. Amphibious operations are faster and, because of the threat of nuclear and chemical weapons, plan on being smaller than those during World War II. Marines no longer plan to land on an enemy-held beach, but to fly over it and kick the enemy in the butt.

AIR DEFENSE

Current air-defense composition is an odd mixture of the familiar World War II and a form of science fiction known as SAM (surface-to-air missiles). The World War II cannon-type of air defense is still used, in some cases with original World War II weapons. More often, the small-caliber (under 75mm) cannon is controlled by radar and computerized fire-control systems. Manual override keeps these systems honest and minimally effective. It still requires several tons of cannon shell for each aircraft brought down. SAMs have great potential. At least one in 50 will hit its target. Radar screens blink, obscure jargon is muttered (at times sounding like prayers), and, far from the darkened rooms, missiles climb skyward by remote control. So far, the electronic-warfare countermeasures and pilot agility have held the upper hand. This is small comfort to pilots, who must entrust their lives to a lot of black boxes. Aircraft are hit by SAMs. And the SAMs are getting better. Most of SAMs' bad reputation comes from the well-publicized failures of Soviet systems in Vietnam and the Middle East. Less well known is how much more effective Western systems have been. The trend is to let pilotless aircraft penetrate areas well covered by SAMs and cannon. Let the machines kill each other off. This may be a portent of the future.

AT THE MOVIES

We gather our impressions of weapon effectiveness from our daily exposure to the media. The worst offenders are films and TV shows. First, films quite naturally depict World War II more frequently than potential contemporary conflict. Because the appearance of World War II weapons does not differ radically from current ones, we tend to equate their performance with what we can expect in current wars. This is not too far off the mark, as the rest of this chapter demonstrates. But weapons have changed. To further muddle our perceptions, films enhance weapons effect in order to increase their visual impact on the screen. Weapons effects in films are more like fireworks displays than reality. For example, artillery explosions are smaller and lack flames. When bullets pass close by, they make a pronounced *crack* as they break the sound barrier, a sound that is no doubt deleted so as not to disturb the dialogue. Films show bullets hitting the ground and walls with little explosions. This is because small explosives are used to produce this effect. In reality, most of those bullets hit with dull little thuds. Some of those thuds are people getting hit. Of course, films cannot re-create the most crucial elements of combat, such as fatigue, the smell, and paralyzing fear. All this extra noise is no doubt suppressed so that the dialogue can be heard. Real combat is noisy, although all many soldiers hear is their hearts pounding loudly. Real combat is distracting, making it difficult to follow any plot. Real combat is not very entertaining, even if you are only an observer. Worst of all, soldiers always appear more in control of the situation in films than they are in real battles. This is a dangerous misconception for young soldiers entering their first battle. *Saving Private Ryan* and a few similar films have come close to reality. But most movies go for the staged version of combat. Watching Rambo is misleading; watching a movie like *Platoon* is a lot more accurate. *Platoon*'s combat sequences may appear confusing, but that's what combat is all about. Those who rise above the confusion most effectively generally win.

Theory and Practice

Don't put a lot of faith in press releases about weapons with no past. Nearly all modern weapons have experienced problems, just as many weapons introduced during World War II did. The primary flaw in most weapons development is the reluctance to go as far as one should in testing. It's quite common for testing to be one of the first items reduced when development budgets come under pressure. Realistic testing is not only expensive but requires a fair amount of imagination to mimic battlefield realities adequately. There is also the political pressure to get the weapon into service with a minimum of fuss and embarrassment. Because most shortcomings are discovered during a war, the urgency to get things working correctly overwhelms any desire to hold an inquest and punish the guilty. During World War II, there were new machine gun designs that jammed with the least amount of dirt; tank-gun stabilization systems that were more trouble than they were worth; torpedo warheads that didn't explode; and aircraft more dangerous to their pilots than to the enemy. All of these failures could have been avoided with a little more diligent testing. No matter, few remember these disasters. We tend to recall only the good things. This is one aspect of human nature that becomes very expensive if no one maintains a memory of the failures. The opportunity for rapid technological change has produced sprinters and plodders, as well as many nations that simply sit out the race. On the fast track is the United States, being first in most weapon technologies. The leading edge of technology is often the bleeding edge. Compounding this is the American tendency to ignore the greater military experience of its friends and allies. A "we can do it better" attitude escalates this hubris into an unending stream of marginal weapons. This expensive and often humbling experience has produced better systems in the last 10 years. But old habits die hard. A lot of gold-plated lemons still exist, waiting to bedevil the troops these overpriced clunkers are intended to help. Being first in a dark room will always be risky, and easier for those who follow. U.S. allies, especially Europeans, take a more circumspect approach. They have the additional advantages of greater experience in military matters, and America's technological leadership to show what to avoid.

But a lot of new weapons aren't new at all. Electronic warfare and smart bombs have been around since the mid-1940s. All the electronic-warfare techniques used today were to be found at work in the skies over Germany in 1944. Back then, the tools were primitive by today's standards, but they were doing the same thing. Smart bombs also got their start during World War II, taking out bridges and sinking warships with individual bombs. Again, the 1940s smart bomb was more difficult to use, more prone to breakdown, and a lot more expensive than today's models. But they did the same job and were simply improved over time. Unfortunately, improvements in older weapons often aren't. So watch out for new models that may turn out to be a step backward.

An ominous development that arose from the 1991 Gulf War, one that did not generate a lot of attention, was the tradeoff between high defense expenditures and low casualties. The U.S. military had, for most of the twentieth century, expended material in return for lower casualties to their own troops. The Gulf War was the pinnacle of that approach, being the first war in nearly a century where a Western army had suffered more deaths from noncombat causes (in this case, accidents rather than disease) than from enemy fire. The trillion dollars the U.S. spent on defense during the 1980s bought unprecedented amounts of training as well as high-tech weapons. This "bought" the lives of hundreds, if not thousands, of American and coalition troops. In the wake of this striking victory, no one made an issue of this, even though the United States was even then cutting its defense budgets in response to the Cold War's ending. Few politicians want to put this hot potato into play. The lives of the troops is a very sensitive issue, and one that has existed as long as there have been organized armed forces. Part of the sensitivity comes from the reluctance of the military and political leaders to take responsibility for screwing up before the war. There is usually a lot of blame to go around, especially when it comes to buying the wrong weapons and not spending enough on training. This became an issue throughout the rest of the 1990s. Despite all the military and civilian leaders proclaiming that training was all-important, the training budgets were cut to keep unneeded bases open and questionable new weapons projects going. There were no big wars. And what conflicts there were saw the fighting done by high-flying warplanes using smart bombs.

Another aspect of the Gulf War was that it was a relatively cheap "reality check" on the effectiveness of the armed forces of the major powers. It has been nearly half a century since the major powers have gone to war with one another, an unprecedented period of peace in this millennium. With the end of the Cold War, it might have been several decades before there would have been a battlefield test of how effective all those decades of military spending had been. The Gulf War allowed the Western powers, particularly the United States, to take their Cold War forces and run what amounted to a live-fire battlefield test against an army using their Cold War opponents' weapons. Of course, it wasn't a perfect test, as the Iraqis were not Soviets. Moreover, the war was fought in a desert, not the rolling woodlands and urban areas of central Europe. But, despite all that, it was possible to measure the effectiveness of Western military forces. The results revealed that Soviet military doctrine was nearly as remiss as their economic and social policies. Going into what, one hopes, is another half century of major-power peace, the world's armed forces will look to the Gulf War as a proof of the success of the NATO style of warfare. Combat is the final arbiter of what military doctrine is correct and worth emulating, and the Gulf War was a convincing demonstration.

The Future

Weapons developments go through cycles of quality and quantity. First there is the development of a new weapon, which represents an increase in performance quality. These new weapons are expensive and not as reliable as existing ones, so they are not produced in large quantities. As the bugs are worked out, more are produced and older models are replaced. This cycle has been quite stable for the last century, the only variation being an understandable speedup during major wars. To demonstrate this, let us consider the changes at 20-year intervals since 1900:

1900. At the beginning of this century, the principal land weapons were masses of infantry armed with bolt-action rifles, not too many machine guns, and somewhat more light artillery pieces (primarily 75mm). At sea, the principal weapon was the armored cruiser equipped with 155mm guns.

1920. The ground forces still had a lot of people walking around with bolt-action rifles, but there were a lot more machine guns, plus many mortars and heavier artillery (105mm). There were also primitive armored vehicles and many trucks. Chemical weapons had been developed and used, but few wanted to use them again. Horses still hauled most of the heavy equipment. At sea, the principal ship was the battleship. The new weapon was the submarine, which was basically a small torpedo boat that could travel submerged for a few hours. Surface ships had only a primitive form of sonar and depth charges to deal with subs. In the air, there were totally new weapons: wood and fabric biplanes carrying machine guns and a few small bombs. All services made extensive use of radio and telephones.

1940. Ground forces had more and better armored vehicles, and 5–10 percent of the troops were in mechanized units that moved about without horses or walking. At sea, there were now aircraft carriers and a lot more submarines. The battleships were on their way out. In the air, there were metal, prop-driven predecessors of modern fighters, as well as four-engine bombers. The ground forces and Navy had thousands of machine guns and cannon for the express purpose of destroying aircraft. There were a lot more radios, along with the newly developed radar and improved sonar.

1960. The horse was gone, and nuclear weapons were all over the place. Armored vehicles had gotten bigger and more numerous. Major nations had completely mechanized armies. The average artillery caliber was 155mm, and much of it was self-propelled. The army was using a lot more electronics, especially radar and more capable radios. The navies had recognized the supremacy of the aircraft carrier, but the first nuclear submarines had put to sea, and change was at hand. Antisubmarine warfare had reached new heights of effectiveness with hundreds of four-engine, computer-equipped patrol aircraft, plus stationary underwater sensors. The Air Force was beginning to develop long-range nuclear missiles and already had supersonic fighters armed with missiles as well as heavy, jet-propelled bombers.

1980. Ground forces had introduced more capable versions of 1960s weapons and equipment. New items were antitank guided missiles and efficient body armor. The major navies had more nuclear submarines than aircraft carriers. The air forces had more capable, and expensive, aircraft. The missiles were more complex and effective. Long-range bombers had been supplanted by ICBMs and other missiles of various ranges. All services were beginning to introduce robotic weapons that could fight on their own.

2000. The generals and admirals talk excitedly about revolution in warfare. These don't come along very often, although there were two in the twentieth century. The first was seen during World War I, when machine guns, modern artillery, aircraft, and electronic communications changed warfare dramatically. A mere 20 years later came another revolution. During World War II we saw mechanized warfare, aircraft carriers, paratroopers, strategic bombing, and atomic weapons change the way of war once more. Now, after half a century of incremental improvements in the World War II model, a new one looms. Computerized weapons are maturing along with the technology that spawned them. Robotic weapons are appearing in growing numbers. Combat between machines, without human intervention, will soon be possible. As history has repeatedly shown, long periods of inactivity between major wars create wide gaps between the theory and reality of actual combat. There has never been so large a quantity of automated weapons available before. In the past, when the troops quickly realized that the battlefield was not like they were told it would be, the survivors quickly adapted. Machines have to be modified. This is going to be interesting.

But What About 2020?

You can see how trends in military equipment work. Large wars force things to happen more quickly. Long periods of peacetime are more evolutionary. We are living in one of the longer evolutionary periods ever experienced. The last evolutionary period extended from 1871 to 1914: 43 years. The current one is over 60 years old and likely to continue for a while yet. Now, consider the surprises encountered during the opening battles of 1914. World War I is largely remembered for the stalemates resulting from faulty understanding of new technology. Despite the experience of the Gulf War, it's still possible to forget. It's happened before; it will happen again.

Most generals and admirals have been giving the impact of new technology a lot of thought. Currently, the most popular view of future battlefields is based on robots and the Internet. The robots have been around for a long time. Torpedoes were turned into robots during World War II when they were equipped with seekers to chase after their targets. Next came cruise missiles, programmed to fly off and hit a specific target. Now there are thousands of GPS-guided bombs. Give the GPS bomb the coordinates of the target and drop it; the bomb goes and delivers itself. The U.S. Army has an antitank mine system that is robotic. The Air Force is building robotic fighters and bombers. Everyone has "fire-and-forget missiles." You can see the pattern. Just as electronic warfare and guided bombs got started in the 1940s and were continuously improved after that, robotic weapons are now becoming a lot cheaper, and smarter.

The Internet effect came on everyone a lot more quickly. Radio nets (allowing several people to talk to everyone else at once) were common during World War II. While the nets allowed for immediate communication, they also easily lapsed into confusion. So strict protocol had to be used—who could talk, when and how to say it. Moreover, there's only so much information you can move around quickly with words. When the Internet became widely available, and a lot of neat software appeared taking advantage of instant communication, the troops saw their opportunity. Multiplayer computer games showed how it could be done, and warriors began to look for ways to use this sort of instant communication (with pictures, data, and sound) on the battlefield. The Army and Air Force called it "digitalization"; the Navy called it "net-centric warfare." Everyone acknowledged that whoever used this stuff first would be able to operate a lot faster. To put it simply, if you can find and hit the enemy faster than he can, you will win. This became the basis of what is called information warfare. Data becomes a weapon, or, rather, ammunition. The battlefield intranet equipment becomes a weapon. Collect more information more quickly, analyze it faster, and act on it long before the other guy figures out what you're up to. But there's more. Figure out ways to cripple the enemy's use of information and make it hard for him to do the same to you. So we have a new kind of warfare, based on space satellites, reconnaissance drones, and many other sources (like eyepiece cams on infantrymen and gunsight cams on tanks) providing information. Software sorts it all out and warns troops in imminent danger while commanders make quick decisions based on the flood of data.

But here's the catch. In 1914, the generals thought they had all the new weapons figured out. OK, aircraft had only been available to the troops for about five years, and radio was less than 20 years old. But telephones had been in use for over three decades. Modern rifles, artillery, and machine guns were nearly as old (or new, depending on how you look at it). And there had been a bunch of smaller wars to give all this new stuff some combat experience. But once all this stuff was put to work in a big war, things didn't work out like anyone expected. It took two years and a lot of dead soldiers for solutions to appear. Everyone had pretty much the same weapons and equipment in 1918 that they had in 1914, but the ideas for using this stuff were a lot more effective after four years of heavy use under fire.

Even with the World War I experience behind them, and a few little wars in between, 21 years later World War II broke out, and many major armed forces had not figured out how best to handle the innovations of the previous two decades. In that time, armored vehicles, used at the tail end of World War I, matured. So did aircraft, with the wooden aircraft of 1918 being replaced by faster and larger metal warplanes. Oh, there had been a lot of theorizing in the 1920s and 1930s, but the sharp reality checks of the first battles were bloody and shocking.

So what's war going to be like in 2020? Not exactly like what any of the experts tell you it will be like. The little wars between now and then will give some solid clues and a lot of false leads. Like any mystery, we won't know which clues are real and which are dead ends. But there are some trends that will continue, if only because they have been moving along for the last century.

Warfare will become faster. The advantage will go to the side that is first out of the gate and takes the initiative.

Victory will go, as it usually does, to the bigger battalions. Not just the side with more armed men, but the side with more well-trained and -led troops. The next big war will involve a lot more robotic weapons, so victory will also favor the side with the greater capacity to turn out the killer droids.

Information war is real, but it always has been. Critical information has, for thousands of years, often proved decisive. But never before have societies and armies been held together by such large and complex webs of information. Keeping your web together, while tearing up your opponents', will be another battlefield. Without adequate information, all your combat forces are more likely to be targets than anything else.

Expect the unexpected. Whoever is flexible enough, and capable enough, to deal with the enemy's surprises will come out ahead and might even find this edge the critical one for victory.

Beware the doomsday weapon. Weapons of mass destruction are another legacy of World War II. A foe, especially one largely driven by ideology and on the brink of final defeat, now has things like biological and nuclear weapons to help him get one last shot in. Since 1945, possessing nukes has largely kept the peace between the major powers. But as more nations get nuclear weapons, or effective biological ones, the final battle could have a bitter aftertaste.

29

The Armed Forces of the World

Armed forces exist primarily, or at least initially, for self-defense. Some nations go overboard, and some feel the best way to defend against a real or imagined threat is to attack it. Armed forces also serve as one more bargaining chip in a state's international diplomacy. If war comes, the armed forces have failed in their primary purpose: to appear too strong to be successfully attacked. Therefore, armed forces pay a lot of attention to appearing strong. If substance is sacrificed to enhance apparent strength, why not? An apparently stronger armed force is more valuable in diplomacy than a less capable-appearing one. Actual combat capability is difficult to measure. It is too easy just to count the number of tanks, ships, aircraft, and men in uniform. Numbers make the loudest noise when you must rattle the saber. Should bluff fail, and you are forced to wage war, well, that's another set of problems.

Doctrine Versus Reality

Doctrine is the plan; reality is the performance. Most nations' military planning rests on their appraisals of their own military ability. This appraisal reaches a low point just before arms budgets are voted on and rises swiftly during international crises and reelection campaigns.

When actual warfare approaches, the military becomes more realistic. It is always a touchy matter when the generals must confront the national leader, who is either inflamed by patriotic optimism or crestfallen by doubt, to present a sober appraisal of the situation. One of the more poignant examples was in 1914. The German kaiser, after declaring war, began to realize the enormity of his action. He asked his generals to stop the mobilization. They informed him that this would put Germany at a grave disadvantage, as it would totally disorganize the armed forces. The war proceeded, and millions of lives were lost.

The peacetime gap between doctrine and reality is recognized, if only vaguely, by most national leaders. Unfortunately, people sometimes forget or are overtaken by events. Most nations have traditional armed forces, capable of some form of warfare. Countries look at their neighbors' past history and finances and build up their armed forces accordingly. The usual idea is to have forces that can successfully resist one or more potentially unfriendly neighbors. Border disputes and excess wealth are the most common causes of building up armed forces above the levels needed for self-defense. The Middle East is a good example; in the eyes of Arab nations, Israel's existence is a border dispute. The size of armed forces in the region has grown accordingly. Excess wealth in the region has also led to excessive armed forces. The more wealth one has, the more concerned one becomes about keeping it. Like good health, no price is too high for security, particularly if you have deep pockets. As doctors are concentrated in wealthy neighborhoods, so arms dealers flock to the oil-rich Middle East. It was just such a case of envy that caused Iraq to invade Kuwait in 1990.

As a nation's apparent military capabilities grow, doctrine tends to follow. One defensive plan is to have armed forces mobilize near the borders to repel invaders. Increasing strength leads one to contemplate taking the war to the aggressor's homeland. An invasion has three attractions:

- The fighting is shifted to the enemy's territory.
- Your forces are have something to negotiate with (enemy territory).
- Retribution is made. Never underestimate the power of revenge in world affairs.

Most armed forces are capable of mustering a defense. An attack, especially an invasion into hostile territory, is considerably more difficult. In the defense, you dig trenches and wait. An attack requires moving large numbers of troops and all their equipment. Eventually defenders start shooting at you. Troops, difficult to control under any circumstances, are more so while moving and being shot at. Keeping large numbers of troops fed and healthy becomes more difficult in unfriendly territory. More supplies must be moved farther. Enemy attacks on these supplies create still more problems. All that movement uses and wastes more supply than if you stay in your own territory. Thus, attacking usually consumes more supply than defending. Commanding, controlling, and communicating with moving forces in enemy territory is enormously more difficult than defending. Gathering information on enemy forces is obviously easier for the defenders in their homeland. It is common for a defender to defeat an invader soundly and then suffer an equally disastrous defeat during a pursuit into the invader's homeland. A recent example of this was Iraq's 1980 invasion of Iran, which was followed by Iran's seven-year attempt to invade Iraq in turn.

Attrition Versus Maneuver

There are two ways to fight a war: plain (attrition) and fancy (maneuver). The stronger military power has the option of which method to use. If the stronger power has little military experience, they simply opt for the meat-grinder approach known as attrition. Any nation with solid military experience and a desire to do it right will choose the maneuver approach. Maneuver kills fewer people on both sides and gets the job done more quickly, if you do it right. Through most of its wars, the United States successfully used the attrition approach. It is easier to be proficient at attrition warfare. You need master only the simplest military skills and possess enormous quantities of arms and munitions. Russia has also opted for attrition through most of its wars, despite continuing efforts to master maneuver warfare on a more than temporary basis. Maneuver warfare means being more agile and efficient than your opponent. Instead of engaging in a mutual slaughter, you destroy your opponent's will to fight. This involves everything from stunning him into surrender with your fancy footwork to the more mundane destruction of enemy headquarters and supplies. Maneuver warfare is waged against leadership, the troops' confidence, and their sense of security. Maneuver warfare also implies a degree of success. Unsuccessful attempts at maneuver warfare are simply failure, and often disastrous failure at that. Maneuver warfare is for able players only. Inept practitioners need not apply. Most nations recognize their limitations in this area and go with attrition. Most nations have no choice.

Maneuver warfare is very risky, a gambler's game. Attrition is slower, plodding, and more predictable—just the sort of thing your average bureaucrat leans toward. The United States has managed to practice maneuver warfare in several smaller conflicts or portions of larger wars. In the war with Mexico in the 1840s, small U.S. forces invaded and outmaneuvered the opposition. During the American Civil War, several campaigns were notable for their successful application of maneuver warfare. But that entire conflict was permeated by, and won with, attrition. In particular, the Confederate forces managed to keep the war going by successful use of maneuver warfare. They won many battles but were ground down by attrition. Like any superior technique, maneuver warfare is not a panacea if you are grossly outnumbered. In one of the more interesting ironies of military affairs, the Soviets were a fervent proponent of maneuver warfare. The Soviet Union was one of the first nations to mechanize portions of its armed forces in the 1930s. They used British theory, American engineering, and German advisers. All of this fell apart when the Germans invaded in 1941. But the Soviets were resilient, and industrious, pupils. By 1943 they were demonstrating their growing prowess in mobile warfare. By 1945, Soviet troops were quite good at maneuver warfare. They were mindful of their teachers and adopted still more German organization, techniques, and weapons after 1945. Soviet commanders were also mindful that they defeated the Germans primarily through a mobile war of attrition. The most crucial lesson the Soviets learned in World War II was that despite their massive preparations for mobile warfare in the 1930s, they still had to relearn all they thought they knew once the war began. The experience in World War II merely confirmed what military leaders have known for thousands of years: military power is mass times velocity. All things being equal, the more mobile force will prevail. Up to a point, a smaller, more mobile force will defeat a larger one. But only up to a point. Unless the smaller, more mobile force wins quickly, the proverbial big battalions will prevail.

The Difference Between Wars and Disorder

There are wars and there are wars. Much of what we currently call war is merely well-armed disorder. It is simply insurrection, guerrilla activity, or general disorder involving the armed forces. This is an important distinction, as a great deal of military skill is not needed to create armed disorder. You don't need trained troops to create a proper insurrection or civil war. All you need are angry people and some weapons.

A war, as is meant in this book, is more than slaughter, mayhem, and senseless destruction. A certain amount of skill is implied, perhaps even a reasonable excuse for the exercise. Not all the armed forces described in this chapter possess skill. Military skill is more than uniforms, display, and awesome-looking equipment. Most of the military violence in the world is nothing more than large-scale disorder, banditry, or worse. Uganda, Lebanon, El Salvador, the Balkans, Mozambique, the Caucasus, and Afghanistan are examples of disorder, even if some of the participants are trying to put up an organized fight. In such conflicts, combat takes on a different meaning. For example, during a disorder in which one side is clearly stronger than the other, the weaker side fights when and where it has a chance of success. When faced with overwhelming military power, the weaker force will turn into civilians, or otherwise seek sanctuary. Afghanistan again comes to mind. If the Soviets had put a million troops into the country, ten times the initial number sent in, the Afghans would still have simply waited them out. Sufficient outrages would have occurred to keep the populace in a properly hateful frame of mind.

A war is fought to a conclusion. Disorders may go on for years, decades, or centuries. Wars are fought by powerful and expensive armed forces. Disorders are fought with whatever deadly force is handy, plus the legendary hearts and minds. Making disorder is simpler than making war, which why it is more common.

The Future

For the last 30 years, and into the foreseeable future, each major world region is dominated by one local superpower. The chart shows this rather vividly. The degree of dominance can be expected to change in the future.

Europe. The NATO alliance, having come out on the winning side of the Cold War, now dominates Europe militarily. But that doesn't mean a whole lot. After suffering wars and threats of wars for most of this century, Europeans are making the most of the first true peace in the continent since, well, since before written records were kept. While fighting broke out in the Balkans in the wake of the Cold War ending, this is normal by European standards. There has *always* been some kind of conflict going on in the Balkans. That's been an ugly condition, but an ancient and persistent one just the same. As Europe moved inexorably to economic and political unification in the 1990s, there were also attempts to form permanent multinational armed forces. It's a new era for Europe, and even the successor states of the Soviet Union want to join in. German reunification raised some fears of a German military hegemony. Germany has shown no interest in this, and, without nuclear weapons, Germany would stand little chance against nuclear-armed Britain, France, and Russia.

Middle East. Israel has been increasing its military domination of the Middle East throughout the 1980s. This has been accomplished more by increasing technical skill and technology than by adding weapons. The Iran-Iraq and Lebanese wars, plus the decline of oil prices, have sapped Arab military and economic resources. The Iraqi invasion of Kuwait in 1990 shattered what anti-Israeli cohesion there was among Arab nations. That war also set back Iraqi military power a decade or more. The end of the Cold War also denied many Arab nations a major patron. The successor states of the Soviet Union have shown no enthusiasm for Middle Eastern politics. On the down side, the end of the Cold War has also led to a lessening of support from Israel's major ally, the United States. But on balance, the Israelis have come out ahead and will likely continue to be the leading military power in the region.

East Asia. The situation in Asia is a bit more complex. As a result of the 40 years of fighting in Indochina, Vietnam emerged as an uncharacteristically strong regional military power. This has been done at the expense of their economy, leaving the Vietnamese one of the poorest nations in the world. Meanwhile, China is undergoing an economic renaissance. Vietnam's military power can be expected to decline while China's will grow, restoring the more normal balance of military capability in the region.

South Asia. India continues to maintain its relative dominant position and even improve it against its primary antagonist, Pakistan. With Pakistan acquiring nuclear weapons, we also have a situation where two antagonistic nuclear powers glare at each other across contested borders. So far, both sides have shown considerable restraint. Indeed, commentators on both sides of the border have made much of the fact that neither nation can afford the economic disruption that even a war with conventional weapons would entail.

Africa. South Africa's well-trained and well-equipped armed forces dominate the less well turned-out troops of neighboring countries. South Africa's major danger is internal disorder, which will likely increase as that nation approaches full democracy. Multiculturalism is the curse of Africa, and South Africa is no different. The Afrikaner tribe has kept the lid on things for many generations, but this tribal-domination approach has its limitations. Democracy is a much sought-after goal, but it is a slippery beast. If you go for it but can't hold it together, you end up with armed disorder.

Americas. The United States will continue to be the dominant power, although Brazil's military power continues to increase along with its economy.

Top Ten Nations in Terms of Land Combat Power

These ten nations possess some 65 percent of the combat power on the planet. They also possess 51 percent of the population, 47 percent of the GDP, 45 percent of the 20 million troops, 40 percent of the armored vehicles, 56 percent of the combat vehicles, and 57 percent of the $900 billion in annual military spending. The United States alone has 35 percent of the world's land combat power (which includes land-based air power) and 37 percent of the defense spending.

Nation	Combat power
United States	2,488
China	827
Israel	617
India	564
Russia	369
South Korea	289
North Korea	274
United Kingdom	259
Turkey	240
Pakistan	235

Armed Forces of the World

This chart gives evaluations of the quantity and quality of each nation's armed forces. The quantity of each combat unit has been derived from various open sources. Quality has been determined by evaluating historical performance. All armed forces are not equal, and this inequality has been expressed numerically. In calculating the numerical value of total strength, it is important to differentiate between what floats and what doesn't. Aircraft carriers and tank divisions are very different instruments of destruction. Both cost about the same, but a carrier cannot march on Moscow, nor can a tank division hunt submarines in the Atlantic. For this reason, land and naval force capabilities are listed separately. In reality, they are not entirely separate. Naval forces, particularly carriers, can support ground combat. Tank divisions can seize ports needed by naval forces for their sustenance. Destructive effect was the main consideration in assigning values. This was modified by the mobility and flexibility of the system. Tank divisions can move over a wide area to fight, while most air-defense forces are limited in their capabilities and mobility. While the numbers of men and weapons are fairly accurate, estimates of quality factors are subjective. Readers may impose their own evaluations. The assessments given are based on current conditions and historical experience. Don't underestimate the historical trends.

Naval forces are shown in detail on their own chart, while on the armed-forces chart they are shown as a component of total nation power. Naval power is difficult to compare to land power, as it is with land power that you ultimately defend yourself or overwhelm an opponent. For nations that are not dependent on seaborne trade, naval power is less important than those that are. For most industrial nations, and many Third World countries that have periodic food shortages, loss of sea trade is a serious problem. Fortunately for the nations dependent on seaborne trade, they have a substantial naval advantage over less dependent nations. In other words, Western navies are collectively considerably larger than those controlled by continental powers.

Country lists every nation with a combat value of one or more. Nations with a combat value of less than one have little more than national police capability. Many smaller countries, especially those that lack a threatening neighbor, use their forces primarily for internal security. These lesser military powers often repel an invasion most effectively simply by arming the population. Nations are grouped into six regions: Europe, Middle East, Africa, east Asia, south Asia, and the Americas.

Rank is the ranking of each nation within its region.

Armed Forces of the World

Country	Rank	Land combat power	Tot. qual.	Tot. pop.	GDP	Act. men.	Mil. bud.	Bud. man	AFV	Aircraft combat
Middle East nations										
Israel	1	617	61%	6.4	$48.0	550	$5,500	$10	10,500	570
Iran	2	204	25%	69.0	$100.0	510	$7,500	$15	3,500	210
Egypt	3	149	26%	71.0	$93.0	440	$3,000	$7	7,400	680
Syria	4	85	19%	16.0	$14.0	310	$700	$2	8,500	600
Iraq	5	84	15%	22.0	$20.0	420	$1,500	$4	5,200	400
Saudi Arabia	6	82	45%	23.0	$190.0	200	$72,000	$360	5,700	350
Algeria	7	41	27%	33.0	$45.0	125	$3,000	$24	3,200	220
Jordan	8	38	25%	6.9	$7.8	100	$500	$5	2,500	110
Morocco	9	28	11%	29.0	$34.0	196	$1,600	$8	1,900	110
Sudan	10	23	13%	29.0	$17.0	115	$600	$5	700	40
Lebanon	11	16	19%	3.3	$6.6	70	$600	$9	1,400	0
Yemen	12	13	18%	19.0		52	$550	$11	1,600	75
Libya	13	13	10%	5.7	$40.0	75	$600	$8	2,900	320
United Arab Emirates	14	12	19%	2.6	$60.0	65	$3,500	$54	1,500	140
Azerbaijan	15	10	11%	7.8	$5.0	70	$200	$3	600	35
Uzbekistan	16	10	17%	24.0	$20.0	52	$1,400	$27	900	160
Kazakhstan	17	9	9%	16.3	$20.0	65	$380	$6	1,600	150
Oman	18	9	28%	2.7	$18.0	42	$1,800	$43	390	40
Tunisia	19	6	21%	9.7	$20.0	33	$440	$13	450	55
Kuwait	20	6	26%	2.1	$35.0	15	$3,400	$227	740	100
Turkmenistan	21	5	13%	4.5	$4.8	17	$180	$11	2,100	80
Bahrain	22	3	22%	0.6	$7.0	11	$450	$41	460	72
Qatar	23	3	24%	0.6	$13.0	12	$1,400	$117	350	36
Kyrgyzstan	24	2	9%	4.8	$1.5	9	$35	$4	700	100
Mauritania	25	1	7%	2.8	$1.0	15	$25	$2	130	6
Tajikistan	26	1	13%	6.3	$1.4	6	$90	$15	80	0

Country	Rank	Land combat power	Tot. qual.	Tot. pop.	GDP	Act. men.	Mil. bud.	Bud. man	AFV	Aircraft combat
East Asian Nations										
China	1	827	32%	1300.0	$800.0	2100	$40,000	$19	14,500	3,300
South Korea	2	289	31%	47.4	$450.0	680	$13,000	$19	5,600	650
North Korea	3	274	20%	24.0	$15.0	1000	$1,200	$1	5,500	600
Taiwan	4	155	41%	22.2	$320.0	350	$18,000	$51	3,200	520
Japan	5	150	73%	127.0	$4,600.0	240	$47,000	$196	2,100	380
Vietnam	6	150	23%	81.0	$32.0	480	$1,400	$3	2,800	200
Indonesia	7	56	16%	212.0	$165.0	290	$1,200	$4	840	120
Thailand	8	45	12%	62.0	$130.0	300	$2,400	$8	1,600	150
Australia	9	33	54%	19.1	$400.0	50	$7,200	$144	640	140
Singapore	10	26	33%	3.7	$100.0	60	$4,800	$80	1,400	170
Philippines	11	25	19%	78.0	$85.0	110	$1,600	$15	480	135
Malaysia	12	23	25%	22.0	$90.0	98	$3,000	$31	450	70
Cambodia	13	16	12%	11.5	$3.3	110	$600	$5	260	22
New Zealand	14	4	39%	4.0	$55.0	9	$1,400	$156	80	36
Laos	15	3	6%	5.5	$1.6	28	$20	$1	120	12
Mongolia	16	2	10%	2.8	$1.1	9	$20	$2	1,400	20
Brunei	17	1	19%	0.3	$6.0	6	$380	$66	55	5
Papua New Guinea	18	1	13%	5.0	$4.8	4	$55	$13	0	0
Fiji	19	0	12%	0.8	$1.4	3	$32	$9	0	0
European Nations										
Russia	1	369	40%	142.0	$1,400.0	850	$70,000	$82	18,000	2,100
United Kingdom	2	259	77%	59.0	$1,400.0	210	$37,000	$176	4,100	420
Turkey	3	240	33%	68.0	$220.0	510	$2,050	$4	5,900	500
Germany	4	190	64%	83.0	$1,900.0	280	$30,000	$107	6,600	400
France	5	147	49%	59.0	$1,400.0	250	$36,000	$144	5,500	450
Italy	6	102	43%	57.0	$1,100.0	220	$22,000	$100	2,600	310
Switzerland	7	88	37%	7.5	$250.0	350	$3,000	$9	2,600	130
Poland	8	83	31%	39.0	$180.0	200	$3,400	$17	5,400	200
Spain	1	65	35%	40.0	$570.0	140	$7,400	$53	3,200	200

Country	Rank	Land combat power	Tot. qual.	Tot. pop.	GDP	Act. men.	Mil. bud.	Bud. man	AFV	Aircraft combat
European Nations										
Ukraine	2	65	19%	50.0	$35.0	300	1000	$3	6,000	510
Greece	3	57	26%	10.7	$120.0	150	$2,000	$13	2,900	450
Netherlands	4	31	48%	15.9	$380.0	51	$6,600	$129	1,500	150
Rumania	5	30	20%	23.0	$40.0	100	$880	$9	2,800	280
Serbia	6	30	25%	10.5	$20.0	95	$1,200	$13	1,500	100
Sweden	7	28	39%	9.0	$240.0	55	$5,200	$95	2,100	200
Bulgaria	8	22	13%	8.2	$13.0	70	$350	$5	3,200	160
Czech Republic	9	20	26%	10.1	$54.0	52	$1,200	$23	2,200	70
Finland	10	20	43%	5.2	$125.0	33	$1,500	$45	1,400	75
Austria	11	19	39%	8.2	$200.0	38	$1,600	$42	800	120
Hungary	12	16	28%	10.0	$50.0	34	$800	$24	1,900	44
Portugal	13	16	30%	10.0	$105.0	42	$2,400	$57	550	50
Belarus	14	15	11%	10.1	$10.0	80	$350	$4	3,300	200
Belgium	15	14	37%	10.0	$240.0	40	$3,500	$88	750	120
Norway	16	13	39%	4.5	$160.0	27	$2,800	$104	600	60
Denmark	17	12	39%	5.2	$165.0	22	$2,200	$100	880	66
Croatia	18	10	13%	4.5	$20.0	55	500	$9	440	30
Armenia	19	9	17%	3.5	$2.0	40	70	$2	300	20
Slovakia	20	6	14%	5.3	$20.0	32	320	$10	1,300	65
Albania	21	4	12%	3.2	$4.0	26	$150	$6	300	36
Cyprus (Greek)	22	4	19%	0.8	$10.0	20	$270	$14	500	0
Georgia	22	2	12%	5.0	$5.0	15	120	$8	270	15
Bosnia	23	2	10%	3.8	$5.5	36	200	$6	550	0
Ireland	24	2	22%	4.0	$100.0	10	$700	$70	110	0
Lithuania	25	2	14%	3.7	$12.0	12	200	$17	90	0
Macedonia	26	2	7%	2.0	$5.0	15	75	$5	250	10
Moldova	26	1	9%	4.2	$1.5	8	24	$3	350	0
Cyprus (Turkish)	27	1	13%	0.2	$1.0	5	$20	$4	20	0
Latvia	28	1	14%	2.3	$8.0	6	80	$13	20	0
Estonia	29	1	14%	1.4	$6.0	5	85	$19	40	0
Slovenia	30	0	14%	2.0	$19.0	8	55	$7	150	8

Country	Rank	Land combat power	Tot. qual.	Tot. pop.	GDP	Act. men.	Mil. bud.	Bud. man	AFV	Aircraft combat
American Nations										
United States	1	2,488	93%	285.0	$11,000	1400	$340,000	$243	32,000	7,600
Brazil	2	94	33%	172.0	$1,200	285	$18,000	$63	1,700	320
Canada	3	45	49%	32.0	$730.0	56	$8,200	$146	2,400	140
Colombia	4	35	23%	43.0	$80.0	160	$2,400	$15	290	115
Mexico	5	33	21%	101.0	$580.0	190	$5,500	$29	1,100	170
Chile	6	26	25%	15.6	$88.0	86	$2,100	$24	1,000	80
Argentina	7	23	28%	37.0	$280.0	70	$4,600	$66	1,000	140
Peru	8	22	18%	26.0	$70.0	100	$880	$9	500	110
Venezuela	9	17	20%	25.0	$95.0	82	$1,800	$22	550	160
Cuba	10	14	22%	11.3	$16.0	45	$700	$16	1,600	45
Ecuador	11	7	11%	13.0	$20.0	60	$400	$7	330	75
Bolivia	12	5	16%	8.5	$10.0	34	$820	$24	120	50
Nicaragua	13	4	19%	5.4	$3.2	16	$370	$23	170	15
El Salvador	14	3	14%	6.4	$11.0	17	$180	$11	50	42
Guatemala	15	3	7%	11.7	$15.0	32	$150	$5	50	16
Uruguay	16	3	12%	3.5	$14.4	23	$370	$16	250	27
Dominican Republic	17	3	15%	8.7	$14.0	23	$110	$5	45	6
Paraguay	18	2	12%	5.7	$10.0	16	$100	$6	50	25
Honduras	19	1	14%	6.6	$6.0	8	$90	$11	75	40
Panama	20	1	11%	2.9	$10.5	11	$140	$13	0	0
Costa Rica	21	1	11%	4.2	$11.3	8	$85	$11	0	0
Haiti	22	1	11%	8.5	$3.5	7	$50	$7	0	0
Jamaica	23	0	14%	2.7	$7.0	3	$50	$18	10	0
Trinidad	24	0	12%	1.3	$7.5	3	$66	$24	0	0
Suriname	25	0	12%	0.4	$0.4	2	$12	$6	20	6
Guyana	26	0	8%	0.9	$0.9	2	$8	$5	8	0
Belize	27	0	19%	0.3	$1.3	1	$17	$28	0	0

Country	Rank	Land combat power	Tot. qual.	Tot. pop.	GDP	Act. men.	Mil. bud.	Bud. man	AFV	Aircraft combat
African Nations										
Ethiopia	1	40	13%	64.0	$7.0	170	$420	$2	500	70
Eritrea	2	32	15%	4.0	$0.8	90	$200	$2	180	18
South Africa	3	30	35%	41.0	$125.0	60	$2,000	$33	2,000	90
Angola	4	20	11%	13.0	$7.0	110	$900	$8	1,200	130
Rwanda	5	16	12%	8.9	$2.5	75	$110	$1	180	4
Nigeria	6	15	14%	114.0	$55.0	80	$350	$4	950	90
Dem. Rep. Congo	7	9	10%	52.0	$5.0	80	$400	$5	230	10
Uganda	8	8	10%	22.0	$9.0	55	$120	$2	310	1
Chad	9	6	12%	7.5	$1.8	28	$45	$2	250	4
Zimbabwe	10	5	6%	12.0	$5.0	41	$150	$4	320	70
Burundi	11	5	5%	6.8	$1.3	46	$48	$1	90	5
Kenya	12	4	16%	31.0	$11.0	24	$300	$13	210	50
Tanzania	13	4	10%	35.0	$8.0	26	$115	$4	170	18
Cameroon	14	2	9%	15.0	$12.0	21	$165	$8	50	18
Zambia	15	2	8%	9.0	$4.0	20	$65	$3	130	50
Mozambique	16	2	9%	15.3	$2.0	10	$80	$8	280	5
Madagascar	17	2	10%	16.0	$6.0	13	$45	$3	100	12
Ivory Coast	18	2	13%	15.0	$15.0	13	$130	$10	60	4
Senegal	19	2	15%	9.9	$6.0	10	$65	$6	80	6
Congo	20	1	14%	3.0	$3.0	10	$75	$8	140	12
Nambia	21	1	14%	1.8	$3.0	9	$85	$9	70	4
Burkina Faso	22	1	12%	12.0	$4.0	10	$70	$7	80	6
Botswana	23	1	11%	1.7	$5.0	9	$240	$27	130	25
Djibouti	24	1	10%	0.8	$0.5	9	$24	$3	30	0
Ghana	25	1	10%	21.0	$11.0	7	$40	$6	50	18
Guinea	26	1	7%	7.6	$4.0	10	$50	$5	110	8
Togo	27	1	7%	4.6	$1.6	9	$30	$3	120	15
Mali	28	1	9%	11.6	$3.5	7	$30	$4	110	14
Guinea-Bisseau	29	1	6%	1.3	$0.4	8	$6	$1	70	3
Gabon	30	1	12%	1.6	$7.0	5	$90	$19	90	15
Sierra Leone	31	1	11%	4.7	$0.8	5	$10	$2	0	0

Country	Rank	Land combat power	Tot. qual.	Tot. pop.	GDP	Act. men.	Mil. bud.	Bud. man	AFV	Aircraft combat
African Nations										
Niger	32	1,997	9%	11.1	$2.0	5	$20	$4	140	0
Liberia	33	1,471	10%	3.2	$0.5	5	$15	$3	0	0
Benin	34	2,082	12%	6.3	$2.7	5	$40	$9	40	0
Malawi	35	2,830	7%	11.2	$1.5	5	$20	$4	40	0
Central Afr. Rep.	36	221	11%	3.7	$1.1	4	$45	$11	50	0
Swaziland	37	947	11%	1.1	$0.5	3	$20	$7	0	0
Lesotho	38		13%	2.2	$0.7	2	$20	$10	20	0
Equatorial Guinea	39		13%	0.5	$0.5	1	$11	$8	15	0
Somalia	40		6%	10.0	$1.0	1	$5	$2	0	0
Cape Verde Is.	41		11%	0.4	$0.3	1	$8	$7	8	0
Gambia	42		13%	1.4	$0.5	1	$14	$18	0	0
South Asian Nations										
India	1	564	35%	1100	$480.0	1250	$15,000	$12	5,100	750
Pakistan	2	235	24%	145	$65.0	610	$3,600	$5	3,600	370
Myanmar	3	74	12%	45.0	$38.0	420	$2,000	$5	550	140
Sri Lanka	4	31	18%	18.0	$17.0	110	$800	$7	300	50
Bangladesh	5	31	20%	131	$40.0	135	$680	$5	370	80
Nepal	6	10	9%	25.0	$5.0	50	$55	$1	50	0
Afghanistan	7	2	8%	19.0	$3.0	10	$50	$5	200	0
Regional Summary										
European Nations				801	$10,596	4,491	$247,299		90,970	7,549
Middle East Nations				418	$832	3,575	$110,950		65,000	4,659
East Asian Nations				2,028	$7,260	5,928	$143,307		41,025	6,530
American Nations				839	$14,285	2,739	$387,198		43,318	9,182
African Nations				614	$339	1,103	$6,676		8,603	775
South Asian Nations				1,483	$648	2,585	$21,585		10,170	1,390
World Totals		9,547		6,183	$33,960	20,419	$917,015		259,086	30,085

Land combat power is the total combat capability of the nations' armed forces except for their navies. Certain nations like Israel, Sweden, and Switzerland have a rapid-mobilization capability that achieves the combat value shown within three days of mobilization. Their normal, unmobilized combat value is less than one-third of the value shown. As explained elsewhere, combat value is modified by geographical, climatic, and political factors. The value given here is a combination of the quantity and quality of manpower, equipment, and weapons. This raw combat value is then multiplied by the force multiplier (see below) to generate the combat value shown in this column.

Naval capability is separate from land value and is found on the naval-forces chart.

Tot. qual. (total force quality) is a fraction by which raw (theoretical) combat power should be multiplied to account for imperfect leadership, component of force quality, support, training, and other "soft" factors. Think of it as an efficiency rating, with 100 being perfect and 55 being a more common 55 percent efficiency.

Tot. pop. (population in millions) indicates the nation's relative military manpower resources. Population is also a more meaningful indicator of a nation's size than territory.

GDP (Gross Domestic Product) is a rough gauge of the nation's economic power. This does not translate immediately into military power because of the time needed to convert industry from civilian to military production. Mobilization of some types of military equipment takes years. Other types of weapons, especially those using electronics, can be brought to bear in months.

Act. men. (active military manpower in thousands) is the total uniformed, paid manpower organized into combat and support units. Because of the widely varying systems of organizing military manpower, this figure is at best a good indicator of the personnel devoted to the military. Industrialized nations hire many civilians to perform support duties, while other nations flesh out skeleton units with ill-prepared reserves. The use of reserve troops varies considerably.

Mil. bud. (military budget in millions of dollars) is the current annual armedforces spending of that nation. All nations use somewhat different accounting systems for defense spending. Efforts are made to eliminate some of the more gross attempts at hiding arms expenditures. Some of the figures, particularly for smaller nations, may be off by 10 percent either way.

Bud. man is the annual cost per man for armed forces in dollars. This is an excellent indicator of the quantity and, to a lesser extent, the quality of weapons and equipment. Some adjustments should be made for different levels of personnel costs, research and development, strategic weapons, and waste. The United States, in particular, is prone to all four afflictions. The precise adjustments for these factors are highly debatable. One possible adjustment would be to cut the U.S. cost per man by at least one-third. Other nations with strategic programs and large R&D establishments (Russia, Britain, France, China, etc.) should be adjusted with deductions of no more than 15 percent. Britain could also take another 5 or 10 percent cut because of its all-volunteer forces' higher payroll. At the other extreme, many nations produce a credible defense force using far less wealth. Low-paid conscripts, good leadership, and the sheer need to improvise enables many of these poorer nations to overcome their low budgets. However, most nations end up with what they pay for.

AFV (armored fighting vehicles). These include tanks, armored personnel carriers, and most other armored combat and support vehicles. AFVs are the primary components of a ground offensive and greatly enhance chances of success.

Aircraft combat are the number of combat aircraft devoted to land operations. This, like AFV, is a good indicator of raw power. The quality of the aircraft, their pilots, ground crew, and leadership are the most important factors in the air power's overall value.

Current Potentials for War

Each region varies in its potential for war and in the type of war likely to be fought there.

Europe is an area that has had more potential for wars since the end of the Cold War and is one place where a conflict would be extremely destructive. There is more combat power concentrated in Europe than in any other region. The nations controlling these forces are keenly aware of the powder keg they have created. Much diplomatic effort is spent ensuring that the situation remains calm. The potential for war between Greece and Turkey festers as it has for the past 1,000 years. Yugoslavia's internal problems finally boiled over in the early 1990s and going into the twenty-first century continue to provoke the intervention of other European powers. Eastern Europe's liberation from four decades of Soviet hegemony has a dark side. The region is a hodgepodge of multicultural animosity. Ethnic populations are dispersed across national borders, and the borders themselves are not as settled as those in Western Europe. Yugoslavia was simply the worst of the multicultural catastrophes waiting to happen. Romania and Hungary have much potential for outright warfare. Czechoslovakia split into its Czech and Slovak parts. Bulgaria and Poland both have claims on their neighbors, as do Belarus and Ukraine. The successor states of the Soviet Union all have substantial Russian minorities. There may be no major war in Europe's future, but there is a lot of potential for a number of little wars.

The Middle East is the most volatile region. Arab animosity toward Israel runs a close second to their disputes with each other and non-Arab groups like Iran, the Kurds, and black Africans. While there have been five Arab-Israeli wars, there have been many other wars between Arabs and other groups. The most persistent conflict is the one between Israel and the Palestinians, which shows signs of smoldering on for the foreseeable future. The industrial nations have an interest in Middle Eastern unrest because the West gets much of its oil from the region. It is quite likely that more wars will occur in this area. Because none of the nations are major military powers, it is possible for these wars to be restricted. Iraq and Iran's attempt to acquire nuclear weapons will eventually succeed, but these weapons are most likely to be used locally, if at all.

Asia is an area where things can get out of hand. The biggest danger is the major military power in the region, China. Korea, Vietnam, Japan, and even India have reason to fear persistent Chinese ambitions. There is also Taiwan, the wayward province now held by the wealthy and powerful losers of the last Chinese civil war. China now hopes to recover Taiwan by negotiation and has played down (but not renounced) a military attempt. The border with India, astride the world's tallest mountains, is relatively quiet. Vietnam is another matter, with troops on the border and low-level but persistent fighting. Vietnam is hardly the victim, having fought with Cambodia for centuries over who will control Indochina. China's borders have never been peaceful and are not likely to be in the future. The central Asian tribes have been waging war with anyone within reach for thousands of years. Only in the last century has Russia finally subdued and conquered them, and now these central Asian peoples are once more independent. Except for Russia and Japan, most of the armed forces in Asia are low-tech. Warfare consists of a lot of infantry and some artillery flailing away at each other. Any war in Asia could easily become nuclear, because the two major powers, Russia and China, have lots of nuclear weapons.

India is a nation similar in size and population to Europe. India also has the same ethnic diversity but has managed to remain united. This unity is always threatened by ethnic and/or regional disputes. There is also the ancient antagonism with the peoples of the northwest (Pakistan), who, for thousands of years, have periodically invaded India. India's immediate neighbors have also been drawn into conflicts that have their origins in India. The civil war in Sri Lanka (between natives and migrants from southern India) is one such war. For all this, India has been significantly more peaceful than any other region of the world. Warfare in this subcontinent is most likely to be in the form of civil disorder.

Africa, south of the Sahara, is a political and economic mess. The region is dominated by South Africa. This nation monopolizes military and economic power in the region and is the most politically stable country around. South Africa underwent a political transformation in the 1990s as all elements were allowed to vote. It's still up in the air what this will do to South Africa's political stability and economic viability. Militarily, Africa presents lots of opportunity for low-level wars. Most of these wars are wars in name only. Civil disorders are a more apt description. There is also a lot of random violence by one ethnic group against another. When one ethnic group is in power, which is a common occurrence, the violence against the civilian population tends to be more systematic and relentless.

The Americas are insulated from the rest of the world by two oceans and the United States. Most of the warfare has, and will probably continue to be, internal disorder. There is some revolutionary activity. Large-scale military activity is discouraged by the generally small armed forces maintained by all nations except the United States. The United States has actively discouraged large wars and foreign intervention for nearly two centuries. This has had a lasting effect in disposing most nations toward negotiation rather than sustained combat. Not having used their armed forces in a war for many decades has left most nations with suspect combat capability. Argentina's performance against Britain in the 1982 Falklands war is indicative of this. But local wars and civil disorder are still present. The war in Colombia and serious civil disorder in other nations will be a source of "little wars" that America may get drawn into.

How to Determine the Losers of Future Wars

In predicting who will win a war, the past is indeed a window to the future. Past performance, however, is not enough. Several problems must be overcome. For example, armed forces are used infrequently. Yet they must train constantly, practicing every task except the most crucial one: combat. This appears to keep military thought and practice essentially conservative. The troops are always more prepared to refight their last war. This makes the task of prediction easier. Uncertainties still exist, but applying proven techniques with some precision, common sense, and systematic persistence will make the results quite accurate. These techniques have been used by military analysts and historical war-game designers successfully. I used it successfully during the 1991 Gulf War (as well as during the 1973 Arab-Israeli war, not to mention the Cold War). The major stipulation is not to become mesmerized by numbers. Counting resources and computing odds will take you only so far. The following procedure will take you a little further.

Select the nations that will go to war and what they are fighting over. Determining the causes of a war, and what each side's goals are, is often difficult. It is essential to find out why this war is happening so you can calculate how far each nation will go in supporting the conflict. A minor border squabble is less likely to escalate than an attempt by one nation to take over a neighbor completely. More important issues encourage a nation to keep at it longer and to resist efforts to settle the matter peacefully.

Determine the mode of combat. Will it be land, naval, or both? Which side will initially be attacking? A large army will be no help to a nation fighting a naval war. The attacker, as we have already learned, must be significantly stronger than the defender in order to succeed.

How much of a nation's forces will be committed to this war, and why? Nations at war generally do not, and often cannot, commit the whole of their armed strength against one enemy. There are often other threats, internal as well as external. It is also prudent to retain substantial forces as a reserve to reinforce some unanticipated success, or to recover from an unexpected disaster. Moreover, a nation's armed forces are not normally concentrated together as they would be for combat. In peacetime, combat units are scattered throughout the nation. This is done for political and economic reasons. Going to war means gathering a substantial portion of these forces on another nation's border. This is usually considered an unfriendly act. The other guy will start mobilizing his forces. Therefore, this "mobilization on the frontiers" must be done as quickly as possible lest you end up facing a defender larger than yourself. When waging an offensive war, you cannot expect to be capable of gathering more than 40–70 percent of your forces for the initial attack. A defender will often gather an even larger portion of his forces. After all, he is basically going to stand still and resist your advance. Another problem with marshaling forces for an attack is the need to occupy enemy territory. Unfriendly civilians can be troublesome unless sufficiently cowed by armed force. Occupation forces, such as your own police or locals acting as collaborators, often can be used instead of troops. In the best of circumstances, 200 troops per million enemy civilians will be needed to keep the conquered population under control. In a worst-case scenario, 2,000 troops per million will be needed.

Look at the combat values for each nation as shown on the charts. The objective of an attacker is to obtain better than 1:1 ratio of his strength to the defenders. A ratio of over 6:1 assures an almost instant victory. Anything below 1:1 means almost certain failure. But doing this simple calculation requires the armchair strategist to take into account the probable effect of geography, surprise, and human factors. Note that most human factors (training, leadership, etc.) have already been calculated to produce the combat values on the charts.

Calculate the effect of combined operations. Most nations have separate ground, air, and naval forces. Each of these forces fights a separate war while simultaneously cooperating with one another. If one nation can obtain air superiority, it can more than double the effectiveness of its ground and naval forces. The degree of increased effectiveness depends on the terrain. It's lower if the war is being fought over "busy" terrain (forests, urban areas, jungle) and higher if the terrain is more open (plains, unforested mountains, and especially deserts). Air superiority also guarantees naval superiority. Control of the air goes to the force with more and higher-quality aircraft.

Account for the effect of climate and geography. Some terrain favors defense; other terrain makes it easier for the attacker. Severe terrain conditions can double the effectiveness of defending troops. Add severe climactic conditions and the defender's combat value can be tripled. An attacker would be handicapped by invading Switzerland or Afghanistan in the winter. Other environments that favor the defender are the urban sprawl that covers most of Germany. Jungles or other thick forests also make defense more effective. An attacker coming across open terrain in dry weather has an advantage. Deserts are particularly difficult to defend.

Estimate the effect of surprise, if any. Surprise can benefit anyone, but the attacker normally has it. A maximum degree of surprise can multiply the attacker's combat capability five times. This is rarely attained. The Japanese came close in 1941. A more likely degree of surprise will multiply the attacker's strength two or three times. At the start of a war, the side that opens hostilities will usually obtain some surprise advantage, at least 10–50 percent. Basically, surprise means attacking enemy forces before they are prepared to resist. Examples are air attacks that catch enemy aircraft still on the ground. At sea, submarines are the preeminent surprise weapon. Ground combat finds surprise more difficult, but not impossible, to achieve. At the start of a war, the defender first has to determine that there is a war going on. After that, there are the problems of:

- Alerting the combat units,
- Getting them on the road,

- Getting them to the border, and
- Establishing defensive positions.

If the attacker has concealed his preparations, the invader can be crossing the frontier before the hapless defender knows what is going on. Such a degree of surprise depends on defender deficiencies as well as energetic moves on the attacker's part. Such surprise is not unknown. Iraq achieved it in 1990, the anti-Iraq coalition in 1991, Egypt in 1973, Israel in 1967, North Korea in 1950, and Germany in 1941. Difficult, but not impossible. Surprise does not end when the attacker's intentions are revealed. Carefully planned attacks on the defender's airfields and transportation network can sustain the surprise effect. If the defender does not have a well-thought-out plan to counter these moves, the effects of the surprise will endure. In the age of technology, there are surprises of a purely technological nature. Underestimating or being ignorant of enemy technical accomplishments can deal out lethal surprises. Israel misread the effectiveness of Egyptian antiaircraft weapons in 1973 and paid a high price in aircraft and lives. The Germans misread the allied use of radar several times during World War II, both in the air and at sea, and took higher losses because of it. The Germans demonstrated another form of surprise when they unleashed the blitzkrieg tactics on their opponents. This was doctrinal surprise. Future wars will be full of opportunities for doctrinal and technological surprise. Some of the surprise will be self-inflicted as nations use untried weapons and techniques. Even the Germans tripped over themselves when they first used their blitzkrieg tactics, but they were fortunate in that they had a few smaller actions to help them get the bugs out before they went up against a major opponent. During the first battles of World War I, everyone was green. Thus 1914 was full of bloody embarrassments. Future wars will likely open with the same errors of inexperience. Whoever is better prepared to cope with these surprises will have an edge.

What is the quality of the armed forces leader on each side? This is typically a factor only in a small armed force, say, under 100,000. A very good or bad leader of a smaller force will have a greater impact on a smaller force. Larger armed forces tend to be institutional, where individuals have less effect and then only over a long time. You apply this factor by multiplying the combat value by anything from .9 (exceptionally good leader) to .1 (very bad). An example of this would be Libya's Muammar Qaddafi, a particularly inept military leader who causes Libya's armed forces strength to be multiplied by only .2 or .3. If a better military leader came to power in Libya, he would improve the situation by replacing many unit commanders with more capable people and introducing new training methods, doctrine, and other practices. This can turn things around in weeks. Within a few months, the multiplier can go up to .6 or .7. Quite a difference. When in doubt, and for larger armed forces not affected by this, multiply by .5.

What impact will time have on the war? Time is the defender's strongest ally. If the attacker doesn't win quickly, several problems inevitably arise. First, the effects of whatever surprise the attacker had wear off. Next, if the attacker has penetrated into the defender's territory, the attacking force is operating under the adverse conditions one would expect in unfriendly territory. The attacking troops are somewhat demoralized by the fact that they have not quickly won, and the defending troops are likewise encouraged by this lack of success. The attacker's failure to win quickly does not assure a defender victory, but it does guarantee a longer war. In a long war, victory goes to the nation with the more robust economic strength. An extreme example of how this works can be seen in Israel, Sweden, and Switzerland. Each of these nations mobilizes a large segment of their male population in wartime. This mobilization strips key people from most economic activities in the nation. As a result, these nations cannot continue fighting at their fully mobilized strength for more than a few months without substantial outside assistance.

Examples

The Arab-Israeli war of 1973 found Israel weaker and Egypt stronger than they are today. Still, Israel had a value of 200, Egypt about 75, and Syria 20. If Israel had launched a surprise attack, as it had in 1967, it would have had an advantage of over 4:1 and virtual assurance of quick victory. However, it was Syria, and especially Egypt, that launched the surprise attack. Moreover, only a small portion of Israel's strength was on the border. Although the Israelis were sitting in bunkers behind the Suez Canal, it was not enough. Egypt had an advantage of over 6:1 on the first day of the attack. Israel recovered quickly, the Arab advantage quickly evaporated, and the advantage shifted to Israel within a week. Part of this rapid shift has to do with the structure of Israel's armed forces. Less than 30 percent of their strength is active in peacetime. Within 24 hours their peacetime strength doubles, and after 72 hours it triples. Most of the fighting took place on flat, largely hard desert terrain, giving the counterattacking Israelis the advantage. The method the Egyptians used initially to deceive the Israelis was quite simple: several times in the past, they had sent their forces to the border and gone through the preparations for an attack. Each time they then withdrew these forces, except on the last occasion, when they actually launched the attack. Israel could not afford to mobilize their forces partially each time Egypt went through this "practice" drill. The last time Egypt did it, the drill turned into the real thing. However, the Arabs were not able to withstand the Israeli counterattack. The final battles of this war saw the Israelis maintaining a combat ratio of better than 3:1. The Arabs had no reserves left, except possibly Soviet paratroopers, and the war soon ended.

A more recent example was the Falklands in 1982. Argentina sent a small portion of its ground forces to occupy the Falkland Islands. These troops were supported by air power from the mainland, plus a few aircraft stationed on the islands. Britain sent a large naval task force whose ground troops retook the islands. On paper (the first edition of this book), Britain had a land value of 98 and a naval value of 88 and a value per man of 54. Argentina had land value of 7, naval value of 15, and value per man of 15. Argentina put 11,000 men on the island and provided support with mainland-based aircraft representing another 10,000 men. The aircraft were the most effective, sinking and damaging 16 British ships. The Argentine navy was kept at bay by British nuclear submarines. It came down to the 28,000-man British task force versus the 21,000 Argentine defenders. Although Argentina had another quarter million men under arms, they could not get them past the British nuclear submarines. British ship-based aircraft prevented significant reinforcement of the islands. All the Argentines could do from the mainland was launch air strikes. The British put 7,000 men ashore and quickly defeated the isolated and demoralized Argentine garrison.

If you use the value-per-man figures (54 and 15), multiplied by the number of men actually involved (28,000 and 21,000), you find the British with a ratio of nearly 5:1. The British could have lost, but it would have been very unlikely.

An even more recent example was the Persian Gulf in 1990–91. This was actually two wars. The first was Iraq's invasion of Kuwait in the summer of 1990, followed by five months of inaction. In January, the anti-Iraq coalition began its six-week air bombardment of Iraqi forces in Kuwait, followed by a three-day ground offensive. Using the data from the second (1988) edition of this book, we have a land-combat value for the Iraqis of 356. This was the value of the Iraqis at the height of the Iran-Iraq war, which ended about the time the 1988 edition of this book was published. The Iraqis demobilized much of this army after the war and then remobilized the discharged veterans in 1990. Between 1988 and 1990, the Iraqis lost some of their combat edge, giving them a 1990 value of about 300. The Kuwaitis were only 9 and the United States was 1,412. Iraq put about 20 percent of its combat forces into the initial invasion of Kuwait, giving them a superiority of 60 to 9. It was actually higher (more like 100 to 9), as the Iraqis had achieved surprise. A subsequent invasion of Saudi Arabia was a real possibility, as the Saudis and the other Gulf nations could muster no more than 20–30 in combat value to oppose the Iraqis. After the Iraqis took Kuwait, they immediately began pouring in additional forces to occupy the country. This left the initial attack force free to continue on to Saudi Arabia. Fortunately, the Iraqi troops were not well organized or efficient (as shown by their total quality rating of 38 percent). The U.S. total quality rating was only 26 percent higher (48 versus 38 percent). But as the 1988 edition pointed out, the U.S. military was in the midst of reforming itself, and, until these reformed forces were put to the test, the new value was uncertain (although a 10–40 percent increase could be expected). It was higher, by about a third, but this was not the principal reason the Iraqis were outclassed. The United States put about 30 percent of its total ground combat power into the Gulf. That gave the United States a combat value of 420 (plus another 100 from allies) using the 1988 values. Using 1990 values, the United States had a 560 combat value, plus the 100 from the allies. Against the 660 of combat value, about 600 was used for the liberation of Kuwait. The Iraqis built up their forces in Kuwait and southern Iraq. By the end of 1990, Iraq had sent about half its armed forces to the Kuwait theater of operations (KTO). Most of these troops were ordered to the Saudi border, which was desert wasteland. Most of the allied troops were stationed under far less rigorous conditions. The Iraqis lacked the logistical and technical support for their troops, who suffered much while building fortifications in the desert summer. Opposite these Iraqi lines were, for the most part, a thin screen of Saudi desert troops who found the horrid climate quite normal. The Iraqis were not desert people, coming from the mountains up north or the Tigris-Euphrates river valleys. By the time the allied air offensive began in January 1991, the Iraqi force had a combat value of about 100. Desertions, illness, and the wear and tear of living in the summer desert had taken its toll. After six weeks of allied bombing, the Iraqi combat strength had been reduced to about 50. The allies then unleashed the ground offensive that, because of the element of surprise, sent a combat value of about 800 against an Iraqi strength of 50. At odds of 16:1, it's no surprise that the battle was over in less than a week. What was surprising was the amount of misinformation spread around in the media between August 1990 and February 1991. Myths such as the "million-man, battle-hardened Iraqi desert army" and the "huge U.S. casualties expected" stayed fresh and credible for a long time. This despite published accounts throughout the 1980s that convincingly disproved these myths. Apparently a lot of people don't read much any more, not counting you and me, of course.

The most recent example is the 2001 war in Afghanistan. This was an ongoing civil war, where one faction (the Taliban) had defeated, but not eliminated, all the other factions. Two things were going on during this war. First, the Taliban were running a religious police state and most Afghans didn't care for it. But the Taliban had imported thousands of fanatic fighters from other Muslim nations, and these guys kept most Afghans in line. Then along came the revenge-minded Americans. The Americans had one thing that the Afghans respected, a lot of bombers that were too high up to shoot back at. The damage the bombers did to the fragile Taliban army was just enough to get most Afghans off their butts and out in the street firing their rifles. The Taliban's foreign troops were really, really disliked by most Afghans, and American propaganda operations made much of this. One might say this was a war of intangibles. But it wasn't. An angry population and a hated occupying army are very tangible. As are the bombs you drop.

Armed Forces of the World: Naval Forces

This chart shows the world's 40 most powerful fleets, which represent 98 percent of the world's naval power.

Nation	Combat value	% of total	1,000 tons	Ships	Qual.
Argentina	2	0.41%	39	17	60%
Australia	5	0.81%	57	16	80%
Belgium	1	0.09%	7	3	75%
Brazil	6	0.99%	86	24	65%
Britain	46	8.11%	510	102	90%
Bulgaria	0	0.04%	4	7	60%
Canada	7	1.17%	78	20	85%
Chile	3	0.56%	45	21	70%
China	16	2.75%	346	219	45%
Colombia	0	0.08%	9	6	50%
Denmark	0	0.07%	6	8	70%
Egypt	2	0.41%	36	13	65%
France	14	2.44%	197	43	70%
Germany	9	1.59%	120	110	75%
Greece	6	1.03%	73	37	80%
India	10	1.74%	164	57	60%
Indonesia	2	0.29%	33	22	50%
Iran	1	0.17%	16	16	60%
Israel	1	0.21%	13	15	90%
Italy	9	1.61%	140	68	65%
Japan	26	4.66%	310	124	85%
North Korea	3	0.59%	56	103	60%
South Korea	6	0.98%	85	65	65%
Malaysia	1	0.14%	13	17	60%
Mexico	2	0.30%	28	8	60%
Netherlands	5	0.88%	62	19	80%
Norway	1	0.25%	18	29	80%
Pakistan	2	0.41%	39	21	60%
Peru	2	0.34%	32	17	60%
Philippines	1	0.13%	12	13	60%
Poland	1	0.18%	16	16	65%
Portugal	1	0.24%	19	9	70%
Romania	1	0.20%	19	11	60%
Russia	45	8.03%	908	187	50%
South Africa	0	0.06%	5.5	11	60%
Spain	5	0.93%	75	26	70%
Sweden	1	0.23%	17	32	75%
Taiwan	10	1.73%	140	99	70%
Thailand	2	0.43%	41	19	60%
Turkey	7	1.25%	118	60	60%
United States	302	53.46%	3,024	201	100%

Nation is the nation of the ships displayed. The figures include coast-guard ships if they have a wartime combat capability. Amphibious shipping is included (for details see Chapter 9).

Combat value is the numerical combat value of the nation's fleet. This value reflects the overall quantity and quality of ships and crew when used only for naval combat. Included is the effectiveness of support and the fleet's system of bases. Aside from the known quantities of ship numbers, tonnages, and manpower, less firm data on quality have been taken in consideration. To put it more crudely, it comes down to who is more capable of doing what they say they can do. The quality factor was derived from historical experience, a less-than-perfect guide.

% of total is the percentage of the world's total combat value each fleet represents.

1,000 tons is the full-load displacement tonnage of the combat fleet, in thousands of tons.

Ships is the total number of ships.

Qual. is the quality of crews and equipment for that fleet, using the U.S. Navy as a baseline.

Victory at Sea

The end of the Cold War has made the U.S. Navy the preeminent maritime power on the planet. No other navy or combination of navies can match the U.S. Navy. Moreover, the U.S. Navy is a truly global force. Even with the elimination of many overseas bases, the U.S. Navy still has sufficient presence and reach to make its power felt in any corner of the globe. Post–Cold War budget cuts may eventually reduce the U.S. fleet to less than half its late-1980s size. Cuts of that magnitude still won't change the U.S. Navy's position of naval superiority. The Soviet Union was always a long shot as a naval superpower. With the Soviet Union gone, Russia no longer has the Black Sea and Baltic bases that supported a third of its naval power. In the Pacific, the enormous expense of maintaining a major fleet far from the Russian heartland can no longer be supported. Russia's northern fleet in sub-Arctic Murmansk is another economic burden that will have to be sacrificed to economic viability and political stability on the home front.

The only remaining continental power potentially capable of creating a large fleet, China, has shown some interest in doing so but is proceeding slowly.

The series of twentieth-century wars (1914–91: World Wars I and II, the Cold War) that saw Britain as the principal naval power at the beginning finds the U.S. Navy holding that position at the end. The planet has gotten a lot smaller during that 77-year period. In the future, "victory at sea" will lose its meaning as future fleets head for orbital space.

Glossary:
Dictionary of Military Terms
(Official and Otherwise)

AAM—Air-to-Air Missile
ABM—Antiballistic Missile
AGM—Air-to-Ground Missile
ALCM—Air Launched Cruise Missile
AM-39—Exocet Missile
APDS—Armor-Piercing Discarding Sabot
APS—Armor-Piercing Shot
ARM—Anti-Radiation Missile
ASW—Anti-Submarine Warfare
ATACMS—Army Tactical Missile System
ATGM—Anti-Tank Guided Missile
AWACS—Airborne Warning and Control System
BB—Battleship
BMD—Ballistic Missile Defense
CA—Cruiser, Armored
CAS/BAI—Close Air Support/Battlefield Interdiction
CEP—Circular Error Probable
DD—Destroyer
DIVAD—Division Air Defense System
ECM—Electronic Countermeasures
ELINT—Electronic Intelligence
EW—Electronic Warfare
FAAD—Forward-Area Air Defense
flak—anti-aircraft guns (from German word)

FLOT—Forward Line of Own Troops
FROG—Free Rocket over Ground (NATO name for Soviet-designed system)
GRT—Gross Register Tons
GTO—Geosynchronous Transit Orbit, high stationary orbit
grunt—U.S. infantryman
HEAT—High Explosive Anti-Tank shell (shaped charge)
ICBM—Intercontinental Ballistic Missile
ICM—Improved Conventional Munitions
JSOC—Joint Special Operations Command
JSTARS—Joint Surveillance And Target Attack Radar System
MARV—Maneuverable Reentry Vehicle
MBT—Main Battle Tank
MIRV—Multiple Independently Targetable Reentry Vehicle
MRBM—Medium Range Ballistic Missile
MTBF—Mean Time Between Failure
NCO—Noncommissioned Officer (sergeants and corporals)
NGO—Non-governmental Organization
NRO—National Reconnaissance Office, controls US recon satellites
OOTW—Operations Other Than War
OTH Radar—Over the Horizon radar
radar—Detects objects by interpreting microwaves it bounces off them
ROE—Rules of Engagement
RV—Reentry Vehicle
SAM—Surface-to-Air Missile
SDI—Strategic Defense Initiative, Star Wars
SEAL—("Sea, Air, Land") U.S. Navy Commandos
SIGINT—Signal Intelligence
SLBM—Sea Launched Ballistic Missile
SLCM—Sea Launched Cruise Missile
SOF—Special Operations Forces (commandos, Rangers, etc.)
sonar—Underwater radar, uses sound instead of microwaves
SOSUS—U.S. sonar system on the continental shelf
SS—Nonnuclear attack submarine
SSBN—Nuclear ballistic missile submarine
SSM—Surface-to-Surface Missile
SSN—Nuclear attack submarine
TOT—Time on Target
WWMCCS—World Wide Military Command and Control System

Sources and Suggested Readings

Information for a work such as this is highly perishable. Your best overall source of information is the World Wide Web. If you want to a good place to start using the Web to search for information, surf on over to a site I founded in 1999: StrategyPage.com. Here you will find daily updates on wars and armed forces. You will also find links to periodicals and related web sites.

BOOKS

Books on modern warfare are a problem, as they are quickly out of date. Most of the truly useful books are periodically updated. When books on modern warfare are published, they usually don't stay in print very long and are thereafter available only in specialized libraries. Your best source of other books on modern warfare are in major research libraries. Large cities have these, as well as many major universities. A stroll through the stacks would present most of what is currently available. Governments are often a source of useful publications. The U.S. Government Printing Office offers catalogs of books on military matters. The U.S. *Congressional Record* is also a treasure trove of material but requires a lot of digging. The CIA has prepared numerous Fact Books that can be obtained through the U.S. government.

There are certain authors who continually put out material of use to anyone in this area. A partial list would include John Keegan, Trevor Dupuy, Martin van Crevald, Harriet Scott, Albert A. Nofi, Stephen Patrick, and many others.

OFFICIAL PUBLICATIONS

Government publications are often a good source of detail on modern military affairs. The U.S. Government Printing Office offers regularly updated lists of what it has available. The publications can be ordered by mail. The U.S. military also has numerous unclassified publications that civilians can legally possess. Unfortunately, the official drill is to make a Freedom of Information Act request, which can turn into a tedious process.

PEOPLE IN THE BUSINESS

It's become something of an open secret that secrets are not always kept very secret. Classified military information is regularly leaked to journalists in order to further one political agenda or another. Vows are regularly taken to tighten up on the flow of sensitive data, but it never seems to work. As a result, people in the business are frequently more talkative than they are supposed to be. As long as you don't ask for secret information, you are fairly safe while it is being dumped into your lap.

Index

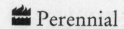 Perennial Quill

Books by James F. Dunnigan:

HOW TO MAKE WAR (FOURTH EDITION)
A Comprehensive Guide to Modern Warfare in the Twenty-first Century
ISBN 0-06-009012-X (paperback)

James F. Dunnigan's classic text on the principles of war has been revised to reflect the latest in technology and international political developments. The book presents a clear picture of the world's complex weapons, armed forces, and tactics.

VICTORY AT SEA
World War II in the Pacific
ISBN 0-688-14947-2 (paperback)

This single volume reference covers the major and lesser-known operations of the largest naval war in history, with extensive data on the ships and aircraft that were used, strategies that were employed, and biographical sketches of major participants.

DIRTY LITTLE SECRETS
Military Information You're Not Supposed To Know
ISBN 0-688-11270-6 (paperback)

Dunnigan fearlessly takes aim at all branches of the armed services to dispel myths, solve mysteries, expose boondoggles, and intrepidly reveal the muck that is kept "secret"— more than 900 entertaining and informative short takes about war making around the world.

DIRTY LITTLE SECRETS OF THE TWENTIETH CENTURY
ISBN 0-688-17068-4 (paperback)

In a concise, easy-to-read format, Dunnigan divulges 150 of the biggest misconceptions about the twentieth century, organizing them under a broad range of such categories as the military, entertainment, technology, and politics.

DIRTY LITTLE SECRETS OF WORLD WAR II
Military Information No One Told You About the Greatest,
Most Terrible War in History
ISBN 0-688-12288-4 (paperback)

More than three hundred historical entries capture aspects of World War II that no one knows, exposing the dark, misunderstood, and tragicomic aspects of the war and showing how today's high-tech weapons had their beginnings sixty years ago.

Available wherever books are sold, or call 1-800-331-3761 to order.